SENTENCING

LAW AND PRACTICE
IN SCOTLAND

SENTENCING
LAW AND PRACTICE IN SCOTLAND

GORDON NICHOLSON
Q.C., M.A., LL.B.
Sheriff Principal of Lothian and Borders

SECOND EDITION

W.GREEN/Sweet & Maxwell
EDINBURGH
1992

Published by W.Green,
The Scottish Law Publisher,
21 Alva Street, Edinburgh.

First edition..........1981
Supplement...........1985
Second edition........1992

© 1992. W. Green & Son Ltd.

ISBN 0 414 01011 6

A catalogue record for
this book is available
from the British Library.

Typeset by
Mendip Communications Ltd.,
Frome, Somerset.
Printed in Great Britain by
Hartnolls Ltd.,

To Hazel, whose patience and forbearance are
undiminished.

PREFACE TO SECOND EDITION

More than ten years have elapsed since the first edition of this work was published. In that time the law and practice of sentencing in Scotland have undergone many changes, partly as a result of new statutory provisions, and partly by reason of decisions reached, and opinions delivered, by the High Court. Moreover, many more of the High Court's decisions on sentencing matters are now reported than was formerly the case.

In the result much new material has been incorporated in this new edition. The general layout is substantially the same as in the first edition, but some sections have been substantially rewritten, some have been relocated in order to make the treatment of particular topics more cohesive, and a few sections have been omitted altogether.

In general, the aim in this edition has been to make the work as useful as possible to all judges and practitioners in the courts. To that end the work is divided into three parts. Part I describes all the law which is relevant to sentencing. Part II seeks to describe the approach to sentencing, and to analyse the considerations which may influence sentencing decisions, or the choice and use of particular sentencing disposals. Additionally, Part II contains (in Chapter 11) a detailed and comprehensive analysis of recent cases illustrating the range of sentences which the High Court has held to be appropriate for all the major crimes and offences which come before the criminal courts. Finally, Part III sets out the text of all the primary and secondary legislation which relates to the subject of sentencing.

The law is stated as at December 31, 1991. Reference is made in the text to two important statutes which received the Royal Assent in July 1991. These are the Criminal Justice Act 1991 and the Road Traffic Act 1991. As at the date of writing this Preface neither of those Acts has yet been brought into force, at least in respect of those parts which affect the law and practice of sentencing. However, the prospective changes made by the Criminal Justice Act are noted in the appropriate parts of the text; and the far-reaching changes to be introduced by the Road Traffic Act are set out in Part III where the text of the relevant sections is accompanied by a tentative commentary.

Since it is likely that sentencing law and practice will continue to develop and change in the future with the same rapidity as has been seen in the last ten years, ways are being explored whereby it may be possible to keep this edition up-dated on several occasions each year. It is hoped that this issue will have been resolved by the time this edition is published.

Finally, I should like to express my thanks to Peter Nicholson of W. Green for the help and encouragement which he has given to me in the preparation of this edition.

Gordon Nicholson
Edinburgh, December 1991

PREFACE TO FIRST EDITION

From the earliest days the sentencing of convicted offenders has played a major part in our criminal justice system but, despite the increasing complexity of the law and procedural rules relating to it, despite its growing social and economic consequences, and despite the enhanced public interest that now surrounds it, there has so far been no textbook in Scotland which has treated sentencing as a subject in itself, separate from other aspects of general criminal law and procedure. This book is an attempt to repair that omission.

Much of the book is purely factual and sets out — I hope accurately — the relevant law and rules of procedure. In addition I have, from time to time, ventured an opinion on certain problems of interpretation and practice which have, I know, been encountered not only by myself but also by others. In particular, I have attempted, in Chapter 10, to analyse and describe the sentencing process itself. I do not expect everyone to agree with all of the opinions that I have expressed throughout the book, and especially in Chapter 10. I hope, however, that, by drawing attention to some of the problems that arise, and by offering a view as to their possible solution, I may at least slightly ease the task of all who have to deal with such problems in practice.

I have drafted the book as if the whole of the Criminal Justice (Scotland) Act 1980 has been brought into effect, though I understand that section 45 (detention of young offenders), and the related Schedule 5, are unlikely to be introduced before the spring of 1982. I have also attempted to take note of the far-reaching changes relating to "totting-up" disqualifications introduced by the Transport Act 1981. That Act was passed just as the book was about to go to press, and consequently the relevant provisions, together with a tentative commentary, have been incorporated as an Appendix to Chapter 6.

In the preparation of this book I have received invaluable assistance and advice from a great many people including, in particular, the Crown Agent, Mr W.G. Chalmers (and through him the regional procurators fiscal), Mr R.C. Allan of Prisons Division, Scottish Home and Health Department, Mr C.J. Wood and Miss Susan Morris of Lothian Region Social Work Department, and, above all, my colleague, Sheriff Caplan, who read the whole book in draft form and who offered many helpful and provocative comments on a wide range of topics. Assistance in the typing of some of my manuscript was undertaken in their spare time by Miss Helen Dignan and especially by Miss Veronica Heaney, to both of whom I am most grateful. Finally, but by no means least, I acknowledge with gratitude the courtesy extended to me by the Lord Justice-General, Lord Emslie, in permitting me to reproduce in full, as an appendix to Chapter 7, the memorandum on contempt of court which he circulated to judges in 1975.

Despite all the assistance I have received, the errors and omissions that remain in the book, together with any opinions expressed therein, are of course entirely my own responsibility.

I have attempted to state the law as at 30 September, 1981.

C.G.B.N.
Edinburgh, 1981

CONTENTS

TABLE OF CASES

[Paragraph references in **bold** indicate that the case is summarised in Chapter 11.]

xiii

TABLE OF STATUTES

TABLE OF STATUTORY INSTRUMENTS

LIST OF ABBREVIATIONS

(excluding standard law reports)

Textbooks

Alison   *Principles and Practice of the Criminal Law of Scotland*, by A.J. Alison, 1832 and 1833.

Gordon   *The Criminal Law of Scotland*, by G.H. Gordon, 2nd edition, 1978, and 1st supplement, 1984.

Hume   *Commentaries on the Law of Scotland Respecting Crimes*, by Baron Hume, 4th edition by B.R. Bell, 1844.

Macdonald   *A Practical Treatise on the Criminal Law of Scotland*, by J.H.A. Macdonald (Lord Kingsburgh), 5th edition by J. Walker (later Lord Walker) and D.J. Stevenson, 1948.

Renton and Brown   *Criminal Procedure according to the Law of Scotland*, by J.W. Renton and H.H. Brown, 5th edition by G.H. Gordon, 1983.

Statutes (except where the context requires otherwise)

1907 Act	Probation of Offenders Act 1907
1926 Act	Criminal Appeal (Scotland) Act 1926
1949 Act	Criminal Justice (Scotland) Act 1949
1954 Act	Summary Jurisdiction (Scotland) Act 1954
1967 Act	Criminal Justice Act 1967
1968 Act	Social Work (Scotland) Act 1968
1975 Act	Criminal Procedure (Scotland) Act 1975
1978 Act	Community Service by Offenders (Scotland) Act 1978
1980 Act	Criminal Justice (Scotland) Act 1980
1982 Act	Criminal Justice Act 1982
1984 Act	Mental Health (Scotland) Act 1984
1985 Act	Law Reform (Miscellaneous Provisions) (Scotland) Act 1985
1987 Act	Criminal Justice (Scotland) Act 1987
1989 Act	Prisons (Scotland) Act 1989
1990 Act	Law Reform (Miscellaneous Provisions) (Scotland) Act 1990
1991 Act	Criminal Justice Act 1991

BIBLIOGRAPHY

Only a few of the following works are expressly referred to in the text of this volume. However, they have all, to a greater or lesser extent, helped to shape the author's general thinking on the subject of sentencing; and they are all recommended to those who seek to know more about the development of sentencing theory and practice both in the United Kingdom and elsewhere.

United Kingdom

Ashworth, Andrew, *Sentencing and Penal Policy*, Weidenfeld and Nicolson, 1983.

Bing, Inigo, *Criminal Procedure and Sentencing in the Magistrates' Courts*, Sweet and Maxwell, 1990.

Coyle, Dr. Andrew, *Inside: Rethinking Scotland's Prisons*, Scottish Child, 1991.

Cross, Sir Rupert, *The English Sentencing System*, Butterworths, 1975.

Emmins, Christopher J., *A Practical Approach to Sentencing*, Financial Training Publications Ltd., 1985.

Garland, D. and Young, P., eds., *The Power to Punish*, Heinemann, 1983.

Garland, D., *Punishment and Welfare*, Gower, 1985.

Henham, Ralph J., *Sentencing Principles and Magistrates' Sentencing Behaviour*, Avebury, 1990.

Home Office, *The Sentence of the Court*, H.M.S.O. 1986.

Home Office, White Paper on *Crime, Justice and Protecting the Public*, H.M.S.O., Cm. 965, 1990.

Pennington, D.C., and Lloyd-Bostock, Sally, eds., *The Psychology of Sentencing*, Centre for Socio-Legal Studies, Oxford, 1987.

Stockdale, Eric, and Devlin, Keith, *Sentencing*, Waterlow Publishers, 1987.

Thomas, D.C., *Encyclopaedia of Current Sentencing Practice*, Sweet and Maxwell.

Walker, Nigel, *Sentencing in a Rational Society*, Penguin Books Ltd., 1969.

Walker, Nigel, *Sentencing: Theory, Law and Practice*, Butterworths, 1985.

Australia

Australian Law Reform Commission, *Sentencing*, Report No. 44, 1988.

Victorian Sentencing Committee, *Sentencing* (3 vols.), 1988.

Lovegrove, Austin, *Judicial Decision Making, Sentencing Policy, and Numerical Guidance*, Springer-Verlag, 1989.

Canada

Canadian Sentencing Commission, *Sentencing Reform: A Canadian Approach*, 1987.

Taking Responsibility, Report of Standing Committee on Justice and Solicitor General on its Review of Sentencing, Conditional Release and Related Aspects of Corrections, 1988.

Scandinavia

Jareborg, Nils, *Essays in Criminal Law*, Iustus Förlag, 1988.

United States of America

Frankel, Marvin E., *Criminal Sentences: Law Without Order*, Hill and Wang, 1972.

Morris, Norval, and Tonry, Michael, *Between Prison and Probation*, Oxford University Press, New York, 1990.

U.S. Sentencing Commission, *Draft Sentencing Guidelines*, 1987.

U.S. Sentencing Commission, *Guidelines Manual*, 1990.

von Hirsch, Andrew, *Past or Future Crimes: Deservedness and Dangerousness in the Sentencing of Criminals*, Rutgers University Press, 1985.

von Hirsch, Andrew, Knapp, Kay A., and Tonry, Michael, *The Sentencing Commission and its Guidelines*, Northeastern University Press, 1987.

General

Bluglass, Robert, and Bowden, Paul, eds., *Principles and Practice of Forensic Psychiatry*, Churchill Livingstone, 1990.

Part I

Substantive Law

CHAPTER 1

NON-CUSTODIAL DISPOSALS

3

Introduction

1–01 This chapter examines the legal characteristics of all the non-custodial disposals which are available to courts in Scotland. These disposals are, on a roughly ascending scale—absolute discharge, admonition, deferred sentence, probation, fines, caution, compensation orders, and community service orders. Each will now be examined in detail.

ABSOLUTE DISCHARGE

1–02 Where, under solemn jurisdiction, a person is convicted of an offence, or where a person is charged before a court of summary jurisdiction with an offence and the court is satisfied that he committed the offence, the court, if it is of opinion, having regard to the circumstances, including the nature of the offence and the character of the offender, that it is inexpedient to inflict punishment and that a probation order is not appropriate, may, instead of sentencing him (under solemn jurisdiction) or without proceeding to conviction (under summary jurisdiction), make an order discharging him absolutely.[1] This disposal is available to all courts, both solemn and summary, and may be used in respect of all offenders regardless of their age.

1–03   Generally a conviction on indictment of an offence for which an order is made discharging the offender absolutely is to be deemed not to be a conviction for any purpose other than the purposes of the proceedings in which the order is made and of laying it before a court as a previous conviction in subsequent proceedings for another offence.[2] Furthermore, and without prejudice to the foregoing, the conviction of an offender who is discharged absolutely is generally to be disregarded for the purposes of any enactment which imposes any disqualification or disability upon convicted persons, or authorises or requires the imposition of any such disqualification or disability.[3] An exception to this general rule is, however, to be found in section 46(3) of the Road Traffic Offenders Act 1988 which provides that a person granted an absolute discharge is to be treated as if he had been convicted for the purpose of ordering

---

[1] 1975 Act, ss. 182, 383. For an example of a case where an absolute discharge was held to be more appropriate than an admonition, see *Galloway* v. *Mackenzie*, 1991 S.C.C.R. 548.

[2] *Ibid.* s. 191(1), but see, for example, Law Reform (Miscellaneous Provisions) (Scotland) Act 1968, s. 10, under which this provision is excluded.

[3] *Ibid.* s. 191(2).

endorsement of his driving licence, or disqualification from driving. A further exception is provided by the Licensed Premises (Exclusion of Certain Persons) Act 1980 (see paragraph 6–33 below).

1–04   So far as forfeiture of property used in the commission of an offence is concerned, the view was expressed in the first edition of this book that this would not be competent in solemn proceedings where an offender is granted an absolute discharge since, although an order for forfeiture is probably not a "disqualification or disability" within the meaning of section 191(2) of the 1975 Act, such an order, which can proceed only upon a conviction,[4] would be excluded by the provisions of section 191(1), which deem an order for absolute discharge not to be a conviction except for certain limited purposes. It is now suggested that that earlier view was wrong. One of the limited purposes just referred to is "the proceedings in which the order is made," and that appears to suggest that, within those proceedings, an order for absolute discharge will be treated as a conviction so as to entitle a court to order forfeiture of property where that would otherwise be appropriate. In summary proceedings, by contrast, where an order for forfeiture must also follow upon conviction,[5] such an order would not be competent since an order for absolute discharge in such proceedings is made "without proceeding to conviction."[6] However, an order for forfeiture may be made under section 58(3) of the Civic Government (Scotland) Act 1982 where, in summary proceedings, a person is discharged absolutely in respect of an offence under that section. So far as compensation orders are concerned, however, under section 58(1) of the Criminal Justice (Scotland) Act 1980 a compensation order is not competent against a person who has been granted an absolute discharge.

1–05   The provisions mentioned in paragraph 1–03 above do not affect:

(a) any right of such offender to appeal against his conviction; or
(b) the operation, in relation to any such offender, of any enactment which was in force as at the commencement of section 9(3)(*b*) of the Criminal Justice (Scotland) Act 1949 and is expressed to extend to persons dealt with under section 1(1) of the Probation of Offenders Act 1907 as well as to convicted persons.[7]

The whole of the Probation of Offenders Act 1907 was repealed by the 1949 Act, and it is thought that the provision in (b) above is now of only historical interest.

1–06   Where an offender is discharged absolutely by a court of summary jurisdiction he is, as already noted, not convicted, but he has the like right of appeal against the finding that he committed the offence as if that finding were a conviction.[8] Where a person charged with an offence has at any time previously been discharged absolutely in respect of the commission by him of an offence, it is competent in the proceedings for the current offence to bring before the court the order of absolute

---

[4] 1975 Act, s. 223(1).
[5] *Ibid.* s. 436.
[6] *Ibid.* s. 383.
[7] *Ibid.* s. 191(3).
[8] *Ibid.* s. 392(4).

discharge in like manner as if the order were a conviction.[9] Formerly, an absolute discharge ordered by a court of summary jurisdiction in respect of an offender of or over the age of 17 was to be regarded as a conviction for the purpose of determining whether that person subsequently fell to be regarded as a first offender. That provision was repealed by the 1980 Act.[10]

1–07   The provisions of sections 191 and 392 of the 1975 Act apply equally, with the addition of one proviso, to offenders who are placed on probation (see paragraph 1–63 below). It was held in one case[11] that the corresponding provisions in section 9 of the Criminal Justice (Scotland) Act 1949 did not, in a question whether an accused person had the character of a known thief, prevent regard being had to previous convictions which had resulted in the offender being placed on probation. It is submitted that previous convictions resulting in an absolute discharge could be regarded in the same way.

ADMONITION

1–08   Any court may, if it appears to meet the justice of the case, dismiss with an admonition any person found guilty by the court of any offence.[12] This disposal may be used in respect of all offenders regardless of their age. Under both solemn and summary jurisdiction an admonition follows upon conviction and, unlike an order for absolute discharge, is not subject to any statutory limitation as to its effects. Consequently, it may in appropriate cases be used both under solemn and summary procedure in conjunction with an order for forfeiture, or an order imposing a disqualification or disability. While an admonition may simply be ordered by a court without any further comment it is common and, it is submitted, perfectly proper for a court to elaborate on the order by a suitable verbal warning.

DEFERRED SENTENCE

Power to defer sentence

1–09   It is competent for a court to defer sentence after conviction for a period and on such conditions as the court may determine.[13] Statutory authority for what had long been a well-established practice in Scottish courts was first provided by section 47 of the Criminal Justice (Scotland) Act 1963. There is no restriction on the length of time for which sentence may be deferred, and it may be—and commonly is—deferred more than once in respect of a single indictment or complaint. Formerly, when sentence had been deferred in a summary case, no appeal by stated case was competent until the cause had been finally determined and sentence pronounced.[14] This rule was altered by the amendments to sections 442 and 451 of the

---

[9] 1975 Act, ss. 191(4), 392(5).

[10] *Ibid.* s. 417, repealed by 1980 Act, Sched. 8.

[11] *Johnston* v. *Heatly*, 1960 J.C. 26.

[12] 1975 Act, ss. 181, 382.

[13] *Ibid.* ss. 219, 432.

[14] *Walker* v. *Gibb*, 1965 S.L.T. 2; *Lee* v. *Lasswade Local Authority* (1883) 5 Couper 329; *Torrance* v. *Miller* (1892) 3 White 254.

1975 Act contained in Schedule 3 to the 1980 Act. These amendments give a right of appeal to "any person convicted," and an appeal is accordingly competent notwithstanding that sentence has been deferred. The statutory provisions relating to appeals under solemn procedure[15] also refer to "a person convicted" and consequently the position is the same in that case. In summary cases it is competent to make a probation order after a period of deferred sentence notwithstanding that in such a case the offender has been convicted.[16]

Use of deferred sentence

1–10 Sometimes a sentence is deferred as a matter of convenience as, for example, when a court is informed that an offender is to answer other charges at a later date and it is considered appropriate that all outstanding matters should be dealt with at the same time.[17] More frequently, some sort of condition is attached to a deferred sentence. This may simply be that the offender should be of good behaviour, but it may be more specific, for example that the offender should pay for the cost of repairing something damaged by him. There is, however, no limitation on the nature of any condition that may be imposed.[18] The court cannot in a strict sense enforce compliance with a condition attached to a deferred sentence but, since at the deferred diet the court has the same power of sentence as at the time of conviction, there are compelling reasons why an offender should comply with the condition which has been imposed. If he does comply, the court will generally be more lenient than would otherwise be the case. Where an offender is convicted of more than one charge it has been held inappropriate to sentence him in respect of one of these charges and to defer sentence on another,[19] though the same principle may not apply where two or more complaints are dealt with simultaneously on the same day. When sentence has been deferred, and particularly where there has been a condition of good behaviour, it is common, and frequently helpful, to have a supplementary social inquiry report available at the deferred diet.

Commission of further offence

1–11 Normally, where a court has deferred sentence on a person, he may not be sentenced in respect of the offence concerned until the expiry of the period of deferment. However, there are two exceptions to this. These are:

(1) if it appears to the court which deferred sentence that the person has been convicted, during the period of deferment, by a court in

---

[15] 1975 Act, s. 228.

[16] *Ibid.* s. 228.

[17] Sentence should not be deferred as a matter of convenience when the purpose in doing so is to extend beyond three weeks the period of adjournment allowed for the purpose of obtaining social inquiry and other reports under ss. 179 and 380 of the 1975 Act, notwithstanding the fact that many clerks of court insist on describing and minuting any such adjournment as a deferment of sentence: *H.M. Advocate* v. *Clegg*, 1990 S.C.C.R. 293; *McRobbie* v. *H.M. Advocate*, 1990 S.C.C.R. 767.

[18] The use of the deferred sentence is considered in greater detail at para. 10–03 *et seq.* below.

[19] *Lennon* v. *Copeland*, 1972 S.L.T. (Notes) 68; *cf. Downie* v. *Irvine*, 1964 J.C. 52.

any part of Great Britain of an offence committed during that period and has been dealt with for that offence, the court which deferred sentence may issue a warrant for the arrest of that person, or may, instead of issuing such a warrant in the first instance, issue a citation requiring his appearance; and on his appearance or on his being brought before the court it may deal with him in any manner in which it would be competent for it to deal with him on the expiry of the period of deferment; and

(2) where a court which has deferred sentence on a person convicts that person of another offence during the period of deferment, it may deal with him for the original offence in any manner in which it would be competent for it to deal with him on the expiry of the period of deferment, as well as for the offence committed during that period.[20]

1–12 Since there is at present no means for ensuring that courts are, as a matter of course, informed of subsequent convictions of persons on whom sentence has been deferred, the first of the above provisions is unlikely to be much used. On the other hand, the situation will frequently arise where a person is convicted by the same court that has previously deferred sentence, and in that situation two points should be noted. The first is that, while it is normally desirable that a deferred case should be finally disposed of by the judge who deferred sentence in the first instance,[21] this may rarely be practicable if the subsequent conviction has occurred before a different judge, because only he can properly determine the sentence for that offence. The answer to this problem is probably to be found in the fact that the power to deal with the old and the new offence simultaneously is permissive rather than mandatory: consequently, if the judge who is dealing with the subsequent conviction considers that there are features in the case which make it desirable that the question of sentence for the original offence should be dealt with by the judge who deferred sentence, he may leave it to be disposed of at the end of the period of deferment. The second point to be noted is that the provision allowing a deferred sentence and a new conviction to be dealt with at the same time contains no express provision as to whether any sentences, if custodial, should be consecutive or concurrent. It seems likely, however, that any such sentences would be made consecutive since otherwise a person on whom sentence had been deferred might conclude that he could thereafter commit further offences with impunity secure in the knowledge that in that event he would not be subjected to a higher sentence than he could have received in the first instance.[22]

PROBATION

Nature of order

1–13 A probation order is an order requiring an offender to be under supervision for a period to be specified in the order of not less than six months nor more than three years. Such an order may be made by any

---

[20] 1975 Act, ss. 219(2) and (3), 432(2) and (3).
[21] See, further, para. 10–16 *et seq.* below.
[22] For a general discussion of consecutive sentences, see para. 7–50 *et seq.* below.

court of solemn or summary jurisdiction in relation to any offence other than one the sentence for which is fixed by law. If the order is made by a court of solemn jurisdiction it may be made after conviction: if by a court of summary jurisdiction it may be made where the court is satisfied that the person charged committed the offence in question. In that event the order is made without proceeding to conviction except where sentence has previously been deferred following upon a conviction (see paragraph 1–09 above). In both cases the court should be of opinion, having regard to the circumstances, including the nature of the offence and the character of the offender, that it is expedient to make such an order.[23] A court must not make a probation order unless it is satisfied that suitable arrangements for the supervision of the offender can be made by the local authority in whose area he resides or is to reside.[24]

Background enquiry

1–14   Before making a probation order a court must obtain a report as to the circumstances and character of the offender.[25] Previously, such a course was merely desirable,[26] but it became mandatory by virtue of amendments contained in the Criminal Justice (Scotland) Act 1987.[27] A case may be adjourned to enable a social inquiry report to be obtained but any such adjournment should not be for any single period exceeding three weeks.[28] When a social inquiry report has been obtained a copy of it must be given by the clerk of court to the offender or his solicitor or, in the case of an offender under 16 years of age who is not represented by counsel or a solicitor, to his parent or guardian if present in court.[29] Sometimes a social inquiry report may disclose previous convictions which have not been libelled by the prosecutor. The court may competently take these into account when considering sentence, but should first give the offender an opportunity to admit or deny them.[30]

Restrictions on use of probation

1–15   Probation and imprisonment are quite inconsistent. Thus, where a person is found guilty of two or more charges on the same complaint or indictment, he should not be imprisoned in respect of one charge and placed on probation in respect of another.[31] Formerly it was not competent, where an offender was placed on probation, to make an order for endorsement of a driving licence or for disqualification from driving.

---

[23] 1975 Act, ss. 183(1), 384(1).
[24] *Ibid.* ss. 183(1A), 384(1A), as added by 1990 Act, s. 61(1). For the future, where the offender resides in England, the suitable arrangements are to be made by the probation committee for the area which contains the petty sessions area which would be named in the order: prospective amendment to ss. 183(1A) and 384(1A) contained in Criminal Justice Act 1991, Sched. 3, para. 7 (see para. 1–51 *et seq.* below).
[25] *Ibid.* ss. 183(1), 384(1).
[26] *Jamieson* v. *Heatly*, 1959 J.C. 22.
[27] Sched. 1, para. 10.
[28] 1975 Act, ss. 179, 380. The device of deferring sentence should not be used as a means of circumventing the three-week maximum period for adjournment: *H.M. Advocate* v. *Clegg*, 1990 S.C.C.R. 293; *McRobbie* v. *H.M. Advocate*, 1990 S.C.C.R. 767.
[29] *Ibid.* ss. 192, 393; and see para. 7–30 *et seq.* below.
[30] *Sillars* v. *Copeland*, 1966 S.L.T. 89.
[31] *Downie* v. *Irvine*, 1964 J.C. 52.

However, that is now competent.[32] Under section 58(1) of the 1980 Act a compensation order may not be made along with a probation order. In relation to forfeiture of articles used in the commission of an offence, express statutory provision no longer exists to enable this to be ordered where a probation order has been made by a court of summary jurisdiction.[33] However, notwithstanding the terms of section 436 of the 1975 Act, forfeiture may be ordered in cases falling under section 58 of the Civic Government (Scotland) Act 1982. The provisions of the Licensed Premises (Exclusion of Certain Persons) Act 1980 apply to probation orders as they do to absolute discharge (see paragraph 6–34 below).

Contents of probation orders

1–16   A probation order must be as nearly as possible in the form prescribed by Act of Adjournal.[34] There are certain provisions which the order must contain, and others which it may contain. Those in the first category are as follows:

(1) The order must name the local authority area in which the offender resides or is to reside, and must make provision for the offender to be under the supervision of an officer of the local authority for that area.[35]

(2) Where the offender resides or is to reside in a local authority area in which the court has no jurisdiction (except where that area is in England, see paragraph 1–51 *et seq.* below) the court must name the appropriate court[36] in the area of residence or intended residence, and that court must require the local authority for that area to arrange for the offender to be under the supervision of an officer of that authority.[37]

(3) In either of the foregoing cases the offender must be required to be under the supervision of an officer of the appropriate local authority.[38]

(4) The offender must be ordered to be of good behaviour, to conform to the directions of an officer of the local authority, and to inform that officer of any change of address or employment.[39]

The provisions which a probation order may contain are as follows:

(1) The order may require the offender to comply during the whole or any part of the probation period with such requirements as the

---

[32] Road Traffic Offenders Act 1988, s. 46(3).
[33] 1975 Act, s. 436; and see para. 6–03 below.
[34] *Ibid.* ss. 183(2), 384(2); Act of Adjournal (Consolidation) 1988, paras. 76, 126, and Sched. 1, Form 35.
[35] *Ibid.*
[36] The "appropriate court" is to be a sheriff or district court exercising jurisdiction in the place where the probationer is to reside according to whether the probation order is made by a sheriff or district court, provided that, if there is no district court exercising jurisdiction in that place, the appropriate court will be the sheriff court: 1975 Act, Sched. 5, para. 2.
[37] See n. 34 above.
[38] 1975 Act, ss. 183(3), 384(3).
[39] Act of Adjournal, above.

court, having regard to the circumstances of the case, considers (a) conducive to securing the good conduct of the offender or to preventing a repetition by him of the offence or the commission of other offences or (b) where the probation order is to include a requirement relating to the performance of unpaid work or the payment of compensation (see paragraphs 1–18 and 1–22 below), conducive to securing or preventing the aforesaid matters.[40] Any court may, if it thinks that such a course is expedient for the purpose of the order, require the offender to give security for his good behaviour.[41] Such security may be given by consignation with the clerk of the court or by entering into an undertaking to pay the amount, but not otherwise, and such security may be forfeited and recovered in the same manner as caution.[42] Although there is no statutory provision for the payment of caution by instalments it is submitted, since the reference to caution is only to forfeiture and recovery, that security under a probation order may be paid by instalments if the court considers that to be appropriate.

(2) The order may also include requirements relating to the residence of the offender, provided that

    (a) before making an order containing any such requirements, the court must consider the home surroundings of the offender,[43] and

    (b) where the order requires the offender to reside in any institution or place, the name of the institution or place and the period for which he is so required to reside must be specified in the order, and that period must not extend beyond 12 months from the date of the requirement or beyond the date when the order expires.[44] It is submitted that the last part of the above proviso would apply when a requirement as to residence was added to a probation order by amendment less than 12 months before the expiry of the order.

(3) A probation order may include requirements as to treatment of an offender's mental condition. This is dealt with in detail in paragraphs 1–24 to 1–33 below.

(4) As mentioned in (1) above a probation order may include requirements as to the performance by the offender of unpaid work, and as to the payment of compensation by him. These are dealt with in detail in paragraphs 1–18 and 1–22 below.

The making of probation orders

1–17   Before making a probation order the court must explain to the offender in ordinary language the effect of the order (including any additional requirements proposed to be inserted) and that if he fails to comply therewith or commits another offence during the probation period he will, under summary jurisdiction, be liable to be convicted of the original

---

[40] 1975 Act, ss. 183(4), 384(4).
[41] *Ibid.* ss. 190(1), 391(1).
[42] *Ibid.* ss. 190(2), 391(2); see para. 1–134 below.
[43] *Ibid.* ss. 183(5)(*a*), 384(5)(*a*).
[44] *Ibid.* ss. 183(5)(*b*), 384 (5)(*b*).

offence and in that event, and under solemn jurisdiction also, be sentenced for it.[45] The court must ask the offender if he is willing to comply with the requirements of the order, and must not make the order unless he expresses such willingness.[46] When an order has been made the clerk of the court by which the order was made, or of the appropriate court, as the case may be, must have copies given to the officer of the local authority who is to supervise the probationer, to the probationer himself, and to the person in charge of any institution or place in which the probationer is required to reside under the order.[47]

Probation orders requiring performance of unpaid work

1–18   After an experimental period when, in four selected areas in Scotland, arrangements were made enabling a requirement for the performance of community service by offenders to be included in probation orders, the Community Service by Offenders (Scotland) Act 1978 was enacted, giving statutory authority to the experiment, as well as providing for the making of community service orders which are independent of probation orders.[48] Where the requirement is contained in a probation order the community service is referred to as "unpaid work."

1–19   A court which is considering making a probation order may include in the order, in addition to any other requirement, a requirement that the offender shall perform unpaid work where the court:

   (a) is satisfied that the offender is of or over 16 years of age and has committed an offence punishable with imprisonment and that the conditions for the making of a community service order under section 1(2)(*a*) and (*c*) of the 1978 Act have been met[49];

   (b) has been notified by the Secretary of State that arrangements exist for persons who reside in the locality where the offender resides, or will be residing when the probation order comes into force, to perform unpaid work as a requirement of a probation order; and

   (c) is satisfied that provision can be made under the arrangements mentioned in (b) above for the offender to perform unpaid work under the probation order.[50]

It is to be noted that, where a requirement of performance of unpaid work is to be attached to a probation order, it is not necessary that the court should otherwise be considering the imposition of a custodial sentence, as is now required for a direct community service order.[51] This is no doubt because a probation order, with or without a requirement as to the

---

[45] 1975 Act, ss. 183(6), 384(6).
[46] *Ibid.*
[47] *Ibid.* ss. 183(7), 384(7).
[48] See para. 1–145 *et seq.* below.
[49] Section 1(2) of the 1978 Act provides *inter alia* that a court is not to make a community service order unless "(*a*) the offender consents" and "(*c*) the court is satisfied, after considering a report by an officer of a local authority about the offender and his circumstances, and, if the court thinks it necessary, hearing that officer, that the offender is a suitable person to perform work under such an order."
[50] 1975 Act, ss. 183(5A), 384(5A).
[51] 1978 Act, s. 1(1), as amended by Law Reform (Miscellaneous Provisions) (Scotland) Act 1990, s. 61(3).

performance of unpaid work, is clearly an alternative to other non-custodial disposals.

1–20 The number of hours of unpaid work which may be required in a probation order is, in total, not less than 40 or more than 240. The precise number must be specified in the order.[52] The Secretary of State may by order amend the maximum and minimum number of hours that may be required.[53]

1–21 Although it is competent to make a community service order in respect of an offender resident in Northern Ireland,[54] it is not competent to make a probation order requiring the performance of unpaid work in respect of such an offender.[55]

Probation orders requiring payment of compensation
1–22 Where a court is considering making a probation order it may include in the order, in addition to any other requirement, a requirement that the offender should pay compensation either in a lump sum or by instalments for any personal injury, loss or damage caused by the acts which constituted the offence. As appropriate, the provisions of the Criminal Justice (Scotland) Act 1980 relating to compensation orders[56] apply to such requirements.[57] In particular a court must give consideration to an offender's means in deciding whether to make a compensation requirement, and in determining its amount.

1–23 Where a compensation requirement is attached to a probation order, it must be a condition of the order that payment of the compensation will be completed not more than 18 months after the making of the order, or not later than two months before the end of the period of probation, whichever first occurs.[58] On the application of the offender, or of the officer of the local authority responsible for supervising the offender, the court may vary the terms of the requirement, including the amount of any instalments, in consequence of any change which may have occurred in the circumstances of the offender.[59] In any proceedings for breach of a probation order, where the breach consists only in failure to comply with a requirement to pay compensation, a document purporting to be a certificate signed by the clerk of the court for the time being having jurisdiction in relation to the order that the compensation or, where payment by instalments has been allowed, any instalment has not been paid is to be sufficient evidence of such breach.[60]

Probation orders requiring treatment for mental condition
1–24 Where the court is satisfied, on the evidence of a registered medical practitioner approved for the purposes of section 20 or 39 of the Mental Health (Scotland) Act 1984, that the mental condition of an offender is

---

[52] 1975 Act, ss. 183(5A), 384(5A).
[53] 1978 Act, ss. 1(5), 7.
[54] *Ibid.* s. 6A.
[55] 1975 Act, ss. 183(5A)(i), 384(5A)(i).
[56] Ss. 58 to 67.
[57] 1975 Act, ss. 183(5B), 384(5B).
[58] *Ibid.* ss. 183(5C)(*a*), 384(5C)(*a*).
[59] *Ibid.* ss. 183(5C)(*b*), 384(5C)(*b*).
[60] *Ibid.* ss. 183(5C)(*c*), 384(5C)(*c*).

such as requires and may be susceptible to treatment, but is not such as to warrant his detention in pursuance of a hospital order under Part VI of that Act, or under the 1975 Act, the court may, if it makes a probation order, include therein a requirement that the offender should submit, for such period not extending beyond 12 months from the date of the requirement as may be specified therein, to treatment by or under the direction of a registered medical practitioner with a view to the improvement of the offender's mental condition.[61] The corresponding provision in section 3 of the Criminal Justice (Scotland) Act 1949 (as amended by the Mental Health (Scotland) Act 1960) was considered in the case of *Isaacs* v. *H.M. Advocate*[62] when the Lord Justice General (Clyde) observed: "the section does not mean that the determination of sentence is taken out of the hands of the court and left to the decision of either a probation officer or a psychiatrist. Their views are only facets of the problem which the court has to determine."

1–25 The rules governing the giving of medical evidence for the purposes of a probation order are (with one exception, noted in paragraph 1–26 below) the same as those which apply where a hospital order is being made.[63] These rules are:

(a) a report in writing purporting to be signed by a medical practitioner may be received in evidence without proof of the signature or qualifications of the practitioner;

(b) the court may, however, in any case require that the practitioner by whom such a report was signed be called to give oral evidence;

(c) in any case the accused may require that the practitioner be called to give oral evidence;

(d) where any such report is tendered in evidence otherwise than by or on behalf of the accused, and the accused is represented by counsel or solicitor, a copy of the report must be given to his counsel or solicitor. If he is not so represented, the substance of the report must be disclosed to the accused or, where he is under 16 years of age, to his parent or guardian if present in court;

(e) evidence to rebut the evidence contained in the report may be called by or on behalf of the accused;

(f) if the court is of opinion that further time is necessary in the interests of the accused for consideration of the report, or the substance of any such report, it must adjourn the case; and

(g) for the purpose of calling evidence to rebut the evidence contained in any such report, arrangements may be made by or on behalf of an accused person detained in a hospital for his examination by any medical practitioner, and any such examination may be made in private.

1–26 Curiously, the provisions of sections 176(1A) and 377(1A) of the 1975 Act have not been applied to sections 184 and 385 in relation to the rules governing the giving of medical evidence for the purposes of a probation

---

[61] 1975 Act, ss. 184(1), 385(1).
[62] 1963 J.C. 71.
[63] 1975 Act, ss. 176, 377, applied by ss. 184(7), 385(7): for hospital orders, see Chap. 3 below.

order. In that case, accordingly, it does not appear to be necessary for the medical practitioner to make any declaration as to his relationship to the accused or as to any pecuniary interest which he may have in that person's admission to hospital.

1–27   The treatment which may be required by a probation order must be specified in the order and must be one of the following kinds:

(a) treatment as a resident patient in a hospital within the meaning of the Mental Health (Scotland) Act 1984, not being a state hospital within the meaning of that Act;

(b) treatment as a non-resident patient at such institution or place as may be specified in the order; or

(c) treatment by or under the direction of such registered medical practitioner as may be specified in the order.

Apart from the foregoing, the nature of the treatment is not to be specified in the order.[64]

1–28   A court must not make an order containing a requirement of treatment for a mental condition unless it is satisfied that arrangements have been made for the treatment intended to be specified in the order and, if the offender is to be treated as a resident patient, for his reception.[65]

1–29   Where the medical practitioner by whom or under whose direction a probationer is receiving any of the kinds of treatment to which he is required to submit in pursuance of a probation order is of the opinion—

(a) that the probationer requires, or that it would be more appropriate for him to receive, a different kind of treatment (whether in whole or in part) from that which he has been receiving, being treatment of a kind which, subject to what is stated in paragraph 1–30 below, could have been specified in the probation order; or

(b) that the treatment (whether in whole or in part) can be more appropriately given in or at a different institution or place from that where he has been receiving treatment in pursuance of the probation order,

he may, subject to what is stated in paragraph 1–31 below, make arrangements for the probationer to be treated accordingly.[66]

1–30   Arrangements made under the foregoing provisions may provide for the probationer to receive his treatment (in whole or in part) as a resident patient in an institution or place notwithstanding that it is not one which could have been specified in the probation order.[67]

1–31   Arrangements to the effect described in paragraph 1–29 above may not be made unless—

(a) the probationer and any officer responsible for his supervision agree;

(b) the treatment will be given by or under the direction of a registered medical practitioner who has agreed to accept the probationer as his patient; and

---

[64] 1975 Act, ss. 184(2), 385(2).
[65] *Ibid.* ss. 184(3), 385(3).
[66] *Ibid.* ss. 184(5), 385(5).
[67] *Ibid.* ss. 184(5A), 385(5A).

(c) where such treatment entails the probationer's being a resident patient, he will be received as such.[68]

1-32   Where any such arrangements as are described in paragraph 1–29 above are made for the treatment of a probationer, any officer responsible for the probationer's supervision must notify the appropriate court of the arrangements; and the treatment provided for by the arrangements is to be deemed to be treatment to which the probationer is required to submit in pursuance of the probation order.[69]

1-33   Except as provided by sections 184 and 385 of the 1975 Act, a court must not make a probation order requiring a probationer to submit to treatment for his mental condition.[70]

Discharge and amendment of probation orders

1-34   The discharge and amendment of probation orders are governed by the provisions contained in Schedule 5 to the 1975 Act.[71] Where, under either section 186 or 387 of that Act, a probationer is sentenced for the offence for which he was placed on probation, the probation order will cease to have effect.[72]

1-35   A probation order may, on the application of the officer supervising the probationer, or of the probationer himself, be discharged:

(a) by the appropriate court, or
(b) if no appropriate court has been named in the original or in any amending order, by the court which made the order.[73]

1-36   If the court by which a probation order was made, or the appropriate court, is satisfied that the probationer proposes to change or has changed his residence from the area of a local authority named in the order to another area of a local authority, the court may, and if application is made in that behalf by the officer supervising the probationer must, by order amend the probation order by:

(a) substituting for the area named therein that other area, and
(b) naming the appropriate court to which all the powers of the court by which the order was made are to be transferred, and by requiring the local authority for that other area to arrange for the probationer to be under the supervision of an officer of that authority.[74]

If the probation order contains requirements which in the opinion of the court cannot be complied with unless the probationer continues to reside in the local authority area named in the order, the court must not amend the order as above unless it cancels those requirements or substitutes therefor other requirements which can be so complied with.[75]

1-37   When a probation order is so amended as to local authority area

---

[68] 1975 Act, ss. 184(5B), 385(5B).
[69] *Ibid.* ss. 184(6), 385(6).
[70] *Ibid.* ss. 184(8), 385(8).
[71] *Ibid.* ss. 185(1), 386(1).
[72] *Ibid.* ss. 185(2), 386(2).
[73] *Ibid.* Sched. 5, para. 1. For definition of "appropriate court" see para. 1–16, n. 36, above.
[74] *Ibid.* para. 2(1).
[75] *Ibid.* para. 2(2)(ii).

(except where the amendment has been made by the High Court: see paragraph 1–38 below) the clerk of the court amending it must send to the clerk of the appropriate court four copies of the order together with such documents and information relating to the case as the court amending the order considers likely to be of assistance to the appropriate court. The clerk of the appropriate court must send one copy of the probation order to the local authority of the substituted local authority area and two copies to the officer supervising the probationer. That officer must give one of these copies to the probationer.[76]

1–38   Special provisions apply where a probation order has been made by the High Court and is to be amended as to local authority area. In that event:

    (a) the court does not name an appropriate court, but may substitute for the local authority named in the order the local authority for the area in which the probationer is to reside; and

    (b) the Clerk of Justiciary must send to the director of social work of that area in which the probationer is to reside three copies of the amending order together with such documents and information relating to the case as are likely to be of assistance to the director. The director must send two copies of the amending order to the officer supervising the probationer, and that officer must give one of these copies to the probationer.[77]

1–39   The court by which a probation order was made or the appropriate court may, upon application made by the officer supervising the probationer or by the probationer himself, by order amend a probation order by cancelling any of the requirements thereof or by inserting therein (either in addition to or in substitution for any such requirement) any requirement which could be included in the order if it were then being made by that court in accordance with the provisions of sections 183, 184, 384, and 385 of the 1975 Act.[78] This could include a requirement as to the performance of unpaid work or as to the payment of compensation. The power to amend an order in this way is subject to three limitations:

    (a) the court must not amend a probation order by reducing the probation period, or by extending that period beyond the end of three years from the date of the original order;

    (b) the court must not so amend a probation order that the probationer is thereby required to reside in any institution or place, or to submit to treatment for his mental condition, for any period or periods exceeding 12 months in all; and

    (c) the court must not amend a probation order by inserting therein a requirement that the probationer is to submit to treatment for his mental condition unless the amending order is made within three months after the date of the original order.[79]

1–40   Where the medical practitioner by whom or under whose direction a probationer is being treated for his mental condition in pursuance of any requirement of the probation order is of opinion:

---

[76] 1975 Act, Sched. 5, para. 2(3).
[77] *Ibid.* para. 2(4).
[78] *Ibid.* para. 3.
[79] *Ibid.*

(a) that the treatment of the probationer should be continued beyond the period specified in that behalf in the order; or

(b) that the probationer needs a different kind of treatment (whether in whole or in part) from that which he has been receiving in pursuance of the probation order, being treatment of a kind which could have been specified in the probation order but to which the probationer or his supervising officer has not agreed under section 184(5B) or 385(5B) of the 1975 Act (see paragraph 1–31 above); or

(c) that the probationer is not susceptible to treatment; or

(d) that the probationer does not require further treatment,

or where the practitioner is for any reason unwilling to continue to treat or direct the treatment of the probationer, he must make a report in writing to the officer supervising the probationer. That officer must then apply to the court which made the order, or the appropriate court, for the variation or cancellation of the requirement.[80] In practice these provisions are rarely required since courts frequently insert in a probation order an open-ended and unspecific requirement such as "to submit, for a period not exceeding 12 months, to such treatment for his mental condition as may be prescribed by Dr X." It may, however, be argued with some force that, in taking such a course, courts are yielding to doctors a power of decision which ought properly to remain in the hands of the court.

1–41   Where the court which made the order or the appropriate court proposes to amend a probation order, otherwise than on the application of the probationer, it must cite him to appear before the court, and the order must not be amended unless the probationer expresses his willingness to comply with the requirements of the order as amended. This provision does not, however, apply to an order cancelling a requirement of the probation order or reducing the period of any requirement, or substituting a new area of local authority for the area named in the probation order.[81]

1–42   On the making of an order discharging or amending a probation order, the clerk of the court must forthwith give copies of the discharging or amending order to the officer supervising the probationer. The officer must then give a copy to the probationer and to the person in charge of any institution in which the probationer is or was required by the order to reside.[82]

Failure to comply with requirements

1–43   If, on information on oath from (a) the officer supervising the probationer, (b) the director of social work of the local authority whose officer is supervising the probationer, or (c) an officer appointed by the director of social work to act on his behalf, it appears to the court by which the order was made or to the appropriate court that the probationer has failed to comply with any of the requirements of the order, that court may issue a warrant for the arrest of the probationer, or may, if it thinks fit, instead of issuing such a warrant in the first instance,

---

[80] 1975 Act, Sched. 5, para. 4.
[81] *Ibid.* para. 5.
[82] *Ibid.* para. 6.

issue a citation requiring the probationer to appear before the court at such time as may be specified in the citation.[83] It is to be noted that the definition of "probationer" in section 462(1) of the 1975 Act makes breach of probation proceedings competent even after a probation order has expired, provided of course that the breach itself occurred during the currency of the order.

1–44   If it is proved to the satisfaction of the court before which a probationer appears or is brought in pursuance of the foregoing provisions that he has failed to comply with any of the requirements of the probation order, the court may:

(a) except in the case of a failure to comply with a requirement to pay compensation, and without prejudice to the continuance in force of the probation order, impose a fine not exceeding level 3 on the standard scale (currently £400: see paragraph 1–67 below); or

(b)   (i)   where the probationer has been convicted for the offence for which the order was made, sentence him for that offence;

(ii)   where the probationer has not been so convicted, convict him and sentence him as aforesaid; or

(c) vary any of the requirements of the probation order, so however that any extension of the probation period shall terminate not later than three years from the date of the probation order; or

(d) without prejudice to the continuance in force of the probation order, in a case where the conditions required by the Community Service by Offenders (Scotland) Act 1978 are satisfied, make a community service order. The provisions of that Act are to apply to such an order as if the failure to comply with the requirement of the probation order were the offence in respect of which the order had been made.[84]

1–45   The 1975 Act is silent as to how, and by whom, any failure by a probationer to comply with a requirement of the order is to be proved. By local arrangement this task is usually in practice undertaken by the procurator fiscal. It is submitted that the standard of proof in such a case should be the same as applies in criminal trials. It is imperative that the correct procedure should be followed.[85] By an amendment to the Community Service by Offenders (Scotland) Act 1978 contained in the Law Reform (Miscellaneous Provisions) (Scotland) Act 1990[86] it is now possible for a failure to comply with a community service order to be proved by the evidence of a single witness. There does not appear to be any comparable provision in relation to proving a failure to comply with a requirement of a probation order.

1–46   A fine imposed under the above provisions in respect of a failure to comply with the requirements of a probation order is to be deemed for the purposes of any enactment to be a sum adjudged to be paid by or in

---

[83] 1975 Act, ss. 186(1), 387(1), as amended by Law Reform (Miscellaneous Provisions) (Scotland) Act 1990, s. 61(2).

[84] *Ibid.* ss. 186(2), 387(2).

[85] *Roy* v. *Cruickshank*, 1954 S.L.T. 217.

[86] Sched. 8, para. 28.

respect of a conviction or a penalty imposed on a person summarily convicted.[87]

1-47   A probationer who is required by a probation order to submit to treatment for his mental condition is not to be deemed for the purpose of these provisions to have failed to comply with that requirement on the ground only that he has refused to undergo any surgical, electrical or other treatment if, in the opinion of the court, his refusal was reasonable having regard to all the circumstances.[88]

1-48   Without prejudice to the provisions of sections 187 and 388 of the 1975 Act (see paragraphs 1–49 and 1–50 below) a probationer who is convicted of an offence committed during the probation period is not on that account to be liable to be dealt with under sections 186 and 387 for failing to comply with any requirement of the probation order.[89] It has been observed that, where circumstances permit, it is preferable to proceed under what are now sections 187 and 388 rather than under sections 186 and 387.[90]

Commission of further offence

1-49   If it appears to the court by which a probation order has been made, or to the appropriate court, that the probationer to whom the order relates has been convicted by a court in any part of Great Britain of an offence committed during the probation period and has been dealt with for that offence, the first-mentioned court, or the appropriate court, may issue a warrant for the arrest of the probationer, or may, if it thinks fit, instead of issuing such a warrant in the first instance issue a citation requiring the probationer to appear before that court at such time as may be specified in the citation. On his appearance or on his being brought before the court, the court may, if it thinks fit, deal with him under section 186(2)(*b*) or 387(2)(*b*) of the 1975 Act, as the case may be (*i.e.* sentence him for the original offence: see paragraph 1–44 above).[91]

1-50   Where a probationer is convicted by the court which made the probation order, or by the appropriate court, of an offence committed during the probation period, that court may, if it thinks fit, deal with him as above for the offence for which the order was made as well as for the offence committed during the period of probation.[92] Any such sentences, if custodial, might well be made consecutive to each other (see paragraph 7–50 *et seq.* below).

Probation orders relating to persons residing in England[93]

(a) Persons aged 17 and over

1-51   Where the court by which a probation order (other than one including a requirement that the offender should perform unpaid work) is made

---

[87] 1975 Act, ss. 186(3), 387(3).

[88] *Ibid.* ss. 186(4), 387(4).

[89] *Ibid.* ss. 186(5), 387(5).

[90] *Roy* v. *Cruickshank*, above.

[91] 1975 Act, ss. 187(1), 388(1). Note the reference to the definition of "probationer" in para. 1–43 above.

[92] *Ibid.* ss. 187(2), 388(2).

[93] The Criminal Justice Act 1991 contains provision for a range of new requirements which may be inserted in a probation order made by a court in England and Wales (Sched. 1). As

under the 1975 Act is satisfied that the offender has attained the age of 17 and resides or will reside in England, sections 183(2) and 384(2) do not apply, that is there is no nomination of a local authority area or an appropriate court, and no provision for the offender to be under the supervision of an officer of the local authority. Instead the order should contain a requirement that the offender is to be under the supervision of a probation officer appointed for or assigned to the petty sessions area in which the offender resides or will reside. That area must be named in the order.[94]

1–52 Where a probation order has been made under the 1975 Act and the court in Scotland by which the order was made, or the appropriate court, is satisfied that the probationer has attained the age of 17 and proposes to reside or is residing in England, the power of that court to amend the order under Schedule 5 to the Act is to include power to insert the provisions set out in paragraph 1–51 above. Such an amendment may be made without summoning the probationer and without his consent.[95]

1–53 A probation order made or amended by virtue of the foregoing provisions may include a requirement that the probationer must submit to treatment for his mental condition. In that event the provisions of sections 184 and 385 of the 1975 Act and section 3 of the Powers of Criminal Courts Act 1973 (which governs the making in England of a probation order containing such a requirement) are in effect assimilated in relation to the making of such orders and the functions of supervising officers and medical practitioners.[96]

1–54 The provisions of the 1975 Act relating to the discharge and amendment of probation orders, and to the procedure where it appears that a probationer has failed to comply with a requirement of the order,[97] do not apply to an order made or amended as above. Subject to certain exceptions the provisions of the Powers of Criminal Courts Act 1973 apply instead.[98]

1–55 If it appears on information to a justice, acting for the petty sessions area for which the supervising court within the meaning of the Powers of Criminal Courts Act 1973 acts, that a person in whose case a probation order has been made or amended as above has been convicted by a court in any part of Great Britain of an offence committed during the period specified in the order, he may issue a summons requiring that person to appear, at the place and time specified therein, before the court in Scotland by which the probation order was made or, if the information is

---

a consequence, that Act also contains detailed amendments to those parts of the 1975 Act which provide for the making or transfer in Scotland of orders in respect of offenders who are resident in England, and for the reciprocal enforcement of orders (Sched. 3). Since it is not known when those provisions will be brought into force, this and the following paragraphs describe the relevant statutory provisions as they were prior to the passing of the 1991 Act. Incidentally, "England" is defined in section 462(1) of the 1975 Act as including Wales.

[94] 1975 Act, ss. 188(1), 389(1).
[95] *Ibid.* ss. 188(2), 389(2). But see para. 1–62 below.
[96] *Ibid.* ss. 188(3), 389(3).
[97] *Ibid.* ss. 185(1), 186(1), 386(1), 387(1).
[98] *Ibid.* ss. 188(4), 389(4).

in writing and on oath, may issue a warrant for his arrest, directing that person to be brought before the Scottish court.[99]

1–56   If a warrant for the arrest of a probationer issued under section 187 or 388 of the 1975 Act (*i.e.* on commission of a further offence) is executed in England, and the probationer cannot forthwith be brought before the court which issued the warrant, the warrant has effect as if it directed him to be brought before a magistrates' court for the place where he is arrested. The magistrates' court must commit him to custody or release him on bail (with or without sureties) until he can be brought or appear before the court in Scotland.[1]

1–57   The court by which a probation order is made or amended in accordance with the foregoing provisions must send three copies of the order to the clerk to the justices for the petty sessions area named therein, together with such documents and information relating to the case as it considers likely to be of assistance to the court acting for that petty sessions area.[2]

1–58   Section 10 of the Powers of Criminal Courts Act 1973 makes provision for the transfer of English probation orders to courts in Scotland when the probationer resides there. The court to be specified is a court of summary jurisdiction but, where the order was made on indictment, the court is to be the appropriate sheriff court. Subject to certain exceptions, the provisions of the 1975 Act apply to such transferred orders as though they had been made by the appropriate court in Scotland. However, where an order is so transferred and is then amended under section 188(2) or 389(2) of the 1975 Act (because the offender is or is to be resident in England) the order is in that event to have effect, as from the date of the amendment, as if it were an order made by a court in England in the case of a person residing there.[3]

1–59   Where the appropriate court in Scotland, dealing with an order transferred from England, is satisfied that the probationer has failed to comply with a requirement of the order it may, instead of dealing with him under the 1975 Act, commit him to custody or release him on bail until he can appear before the English court which made the order. A certificate by the clerk of the Scottish court is evidence of the failure to comply with the requirement of the order which is specified in the certificate.[4]

(b) Persons under the age of 17

1–60   Where the court by which a probation order is made is satisfied that the person to whom the order relates is under the age of 17 and resides or will reside in England, similar provisions apply as in the case of probation orders relating to persons above that age so far as the making and amendment of such orders is concerned.[5] It is the duty of the clerk to the justices for the area where the probationer resides, upon receiving notification of the order, to refer the notification to a juvenile court acting

---

[99] 1975 Act, ss. 188(5), 389(5).

[1] *Ibid.* ss. 188(6), 389(6).

[2] *Ibid.* ss. 188(7), 389(7).

[3] *Ibid.* ss. 188(8), 389(8).

[4] Powers of Criminal Courts Act 1973, s. 10(5).

[5] 1975 Act, ss. 189(1) to (3), 390(1) to (3); see paras. 1–51, 1–52, and 1–57 above.

for the petty sessions area named in the order, and on such a reference the court:

> (a) may make a supervision order under the Children and Young Persons Act 1969 in respect of a person to whom the notification relates; and
>
> (b) if it does not make such an order, must dismiss the case.[6]

When a juvenile court disposes of a case referred to it in either of the above ways, the probation order in consequence of which the reference was made ceases to have effect.[7]

1–61   When a person who is subject to a supervision order made in England moves to Scotland, and his case is referred to a Scottish court under section 73(1) of the Social Work (Scotland) Act 1968, that court:

> (a) may, if it is of opinion that the person to whom the notification relates should continue to be under supervision, make a probation order in respect of him for a period specified in the order; and
>
> (b) if it does not make such an order, must dismiss the case.

When the court disposes of a case in either of the above ways the supervision order ceases to have effect.[8] Provided that the probation order includes only requirements having the like effect as any requirement or provision of the supervision order, it may be made without summoning the person concerned and without his consent. Any such probation order must not be made for a period which would extend beyond the date when the supervision order would have expired.[9]

(c) Orders with a requirement to perform unpaid work

1–62   No facilities exist in England for the carrying into effect of probation orders made in Scotland which contain a requirement that the probationer should perform a number of hours of unpaid work, and they are expressly excluded from the provisions of sections 188(1) and 389(1) of the 1975 Act by paragraphs 2 and 3 of Schedule 2 to the 1978 Act. Consequently, no such requirement should be included in an order being made under either section 188(1) of 389(1); and, when an existing order containing such a requirement is to be transferred to England under subsection (2) of these sections, it should first be amended so as to remove that requirement.

Effects of probation

1–63   A probation order has the same effect as an absolute discharge in so far as it does or does not fall to be treated as a conviction for the purposes of an appeal or other proceedings (see paragraphs 1–06 and 1–07 above).[10] There is, however, one provision which applies only in relation to probation orders. Where an offender, being not less than 16 years of age at the time of his conviction of an offence for which he is placed on probation, is subsequently sentenced under the 1975 Act for that offence,

---

[6] 1975 Act, ss. 189(4), 390(4).
[7] *Ibid.* ss. 189(5), 390(5).
[8] *Ibid.* ss. 189(6), 390(6).
[9] *Ibid.* ss. 189(7), 390(7).
[10] *Ibid.* ss. 191, 392.

the provisions of subsection (1) of sections 191 and 392 do not apply, that is to say that the effect of a conviction on indictment is not then restricted in any way.[11]

FINES

Maximum amounts[12]

1–64 The rules for determining the maximum fine which may be imposed in different courts were substantially altered by the Criminal Justice Act 1982 which inserted into the 1975 Act new (and complicated) sections 289B, 289F and 289G. Since then those rules have been further altered as a result of amendments made by several later statutes, including in particular the Criminal Justice (Scotland) Act 1987 and the Criminal Justice Act 1988. The result is a complex mass of legislation which is extremely difficult to follow or to explain, and it is to be hoped that at some time in the near future an opportunity may be found to introduce simplifying legislation. Mercifully, it is not necessary in a work on sentencing to probe all the finer details of this legislation, and in the paragraphs which follow an attempt is simply made to describe the main structure of the provisions in question. An important distinction which must be made is between common law offences, indictable statutory offences, and offences which are triable only summarily.

(1) Common law offences

1–65 There is no limit to the amount of the fine which may be imposed in respect of a common law offence where conviction is on indictment in either the High Court or the sheriff court.[13] On summary conviction in the district court the maximum fine in respect of a common law offence is level 4 on the standard scale (presently £1,000).[14] On summary conviction in the sheriff court the maximum fine in respect of a common law offence is "the prescribed sum" which is at present £2,000.[15]

(2) Indictable statutory offences

1–66 There is no limit to the maximum fine which may be imposed on conviction of an indictable statutory offence on indictment in the High Court or the sheriff court. That is so regardless of whether the enactment creating the offence originally provided a maximum amount.[16] Where a statutory offence is triable either on indictment or summarily, the maximum fine available on summary conviction is regulated by the rather complex provisions of section 289B of the 1975 Act. It is to be noted that, where different fines are provided for on a first and on subsequent

---

[11] 1975 Act, ss. 191(1), 392(1).
[12] The Criminal Justice Act 1991 (by s. 17) increases the maximum fines in the standard scale (see para. 1–67 below) and the amount of the prescribed sum (see para. 1–65 below) to a new maximum of £5,000. Since it is not known when the provisions of the 1991 Act will come into force, the following paragraphs describe the position as it was prior to the 1991 Act.
[13] 1975 Act, s. 193A(1).
[14] *Ibid.* s. 284(*b*), and see para. 1–67 below.
[15] *Ibid.* ss. 289(*a*), 289B(6).
[16] *Ibid.* s. 193A.

summary convictions, the largest fine is now available on any conviction.[17]

(3) Offences triable only summarily

1–67   Section 289G of the 1975 Act makes provision for a standard scale of fines for offences which are triable only summarily. By a somewhat complex process maximum fines for most summary offences which were in existence prior to April 11, 1983 were first increased in monetary value and then, as it were, translated to the appropriate level on the standard scale. New offences created since that date have expressed their maximum fine by reference to a level on that scale. The result is that when the monetary values of each level on the standard scale are changed, as they can be by statutory instrument, it is not necessary to amend all the offence-creating statutes concerned. The standard scale, as set out in section 289G of the 1975 Act is:

Standard Scale

Level	*Amount*
1	£50
2	£100
3	£400
4	£1,000
5	£2,000

1–68   As is the case with indictable statutory offences, where a statute contains different maximum penalties for a first conviction and for a second or subsequent conviction of a summary offence, the maximum penalty provided for any conviction is to be the maximum penalty for all convictions.[18]

(4) Where no fine provided for in statute

1–69   Where a statute provides only for imprisonment a court of solemn jurisdiction may substitute (either with or without caution for good behaviour, not exceeding the amount of the prescribed sum for the time being and a period of 12 months) a fine of any amount.[19] In a summary prosecution for the contravention of a statute which provides only for imprisonment the court may, where the offence is triable either summarily or on indictment, substitute a fine not exceeding the prescribed sum; and, where the offence is triable only summarily, it may substitute a fine not exceeding level 4 on the standard scale. In either case the fine may be imposed with or without caution for good behaviour.[20] Where a statute provides for a minimum penalty it has been held competent to modify the penalty still further.[21]

---

[17] 1975 Act, s. 289B(2).
[18] *Ibid.* s. 289E.
[19] *Ibid.* s. 193(2).
[20] *Ibid.* s. 394(*b*).
[21] *Lambie* v. *Mearns* (1903) 4 Adam 207; and see *Paton* v. *Neilson* (1903) 4 Adam 268; *McDonald* v. *Wood and Bruce*, 1950 J.C. 72.

Imposition and payment of fines

1–70   Prior to the passing of the 1980 Act the rules regulating the imposition and payment of fines were substantially different depending on whether the fines arose from a conviction on indictment or summarily. Section 47 of that Act, however, effectively assimilated the two procedures, and since then it has been possible to describe a substantially uniform system by reference, mainly, to those parts of the 1975 Act which previously related only to fines imposed under summary procedure.[22]

Determination of amount of fine

1–71   Any court, in determining the amount of any fine to be imposed on an offender, must take into consideration, amongst other things, the means of the offender so far as known to the court.[23] The effect of this provision has been considered by the High Court on many occasions.[24]

Application of money in offender's possession

1–72   Where a court of summary jurisdiction imposes a fine it may order the offender to be searched, and any money found on him on apprehension or search, or when taken to prison or to a young offenders institution in default of payment of the fine, may, unless the court otherwise directs, be applied towards payment of the fine. Such money is not to be so applied if the court is satisfied that it does not belong to the person on whom it is found, or that the loss of the money will be more injurious to his family than his imprisonment or detention.[25]

1–73   When a court of summary jurisdiction, which has adjudged that a sum of money is to be paid by an offender, considers that any money found on him on apprehension, or after he has been searched by order of the court, should not be applied towards payment of such sum, the court must make a direction in writing to that effect. That direction is to be written on the extract of the sentence which imposes the fine before that is issued by the clerk of court.[26]

1–74   An accused may make an application to such a court either orally or in writing, through the governor of the prison in whose custody he may be at the time, that any sum of money found on his person should not be applied in payment of the fine adjudged to be paid by him.[27] A person who alleges that any money found on the person of an offender is not the property of the offender, but belongs to such person, may apply to the court either orally or in writing for a direction that such money should not be applied in payment of the fine; and the court after inquiry may so direct.[28]

1–75   A court of summary jurisdiction may order the attendance in court of the offender, if he is in prison, for the purpose of ascertaining the ownership of money found on his person.[29] In such a case a notice, of the

---

[22] See 1975 Act, s. 194.
[23] 1975 Act, s. 395(1).
[24] See, further, para. 10–26 *et seq.* below.
[25] 1975 Act, s. 395(2).
[26] *Ibid.* s. 395(3).
[27] *Ibid.* s. 395(4).
[28] *Ibid.* s. 395(5).
[29] *Ibid.* s. 395(6).

appropriate form contained in an Act of Adjournal,[30] addressed to the governor of the relevant prison, and signed by the judge of the court, is sufficient warrant to the governor for conveying the offender to the court.[31]

Remission of fine

1–76   A fine may at any time be remitted in whole or in part by:

   (a) in a case where a transfer of fine order is effective (see paragraph 1–92 *et seq.* below) and the court by which payment is enforceable is, in terms of the order, a court of summary jurisdiction in Scotland, that court; or
   (b) in any other case, the court which imposed the fine or (where that court was the High Court) the court by which payment was first enforceable.[32]

Where the court remits the whole or part of a fine after imprisonment has been imposed in default, it must also remit the whole period of imprisonment or reduce the period by an amount which bears the same proportion to the whole period as the amount remitted bears to the whole fine.[33] The above power to remit a fine in whole or in part may be exercised without requiring the attendance of the accused.[34]

Time to pay

1–77   Unless payment of a fine is tendered at the time of its imposition a court must normally allow an offender at least seven days to pay the fine or the first instalment thereof.[35] A court may allow time for payment even where that has not been requested by an accused.[36]

Refusal of time to pay

1–78   The court may refuse to allow time for payment if:

   (a) the offender appears to possess sufficient means to enable him to pay the fine forthwith; or
   (b) on being asked whether he wishes to have time for payment he does not ask for time; or
   (c) he fails to satisfy the court that he has a fixed abode; or
   (d) the court is satisfied for any other special reason that no time should be allowed for payment.

If, in any of these events, the offender fails to pay, the court may exercise its power to impose imprisonment but, if it does so, it must state the

---

[30] Act of Adjournal (Consolidation) 1988, Form 61. It is to be noted that, notwithstanding the terms of s. 395(7) of the 1975 Act, this Form provides for signature by the clerk of court, and not by the judge.
[31] 1975 Act, s. 395(7).
[32] *Ibid.* s. 395A(1). When an offender's means are unknown, it is improper to impose the maximum fine on the basis that the offender can subsequently apply to have that fine remitted: *McCandless* v. *MacDougall*, 1987 S.C.C.R. 206.
[33] *Ibid.* s. 395A(2).
[34] *Ibid.* s. 395A(3).
[35] *Ibid.* s. 396(1).
[36] *Fraser* v. *Herron*, 1968 J.C. 1.

special reason for its decision.[37] This power is now restricted by the provisions of section 41 of the 1980 Act which provide *inter alia* that, unless certain conditions are satisfied, imprisonment is not to be imposed in such a case on an accused who is not legally represented and has not been previously sentenced to imprisonment or detention by a court in any part of the United Kingdom. This provision is examined more fully in Chapter 2. The nature of the offence is not a relevant consideration when determining whether time should be allowed for payment. Where the nature of the offence is such as to warrant a sentence of imprisonment the proper course is to impose such a sentence in the first instance.[38] Also, the fact that an accused is currently serving a sentence of imprisonment is not a special reason for refusing time to pay.[39] In all cases where time is not allowed for payment of a fine the reasons of the court must be stated in the extract of the finding and sentence as well as in the finding and sentence itself.[40] A failure to record the reasons, provided that they were in any event valid and had been stated in the presence of the offender, may not invalidate the sentence.[41]

Restrictions on imprisonment after fine

1–79   Where time is allowed for payment of a fine or payment by instalments is ordered, a court must not, on the occasion of the imposition of the fine, impose imprisonment in the event of a future default unless the offender is before it and the court determines that, having regard to the gravity of the offence or to the character of the offender, or to other special reason, it is expedient that he should be imprisoned without further inquiry in default of payment. Where a court so determines it must state the special reason for its decision.[42] The nature of the offence is not a relevant ground for imposing imprisonment in the event of future default.[43] An offence of careless driving, which is not punishable with imprisonment in the first instance, is not an offence of gravity within the meaning of section 396(4) of the 1975 Act,[44] but the mere fact that an offence is not punishable with imprisonment in the first instance is not of itself a complete bar to the imposition of imprisonment in the event of future default: that may be justified having regard to the character of the offender or to other special reason.[45] By contrast, a charge of shoplifting which the sheriff described as "barefaced" was held on appeal to be the very case in which it was appropriate to impose imprisonment under the subsection.[46] If a court has imposed imprisonment in the event of future default then, if at any time the offender asks the court to commit him to prison, the court may do so.[47]

---

[37] 1975 Act, s. 396(2); and see *Sullivan* v. *McLeod*, 1980 S.L.T. (Notes) 99.
[38] *Barbour* v. *Robertson, Ram* v. *Robertson*, 1943 J.C. 46; *cf. Buchanan* v. *Hamilton*, 1988 S.C.C.R. 379.
[39] *Robertson* v. *Jessop*, 1989 S.L.T. 843; 1989 S.C.C.R. 387.
[40] 1975 Act, s. 396(3).
[41] *Bruce* v. *Hogg*, 1966 J.C. 33, distinguishing *Winslow* v. *Farrell*, 1965 J.C. 49.
[42] 1975 Act, s. 396(4).
[43] *Buchanan* v. *Hamilton*, 1988 S.C.C.R. 379.
[44] *Dunlop* v. *Allan* 1984 S.C.C.R. 329; followed in *Simmons* v. *Lowe*, 1990 G.W.D. 17–973.
[45] *Paterson* v. *McGlennan*, 1991 S.C.C.R. 616.
[46] *Finnie* v. *McLeod*, 1983 S.C.C.R. 387.
[47] 1975 Act, s. 396(5).

1–80 Where time has been allowed for payment of a fine the court may, on an application by or on behalf of the offender, and after giving the prosecutor an opportunity of being heard, allow further time for payment.[48] Such an application, which may be made orally or in writing,[49] should be made to the court which imposed the fine unless there has been a transfer of fine order in which event the application should be made to the court specified therein.[50] A court to which such an application is made must allow further time for payment unless it is satisfied that the failure to make payment has been wilful or that the offender has no reasonable prospect of being able to pay if further time is allowed.[51] Two points arising from the foregoing may be mentioned. The first concerns the requirement that the prosecutor should be given an opportunity of being heard. This is a curious provision since traditionally the prosecutor is not concerned with matters relating to sentence, and moreover there is no comparable provision in relation to cases where an offender who has not paid timeously is brought to court to explain the reasons for the non-payment (see paragraph 1–81 below). In practice, it is thought, this provision is regularly ignored, and probably most prosecutors would be rather surprised to be offered an opportunity to be heard. The second point is that section 396(7) of the 1975 Act does not in terms apply to a case where imprisonment has already been imposed in the event of future default. It is submitted, however, that the subsection applies in such a case also, though probably only at a stage prior to the issue of an extract warrant to enforce the sentence of imprisonment.

Means inquiry procedure

1–81 Where a court has imposed a fine without imposing imprisonment in default of payment, it must not impose imprisonment for failing to make payment unless, on an occasion subsequent to that sentence, the court has inquired, in the offender's presence, into the reason why the fine has not been paid. This requirement does not apply where the offender is in prison.[52] Under earlier legislation this procedure was known as an inquiry into the offender's means, and the hearing under present legislation is still commonly referred to as a means inquiry court.

1–82 For the purpose of enabling such an inquiry to be made a court may issue a citation requiring the offender to appear at an appointed time and place, or may issue a warrant of apprehension.[53] Such a warrant may also be issued if an offender fails to appear in response to a citation.[54] The form of warrant and the form of minute of procedure in such cases are prescribed by Act of Adjournal.[55] It is normal practice in most courts for the clerk of court to send a warning letter to an offender who is in default before the inquiry procedure is initiated.

1–83 For many years it was common practice at means inquiry courts for an

[48] 1975 Act, s. 396(7).
[49] *Ibid.* s. 397(3).
[50] *Ibid.* s. 397(1).
[51] *Ibid.* s. 397(2).
[52] *Ibid.* s. 398(1).
[53] *Ibid.* s. 398(2).
[54] *Ibid.* s. 398(3).
[55] *Ibid.* s. 398(4) and (5). Act of Adjournal (Consolidation) 1988, para. 124, Forms 57 to 59.

offender to be allowed further time for payment of a fine, but for imprisonment to be imposed at the same time in the event of future default (on the analogy of, and by extrapolation from, the provisions of section 396(4) of the 1975 Act: see paragraph 1–79 above). However, in the course of 1989 and 1990 this practice was called into question, first in the case of *Stevenson* v. *McGlennan*,[56] and finally in *Craig* v. *Smith*[57] where it was held that the practice was unlawful. The High Court held that, under section 407(1) of the Act, a court has power to impose imprisonment in the event of future default only at the time when a fine is imposed, and not on the occasion of a means inquiry court (though there is power to impose immediate imprisonment at that stage). Happily, the effects of that decision were short-lived since the Law Reform (Miscellaneous Provisions) (Scotland) Act 1990[58] amended section 407(1) to make it clear that, at a means inquiry court, imprisonment can be imposed to take effect in the event of subsequent default in payment of the fine or any instalment thereof (see, further, paragraph 1–96 *et seq.* below).

Payment by instalments

1–84   Without prejudice to a court's right under section 396(2) of the 1975 Act to refuse time for payment of a fine (see paragraph 1–78 above), a court may, of its own accord or on the application of the offender, order payment of the fine by instalments of such amounts and at such times as it may think fit.[59] Where payment by instalments has been ordered the court, without requiring the attendance of the accused, may allow further time for payment of any instalment, or may order payment by instalments of lesser amounts or at longer intervals than those originally fixed.[60] Although this provision does not empower a court to increase the instalments originally fixed, it is submitted that it is open to a court to take that course where the offender is in default and has been brought before the court for inquiry under section 398 of the 1975 Act.

Supervision

1–85   Where an offender has been allowed time for payment of a fine the court may, either on the occasion of the imposition of the fine or on a subsequent occasion, order that he be placed under the supervision of such person as the court may from time to time appoint for the purpose of assisting and advising the offender in regard to payment of the fine.[61] This task is normally given to a member of a local social work department. A supervision order remains in force so long as the offender to whom it relates remains liable to pay the fine or any part of it,[62] but the court may discharge the order within that period and, in any event, the order ceases to have effect on the making of a transfer of fine order (see paragraph

---

[56] 1990 S.L.T. 842; 1989 S.C.C.R. 711.
[57] 1990 S.C.C.R. 328.
[58] Sched. 8, para. 27(3).
[59] 1975 Act, s. 399(1).
[60] *Ibid.* s. 399(2) and (3).
[61] *Ibid.* s. 400(1).
[62] *Ibid.* s. 400(2).

1–92 *et seq.* below). In either case the court may, if it wishes, make a new order.[63]

1–86   Where an offender under 21 years of age has been allowed time for payment of a fine the court must not order the form of detention appropriate to him in default of payment unless he has been placed under supervision in respect of the fine, or the court is satisfied that it is impracticable to place him under supervision.[64] In the latter event the court must state the grounds on which it is satisfied that supervision is impracticable and these must be entered in the record of proceedings.[65] The general requirement in relation to offenders under 21 means in practice that, if a supervision order is not made at the time when a fine is imposed, and the offender subsequently defaults, he will have to be brought before the court for an inquiry under section 398 of the 1975 Act and will then, generally, have to be placed under a supervision order (no detention then being competent) and allowed further time to pay. To avoid this process, which some believe encourages young offenders to be dilatory in the payment of fines, it is thought to be the practice in some courts to place all such offenders under a supervision order at the time when a fine is imposed. Such a practice, however, places a considerable burden on the social work departments concerned and thereby reduces any likelihood of effective supervision being carried out. It is submitted that it is generally better practice to make a supervision order at the time of imposing a fine only when special features are present, *e.g.* the fine is substantial, the offender has a considerable criminal record, or there are indications that he will have difficulty in efficiently managing his finances. It is also submitted that the provision about impracticability should be used sparingly. Although there is no authority on the matter it is suggested that supervision could properly be considered impracticable where an offender was employed in a place where contact with a supervising officer would be difficult or impossible, *e.g.* at sea, or where there was evidence that, on a previous occasion, the offender had failed to co-operate with the terms of a supervision order.

1–87   Where a supervision order is in force the court must not impose imprisonment or detention in default of payment of the fine unless it has, before so doing, taken such steps as may be reasonably practicable to obtain from the person appointed for the supervision of the payment of the fine a report, which may be oral, on the offender's conduct and means. The court must consider any such report in a case where inquiry is required under section 398 of the 1975 Act in addition to the inquiry called for by that section.[66]

1–88   Upon the making of a supervision order the clerk of court must send a notice to the offender in, as nearly as may be, the form contained in an Act of Adjournal.[67] The person appointed to supervise the offender must communicate with him with a view to assisting and advising him in regard to payment of the fine, and unless the fine or any instalment has been paid

---

[63] 1975 Act, s. 400(3).
[64] *Ibid.* s. 400(4).
[65] *Ibid.* ss. 400(5), 401(1).
[66] *Ibid.* s. 400(6).
[67] *Ibid.* s. 400(7); Act of Adjournal (Consolidation) 1988, para. 124, Form 60.

within the time allowed that person must report to the court without delay as to the conduct and means of the offender.[68]

1–89　In many courts the payment of fines, or instalments of fines, is now assisted by fines enforcement officers who are members of court staff. Their main functions are, as necessary, to visit offenders at home or elsewhere in order to receive payment of fine instalments, and to provide reports to the court at the stage of a means inquiry as to the offender's means and the likelihood of the fine being paid if further time were to be allowed. Although fines supervision in the statutory sense is not part of the function of fines enforcement officers, in practice many of them offer advice and guidance to offenders in relation to their financial affairs where this seems likely to result in more effective payment of the fine.

Enforcement in other districts, and enforcement of High Court fines
1–90　Any sentence or decree for any fine or expenses (see paragraph 6–11 below) pronounced by any court may be enforced against the person or effects of any party against whom any such sentence or decree has been awarded in any other sheriff court district, as well as in the district where the sentence or decree was pronounced. However, such sentence or decree, or an extract thereof, must first be produced to and endorsed by the sheriff or justice of the other district competent to have pronounced the sentence or decree in that other district.[69]

1–91　A fine imposed by the High Court is to be remitted for enforcement:

(a) where the person upon whom the fine was imposed resides in Scotland, to the sheriff for the district where the person resides;

(b) where the person resides outwith Scotland, to the sheriff before whom he was brought for examination in relation to the offence for which the fine was imposed.[70]

Transfer of fine orders
1–92　Where a court has imposed a fine and it appears to the court charged with the enforcement of that fine that the offender is residing within the jurisdiction of another court of summary jurisdiction in Scotland, or in any petty sessions area in England or Wales, or in any petty sessions district in Northern Ireland, the court may order that payment of the fine is to be enforceable by that other court of summary jurisdiction or in that petty sessions area or district.[71] Such an order may be made notwithstanding that imprisonment has been imposed in default of payment of the fine.[72] A transfer of fine order must specify the court by which, or the petty sessions area or district in which, payment is to be enforceable. If a court is specified it must be a sheriff court where the transfer of fine order is itself made by a sheriff court.[73]

1–93　A fine imposed in England or Wales, or in Northern Ireland, may be transferred, under the Magistrates' Courts Act 1980 or the Magistrates'

---

[68] 1975 Act, s. 400(8).
[69] *Ibid.* ss. 196(1), 402(1).
[70] *Ibid.* s. 196(2).
[71] *Ibid.* s. 403(1).
[72] Criminal Law Act 1977, Sched. 7, para. 2.
[73] 1975 Act, s. 403(2).

Courts Act (Northern Ireland) 1964 as the case may be, for enforcement to a court of summary jurisdiction in Scotland, in which event that court has the same functions and powers as if the fine had been imposed by that court. However, in the event of imprisonment being imposed by the court in Scotland for default in payment, the period that may be imposed is to be that provided for in paragraph 1 of Schedule 4 to the Magistrates' Courts Act 1980 where the fine was originally imposed by a magistrates' court, and that provided for in section 31 of the Powers of Criminal Courts Act 1973 where the fine was originally imposed by a Crown Court.[74] In fact, since the passing of the 1980 Act the periods which may be imposed in Scotland have been the same as those competent under English legislation (see paragraph 1–97 below).

1–94   Where a transfer of fine order has been made as above the clerk of the court must send to the clerk of the court specified in the order a notice in a form prescribed by Act of Adjournal[75] together with any other relevant information relative to the fine.[76] The clerk of the court where the fine was originally imposed is to be kept informed of any further transfer of fine orders, and of any enforcement of the fine otherwise than by payment. Where any payment of the fine is received the clerk of the court specified in the transfer of fine order must remit or otherwise account for it to the clerk of the court by which the fine was imposed.[77] On receipt of a transfer of fine order the clerk of the receiving court must send intimation of the transfer to the offender in a form prescribed by Act of Adjournal.[78]

Default by a child in payment of a fine
1–95   Where a child would, if he were an adult, be liable to be imprisoned in default of payment of a fine, damages or expenses, the court may, if it considers that none of the other methods by which the case may legally be dealt with is suitable, order that the child be detained for a period not exceeding one month in a place chosen by the local authority in whose area the court is situated.[79] It is thought that this power is rarely used since, subsequent to the introduction of the children's hearing system under the Social Work (Scotland) Act 1968, very few children are prosecuted and, when they are, it is very unlikely that a fine would be a suitable disposal.

Imprisonment for non-payment of fine
1–96   Subject to sections 396 to 401 of the 1975 Act (see above):

(a) a court may, when imposing a fine, impose a period of imprisonment in default of payment; or
(b) where no such order has been made, and a person fails to pay a fine or any part or instalment of a fine by the time ordered, the court may impose a period of imprisonment for that failure,

---

[74] 1975 Act, s. 403(4) and (6).
[75] Act of Adjournal (Consolidation) 1988, para. 124, Forms 62 to 64.
[76] 1975 Act, s. 404(1).
[77] *Ibid.* s. 404(2) and (4).
[78] Act of Adjournal, above, Form 65.
[79] 1975 Act, s. 406.

whether or not the fine is imposed under an enactment which makes provision for its enforcement or recovery.[80]

1–97 The maximum period of imprisonment which may be imposed for such failure is as follows:

Amount of Fine	*Maximum Period of Imprisonment*
Not exceeding £50	7 days
Exceeding £50 but not exceeding £100	14 days
Exceeding £100 but not exceeding £400	30 days
Exceeding £400 but not exceeding £1,000	60 days
Exceeding £1,000 but not exceeding £2,000	90 days
Exceeding £2,000 but not exceeding £5,000	6 months
Exceeding £5,000 but not exceeding £10,000	9 months
Exceeding £10,000 but not exceeding £20,000	12 months
Exceeding £20,000 but not exceeding £50,000	18 months
Exceeding £50,000 but not exceeding £100,000	2 years
Exceeding £100,000 but not exceeding £250,000 ...	3 years
Exceeding £250,000 but not exceeding £1 million ..	5 years
Exceeding £1 million	10 years[81]

1–98 Where an offender is fined on the same day before the same court for offences charged in the same complaint or in separate complaints, the amount of the fine, for the purpose of fixing a period of imprisonment, is to be taken to be the total of the fines imposed.[82] This provision, introduced by the 1980 Act, substantially altered a summary court's powers of imprisonment in the event of default. Previously, when there were separate tables of maximum periods of imprisonment in respect of fines imposed summarily and on indictment, it was the case that, if an offender was being dealt with in respect of two or more complaints on the same day, any periods of imprisonment in default of payment should not cumulatively exceed the summary court maximum, which was 90 days.[83] The provision in section 407(1B) of the 1975 Act alters that rule by providing that, if, for example, a court on the same day imposes periods of imprisonment in respect of two fines of £1,500, for offences in separate complaints, the maximum period of imprisonment which can be imposed will be six months rather than 90 days.[84]

---

[80] 1975 Act, s. 407(1).

[81] *Ibid.* s. 407(1A). The Criminal Justice Act 1991 provides (s. 23(2)) a new table of maximum periods of imprisonment appropriate for fines of specified amounts. That Act is not yet in force.

[82] *Ibid.* s. 407(1B).

[83] See, for example, *Kesson* v. *Heatly*, 1964 J.C. 40.

[84] For further discussion of this, see para. 1–109 below.

1–99   Where a period of imprisonment has been imposed in default of payment of a fine and an instalment is not paid at the time ordered, or part only of the fine has been paid within the time allowed, the offender becomes liable to imprisonment for a period proportionate to the amount of the fine then outstanding.[85]

1–100   When a period of imprisonment is imposed subsequent to a default of payment of part of a fine, part having already been paid, the maximum period of imprisonment to be imposed should bear to the period that might have been imposed in respect of the whole fine the same proportion as the outstanding balance bears to the original fine.[86] The statutory provision in this regard is not very clearly expressed, but it is submitted that the foregoing represents its meaning. The provision was added by the 1980 Act presumably because, prior to that time, there was some uncertainty about whether, when imposing a period of imprisonment at a stage when part of a fine had already been paid, the court should state a period appropriate to the whole of the original fine, leaving it to administrative action to calculate the proportion thereof applicable to the unpaid balance, or do the calculation itself and state the period applicable only to that balance. It is now clear that the latter is the proper course.

1–101   If in any sentence or extract of sentence the period of imprisonment inserted in default of payment of a fine is in excess of that competent under the 1975 Act, such period is to be reduced to the maximum permissible; and the judge who pronounced the sentence has power to order the sentence or extract to be corrected accordingly.[87]

1–102   The statutory provisions relating to imprisonment for non-payment of fines contain an important exception to the general practice whereby all fines, whether imposed in a sheriff court or in the High Court, are to be enforced in the sheriff court. Where, in a case coming before a sheriff for imposition of imprisonment in default, he considers that the imposition of imprisonment for a period of three years (the maximum available to a sheriff under solemn jurisdiction) would be inadequate, and the maximum period of imprisonment available under section 407 (see paragraph 1–97 above) exceeds that number of years, he must remit the case to the High Court for sentence.[88] This restriction on the sheriff's own sentencing powers applies not only in respect of fines but also in respect of compensation orders and in respect of confiscation orders made under the Criminal Justice (Scotland) Act 1987.

1–103   All warrants of imprisonment for non-payment of a fine must specify a period at the expiry of which the person sentenced is to be discharged notwithstanding that the fine has not been paid.[89]

1–104   A person committed to prison or detention for failure to pay a fine may make payment to the governor of the prison of all or part of the outstanding amount due by him. If only part payment is made the term of imprisonment is to be reduced by the same proportion that the payment made bears to the amount outstanding when the period of imprisonment commenced. However, the day on which any sum is paid is not to be

---

[85] 1975 Act, s. 407(1C).
[86] *Ibid.* s. 407(1D).
[87] *Ibid.* s. 407(2).
[88] *Ibid.* s. 407(4).
[89] *Ibid.* s. 408.

regarded as a day served by the prisoner as part of his sentence.[90] This proviso avoids the former abuse whereby a fine defaulter could, at no inconsiderable public expense, spend only a few hours in prison and then secure his release by payment of a lesser amount than would have prevented his being taken to prison in the first place.

Consecutive sentences of imprisonment for non-payment of fines

1–105   From time to time questions may arise as to the competency of making terms of imprisonment for non-payment of fines consecutive to each other, or consecutive to direct sentences of imprisonment imposed at the same time, or consecutive to a period of imprisonment then being served. The statutory provisions in the 1975 Act do not by themselves clearly answer all such questions, and in some instances common law principles apply along with, or instead of, the statutory provisions. The law on this subject is now relatively clear, but it is the consequence of a period of rapid, and at times contradictory, development over the space of a very few years.

1–106   Where imprisonment in default is imposed at the same time as the imposition of a fine, and the offender is subsequently imprisoned on another matter and then asks the court to order the imprisonment in default to be served concurrently, that imprisonment may be ordered to be served consecutively but that must be done in open court in the presence of the offender.[91] In the case establishing the foregoing principle the High Court held that, in determining whether the period of imprisonment in default was to be concurrent or consecutive, the court was exercising a sentencing function, something which, in terms of section 433 of the 1975 Act,[92] requires a hearing in open court in the presence of the offender. The principle established in this case appears still to represent the law.

1–107   In contrast to the situation described in the foregoing paragraph, where imprisonment in default was ordered subsequent to the offender being imprisoned on another matter, it was at one stage held not to be competent to impose imprisonment in default and to order that it should be consecutive to the period of imprisonment then being served by the offender.[93] The basis for that proposition was that, while section 430(4) of the 1975 Act provides that a sentence of imprisonment may be framed so as to take effect on the expiry of any sentence the accused is undergoing at the time of his conviction, the definition of "sentence" in section 462(1) excludes an order for committal in default, and consequently section 430(4) does not apply in such a case (but see the next paragraph).

1–108   In *Cartledge* v. *McLeod*[94] it was held that, where a court is imposing imprisonment in default of payment of separate fines imposed on different days, it may order those periods to be served consecutively to

---

[90] 1975 Act, s. 409(1).
[91] *Campbell* v. *Jessop*, 1988 S.L.T. 160; 1987 S.C.C.R. 670. In this situation the position in England appears to be the same: *Re Hamilton and Another* [1981] 3 W.L.R. 79.
[92] "Every sentence imposed by a court of summary jurisdiction shall unless otherwise provided be pronounced in open court in the presence of the accused."
[93] *Cain* v. *Carmichael*, 1991 S.L.T. 442; 1990 S.C.C.R. 369 (a case dealing with the enforcement of a compensation order).
[94] 1988 S.L.T. 389, 1988 S.C.C.R. 129.

each other. Furthermore, if the court is at the same time imposing a direct sentence of imprisonment in respect of another matter, it may order that the consecutive periods of imprisonment imposed in default should also be consecutive to the direct sentence of imprisonment.[95] In reaching the foregoing conclusions the High Court noted that section 430(4) of the 1975 Act had no application because of the definition of "sentence" noted above. However, in *Cartledge* v. *McLeod* the challenge to the consecutive sentences had been founded solely on section 430(4), and the court did not find it necessary to express any more general views on the question of consecutive sentences. The whole matter was considered more widely in the later cases of *Young* v. *McGlennan*,[96] *Beattie* v. *McGlennan*,[97] and *Russell* v. *Macphail*.[98] As a result of these cases (the last of which was heard by a court of five judges) the law now appears to be that, although section 430(4) does not apply to imprisonment in default, the court has a common law power to impose consecutive periods of imprisonment which is not affected by the definition of "sentence" in section 462(1). Consequently, periods of imprisonment in default may be consecutive to each other and consecutive to a direct sentence of imprisonment being imposed on the same occasion or to a sentence of imprisonment already being served. Any such periods may cumulatively exceed a court's maximum sentencing powers in respect of a single complaint subject to a general test of fairness and equity.[99]

1–109   It is to be noted that the power to order periods of imprisonment in default to be consecutive to each other applies only where the fines in question were imposed on separate occasions on different days. Where the fines have been imposed on the same complaint, or on different complaints on the same day, the fines must be aggregated in order to determine the maximum period of imprisonment which is competent.[1]

1–110   The whole matter of consecutive sentences is quite complex, and is dealt with generally at paragraphs 7–50 to 7–66 below.

Supervised attendance orders

(1) Nature of supervised attendance orders

1–111   As an alternative to imprisonment in default of payment of a fine (but not a compensation order) a court may make a supervised attendance order.[2] Such an order is an order made by a court with the consent of an offender requiring him:

  (a) to attend a place of supervision for such time, being 10, 20, 30, 40, 50 or 60 hours, as is specified in the order; and

  (b) during that time to carry out such instructions as may be given to him by the supervising officer.[3]

---

[95] *Cartledge* v. *McLeod*, above.
[96] 1991 S.L.T. 375; 1990 S.C.C.R. 373.
[97] 1991 S.L.T. 384; 1990 S.C.C.R. 497.
[98] 1991 S.L.T. 449; 1990 S.C.C.R. 628.
[99] *Thomson* v. *Smith*, 1982 J.C. 40; 1982 S.L.T. 546; 1982 S.C.C.R. 57.
[1] 1975 Act, s. 407(1B); and see para. 1–98 above.
[2] 1990 Act, s. 62(1).
[3] *Ibid.* s. 62(2). The number of hours may be amended by order of the Secretary of State: 1990 Act, Sched. 6, para. 1(3) and (4).

1–112   A supervised attendance order may be made only in certain circumstances. These are where:

(a) the offender is of or over 16 years of age; and
(b) having been convicted of an offence, he has had imposed on him a fine which (or any part or instalment of which) he has failed to pay and either of the following subparagraphs applies—
  (i) the court, prior to the date when section 62 of the 1990 Act comes into force, has imposed on him a period of imprisonment under section 407(1)(*a*) of the 1975 Act but he has not served any of that period of imprisonment;
  (ii) the court, but for this provision, would also have imposed on him a period of imprisonment under section 407(1)(*a*) or (*b*); and
(c) the court considers a supervised attendance order more appropriate than the serving of or, as the case may be, imposition of such a period of imprisonment.[4]

Where a supervised attendance order is made in the circumstances set out in (i) above, the making of that order has the effect of discharging the sentence of imprisonment imposed on the offender.[5]

1–113   For the purposes of the foregoing, "place of supervision" means such place as may be determined by the supervising officer, and "supervising officer" means a person appointed or assigned by the local authority whose area includes the locality in which the offender resides or will be residing when the order comes into force.[6]

(2) Further requirements as to supervised attendance orders
1–114   A court is not to make a supervised attendance order unless:

(a) it has been notified by the Secretary of State that arrangements exist for persons who reside in the locality in which the offender resides, or will be residing when the order comes into force, to carry out the requirements of such an order;
(b) it is satisfied that provision can be made under the above arrangements for the offender to carry out such requirements.[7]

1–115   Before making a supervised attendance order the court must explain to the offender in ordinary language:

(a) the purpose and effect of the order and in particular the obligations on the offender as specified in paragraph 1–119 below;
(b) the consequences, as set out in paragraph 1–120 below, which may follow if he fails to comply with any of those requirements; and
(c) that the court has the power to review the order on the application either of the offender or of an officer of the local authority in whose area the offender for the time being resides[8] (see paragraph 1–122 below).

---

[4] 1990 Act, s. 62(3).
[5] *Ibid.* s. 62(4).
[6] *Ibid.* s. 62(6).
[7] *Ibid.* Sched. 6, para. 1(1).
[8] *Ibid.* para. 1(2).

1–116   A supervised attendance order must:

(a) specify the locality in which the offender resides or will be residing when the order comes into force; and

(b) require the local authority in whose area the locality specified as above is situated to appoint or assign a supervising officer.[9]

1–117   Where, whether on the same occasion or on separate occasions, an offender is made subject to more than one supervised attendance order, the court may direct that the requirements specified in any of those orders are to be concurrent with or additional to those specified in any other of those orders. However, at no time should the offender have an outstanding number of hours during which he must carry out the requirements of those orders in excess of the largest number specified in section 62(2)(*a*) of the 1990 Act[10] (see paragraph 1–111 above).

1–118   Upon making a supervised attendance order the court must:

(a) give a copy of the order to the offender;

(b) send a copy of the order to the director of social work of the local authority in whose area the offender resides or will be residing when the order comes into force; and

(c) where it is not the appropriate court, send a copy of the order (together with such documents and information relating to the case as are considered useful) to the clerk of the appropriate court.[11]

(3) Obligations on offender and operation of order

1–119   An offender in respect of whom a supervised attendance order is in force must report to the supervising officer and notify him without delay of any change of address or in the times, if any, at which he usually works.[12] Instructions given under a supervised attendance order must be carried out during the period of 12 months beginning with the date of the order. Unless revoked, however, the order will remain in force until the offender has carried out the instructions given under it for the number of hours specified therein.[13] The instructions given by the supervising officer must, so far as practicable, be such as to avoid any conflict with the offender's religious beliefs and any interference with the times, if any, at which he normally works or attends a school or other educational establishment.[14]

(4) Breach of supervised attendance order

1–120   If, at any time while a supervised attendance order is in force in respect of any offender, it appears to the appropriate court, on evidence on oath from the supervising officer, that that offender has failed to comply with

---

[9] 1990 Act, Sched. 6, para. 2(1).

[10] *Ibid.* para. 2(2).

[11] *Ibid.* para. 2(3). "Appropriate court" means the court having jurisdiction in the locality for the time being specified in the order, being a sheriff or district court according to whether the order has been made by a sheriff or a district court, but in a case where the order has been made by a district court and there is no district court in that locality, the sheriff court: 1990 Act, Sched. 6, para. 9(1).

[12] *Ibid.* para. 3(1).

[13] *Ibid.* para. 3(2).

[14] *Ibid.* para. 3(3).

any of the requirements specified in paragraph 1–119 above or of the order (including any failure satisfactorily to carry out any instructions which he has been given by the supervising officer under the order), the court may issue a warrant for the arrest of that offender, or may, if it thinks fit, instead of issuing a warrant in the first instance issue a citation requiring the offender to appear before that court at such time as may be specified in the citation.[15]

1–121   If it is proved to the satisfaction of the court before which an offender is brought or appears under the foregoing procedure that he has failed without reasonable excuse to comply with any of the requirements mentioned above, the court may:

   (a) revoke the order and impose such period of imprisonment as could, in respect of the original default or failure, have been imposed by the court which made the order if the order had not been made; or
   (b) subject to the maximum number permitted under the Act, vary the number of hours specified in the order.[16]

For the foregoing purposes the evidence of one witness is to be sufficient evidence.[17]

(5) Variation of supervised attendance order

1–122   Where a supervised attendance order is in force in respect of any offender and, on the application of that offender or of the supervising officer, it appears to the appropriate court that it would be in the interests of justice to do so, having regard to circumstances which have arisen since the order was made, the court may:

   (a) extend, in relation to the order, the period of 12 months specified in paragraph 1–119 above;
   (b) subject to the maximum number permitted under the Act, vary the number of hours specified in the order;
   (c) revoke the order; or
   (d) revoke the order and impose such period of imprisonment as could, in respect of the original default or failure, have been imposed by the court which made the order if the order had not been made.[18]

1–123   If the appropriate court is satisfied that the offender proposes to change, or has changed, his residence from the locality for the time being specified in the order to another locality and

   (a) the court has been notified by the Secretary of State that arrangements exist for persons who reside in that other locality to carry out instructions under supervised attendance orders; and
   (b) it appears to that court that provision can be made under those arrangements for him to carry out instructions under the order;

that court may, and on application of the supervising officer must, amend

---

[15] 1990 Act, Sched. 6, para. 4(1).
[16] *Ibid.* para. 4(2).
[17] *Ibid.* para. 4(3).
[18] *Ibid.* para. 5(1).

the order by substituting that other locality for the locality for the time being specified in the order.[19]

1–124   Where the court proposes to exercise its powers under heads (a), (b) or (d) as set out in paragraph 1–122 above otherwise than on the application of the offender, it must issue a citation requiring him to appear before the court and, if he fails to appear, may issue a warrant for his arrest.[20]

(6) General comment on supervised attendance orders

1–125   Supervised attendance orders are a new means of trying to ensure that fewer offenders are imprisoned for non-payment of fines. For the moment the way in which they will be used in practice remains to be seen. However, some possible difficulties suggest themselves at once.

1–126   First, it is uncommon for a court to impose a term of imprisonment in the event of default at the time when a fine is imposed, and it may be assumed that it will be equally uncommon for a court to make a supervised attendance order at that stage in the event of future default. What is much more common is for a court, at the means inquiry stage, to allow further time for payment of a fine and at the same time to order a term of imprisonment in the event of further default.[21] It may be questionable whether, at that stage, a court will wish to make a supervised attendance order, rather than ordering a term of imprisonment, in the event of further default if only because many courts are likely, it is thought, to take the view that a threat of future imprisonment is more likely to secure payment of the fine than a threat of having to comply with a supervised attendance order. If that is right, it may be that supervised attendance orders will be little used in practice. It would, of course, be possible for courts, at the means inquiry stage, to allow further time for payment without imposing any alternative in the event of further default so that the alternatives of imprisonment or a supervised attendance order could be considered later should that become necessary. However, it is thought that courts may be reluctant to follow that course since it is likely to result in a significant increase in their workload.

1–127   A second feature of supervised attendance orders which is worth noting is that the statute offers no guidance as to the circumstances in which such an order is to be preferred to the imposition of a term of imprisonment. It merely states that it may be made where the court considers it "more appropriate."[22] No doubt the gravity of the offence, the offender's age and record, and the amount of the fine will be factors which a court will take into account, but in practice other factors may emerge as equally important. It may be that a practice will develop whereby courts will call for social inquiry reports at the enforcement stage (though the statute is silent about that); and in that event social factors peculiar to the offender may also come to be taken into account.

1–128   A final feature of supervised attendance orders which falls to be noted

---

[19] 1990 Act, Sched. 6, para. 5(2).
[20] *Ibid.* para. 5(3).
[21] A practice which has, as it were, been officially reinstated by virtue of the amendment to s. 407(1)(*b*) of the 1975 Act contained in the 1990 Act, Sched. 8, para. 27(3): see para. 1–83 above.
[22] 1990 Act, s. 62(3)(*c*).

is that the statute offers no guidance as to the circumstances in which a particular number of hours out of those specified in section $62(2)(a)$[23] ought to be selected. In relation to imprisonment in default courts are familiar with the statutory table[24] which indicates the maximum periods of imprisonment which may be imposed for non-payment of fines of differing amounts, but no comparable guidance is offered in relation to the range of hours, from 10 to 60, which may be ordered in supervised attendance orders. This suggests that, unless the High Court is given, and is prepared to take, the opportunity to set parameters and guidelines, there may be a considerable amount of disparity in the way in which the provisions are applied in different courts.

Recovery of fine by deductions from income support

1-129   Section 24 of the Criminal Justice Act 1991 empowers the Secretary of State to provide by regulations that, where a fine or compensation order has been imposed on an offender and that offender is entitled to income support, the court may apply to the Secretary of State asking him to deduct sums from any amounts payable to the offender by way of income support towards payment of the fine or compensation order. At the time of writing, the provisions of section 24 are not yet in force.

Recovery of fine by civil diligence

1-130   A court may order recovery of a fine by civil diligence. This may be ordered at any time after a fine has been imposed, including after imprisonment in default of payment has been ordered, provided that imprisonment has not in fact taken place.[25] Equally, imprisonment may be imposed at a later stage notwithstanding that recovery by civil diligence has previously been ordered.[26] Prior to 1980 that was incompetent but the provision in section 411 of the 1975 Act which had that effect was repealed by the 1980 Act. Of course, when imprisonment is ordered at a later stage, that order will not be carried into effect if the civil diligence is effective in producing payment of the fine, or if the fine is otherwise paid.

1-131   Where civil diligence is ordered the extract of the sentence should include a warrant for execution in the following terms: "and the sheriff [or justice(s)] grant(s) warrant for all lawful execution hereon."[27] That has the effect of authorising the charging[28] of the offender to pay the fine within the period specified in the charge and, in the event of failure to make such payment within that period, the execution of an earnings arrestment and a poinding. It also authorises an arrestment other than an arrestment of earnings in the hands of the offender's employer.[29] Any such diligence, whatever the amount of the fine, may be executed in the

---

[23] See para. 1–111 above.
[24] See para. 1–97 above.
[25] 1975 Act, s. 411(1) and (3).
[26] 1980 Act, s. 52.
[27] Act of Adjournal (Consolidation) 1988, para. 126A.
[28] For style of charge, see Act of Adjournal above, Form 36A.
[29] 1975 Act, s. 411(1).

same manner as if the proceedings were on an extract decree of the sheriff in a summary cause.[30]

1–132   Civil diligence is the only means of recovering a fine imposed in proceedings taken against a company, association, incorporation or body of trustees.[31] However, it has been little used against individuals partly because, until the passing of the 1980 Act, a decision to recover in this way was final and could not be followed by the imposition of imprisonment, even if the diligence was unsuccessful. No doubt, also, the cumbersome state of the Scots law of diligence which existed for many years contributed to the court's reluctance to use this method of recovery. There was also some stern, if elderly, judicial disapproval. In the case of *Moffat* v. *Shaw*[32] Lord McLaren laid down a principle for the guidance of judges in the inferior courts. In that case a question arose as to the use of civil diligence in place of imprisonment in a case under the Vaccination Act 1863. His lordship stated: "In the enforcement of the penalty the statute requires that the more humane and effective alternative of imprisonment for a short period should be adopted in preference to the civil remedy of poinding, which might be ruinous to a poor man." Given that there is now a widespread feeling that fine defaulters should not be imprisoned unless that is absolutely necessary, it seems likely that Lord McLaren's views would find little favour today. Indeed, the availability of earnings arrestments, under the Debtors (Scotland) Act 1987, as a means of recovering fines from offenders who are in employment seems likely to make recovery by civil diligence more, rather than less, attractive in some cases.

Persons to whom fines are to be paid

1–133   Any fine imposed in the High Court is payable to H.M. Exchequer.[33] Otherwise, all fines and expenses are to be paid to the clerk of court, to be accounted for by him to the person entitled to them.[34] However, where a warrant has been issued for the apprehension of an offender for non-payment of a fine, he may pay the fine in full to a police constable; and in that event the warrant will not be enforced, and the constable is obliged to remit the fine to the clerk of court.[35] Similarly, any part payment of a fine made to the governor of a prison under section 409 of the 1975 Act must be remitted by him to the clerk of the court in which the conviction was obtained.[36]

CAUTION

1–134   Summary courts have power on convicting of a common law offence to ordain an offender to find caution for good behaviour for any period not exceeding 12 months in the case of the sheriff court, and six months in the case of the district court. This may be ordered in lieu of, or in addition to,

---

[30] 1975 Act, s. 411(1).
[31] *Ibid.* s. 333.
[32] (1896) 2 Adam 57.
[33] 1975 Act, s. 203.
[34] *Ibid.* s. 412.
[35] *Ibid.* s. 401(3).
[36] *Ibid.* Sched. 7.

imprisonment or a fine. The maximum amount of caution which may be required is an amount not exceeding, in the case of the district court, level 4 on the standard scale (at present £1,000) and, in the case of the sheriff court, the prescribed sum (at present £2,000).[37]

1–135   Imprisonment in accordance with section 407 of the 1975 Act may be imposed for failure to find caution,[38] but since caution is not mentioned in section 400 of the 1975 Act it would seem that a supervision order pending payment is not competent. Caution may be found by consignation of the amount with the clerk of court, or by bond of caution which may be signed by the mark of the cautioner. Where caution becomes liable to forfeiture, that may be granted by the court on the motion of the prosecutor and, where necessary, warrant may be granted for its recovery. In the event of the cautioner failing to pay the amount due under his bond within six days of receiving a charge to that effect, the court may order him to be imprisoned for the maximum period applicable under section 407 of the 1975 Act, or may grant time for payment, or may order recovery by civil diligence.[39] "Good behaviour" is not defined in the Act, but in practice it is generally taken to mean no more than refraining from committing further offences. Consequently, forfeiture will generally be ordered only where the offender has committed a further offence during the relevant period. Because of the current delays in many courts in bringing cases to trial, difficulties can arise if an offence alleged to have been committed during the relevant period is not to be the subject of a trial until after that period has expired. It is submitted that, in such a case, the court would be entitled, where consignation had taken place, to retain the sum concerned until the outcome of the trial became known.

1–136   When caution is to be found other than by way of a bond of caution similar procedures apply as in the case of fines to the allowance of time for payment, and recovery in the event of non-payment. However, no provision is made for the payment of caution by instalments, and accordingly that is not competent: the full amount of caution must be paid at one time.

COMPENSATION ORDERS

1–137   Where a person is convicted of an offence a court, except when granting an absolute discharge or making a probation order or deferring sentence, instead of or in addition to dealing with the offender in any other way, may make a compensation order requiring him to pay compensation for any personal injury, loss or damage caused (whether directly or indirectly) by the acts which constituted the offence.[40] In solemn proceedings there is no limit to the amount of such an order.[41] In summary proceedings a sheriff or stipendiary magistrate may make a compensation order in respect of each offence to an amount not

---

[37] 1975 Act, ss. 284, 289; but see prospective changes to the standard scale and to the prescribed sum in Criminal Justice Act 1991, s. 17.

[38] *Ibid.* ss. 284(*d*), 289(*c*).

[39] *Ibid.* s. 303.

[40] 1980 Act, s.58(1). For discussion of the use of compensation orders see para. 10–50 *et seq.* below.

[41] *Ibid.* s. 59(2).

exceeding the prescribed sum (at present £2,000). The limit in the case of the district court is level 4 on the standard scale (at present (£1,000).[42]

1–138   Where, in the case of an offence involving the dishonest appropriation, or the unlawful taking and using, of property or a contravention of section 175(1) of the Road Traffic Act 1972,[43] the property is recovered, but has been damaged while out of the owner's possession, that damage (however and by whomsoever it was in fact caused) is to be treated for the purpose of making a compensation order as having been caused by the acts which constituted the offence.[44]

1–139   In two cases a compensation order may not be made. These are:

(a) in respect of loss suffered in consequence of the death of any person, and
(b) in respect of injury, loss or damage due to an accident arising out of the presence of a motor vehicle on a road, except such damage as is treated, as under paragraph 1–138 above, as having been caused by the convicted person's acts.[45]

1–140   As is made clear by the statutory provisions,[46] a compensation order is competent in respect of injury or damage caused *indirectly* by the acts which constituted the offence. Thus, it has been held that such an order is competent against a shopkeeper who unlawfully sold fireworks to a young boy who was subsequently injured when one of the fireworks was lit by a friend.[47] It also appears to be competent to make a compensation order where the victim has died prior to the making of the order, provided he had sustained personal loss prior to his death.[48] However, a compensation order is not appropriate in respect of an offence of violence in circumstances where, by reason of his own conduct, a complainer would not be entitled to compensation from the Criminal Injuries Compensation Board[49]: and a compensation order is not competent in respect of alarm caused by a breach of the peace since alarm alone does not sound in damages.[50]

1–141   Given the provision[51] that a compensation order may be made "instead

---

[42] 1980 Act, s. 59(3). The Criminal Justice Act 1991 has prospectively increased the amount of the prescribed sum and the maximum fines under the standard scale (s. 17). When that Act is brought into force the prescribed sum will be £5,000, and level 4 on the standard scale will be £2,500.

[43] Section 175(1) of the 1972 Act has now been replaced by section 178(1) of the Road Traffic Act 1988. The Road Traffic (Consequential Provisions) Act 1988, which contains all the amending provisions consequential upon the consolidation of road traffic legislation in 1988, contains no provision to update the reference to the 1972 Act in section 58(2) of the 1980 Act. It is submitted, however, that courts would be entitled to apply the latter provision in the case of contraventions of the corresponding provision in the Road Traffic Act 1988 given the general provisions which are contained in section 2 of the Road Traffic (Consequential Provisions) Act.

[44] 1980 Act, s. 58(2).

[45] *Ibid.* s. 58(3).

[46] *Ibid.* s. 58(1).

[47] *Carmichael* v. *Siddique*, 1985 S.C.C.R. 145 (a sheriff court decision).

[48] *Tudhope* v. *Furphy*, 1984 S.L.T. (Sh.Ct.) 33; 1982 S.C.C.R. 575.

[49] *Brown* v. *Normand*, 1988 S.C.C.R. 229; but see *McPhail* v. *Hamilton*, 1991 G.W.D. 24–1375.

[50] *Smillie* v. *Wilson*, 1990 S.L.T. 582; 1990 S.C.C.R. 133.

[51] 1980 Act, s. 58(1).

of or in addition to" any other sentence, it is plainly competent to combine such an order with a sentence of imprisonment, and this has been approved by the High Court both tacitly and explicitly.[52] It is thought, however, that there could be a problem in relation to enforcement if a compensation order were to be made in addition to the maximum sentence of imprisonment for the offence[53] since, in a case[54] where the maximum sentence of imprisonment was imposed on one charge on a complaint and a fine on another, it was held to be incompetent to impose further imprisonment in default of payment of the fine since the court's maximum power of imprisonment in respect of the complaint had already been exhausted. There seems to be no reason why the same principle should not apply in respect of imprisonment and a compensation order in respect of the same offence.[55] In *Fraser* v. *Herron*, however, it was observed that in the circumstances the fine could have been recoverable by civil diligence.

1–142   In determining whether to make a compensation order against any person and in determining the amount of any such order, the court must take into consideration that person's means so far as known to the court. However, where the person is serving, or is to serve, a period of imprisonment or detention, no account is to be taken, in assessing such means, of earnings contingent upon his obtaining employment after release.[56] Where a court considers that it would be appropriate to impose a fine and to make a compensation order, but the convicted person has insufficient means to pay both, the court should prefer a compensation order.[57]

1–143   Where a person has been both fined and had a compensation order made against him in respect of the same offence or different offences in the same proceedings, the compensation order takes precedence over the fine in respect of payments made by the offender.[58] Payments under a compensation order are to be made to the clerk of court who has to account for them to the person entitled thereto, but only the court has power to enforce compensation orders.[59] The provisions of the 1975 Act relative to the payment, remission, transfer and enforcement of fines apply, subject to any necessary modifications, to compensation orders. However, a court may impose imprisonment in respect of a fine and decline to impose imprisonment in respect of a compensation order, but not vice versa, and, where a court imposes imprisonment in respect of both a fine and a compensation order the amounts are to be aggregated for the purpose of calculating the maximum period allowed.[60]

---

[52] *Clark* v. *Cardle*, 1989 S.C.C.R. 92; *Collins* v. *Lowe*, 1990 S.C.C.R. 605.

[53] As happened in *Clark* v. *Cardle* above, though the problem did not emerge there since, on appeal, the High Court quashed the compensation order.

[54] *Fraser* v. *Herron*, 1968 J.C. 1.

[55] But see *Beattie* v. *H.M. Advocate*, 1986 S.C.C.R. 605, and see para. 10–54 *et seq.* below.

[56] 1980 Act, s. 59(1). Notwithstanding the prohibition in this subsection against taking account of post-imprisonment earnings, it appears to be competent to take account of the likely amount of benefits which the offender will receive after his release: see *Collins* v. *Lowe*, 1990 S.C.C.R. 605.

[57] *Ibid.* s. 61.

[58] *Ibid.* s. 62.

[59] *Ibid.* s. 60.

[60] *Ibid.* s. 66.

1–144   At any time before a compensation order has been complied with or fully complied with a court of summary jurisdiction in Scotland to which the order has been transferred, or the court which made the order, or (where that court was the High Court) the appropriate sheriff court, may, on the application of the offender, discharge the compensation order or reduce the amount that remains to be paid. This may be done if it appears to the court either that the injury, loss or damage has been held in civil proceedings to be less than it was taken to be for the purposes of the order, or that property, the loss of which was reflected in the order, has been recovered.[61] This provision does not appear to allow a court to discharge or reduce the amount of a compensation order where the injury, loss or damage turns out, otherwise than in civil proceedings, to be less than it was taken to be for the purposes of the order.

COMMUNITY SERVICE ORDERS

Nature and making of community service orders

1–145   In addition to empowering courts, when making a probation order, to include a condition that the offender should perform a number of hours of unpaid work,[62] the Community Service by Offenders (Scotland) Act 1978 also gives power in certain circumstances to make community service orders which stand on their own and do not form part of a probation order.

1–146   Where a person of or over 16 years of age is convicted of an offence punishable by imprisonment, other than an offence the sentence for which is fixed by law, the court, instead of imposing on him a sentence of, or including, imprisonment or any other form of detention, may make an order, referred to as "a community service order," requiring him to perform unpaid work for such number of hours (being in total not less than 40 nor more than 240) as may be specified in the order.[63] A court must not make a community service order in respect of any offender unless:

(a) the offender consents;

(b) the court has been notified by the Secretary of State that arrangements exist for persons who reside in the locality in which the offender resides, or will be residing when the order comes into force, to perform work under such an order;

(c) the court is satisfied, after considering a report by an officer of a local authority about the offender and his circumstances, and, if the court thinks it necessary, hearing that officer, that the offender is a suitable person to perform work under such an order; and

(d) the court is satisfied that provision can be made under the arrangements mentioned in (b) above for the offender to perform work under such an order.[64]

---

[61] 1980 Act, s. 64.

[62] See paras. 1–18 to 1–21 above.

[63] 1978 Act, s. 1(1), as amended by 1990 Act, s. 61(3). Where a person is being sentenced in respect of two complaints on the same day, it is competent to impose detention in respect of one complaint and to order community service in respect of the other: *McQueen* v. *Lockhart*, 1986 S.C.C.R. 20.

[64] *Ibid.* s. 1(2).

A copy of the report mentioned in (c) above must be supplied to the offender or his solicitor.[65]

1–147   Before making a community service order the court must explain to the offender in ordinary language:

(a) the purpose and effect of the order and in particular the obligations on the offender as specified in section 3 of the Act[66];
(b) the consequences which may follow under section 4 of the Act if he fails to comply with any of those requirements[67];
(c) that the court has, under section 5 of the Act,[68] the power to review the order on the application either of the offender or of an officer of the local authority in whose area the offender for the time being resides.[69]

1–148   The Secretary of State may by order amend the minimum and maximum number of hours specified in paragraph 1–146 above, and may specify a different maximum or minimum number of hours for different classes of case.[70] Any such order is subject to positive resolution by both Houses of Parliament.[71]

1–149   The making of a community service order does not affect the court's power, at the same time: (a) to impose any disqualification on an offender; (b) to make an order for forfeiture in respect of the offence; and (c) to order the offender to find caution for good behaviour.[72]

1–150   A community service order must:

(a) specify the locality in which the offender resides or will be residing when the order comes into force;
(b) require the local authority in whose area the locality specified is situated to appoint or assign an officer (referred to in the Act as "the local authority officer") who will discharge the functions assigned to him by the Act; and
(c) state the number of hours of work which the offender is required to perform.[73]

1–151   Where, whether on the same occasion or on separate occasions, an offender is made subject to more than one community service order, or to both a community service order and a probation order which includes a requirement that the offender is to perform unpaid work, the court may direct that the hours of work specified in any of those orders shall be concurrent with or additional to those specified in any other of those orders. At no time, however, must the offender have an outstanding number of hours of work to perform in excess of the maximum provided for in section 1(1) of the Act.[74]

---

[65] 1978 Act, s. 1(3).
[66] See paras. 1–153 and 1–154 below.
[67] See paras. 1–155 and 1–156 below.
[68] See paras. 1–157 and 1–158 below.
[69] 1978 Act, s. 1(4).
[70] *Ibid.* s. 1(5).
[71] *Ibid.* s. 1(6).
[72] *Ibid.* s. 1(7).
[73] *Ibid.* s. 2(1).
[74] *Ibid.* s. 2(2).

1–152   Upon making a community service order the court must:

(a) give a copy of the order to the offender;

(b) send a copy of the order to the director of social work of the local authority in whose area the offender resides or will be residing when the order comes into force; and

(c) where it is not the appropriate court,[75] send a copy of the order (together with such documents and information relating to the case as are considered useful) to the clerk of the appropriate court.[76]

Where there is an appeal against conviction in a case where the court has made a community service order, it is not competent to suspend the community service order pending the hearing of the appeal.[77]

Obligations on the offender

1–153   An offender in respect of whom a community service order is in force must:

(a) report to the local authority officer and notify him without delay of any change of address or in the times, if any, at which he usually works; and

(b) perform for the number of hours specified in the order such work at such times as the local authority officer may instruct.[78]

1–154   Subject to section 5(1) of the Act (see paragraph 1–157 below), the work required to be performed under a community service order must be performed during the period of 12 months beginning with the date of the order. Unless revoked, however, the order will remain in force until the offender has worked under it for the number of hours specified in it.[79] The instructions given by the local authority officer in relation to the work must, so far as practicable, be such as to avoid any conflict with the offender's religious beliefs and any interference with the times, if any, at which he normally works or attends a school or other educational establishment.[80]

Failure to comply with requirements of order

1–155   If at any time while a community service order is in force it appears to the appropriate court, on evidence on oath from the local authority officer, that the offender has failed to comply with any of the requirements set out in paragraphs 1–153 and 1–154 above (including any failure satisfactorily to perform the work which he has been instructed to do), that court may issue a warrant for the arrest of that offender, or may,

---

[75] "Appropriate court" means (a) where the relevant community service order has been made by the High Court, the High Court; (b) in any other case the sheriff or district court having jurisdiction in the relevant locality according to whether the order was made by the sheriff or district court but, where there is no district court in the locality, the sheriff court: 1978 Act, s. 12(1).

[76] 1978 Act, s. 2(3).

[77] *Farmer* v. *Guild*, 1991 S.C.C.R. 174.

[78] 1978 Act, s. 3(1).

[79] *Ibid.* s. 3(2). Work under an order can be required after the expiry of 12 months only where that period has been extended in terms of section 5(1)(*a*) of the 1978 Act: *H.M. Advocate* v. *Hood*, 1987 S.C.C.R. 63.

[80] *Ibid.* s. 3(3).

if it thinks fit, instead of issuing a warrant in the first instance issue a citation requiring that offender to appear before that court at such time as may be specified in the citation.[81]

1–156   If it is proved[82] to the satisfaction of the court before which an offender appears or is brought that he has failed without reasonable excuse to comply with any of the requirements of section 3 of the Act, that court may:

(a) without prejudice to the continuance in force of the order, impose on him a fine not exceeding level 3 on the standard scale (at present £400);

(b) revoke the order and deal with the offender in any manner in which he could have been dealt with for the original offence by the court which made the order if the order had not been made; or

(c) subject to the restrictions on the minimum and maximum number of hours that may be ordered, vary the number of hours specified in the order.[83]

Amendment and revocation of orders

1–157   Where a community service order is in force in respect of any offender and, on the application of that offender or of the local authority officer, it appears to the appropriate court that it would be in the interests of justice to do so, having regard to circumstances which have arisen since the order was made, that court may:

(a) extend, in relation to the order, the period of 12 months specified in paragraph 1–154 above;

(b) subject to the restrictions on the minimum and maximum number of hours that may be ordered, vary the number of hours specified in the order;

(c) revoke the order; or

(d) revoke the order and deal with the offender for the original offence in any manner in which he could have been dealt with for that offence by the court which made the order if the order had not been made.[84]

Where the court proposes to exercise its powers under head (a), (b) or (d) of the above provisions otherwise than on the application of the offender, it must issue a citation requiring him to appear before the court and, if he fails to appear, may issue a warrant for his arrest.[85]

1–158   If the appropriate court is satisfied that the offender proposes to change, or has changed, his residence from the locality for the time being specified in the order to another locality and:

---

[81] 1978 Act, s. 4(1).

[82] As in the 1975 Act in relation to failure to comply with requirements under a probation order, the 1978 Act is also silent about how and by whom a failure is to be proved. Once again procurators fiscal usually come to the rescue. See para. 1–45 above. It is to be noted that the evidence of one witness is sufficient evidence for the purposes of section 4(2): 1978 Act, s. 4(3), added by 1990 Act, Sched. 8, para. 28.

[83] 1978 Act, s. 4(2). It is not competent to pass sentence under s. 4(2)(*b*) unless the principal complaint is before the court: *O'Brien* v. *Dowdells*, 1991 S.C.C.R. 912.

[84] *Ibid.* s. 5(1).

[85] *Ibid.* s. 5(3).

(a) that court has been notified by the Secretary of State that arrangements exist for persons who reside in that other locality to perform work under community service orders; and

(b) it appears to that court that provision can be made under those arrangements for him to perform work under the order;

that court may, and on the application of the local authority officer must, amend the order by substituting that other locality for the locality for the time being specified in the order.[86]

Persons resident in England or Wales

1–159   Where a court is considering the making of a community service order under section 1(1) of the 1978 Act and it is satisfied that the offender has attained the age of 16 years and resides, or will be residing when the order comes into force, in England or Wales, it may make an order but it must be satisfied as to the following. First, where the offender is under the age of 17 years, it must have been notified by the Secretary of State that arrangements exist for persons of the offender's age who reside in the petty sessions area in which the offender resides, or will be residing when the order comes into force, to perform work under community service orders made under section 14 of the Powers of Criminal Courts Act 1973. Second, it must appear to the court that provision can be made for the offender to perform work under the order under the arrangements which exist in the petty sessions area in which he resides or will be residing for persons to perform work under community service orders made under section 14 of the above Act of 1973. The order must specify that the unpaid work is to be performed under the above arrangements.[87]

1–160   Where a community service order has been made in respect of an offender who is resident in Scotland, and the appropriate court is satisfied that the offender has attained the age of 16 years and proposes to reside, or is residing, in England or Wales, the court may amend the order to the same effect, and subject to the same conditions, as an order made in the manner described in the foregoing paragraph.[88]

1–161   A community service order made in accordance with the procedure described in paragraph 1–159 above, or amended in accordance with the procedure described in paragraph 1–160 above, must specify the petty sessions area in England or Wales in which the offender resides or will be residing when the order or amendment comes into force. Additionally, it must require the probation committee for that area to appoint or assign a probation officer who will discharge in respect of the order the functions in respect of community service orders conferred on relevant officers by the Powers of Criminal Courts Act 1973.[89]

Persons resident in Northern Ireland

1–162   Where a court is considering the making of a community service order

---

[86] 1978 Act, s. 5(2).
[87] *Ibid*. s. 6(1). The Criminal Justice Act 1991 contains provisions (Sched. 3, para. 8) which, when they come into force, will make certain amendments to s. 6 of the 1978 Act. What is stated here, however, represents the position prior to the passing of the 1991 Act.
[88] *Ibid*. s. 6(2).
[89] *Ibid*. s. 6(2A).

under section 1(1) of the 1978 Act and it is satisfied that the offender has attained the age of 17 years and resides, or will be residing when the order comes into force, in Northern Ireland, then, without having to receive any notification from the Secretary of State as to the existence of appropriate arrangements, it may make the order. It must, however, appear to the court that provision can be made by the Probation Board for Northern Ireland for the offender to perform work under such an order. The order must specify that the unpaid work required to be performed by the order is to be performed under the provision made by the Probation Board for Northern Ireland.[90]

1–163   Where a community service order has been made under section 1(1) of the 1978 Act in respect of an offender who is resident in Scotland, and the appropriate court is satisfied that the offender has attained the age of 17 years and proposes to reside or is residing in Northern Ireland, the court may amend the order by specifying that the unpaid work required to be performed by the order is to be performed under provision made by the Probation Board for Northern Ireland. Before such amendment is made it must appear to the court that provision can be made by the Probation Board for Northern Ireland for the offender to perform work under the order.[91]

1–164   A community service order made or amended in accordance with the procedure described in paragraphs 1–162 and 1–163 above must specify the petty sessions district in Northern Ireland in which the offender resides or will be residing when the order or amendment comes into force. Additionally, it must require the Probation Board for Northern Ireland to select an officer who will discharge, in respect of the order, the functions in respect of community service orders conferred on the relevant officer by the Treatment of Offenders (Northern Ireland) Order 1976.[92]

General provisions relating to community service orders in respect of offenders residing in England or Wales or Northern Ireland

1–165   Where a community service order is made or amended in the circumstances described in paragraphs 1–159 to 1–164 above the court making or amending the order should send three copies of it, as made or amended, to what is described as the "home court," together with such documents and information relating to the case as it considers likely to be of assistance to that court.[93]

1–166   "Home court" means, if the offender resides in England or Wales, or will be residing there at the relevant time, the magistrates' court acting for the petty sessions area in which he resides or proposes to reside, and, if he resides in Northern Ireland, or will be residing there at the relevant time, the court of summary jurisdiction acting for the petty sessions district in which he resides or proposes to reside. In this context "the relevant time" means the time when the order or the amendment to it comes into force.[94]

---

[90] 1978 Act, s. 6A(1).
[91] *Ibid.* s. 6A(2).
[92] *Ibid.* s. 6A(3).
[93] *Ibid.* s. 6B(1).
[94] *Ibid.* s. 6B(2).

1–167   Subject to what is stated in paragraphs 1–168 to 1–171 below, a community service order made or amended in the circumstances described in paragraphs 1–159 to 1–164 above is to be treated as if it were a community service order made in the part of the United Kingdom in which the offender resides, or will be residing, at the relevant time. The legislation relating to community service orders which has effect in that part of the United Kingdom is to apply accordingly.[95] So far as England and Wales are concerned this means that the Powers of Criminal Courts Act 1973 will apply; and in relation to Northern Ireland the relevant legislation is the Treatment of Offenders (Northern Ireland) Order 1976.

1–168   Before making or amending a community service order in the above circumstances the court must explain to the offender in ordinary language:

   (a) the requirements of the legislation relating to community service orders which have effect in the part of the United Kingdom in which he resides or will be residing at the relevant time;
   (b) the powers of the home court under that legislation, as modified by section 6B of the 1978 Act; and
   (c) its own powers under that section.

An explanation in accordance with the foregoing will be sufficient without the addition of an explanation under section 1(4) of the 1978 Act.[96]

1–169   Subject to three exceptions noted below the home court may exercise in relation to the community service order any power which it could exercise in relation to a community service order made by a court in the same part of the United Kingdom, by virtue of the legislation having effect in that part of the United Kingdom. The powers which are excepted from this are:

   (a) the power to vary the order by substituting for the number of hours' work specified in it any greater number than the court which made the order could have specified;
   (b) the power to revoke the order; and
   (c) the power to revoke the order and deal with the offender for the offence in respect of which it was made in any manner in which he could have been dealt with for that offence by the court which made the order if the order had not been made.[97]

1–170   In certain circumstances the home court may require an offender who is subject to a community service order to appear before the court by which the order was made. These circumstances are, first, where it appears to the home court, on information or complaint made to a justice of the peace, that the offender has failed to comply with any of the requirements of the legislation applicable to the order; or, second, where it appears to the home court, on the application of the offender or the relevant officer under the Powers of Criminal Courts Act 1973 or the Treatment of Offenders (Northern Ireland) Order 1976, that it would be

---

[95] 1978 Act, s. 6B(3).
[96] *Ibid.* s. 6B(4).
[97] *Ibid.* s. 6B(5).

in the interests of justice to exercise the power under (b) or (c) in paragraph 1–169 above.[98]

1–171 Where an offender is so required to appear before a court which made a community service order, that court may issue a warrant for his arrest, and may exercise any power which it could exercise in respect of the community service order if the offender resided in the part of the United Kingdom where the court has jurisdiction.[99]

Community service orders made or amended by courts in England or Wales or Northern Ireland in respect of offenders resident in Scotland

1–172 Schedule 13 to the Criminal Justice Act 1982 (Parts I and III) makes detailed provision for cases where a court in England or Wales or Northern Ireland makes or amends a community service order in respect of an offender who resides or proposes to reside in Scotland. Apart from necessary modifications this provision is in the same terms and to the same effect as the provisions described in paragraphs 1–159 to 1–171 above.[1]

---

[98] 1978 Act, s. 6B(6).

[99] *Ibid.* s. 6B(7).

[1] Those provisions have been prospectively amended by the Criminal Justice Act 1991 (Sched. 3, para. 3).

CUSTODIAL DISPOSALS

Introduction

2–01 With the exception of the rarely used power enjoyed by a summary court to order detention in the precincts of a court or in legalised police cells,[1] the only custodial sentence for persons of the age of 21 or over is now imprisonment. The only custodial sentence for persons who are not less than 16 but under 21 years of age is detention. The obsolescent sentences of preventive detention and corrective training were finally swept away by the 1980 Act,[2] and specific types of imprisonment, namely penal servitude and imprisonment with hard labour, had previously been abolished by the Criminal Justice (Scotland) Act 1949.[3] Any enactment conferring a power to pass a sentence of penal servitude or imprisonment with hard labour is to be construed as conferring power to pass a sentence of imprisonment for a term not exceeding the term for which a sentence of the former kind could have been passed prior to June 12, 1950: but this is not to be construed as permitting a court other than the High Court to pass a sentence of imprisonment for a term exceeding three years.[4]

---

[1] See paras. 2–06 and 2–07 below.
[2] S. 83(3) and Sched. 8.
[3] S. 16: now 1975 Act, s. 221.
[4] 1975 Act, s. 221(1) and (2).

MAXIMUM SENTENCES

High Court

2–02 Except where otherwise provided by a particular statute under which an accused is convicted, the High Court has no upper limit to its power to impose imprisonment or detention, and it may impose a sentence of any determinate period, or for life. Apart from the life sentence no other indeterminate sentence is competent. A person convicted of murder, unless he is under the age of 21,[5] must be sentenced to imprisonment for life.[6] On sentencing any person convicted of murder a judge may make a recommendation as to the minimum period which should elapse before, under section 26 of the Prisons (Scotland) Act 1989, the Secretary of State releases that person on licence.[7] When making such a recommendation the judge must state his reasons for so recommending.[8] Notwithstanding the proviso to section 228(1) of the 1975 Act, such a recommendation may be made the subject of an appeal, and may be dealt with on appeal in the same manner as any other sentence.[9] Where a person is already serving a sentence of life imprisonment, and is sentenced to a determinate period of imprisonment in respect of a subsequent offence, it is inappropriate to make that latter sentence consecutive to the sentence of life imprisonment.[10]

Sheriff court under solemn jurisdiction

2–03 The maximum period of imprisonment or detention which may be imposed on indictment in the sheriff court is three years.[11] However, if the sheriff holds that any competent sentence which he can impose is inadequate so that the question of sentence is appropriate for the High Court, there is a power of remit to that court for sentence.[12]

Sheriff court under summary jurisdiction

2–04 A sheriff, when sitting summarily, has power on convicting a person of a common law offence to impose imprisonment for any period not exceeding three months.[13] Where that power is exercised it is incompetent to impose a fine in addition.[14] The above period of three months may be increased to six months where a person is convicted of (a) a second or subsequent offence inferring dishonest appropriation of property, or attempt thereat, or (b) a second or subsequent offence inferring personal violence.[15] It is to be noted that the statute refers to conviction of a second or subsequent offence, and not to a second or subsequent conviction. Consequently, it is submitted, a court would not

---

[5] See para. 2–09 below.
[6] 1975 Act, s. 205(1).
[7] *Ibid.* s. 205A(1).
[8] *Ibid.* s. 205A(2).
[9] *Ibid.* s. 205A(3). Generally, on appeals against sentence, see Chap. 8.
[10] *McRae* v. *H.M. Advocate*, 1987 S.C.C.R. 36; *McPhee* v. *H.M. Advocate*, 1990 S.C.C.R. 313.
[11] 1975 Act, s. 2(2).
[12] *Ibid.* s. 104(1); and see para. 7–35 *et seq.* below for the procedure to be followed.
[13] *Ibid.* s. 289(d).
[14] *McGunnigal* v. *Copeland*, 1972 S.L.T. (Notes) 70.
[15] 1975 Act, s. 290.

be entitled to impose a sentence of more than three months' imprisonment on a second conviction if the offence to which that conviction related was earlier in date than the offence which was the subject of the first conviction. A charge of breach of the peace, even where it involves threats of violence and malicious damage, is not an offence inferring personal violence for the above purpose,[16] nor are the offences of possession of an offensive weapon and reckless discharge of an air pistol.[17] Where, in the case of a summary statutory offence, a statute provides for a different maximum penalty on a first and on a subsequent conviction, the maximum penalty available is the maximum available on any conviction.[18] Thus, for example, the maximum penalty for both the first and any subsequent conviction for a contravention of section 41 of the Police (Scotland) Act 1967 (obstruction, *etc.*, of police officers) is now nine months' imprisonment.

District court

2–05   A district court has power on convicting a person of a common law offence to impose imprisonment for any period not exceeding 60 days.[19] The same limit applies in relation to statutory offences, and it is not competent for a statutory offence to be tried in the district court where the maximum penalty which may be imposed for that offence exceeds 60 days' imprisonment or a fine of level 4 on the standard scale.[20]

DETENTION IN PRECINCTS OF COURT

2–06   Where a court of summary jurisdiction has power to impose imprisonment on an offender it may, in lieu of so doing, order that he be detained within the precincts of the court or at any police station till such hour, not later than eight in the evening, on the day on which he is convicted, as the court may direct. Before making such an order the court must take into consideration the distance between the proposed place of detention and the offender's residence (if known to, or ascertainable by, the court) and must not make any such order as would deprive the offender of a reasonable opportunity of returning to his residence on the day on which the order is made.[21] It is believed that this power is little, if at all, used, and its contemporary usefulness may be doubted.

NO IMPRISONMENT FOR LESS THAN FIVE DAYS

2–07   No person may be sentenced to imprisonment by a court of summary jurisdiction for a period of less than five days.[22] Where a court of summary jurisdiction has power to impose imprisonment on an offender it may sentence the offender to be detained, for such period not exceeding four

---

[16] *Adair* v. *Morton*, 1972 S.L.T. (Notes) 70.
[17] *Sharp* v. *Tudhope*, 1986 S.C.C.R. 64.
[18] 1975 Act, s. 289E.
[19] *Ibid.* s. 284.
[20] 1980 Act, s. 7(1).
[21] 1975 Act, s. 424.
[22] *Ibid.* s. 425(1).

days as the court thinks fit, in what are known as legalised police cells.[23] The main purpose of this provision is to ensure that, mainly in the more remote areas, prisoners can be detained in secure conditions for periods before, during, and after a trial. As a short custodial sentence it is thought that detention in legalised police cells is little used. It may not be used in the case of females unless provision is made for their supervision by female officers.[24]

CONSIDERATION OF TIME SPENT IN CUSTODY

2–08 A court, in passing a sentence of imprisonment or detention on a person for any offence, must, in determining the period of imprisonment or detention, have regard to any period of time spent in custody by that person on remand awaiting trial or sentence.[25]

YOUNG OFFENDERS

Sentence for murder

2–09 Where a person convicted of murder is under the age of 18 years he must not be sentenced to imprisonment for life but should be sentenced to be detained without limit of time. When so sentenced he is liable to be detained in such place, and under such conditions, as the Secretary of State may direct.[26] Where a person convicted of murder has attained the age of 18 years but is under the age of 21 years he must not be sentenced to imprisonment for life but should be sentenced to be detained in a young offenders' institution. Such a person is liable to be detained for life.[27] The power to make a recommendation in relation to a person convicted of murder as to the minimum period which should elapse before the Secretary of State releases that person on licence applies equally to young offenders as it does to adult offenders.[28]

Sentence in cases other than murder

2–10 It is not competent to impose imprisonment on a person under 21 years of age.[29] A sentence of detention is the only competent custodial sentence which may be imposed on a person who is not less than 16 but under 21 years of age. Detention (whether by way of sentence or otherwise) may be imposed where, but for the above prohibition, the court would have power to impose a period of imprisonment. The period of such detention must not exceed the maximum period of imprisonment which might otherwise have been imposed.[30] The slightly obscure phrase "whether by way of sentence or otherwise" seems to take account of the definition of "sentence" in the 1975 Act[31] and distinguishes between a period of

---

[23] 1975 Act, s. 425(2) to (4).
[24] *Ibid.* s. 425(5).
[25] *Ibid.* ss. 218, 431: for a discussion of the effect of this provision, commonly referred to as backdating, see para. 7–67 *et seq.* below.
[26] *Ibid.* s. 205(2).
[27] *Ibid.* s. 205(3).
[28] *Ibid.* s. 205A; and see para. 2–02 above.
[29] *Ibid.* ss. 207(1) and 415(1).
[30] *Ibid.* ss. 207(2) and 415(2).
[31] *Ibid.* s. 462(1).

detention imposed under a direct sentence in respect of a crime or offence and a period of detention imposed in default of payment of any sum of money or for contempt of court.

2–11   Detention, whether upon a direct sentence, or in default of payment of a sum of money, or for contempt of court, must not be imposed unless the court is of the opinion that no other method of dealing with the person is appropriate: and the court must state its reasons for that opinion and, except in the case of the High Court, those reasons must be entered in the record of proceedings.[32] To enable the court to form such an opinion it must obtain (from an officer of a local authority or otherwise) such information as it can about the offender's circumstances. It must also take into account any information before it concerning the offender's character and physical and mental condition.[33] In practice this means that a court must at least obtain a social inquiry report before imposing a sentence of detention, and may also find it advisable to obtain a report as to the offender's suitability for a community service order. Information obtained only from the Crown or the defence is probably not sufficient.[34] The court is obliged to consider anything contained in a social inquiry report, but is not obliged to follow any recommendations therein.[35] A sentence of detention imposed as above means a sentence of detention in a young offenders' institution.[36]

Recall to young offenders' institution on reconviction

2–12   Where a person who has been sentenced to detention under either section 207 or section 415 of the 1975 Act, and who is under supervision following on his release, is convicted of an offence punishable with imprisonment, the court may make an order for his recall. This power is not available where the person is subject to a licence granted under section 60(1) or section 61 of the Criminal Justice Act 1967 or section 22(1) or section 26 of the Prisons (Scotland) Act 1989.[37] Any such order for recall has the like effect as an order for recall made by the Secretary of State under section 32 of the Prisons (Scotland) Act 1989, that is to say the recall may be for a period not exceeding three months.[38] It is thought that courts rarely, if ever, make use of this power preferring, if a custodial sentence is to be imposed, to impose a direct sentence of detention for whatever period seems appropriate.

RESTRICTIONS ON PASSING SENTENCES OF IMPRISONMENT OR DETENTION

Imprisonment of person not previously so dealt with

2–13   A court must not pass a sentence of imprisonment on a person of or over 21 years of age who has not been previously sentenced to imprisonment

---

[32] 1975 Act, ss. 207(3) and 415(3); *Dunsmore* v. *Allan*, 1991 S.C.C.R. 946.
[33] *Ibid*. ss. 207(4) and 415(4).
[34] *Auld* v. *Herron*, 1969 J.C. 4.
[35] *Scott* v. *MacDonald*, 1961 S.L.T. 257; *Kyle* v. *Cruickshank*, 1961 J.C. 1; *Hogg* v. *Heatlie*, 1962 S.L.T. 39.
[36] 1975 Act, ss. 207(5) and 415(5).
[37] *Ibid*. ss. 212(1) and 421(1). For a description of parole and licence law and practice, see para. 2–23 *et seq*. below.
[38] *Ibid*. ss. 212(2) and 421(2).

or detention by a court in any part of the United Kingdom unless the court considers that no other method of dealing with him is appropriate. For the purpose of determining whether any other method of dealing with such a person is appropriate the court must obtain (from an officer of a local authority or otherwise) such information as it can about the offender's circumstances. It must also take into account any information before it concerning the offender's character and physical and mental condition.[39]

2–14   The foregoing provisions replaced prior legislation restricting the imprisonment of first offenders, and now restrict the imprisonment of any adult, whether a first offender or not, who has not previously been sentenced to imprisonment or detention. It is to be noted that the restriction applies where a court is passing a *sentence* of imprisonment, and where the offender has not previously been *sentenced* to imprisonment or detention. The definition of "sentence" in the 1975 Act is applied to the 1980 Act,[40] and consequently the restriction does not apply where imprisonment is being imposed in default of payment of a sum of money or for contempt of court, but does apply where any previous imprisonment or detention was imposed for either of these reasons.[41] A possible difficulty may be thought to arise where a person has not been sentenced to imprisonment or detention prior to the date of the current offence, so that any schedule of previous convictions does not disclose such a sentence, but it transpires that he has subsequently received such a sentence, and may indeed still be serving it at the date in question. It is submitted that the wording of section 42(1) is such that its restrictions would not apply in such a case since the reference to a previous sentence of imprisonment is not restricted in any way as to the date of that sentence save that it must be previous to the new sentence being imposed. It might nonetheless be wise, where a person is presently serving a sentence of imprisonment or detention, for the court to ascertain whether or not that sentence, or the conviction to which it relates, is under appeal and, if it is, to proceed as if section 42(1) did apply; for, if the appeal were to be successful, it could be argued that the spirit if not the letter of the section had not been taken into account in the later case.

2–15   Where a court of summary jurisdiction passes a sentence of imprisonment on any person to whom the above restrictions apply, the court must state the reason for its opinion that no other method of dealing with him is appropriate, and must have that reason entered in the record of the proceedings.[42]

2–16   For the purpose of determining whether a person has been previously sentenced to imprisonment or detention by a court in any part of the United Kingdom the court should (a) disregard a previous sentence of imprisonment which, having been suspended, has not taken effect under

---

[39] 1980 Act, s. 42(1); and see para. 2–11 above and cases referred to therein.

[40] *Ibid.* s. 81(2).

[41] See observations on the purpose of the 1975 Act definition of "sentence" in *Russell* v. *MacPhail*, 1991 S.L.T. 449; 1990 S.C.C.R. 628. Those observations were made in relation to s. 41 of the 1980 Act (see para. 2–18 *et seq.* below), but it is submitted that they also apply *mutatis mutandis* in respect of s. 42.

[42] 1980 Act, s. 42(2).

section 23 of the Powers of Criminal Courts Act 1973 or under section 19 of the Treatment of Offenders Act (Northern Ireland) 1968; and (b) construe detention as meaning (i) in relation to Scotland, detention in a young offenders' institution or detention centre, (ii) in relation to England and Wales, a sentence of youth custody, borstal training or detention in a young offenders' institution or detention centre, and (iii) in relation to Northern Ireland, detention in a young offenders' centre.[43] The absence of any reference in (i) above to borstal training would seem to imply that a previous sentence of borstal training in Scotland is not to be taken as a previous sentence of detention with the result that in such a case the court would be bound to comply with the restrictions imposed by section 42(1) of the 1980 Act.

2–17   The foregoing restrictions do not affect the power of a court to pass sentence on any person for an offence the sentence for which is fixed by law.[44]

Imprisonment or detention of person not legally represented

2–18   A court must not pass a sentence of imprisonment or of detention in respect of any offence, nor impose imprisonment or detention under section 396(2) of the 1975 Act in respect of failure to pay a fine, on an accused who is not legally represented in that court and has not been previously sentenced to imprisonment or detention by a court in any part of the United Kingdom,[45] unless the accused either (a) applied for legal aid and the application was refused on the ground that he was not financially eligible, or (b) having been informed of his right to apply for legal aid, and having had the opportunity, failed to do so.[46] To satisfy the foregoing requirements it is not enough merely to ask an accused if he wishes the services of a solicitor: he must be advised of his right to apply for legal aid.[47]

2–19   Section 396(2) of the 1975 Act provides for the situation where, on the occasion of the imposition of a fine, a court refuses time to pay and imposes imprisonment or detention when the offender fails to pay. The above restriction, accordingly, does not apply in any other circumstances where a court imposes imprisonment or detention in default of payment of a fine.[48]

2–20   As with the restriction on imprisoning persons not previously sentenced to imprisonment or detention, the above restriction does not affect the power of a court to pass sentence on any person for an offence the sentence for which is fixed by law.[49]

2–21   In relation to the above restriction "legal aid" means legal aid for the purposes of any part of the proceedings before the court, and "legally represented" means represented by counsel or a solicitor at some stage

---

[43] 1980 Act, s. 41(2) as applied by s. 42(3).
[44] *Ibid.* s. 41(3) as applied by s. 42(3).
[45] These words have the meaning described in para. 2–16 above.
[46] 1980 Act, s. 41(1).
[47] *Milligan* v. *Jessop*, 1988 S.C.C.R. 137.
[48] See comment in para. 2–14 above, and in note 41 thereto.
[49] 1980 Act, s. 41(3).

after the accused is found guilty and before he is dealt with by the passing of a sentence of, or by the imposition of, imprisonment or detention.[50]

CHILDREN

2–22 The subjects of children, and the imposition of custodial sentences on children, are dealt with in Chapter 4.

PAROLE AND RELEASE ON LICENCE

2–23 Parole, which is a method by which a person serving a sentence of imprisonment or detention may be released, under specified conditions, to serve part of that sentence under supervision in the community, was introduced simultaneously in England and Wales, and in Scotland, by the Criminal Justice Act 1967.[51] Under that Act the Parole Board for Scotland was created, whose duty it is to advise the Secretary of State on those cases which may be suitable for release on licence. The board must consist of a chairman and not less than four other members.

2–24 The consequence of the present parole arrangements is, briefly, that those serving determinate sentences become eligible for release on licence after they have completed one third of their sentence or one year, whichever is the longer period. If released on parole such persons remain on licence, and subject to recall, until the date when they would otherwise have been released with remission of sentence. Those who have been sentenced to life imprisonment may be released on licence by the Secretary of State on the recommendation of the Parole Board and after consultation with the Lord Justice-General and, if he is still available, the trial judge. Such persons remain on licence for the remainder of their lives.

2–25 Current arrangements for parole in Scotland were reviewed in 1988 and 1989 by a committee under the chairmanship of Lord Kincraig, and many of that committee's recommendations[52] have since been accepted by government.[53] It is therefore likely that there may be substantial changes to parole arrangements in Scotland in the near future.

---

[50] 1980 Act, s. 41(4).
[51] Ss. 59 to 62; now replaced for Scotland by Prisons (Scotland) Act 1989, ss. 22 to 26.
[52] *Parole and Related Issues in Scotland*, 1989, Cm. 598.
[53] *Parole and Related Issues in Scotland*, S.H.H.D., July, 1990.

MENTALLY DISORDERED OFFENDERS

Duty on prosecutor—remit to sheriff court

3–01 Where it appears to the prosecutor in any court before which a person is charged with an offence that the person may be suffering from mental disorder, the prosecutor must bring before the court such evidence as may be available of the mental condition of that person.[1] If the person is charged before a court of summary jurisdiction other than a sheriff court, and the offence charged is one punishable with imprisonment, then, if it appears to the court that the person may be suffering from mental disorder, he must be remitted to the sheriff court in the manner provided by section 286 of the 1975 Act.[2] Mental disorder means mental illness or mental handicap however caused or manifested.[3] However, no person is to be treated under the Mental Health (Scotland) Act 1984 as suffering from mental disorder by reason only of promiscuity or other immoral conduct, sexual deviancy or dependence on alcohol or drugs.[4]

Remand in hospital

3–02 Where a court remands or commits for trial a person charged with any offence who appears to the court to be suffering from mental disorder, and the court is satisfied that a hospital is available for his admission and suitable for his detention, the court may, instead of remanding him in custody, commit him to that hospital.[5] Such an order may only be made on the written or oral evidence of a medical practitioner.[6] No provision is made, however, requiring that medical practitioner to possess any special qualification under the Mental Health (Scotland) Act 1984.[7] When such

---

[1] 1975 Act, ss. 175(2), 376(5).
[2] *Ibid.* s. 376(4); and see *Herron* v. *McCrimmon*, 1969 S.L.T. (Sh.Ct.) 37.
[3] 1984 Act, s. 1(2).
[4] *Ibid.* s. 1(3).
[5] 1975 Act, ss. 25(1), 330(1); for remands other than for trial, see para. 7–19 *et seq.* below.
[6] *Ibid.* ss. 25(4), 330(4).
[7] *Cf.* para. 3–11 below.

an order is made the hospital must be specified in the warrant and, if the responsible medical officer is satisfied that the person concerned is suffering from mental disorder of a nature or degree which warrants his admission to a hospital under Part V of the 1984 Act,[8] he must be detained there for the period for which he is remanded or the period of committal, unless previously liberated in due course of law.[9] When the responsible medical officer has examined the person so detained he must report the result of that examination to the court. If the report is to the effect that the person is not suffering from mental disorder of the above nature or degree the court may commit him to any appropriate prison or other institution or otherwise deal with him according to law.[10] The responsible medical officer is any medical practitioner on the staff of the hospital authorised to act as such by the board of management.[11]

Insanity

(a) In bar of trial

3–03   Insanity at the time of a trial is a bar to the trial taking place if the effect of the insanity is to render the accused unfit either to tender a rational plea, or properly to instruct his defence.[12] It is outwith the scope of this work to examine what may or may not amount to insanity in any particular case. However, the procedures which may lead up to a disposal in a case of insanity in bar of trial fall to be mentioned.

3–04   The plea of insanity in bar of trial is normally taken by the defence, in which case it should be intimated as a special defence.[13] It may, however, be put in issue by the prosecutor, or by the court itself. There is authority[14] that the question whether or not an accused is capable of pleading may be left to the jury, but the normal practice is for the court to conduct an inquiry before the accused is called on to plead. If, as a result of that inquiry, the court concludes that an accused is fit to plead, it is not then competent to put that matter to a jury.[15] Evidence at a preliminary inquiry is normally led from two or more psychiatrists who have each independently examined the accused. Where it appears to a court that it is

---

[8] In general, a person may be admitted under Part V of the Act on the grounds that (a) he is suffering from mental disorder of a nature or degree which makes it appropriate for him to receive treatment in a hospital, and (i) in the case where the mental disorder from which he suffers is a persistent one manifested only by abnormally aggressive or seriously irresponsible conduct, such treatment is likely to alleviate or prevent a deterioration of his condition, or (ii) in the case where the mental disorder from which he suffers is a mental handicap, the handicap comprises mental impairment (where such treatment is likely to alleviate or prevent a deterioration of his condition) or severe mental impairment; and (b) it is necessary for the health or safety of that person or for the protection of other persons that he should receive such treatment and it cannot be provided unless he is detained under Part V of the Act (1984 Act, s. 17(1)). A previous distinction between patients over and under the age of 21 no longer applies.

[9] 1975 Act, ss. 25(2), 330(2).

[10] *Ibid.* ss. 25(3), 330(3).

[11] *Ibid.* s. 462(1); 1984 Act, ss. 59(1), 125.

[12] Hume, ii.143; Macdonald, *Criminal Law*, 5th ed., pp. 9, 10, 271; Gordon, *Criminal Law*, 2nd ed., paras. 10–42 *et seq.*; and see *H.M. Advocate* v. *Brown* (1907) 5 Adam 312.

[13] *H.M. Advocate* v. *Brown*, above; *H.M. Advocate* v. *Cunningham*, 1963 J.C. 80; and see *Ross* v. *H.M. Advocate*, 1991 S.L.T. 564, 1991 S.C.C.R. 823.

[14] *H.M. Advocate* v. *Brown*, above.

[15] *Russell* v. *H.M. Advocate*, 1946 J.C. 37.

not practicable or appropriate for the accused to be brought before it for the purpose of determining whether he is insane in bar of trial, the court may order that the case be proceeded with in his absence provided that no objection to such a course is taken by or on behalf of the accused.[16]

3–05   Where any person charged on indictment is found insane so that the trial cannot proceed, or if in the course of the trial it appears to the jury that he is insane, the court must direct a finding to that effect to be recorded.[17] In such a case the court must then order that the person concerned is to be detained in a state hospital, or such other hospital as for special reasons the court may specify.[18] Such an order has the same effect as a hospital order under section 175 of the 1975 Act (see below) together with a restriction order restricting the person's discharge, made without limitation of time.[19] The restriction order will remain in force until the restriction is removed by the Secretary of State. He must be satisfied that the restriction is no longer required for the protection of the public from serious harm.[20]

3–06   In general the rules relating to insanity in bar of trial apply equally to a person charged summarily in the sheriff court.[21] Where the court is satisfied that the person is insane so that his trial cannot proceed, the court must direct a finding to that effect, and the reasons for that finding, to be recorded. The court then deals with the person by the making of a hospital order under section 376(2) of the 1975 Act.[22] It is not competent for a person to found on a plea of insanity in bar of trial unless, before the first witness for the prosecution is called, he gives notice to the prosecutor of the plea and of the witnesses by whom he proposes to maintain it. Upon such notice being given the court must, if the prosecutor so moves, adjourn the case.[23] A summary court has the same power as a court of solemn jurisdiction to inquire into an accused person's sanity in his absence (see para. 3–04 above).[24]

3–07   A person who has been found insane in bar of trial, and has been dealt with accordingly, has not thereby tholed his assize. Should he recover his sanity he may again be put on trial.[25]

(b) At the time of commission of the offence

3–08   When a person is charged on indictment and is found to have committed the act libelled, but to have been insane at the time, he may not be convicted. The jury should be directed to find whether the person

---

[16] 1975 Act, ss. 174(5), 375(4).
[17] *Ibid.* s. 174(1); but see *H.M. Advocate* v. *Brown and Foss*, 1966 S.L.T. 341.
[18] *Ibid.* s. 174(3).
[19] *Ibid.* s. 174(4).
[20] 1984 Act, s. 68(1).
[21] 1975 Act, s. 375(1).
[22] *Ibid.* s. 375(2); *Barr* v. *Herron*, 1968 J.C. 20; *Bain* v. *Smith*, High Court, 19 February 1980. The provisions of section 375 were not altered by amendments made to mental health legislation in the 1980s, and in particular the direction in section 375(2) requiring the court to deal with a person in the manner provided by section 376(2) was not amended. The effect appears to be to preclude a court from making an interim hospital order under section 375A (see below) notwithstanding that, under section 376(7) a state hospital may be specified in a hospital order under that section.
[23] *Ibid.* s. 375(3).
[24] *Ibid.* s. 375(4).
[25] *H.M. Advocate* v. *Bickerstaff*, 1926 J.C. 65.

was insane at the time, and to declare whether the person has been acquitted by them on account of that insanity.[26] If insanity at the time of commission of the offence is being founded on by the accused he must lodge a special defence to that effect.[27] Where a jury declares that it has acquitted a person on account of his insanity at the time of committing the offence, the court should proceed in the same manner as if the accused had been found insane in bar of trial, that is by ordering his detention in a state hospital, or such other hospital as for special reasons the court may specify.[28]

3–09 Curiously, there are no express statutory provisions to deal with the case where a person is charged summarily in the sheriff court and is found to have committed the act alleged but to have been insane at the time. Section 376(3) of the 1975 Act provides that, where a person is so charged and the court would have power on convicting him to make an order under section 376(1) (a hospital or guardianship order), then, if the court is satisfied that the person did the act charged, it may, if it thinks fit, make such an order without convicting him. This has been construed[29] as meaning that, if a court is satisfied that an offender committed the act charged, but was insane at the time, it should acquit him and proceed to make a hospital or guardianship order. It is submitted that this interpretation of section 376(3) is not really tenable. The section makes no mention of insanity, and in particular makes no mention of insanity at the time of commission of an offence. In so far as it deals with any form of mental disorder it does so only in respect of an offender who is suffering from mental disorder at the time when he appears for trial and sentence. Furthermore, to make an order "without convicting" a person is not the same as to acquit that person.[30]

3–10 It is submitted, accordingly, that there is no statutory provision to deal with the situation where an accused person in a summary prosecution establishes that he was insane at the time of commission of the alleged offence but is sane by the date of the trial. Nor, it is also submitted, has there ever been any such statutory provision. The provisions to be found in the Lunatics (Scotland) Act 1857, the Criminal Justice (Scotland) Act 1949, and the Mental Health (Scotland) Acts 1960 and 1984 all relate to cases on indictment only and are silent with regard to summary procedure. Inquiries through the Crown Office suggest that the normal practice in cases where it is known that a defence of insanity at the time of commission of the offence is likely to be put forward (and they are very rare) is either to take no proceedings at all or, if it appears to be in the public interest, to proceed by way of petition. There is no statutory provision requiring a defence of insanity at the time of commission of the offence to be intimated before a trial begins.[31] In such a case, if the

---

[26] 1975 Act, s. 174(2); *H.M. Advocate* v. *Mitchell*, 1951 J.C. 53.

[27] *H.M. Advocate* v. *Cunningham*, 1963 J.C. 80; and see *Ross* v. *H.M. Advocate*, 1991 S.L.T. 564, 1991 S.C.C.R. 823.

[28] 1975 Act, s. 174(3).

[29] Renton and Brown, *Criminal Procedure*, para. 20–17.

[30] Compare, for example, the statutory provisions relating to absolute discharge and probation in the 1975 Act, ss. 383, 384.

[31] Compare 1975 Act, ss. 339 and 375(3); and see *Lambie* v. *H.M. Advocate*, 1973 J.C. 53. See, also, para. 8–91 below.

defence were established, a question would arise as to how the case should be disposed of. It is submitted that the proper course would simply be to find the accused not guilty on the ground that his insanity prevented him from having the necessary *mens rea*. In the absence of statutory provision it would not be competent to proceed to make any kind of hospital order.[32]

Hospital orders and guardianship orders

3–11   Where a person is convicted in the High Court or the sheriff court of an offence, other than an offence the sentence for which is fixed by law, punishable by that court with imprisonment, the court may, subject to certain conditions, make an order (a "hospital order") authorising his admission to and detention in such hospital as may be specified in the order, or place him under the guardianship of such a local authority or such other person approved by a local authority as may be so specified (a "guardianship order"). The conditions are:

(a) the court must be satisfied, on the written or oral evidence of two medical practitioners, that the grounds set out in section 17(1) or, as the case may be, the ground set out in section 36(*a*) of the 1984 Act apply in relation to the offender. (The provisions of section 17(1) are set out in footnote 8 to paragraph 3–02 above.) Section 36(*a*) provides, in relation to reception into guardianship, that a person may be received into guardianship on the grounds that he is suffering from mental disorder of a nature or degree which warrants his reception into guardianship; and

(b) the court must be of the opinion, having regard to all the circumstances, including the nature of the offence and the character and antecedents of the offender, and to the other available methods of dealing with him, that the most suitable method of disposing of the case is by means of such an order.[33]

Of the two medical practitioners at least one must be approved for the purposes of section 20 or section 39 of the 1984 Act by a health board as having special experience in the diagnosis or treatment of mental disorder.[34] The power to make an order is exercisable by the High Court in cases remitted to it from the sheriff court as well as in cases originating in that court.[35] A hospital order should not be made unless the court is satisfied that the hospital in question is available for the person's admission within 28 days of the making of such an order.[36] Similarly, a guardianship order should not be made unless the court is satisfied that the local authority, or any other person involved, is willing to receive the

---

[32] This approach was followed in *Smith* v. *M.*, 1984 S.L.T. (Sh.Ct.) 28; 1983 S.C.C.R. 67. Although that case supports the present author's views, the time has probably come when Parliament ought to clear up this area of uncertainty.

[33] 1975 Act, ss. 175(1), 376(1). Written or oral evidence given for the purposes of section 175(1)(*a*) or section 376(1)(*a*) must include a statement as to whether the person giving the evidence is related to the accused and of any pecuniary interest which that person may have in the admission of the accused to hospital or his reception into guardianship (1975 Act, ss. 176(1A), 377(1A)).

[34] *Ibid.* ss. 176(1), 377(1).

[35] *Ibid.* s. 175(1).

[36] *Ibid.* ss. 175(3), 376(6).

offender into guardianship. Additionally, a guardianship order should not be made unless the court is satisfied, after taking into consideration the evidence of a mental health officer, that it is necessary in the interests of the welfare of the person that he should be placed under guardianship.[37]

3–12   A state hospital should not be specified in a hospital order unless the court is satisfied that the offender, on account of his dangerous, violent or criminal propensities, requires treatment under conditions of special security, and cannot suitably be cared for in a hospital other than a state hospital. Evidence to that effect must be given by the medical practitioners whose evidence is taken into account when deciding whether or not to make a hospital order.[38] An order for admission to a state hospital may be made in an interim hospital order, or may follow after the making of such an order (see para. 3–16 *et seq.* below).

3–13   A hospital order or guardianship order must specify the form of mental disorder, being mental illness or mental handicap or both, from which the offender is found by the court to be suffering. No such order may be made unless the offender is described by each of the medical practitioners whose evidence is taken into account as suffering from the same form of mental disorder, whether or not he is also described by either of them as also suffering from another form.[39]

3–14   Where a hospital order or guardianship order is made the court may not pass sentence of imprisonment (which includes any sentence or order for detention), or impose a fine or make a probation or a community service order. It may, however, make any other order which it would otherwise have power to make.[40] That is to say, it may, for example, make an order for forfeiture of an article, or for disqualification from holding or obtaining a driving licence.

3–15   The court by which a hospital order is made may give such directions as it thinks fit for the conveyance of the patient to a place of safety and his detention therein pending his admission to the hospital within the period of 28 days mentioned above. However, a direction for the conveyance of a patient to a residential establishment provided by a local authority under Part IV of the Social Work (Scotland) Act 1968 must not be given unless the court is satisfied that the authority is willing to receive the patient therein.[41]

Interim hospital orders

3–16   Provision exists in certain circumstances for the making of interim hospital orders. Where a person is convicted in the High Court or on indictment in the sheriff court of an offence punishable with imprisonment (other than an offence the sentence for which is fixed by law) and the court before or by which he is convicted is satisfied on the written or oral evidence of two medical practitioners—

---

[37] 1975 Act, ss. 175(5), 376(8).
[38] *Ibid.* ss. 175(4), 376(7).
[39] *Ibid.* ss. 175(6), 376(9).
[40] *Ibid.* ss. 175(7), 376(10).
[41] *Ibid.* ss. 177, 378.

(a) that the offender is suffering from mental disorder within the meaning of section 1(2) of the 1984 Act; and
(b) that there is reason to suppose—
  (i) that the mental disorder from which the offender is suffering is such that it may be appropriate for a hospital order to be made in his case; and
  (ii) that, having regard to the provisions of section 175(4) of the 1975 Act, the hospital to be specified in any such hospital order may be a state hospital,

the court may, before making a hospital order or dealing with the offender in some other way, make an order ("an interim hospital order") authorising his admission to and detention in a state hospital or such other hospital as for special reasons the court may specify in the order. This power may also be exercised by the High Court where, under any enactment, an offender is remitted to that court for sentence by a sheriff.[42]

3–17 Similar provision to the foregoing exists in the case of any person charged summarily in the sheriff court but in that event the power is exercisable not only where the person is convicted but also where the sheriff is satisfied that the person did the act or made the omission charged but does not convict him.[43] Where a person is remitted to the sheriff court from the district court under section 376(4) of the 1975 Act, the sheriff may make an interim hospital order if satisfied as to the conditions in section 375A(1).[44]

3–18 The two medical practitioners whose evidence is taken into account must comply with section 176 or section 377 of the 1975 Act (see paragraph 3–11 above), and, additionally, at least one of them must be employed at the hospital which is to be specified in the order.[45]

3–19 An interim hospital order should not be made unless the court is satisfied that the hospital to be specified in the order, in the event of such an order being made, is available for the admission of the offender within 28 days of the making of the order.[46] Where a court makes an interim hospital order it must not make any other order for detention, or impose a fine, or pass sentence of imprisonment, or make a probation order or a community service order in respect of the offence. It may, however, make any other order which it has power to make.[47] As with hospital orders this means that in appropriate cases a court could make an order for forfeiture of an article or for disqualification from holding or obtaining a driving licence (see paragraph 3–14 above).

3–20 The court by which an interim hospital order is made may include in the order such direction as it thinks fit for the conveyance of the offender to a place of safety and his detention therein pending his admission to the hospital within the period of 28 days referred to above.[48]

---

[42] 1975 Act, s. 174A(1).
[43] *Ibid.* s. 375A(1). This provision is similar to s. 376(3) of the 1975 Act (see paras. 3–09 and 3–10 above), and gives rise to the same problems of interpretation.
[44] *Ibid.* s. 375A(2).
[45] *Ibid.* ss. 174A(1) and (2), 375A(1) and (3).
[46] *Ibid.* ss. 174A(3), 375A(4).
[47] *Ibid.* ss. 174A(4), 375A(5).
[48] *Ibid.* ss. 174A(5), 375A(6).

3–21   An interim hospital order will remain in force for such period not exceeding 12 weeks as is specified by the court when making the order; but it may be renewed for further periods of not more than 28 days at a time if it appears to the court on the written or oral evidence of the responsible medical officer that the continuation of the order is warranted. However, no such order is to continue in force for more than six months in all, and the court must terminate the order if it makes a hospital order in respect of the offender, or if it decides, after considering the written or oral evidence of the responsible medical officer, to deal with the offender in some other way.[49] The foregoing power to renew an interim hospital order may be exercised without the offender being brought before the court if he is represented by counsel or a solicitor and such representative is given an opportunity of being heard.[50]

3–22   If an offender absconds from a hospital in which he is detained under an interim hospital order, or while being conveyed to or from such a hospital, he may be arrested without warrant by a constable. If so arrested, he must be brought as soon as practicable before the court which made the order, and the court may thereupon terminate the order and deal with him in any way in which it could have dealt with him if no such order had been made.[51]

3–23   Where an interim order ceases to have effect in relation to an offender the court may deal with him in any way (other than by making a new interim hospital order) in which it could have dealt with him if no such order had been made.[52]

3–24   The power to make interim hospital orders is without prejudice to the power of the court under section 180(1) or section 381(1) of the 1975 Act to remand a person in order that an inquiry may be made into his physical or mental condition.[53]

3–25   The procedures and forms relevant to interim hospital orders are prescribed in the Act of Adjournal (Consolidation) 1988, paragraphs 62 and 112, and Schedule 1, Forms 29 and 30.

Medical evidence

3–26   Apart from the requirement that has already been noted concerning the qualifications of at least one of the medical practitioners (see paragraph 3–11 above), there are certain other statutory requirements in relation to medical evidence taken into account for the purposes of making a hospital order, a guardianship order, or an interim hospital order.

3–27   A report in writing purporting to be signed by a medical practitioner may be received in evidence without proof of the signature or qualifications of the practitioner. The court may, however, in any case require that the practitioner by whom such a report was signed be called to give oral evidence.[54]

3–28   Where a written report is tendered in evidence otherwise than by or on

---

[49] 1975 Act, ss. 174A(6), 375A(7).
[50] *Ibid.* ss. 174A(7), 375A(8).
[51] *Ibid.* ss. 174A(8), 375A(9).
[52] *Ibid.* ss. 174A(9), 375A(10).
[53] *Ibid.* ss. 174A(10), 375A(11); and see para. 7–19 *et seq.* below.
[54] *Ibid.* ss. 176(2), 377(2).

behalf of the accused, a copy of it must be given to his counsel or solicitor. If the accused is unrepresented, the substance of the report must be disclosed to him or, where he is a child under 16 years of age, to his parent or guardian if present in court. In any case the accused may require that the practitioner by whom the report was signed be called to give oral evidence. Furthermore, evidence to rebut that contained in the report may be called by or on behalf of the accused. Where the court is of opinion that further time is necessary in the interests of the accused for consideration of a report or its substance the case must be adjourned.[55]

3–29 For the purpose of calling evidence to rebut the evidence contained in a report that has been tendered otherwise than by or on behalf of the accused arrangements may be made by him or on his behalf, where he is detained in a hospital, for his examination by any medical practitioner. Any such examination may be made in private.[56]

Restriction on discharge from hospital

3–30 Where a hospital order is made and it appears to the court, having regard to the nature of the offence, the antecedents of the person concerned, and the risk that as a result of his mental disorder he would commit offences if set at large, that it is necessary for the protection of the public from serious harm so to do, the court may make an order, known as a restriction order,[57] restricting that person's discharge. Such an order may be made either without limit of time or for such period as may be specified in the order.[58] A restriction order must not be made unless the medical practitioner approved by the health board for the purposes of section 20 or section 39 of the 1984 Act has given evidence orally before the court.[59]

3–31 A restriction order has the effect of subjecting the patient to the special restrictions set out in section 62(1) of the 1984 Act. These are:

(a) none of the provisions of Part V of that Act relating to the duration, renewal and expiration of authority for the detention of patients apply, and the patient continues to be liable to be detained until he is absolutely discharged by the Secretary of State;

(b) power to grant leave of absence to the patient, and power to transfer the patient to another hospital, may be exercised only with the consent of the Secretary of State; and

(c) the power to take an absconding patient into custody and to return him to hospital may be exercised at any time, and cannot be defeated by the length of time that the patient contrives to remain at large.[60]

3–32 Where a restriction order is in force it is not competent to make a guardianship order in respect of the same person. Where, under section 60(4) of the 1984 Act, the hospital order containing the restriction order ceases to have effect upon the making of another hospital order, that

---

[55] 1975 Act, ss. 176(3), 377(3).
[56] *Ibid.* ss. 176(4), 377(4).
[57] *Ibid.* ss. 178(2), 379(2).
[58] *Ibid.* ss. 178(1), 379(1).
[59] *Ibid.* ss. 178(2), 379(2).
[60] Compare 1984 Act, s. 28(3).

subsequent order is to have the same effect in relation to the restriction order as the previous hospital order. It is, however, competent in such a case for the court making the subsequent order to make another restriction order to have effect on the expiration of the previous such order.[61]

---

[61] 1975 Act, ss. 178(3), 379(3).

CHILDREN

Definition of "child"

4–01 For the purposes of the 1975 Act the word "child" has, with a few exceptions, the meaning assigned to it by section 30 of the 1968 Act.[1] A child is there stated to mean—

(a) a child who has not attained the age of 16 years;

(b) a child over the age of 16 years who has not attained the age of 18 years and in respect of whom a supervision requirement of a children's hearing is in force under Part III of the 1968 Act; and

(c) a child whose case has been referred to a children's hearing in pursuance of Part V of that Act. That is, generally, a child whose case has been transferred from a juvenile court in England or Wales.

Prosecution of children

4–02 Since the coming into force of the 1968 Act most children who have committed offences are dealt with by being referred to a children's hearing, and therefore do not appear in court. Indeed, no child may be prosecuted for any offence except on the instructions of the Lord Advocate, or at his instance; and any such prosecution is competent only in the High Court or in the sheriff court.[2] In practice children under the age of 16 are rarely prosecuted unless the offence is sufficiently serious to merit being taken on indictment, though they may on occasions be prosecuted summarily when the offence is one where the prosecutor wishes to seek some particular penalty which cannot be imposed by a children's hearing, such as forfeiture or disqualification for holding or obtaining a driving licence. Prosecution is more common in the case of children between the ages of 16 and 18 who are subject to a supervision requirement. On occasions a child may be prosecuted, either summarily

---

[1] 1975 Act, s. 462.
[2] 1968 Act, s. 31(1).

or on indictment, along with an adult in respect of an offence or offences alleged to have been committed by them jointly. However, it is not obligatory to prosecute a child in such circumstances,[3] and the matter is one for the discretion of the prosecutor.

Finding of guilt

4–03 The words "conviction" and "sentence" must not be used in relation to children dealt with summarily. Instead they are to be replaced by "a finding of guilt" and "an order made upon such a finding.[4]" Every court in dealing with a child who is brought before it as an offender must have regard to the welfare of the child and must, in a proper case, take steps for removing him from undesirable surroundings.[5]

Remit to children's hearing

4–04 Where a child who is not subject to a supervision requirement is charged with an offence and pleads guilty to, or is found guilty of, that offence the court, instead of making an order on that plea or finding, may remit the case to the reporter of the local authority to arrange for the disposal of the case by a children's hearing. Alternatively, the court may request the reporter to arrange a children's hearing for the purpose of obtaining their advice as to the treatment of the child.[6] In that event the court, after consideration of the advice received, may either dispose of the case itself or remit the case to the hearing for disposal.[7]

4–05 Where a child who is subject to a supervision requirement is charged with an offence and pleads guilty to, or is found guilty of, that offence the High Court may, and the sheriff court must, request the reporter to arrange a children's hearing for the purpose of obtaining their advice. Where that is done the case may be disposed of in either of the ways mentioned above.[8]

4–06 A summary court may also follow the same procedure in the case of a person who is not subject to a supervision requirement but who is over the age of 16 and is not within six months of attaining the age of 18. If, however, in such a case the court wishes to remit the case to the hearing for disposal, it may only do so where the hearing have so advised.[9]

4–07 Where a court has remitted a case to the reporter the jurisdiction of the court in respect of the child or person ceases, and his case stands referred to a children's hearing.[10]

4–08 None of the foregoing disposals applies to a case in respect of an offence the sentence for which is fixed by law.[11]

---

[3] 1968 Act, Sched. 2, para. 10, repealing s. 50 of the Children and Young Persons (Scotland) Act 1937.
[4] 1975 Act, s. 429.
[5] *Ibid.* ss. 172, 371.
[6] *Ibid.* ss. 173(1), 372(1).
[7] *Ibid.* ss. 173(2), 372(2).
[8] *Ibid.* ss. 173(3), 372(3).
[9] *Ibid.* s. 373.
[10] *Ibid.* ss. 173(4), 372(4).
[11] *Ibid.* ss. 173(5), 372(5).

Powers of court where child not remitted to children's hearing

4–09   Where a court decides, with or without a prior remit for advice, to deal with a case involving a child itself, its powers of disposal will depend on the age of the child. If the child is over the age of 16 all of the powers of disposal applicable to young offenders will be available to the court. These are dealt with in Chapters 1 and 2 above. If, however, the child is under the age of 16 some, but not all, of those powers will be available, and others, applicable only to children under the age of 16, will also be available. The following are the powers which are applicable to such children.

(a) Non-custodial disposals

4–10   A court may deal with a child by an absolute discharge, by an admonition, by the making of a probation order, or by the imposition of a fine. Further, a court may defer making an order in respect of a child just as it may defer sentence in the case of an older offender. Although in general the above powers may be exercised in the manner appropriate to older offenders, two special features applicable to children should be noted. In the first place, where a social inquiry report has been prepared for the assistance of the court and the child is not represented by counsel or solicitor, a copy of the report need not be given to the child but one must be given to his parent or guardian if present in court.[12] In the second place, where a child has been fined and would, if he were an adult, be liable to be imprisoned in default of payment, the court may, if it considers that none of the other methods by which the case may legally be dealt with is suitable, order that the child be detained for such period, not exceeding one month, as may be specified in the order in a place chosen by the local authority in whose area the court is situated.[13] It should be added that, since a child is by definition also a person under the age of 21, the general restrictions applicable in such cases before any form of detention can be ordered in default of payment of a fine will also apply.[14] It is submitted that section 41(1) of the 1980 Act (restriction on imprisonment of person not legally represented) will also apply in the case of a child.

4–11   Prior to the passing of the 1968 Act it was competent to deal with cases involving children by fining the parent, but that is no longer competent.[15] However, there still remains a power to order a parent or guardian to give security for his co-operation in securing a child's good behaviour. Except where a parent or guardian has been required to attend court and has failed to do so, no such order is to be made without giving the parent or guardian an opportunity of being heard. Where any such security is forfeited, the sum in question may be recovered from the parent or guardian by civil diligence or by imprisonment as if the order had been made on conviction of the parent or guardian of the offence with which the child was charged.[16] It is thought that this power is now rarely used.

---

[12] 1975 Act, ss. 192, 393; but, see further para. 7–30 *et seq.* below.
[13] *Ibid.* s. 406 (made applicable to fines on indictment by 1980 Act, s. 47(2)).
[14] See para. 1–86 above.
[15] 1968 Act, Sched. 9; 1975 Act, Sched. 10.
[16] 1975 Act, ss. 37, 304.

(b) Custodial disposals

4–12   Where any person under the age of 18 is convicted of murder he must be sentenced to be detained without limit of time, and is liable to be detained in such place, and under such conditions, as the Secretary of State may direct.[17]

4–13   Apart from the foregoing case, where a child is convicted on indictment and the court is of opinion that no other method of dealing with him is appropriate, it may sentence him to be detained for a period which must be specified in the sentence. During that period the child is liable to be detained in such place and on such conditions as the Secretary of State may direct.[18] It has been held that, where a child is sentenced under section 206 and is ordered to be detained "without limit of time", that is an order for detention "for a period", and therefore a competent sentence.[19]

4–14   Where a child appears before the sheriff in summary proceedings and pleads guilty to, or is found guilty of, an offence in respect of which it is competent to impose imprisonment on a person of the age of 21 years or more, the sheriff may order that he be detained in residential care by the appropriate local authority for such period, not exceeding one year, as the sheriff may determine and in such place (in any part of the United Kingdom) as the local authority may, from time to time, consider appropriate.[20] For the foregoing purposes "the appropriate local authority" means—

(a) where the child usually resides in Scotland, the regional or islands council for the area in which he usually resides;

(b) in any other case, the regional or islands council for the area in which the offence was committed.[21]

Also for the foregoing purposes "care" is to be construed in accordance with section 32(3) of the 1968 Act, and the provisions specified in section 44(5) of that Act are to apply in respect of a child who is detained in residential care as they apply in respect of a child who is subject to a supervision requirement.[22]

4–15   Where a child has been ordered to be detained in residential care the place where that detention is to take place, and the conditions of the detention, are subject to review by the local authority.[23]

Consecutive period of detention on child sentenced under section 206

4–16   Where a child who is serving a sentence of detention imposed under section 206 is subsequently sentenced to a period of detention of the kind appropriate to a young offender (he having by then reached an age where such a sentence is competent), the latter sentence should not be made consecutive to the former. This is because there is no statutory provision to enable a sentence under section 206 to be aggregated with another

---

[17] 1975 Act, s. 205(2).
[18] *Ibid.* s. 206.
[19] *K.* v. *H.M. Advocate*, 1991 S.C.C.R. 703.
[20] 1975 Act, s. 413(1) and (2).
[21] *Ibid.* s. 413(3).
[22] *Ibid.*
[23] *Ibid.* s. 413(6) and (7).

sentence so as to enable a date for release on licence to be calculated (as happens with other consecutive sentences), with the result that a child sentenced under section 206 and subsequently to a consecutive sentence of detention would require to serve the first sentence in full.[24]

---

[24] *Clayton, Petr.*, 1991 S.C.C.R. 261.

ROAD TRAFFIC OFFENCES

[The Road Traffic Act 1991, which received the Royal Assent on July 25, 1991, creates several new offences, increases the sentencing powers of courts, and makes a number of other modifications to the law as contained in the Road Traffic Act 1988 and the Road Traffic Offenders Act 1988. Since (a) those new provisions appear likely to be introduced by stages, and (b) the earlier law will continue to apply for some time in respect of offences committed prior to the coming into force of the 1991 Act, this chapter has been written without regard to the provisions of that Act. However, the relevant provisions of the 1991 Act, together with some tentative commentary, are set out in Part III of this volume.]

Introduction

5–01 It is not the intention in this chapter to attempt to set out the financial and custodial penalties which are available to courts dealing with road traffic offences. These are many and various, and are moreover subject to frequent change by the passage of new legislation. For those who seek to know the maximum penalty for a particular offence there is really no alternative to a diligent study of the relevant statutes. Instead, this chapter will concentrate mainly on the two orders which are peculiar to road traffic cases, and which have generated over the years a considerable volume of judicial decision, and on occasions misunderstanding: these are endorsement and disqualification. The problems engendered by these matters were added to by the introduction of new "totting-up" provisions in the Transport Act 1981 (now the Road Traffic Offenders Act 1988, section 35). Some of those provisions have been the subject of judicial decision in the years since 1981, while others still await judicial interpretation.

5–02   Although in many instances the rules governing endorsement and disqualification are the same, there are also important differences, and these must always be kept clearly in mind. Thus, although disqualification may sometimes be obligatory, and sometimes discretionary, endorsement, where appropriate at all, is always obligatory. So too, although a court may sometimes order endorsement without disqualification, it may never order disqualification without endorsement. Again, although in one instance (totting-up cases) a court may refrain from disqualification if mitigating circumstances are present, in all other obligatory disqualification cases, and always in cases of endorsement, it may refrain from making the order only if special reasons are established.

ENDORSEMENT

Offences involving obligatory endorsement

5–03   The offences which involve obligatory endorsement are set out in Schedule 2 of the Road Traffic Offenders Act 1988. The general scheme of Schedule 2 is to set out in columns the various offences created by the Traffic Acts,[1] and to indicate as appropriate those where endorsement is obligatory. In some instances the word "obligatory" in relation to a particular offence is qualified in some way. In such cases endorsement is obligatory only if the condition or conditions referred to in the qualification are satisfied. That does not mean, however, that endorsement becomes discretionary if the conditions are not satisfied. There is no statutory provision for discretionary endorsement and, if there is to be no obligatory endorsement, there should be no endorsement at all.

Endorsement of licence

5–04   Where a person is convicted of an offence involving obligatory endorsement the court must order that particulars of the conviction and, if the court orders him to be disqualified, particulars of the disqualification, should be endorsed on any licence held by him. If the court does not order him to be disqualified, it must order that particulars of the offence, including the date when it was committed, and the penalty

---

[1] The Traffic Acts for this purpose are the Road Traffic Regulation Act 1984, the Road Traffic Act 1988, the Road Traffic Offenders Act 1988, and the Road Traffic (Consequential Provisions) Act 1988: Road Traffic Offenders Act 1988, s. 98(1).

points to be attributed to the offence should be endorsed on any licence held by the offender.[2] Where a person is convicted of an offence involving obligatory endorsement, and his licence is produced to the court, any existing endorsement on his licence is prima facie evidence of the matters endorsed, and the court may, in determining what order to make in pursuance of the conviction, take those matters into consideration.[3] This is so notwithstanding sections 311(5) and 357(1) of the 1975 Act (requirements as to notices of penalties and previous convictions).[4] If no order for disqualification is made the conviction need not be endorsed if, for special reasons, the court thinks fit not to do so.[5]

5–05   Although the Act refers to endorsement of "any" licence held by the offender, it is submitted that this can refer only to full or provisional licences issued under the Road Traffic Act 1988.[6] Thus an endorsement may not be made on a heavy goods vehicle licence or a foreign licence. However, whether an offender is at the time of conviction the holder of a licence under the 1988 Act or not, an order for endorsement operates as an order that any licence he may then hold or may subsequently obtain shall be so endorsed.[7] Consequently, although no actual endorsement may be made on, for example, a foreign licence, the order should be made since it will be effective in the event of the offender subsequently obtaining a British licence. It may also prove to be of significance at a later date in relation to a totting-up disqualification.

Penalty points

5–06   Where a person is convicted of an offence involving obligatory or discretionary disqualification, the number of penalty points to be endorsed on his licence will be the number provided for in Schedule 2 to the Road Traffic Offenders Act 1988. Depending on the offence concerned that will either be a fixed number or a number selected by the court from within a prescribed range.[8] In the case of an offence committed by aiding, abetting, counselling or procuring, or inciting to the commission of, an offence involving obligatory disqualification, the number of penalty points to be attributed to the offence is 10.[9]

5–07   Where a person is convicted of two or more offences, the number of penalty points to be attributed to those of them that were committed on the same occasion is the number or highest number that would be attributed on a conviction of one of them.[10] In England it has been held that the offences of failing to stop after an accident, and failing to report the accident, were committed "on the same occasion."[11] It has also been held to be the same occasion when a person was convicted of having two uninsured vehicles outside his house at the same time.[12] It would appear

---

[2] Road Traffic Offenders Act 1988, s. 44(1).
[3] *Ibid.* s. 31(1).
[4] *Ibid.* s. 31(2), *Urry* v. *Gibb*, 1979 S.L.T. (Notes) 19.
[5] *Ibid.* s. 44(2); for "special reasons" see paras. 5–30 to 5–36 below.
[6] Definition of "licence" in Road Traffic Offenders Act 1988, s. 98(1).
[7] Road Traffic Offenders Act 1988, s. 45(1).
[8] *Ibid.* s. 28(1)(*a*).
[9] *Ibid.* s. 28(1)(*b*).
[10] *Ibid.* s. 28(2).
[11] *Johnson* v. *Finbow* [1983] 1 W.L.R. 879.
[12] *Johnston* v. *Over* [1985] R.T.R. 240.

to follow that, if a person is convicted of two or more offences committed on *different* occasions, the number of penalty points to be endorsed on his licence is the total of those appropriate for each offence.

Production of licence

5–08   When a person who is the holder of a licence is prosecuted for an offence involving obligatory endorsement he must produce it to the court. He may do this in one of three ways—by causing it to be delivered to the clerk of the court not later than the day before the date of the hearing, by posting it by registered or recorded delivery so as to reach the clerk of court not later than the day before the hearing, or by having it with him at the hearing.[13] If he is convicted of the offence the court must, before making any order for endorsement, require the licence to be produced to it,[14] and, if the offender fails to do so, a constable may require him to produce it and, upon its being produced, may seize it and deliver it to the court.[15] The requirement to have a licence produced may cause some uncertainty as to the procedure which should be followed when an offender pleads guilty by letter but has not complied with any of the requirements as to production of his licence. If, notwithstanding his written plea of guilty, he still attends court in person, there is no problem: he can then be required to produce his licence. But what if he does not attend court? The papers which accompany the complaint which is sent to a person charged with an offence involving obligatory endorsement contain instructions about production of the licence, and the view may be held in some quarters that this amounts to a "requirement" to produce the licence with the result that, if the licence is not produced, the court may nonetheless proceed to sentence the offender in absence, and to order endorsement of penalty points on his licence. It is submitted that such a view is erroneous. The obligation on the court to require production of the licence arises only if the offender is convicted, and that cannot take place until the hearing of the case in court, which will inevitably be some time after the prosecutor has sent the complaint and the accompanying instructions to the accused person. Consequently, it is submitted that the proper practice in such cases is to record the conviction and to defer sentence for a week or two so that the requirement to produce his licence can be intimated to the offender. If, at the adjourned diet, he has still failed to produce his licence the court may then order its endorsement, and the consequences of non-production will come into effect.

Consequences of non-production

5–09   If an offender fails to produce his licence in any of the ways described above he is guilty of an offence unless he satisfies the court that he has applied for a new licence and has not received it. If he fails so to satisfy the court his licence must be suspended from the time when its production was required until it is produced to the court and, while suspended, it is of

---

[13] Road Traffic Offenders Act 1988, s. 7.
[14] *Ibid.* s. 27(1).
[15] Road Traffic Act 1988, s. 164(5).

no effect.[16] The consequence of this is that a person who drives a motor vehicle while his licence is so suspended will be guilty of an offence under section 87 of the Road Traffic Act 1988. Quite frequently an offender who has failed to produce his licence will say, by way of explanation, that he has lost it. Not only is this not an excuse sanctioned by the statute, but it may well be no more than a device to prevent the court from seeing the endorsements which the licence may contain. It is submitted that in such a case the proper course is to suspend the offender's licence until it is produced to the court: if it is genuinely lost the offender will then have to apply for a new licence, and produce it as soon as it is received.

Examination of extract from licensing records

5–10   Where a person is convicted but his licence is not produced to the court, the court may be able to discover details of previous endorsements from a notice of previous convictions served on the accused by the prosecutor. However, the court is also entitled to have regard to any previous convictions and penalty points which are specified in a document purporting to be a note of information contained in the records maintained by the Secretary of State in connection with his functions under Part III of the Road Traffic Act 1988.[17] Such a document is often referred to as a "D.V.L.A. print-out." If such a print-out is laid before the court by the prosecutor, the court or the clerk of court must ask the accused if he admits the accuracy of the particulars relating to him.[18] If the accused admits the accuracy of the particulars, the prosecutor need not adduce evidence in proof of them, and the admission must be entered in the record of the proceedings; but, if the accused does not admit the accuracy of any particulars, the prosecutor must, unless he withdraws them, adduce evidence in proof of those particulars either then or at any other diet.[19] The foregoing provisions have effect notwithstanding anything in sections 311(5) and 357(1) of the Criminal Procedure (Scotland) Act 1975 (requirements as to notices of penalties and previous convictions).[20]

Absolute discharge and probation orders

5–11   Although, under sections 191 and 392 of the Criminal Procedure (Scotland) Act 1975, orders granting an absolute discharge and probation orders are not generally to be treated as convictions, where a person is charged with an offence involving obligatory or discretionary disqualification, and the court makes any such order in respect of him, he is to be treated as if he had been convicted for the purposes of endorsement of his licence and of disqualification from holding or obtaining a driving licence.[21]

---

[16] Road Traffic Offenders Act 1988, s. 27(3).
[17] *Ibid*. s. 32(2).
[18] *Ibid*. s. 32(3), adopting the view earlier expressed by the High Court in *McCallum* v. *Scott*, 1987 S.L.T. 491; 1986 S.C.C.R. 645. What is now s. 32 of the Road Traffic Offenders Act 1988 was first introduced by the Criminal Justice (Scotland) Act 1987, Sched. 1, para. 3.
[19] *Ibid*. s. 32(4) and (5).
[20] *Ibid*. s. 32(6).
[21] *Ibid*. s. 46(3).

Endorsement and disqualification as penalties

5–12   If, through oversight, a prosecutor fails to serve a notice of penalties on a person who is subsequently convicted summarily of an offence involving obligatory endorsement, there has for many years been clear authority for the proposition that an order for disqualification may not be made.[22] Disqualification is a penalty and, as such, notice of its possible imposition must be given. For some years there was a measure of uncertainty as to whether or not the same rule applied in relation to endorsement.[23] However, the matter was finally settled in 1983 when a court of five judges held that penalty points cannot be endorsed on a licence unless notice of that possibility has been given in a notice of penalties.[24] It is also to be noted that this requirement cannot be circumvented by endorsing particulars of an offence without any attribution of penalty points: an endorsement must also award the appropriate number of penalty points.[25] Notwithstanding the foregoing, it has been held[26] that, where a notice of penalties warns that an accused may be disqualified for a minimum of 12 months, the court may nonetheless impose a higher minimum (*e.g.* for a second drink/driving offence) albeit that that higher minimum is not referred to expressly in the notice.

Exemptions from endorsement and disqualification for offences against construction and use regulations

5–13   Where a person is convicted of a contravention of construction and use regulations committed in a manner described against section 42(1) of the Road Traffic Act 1988 in column 5 of Part I of Schedule 2 to the Road Traffic Offenders Act 1988, the court must not order him to be disqualified or order any particulars or penalty points to be endorsed on any licence held by him if he proves that he did not know, and had no reasonable cause to suspect, that the facts of the case were such that the offence would be committed.[27] In such a case it is for the accused to prove that he did not know, and had no reasonable cause to suspect, that the facts of the case were such that the offence would be committed; and the question is not what caused the defect in question but whether or not the accused has proved that he had no reasonable cause to suspect its presence.[28]

DISQUALIFICATION

General

5–14   Orders for disqualification fall generally into two categories: those where the disqualification is obligatory, and those where the disqualification is discretionary. With the exception of a totting-up disqualification all offences involving disqualification are also offences involving obligatory

---

[22] *Coogans* v. *MacDonald*, 1954 J.C. 98.
[23] See, for example, *Pirie* v. *Rivard*, 1976 S.L.T. (Sh.Ct.) 59; *Scott* v. *Annan*, 1982 S.L.T. 90; 1981 S.C.C.R. 172; *Donnelly* v. *Shotton*, 1983 S.L.T. 657; 1983 S.C.C.R. 237.
[24] *Tudhope* v. *Eadie*, 1984 S.L.T. 178; 1983 S.C.C.R. 464.
[25] *Miller* v. *Allan*; *England* v. *Allan*, 1984 S.L.T. 280; 1984 S.C.C.R. 28.
[26] *Campbell* v. *McLeod*, 1975 S.L.T. (Notes) 6.
[27] Road Traffic Offenders Act 1988, s. 48.
[28] *Forrest* v. *Annan*, 1990 S.C.C.R. 619.

endorsement. The scheme of the Road Traffic Offenders Act 1988 in relation to disqualification is similar to that in relation to endorsement, that is to say that the appropriate column of Part I of Schedule 2 shows, as appropriate, those offences in respect of which disqualification is either obligatory or discretionary. As with endorsements certain of those entries are qualified by conditions or circumstances relating to the offence. Certain other offences involving obligatory and discretionary disqualification are listed in Part II of the Schedule.

Obligatory disqualification

5–15　　　Where a person is convicted of an offence involving obligatory disqualification the court must order him to be disqualified for such period not less than 12 months as the court thinks fit unless the court for special reasons thinks fit to order him to be disqualified for a shorter period or not to order him to be disqualified.[29] Where the conviction is for causing death by reckless driving, the minimum period of disqualification is two years.[30] It follows from the wording of this section in the Act that, in such cases, the court may order the offender to be disqualified for more than 12 months or, as the case may be, two years if it thinks fit.

5–16　　　Where a person is convicted of certain offences, and he has within the 10 years immediately preceding the commission of that offence been convicted of any such offence, he must, in the absence of special reasons, be disqualified for a minimum of three years.[31] The offences in question are (a) driving or attempting to drive while unfit, (b) driving or attempting to drive with excess alcohol, and (c) failing to provide a specimen where that involves obligatory disqualification. By virtue of section 46(3) of the Road Traffic Offenders Act 1988 the obligation to disqualify for at least three years will arise even where, on the previous occasion, the offender was granted an absolute discharge or placed on probation. It is to be noted that, so far as the previous offence is concerned, the section refers only to the offender having been convicted. It would appear to follow, therefore, that a minimum three year disqualification must be imposed even where, on the previous occasion, no disqualification was ordered because of special reasons. It is also to be noted that the period of 10 years is calculated back from the date of *commission* of the second offence though, so far as the earlier offence is concerned, the qualifying date is the date of *conviction*. Thus an offender could be liable to a three year disqualification even where more than 10 years had elapsed between the dates of commission of the two relevant offences.

Discretionary disqualification

5–17　　　Where a person is convicted of an offence involving discretionary disqualification the court may order him to be disqualified for such period as the court thinks fit.[32]

---

[29] Road Traffic Offenders Act 1988, s. 34(1).
[30] *Ibid.* s. 34(4).
[31] *Ibid.* s. 34(3).
[32] *Ibid.* s. 34(2).

Exemption from endorsement and disqualification for offences against construction and use regulations

5–18   As in the case of endorsement, a person may escape disqualification for a contravention of construction and use regulations if he can prove that he did not know, and had no reasonable cause to suspect, that the facts of the case were such that the offence would be committed (see paragraph 5–13 above).

Totting-up disqualification

5–19   For many years it has been the policy of the Road Traffic Acts to seek to deter repetitive offending by requiring the imposition of a mandatory disqualification whenever a certain number of convictions is exceeded within a period of around three years. The manner in which effect is given to this policy underwent a radical change with the introduction of the penalty points system under the Transport Act 1981, and the present position is as follows.

5–20   Where a person is convicted of an offence involving obligatory or discretionary disqualification, and the penalty points to be taken into account on that occasion number 12 or more, the court must order him to be disqualified for not less than the minimum period unless the court is satisfied, having regard to all the circumstances, that there are grounds for mitigating the normal consequences of the conviction and thinks fit to order him to be disqualified for a shorter period or not to order him to be disqualified.[33]

5–21   For the foregoing purposes the penalty points which are to be taken into account are (a) any that are to be attributed to the offence or offences of which he is convicted, and (b) any that were on a previous occasion ordered to be endorsed on any licence held by him, unless the offender has since that occasion and before the conviction been disqualified either directly or under the totting-up procedure. However, if any of the offences was committed more than three years before another, the penalty points in respect of that offence are not to be added to those in respect of the other. It is to be noted that for the purposes of the foregoing calculation the relevant dates are the dates when the offences in question were committed.[34] This is in distinction to the calculation which must be carried out to ascertain whether or not a minimum three year disqualification is obligatory in respect of certain offences: in such cases the relevant date is the date of conviction of the earlier offence (see paragraph 5–16 above). It has been held that a disqualification occurring within the three year period "wipes the slate clean" so that "any penalty points acquired prior to that disqualification are written off."[35]

5–22   For the purposes of the provision described in paragraph 5–20 above the minimum period for which an offender must be disqualified is (a) six months if no previous disqualification imposed on the offender is to be taken into account, and (b) one year if one, and two years if more than

---

[33] Road Traffic Offenders Act 1988, s. 35(1).

[34] *Ibid.* s. 29. The calculation is to be made *de die in diem* so that an offence committed on July 25 three years before a subsequent offence, also committed on July 25, will fall to be included in the calculation: *Keenan* v. *Carmichael*, 1991 S.C.C.R. 680.

[35] *Drummond* v. *MacKinnon*, 1983 S.L.T. 681, 1983 S.C.C.R. 289.

one, such disqualification is to be taken into account. A previous disqualification is to be taken into account if it was imposed within the three years immediately preceding the commission of the latest offence in respect of which penalty points are taken into account.[36]

5–23   Where an offender is convicted on the same occasion of more than one offence involving obligatory or discretionary disqualification, not more than one totting-up disqualification is to be imposed on him. However, in determining the period of disqualification the court must take into account all of the offences; and, for the purposes of any appeal, any such totting-up disqualification is to be treated as an order made on the conviction of each of the offences[37]: that is to say, a totting-up disqualification will not be disturbed merely because an offender appeals successfully against one of several convictions in respect of which that disqualification was imposed.

5–24   In determining whether or not to impose a totting-up disqualification, and in determining the length of any such disqualification, certain circumstances must *not* be taken into account. These are:

(a) any circumstances that are alleged to make the offence or any of the offences not a serious one;

(b) hardship, other than exceptional hardship; or

(c) any circumstances which, within the three years immediately preceding the conviction, have been taken into account in ordering the offender to be disqualified for a shorter period or not ordering him to be disqualified.[38]

5–25   So far as (a) is concerned, there is one reported case[39] in which the High Court did take account of the fact that the instant offence was not a serious one. However, the court's attention does not appear to have been directed to the statutory provision on that occasion, and it seems likely that in future the court would follow the clear words of the statute. Certainly, in cases where the instant offence was itself serious, the High Court has held that it is improper to use a totting-up disqualification to mark the gravity of that offence: the proper course is to determine the appropriate penalty for the instant offence, and then to go on to consider the matter of a totting-up disqualification.[40]

5–26   Not surprisingly, sub-paragraph (b) of section 35(4) has generated the largest volume of case law relating to the totting-up legislation. Since the introduction of that legislation the High Court has gradually adopted a stricter view as to what will constitute "exceptional" hardship, and it is now clear that considerably more than, for example, loss of employment will be required.[41]

5–27   Sub-paragraph (c) is clearly intended to prevent repeated avoidance of disqualification upon the same grounds. It is not clear how this can be established in practice, and as yet there are no reported Scottish cases on the point. However, it has been held in England that, where it is clear that

---

[36] Road Traffic Offenders Act 1988, s. 35(2).
[37] *Ibid.* s. 35(3).
[38] *Ibid.* s. 35(4).
[39] *North* v. *Tudhope*, 1985 S.C.C.R. 161.
[40] *Briggs* v. *Guild*, 1987 S.C.C.R. 141; *Gray* v. *Jessop*, 1988 S.C.C.R. 71.
[41] The reported cases dealing with this are summarised at para. 11–72 below.

a disqualification has been avoided within the relevant period, it is for the accused to establish what were the grounds relied upon on that occasion.[42]

5–28 Totting-up disqualification may competently be imposed by a district court.[43] This is the only situation in which that court has a power of disqualification.

5–29 Since the introduction of the new form of totting-up disqualification in 1981 the High Court has clarified certain matters in relation to it. A disqualification under section 35(1) has immediate effect, and it is incompetent to order it to run consecutively to any other period of disqualification then being imposed or already in existence.[44] Where an accused seeks to persuade a court that a totting-up disqualification should not be imposed, or that less than the normal minimum period should be imposed, it is for him to put proper material before the court in support of that plea. Thereafter, in the event of an appeal, the sentencing judge should state fully and clearly what representations were made to him, and what view he took of them.[45] If an accused requests a proof in mitigation, and that request is concurred in by the prosecutor, it is incumbent on the court to allow it to take place.[46]

Special reasons

5–30 In cases involving obligatory endorsement or obligatory disqualification the court may refrain from making the appropriate order only where there are special reasons for taking that course. Whether it is disqualification or merely endorsement which is in issue the criteria are the same and, it is submitted, it is not open to a court to apply a less stringent test in the latter case than in the former one. For those reasons any decided cases dealing with special reasons for not disqualifying are relevant to cases involving endorsement only, and vice versa. It is, however, important when considering special reasons to be clear about the precise nature of the offence in question. Thus, on a charge of failing to provide specimens of breath for analysis it is not relevant to have regard to the reasons which the offender may have had for driving his car in the first place, since the charge against him does not involve a driving offence.[47]

5–31 What will amount to special reasons is essentially a question of law but will always depend first and foremost on the facts of the particular case; and the number of decided cases on the subject amply demonstrates the wide variety of circumstances which can and do arise. However, several principles which must be applied in such cases are now clearly established. The most fundamental is that, for a reason to be special, it must be special to the particular offence itself and not to the offender.[48] It has been held to amount to a special reason, on a charge of failing to

---

[42] *R.* v. *Sandbach Justices, ex p. Pescud* (1983) 5 Cr.App.Rep. (S.) 177.
[43] Road Traffic Offenders Act 1988, s. 35(6).
[44] *Middleton* v. *Tudhope*, 1986 S.C.C.R. 241.
[45] *McFadyen* v. *Tudhope*, 1986 S.C.C.R. 712.
[46] *Kyle* v. *McNaughton*, 1990 S.C.C.R. 450.
[47] *Smith* v. *Nixon*, 1985 S.L.T. 192; 1984 S.C.C.R. 373; and see *Anderton* v. *Anderton* [1977] R.T.R. 424.
[48] *Adair* v. *Munn*, 1940 J.C. 69; *Whittall* v. *Kirby* [1946] 2 All E.R. 552.

supply a specimen for analysis, that the accused was a teetotaller[49]; but it is submitted that that must be regarded as a very special case which does not derogate from the general principle. As was said by the Court of Appeal in England, in *R.* v. *Jackson*,[50] "it is difficult to envisage what could be a special reason in relation to an unreasonable refusal." Factors giving rise to the detection of the offence (*e.g.* a "random check") as opposed to its commission will not amount to a special reason.[51]

5–32   It follows that, in distinction to cases involving a totting-up disqualification, considerations of hardship affecting the offender or his family can never be a special reason. Thus, the possible loss of a university place is not a special reason.[52] Nor is it a special reason that a disqualification may cause public prejudice where the offender is an officer supervising the organisation of the Territorial Army throughout a county.[53] Furthermore, it is not a special reason that an offender has an otherwise good driving record.[54]

5–33   So far as factors pertaining to the offence itself are concerned it has been held, in a careless driving case, that a special reason may be found where there has only been a small degree of carelessness.[55] However, the case of *Smith* v. *Henderson* has been disapproved in England,[56] and it is submitted that it might not readily now be followed in Scotland. Where a sheriff purported to find special reasons for not endorsing in a case under the Pelican Crossings Regulations on the basis that the offence was trivial, and there had been no evidence that it had caused actual danger to anyone, it was held on appeal that he had erred: the offence was an absolute one and was designed to protect the public from potential as distinct from actual danger.[57] So too, in relation to an offence under section 6(1) of the Road Traffic Act 1972 (driving with more than the permitted amount of alcohol) it was held not to be a special reason for not disqualifying that the offender had only a very small excess over the limit.[58]

5–34   It may be a special reason for not disqualifying in a drink/driving case that the offender did not know, and had no reasonable grounds for suspecting, that he was committing the offence.[59] This is probably more difficult to establish in an unfitness case than in a case of exceeding the prescribed limit (at least where the excess is quite small). In such a case a not uncommon assertion is that the offender was given a "laced" drink. If

[49] *Tudhope* v. *O'Kane*, 1986 S.C.C.R. 538.

[50] [1970] 1 Q.B. 647, at 658; and see *McDade* v. *Jessop*, 1990 S.L.T. 800; 1990 S.C.C.R. 156, where the High Court approved of the views expressed in *Jackson*, and confirmed that *Tudhope* v. *O'Kane* is a very special case.

[51] *Smith* v. *Peaston*, High Court, September 16, 1977, unreported.

[52] *Carnegie* v. *Clark*, 1947 J.C. 74.

[53] *McFadyean* v. *Burton*, 1954 J.C. 18.

[54] *Muir* v. *Sutherland*, 1940 J.C. 66.

[55] *Smith* v. *Henderson*, 1950 J.C. 48.

[56] *Nicholson* v. *Brown* [1974] R.T.R. 177; and see *Holden* v. *MacPhail*, 1986 S.C.C.R. 486, where the High Court referred to *Smith* v. *Henderson* but neither approved nor disapproved of it.

[57] *Tudhope* v. *Birbeck*, 1979 S.L.T. (Notes) 47.

[58] *Herron* v. *Sharif*, 1974 S.L.T. (Notes) 63; *Delaroy-Hall* v. *Tadman* [1969] 2 Q.B. 208.

[59] *Brewer* v. *Metropolitan Police Commissioner* [1969] 1 All E.R. 513.

accepted, that will amount to a special reason for not disqualifying.[60] Before such a plea can be accepted, however, it must be established, firstly, that the offender did not know, and had no reasonable grounds for suspecting, that his drink had been "laced" and, secondly, that the alcohol surreptitiously provided was responsible for the excess over the prescribed limit. The latter requirement may be difficult to establish in cases where it is proved, or the offender admits, that he knew he was consuming some alcohol, but asserts that more was added without his knowledge.

5–35　　If a person drives in circumstances which would normally attract an obligatory disqualification (*e.g.* with more than the permitted amount of alcohol), or an obligatory endorsement, but does so because of a sudden emergency, that may amount to a special reason for not disqualifying him or not endorsing his licence.[61] In such cases the emergency should normally be shown to be such as to provide a compelling reason for the offender having driven, and it should normally be shown that he had no real alternative but to do so.[62] The need to escape an assailant has been held to amount to special reason.[63] In *Riddell* v. *MacNeill*[64] the accused had been a passenger in his own car when it became embedded in a snowdrift. Being more familiar with the car than the person who was driving it, the accused drove it out of the snowdrift and continued some 200 yards along the road to the nearest parking spot. The circumstances were held to amount to a special reason. And, in *Ortewell* v. *Allan*[65] it was held that there were special reasons for reducing an otherwise mandatory three year disqualification to one year where the owner of a car, which had broken down on a main road, returned to it after two hours, manhandled it up an incline with the help of a passer-by, and then free-wheeled it into a parking place where it collided with another car.

5–36　　On a charge of failing to provide specimens it is not a special reason that the accused did not drink until after the accident.[66] Premenstrual syndrome is not a special reason.[67] And, the fact that an accused has driven for only a very short time or distance is not a special reason.[68]

PROCEDURE

Attendance of offender in court

5–37　　There is no statutory obligation on a court to require the attendance of an offender in court when an order for disqualification is being made. However, it is good practice to do so, if necessary by deferring sentence

---

[60] *Skinner* v. *Ayton*, 1977 S.L.T. (Sh.Ct.) 48, following *Pugsley* v. *Hunter* [1973] 1 W.L.R. 578.
[61] *Graham* v. *Annan*, 1980 S.L.T. 29; *Watson* v. *Hamilton*, 1988 S.L.T. 316; 1988 S.C.C.R. 13; and see *Brown* v. *Dyerson* [1969] 1 Q.B. 45.
[62] *Copeland* v. *Sweeney*, 1977 S.L.T. (Sh.Ct.) 28.
[63] *McLeod* v. *MacDougall*, 1989 S.L.T. 151; 1988 S.C.C.R. 519.
[64] 1983 S.C.C.R. 26.
[65] 1984 S.C.C.R. 208.
[66] *Emms* v. *Lockhart*, 1988 S.L.T. 222; 1987 S.C.C.R. 622.
[67] *Scott* v. *Hamilton*, 1988 S.C.C.R. 262; but premenstrual tension may be a mitigating factor in relation to a discretionary disqualification: *Thomas* v. *Lowe*, 1991 S.C.C.R. 943.
[68] *Lamb* v. *Heywood*, 1988 S.L.T. 728; 1988 S.C.C.R. 42; *Mackay* v. *MacPhail*, 1989 S.C.C.R. 622; but see *Lowe* v. *Mulligan*, 1991 S.C.C.R. 551.

for that purpose.[69] This is particularly desirable if a court is contemplating the imposition of a discretionary disqualification or a disqualification for more than a minimum period since it will allow the offender an opportunity to make appropriate representations to the court. However, much will depend on the circumstances of a particular case: it has been held to be unreasonable for a court to require a personal appearance by an accused who was in the Middle East, whose passport was in the hands of the authorities there, and who had lost his licence.[70]

Statement of grounds for not disqualifying or endorsing

5–38   In any case where a court exercises its power under section 34, 35 or 44 of the Road Traffic Offenders Act 1988 not to order any disqualification or endorsement, or to order disqualification for a shorter period than would otherwise be required, it must state the grounds for doing so in open court and, if it is a court of summary jurisdiction, it must cause those grounds to be entered in the record of proceedings.[71] It has been said that a failure to comply with this requirement may put a refusal to disqualify in peril.[72]

Procedure in "special reasons" cases

5–39   The existence of special reasons for not disqualifying or not endorsing as the case may be should not be put in issue *ex proprio motu* by the court: it is for the accused to plead, and to establish if he can, that such reasons are present.[73] The principal reason for this is that the Crown may otherwise be given no proper opportunity to argue that special reasons should not be found. However, where an accused pleads guilty by letter and, in that letter, sets out facts and circumstances which are capable of amounting to special reasons for not endorsing (though without expressly mentioning "special reasons"), it is open to a court, after giving the prosecutor an opportunity to challenge the facts and circumstances set out in the letter, to refrain from endorsing.[74] If, in a case involving obligatory disqualification or endorsement, an accused does not put forward special reasons at the time of sentence, he may not do so later.[75] If the facts which are to be founded on as establishing the special reasons are not admitted by the prosecutor, evidence should be led by and, if necessary, on behalf of the accused in an attempt to prove them.[76] Where an accused seeks a proof in mitigation, and that is not opposed by the prosecutor, it is incumbent on the court to allow a proof to take place.[77]

---

[69] *Stephens* v. *Gibb*, 1984 S.C.C.R. 195; *MacDonald* v. *MacGillivray*, 1986 S.C.C.R. 28; *Buchan* v. *Ingram*, 1987 S.C.C.R. 509; *Urquhart* v. *Hingston*, 1990 G.W.D. 28–1641.

[70] *Imrie* v. *McGlennan*, 1990 S.C.C.R. 218.

[71] Road Traffic Offenders Act 1988, s. 47(1).

[72] *McNab* v. *Pyper*, High Court, December 14, 1977, unreported; *cf. Winslow* v. *Farrell*, 1965 J.C. 49, but see also *Bruce* v. *Hogg*, 1966 J.C. 33; *Binnie* v. *Farrell*, 1972 J.C. 49.

[73] *McLeod* v. *Scoular*, 1974 J.C. 28; *Tudhope* v. *Birbeck*, 1979 S.L.T. (Notes) 47; *McNab* v. *Feeney*, 1980 S.L.T. (Notes) 52; *Donald* v. *MacPhail*, 1991 G.W.D. 2–129.

[74] *Keane* v. *Perrie*, 1983 S.L.T. 63; 1982 S.C.C.R. 377.

[75] *Hynd* v. *Clark*, 1954 S.L.T. 85.

[76] *McLeod* v. *Scoular*, above.

[77] *Kyle* v. *McNaughton*, 1990 S.C.C.R. 450.

Proof is required on a balance of probabilities.[78] In such a proof it is open to the prosecutor to cross-examine the accused and his witnesses and, if so advised, to lead evidence in rebuttal. If no evidence is led and the court is faced with conflicting statements from the prosecutor and the accused, neither should be preferred: all such statements should simply be ignored.[79]

5–40   In cases where disqualification is discretionary only, and submissions are made that there are special reasons for not ordering endorsement, it is important that the court should approach its task correctly. Where, in such a case, a sheriff decided that special reasons for not endorsing had not been established, and then went on not only to order endorsement but also to impose a period of disqualification, it was held that he had dealt with matters in the wrong order.[80] What should have been done was to decide what monetary penalty was appropriate and whether any period of disqualification ought to be ordered in the circumstances established in the proof in mitigation of penalty. Only after a proper decision had been reached on those matters should the question of endorsement have been considered. The need to follow such a course arises because, if the court in its discretion decides to order disqualification, endorsement must then follow. It is only where the court has decided not to disqualify that it may then competently consider whether or not there are special reasons for not endorsing.

Procedure where disqualifying on several charges and where accused already disqualified

5–41   Where an offender is being disqualified in respect of several charges in the same complaint or indictment the proper course is to impose in respect of each charge the period of disqualification appropriate to that charge. It is not appropriate to apply the longest period to every charge on the basis that, since all the periods will in any event be concurrent (there being no power to make them consecutive), there is no need to distinguish between the periods.[81] Unless the proper practice is followed it may be difficult for the High Court on appeal to deal with the matter if, for example, conviction were to be quashed in respect of some but not all the charges. It is also improper to attempt to get round the fact that periods of disqualification cannot be made consecutive to each other by looking at an offender's conduct as a whole and, on that basis, imposing on each charge a longer period of disqualification than would be warranted if each charge were dealt with on its own.[82]

5–42   Where an offender is already subject to a disqualification, and is being disqualified in respect of a fresh offence, it is improper to make the period of disqualification for that offence longer than would otherwise be

---

[78] *Farrell* v. *Moir*, 1974 S.L.T. (Sh.Ct.) 89; *Keane* v. *Perrie*, above, *per* Lord Hunter, in the last paragraph of his opinion.

[79] *Galloway* v. *Adair*, 1947 J.C. 7; *Barn* v. *Smith*, 1978 J.C. 17.

[80] *Graham* v. *Annan*, 1980 S.L.T. 29.

[81] *Austin* v. *Carnegie*, High Court, July 21, 1982, unreported.

[82] *McMurrich* v. *Cardle*, 1988 S.C.C.R. 20; and see *Patterson* v. *Whitelaw*, 1990 G.W.D. 23–1308.

appropriate simply to give it some effect after the expiry of the existing disqualification.[83]

DISQUALIFICATION UNTIL PASSING OF DRIVING TEST

5–43 Where a person is convicted of an offence involving obligatory or discretionary disqualification the court may, whether or not he has previously passed the driving test, order him to be disqualified until he has, since the date of the order, passed the test. Such an order may be made whether or not any other order of disqualification has been made.[84] Where such an order is made, and provided that the offender is not subject to any other period of disqualification, he is entitled to hold a provisional licence and to drive in accordance with its conditions.[85] A disqualification until the driving test is passed is expressly excluded from the categories of disqualification which may subsequently be removed by the court which made the order.[86]

5–44 An order disqualifying until the driving test is passed should not be imposed as a punishment, but should be imposed where to do so is in the public interest.[87] The desirability of such an order could arise in various circumstances, but three in particular may be mentioned. The first is where the driver is inexperienced and the circumstances of the case tend to cast doubts on his competence, maturity or judgment.[88] However, momentary inattention on the part of the driver, even to a gross degree, does not of itself demonstrate such incompetence as to justify an order to resit the test.[89] The second circumstance which may justify an order is where a lengthy period of disqualification is being imposed, on the basis that, in modern traffic conditions, a long interruption in a driver's experience may prove dangerous if he is not required thereafter to prove his competence.[90] The third circumstance is where the convicted driver is elderly or infirm, and there is reason to suppose that his ability to drive safely is diminishing.[91] Such cases should always be regarded sympathetically, but bearing in mind that the public interest is paramount.

AIDERS AND ABETTORS

5–45 Those who aid, abet, counsel or procure, or incite to the commission of, an offence involving obligatory disqualification may themselves be

---

[83] *Horne* v. *H.M. Advocate*, 1990 G.W.D. 36–2093.
[84] Road Traffic Offenders Act 1988, s. 36(1) and (2).
[85] *Ibid.* s. 37(3).
[86] *Ibid.* s. 42(6).
[87] *Sweeney* v. *Cardle*, 1982 S.L.T. 312; 1982 S.C.C.R. 10.
[88] *Smith* v. *Wilson*, 1990 S.L.T. 582; 1989 S.C.C.R. 395; *Neill* v. *Annan*, 1990 S.C.C.R. 454; *Ramage* v. *Whitelaw*, 1991 G.W.D. 35–2157; but contrast *McLean* v. *Annan*, 1986 S.C.C.R. 52.
[89] *Tariq* v. *Carmichael*, 1982 S.C.C.R. 488.
[90] *Sweeney* v. *Cardle*, above; *Holmes* v. *Stewart*, 1983 S.C.C.R. 446; but a disqualification for two years may not be long enough to justify an order to resit the test: *Morris* v. *Hamilton*, 1990 G.W.D. 28–1637.
[91] *Ashworth* v. *Johnston* [1959] Crim.L.R. 735; *Coull* v. *Lockhart*, 1991 G.W.D. 24–1415.

disqualified if convicted. In such cases, however, their offence is to be regarded as one involving discretionary disqualification.[92]

5–46 Where the holder of a licence is disqualified by an order of a court, his licence is treated as being revoked with effect from the beginning of the period of disqualification.[93] If a person who is disqualified obtains a licence, he is guilty of an offence,[94] and any such licence is of no effect.[95] As previously noted, however, a person who is disqualified until he passes a driving test, and who is not otherwise disqualified, may obtain and hold a provisional licence.[96]

5–47 A disqualification may in certain circumstances be removed by the court which made the original order. The person disqualified must apply to the court, but no application may be made before the expiry of certain periods, depending on the length of the disqualification concerned. Those periods are:

    (a) two years, if the disqualification is for less than four years;
    (b) one half of the period of disqualification if it is for less than ten years but not less than four years;
    (c) five years in any other case.

In determining the relevant period, any time after the conviction during which the disqualification was suspended or the person was not disqualified (*e.g.* pending an appeal) must be disregarded.[97] It is submitted that (c) above includes cases where the disqualification is for life.

5–48 Where an application is made to it the court may, as it thinks proper, either by order remove the disqualification or refuse the application. In exercising that discretion the court must have regard to the character of the person disqualified and his conduct subsequent to the order, the nature of the offence, and any other circumstances of the case[98] The prosecutor will normally submit information to the court regarding the applicant's conduct subsequent to the order. It is to be noted that, where an order is made removing a disqualification, the removal is to be "from such date as may be specified in the order."[99] That means that a court is not obliged to remove a disqualification with instant effect: it may, if it thinks fit, grant the application but postpone the removal to a later date.

5–49 Where an application is refused a further application may be made

---

[92] Road Traffic Offenders Act 1988, s. 34(5).
[93] *Ibid.* s. 37(1).
[94] Road Traffic Act 1988, s. 103(1)(*a*).
[95] *Ibid.* s. 103(2).
[96] Road Traffic Offenders Act 1988, s. 37(3).
[97] *Ibid.* s. 42(3).
[98] *Ibid.* s. 42(2).
[99] *Ibid.*

after the expiry of a period of not less than three months.[1] There is no limitation on the number of applications that may be made provided the three month interval is observed.

5–50   As has already been noted, a disqualification until a driving test is passed may not be removed.[2] However, if such a disqualification has been imposed in addition to one for a determinate period, it has been held in England that the latter may be removed although the former must remain in operation.[3]

5–51   Where a person has been disqualified for at least three years under section 34(3) of the Road Traffic Offenders Act for a second or subsequent drink/driving offence within 10 years, there is no prohibition against his applying for removal of the disqualification at any time after the expiry of two years. It is submitted, however, that in such a case, where the original period of disqualification was mandatory, there should be particularly compelling reasons before a court will exercise its discretion to remove the disqualification.[4]

APPEAL AGAINST DISQUALIFICATION

5–52   A person disqualified by an order of a court in Scotland may appeal against the order in the same manner as against a sentence,[5] and the court by or before which he was convicted may, if it thinks fit, suspend the disqualification pending the appeal.[6] In determining the expiration of the period for which a person is disqualified by an order of a court made in consequence of a conviction, any time after the conviction during which the disqualification was suspended or he was not disqualified is to be disregarded.[7] There is no appeal against the decision of a court in relation to an application for removal of disqualification.[8]

NOTIFICATION OF DISABILITY

5–53   If, in any proceedings for an offence committed in respect of a motor vehicle, it appears to the court that the accused may be suffering from any relevant disability or prospective disability, the court must notify the Secretary of State.[9] The words "relevant disability or prospective disability" have the meaning assigned to them in Part III of the Road Traffic Act 1988.[10] Any notice sent to the Secretary of State must be sent in such manner and to such address and contain such particulars as the Secretary of State may determine.[11] The obligation to notify the Secretary of State would appear to arise even in cases where the accused is not convicted.

---

[1] Road Traffic Offenders Act 1988, s. 42(4).
[2] *Ibid.* s. 42(6).
[3] *R.* v. *Nuttall* [1971] Crim.L.R. 485.
[4] *Damer* v. *Davison* [1976] R.T.R. 44.
[5] Road Traffic Offenders Act 1988, s. 38(2).
[6] *Ibid.* s. 39(2).
[7] *Ibid.* s. 43.
[8] *MacLeod* v. *Levitt*, 1969 J.C. 16.
[9] Road Traffic Offenders Act 1988, s. 22(1).
[10] See Road Traffic Act 1988, s. 92.
[11] Road Traffic Offenders Act 1988, s. 22(2).

MISCELLANEOUS DISPOSALS

Introduction

6–01 In addition to the common sentences of imprisonment, fines, probation, and the like, there are many additional disposals which may be available to courts in certain circumstances. Some of these exist by virtue of the common law while many others are the creation of particular statutes. Some miscellaneous disposals may involve the forfeiture of articles used for the commission of a crime, the imposition of certain incapacities or disqualifications, or a recommendation that a convicted offender should be deported. Given the very large number of special disposals attached to particular statutes,[1] it would not be practicable to attempt to describe every miscellaneous disposal which may be available to Scottish criminal courts. However, this chapter seeks to describe, and to offer some guidance in relation to, those miscellaneous disposals which arise most frequently in practice.

---

[1] The Hodgson Committee (Profits of Crime and their Recovery (1984), p. 18) noted no less than 50 different statutory provisions relating to forfeiture alone.

FORFEITURE

General provisions

6–02   Where a person is convicted of an offence on indictment and the court
which passes sentence is satisfied that any property which was in his
possession or under his control at the time of his apprehension:

(a) has been used for the purpose of committing, or facilitating the
commission, of any offence, or

(b) was intended by him to be used for that purpose,

that property is liable to forfeiture, and any property so forfeited is to be
disposed of as the court may direct.[2] It is to be noted that the above power
extends to property used or intended to be used for the commission of *any*
offence, and not merely the offence of which a person is convicted. The
reference to "facilitating the commission" of an offence includes a
reference to the taking of any steps after it has been committed for the
purpose of disposing of any property to which it relates or of avoiding
apprehension or detection.[3]

6–03   Where a person is convicted of any offence by a court of summary
jurisdiction the same provisions apply as in the case of a person convicted
on indictment.[4] Formerly, somewhat different provisions applicable to
summary procedure applied not only where a person was convicted but
also expressly to cases where a probation order (which does not involve
conviction) was made. The replacement of the old section 436 of the 1975
Act by provisions identical to those in section 223 appears to remove that
power,[5] so that forfeiture of articles may not now be ordered under the
provisions contained in the 1975 Act where a summary case is disposed of
by the making of a probation order. However, where a person is placed
on probation or granted an absolute discharge in respect of a
contravention of section 58(1) of the Civic Government (Scotland) Act
1982 (previously convicted person in possession of tool or any other
object from which the commission or intended commission of theft may
reasonably be inferred), the court may order forfeiture of the tool or
other objects concerned.

Relationship between powers in 1975 Act and powers in specific statutes

6–04   The powers of forfeiture described above are available to the court in
relation both to common law and statutory offences. However, many
statutes contain their own specific provisions for forfeiture. Examples are
the Prevention of Crime Act 1953, the Salmon and Freshwater Fisheries
(Protection) (Scotland) Act 1951, and the Misuse of Drugs Act 1971.
Where a statutory offence is involved, there can be no order for forfeiture
unless that is mentioned in the notice of penalties served on the accused.[6]
From time to time questions may arise as to whether the general

---

[2] 1975 Act, s. 223(1).
[3] *Ibid.* s. 223(2).
[4] *Ibid.* s. 436.
[5] Brought about by 1980 Act, Sched. 7, para. 71.
[6] *Duffy* v. *Lakie*, 1962, S.L.T. 31; but see Renton and Brown, para. 17–44, which suggests
that notice is not required in respect of a statutory offence where any forfeiture is to be
under the 1975 Act.

forfeiture provisions in the 1975 Act may competently be invoked in preference to other, and possibly more limited, forfeiture provisions contained in an offence-creating statute. The position appears to be that the 1975 Act provisions may competently be used to supplement or replace more limited provisions in such a statute,[7] but should not be used where the offence-creating statute expressly prohibits the forfeiture of articles of a certain kind.[8]

Examples of use of forfeiture powers

6–05   The power to order forfeiture is most commonly used in relation to articles such as weapons, firearms, dangerous drugs, a housebreaker's tools, and so on. It has been held, however, that the court has power to order the destruction of indecent or obscene books which were exhibited to view in contravention of section 380(3) of the Burgh Police (Scotland) Act 1892.[9] A power to order forfeiture also implies the right to seize the articles concerned.[10] Without express statutory authority, however, it is not competent to order the forfeiture of a motor car used as a conveyance to and from the scene of an offence against a fishing statute.[11] On the other hand it is competent to order forfeiture of a motor vehicle used to convey stolen property from the scene of a crime,[12] but it is not competent to order forfeiture of a motor vehicle used in the course of the commission of the offence of driving while disqualified.[13]

Possession or control at time of apprehension

6–06   Sections 223 and 436 of the 1975 Act both require that property which is to be forfeited should have been in the offender's "possession or under his control at the time of his apprehension." Identical words in the English Powers of Criminal Courts Act 1973[14] have been construed as precluding forfeiture where property had been in the offender's possession or under his control at the time of committing the offence but was no longer in his possession or under his control at the time of his arrest. Thus, for example, in *R*. v. *Hinde*[15] an offender, along with four others, drove a car to a shop which they burgled. Some of the stolen items were placed in the

---

[7] *Donnelly* v. *H.M. Advocate*, 1984 S.C.C.R. 93 (a case under the Misuse of Drugs Act 1971).

[8] *Aitken* v. *Lockhart*, 1989 S.C.C.R. 368 (a case under the Wireless Telegraphy Act 1949). In this case it does not appear to have been drawn to the attention of the High Court that none of the forfeiture provisions in the 1975 Act apply to offences under the 1949 Act: Telecommunications Act 1984, Sched. 3, para. 3(*b*).

[9] *Galletly* v. *Laird*, 1952 J.C. 16.

[10] *Mauchline* v. *Stevenson* (1878) 4 Couper 20.

[11] *Simpson* v. *Fraser & Ors.*, 1948 J.C. 1.

[12] *Carruthers* v. *MacKinnon*, 1986 S.C.C.R. 643; *McQueeney* v. *Carmichael*, 1991 S.C.C.R. 221; *Wallace* v. *MacDougall*, 1991 S.C.C.R. 962.

[13] *Findlay* v. *McNaughton*, 1991 S.C.C.R. 321. It is submitted that forfeiture of a motor vehicle is incompetent in respect of all other road traffic offences since it could not be said in such cases that the vehicle had "been used for the purpose of committing, or facilitating the commission of, any offence," as required by the provisions in the 1975 Act, such offences not being offences of intent in that sense: but see 1975 Act, ss. 223(1A) and (1B) and 436(1A) and (1B), introduced by Road Traffic Act 1991, s. 37 (reproduced in Part III below).

[14] S. 43, now amended by Criminal Justice Act 1988, s. 69.

[15] [1977] Crim.L.R. 847; and see also *R*. v. *McFarlane* [1982] Crim.L.R. 863.

car, but the offender ran off when police officers arrived, leaving the car behind. The offender was arrested four days later. On appeal it was held that the car could not be forfeited since it had not been in the offender's possession or control at the time of his apprehension. It is submitted that, unsatisfactory as it may be,[16] a similar construction ought to be placed on the words in the 1975 Act.

Ownership of property

6–07   There are sometimes problems when the article which the court wishes to forfeit does not belong to the offender himself. Thus, a third party, whose boat was ordered to be forfeited, successfully petitioned the High Court for recall of the forfeiture.[17] So too, in a prosecution under the Wireless Telegraphy Act 1949 for using a receiver without a licence, it was held to be incompetent to order the forfeiture of the television set in question where it was the subject of a rental agreement.[18] In *Lloyds and Scottish Finance Ltd.* v. *H.M. Advocate,*[19] however, a somewhat different approach was taken. In that case a person was charged on indictment with theft, and pleaded guilty to reset. At the time of the offence he had used a motor vehicle which was the subject of a hire-purchase agreement. Forfeiture of the vehicle was ordered with a direction that it be sold by public auction. The finance company, as owners of the vehicle, sought to have the High Court quash the order for forfeiture and suspend the order for sale. In the event the order for forfeiture was not quashed, but the order for sale was varied to enable the value of the vehicle to be paid to the finance company. The decision in this case was largely influenced by the fact that section 23 of the Criminal Justice Act 1972 (which contained the forfeiture provision which is now section 223 of the 1975 Act) provided, on one view in relation to English cases only, for third parties being able to claim an interest in forfeited goods for up to six months after the date of the order. The High Court saw no reason why the same right should not exist in Scotland, and indeed urged courts to have in mind the interests of third parties when making forfeiture orders. It is suggested that the case of *Lloyds and Scottish Finance* may be distinguished from the others to which reference has been made in that the offender had, under the hire-purchase agreement, a quantifiable interest in the vehicle of which he could properly be deprived by forfeiture, whereas there is no such interest in cases involving mere rental or where the property is wholly owned by a third party.

Search warrants

6–08   Where an order for forfeiture has been made, the court or any justice of the peace may, if satisfied on information on oath:

    (a) that there is reasonable cause to believe that the article is to be found in any place or premises; and

---

[16] But see proposals for reform in Scottish Law Commission, Forfeiture and Confiscation (Discussion Paper No. 82, June 1989), paras. 3.44 to 3.47.

[17] *Loch Lomond Sailings Ltd.* v. *Hawthorn*, 1962 J.C. 8; but see *Bain* v. *Wilson*, 1987 S.C.C.R. 270.

[18] *Semple & Sons* v. *MacDonald*, 1963 J.C. 90.

[19] 1974 J.C. 24.

(b) that admission to the place or premises has been refused or that a refusal of such admission is apprehended,

issue a warrant of search.[20]

Suspension of forfeiture pending appeal

6–09 Where a person is convicted on indictment any disqualification, forfeiture or disability which attaches to that person by reason of the conviction will not so attach for a period of two weeks nor, in the event of an appeal against conviction or sentence, until such appeal is determined.[21] Where any property, matters or things are to be or may be ordered to be destroyed or forfeited, any such order is to be suspended for the same period as noted above.[22] However, the foregoing provisions do not apply in a case where an order for forfeiture or destruction is made under a statute which contains its own provisions for suspension pending the determination of the appeal.[23]

6–10 Formerly, there was no similar provision in respect of disqualifications or forfeitures ordered in summary proceedings. However, that is no longer the case and there is now provision in summary proceedings[24] similar to that described above in relation to proceedings on indictment. It is to be noted, however, that in summary proceedings there is no automatic suspension for two weeks, and suspension pending the determination of an appeal is at the discretion of the court.[25] The reason for those differences is not apparent.

EXPENSES

6–11 In cases on indictment expenses may be awarded only in the extremely rare case of a private prosecution. Such prosecutions are, however, sometimes brought under summary procedure and are then subject to the provisions set out in section 435 of the 1975 Act. These are:

(a) expenses may be awarded to or against a private prosecutor but must not be awarded against any person prosecuting in the public interest unless the statute or order under which the prosecution is brought expressly or impliedly authorises such an award[26];
(b) the finding regarding expenses must be stated in the sentence or judgment disposing of the case;
(c) expenses awarded to the prosecutor are to be restricted to the fees set forth in Schedule 3 to the Summary Jurisdiction (Scotland) Act 1954[27];

---

[20] 1975 Act, ss. 224, 437.
[21] *Ibid.* s. 264(1).
[22] *Ibid.* s. 264(2).
[23] *Ibid.* s. 264(3).
[24] *Ibid.* s. 433A, inserted by Criminal Justice (Scotland) Act 1987, s. 68.
[25] *Ibid.* s. 443A(1).
[26] *Mackirdy* v. *McKendrick* (1897) 2 Adam 435; *Lockwood* v. *Chartered Institute of Patent Agents* (1912) 7 Adam 14.
[27] Schedule 3 to the 1954 Act was replaced by the Act of Adjournal (Fees in the Inferior Courts) 1972, but that Act of Adjournal was subsequently repealed, without replacement, by Schedule 2 to the Act of Adjournal (Consolidation) 1988. The Explanatory Note to the 1988 Act of Adjournal explains that previous rules relating to fees in inferior

(d) the court may award expenses against the accused without imposing any fine or may direct the expenses incurred by the prosecutor, whether public or private, to be met wholly or partly out of any fine imposed;

(e) expenses awarded against the accused, where the fine or fines imposed do not exceed £400, must not exceed £100; provided that if it appears to the court that the reasonable expenses of the prosecutor's witnesses together with the other expenses exceed the sum of £100, the court may direct the expenses of those witnesses to be paid wholly or partly out of the fine;

(f) where a child is himself ordered by a sheriff sitting summarily to pay expenses in addition to a fine, the amount of the expenses so ordered to be paid must in no case exceed the amount of the fine;

(g) any expenses awarded are recoverable by civil diligence in accordance with section 411 of the 1975 Act.[28]

6–12   Subject to what is said in footnote 27, the table of fees referred to in (c) above has been held not to apply where expenses are awarded against a prosecutor, and in such a case the account may be remitted for taxation.[29] Where there are two or more accused the amount of expenses awarded against each must not exceed the permitted limit, although the total expenses may do so.[30]

CONTEMPT OF COURT

Introduction
6–13   Every court has an inherent power to punish those who are in contempt of court. Formerly, at least in the High Court or the Court of Session, the punishment took the form of a sentence of imprisonment for an indefinite period.[31] In more recent times, however, the normal practice has been to impose a determinate sentence either in the form of a term of imprisonment,[32] or a fine[33]; and, by virtue of section 15(1) of the Contempt of Court Act 1981, any sentence of imprisonment must now be for a fixed term.[34]

6–14   A book primarily concerned with sentencing is not the place to discuss at length what is or is not contempt of court. That is fully dealt with in other textbooks.[35] It may, however, be helpful to give some indication of the circumstances in which the problem of sentencing for contempt is most frequently encountered. In this context it must be borne in mind that the need to sentence for contempt may arise in two quite distinct

---

courts have been revoked as unnecessary. That may be so, but it is unfortunate that, as a result, a meaningless provision is now left in the 1975 Act.

[28] *Ross* v. *Stirling* (1869) 1 Couper 336. See commentary on s. 411 of the 1975 Act in para. 1–129 *et seq.* above.

[29] *J. & G. Cox Ltd.* v. *Lindsay,* 1907 S.C. 96.

[30] *Tough & Ross* v. *Mitchell* (1886) 1 White 79.

[31] *Muir* v. *Milligan* (1868) 6 M. 1125; *Leys* v. *Leys* (1886) 13 R. 1223.

[32] *Wylie & Anr.,* v. *H.M. Advocate,* 1966 S.L.T. 149; *Hislop, Petr.,* 1986 S.C.C.R. 268; *Smith, Petr.,* 1987 S.C.C.R. 726.

[33] *H.M. Advocate* v. *Airs,* 1975 J.C. 64; *H.M. Advocate* v. *News Group Newspapers and Ors.,* 1989 S.C.C.R. 156.

[34] See, further, para. 6–20 below.

[35] See, for example, Gordon, *Criminal Law,* 2nd ed., Chap. 51.

types of case. The first is where the offender has been proceeded against for the contempt in question. This may occur in one of two ways. Since contempt of court is not itself a crime or offence, a prosecution for contempt is not competent, but the facts constituting the contempt may themselves amount to a crime or offence, and so be capable of forming the subject of criminal proceedings.[36] Alternatively, the Lord Advocate may proceed by way of petition to bring facts constituting a contempt directly to the attention of a court. In both such cases the offender's guilt will either be admitted or established by evidence in the normal way, and the sentencing problem for the court will be essentially the same as in any other case. The second type of case arises where the court itself proposes summarily to find the offender guilty of the contempt. In such cases difficulties may arise as to whether or not the court should deal with the matter itself or leave it to be dealt with by the prosecutor and, if dealing with it itself, what level of sentence is competent and appropriate. Certain procedural difficulties are also encountered on occasions.

Contempt by a witness in a summary prosecution

6–15   Contempt by a witness in a summary prosecution is to some extent dealt with by statute. Section 344 of the 1975 Act provides:

> (1) If a witness in a summary prosecution shall wilfully fail to attend after being duly cited, or unlawfully refuse to be sworn, or after the oath has been administered to him refuse to answer any question which the court may allow, or to produce documents in his possession when required by the court, or shall prevaricate in his evidence, he shall be deemed guilty of contempt of court and be liable to be summarily punished forthwith for such contempt by a fine not exceeding level 3 on the standard scale or by imprisonment for any period not exceeding 21 days.
>
> (2) Where such punishment as aforesaid is summarily imposed, the clerk of court shall enter in the record of the proceedings the acts constituting the contempt or the statements forming the prevarication.[37]
>
> (3) The foregoing provisions of this section shall be without prejudice to the prosecutor proceeding by way of formal complaint for any such contempt where such summary punishment, as above mentioned, is not imposed.
>
> (4) Any witness who, after being duly cited in accordance with section 315 of this Act—
>
> > (*a*) fails without reasonable excuse, after receiving at least 48 hours' notice, to attend for precognition by a prosecutor at the time and place mentioned in the citation served on him, or
> >
> > (*b*) refuses when so cited to give information within his knowledge regarding any matter relative to the commission of the offence in relation to which such precognition is taken,

---

[36] *Dyce* v. *Aitchison*, 1985 S.L.T. 512; 1985 S.C.C.R. 184.

[37] Care must be taken to comply fully with the requirements of this subsection: *Strang* v. *Annan*, 1991 G.W.D. 23–1315, though it is not necessary, in a case of prevarication, that every question and answer should be minuted *verbatim*: *Sze* v. *Wilson*, 1991 G.W.D. 35–2106.

shall be liable to the like punishment as is provided in the foregoing provisions of this section.

It would appear that, where a prosecutor proceeds by way of summary complaint as provided for in subsection (3) above, the court's powers of punishment will be those provided for in section 15(2)(a) of the Contempt of Court Act 1981, that is to say imprisonment for a maximum period of three months or a maximum fine of level 4 on the standard scale or both.

Contempt at common law

6-16   There are no comparable statutory provisions relative to contempt in cases on indictment and, as can be seen, the provisions in summary procedure relate only to certain classes of contempt and only to two categories of offender. In all other cases, therefore, the matter must be dealt with according to the common law of contempt of court. Generally, any improper or disorderly behaviour in court may be treated as contempt, and it is for the presiding judge to decide whether any particular conduct amounts to contempt of court. Where, however, the conduct itself constitutes a substantial crime or offence, such as an attempt to pervert the course of justice, prevarication, or the carrying of an offensive weapon, the judge will normally seek to ascertain whether the prosecutor proposes to bring criminal proceedings against the offender before dealing himself with the matter as contempt of court.

6-17   The following are some examples of conduct which may be treated as contempt of court:

(a) drunkenness in court by an accused, a witness, a juror, or a spectator[38];

(b) insulting language to the judge[39]; in such a case the court should be slow to regard criticism as contempt unless it is clearly disrespectful or likely to interfere with the proper administration of justice: it should be recognised that "disappointed litigants sometimes feel aggrieved and that some of them are ill-tempered, and that they may say or write things which are foolish and reprehensible"; consequently the contempt process should not "degenerate into an oppressive or vindictive abuse of the court's powers"[40];

(c) failure to attend court when duly cited as a witness or an accused[41]; to amount to contempt such failure must be wilful: it is submitted that a failure by an accused person to attend for his trial may still be treated as contempt notwithstanding that such a person has been granted bail under the Bail, etc., (Scotland) Act 1980, and is therefore liable to prosecution in respect of that failure; in such a case, however, it will be prudent to check whether the accused has been, or will be, charged with the statutory offence so as to avoid any risk of double jeopardy;

(d) prevarication by witnesses[42];

---

[38] *Alex. MacLean* (1838) 2 Swin. 185; *John Allan* (1826) Shaw 172; *Jas. Wemyss* (1840) Bell's Notes 165; *Eliz. Yates* (1847) Ark. 238.

[39] *Robt. Clark or Williamson* (1829) Shaw 215.

[40] *Milburn*, 1946 S.C. 301, *per* L. P. Normand at 315.

[41] *H.M. Advocate* v. *Bell*, 1936 J.C. 89; *Pirie* v. *Hawthorn*, 1962 J.C. 69.

[42] Hume, i. 380; Alison, i. 484; *MacLeod* v. *Speirs* (1884) 5 Couper 387.

(e) refusal by a witness to take an oath or affirmation, or to answer questions.[43]

Procedure and sentence

6–18   When contempt occurs, difficulties may arise as to the appropriate procedure to be followed. In 1975 Lord Justice-General Emslie circulated to all judges a memorandum setting out a suggested procedure, and that has formed the basis for practice in all subsequent cases. That memorandum is still in force and, with the permission of Lord Justice-General Hope, it is printed at the end of this part of this chapter. In dealing with cases of contempt the court must bear in mind that the desirability of dealing with the matter expeditiously must be balanced against the need to allow the offender to consider, and perhaps take advice on, his position, and, where the contempt occurs in the course of a jury trial, the need to avoid the risk of creating any prejudice in the mind of the jury. So far as the formal finding of guilt is concerned this may properly, in the case of contempt by a spectator, be made as soon as the contempt has been committed. In a jury trial, however, the best course is to delay making the formal finding until at least the jury has retired to consider its verdict. Thereafter, unless the contempt is of a trivial nature, further consideration should be deferred to enable the offender to have the opportunity of obtaining professional advice (and, if necessary, legal aid), and considering his position.[44] The period of deferment will depend on circumstances, including perhaps the desirability of obtaining a social inquiry report, and will be at the discretion of the judge. At the adjourned diet the offender should be given a full opportunity of apologising for his conduct, and of making a statement in mitigation.[45] These will, of course, be given such weight as they merit when sentence is being determined. If a custodial sentence is imposed it may be made consecutive to any sentence then being served by the offender. Formerly, a sentence of imprisonment imposed for contempt of court was not eligible for parole. That meant that, if any such sentence was made consecutive to a sentence then being served, the prisoner could not qualify for parole in respect of his original sentence, and had to serve it in full.[46] However, by virtue of provisions contained in the Criminal Justice (Scotland) Act 1987[47] and the Prisons (Scotland) Act 1989[48] a sentence of imprisonment imposed for contempt of court is now treated as a sentence which is eligible for parole.[49]

6–19   If a court is contemplating the imposition of a term of imprisonment on a person found guilty of contempt of court, questions may arise as to the applicability of provisions such as those in sections 41 and 42 of the 1980 Act restricting the imposition of such a sentence on offenders who have not previously been sentenced to imprisonment or who are

---

[43] *Wylie & Anr.* v. *H.M. Advocate*, 1966 S.L.T. 149; *H.M. Advocate* v. *Airs*, 1975 J.C. 64; *Hislop, Petr.*, 1986 S.C.C.R. 268; *Smith. Petr.*, 1987 S.C.C.R. 726.
[44] But, see *Smith, Petr.*, above, and para. 6–19 below.
[45] *Royle* v. *Gray*, 1973 S.L.T. 31.
[46] *Manson, Petr.* (1977) S.C.C.R. Supp. 176.
[47] Sched. 1, para. 19.
[48] Sched. 2, para. 18.
[49] Contempt of Court Act 1981, s. 15(6).

unrepresented. It is submitted that neither of the foregoing provisions apply in the case of a person who is sentenced to imprisonment for contempt of court. Expressions in the 1980 Act are to have the same meanings as in the 1975 Act,[50] and in the 1975 Act "sentence" is expressly defined[51] as excluding a sentence for contempt of court. On the other hand, section 15(3) of the Contempt of Court Act 1981 expressly applies to persons found guilty of contempt of court the provisions of sections 207 and 415 of the 1975 Act (restriction on detention of young offenders),[52] and of sections 175 to 178 and 376 to 379 of that Act (persons suffering from mental disorder).

6–20   Until the passing of the Contempt of Court Act 1981 there were no statutory provisions, other than those mentioned in paragraph 6–15 above, setting out the penalties which may be imposed in respect of a contempt of court. The Act now provides (by section 15(2)) that the maximum penalty which may be imposed by way of imprisonment or fine for contempt of court in Scottish proceedings is two years' imprisonment or a fine or both. That power is, however, restricted in that (a) where the contempt is dealt with by a sheriff in the course of or in connection with proceedings other than criminal proceedings on indictment, the maximum penalty is not to exceed three months' imprisonment or a fine of level 4 on the standard scale or both, and (b) where the contempt is dealt with by a district court the penalty is not to exceed 60 days' imprisonment or a fine of level 4 on the standard scale or both. Where a person is found guilty by a district court of contempt of court and it appears to the court that he may be suffering from mental disorder, it must remit him to the sheriff in accordance with section 286 of the 1975 Act whereupon the sheriff has the same power to make an order under section 376(1) (hospital or guardianship order) in respect of him as if he had been convicted by the sheriff of an offence, or in dealing with him may exercise the like powers as the court making the remit.[53]

"MEMORANDUM TO JUDGES ISSUED BY LORD JUSTICE-GENERAL IN 1975

1. As a consequence of the decision of the Court in *H.M. Advocate* v. *Airs,* 1975 J.C. 64, judges may welcome further guidance as to the procedure to be adopted when the conduct of any party during a trial constitutes, in the opinion of the presiding judge, a contempt of the Court.
2. Only the presiding judge can decide if conduct amounts to contempt. If he is of that opinion, he should normally make the appropriate judicial finding at the appropriate time and, as a matter of record, this finding should be entered in the minutes.
3. The appropriate time to make the judicial finding will vary according to circumstances. In the case of contempt by a spectator, for example,

---

[50] 1980 Act, s. 81(2).
[51] 1975 Act, s. 462(1).
[52] See *Dawes* v. *Cardle*, 1987 S.C.C.R. 135.
[53] Contempt of Court Act 1981, s. 15(5).

the finding may properly be made at once. In the case, however, of contempt by a witness or by a party to the proceedings in a trial, criminal or civil, before a jury, it is important to avoid the risk of creating prejudice in the mind of the jury and the best course will be to delay making the formal finding until at least the jury has retired at the conclusion of the trial.

4. Thereafter in every case it is for the judge to decide whether circumstances warrant an exception to the normal rule that the trial judge ought personally to deal with the contempt of the Court over which he is presiding.

5. If there is to be no exception to the general rule, the judge should not, however, deal with the offender, including a spectator, forthwith. Although an act of contempt should be dealt with expeditiously, it is much more important that it be dealt with—and be seen to be dealt with—objectively. When the judge has made a finding of contempt he should defer further consideration to enable the offender to have the opportunity of obtaining professional advice (and if need be legal aid) and considering his position. The period of deferment will depend upon the circumstances. It would be a matter for judicial determination, in the light of the circumstances of each case, whether the offender should be detained in custody until the adjourned diet, or released either with or without Bail. If the offender is under 21 the judge ought also to bear in mind the propriety of obtaining a Social Inquiry Report.

6. At the adjourned diet the offender should be given a full opportunity of apologising for his conduct, and of making a statement in mitigation. If a custodial sentence is then imposed, it should normally be made to run consecutively to any sentence the offender is currently serving, and this would be a factor in determining severity.

7. If on the other hand the judge feels that the case is of such an exceptional nature that he cannot properly deal with it himself he should, after making the formal finding of contempt, remit the case to the High Court at Edinburgh, on a specified diet, either detaining or releasing the offender as he might think appropriate.

8. If the offence be one of prevarication, the judge should normally ascertain whether the Crown intends to bring criminal proceedings against the offender before deciding to deal with the matter himself as a contempt."

OFFENCES AGAINST CHILDREN—REFERENCE TO REPORTER

6–21 Any court by or before which a person is convicted of having committed any offence:

(a) under section 21 of the Children and Young Persons (Scotland) Act 1937;

(b) mentioned in Schedule 1 to the 1975 Act; or

(c) in respect of a female person aged 17 years or over which constitutes the crime of incest,

may refer (i) the child in respect of whom the offence mentioned in paragraph (a) or (b) above has been committed; or (ii) any child who is, or who is likely to become, a member of the same household as the person who has committed the offence mentioned in paragraph (b) or (c) above, to the reporter.[54] The offences mentioned in Schedule 1 to the 1975 Act are:

(1) Any offence under the Sexual Offences (Scotland) Act 1976.
(2) Any offence under section 80(7) of the Criminal Justice (Scotland) Act 1980 (commission of a homosexual act in certain circumstances).
(3) Any offence under section 12, 15, 22 or 33 of the Children and Young Persons (Scotland) Act 1937.
(4) Any other offence involving bodily injury to a child under the age of 17 years.
(5) Any offence involving the use of lewd, indecent or libidinous practice or behaviour towards a child under the age of 17 years.

INCAPACITIES AND DISQUALIFICATIONS

6–22   Under various statutes courts are empowered, in addition to other penalties, to make orders declaring offenders to be incapable of holding certain offices, or disqualifying them from holding certain permits or licences. Such powers are always to be found in the statutes creating the particular offences. Two examples will illustrate this. For a contravention of section 1 of the Public Bodies Corrupt Practices Act 1889 an offender is liable to be adjudged incapable of holding any public office for five years from the date of conviction (or for ever in the case of a second or subsequent conviction). In addition such an offender may be ordered to forfeit any office held by him at the date of the conviction, and to forfeit any claim he may have to a pension as an employee of a public body. In a more modern statute, section 11 of the Betting, Gaming and Lotteries Act 1963 provides that if the holder of a bookmaker's permit or a betting agency permit is convicted of certain offences the court may forfeit his permit. Forfeiture in such a case involves disqualification from holding a permit of either description for five years or such shorter time as the court may specify. Many other statutes contain comparable provisions, a recent example being the Company Directors Disqualification Act 1986. When a court is considering the imposition of a statutory disqualification, care should be taken to ensure that the offender is in fact liable to the disqualification in question.[55]

REVOCATION OF PAROLE LICENCE

6–23   The Criminal Justice Act 1967 provided for the creation of a Parole Board for Scotland, and gave power to the Secretary of State to release certain prisoners, including those serving life sentences, on licence on the

---

[54] 1975 Act, ss. 168, 364.
[55] *Gregan* v. *Tudhope*, 1987 S.C.C.R. 57. Under the Civic Government (Scotland) Act 1982 a street trading licence holder may be disqualified from holding a licence in the event of being convicted of certain offences, but it is not competent to impose such a disqualification on a street trader who does not in fact hold a licence.

recommendation of the board.[56] Certain courts are empowered, in certain circumstances, to revoke such licences.

6–24   If a person who is subject to a licence under section 60 or 61 of the 1967 Act or section 22 or 26 of the Prisons (Scotland) Act 1989 is convicted by the High Court or by a sheriff, whether summarily or on indictment, of an offence punishable on indictment with imprisonment, the court by which he is convicted may, whether or not it passes any other sentence on him, revoke the licence.[57] The Parole Board itself has certain powers to recommend the recall of persons who are convicted while on licence but, it is submitted, it is not good practice for a court which is considering a disposal other than revocation of the licence to defer sentence on an offender in order to see whether or not the board will recommend his recall: only the court can indicate the view it takes of the offence by passing sentence and, until it does so, the board has no basis on which to exercise its discretion. Consequently the court should impose whatever sentence it deems proper without regard to any action which may subsequently be taken by the Parole Board.

Effects of revocation

6–25   On the revocation of the licence of any person he is liable to be detained in pursuance of his sentence and, if at large, is to be deemed to be unlawfully at large.[58] If, in the case of a person subject to a licence under section 60 of the 1967 Act or section 22 of the 1989 Act, a Crown Court or the High Court or a sheriff revokes that licence under section 62 of the 1967 Act or, as the case may be, under section 28 of the 1989 Act, the Secretary of State must not thereafter release him under section 22(1) of the 1989 Act before the expiration of the specified period[59] from the date of revocation or before the expiration of one-third of the period during which the licence would have remained in force, whichever is the later. However, none of the foregoing affects any other power to release the prisoner concerned.[60]

RECOMMENDATION FOR DEPORTATION

6–26   The right of entry into and abode in the United Kingdom are regulated by the Immigration Act 1971 ("the 1971 Act"), as amended by the British Nationality Act 1981 and the Criminal Justice Act 1982. Under the 1971 Act a person who is not a British citizen is liable to deportation in certain circumstances. One of these is where his deportation is recommended by a court.[61] In Scotland that court must be either the High Court or the sheriff court.[62]

6–27   A Commonwealth citizen who has a right of abode in the United Kingdom is treated as a British citizen for the purposes of section 3(6) of

---

[56] Ss. 60(1) and 61: more generally on parole, see para. 2–23 *et seq.* above.

[57] Prisons (Scotland) Act 1989, s. 28(6).

[58] *Ibid.* s. 28(7).

[59] The "specified period" means 12 months or such period, not more than 12 months, as the Secretary of State may by order provide: Prisons (Scotland) Act 1989, ss. 28(9) and 22(2).

[60] Prisons (Scotland) Act 1989, s. 28(8).

[61] 1971 Act, s. 3(6).

[62] *Ibid.* s. 6(1).

the 1971 Act.[63] A person who was a Commonwealth citizen or a citizen of the Republic of Ireland at the coming into force of the Act, and who was then ordinarily resident in the United Kingdom, is exempt from liability to a recommendation for deportation if at the time of the conviction he had for the last five years been ordinarily resident in the United Kingdom and Islands.[64] European Community law also imposes certain restrictions on the deportation of E.E.C. nationals.[65]

6–28 A person who is not a British citizen is liable to deportation from the United Kingdom if, after he has attained the age of 17, he is convicted of an offence for which he is punishable with imprisonment and on his conviction he is recommended for deportation by a court empowered to do so.[66] However, the court must not recommend a person for deportation unless he has been given not less then seven days' notice in writing stating that a person is not liable to deportation if he is a British citizen, describing the persons who are British citizens, and stating, so far as material, the effects of section 3(8) (onus on person to prove that he is a British citizen) and section 7 (exemption from deportation for certain existing residents). The court has power to adjourn, after convicting an offender, for the purpose of enabling a notice to be given to him or, if a notice was given to him less than seven days previously, to allow the necessary seven days to elapse.[67] A recommendation for deportation may be made in respect of an offender who is sentenced to imprisonment for life.[68] A recommendation may also be made by the High Court on appeal, but cnly where the appeal is against conviction or sentence on indictment.[69] A recommendation for deportation is itself appealable in the same way as a sentence.[70]

6–29 The question whether an offence is one for which a person is punishable with imprisonment is to be determined without regard to any enactment restricting the imprisonment of young offenders or persons not previously sentenced to imprisonment.[71] Furthermore, for the purposes of deportation a person who, on being charged with an offence, is found to have committed it, shall, notwithstanding any enactment to the contrary and notwithstanding that the court does not proceed to conviction, be regarded as a person convicted of the offence. References in the 1971 Act to conviction are to be construed accordingly.[72]

Procedure

6–30 Where a court is considering making a recommendation for deportation, and the offender has been served with the notice required by

---

[63] 1971 Act, ss. 2(1)(*b*) and 2(2).

[64] *Ibid.* s. 7(1)(*c*); and see *R.* v. *Hussain* (1971) 56 Cr.App.R. 165. "Islands" means the Channel Islands and the Isle of Man: Interpretation Act 1978, Sched. 1.

[65] E.E.C. Council Directive (64/221.EEC) Arts. 3 and 9; and see *R.* v. *Secretary of State for Home Department, ex p. Santillo* (1981) 73 Cr.App.R. 71; *R.* v. *Secretary of State for Home Department, ex p. Dannenberg* [1964] 2 W.L.R. 855.

[66] 1971 Act, s. 3(6).

[67] *Ibid.* s. 6(2).

[68] *Ibid.* s. 6(4).

[69] *Ibid.* s. 6(1).

[70] *Ibid.* s. 6(5).

[71] *Ibid.* s. 6(3)(*b*).

[72] *Ibid.* s. 6(3).

section 6(2), he should be given an opportunity to give evidence on matters affecting his eligibility for deportation as set out in the notice. If a recommendation is then made, a certificate of recommendation should be sent as soon as possible to the Home Office, along with a copy of any social inquiry report that was considered by the court. If a person has been convicted of an offence under section 24(1)(*a*) or (*b*) of the Act (illegal entry, overstaying or breach of conditions), but the court decides not to make a recommendation for deportation, the Home Secretary should, when possible, be informed of the reasons for the court's decision.

6–31   Where a person is recommended for deportation by a court he must be detained in custody pending the making of a deportation order unless the court directs otherwise, or unless the Home Secretary subsequently directs his release.[73] If, however, he appeals against his conviction or against the recommendation for deportation, the appeal court may direct him to be released.[74] It is suggested that in determining whether or not to release such a person the court should, in so far as they are appropriate, apply the normal considerations applicable to a grant or refusal of bail. It is to be noted, however, that, in directing release, a court may make the person subject to restrictions as to residence and as to reporting to the police.[75] The person recommended for deportation, a constable, or an immigration officer may apply to the court, if it has not imposed such restrictions, to do so and, if it has imposed such restrictions, to recall or vary them.[76] Such an application may not be made to the High Court where, as an appeal court, it has directed release under paragraph 2(1A) of the Schedule.[77]

Considerations affecting recommendation for deportation
6–32   It has been clearly stated by the High Court that a recommendation for deportation is appropriate only where a person is convicted of a serious charge or where there has been a succession of charges indicating a course of conduct. "The test at the end of the day is whether to allow the offender to remain in this country would be contrary to the national interest."[78] Thus, calculated frauds on banks, which were said to have struck at the root of one aspect of the banking system, were held to be sufficiently serious to merit a recommendation for deportation.[79] On the other hand, a case involving minor shoplifting and giving a false name to the police was held not to be sufficiently serious for that course to be taken.[80]

---

[73] 1971 Act, Sched. 3, para. 2(1).
[74] *Ibid*. Sched. 3, para. 2(1A).
[75] *Ibid*. Sched. 3, para. 4.
[76] *Ibid*. Sched. 3, para. 5.
[77] *Ibid*. Sched. 3, para. 6(5).
[78] *Willms* v. *Smith*, 1982 J.C. 9; 1982 S.L.T. 163; 1981 S.C.C.R. 257, approving *R.* v. *Caird* (1970) 54 Cr.App.R. 499 and *R.* v. *Nazari and Ors.* (1980) 71 Cr.App.R. 87; and see *Klicic* v. *Jessop*, 1991 G.W.D. 9–526; *Caldewi* v. *Jessop*, 1991 S.C.C.R. 323.
[79] *Faboro* v. *H.M. Advocate*, 1982 S.C.C.R. 22.
[80] *Salehi* v. *Smith*, 1982 S.C.C.R. 552.

EXCLUSION FROM LICENSED PREMISES

6–33   Where a court by or before which a person is convicted of an offence committed on licensed premises is satisfied that in committing that offence he resorted to violence or offered or threatened to resort to violence, the court may make an exclusion order prohibiting him from entering those premises or any other specified premises without the express consent of the licensee of the premises or his servant or agent.[81] In summary proceedings the word "convicted" is to be construed, where the court makes a probation order or grants an absolute discharge, as a reference to the court's being satisfied that the person committed the offence.[82]

6–34   An exclusion order may be made either in addition to any sentence which is imposed in respect of the offence of which the person is convicted, or in addition to a probation order or an absolute discharge (notwithstanding the normal provisions relating to them and to their effect). An exclusion order may not be made in any circumstances other than those mentioned.[83] Unless the order is terminated as described below, it is to have effect for such period as is specified in the order, being not less than three months or more than two years.[84] Where a court makes an exclusion order, or an order terminating or varying an exclusion order, the clerk of the court must send a copy of the order to the licensee of the premises to which the order relates.[85]

6–35   Without prejudice to any other right to expel a person from premises, the licensee of licensed premises or his servant or agent may expel from those premises any person who has entered the premises in breach of an exclusion order. A constable must, on the demand of the licensee or his servant or agent, help to expel any person whom the constable reasonably suspects of having entered the premises in breach of an exclusion order.[86]

6–36   A person who enters any premises in breach of an exclusion order is guilty of an offence and is liable, on conviction in a court of summary jurisdiction, to a fine not exceeding £200 or to imprisonment for a term not exceeding one month or both.[87] The court by which a person is convicted of an offence as just described is required to consider whether or not the exclusion order should continue in force. The court may, if it thinks fit, by order terminate the exclusion order or vary it by deleting the name of any specified premises. An exclusion order is not otherwise to be affected by a person's conviction for such an offence.[88]

6–37   In relation to all of the foregoing the term "licensed premises" means premises in respect of which a licence under the Licensing (Scotland) Act 1976 is in force, but does not include premises in respect of which an

---

[81] Licensed Premises (Exclusion of Certain Persons) Act 1980, s. 1(1).
[82] *Ibid.* s. 4(2).
[83] *Ibid.* s. 1(2)(*a*) and (*c*).
[84] *Ibid.* s. 1(3).
[85] *Ibid.* s. 4(3).
[86] *Ibid.* s. 3.
[87] *Ibid.* s. 2(1).
[88] *Ibid.* s. 2(2).

off-sales licence or a licence under Part III of the 1976 Act (licences for seamen's canteens) is in force.[89]

6-38 Two points may be noted in relation to the foregoing provisions. The first is whether or not they can be applied in a case where a person is convicted of a breach of the peace committed on licensed premises. It has been held[90] that a charge of breach of the peace, even where it involves threats of violence and malicious damage, is not an offence inferring personal violence for the purpose of enabling a sheriff summary court to impose more than a three months' sentence of imprisonment. The present Act, however, describes the particulars of a qualifying offence in a specific and factual way, and it is accordingly submitted that an exclusion order may be made where a person is convicted of a breach of the peace, provided that the court is satisfied that, in committing the offence, the offender "resorted to violence or offered or threatened to resort to violence."

6-39 The second point is one relating to practice. The Act contains no provisions enabling the licensee of any premises concerned to state to the court whether or not he would wish an exclusion order to be made: and of course such a provision would be contrary to normal and accepted practice in statutes relating to sentencing powers. On the other hand, an exclusion order is plainly intended to be not so much a penalty imposed on the offender as a benefit conferred on the licensee concerned: and it is clear from the terms of section 1(1) of the Act that the licensee may waive that benefit if he so wishes. There is little point in a court making an exclusion order if it is not to be enforced by the licensee, and this suggests that it may be prudent for a court, where circumstances permit, to seek to ascertain his views before such an order is made.

CONFISCATION OF PROCEEDS OF DRUG TRAFFICKING

6-40 The Criminal Justice (Scotland) Act 1987[91] introduced in Scotland provisions to enable the High Court, upon convicting an offender of certain drug trafficking offences, to make a confiscation order to strip the offender of the proceeds of that drug trafficking. These provisions are analogous to provisions introduced in England and Wales a year earlier.[92]

6-41 The provisions in the 1987 Act are detailed and complex; and since, so far, they have not been the subject of a reported appeal to the High Court, no attempt is made here to describe them in full.[93] Suffice it to say that they contain detailed provisions about, for example, the value of proceeds[94]; rules for assessing proceeds[95]; realisable property[96];

---

[89] Licensed Premises (Exclusion of Certain Persons) Act 1980, s. 4(1).
[90] *Adair* v. *Morton,* 1972 S.L.T. (Notes) 70.
[91] Ss. 1 to 47.
[92] Drug Trafficking Offences Act 1986.
[93] They are, however, set out in Part III below.
[94] 1987 Act, s. 1(1).
[95] *Ibid.* s. 3.
[96] *Ibid.* s. 5.

implicative gifts[97]; enforcement[98]; restraint orders, and the appointment and functions of administrators[99]; and reciprocal arrangements.[1]

6–42   There is, however, one provision in the 1987 Act which should be noted in detail. Subject to the obligation under section 395(1) of the 1975 Act to take an offender's means into consideration when determining the amount of a fine, where a person is convicted on indictment of a drug trafficking offence as defined in section 1 of the 1987 Act and is sentenced to a period of imprisonment or detention, the court must also impose a fine where it is not also making a confiscation order, unless it is satisfied that for any reason it would be inappropriate to do so; and, where the court *is* making a confiscation order, it may also impose a fine.[2] Unlike the provisions relating to confiscation orders this provision is not restricted to the High Court, and accordingly also applies to the sheriff court under solemn procedure. In that case, however, the imposition of a fine in addition to a period of imprisonment or detention will always be mandatory (unless the court is satisfied for any reason that it would be inappropriate to do so) since the sheriff court cannot make a confiscation order.

6–43   In determining the amount of a fine in cases where its imposition is mandatory the court must have regard to any profits likely to have been made by the person from the crime in respect of which he has been convicted.[3] The Act is silent as to how the amount of any such profits is to be determined. Presumably it is anticipated that sufficient information will emerge in the course of a trial or will be provided by the prosecutor in the event of a plea of guilty.

6–44   Any period of imprisonment or detention for non-payment of a fine imposed under the foregoing provisions is to be served consecutively to, and not concurrently with, the period of imprisonment or detention originally imposed, except where the original sentence is one of imprisonment or detention for life.[4]

---

[97] 1987 Act, s. 6.
[98] *Ibid.* s. 7.
[99] *Ibid.* ss. 8 to 22.
[1] *Ibid.* ss. 27 to 32.
[2] *Ibid.* s. 44(1).
[3] *Ibid.* s. 44(2).
[4] *Ibid.* s. 44(4).

CHAPTER 7

PROCEDURE

Introduction

7–01   While it is essential that the correct procedures should be observed by judges and by clerks of court when a sentence is being passed, since otherwise the sentence may be put at risk, the rules governing these procedures are detailed and complex and are, moreover, to be found partly in the common law, partly in a variety of statutes, and partly in directions contained in judgments issued by the appeal court. Consequently the task of finding one's way successfully to the correct

113

procedure in any particular case is not an easy one. This chapter is an attempt to make that path a little simpler to follow.

PROCEDURE IMMEDIATELY AFTER GUILT ESTABLISHED

7–02   Once an offender has pled guilty or has been found guilty by the verdict of a jury or the finding of a court, it is the court's duty to consider and pass sentence provided that it is moved to do so by the prosecutor, and provided that it may competently do so.[1] Unless the court is unable competently to proceed any further it may not "make no order."[2] In cases on indictment the prosecutor must formally move for sentence. If he does not do so, no sentence may be pronounced,[3] and the accused should be discharged from the dock. The motion may, however, be inferred from the prosecutor's actings as where he lays before the court a schedule of previous convictions.[4] In summary cases no formal motion for sentence is required, but here too a prosecutor will normally take some action consistent with asking for sentence by, for example, submitting a notice of penalties or a schedule of previous convictions. However, should he do none of these things, and if the case is not one where a notice of penalties is required, the court may, in contrast to cases on indictment, proceed to sentence.

Plea of guilty

7–03   Where there has been a plea of guilty the prosecutor will narrate the circumstances of the offence and the accused, or his counsel or solicitor, who must in all cases be given an opportunity to address the court in mitigation,[5] will normally give the accused's version of these circumstances. If there is any dispute between the prosecution and the defence concerning any material facts, and if no evidence is led, the proper course for the court is to ignore such disputed facts.[6] This may, of course, give rise to problems. The defence statement of facts may be so inconsistent with that given by the prosecution as to negate the plea of guilty. In that event, if the plea of guilty is not withdrawn, the proper course, it is submitted, is for the court to refuse to proceed on the plea of guilty and to have a plea of not guilty recorded so that the case can proceed to trial. Where that course is followed it may be desirable to ensure that the trial is taken by a different judge. Again, disputes on matters of fact, while not negating the plea of guilty, may be so extensive or material that, if he is to ignore these facts, the judge will be left with insufficient facts to form a satisfactory basis for a decision on sentence. There is no authority to determine the proper procedure in such a case, but it is submitted that it would be open to a judge to require evidence to be led before pronouncing sentence. Similar problems may also arise in

---

[1] See para. 7–08 below. In summary cases it is essential that the principal, and not a copy, complaint should be before the court: *Wilson* v. *Carmichael*, 1991 S.C.C.R. 587; and see *O'Brien* v. *Dowdells*, 1991 S.C.C.R. 912.

[2] *Skeen* v. *Sullivan*, 1980 S.L.T. (Notes) 11.

[3] Macdonald, 348; Hume, ii, 470; Alison, ii, 653; Bell's Notes, 300.

[4] *Noon* v. *H.M. Advocate*, 1960 J.C. 52.

[5] *Falconer* v. *Jessop*, 1975 S.L.T. (Notes) 78.

[6] *Galloway* v. *Adair*, 1947 J.C. 7; *Barn* v. *Smith*, 1978 J.C. 17.

summary cases where an accused has pled guilty by letter and has tendered an explanation which is in some respects inconsistent with the account given by the prosecutor. The proper course in such a case is for the judge to put the accused's explanation to the prosecutor to see if the two accounts can be reconciled: very often they can. However, if they cannot, and the inconsistency is, or may be, material, the case should be continued to a later date so that the accused may appear personally. If the case is one where the court is considering the possibility of making a compensation order, and any dispute relates to, for example, the value of stolen or damaged property, the court may wish to have the case continued so that the true value can be established.

Previous convictions

7–04   Where a person is convicted of an offence, the court may have regard to any previous conviction in respect of that person in deciding on the disposal of the case.[7] Previous convictions should be contained in a notice prepared by the prosecutor, and that notice must conform to, and have been served on the accused in accordance with, the relevant statutory provisions.[8] When moving for sentence in cases on indictment, or after a plea or finding of guilt in summary cases, the prosecutor lays this notice before the court. However, if a notice containing previous convictions is inadvertently seen by a judge prior to conviction, that does not amount to a laying of the notice before him by the prosecutor.[9] In solemn procedure any conviction contained in the notice is held to apply to the accused unless he gives prior written intimation objecting to such a conviction on the ground that it does not apply to him or is otherwise inadmissible.[10] In summary procedure, where a plea of guilty is tendered in writing the accused is deemed to admit any previous conviction set forth in the notice unless he expressly denies it in the writing by which that plea is tendered: in any other case the judge or the clerk of court must ask the accused whether he admits the previous conviction.[11] In both solemn and summary procedure, if a previous conviction is not admitted, the prosecutor may either withdraw it or he may lead evidence in order to prove it. Since, in a summary case, the prosecutor may not know in advance that a previous conviction is to be challenged, he should normally be allowed an opportunity, by adjournment if necessary, to adduce the necessary evidence to prove the conviction.[11a] A previous conviction may be proved, *inter alia*, by an extract conviction, by witnesses including an official of any prison in which the accused may have been confined on such conviction, and by fingerprint evidence.[12]

7–05   Certain detailed rules relating to previous convictions fall to be noted. A previous conviction must be one dated prior to the date of the current

---

[7] 1975 Act, ss. 159(2), 356(2).
[8] *Ibid.* ss. 68, 161, 357.
[9] *O'Neill* v. *Tudhope*, 1984 S.L.T. 424; 1984 S.C.C.R. 276.
[10] 1975 Act, s. 68(2) to (4).
[11] *Ibid.* s. 357(1).
[11a] *Cf. McGlennan* v. *Johnston*, 1991 S.C.C.R. 895.
[12] 1975 Act, ss. 162, 163, 164, 357, 358.

offence.[13] A previous conviction cannot be libelled if it is under appeal.[14] It has also been held to be improper for a prosecutor in moving for sentence to refer to offences not included in the notice of previous convictions.[15] While that, and the rule that a previous conviction must be one dated prior to the current offence, are strictly correct, it would clearly be absurd if a court was not, in appropriate circumstances, informed of a conviction that has occurred subsequent to the current offence and which could not therefore be included in the notice. The most obvious example of this is where the offender has, since the current offence, been sentenced to a long period of imprisonment. In such a case, if the court were not to be informed of this, it might take a course which would be wholly inconsistent with the term of imprisonment, such as asking for a social inquiry report with a view to considering a probation order. Another example is where the accused has, since the current offence, been placed on probation. In such a case it is obviously desirable for the court to be aware of this if it is to make a sensible decision in the case under consideration.

7–06   There is some uncertainty about the propriety of taking note of past offences committed by a person who was under the age of 16 at the time when those offences were committed, and who was dealt with in respect of them by the children's panel. Such previous offences are frequently disclosed in social inquiry reports, and it is thought to have been the practice of most courts for many years to take note of any such history of previous offences even though they did not in the strict sense amount to previous convictions. However, in *Gibson* v. *Annan*[16] the High Court held in such a case that "the sheriff was in error in taking into account what was said in the social enquiry report." By contrast, in the later case of *Curran* v. *Jessop*,[17] in which no reference appears to have been made to *Gibson* v. *Annan*, the court said "the sheriff very properly had regard to the fact that the social enquiry report reveals that there is a long history of bad behaviour and offending." Consequently, this point awaits a final and authoritative decision. For the present, however, it is submitted that it offends against common sense to expect a court which is dealing with a 16- or 17-year-old offender to close its eyes entirely to the fact that that person has a long history of previous offending; and accordingly it is submitted that the approach of the High Court in *Curran* is to be preferred to that in *Gibson*. Apart from cases involving children, it is now clear that a court is entitled to have regard to convictions disclosed in a report, even though these have not been libelled by the prosecutor.[18] Where convictions are disclosed in a report it is proper practice for the court to give the accused an opportunity to admit or deny them. Previous convictions disclosed on a driving licence may also be taken into account when sentencing for road traffic offences (see Chapter 5 above).

7–07   Two other matters relating to previous convictions require to be noticed. First, a previous conviction libelled must apply to the accused.

---

[13] *H.M. Advocate* v. *John Graham* (1842) 1 Brown 445.
[14] *McCall* v. *Mitchell* (1911) 6 Adam 303.
[15] *Ramsay* v. *H.M. Advocate*, 1959 J.C. 86; *Adair* v. *Hill*, 1943 J.C. 9.
[16] 1990 S.C.C.R. 519.
[17] 1991 S.C.C.R. 150.
[18] *Sharp* v. *Stevenson*, 1945 S.L.T. (Notes) 79; *Sillars* v. *Copeland*, 1966 S.L.T. 89.

Thus, it is incompetent in a complaint against the representative of a company as an individual to libel a conviction obtained against the company in its corporate capacity.[19] Second, it has been observed[20] that, where a judge considers a previous conviction, he should look at the conviction and the sentence alone and should not take into account the details that led thereto. There is no modern reported statement to the same effect and, with the growing insistence in recent times on providing a court with the maximum information concerning an offender and his background, it may be doubted whether the view expressed in *Connel* v. *Mitchell* would today gain acceptance in its entirety. Certainly it would probably still be seen as inappropriate to examine all the details of previous offences, and to examine again all the arguments about, for example, provocation, or the pleas in mitigation. On the other hand, given the complete absence of detail that is normal in the Scottish system of recording convictions, it may be helpful for a court to know, in for example a case of wife assault, whether or not previous convictions for assault were of a similar character. In practice this sort of information is frequently given to the court either by the prosecutor or by counsel or solicitor for the defence, and it is submitted that it is neither improper for this to be done nor for the court to seek further information about previous convictions when it is not.[21]

Notice of penalties

7–08   Where any complaint includes a statutory charge a notice of penalties, in the form prescribed by statute,[22] must be served on the accused with the complaint, and a copy of the notice should be laid before the judge after the accused has pled or has been found guilty. Although errors in a notice of penalties may be rectified by amendment,[23] there is no power to serve a notice of penalties on an accused after he has been called on to plead; and, if a prosecutor has failed to serve a notice at the proper time, so that he cannot lay one before the court prior to sentence, it is incompetent for the court to impose any penalty.[24]

7–09   However, if there is no challenge of the fact that a notice of penalties was served on an accused but, at the stage of conviction, the prosecutor does not have a copy to lay before the judge, it is permissible for the prosecutor to prepare a copy during an adjournment and to lay it before the judge thereafter: the copy need not have been made contemporaneously with the principal.[25] Similarly, where an offender who was resident in the Republic of Ireland was served with a complaint and notice of penalties by recorded delivery, and subsequently admitted receipt of those documents, this was held to be a valid service notwithstanding that notices of penalties are not expressly mentioned in sections 316(3) and 334(6) of the 1975 Act.[26] Where a service of a notice of

---

[19] *Campbell* v. *MacPherson* (1910) 6 Adam 394.
[20] *Connel* v. *Mitchell* (1908) 5 Adam 641.
[21] See, for example, *Rozanski* v. *Ingram*, 1981 S.C.C.R. 100.
[22] 1975 Act, s. 311(5).
[23] *Ibid.* s. 335(1).
[24] *Coogans* v. *Macdonald*, 1954 J.C. 98.
[25] *Smith* v. *Moffat*, 1981 S.C.C.R. 291.
[26] *Aitchison* v. *Wringe*, 1985 S.L.T. 449; 1985 S.C.C.R. 134.

penalties has been effected personally, this may be proved by a written execution of service signed by a constable.[27] However, service on an accused's solicitor is not sufficient[28]; and service of a bundle of papers on an accused in prison where it is not possible to say with certainty what was contained in that bundle may also be insufficient.[29]

7–10   Disqualification from holding or obtaining a driving licence is a penalty of which notice must be given in a notice of penalties,[30] as also is endorsement of penalty points on a driving licence.[31] Forfeiture is also a penalty and, unless it is expressly mentioned in the notice of penalties, it cannot competently be ordered.[32]

7–11   A failure by a prosecutor to sign a notice of penalties is not fatal,[33] but he should take care, when referring to the section or sections in which the penalties are set forth, to state the correct sections.[34] However, where a notice of penalties refers to one situation arising under a particular statutory provision, and an accused is found guilty under another situation, the court may still pass sentence.[35] And, where a notice of penalties prescribes the penalties for driving with excess alcohol and the charge relates to a failure to provide specimens (the penalties being identical in each case), it is competent for the court to pass sentence though it would probably be more prudent in such a case for the prosecutor to seek leave to amend the notice.[36]

PLEA IN MITIGATION

7–12 After previous convictions have been admitted or proved, and after a notice of penalties has, where appropriate, been laid before the court, the accused, or his counsel or solicitor, may address the court in mitigation. This is a right which cannot be denied to an accused,[37] and, if an accused is not legally represented, the presiding judge must ask him if he has anything to say,[38] though failure to do this may not constitute a good ground of appeal unless the judge has acted oppressively. Mitigating circumstances may not be a matter of dispute, or may already have emerged in the course of a trial or in the narration of events by the prosecutor.[39] In any other case they should be established by oral evidence on oath.[40] Notwithstanding this rule it is not uncommon in summary cases, and even occasionally in cases on indictment, for the defence to produce a document, such as a letter from an employer or a

---

[27] *Muir* v. *Carmichael*, 1988 S.C.C.R. 79.
[28] *Geddes* v. *Hamilton*, 1986 S.L.T. 536; 1986 S.C.C.R. 165.
[29] *Cowan* v. *Guild*, 1991 S.C.C.R. 424.
[30] *Coogans* v. *Macdonald*, above.
[31] *Tudhope* v. *Eadie*, 1984 S.L.T. 178; 1983 S.C.C.R. 464; overruling *Pirie* v. *Rivard*, 1976 S.L.T. (Sh.Ct.) 59.
[32] *Duffy* v. *Lakie*, 1962 S.L.T. 30.
[33] *McCoull & Anr.* v. *Skeen*, 1974 S.L.T. (Notes) 48.
[34] *Cumming* v. *Frame* (1909) 6 Adam 57; *Galt* v. *Ritchie* (1873) 2 Couper 470.
[35] *Cardle* v. *Campbell*, 1985 S.C.C.R. 309.
[36] *Donnachie* v. *Smith*, 1989 S.C.C.R. 144.
[37] *Falconer* v. *Jessop*, 1975 S.L.T. (Notes) 78.
[38] *Grahams* v. *McLennan* (1911) 6 Adam 315; *Ewart* v. *Strathern*, 1924 J.C. 45.
[39] *Clark* v. *H.M. Advocate*, 1968 J.C. 53; *H.M. Advocate* v. *Murray*, 1969 S.L.T. (Notes) 85.
[40] *Forbes* v. *H.M. Advocate*, 1963 J.C. 68.

minister of religion to establish an accused person's good character. Although, strictly, such documents should not be considered in place of oral evidence, it is submitted that it is not unreasonable to do so provided that the court can be reasonably satisfied as to the authenticity of the documents, and provided that they are not submitted as evidence of material facts as distinct from being expressions of opinion on the general character of the accused. It is also common for all courts to accept, without oral evidence, statements from counsel and solicitors concerning matters such as an accused person's employment, marital status and family position—all of which are factors which may have some mitigating effect on sentence. If all matters relied on in a plea in mitigation had to be established by oral evidence the work of the courts would probably very quickly grind to a halt, and in these circumstances, it is submitted, what a judge must do is to exercise a sensible discretion so as to distinguish between those matters which can reasonably be taken as established without oral evidence and those which cannot.

7–13   Sometimes a judge will be obliged, or will consider it desirable, to obtain reports before deciding on sentence. If the need for this is apparent at an early stage, it may be sensible for the judge to suggest to the accused, or his counsel or solicitor, that any plea in mitigation should be held over until the reports have been made available. Sometimes, indeed, an accused's counsel or solicitor may suggest this course to the judge.

ADJOURNMENT FOR INQUIRY

7–14   The normal power which a court has to adjourn the hearing of a case includes the power, after a person has been convicted or the court has found that he committed the offence and before he has been sentenced or otherwise dealt with, to adjourn the case for the purpose of enabling inquiries to be made or of determining the most suitable method of dealing with his case. Although there may be more than one adjournment for this purpose, no single period of adjournment should exceed three weeks.[41] This power is used on every occasion when reports on an offender are asked for by the court and, although it is sometimes loosely referred to as "deferring sentence" or, in summary courts, by clerks of court, as "deferring conviction and sentence," the power is properly described as one of adjournment. Indeed, it is improper to use the power to defer sentence in order to circumvent the three weeks' time limit imposed by sections 179 and 380 of the 1975 Act.[42] Although there can be several adjournments to enable inquiries to be made, it is generally desirable that the actual date of final disposal should not be postponed more than is necessary and, to that end, it is as well, at the stage of first adjournment, that the court should consider and call for all the reports which appear to be necessary or desirable. This course is particularly to be commended where an offender is being remanded in custody. Where a case is adjourned it is essential that a minute of adjournment should be

---

[41] 1975 Act, ss. 179, 380.
[42] *H.M. Advocate* v. *Clegg*, 1990 S.C.C.R. 293; *McRobbie* v. *H.M. Advocate*, 1990 S.C.C.R. 767: and see paras. 1–10 and 1–14 above.

prepared and signed by the clerk of court: a failure to do this will render future proceedings incompetent.[42a]

Bail or custody

7–15   Generally, a person whose case is adjourned for reports should not be remanded in custody in the absence of special circumstances. This is particularly so in the case of first offenders.[43] If a person is not remanded in custody he must either be released on bail, or be ordained to attend the adjourned diet.[44] The special circumstances which may justify a remand in custody will vary from case to case but may include the fact that the offender is of no fixed abode or, even where he is a first offender, that he has been remanded in custody prior to trial. If, in such a case, the court is obtaining reports in the anticipation that a custodial sentence may be necessary, it would probably not be appropriate to release the offender during the period of adjournment.

Remand of children

7–16   Any court, on remanding or committing for trial a child who is not liberated on bail must, instead of committing him to prison, commit him to the local authority in whose area the court is situated to be detained in a place of safety chosen by the local authority for the period for which he is remanded or until he is liberated in due course of law. However, in the case of a child over 14 years of age it is not obligatory on the court so to commit him if the court certifies that he is of so unruly a character that he cannot safely be so committed or that he is of so depraved a character that he is not a fit person to be so detained.[45] Any commitment as aforesaid may be varied or, in the case of a child over 14 years of age, revoked if he proves to be of so unruly a character that he cannot safely be detained in such custody, or to be of so depraved a character that he is not a fit person to be so detained. Any variation or revocation is to be made by the court which made the order or, if application cannot conveniently be made to that court, by a sheriff sitting summarily having jurisdiction in the place where the court which made the order sat. If the order is revoked, the child may be committed to prison.[46]

7–17   The foregoing provisions are most unsatisfactory in several respects. First, they are duplicated in part, but by no means entirely, by the provisions of sections 23 and 329 of the 1975 Act; but these latter provisions have never been brought into operation notwithstanding that they actually have their origins in the Criminal Justice (Scotland) Act 1949,[47] and that the progenitors of what are now sections 24 and 297 of the 1975 Act were prospectively repealed by the 1949 Act. Second, sections 24 and 297 are in identical terms notwithstanding that some of the terminology which is used (for example, "committing for trial" and "liberated in due course of law") is wholly inappropriate under summary procedure. Third, the words "remanding or committing for trial" do not

---

[42a] *Heywood* v. *Stewart*, 1991 G.W.D. 36–2189.
[43] *Morrison* v. *Clark*, 1962 S.L.T. 113.
[44] 1975 Act, ss. 179, 380.
[45] *Ibid*. ss.24(1), 297(1).
[46] *Ibid*. ss. 24(2), 297(2).
[47] S. 28: and see 1975 Act, s. 464(3).

appear to be apt for cases where a child is to be remanded for sentence after trial[48]: consequently, there appears to be no statutory provision to cover such cases. And fourth, both sections 24 and 297 contain provision that a court is not to certify a child as unruly unless such conditions as the Secretary of State may by order prescribe are satisfied in relation to the child: but that provision, added by section 70 of the Children Act 1975, has never been given effect, and no conditions have ever been prescribed by the Secretary of State. Although in practice few children are prosecuted, and even fewer are remanded in custody, it is nonetheless little short of a disgrace that this part of Scottish criminal procedure legislation should be in such a mess.[48a]

7–18   Where a child is committed to a local authority under section 24 or section 297 of the 1975 Act he may not be placed in secure accommodation in a residential establishment as a place of safety unless the director of social work and the person in charge of the residential establishment providing the secure accommodation are satisfied that it is in the child's best interests and that the criteria specified in section 58A(3)(*a*) or (*b*) of the Social Work (Scotland) Act 1968 apply.[49] Section 58A was added to the 1968 Act by section 8 of the Health and Social Services and Social Security Adjudications Act 1983, and subsection (3) provides that a child may only be kept in secure accommodation where either he has a history of absconding, is likely to abscond unless kept in secure accommodation, and his physical, mental or moral welfare is likely to be at risk if he absconds, or he is likely to injure himself or others unless he is kept in secure accommodation.

Remand for inquiry into physical or mental condition

7–19   Where a person is charged before a court with an offence punishable with imprisonment, and the court is satisfied that he did the act or made the omission charged but is of opinion that an inquiry ought to be made into his physical or mental condition before the method of dealing with him is determined, the court must remand him in custody or on bail for such period or periods as the court thinks necessary to enable a medical examination and report to be made. No single period of remand should exceed three weeks.[50] Where bail is allowed it must be a condition of the bail that the person should undergo a medical examination by a duly qualified medical practitioner or, where the inquiry is into his mental condition and the bail order so specifies, two such practitioners. Furthermore, it must be a condition of bail that he attends at an institution or place, or on any such practitioner specified in the order and, where the inquiry is into his mental condition, that he should comply with

---

[48] Compare, for example, the words "remands or commits for trial or for sentence" in 1975 Act, ss. 23, 329.

[48a] As this book was going to press it became known that ss. 23 and 329 of the 1975 Act are to come into force on January 6, 1992: Criminal Procedure (Scotland) Act 1975 (Commencement No. 1) Order 1991 (S.I. 1991 No. 2883 (c. 89)).

[49] Secure Accommodation (Scotland) Regulations 1983, reg. 13(*a*).

[50] 1975 Act, ss. 180(1), 381(1). Unlike ss. 179 and 380 there is no power to ordain an offender to appear at subsequent diets.

any directions which may be given to him for that purpose by any person so specified or by a person of any class so specified.[51]

7–20   From time to time a court may wish medical reports before deciding on the proper method of disposing of a case but may be of opinion that the offender's mental condition is such that he cannot be relied upon to comply with the above conditions of a bail order, and that it would be better that he should reside in a hospital during the period of remand rather than being committed to prison. Provision exists under sections 25 and 330 of the 1975 Act for committing persons to hospital in certain circumstances, but these sections only deal with the case where a court *remands or commits for trial*, and therefore provide no authority for such a course after trial and before sentence. In that situation the proper course is provided by sections 180(2) and 381(2) which, in addition to the provisions already described, go on to provide that, if arrangements have been made for his reception, it may be a condition of the bail allowed to a person who is to undergo medical examination that he should, for the purpose of the examination, reside in an institution or place specified in the order. In such a case the institution or place will normally be a hospital.

7–21   Where a court exercises any of the above powers it must send a statement of the reasons for which it is of opinion that an inquiry ought to be made into the person's physical or mental condition, and of any information before the court about his condition, to the institution or place where he is remanded in custody or, where he is released on bail, to the institution or place at which or the person by whom he is to be examined.[52]

WHEN REPORTS MUST BE OBTAINED

(a) In connection with non-custodial disposals

7–22   Where a court is considering the making of a probation order it must first obtain a social inquiry report as to the circumstances and character of the offender.[53] This was common practice for many years, and became a statutory requirement in 1987.[54] In cases where the court is considering the insertion in a probation order of a requirement that the offender should perform unpaid work it must be satisfied that provision can be made for the offender to perform such work.[55] That information too can best be obtained in a social inquiry report. Moreover, where a court is considering the making of a community service order, it must obtain and consider a report by an officer of a local authority about the offender and his circumstances.[56] It is improper for a judge to interview a social worker in private.[57]

---

[51] 1975 Act, ss. 180(2), 381(2).
[52] *Ibid.* ss. 180(4), 381(4).
[53] *Ibid.* ss. 183(1), 384(1).
[54] Criminal Justice (Scotland) Act 1987, Sched. 1, para. 10.
[55] 1975 Act, ss. 183(5A), 384(5A).
[56] Community Service by Offenders (Scotland) Act 1978, s. 1(2)(*c*).
[57] *W.* v. *H.M. Advocate*, 1989 S.C.C.R. 461.

(b) In connection with custodial disposals

Children[58]

7–23   There are no statutory provisions which expressly require a court to obtain a social inquiry report when dealing with a child. However, where a child is convicted on indictment and the court proposes to sentence him to detention it must be of opinion that no other method of dealing with him is appropriate.[59] It is submitted that a court could not properly be so satisfied without obtaining and considering at least a social inquiry report. Moreover, where a child who is subject to a supervision requirement is charged with an offence and pleads guilty to, or is found guilty of, that offence the High Court may, and the sheriff court must, request the reporter to arrange a children's hearing for the purpose of obtaining their advice.[60] In practice, since children are seldom prosecuted, at least where they are under the age of 16, unless their offence is a serious one, it is submitted that it is sensible practice to obtain a social inquiry report in all cases, even where a custodial disposal is not in contemplation.

Young offenders

7–24   In the case of a person who is not less than 16 but under 21 years of age a court may not impose detention unless it is of opinion that no other method of dealing with him is appropriate; and to enable the court to form such an opinion it must obtain, from an officer of a local authority or otherwise, such information as it can about the offender's circumstances. It must also take into account any information before it concerning the offender's character and physical and mental condition.[61] It is essential that the foregoing provisions should be complied with.[62]

Adult offenders

7–25   A court must not pass a sentence of imprisonment on a person of or over 21 years of age who has not been previously sentenced to imprisonment or detention by a court in any part of the United Kingdom unless the court considers that no other method of dealing with him is appropriate. Before a court can so determine it must obtain, from an officer of a local authority or otherwise, such information as it can about the offender's circumstances. It must also take into account any information before it concerning the offender's character and physical and mental condition.[63] The foregoing provisions replace previous legislation concerning the imprisonment of first offenders and not only concentrate on the first sentence of imprisonment rather than the first offence but also apply equally to courts of solemn and summary jurisdiction.

---

[58] For a definition of "child" see para. 4–01 above.
[59] 1975 Act, s. 206(1).
[60] *Ibid.* ss. 173(3), 372(3).
[61] *Ibid.* ss. 207(3) and (4), 415(3) and (4).
[62] *Hogg* v. *Heatlie*, 1962 S.L.T. 38; *Deasley* v. *Hogg*, 1976 S.L.T. (Notes) 7. It is also essential, where a court *does* impose a custodial sentence, that it should state clearly why it is of opinion that no other method of dealing with the offender is appropriate: *Dunsmore* v. *Allan*, 1991 S.C.C.R. 946.
[63] 1980 Act, s. 42(1); and see *Dunsmore* v. *Allan*, above.

7–26   For the purpose of determining whether a person has been previously sentenced to imprisonment or detention by a court in any part of the United Kingdom the court must (a) disregard a previous sentence of imprisonment which, having been suspended, has not taken effect under section 23 of the Powers of Criminal Courts Act 1973 or under section 19 of the Treatment of Offenders Act (Northern Ireland) 1968, and (b) construe detention as meaning (i) in relation to Scotland, detention in a young offenders' institution or detention centre, (ii) in relation to England and Wales, a sentence of youth custody, borstal training or detention in a young offenders' institution or detention centre, and (iii) in relation to Northern Ireland, detention in a young offenders' centre.[64]

Mentally disordered offenders[65]

7–27   Before a court may make a hospital order or a guardianship order it must (a) be satisfied, on the written or oral evidence of two medical practitioners, that the grounds set out in section 17(1) or section 36(*a*) of the Mental Health (Scotland) Act 1984[66] apply in relation to the offender, and (b) be of the opinion, having regard to all the circumstances of the offence and the character and antecedents of the offender, and to the other available methods of dealing with him, that the most suitable method of disposing of the case is by means of such an order.[67] If the court does not consider it necessary to proceed on the basis of oral evidence for the purpose of (a) above, it is customary to refer to the written documents produced by the medical practitioners as medical or psychiatric *reports*: it is to be observed, however, that for the purposes of the section these documents are to be regarded as *evidence*, the absence of which will preclude the making of the order. By contrast, no provision is made as to the means by which the court should reach the opinion referred to in (b) above. It is submitted, however, that a social inquiry report will normally be desirable and appropriate for that purpose, in addition to such other information as the court may have obtained in the course of the proceedings.

7–28   Requirements which are similar to the foregoing also apply in cases where a court is considering the making of an interim hospital order under either section 174A or section 375A of the 1975 Act.[68]

WHEN REPORTS MAY BE DESIRABLE

7–29   Apart from cases where a court is obliged by statute to obtain a report of a particular character before disposing of a case, there are many instances where additional information, either as to the offender's background and home circumstances or as to his physical or mental condition, may be of considerable value. The occasions when the desirability of obtaining such information will suggest itself will depend largely on the circumstances of a particular case or particular offender, and to some extent on the views of individual judges. While in general it may be said that, in the interests

---

[64] 1980 Act, s. 41(2), as applied by s. 42(3).
[65] For a general treatment of the subject, see Chapter 3.
[66] For an explanation of those grounds, see para. 3–11 above.
[67] 1975 Act, ss. 175(1), 376(1).
[68] See further para. 3–16 *et seq.* above.

of economy, reports of any kind should not be asked for unless there are some positive indications that they are likely to be helpful, it is nonetheless the case that judges increasingly tend to look for additional information to assist them when making any other than the clearest and most obvious sentencing decisions. Although not intended to be either definitive or exhaustive, the following list shows the circumstances in which the obtaining of reports is frequently desirable.

Social inquiry reports

    (a) cases involving children;
    (b) cases involving young offenders where the offence is of at least moderate gravity;
    (c) cases where the offence is one of violence, and in particular domestic violence, and cases where the offender has a previous record of violence;
    (d) cases where the offence is of at least moderate gravity and the offender either has no previous convictions or has been free of convictions for a substantial period;
    (e) cases where the offence is of at least moderate gravity and the offender is female;
    (f) cases where the offender is presently, or has recently been, the subject of a probation or a community service order.

Psychiatric reports[69]

    (a) cases where the offence is of a sexual nature;
    (b) some, but not all, cases where the offence is related to the misuse of drugs or alcohol;
    (c) cases where the offender has a previous history of mental disorder;
    (d) cases where the offence shows bizarre or unusual behaviour on the part of the offender;
    (e) cases where the offender's behaviour in court is bizarre or unusual;
    (f) some cases where the offence is one of violence, particularly where the offender has a previous record of similar offences.

PROVISION OF REPORTS TO OFFENDER AND OTHERS

7–30   When a social inquiry report has been obtained a copy of it must be given by the clerk of court to the offender or his solicitor. In the case of an offender under 16 years of age, who is not represented by counsel or a solicitor, a copy of the report must be given to his parent or guardian if present in court.[70]

7–31   The foregoing rule in relation to offenders under 16 years of age is subject to modification in cases where the child is dealt with summarily under special rules made under section 366 of the 1975 Act. In such cases, where a report has been received from a local authority, an education

---

[69] If there is reason to suppose that an offender may be suffering from a mental illness so that a hospital order or guardianship order may be appropriate, it is usually sensible to ask for two psychiatric reports at the outset to avoid the necessity of a subsequent adjournment after a single report has been obtained: see para. 7–27 above.
[70] 1975 Act, ss. 192, 393.

authority, or a registered medical practitioner, (i) the child must be told the substance of any part of the report bearing on his character or conduct which the court considers to be material to the disposal of the case; (ii) the child's parent or guardian or other representative, if present, must be told the substance of any part of the report which the court considers to be material and which has reference to his character or conduct, or the character, conduct, home surroundings or health of the child; and (iii) if the child or his parent or guardian or other representative, having been told the substance of any part of a report, desires to produce evidence in relation to any matter contained in it, the court, if it thinks the evidence material, must adjourn the proceedings for the production of further evidence. In the latter event the court must, if necessary, require the attendance at the adjourned hearing of the person who made the report.[71]

7–32   Given the provisions in the Act of Adjournal referred to above, it may be wondered what content is to be given to the provisions relating to offenders under 16 years of age in section 393 of the 1975 Act.[72] The answer appears to be that section 366, and the rules contained in the Act of Adjournal, do not apply in cases where a child is charged with an offence jointly with a person who is not a child.[73] In such cases, consequently, section 393 of the 1975 Act will apply.

7–33   Where a written report from a medical practitioner is tendered in evidence otherwise than by or on behalf of the accused (and otherwise than in the circumstances mentioned in paragraph 7–31 above), a copy of it must be given to the accused's counsel or solicitor. If the accused is unrepresented, the substance of the report must be disclosed to him or, where he is a child under 16 years of age, to his parent or guardian if present in court. Where the court is of opinion that further time is necessary in the interests of the accused for consideration of a report by a medical practitioner, or its substance, the case must be adjourned.[74]

REPORTS IN CASES WHERE THERE ARE SEVERAL ACCUSED

7–34   Where several accused are convicted or found guilty on the same complaint or indictment, it is highly desirable that the same judge should sentence all the accused. Consequently, where the court asks for reports in respect of some, but not all, of the accused, the proper course, it has been held, is to defer sentence on any in respect of whom reports are not being prepared until the adjourned diet when the reports will be available in respect of the others.[75] While this rule can usually be complied with in cases on indictment, and in many summary cases as well, problems may arise in those summary cases where, at the first calling, one of several accused pleads guilty while the others plead not guilty. Similar problems may also arise in cases under solemn procedure where one out of several accused intimates a desire to have his case disposed of at an early stage under section 102 of the 1975 Act. Even in such cases it may be desirable

---

[71] Act of Adjournal (Consolidation) 1988, para. 144(*g*).
[72] See para. 7–30 above.
[73] 1975 Act, s. 370.
[74] *Ibid.* ss. 176(3), 377(3).
[75] *Thom* v. *Smith*, High Court, December 7, 1978 (unreported).

to defer sentence on the one who has pled guilty so that questions of relative culpability can be considered after the trial. On the other hand—and bearing in mind that in some cases the trial may not take place for several weeks or even months—there may be circumstances which make it desirable that the accused who has pled guilty should be dealt with at once. For example, he may be the subject of a probation order which will have terminated before the trial diet, but of which the offence to which he has pled guilty constitutes a breach. Again, it may be clear that he must be dealt with by a custodial sentence, but there is of course no power to remand him in custody until the trial diet. In such cases, it is submitted, it would be appropriate for the court to consider departing from the general rule outlined above.

REMIT TO HIGH COURT FOR SENTENCE

7–35　Where at any diet in proceedings on indictment in the sheriff court sentence falls to be imposed but the sheriff holds that any competent sentence which he can impose is inadequate so that the question of sentence is appropriate for the High Court, he must:

(a) endorse upon the record copy of the indictment a certificate of the plea or the verdict (as the case may be);

(b) by interlocutor written on such record copy remit the convicted person to the High Court for sentence; and

(c) append to such interlocutor a note of his reasons for such remit. Such a remit is sufficient warrant to bring the accused before the High Court for sentence, and it will remain in force until the convicted person is sentenced.[76]

7–36　Prior to the passing of the 1980 Act the necessity of remitting an offender to the High Court for sentence occasionally arose in cases of crimes reserved to the High Court, such as rape. That was because, under the former provisions of section 102 of the 1975 Act, where an accused intimated a desire to have his case at once disposed of, it was indicted in the sheriff court regardless of its nature. However, the amendment to section 102 made by section 16 of the 1980 Act now means that such a case may be indicted directly to the High Court, as also may any other case where, had it gone to trial, the trial would have been in the High Court. Consequently, all cases in which a sheriff is now likely to consider it appropriate to remit to the High Court for sentence will arise under section 104 of the 1975 Act, and they will all be cases where the reason for remitting is that the sheriff considers that any competent sentence which he can impose is inadequate.

7–37　Over the years the procedures for remitting offenders to the High Court for sentence have caused some difficulties, and have on occasions been misunderstood by sheriffs. The following points should therefore be borne in mind:

(a) The statutory provisions relating to the recording of pleas or

---

[76] 1975 Act, s. 104.

verdicts, and the recording of the order for remit, must be strictly adhered to, otherwise the remitted diet may be put in peril.[77]

(b) It is normally desirable, where there has been a trial, that the sheriff who presided at the trial should remit the accused for sentence. However, in a case where sentence was originally deferred for a period, it was held that it was permissible for the remit to be made by a sheriff other than the one who had presided at the trial.[78] While there may occasionally be circumstances which make such a course necessary, it is submitted that it should be avoided if at all possible because difficulties may arise regarding the preparation of the note which is to accompany the interlocutor of remit.

(c) If a case is of such a character that the sheriff considers that any sentence which he can impose is inadequate, but the case also raises the possibility that the offender may be mentally ill so that a hospital order or guardianship order (which are within the sheriff's competence) may be appropriate, the proper course is to remit the accused to the High Court for sentence and to allow that court to consider any evidence relevant to the accused's physical or mental condition.[79] The reason for this is to avoid the necessity of the High Court having to rehear medical evidence which has been considered, but for any reason not acted upon, by the sheriff. It should be added, however, that the case of *H.M. Advocate* v. *Clark* was a rather special one which dealt only with the problems relating to medical *evidence*. It does not mean that in cases where, for example, a social inquiry report must be obtained before a custodial sentence can be imposed, the sheriff should at once remit the case where he has concluded that, in the event of a custodial sentence being necessary, his own powers will be inadequate. The proper course in such a case, it is submitted, is for the sheriff first to obtain such reports as may be either necessary or desirable, and to consider in the light of such information as they may contain whether a sentence within his own competence is appropriate. If the accused is then remitted for sentence, those reports, together with the sheriff's note, should be available to the High Court.

(d) Where two or more accused appear on the same indictment and the sheriff considers that he could deal with one or more of them within the limits of his own powers, but that the others should be remitted to the High Court, the proper procedure is to remit all the accused.[80] This is to enable the same court to consider the appropriate sentence for each accused and, where necessary, to adjust a proper balance between these sentences. If the sheriff considers that there are circumstances which would, in the case of one or more of the accused, have justified a sentence within his own competence, he can refer to those circumstances in his note. The foregoing rule may be departed from in exceptional circumstances

---

[77] *H.M. Advocate* v. *Galloway* (1894) 1 Adam 375; *H.M. Advocate* v. *MacDonald* (1896) 3 S.L.T. 317.

[78] *Borland* v. *H.M. Advocate*, 1976 S.L.T. (Notes) 12.

[79] *H.M. Advocate* v. *Clark*, 1955 J.C. 88.

[80] *H.M. Advocate* v. *Duffy*, 1974 S.L.T. (Notes) 46.

as, for example, where one accused is convicted of an offence which does not involve any of the others. However, this exception to the general rule should be used very sparingly.

(e) Where an accused appears before the court on two separate indictments, one of which contains a charge or charges the maximum penalty for which is within the sheriff's competence, and the other of which contains a charge or charges in respect of which the sheriff considers that any sentence which he can impose is inadequate, the accused must not be remitted for sentence on both indictments. The sheriff should himself deal with the accused on the former indictment, but may refer to that circumstance in his note accompanying the remit of the accused on the other indictment.[81]

SENTENCE

Form of sentence in cases on indictment

7–38 In any case, whether in the High Court or the sheriff court, the sentence to be pronounced must be announced by the judge in open court, and must be entered in the record in the form used in the High Court. It is not necessary to read the entry of the sentence from the record.[82] In recording sentences of imprisonment it is sufficient to minute the term of imprisonment to which the court sentenced the accused without specifying the prison in which the sentence is to be carried out. (Nowadays, the prison in which an offender will serve his sentence is, in any event, a matter for the prison authorities, and not for the court.) Such entries of sentences, signed by the clerk of court, are full warrant and authority for all execution to follow thereon, and for the clerk to issue extracts thereof for carrying the same into execution or otherwise.[83]

Form of sentence in summary cases

7–39 The finding and sentence and any order of a court of summary jurisdiction, as regards both offences at common law and offences under any statute or order, must be entered in the record of the proceedings in the form, as nearly as may be, of the appropriate form contained in Part V of Schedule 2 to the Summary Jurisdiction (Scotland) Act 1954. Such an entry is sufficient warrant for all execution thereon and for the clerk of court to issue extracts containing such executive clauses as may be necessary for implement thereof. When imprisonment forms part of any sentence or other judgment, warrant for the apprehension and interim detention of the accused pending his being committed to prison will, where necessary, be implied.[84]

7–40 It is essential that the forms contained in Part V of Schedule 2 to the 1954 Act should be strictly followed.[85] Normally, where an accused is present, the conviction and sentence will be announced orally by the judge, but this intimation is not sufficient to make them effective. Only

---

[81] *H.M. Advocate* v. *Anderson & Ors.*, 1946 J.C. 81; *H.M. Advocate* v. *Stern*, 1974 J.C. 10.
[82] 1975 Act, s. 217(1).
[83] *Ibid.* s. 217(2).
[84] *Ibid.* s. 430(1).
[85] *Paterson* v. *McLennan* (1914) 7 Adam 428.

the signing of the formal judgment in the record of proceedings has that effect.[86]

7–41   Every sentence imposed by a court of summary jurisdiction must, except where there is provision to the contrary, be pronounced in open court in the presence of the accused, but it need not be written out or signed in his presence.[87] If the sentence is one which cannot competently be pronounced in the accused's absence it will be set aside.[88]

When sentence may be pronounced in absence

7–42   The circumstances where a court may pronounce sentence in the absence of the accused are: (a) where he had tendered a written plea of guilty, or tenders such a plea by a solicitor or any other authorised person,[89] but in such a case the court may not impose a custodial sentence unless it continues the case to another diet when the accused is present[90]; (b) where the trial of a statutory offence for which a sentence of imprisonment cannot be imposed in the first instance has taken place in the absence of the accused[91]; and (c) in cases on indictment against a body corporate.[92] Where imprisonment is being imposed in respect of default in payment of a fine, that may be done in absence only where the offender is already in prison.[93]

Interruption of proceedings

7–43   It is possible in both solemn and summary proceedings to interrupt those proceedings so as to pass sentence on the accused in respect of a conviction arising from other proceedings. This will not cause the instance to fall nor otherwise affect the validity of the proceedings.[94] The provisions in the Act of Adjournal (originally introduced in 1978) give effect to a recommendation by the Thomson Committee[95] following upon a somewhat technical decision in an earlier case[96] where, following a jury trial, the sheriff sentenced the first accused in respect of that indictment, and at the same time sentenced him in respect of an outstanding summary complaint, all before sentencing the second accused on the indictment. It was held that the interruption of the solemn proceedings by consideration of the outstanding summary matter caused the instance to fall so that the conviction of both accused required to be quashed. What took place in that case is now permissible under the Act of Adjournal; and indeed it will frequently be desirable that sentence in one case should be deferred until the date of a forthcoming trial so that, in the event of the accused then being convicted, both cases can be considered simultaneously for the purpose of determining the appropriate sentence.

---

[86] *Cameron* v. *Deans* (1901) 3 Adam 498; *Rintoul* v. *Stewart* (1902) 3 Adam 574.
[87] 1975 Act, s. 433.
[88] *Watson* v. *Argo*, 1936 J.C. 87.
[89] 1975 Act, s. 334(3).
[90] *Ibid.* s. 334(4).
[91] *Ibid.* s. 338(*b*).
[92] *Ibid.* s. 74(4).
[93] *Ibid.* s. 398(1); but see *Proudfoot* v. *Wither*, 1990 S.L.T. 742; 1990 S.C.C.R. 96; *Nash, Petr.*, 1991 S.C.C.R. 978.
[94] Act of Adjournal (Consolidation) 1988, paras. 74, 123.
[95] *Criminal Procedure in Scotland (Second Report)*, 1975, Cmnd. 6218.
[96] *Law and Nicol* v. *H.M. Advocate*, 1973 S.L.T. (Notes) 14.

It is to be noted, however, that interruption of proceedings in terms of the Act of Adjournal is competent only where there is a previous *finding of guilt* in existence: it is not competent where proceedings are interrupted so as to take a plea in respect of a complaint or indictment to which no plea of guilty has previously been tendered.[96a]

Essentials of a valid sentence

7–44   According to Macdonald[97] a valid sentence must contain certain features. These are that it must be consistent with the charge and with the law, and that it must be one which can be passed on the person convicted. Additionally, it must be free from any ambiguity. The last of these essentials has from time to time given rise to difficulties.[98] Two points in particular should be noted. A sentence of imprisonment which does not clearly indicate the date from which that sentence is to run is a fundamental nullity[99]; and, any order for forfeiture must clearly describe the article concerned.[1]

Cumulo **penalties**

7–45   Several problems present themselves where a *cumulo* penalty is imposed: some of these relate to the competency of the sentence itself while some are related to difficulties which may arise in the event of an appeal. Section 430(3) of the 1975 Act expressly provides that where several charges at common law or under any statute or order are embraced in one complaint a *cumulo* fine may be imposed in respect of all or any of such charges of which the accused is convicted. It has been held that the effect of section 56(3) of the Summary Jurisdiction (Scotland) Act 1954 (which is now repeated as section 430(3) of the 1975 Act) is to allow a summary court to impose a *cumulo* fine in respect of several offences which exceeds the maximum provided by the statutes for a single offence.[2] However, it is incompetent, where one of two offences provides only for a penalty of a fine, with imprisonment in default of payment, to impose a *cumulo* sentence of imprisonment, that sentence being competent only in respect of the other offence.[3]

7–46   A point of some interest falls to be noted in relation to the wording of section 430(3) of the 1975 Act. As already noted that section permits a court to impose a *cumulo* fine where several charges are contained in the same complaint, and the question may be asked whether there is any power for a summary court to impose a single sentence of *imprisonment* in similar circumstances. That this is sometimes done there can be no doubt, and it does not appear ever to have been questioned. It is to be noted, however, that there has been some statutory change on the matter. The Summary Jurisdiction (Scotland) Act 1908, by section 53, gave summary courts a similar power to that now contained in section

---

[96a] *Watters and Ors.* v. *H.M. Advocate*, 1991 G.W.D. 38–2304.
[97] Pp. 350, 351.
[98] *Allan* v. *Lamb* (1900) 3 Adam 248; *Macleman* v. *Middleton* (1901) 3 Adam 353; *Cowans* v. *Sinclair* (1905) 4 Adam 585.
[99] *Grant* v. *Grant* (1855) 2 Irv. 277.
[1] *Rankin* v. *Wright* (1901) 3 Adam 483.
[2] *Wann* v. *Macmillan*, 1957 J.C. 20.
[3] *McLauchlan* v. *Davidson*, 1921 J.C. 45.

430(3) of the 1975 Act, but with this difference, that the court was empowered to impose a *cumulo penalty*. Referring to section 53 in the 1908 Act, Lord Justice-General Cooper, in the Full Bench case of *Maguiness* v. *MacDonald*,[4] said: "Section 53 certainly authorises any court to impose a single fine or a single sentence of imprisonment on a multiple complaint." When, however, the 1908 Act was replaced by the Summary Jurisdiction (Scotland) Act 1954, the provision in section 56(3) was reworded so as to allow for the imposition of a *cumulo fine*, a form of words which, as has been seen, now appears in the 1975 Act. Whether this was deliberate or merely an accident on the part of the draftsman is impossible to say.

7–47   Normally, the rules of statutory interpretation would require that effect should be given to a change of words such as that noted above, and in that case the result would have been to exclude the power of a summary court to impose a single sentence of imprisonment on a multiple complaint. It is to be noted, however, that the Act of 1954, like the one of 1975, was a consolidating and not an amending statute, and that fact, coupled with the continuing and unquestioned practice of the courts, tends to confirm that it was not intended to make any change in 1954, that the power has remained unchanged since 1908, and that it is competent to impose a single sentence of imprisonment where there are several charges on one complaint.

7–48   The use of *cumulo* fines and sentences of imprisonment, even where competent, should be considered carefully since, in the event of a successful appeal against conviction in respect of one or more of the charges, it may be difficult for the appeal court to impose an appropriate sentence on the remaining charges.[5] In general it may be said that *cumulo* fines or sentences of imprisonment should be imposed only where the offences are all of a very similar character, and will stand or fall together in the event of an appeal against conviction. It should be added that, in relation to those road traffic offences which attract disqualification, they should also be dealt with separately. Although a court is not empowered to impose a *cumulo* order for disqualification, it may be tempted, when dealing with several charges, to apply to each the longest period of disqualification appropriate to any one of them on the basis that any shorter periods would in any event be concurrent with that longer period. However, the High Court has expressed its disapproval of such a practice,[6] again on the basis that, in the event of a successful appeal against conviction in respect of one or more of the charges, it may be impossible to determine the appropriate period of disqualification on the remaining charges.

Sentence on lesser charges

7–49   Where an accused is convicted on a complaint, or particularly an indictment, which contains one very serious charge and a number of lesser charges, it is better to impose shorter, concurrent, sentences of imprisonment on the lesser charges rather than merely to admonish in

[4] 1953 J.C. 31, at 35.
[5] *Paisley Ice Rink* v. *Hill*, 1944 J.C. 158; *Seaton* v. *Allan*, 1973 J.C. 24.
[6] *Austin* v. *Carnegie*, High Court, July 21, 1982, unreported.

respect of them. The reason for this was highlighted in a case[7] where an accused was convicted of a charge of murder as well as several lesser, though still quite serious, charges. In accordance with what was then Crown practice the advocate-depute moved for sentence on the murder charge alone and, consequently, no sentence was pronounced on the lesser charges. When, subsequently, the accused successfully appealed against his conviction on the charge of murder, the result was that no sentence could be imposed on the lesser charges. By the same token, if a court is considering sentence and is told that the accused has recently been sentenced to a long term of imprisonment for another offence, then, unless the court proposes to impose a consecutive sentence of imprisonment, it is probably better to impose a concurrent sentence rather than merely to admonish because the earlier conviction and/or sentence may be successfully appealed against.

Consecutive sentences

7–50   Under both solemn and summary jurisdiction courts are empowered to order that sentences of imprisonment or detention should be served consecutively. In some instances that power exists at common law, and in others it is conferred by statute. Over the years many appeals have been taken to the High Court in relation to the use of the power to order sentences to be served consecutively. In some instances such appeals have been concerned with the competency of consecutive sentences in certain circumstances, and in others they have been concerned more with questions of reasonableness and appropriateness. Questions as to competency and appropriateness may arise in three distinct situations, namely:

(1) where there are two or more charges in a single complaint or indictment;

(2) where on the same occasion a court is passing sentence in respect of two or more complaints or indictments; and

(3) where, in any case, the accused is already undergoing a sentence of imprisonment imposed on an earlier occasion.[8]

Each of those situations will now be considered in turn.

(1) Where two or more charges in a single complaint or indictment

7–51   Where sentences of imprisonment are imposed in respect of two or more charges in a single complaint or indictment they may be made consecutive to each other. However, this common law power is subject to the limitation that a court may not thereby exceed its normal maximum sentencing power. Thus, the fact that an accused has been convicted of eight separate charges on a summary complaint does not permit a sheriff, by the imposition of consecutive sentences, to exceed his normal maximum sentence of three months' imprisonment.[9] Although there is no

---

[7] *H.M. Advocate* v. *Paterson*, 1974 S.L.T. 53.

[8] A further situation of difficulty can arise in relation to the imposition of consecutive sentences of imprisonment in respect of unpaid fines. This is dealt with at para. 1–105 *et seq.* above.

[9] *Maguiness* v. *MacDonald*, 1953 J.C. 31.

comparable authority in relation to cases on indictment, it is submitted that the same principle applies so that a sheriff would not be entitled, in respect of a single indictment, to exceed his statutory maximum of three years' imprisonment by the imposition of consecutive sentences.

7–52   So far as the appropriateness of imposing consecutive sentences in respect of several charges on a single complaint or indictment is concerned, the general rule appears to be that such sentences are inappropriate where the charges all arise out of the same incident.[10] However, much will depend on the circumstances of a given case. The High Court has approved of consecutive sentences for a charge of possessing an offensive weapon (a razor) and a charge of assault involving that razor, largely on the basis that the statutory charge of possession was committed as soon as the offender set out with the razor, and would have been committed whether or not there had been an assault.[11]

7–53   Where a person is charged on a single complaint or indictment with a substantive offence or offences and, additionally, with a contravention of the Bail etc. (Scotland) Act 1980, it will generally be appropriate to make any sentence of imprisonment in respect of the Bail Act offence consecutive to a sentence or sentences of imprisonment imposed for the substantive offence or offences.[12] However, this is always a matter for the discretion of the court, and that may particularly be so where the commission of a substantive offence gives rise to two or more charges under the Bail Act. In such cases there may be a question as to whether or not sentences of imprisonment in respect of the Bail Act charges should be ordered to be consecutive to each other. The High Court has acknowledged that this is a matter for the discretion of the court of first instance,[13] but in some instances the High Court has held that consecutive sentences for two or more Bail Act offences were inappropriate.[14]

7–54   Where a complaint or indictment contains, in effect, a single charge but that charge is described by reference to a number of sub-charges each of which would by itself be a substantive charge, it is incompetent to impose consecutive sentences in respect of each of the sub-charges so that the total period of imprisonment exceeds the statutory maximum for the single charge.[15] Although the High Court, in *Beattie*, did not say that in such a case it is incompetent to impose separate sentences in respect of each of the sub-charges, it is submitted that the preferable course would be for a court to impose a single sentence in respect of the principal charge, though that sentence would of course reflect the number and the gravity of the sub-charges of which the accused had been convicted.

(2) Where two or more complaints or indictments are dealt with on same occasion

7–55   It is not uncommon for a court to have to sentence an accused on the

---

[10] *McGuigan* v. *Wilson*, 1988 S.C.C.R. 474; *Sillars* v. *H.M. Advocate*, 1990 S.C.C.R. 425; but see *Hunt* v. *Wilson*, 1991 S.C.C.R. 821.

[11] *Campbell* v. *H.M. Advocate*, 1986 S.C.C.R. 516.

[12] *Garner* v. *Lockhart*, 1990 S.C.C.R. 385.

[13] *Whyte* v. *Normand*, 1988 S.C.C.R. 465.

[14] *Allan* v. *Lockhart*, 1986 S.C.C.R. 395; *Montgomery* v. *H.M. Advocate*, 1987 S.C.C.R. 264.

[15] *Beattie* v. *H.M. Advocate*, 1986 S.C.C.R. 605.

same occasion in respect of charges contained in two or more complaints or, less frequently, two or more indictments. Apart from cases where two complaints or indictments have been served on an accused for technical reasons (see paragraph 7–59 below), this may occur because, for example, sentence has been deferred in respect of one complaint in order to await the outcome of a trial in respect of another or, increasingly, because an accused has a succession of complaints to answer, relating to various offences committed over a period of time, and elects to clear everything up by having all outstanding matters dealt with at once (popularly known in some courts as a "roll-up").

7–56   In such cases it is competent to impose consecutive sentences of imprisonment in respect of each complaint even where the effect of doing so is to exceed the court's statutory maximum in respect of a single complaint.[16] However, that general rule is subject to the qualification that consecutive sentences which in total exceed a court's maximum sentencing power in respect of a single complaint should not be imposed where equity demands that in all the circumstances the various complaints should be treated as if they were one. The test is one of fairness in the sense of fairness to the accused and to the public interest. In considering how to apply that test it may be relevant that some of the complaints contain charges in respect of which probation orders (breached by later offences) were made, or sentence was deferred, prior to the date of commission of the offences contained in other complaints.[17] There may also be other circumstances which justify exceeding in total the statutory maximum for one complaint. In *Morgan* v. *Smith*[18] the accused failed to appear in September to answer a charge of driving whilst disqualified committed the previous January. He committed the same offence again in October. In respect of the two complaints he was sentenced to consecutive sentences of four months' imprisonment, making eight months in all, though the maximum penalty for a single contravention of the statute in question is six months' imprisonment. It was held that in the circumstances the sheriff was not bound to treat the offences as if they had been in one complaint, and an appeal against sentence was refused.

7–57   Since the decisions in the cases of *Thomson* and *Morgan* there have been several reported cases in which the High Court has confirmed the imposition of consecutive sentences amounting in total to more than the permitted maximum in respect of a single complaint. In *Haggerty* v. *Tudhope*[19] consecutive sentences of six months' imprisonment were upheld in respect of two offences of housebreaking libelled in separate complaints, and in *O'Lone* v. *Tudhope*[20] three consecutive sentences of six months' imprisonment were upheld in respect of three offences of housebreaking committed at different times and charged in separate complaints.

7–58   Consecutive sentences need not necessarily be of the same kind. Thus,

---

[16] *Thomson* v. *Smith*; *Morgan* v. *Smith*, 1982 J.C. 40; 1982 S.L.T. 546; 1982 S.C.C.R. 57; explaining and, to an extent, enlarging upon *Kesson* v. *Heatly*, 1964 J.C. 40.
[17] See, for example, *Thomson* v. *Smith*, above.
[18] See n. 16 above.
[19] 1985 S.C.C.R. 121.
[20] 1987 S.C.C.R. 211.

it has been held to be competent, where two complaints are dealt with at the same time, to impose a period of detention in respect of one complaint and to make a community service order in respect of the other.[21] However, there is authority to the effect that imprisonment and probation are inconsistent and ought not to be imposed together, at least in respect of charges in the same complaint or indictment[22]; and it may be, now that community service is to be ordered only where a court would otherwise have imposed imprisonment,[23] that a similar view would now be taken in respect of a combination of imprisonment and community service.

7–59   Although the cases of *Thomson* and *Morgan* have clearly established that consecutive sentences, in respect of two or more complaints, may in total exceed the permitted maximum for a single complaint, that general rule is subject to an important exception where charges are libelled in separate complaints for technical reasons. The most common example of this is where a charge, such as that of driving while disqualified, would by its nature disclose that an accused had previously been convicted. The normal practice in such cases is to libel the charge which reveals a previous conviction in a complaint or indictment on its own, and to libel any associated charges on a separate complaint or indictment. In such cases, although consecutive sentences remain competent, they should not in total exceed the maximum which would have been permissible had all the charges been taken on a single complaint or indictment.[24]

(3) Where accused already undergoing a sentence of imprisonment or detention imposed on an earlier occasion

7–60   Where an accused person is already serving a previously imposed sentence of imprisonment, his imprisonment may be ordered to date from the expiry of that sentence.[25] That is so even where the previous sentence of imprisonment was imposed in England.[26] In summary courts the foregoing common law power is given statutory effect by section 430(4) of the 1975 Act. That subsection provides: "A sentence following on a conviction by a court of summary jurisdiction may be framed so as to take effect on the expiry of any previous sentence which at the date of such conviction the accused is undergoing." Both the common law rule and the foregoing statutory provision have on occasions given rise to certain difficulties.

7–61   In 1975 the Thomson Committee[27] drew attention to a possible uncertainty arising from the last 10 words of section 430(4) in cases where an offender is already serving two consecutive sentences of imprisonment but, at the time of sentence on the fresh complaint, has not yet exhausted

[21] *McQueen* v. *Lockhart*, 1986 S.C.C.R. 20.

[22] *Downie* v. *Irvine*, 1964 J.C. 52.

[23] 1990 Act, s. 61(3), amending Community Service by Offenders (Scotland) Act 1978, s. 1(1).

[24] *Williamson* v. *Farrell*, 1975 S.L.T. (Notes) 92; *Ross* v. *McLeod*, 1987 S.C.C.R. 525; *Moore* v. *H.M. Advocate*, 1989 S.L.T. 883; 1989 S.C.C.R. 298; *McGrory* v. *Jessop*, 1990 S.C.C.R. 222; and see *Hunt* v. *Wilson*, 1991 S.C.C.R. 821.

[25] Macdonald, p. 357; *John Graham* (1842) 1 Brown 445.

[26] *Grey* v. *H.M. Advocate*, 1958 S.L.T. 147.

[27] *Criminal Procedure in Scotland (Second Report)*, Cmnd. 6218, paras. 57.06, 57.07.

the first of those sentences. Do the closing words of the subsection mean that in such circumstances the court can do no more than order the new sentence to be consecutive to the first of the existing consecutive sentences (that is to say, concurrent with the second), or can the new sentence be made consecutive to the offender's total period of imprisonment under the earlier sentences? The Thomson Committee recommended that the statute should be amended so as clearly to permit what it termed "the wider interpretation," but no such amendment was contained in the 1980 Act (which gave effect to many of the Committee's other recommendations).

7–62   It may be that those responsible for the 1980 Act thought that no amendment was necessary and that "the wider interpretation" would in fact be followed by the courts. That indeed seems to have happened, and in *Moore* v. *MacPhail*[28] the High Court gave tacit, though not explicit, approval to the view that a sentence of imprisonment can be made consecutive to *all* sentences then being served by the offender. In that case the sole point in issue was how a court should express its sentence so as to make that intention clear. In that regard the High Court recommended that a court should use one of two possible forms of words, namely "consecutive to the total period of imprisonment to which the prisoner is already subject," or "is to take effect on the expiry of all sentences previously imposed."

7–63   The terms of section 430(4) of the 1975 Act have been further explained by the High Court in the case of *Beattie* v. *McGlennan*.[29] In that case two sheriffs in the same court dealt separately with the offender on the same day (in the mistaken belief that it was not competent for all matters to be dealt with by one sheriff). On the first complaint Sheriff C sentenced the accused to five months' detention. The accused thereafter appeared before Sheriff R on a complaint which had previously been continued for the preparation of a social inquiry report. In respect of that complaint Sheriff R sentenced the accused to two months' detention "to date from expiry of any sentence presently liable to be served."

7–64   The accused appealed on the ground that the order pronounced by Sheriff R was incompetent in terms of section 430(4) of the 1975 Act in that he had been *convicted* of the offence for which Sheriff R had sentenced him on the date when the case was continued for a social inquiry report, and that that date was prior to the date when he was sentenced by Sheriff C. In refusing the appeal the High Court held that Sheriff R had a common law power to make the order which he did which was not affected by section 430(4),[30] and that the date of conviction for the purposes of that subsection was not the date of the plea of guilty but the date of the sentence.

7–65   Three further points fall to be noted in respect of sentences which are ordered to be consecutive to sentences already being served. First, it is not appropriate to order that a determinate sentence of imprisonment

---

[28] 1986 S.C.C.R. 669.
[29] 1990 J.C. 391; 1991 S.L.T. 384; 1990 S.C.C.R. 497.
[30] A view subsequently confirmed in *Russell* v. *MacPhail*, 1991 S.L.T. 449; 1990 S.C.C.R. 628.

should be consecutive to a sentence of life imprisonment.[31] Second, where an appeal is abandoned and a sheriff is contemplating the reimposition of the unexpired portion of the sentence of imprisonment originally imposed, he may order that period to be consecutive to any other sentence of imprisonment subsequently imposed on the offender,[32] but before doing so he should give the offender an opportunity to make representations on the matter.[33] Third, there is a particular problem when a court wishes to impose a consecutive period of detention on a child who is currently serving a sentence under section 206 of the 1975 Act.

7–66   That problem came to the attention of the High Court in 1990 in the case of *Clayton, Petitioner*.[34] The petitioner in that case was sentenced in November 1988 to six years' detention under section 206 of the 1975 Act. Later in the same month the petitioner, who was by then 16 years of age, was sentenced by a sheriff to four months' detention, and that sentence was ordered to be served consecutively to the period of detention under section 206. Subsequently it came to be appreciated that the petitioner could not be considered for early release on licence by reason of the fact that, although normally sentences of detention or imprisonment which are consecutive to each other are aggregated for the purpose of determining an early release date on licence, that is not competent where one of the sentences is under section 206 with the result that the sentence under that section must be served in full since otherwise the later sentence would not be given any effect. Accordingly the petitioner appealed to the *nobile officium* of the High Court. The court held that the case was inappropriate for a remedy under the *nobile officium* since the proper course would have been for the petitioner to appeal against the consecutive nature of the sentence of four months' detention. However, the court indicated that an application for leave to appeal late against that sentence might be favourably received. In due course such an application was made, and the court allowed the appeal to the extent of ordering that the sentence of four months' detention should run from the date of its imposition. In disposing of the original petition the High Court observed that in similar cases it would be more appropriate for sheriffs to use some other form of sentence, such as an admonition, or for any custodial sentence to be ordered to be concurrent with the sentence under section 206.

Dating of sentences of imprisonment or detention

7–67   Unless otherwise qualified a sentence of imprisonment will run from the date on which it is pronounced. However, all courts, both solemn and summary, are directed, when determining a period of imprisonment or detention, to have regard to any period of time spent in custody by the offender on remand awaiting trial or sentence.[35] The effect of that provision may be to persuade a court to reduce the length of sentence that

---

[31] *McRae* v. *H.M. Advocate*, 1987 S.C.C.R. 36; *McPhee* v. *H.M. Advocate*, 1990 S.C.C.R. 313.
[32] 1975 Act, s. 446(5).
[33] *Proudfoot* v. *Wither*, 1990 S.L.T. 742; 1990 S.C.C.R. 96; and see *Nash, Petr.*, 1991 S.C.C.R. 978.
[34] 1991 S.C.C.R. 261.
[35] 1975 Act, ss. 218, 431.

would otherwise have been imposed. Alternatively, the full sentence may be imposed, but it may be back-dated so as to span the period, or part of the period, of the remand. There is no express statutory authority for that practice, but it appears to be hallowed by long usage. The practical consequences of this practice, however, fall to be noted. On the one hand, to pronounce the full sentence appropriate to the offence, but to back-date it to take account of a period spent in custody, means that, in the event of a subsequent conviction, the offender's record will accurately reflect the gravity of the offence. On the other hand, the effect of remission may significantly alter the period that the offender actually spends in custody since remission is calculated only by reference to imprisonment under sentence, and takes no account of any period of imprisonment on remand. A simple example will illustrate this. Suppose that a sentence of imprisonment falls to be pronounced on January 1, and the court is informed that the offender has been in custody on remand for three months since October 1. If the court considers that the appropriate sentence for the offence is one of nine months' imprisonment, but wants to take full account of the period spent in custody on remand, it may either impose a sentence of six months' imprisonment dated from January 1, or it may impose a sentence of nine months' imprisonment dated from October 1. Assuming normal remission of one-third, the consequence is that in the former case the offender will be released after four months, that is to say on May 1, whereas in the latter case he will be released six months after October 1, that is to say on April 1. While it is improper for a judge to take remission into account in determining the length of a sentence, it is submitted that it is perfectly proper for a judge to be aware of the above considerations, and to take them into account as he thinks proper.

7–68 Understandably, however, many offenders who have been remanded in custody prior to trial or sentence are anxious that any prison sentence imposed on them should be back-dated so as to cover all, or at least part, of that period, with the consequences for remission which have just been noted. For that reason the High Court has had to deal with many appeals in which the question of back-dating has been in issue.[36]

7–69 Central to all the reported cases on this matter is the principle that back-dating, and in particular the decision whether or not to back-date at all, is very much at the discretion of the sentencing court. Subject to that, however, certain guidelines have emerged over the years. Although in certain respects these are not entirely as clear as one might have wished, they none the less offer a substantial amount of guidance to judges, to practitioners, and to convicted persons. Given the manner in which the most recent cases have been decided, what follows ought to be read subject to the proviso that the first question for a court to determine is whether in all the circumstances to back-date a sentence at all. It is only where a decision to back-date has been taken that some of the following guidelines will become operative. Subject to that, the existing guidelines may be summarised as follows:

---

[36] For an interesting analysis of the reported cases, see "Backdating," 1991 S.L.T. 23, and "Backdating—New Developments," 1991 S.L.T. 93.

(1) Provided that a court does not neglect to have regard to any period spent in custody on remand prior to trial or sentence (as required by sections 218 and 431 of the 1975 Act), it may decline to take any account of that period; it may back-date a sentence in whole or in part; or it may impose with immediate effect a sentence which has been reduced to take account of the earlier period spent in custody.[37] There is no obligation to back-date a sentence in all cases.[38]

(2) Where an offender is charged with a serious charge, but is ultimately convicted of a lesser charge (in respect of which he would have been likely to have been released on bail had it been charged originally), any custodial sentence should probably be back-dated to the start of the remand period.[39]

(3) If an accused has all along been prepared to plead guilty to some charges but not to others, and is ultimately convicted only in respect of the former charges, any sentence of imprisonment should probably be back-dated to cover the whole period in custody on remand.[40] Similarly, where a plea of guilty is tendered under section 102 of the 1975 Act, a court, if it is going to back-date at all, should do so to the date when that plea was first tendered.[41]

(4) At one time it appeared to have been decided that, where a court remands an offender in custody pending the preparation of reports which are required by statute, and thereafter imposes the maximum competent sentence, that sentence ought to be back-dated to the date when the offender was remanded in custody.[42] However, later cases have cast doubt on the general applicability of *Morrison*,[43] at least in cases where an offender has a very bad criminal record.

(5) Whatever may be the position in cases where an offender is remanded in custody pending the preparation of reports which are obligatory, it is clear that back-dating is not considered to be necessary where an offender is remanded for the preparation of reports which are merely discretionary, notwithstanding that the maximum sentence is thereafter imposed.[44]

(6) In any event, "maximum sentence" for the purpose of the foregoing refers only to a sentence which cannot in any circumstances be exceeded. In cases on indictment in the sheriff court there is no obligation, where an offender has been remanded for reports, to back-date a sentence simply because it is at the limit of the sheriff's sentencing powers (three years) since, in any such case, it would be open to the sheriff to remit the offender to the High Court for sentence.[45]

---

[37] *Bellamy* v. *H.M. Advocate*, 1987 S.C.C.R 101.
[38] *Muir* v. *H.M. Advocate*, 1985 S.C.C.R. 402.
[39] *Callaghan* v. *H.M. Advocate*, 1986 S.C.C.R. 563.
[40] *Campbell* v. *H.M. Advocate*, 1986 S.C.C.R. 403; *Tulloch* v. *Annan*, 1991 S.C.C.R. 24.
[41] *Neilson* v. *H.M. Advocate*, 1989 S.C.C.R. 527.
[42] *Morrison* v. *Scott*, 1987 S.C.C.R. 376.
[43] *McDonald* v. *Wilson*, 1991 S.C.C.R. 61; *Brady* v. *McNeill*, 1991 S.C.C.R. 234.
[44] *Plenderleith* v. *Carmichael*, 1990 G.W.D. 14–742.
[45] *Grant* v. *H.M. Advocate*, 1990 G.W.D. 14–743.

(7) The fact that an accused maintains a plea of not guilty and elects to go to trial is not a reason for refusing to back-date a sentence since every accused person is entitled to require the Crown to prove his guilt. Moreover, the fact that an accused has been refused bail on account of his record does not entitle a court to hold that a period in custody on remand is of the accused's own making, and for that reason to refuse to back-date a sentence of imprisonment.[46] The case of *Grummer* appears at first sight to be at odds with the earlier case of *Muir*,[47] and for that reason caused some anxiety to the anonymous author of the articles referred to in footnote 36. Certainly *Muir* appears to support the view that a court is entitled to refuse to back-date simply because an accused has been refused bail on account of his previous record. However, later cases[48] have further explained the decision in *Grummer*, and it now seems to be clear that the mere fact that an accused was refused bail (for whatever reason) is not a sufficient ground for refusing to back-date. However, an accused's previous record may of itself provide a sufficient reason for deciding not to back-date at all. Although this distinction may at first sight appear somewhat artificial, it is submitted that it is both logical and sound since sections 218 and 431 of the 1975 Act inevitably presuppose that an offender has been remanded in custody for *some* reason, which may often involve his previous record. If the mere fact of a remand in custody, whether on account of record or any other cause, were automatically to justify a refusal to back-date, the sections in the Act would be left with little or no content.

(8) The obligation to have regard to time spent on remand does not extend to periods so spent outwith Scotland.[49]

STATEMENT OF REASONS FOR SENTENCE

7–70 There are several circumstances in which a court is obliged to state its reasons for imposing a particular sentence, and to ensure that those reasons are entered in the record of proceedings. The principal circumstances are:

(1) where a young offender is sentenced to detention, the reasons for rejecting any alternative must be stated and, in the case of all courts other than the High Court, must be entered in the record of proceedings[50];

(2) where a sentence of imprisonment is imposed on a person who has not been previously sentenced to imprisonment or detention by a court in any part of the United Kingdom, the reason for deciding that no other method of dealing with the offender is suitable must

---

[46] *Grummer* v. *H.M. Advocate*, 1991 S.C.C.R. 194.
[47] See n. 38 above.
[48] *Nicol* v. *McGlennan*, 1991 G.W.D. 22–1283; *Quigley* v. *McGlennan*, 1991 G.W.D. 24–1377; *McLean* v. *H.M. Advocate*, 1991 G.W.D. 27–1586.
[49] *Geddes* v. *Heywood*, 1991 G.W.D. 22–1299.
[50] 1975 Act, s. 207(3).

be stated, and entered in the record of proceedings, where the sentence is imposed by a summary court[51];

(3) where time is not allowed for payment of a fine, the reasons must be stated and entered in the extract of the finding and sentence as well as in the finding and sentence itself.[52]

While the foregoing requirements should be followed at all times, a failure to record the appropriate reasons may not be fatal provided that the court has given the proper consideration to the matter in issue and has stated its reasons orally to the accused.[53]

ALTERATION AND SIGNATURE OF SENTENCE

Alteration of sentence

7–71   Without requiring the attendance of the accused, it is competent at any time before imprisonment has followed on a sentence for a summary court to alter or modify it. In that case, however, it is not competent to substitute a higher sentence than that originally pronounced.[54] This power has been held sufficient to enable a court to correct mistakes in executorial detail,[55] but that matter is now largely the subject of express statutory provision.[56] If a court has, in error, imposed a sentence which is beyond its competence, it may reduce the sentence to one which is competent,[57] but, where a magistrate had by mistake imposed, in default of payment of a fine, a sentence of imprisonment in excess of the maximum allowed, it was held to be incompetent for him to seek to correct the error by increasing the amount of the fine.[58] Also, the power to modify a sentence must be exercised before any imprisonment has followed on that sentence.[59] However, it has been held that what is now section 434(1) of the 1975 Act does not apply where the original sentence is incompetent, and in that case the court may substitute a competent sentence even where it is of greater severity, for the original sentence is void and the second sentence is not an alteration but a *de novo* imposition.[60]

Signature of sentence

7–72   The sentence of a summary court must be signed either by the judge or by the clerk of court,[61] and the signature of either of them is sufficient also to authenticate the findings on which the sentence proceeds.[62] No time

---

[51] 1980 Act, s. 42(2).
[52] 1975 Act, s. 396(2) and (3); and see *Sullivan* v. *McLeod*, 1980 S.L.T. (Notes) 99.
[53] *Binnie* v. *Farrell*, 1972 J.C. 49, explaining apparently conflicting decisions in *Winslow* v. *Farrell*, 1965 J.C. 49 and *Bruce* v. *Hogg*, 1966 J.C. 33; but see *Dunsmore* v. *Allan*, 1991 S.C.C.R. 946.
[54] 1975 Act, s. 434(1) and (3).
[55] *Mackenzie* v. *Allan* (1889) 2 White 253; *Stewart* v. *Uppleby* (1899) 3 Adam 6; *Renwick* v. *McDougall* (1913) 7 Adam 91.
[56] See para. 7–74 below.
[57] *Renwick* v. *McDougall*, above.
[58] *McRory* v. *Findlay* (1911) 6 Adam 416.
[59] *Skeen* v. *Sim*, High Court, March 19, 1975, unreported.
[60] *Patrick* v. *Copeland*, 1969 J.C. 42.
[61] 1975 Act, s. 309(2).
[62] *Ibid.* s. 434(2).

limit is stated within which a sentence must be signed, but it has been held that it should be signed as soon as reasonably possible, and in almost every case on the day on which the sentence is pronounced.[63] A court is not *functus officio* until a conviction and sentence have been recorded and signed,[64] but, where an agent for an accused (who was absent) tendered a plea of guilty in error and conviction and sentence followed on that plea, it was held to be incompetent for the sheriff, two days later, to "recall" those orders and to proceed to trial: after conviction and sentence the sheriff was held to be *functus* and without any authority thereafter to alter the finding so far as it related to conviction.[65] In that case the sheriff could, provided no imprisonment had followed thereon, have modified the sentence under section 434 of the 1975 Act, but he could not alter the recorded conviction.

7–73   In the case of *MacNeill* v. *MacGregor* the error which created the problem was that of the accused's agent who had erroneously tendered a clear and unambiguous plea of guilty. But what if the error arises in a different way? Summary complaints which are served by a means other than a warrant to apprehend contain a printed form on which an accused may intimate his plea in writing. On occasions a written plea may either be ambiguous, or may be construed as a plea of guilty when in fact the accused intended it to be one of not guilty. In the former case the court will normally continue the case without recording a plea so that the ambiguity can be cleared up, but in the latter case it may proceed to deal with the case in the accused's absence by recording a conviction and passing sentence. The question then is whether, upon receiving the inevitable irate communication from the accused, the court is bound by the decision in *MacNeill* v. *MacGregor*. It is tentatively submitted that the answer to that question is in the negative. Although there is no express statutory authority to deal with the situation above described, it may be that, where the error is one of misinterpretation by the court rather than an erroneous statement by an agent, the statutory provisions concerning correction of entries[66] are sufficiently wide to enable the court to correct the error without the necessity of requiring the accused to have the proceedings reviewed in a higher court.

Correction of entries
7–74   It is competent to correct an entry in (a) the record of proceedings in a solemn or summary prosecution, or (b) the extract of a sentence passed or an order of court made in such proceedings, in so far as that entry constitutes an error of recording or is incomplete.[67] Such an entry may be corrected (a) by the clerk of the court at any time before either the sentence or order of the court is executed or, on appeal, the proceedings are transmitted to the Clerk of Justiciary, (b) by the clerk of the court, under the authority of the court which passed the sentence or made the order, at any time after the execution of the sentence but before

---

[63] *Furnheim* v. *Watson*, 1946 J.C. 99; but see *Cameron* v. *Deans* (1901) 3 Adam 498.
[64] *Tudhope* v. *Campbell*, 1979 J.C. 24; but *cf. Williams and Anr.* v. *Linton* (1878) 6 R. (J.) 12.
[65] *MacNeill* v. *MacGregor*, 1975 J.C. 55.
[66] See para. 7–74 below.
[67] 1975 Act, ss. 227A(1) and 439(1).

transmission on appeal to the Clerk of Justiciary, or (c) by the clerk of the court under the authority of the High Court where that court has, during the course of an appeal, become aware of an erroneous or incomplete entry and has remitted the proceedings for correction.[68] Where a correction is made under the authority of the court which passed the sentence or made the order, that correction must be intimated to the prosecutor and to the former accused or his solicitor.[69] Where, during the course of an appeal, the High Court becomes aware of an erroneous or incomplete entry, it may consider and determine the appeal as if that entry were corrected, and may remit the proceedings for correction, as noted above, either before or after the determination of the appeal.[70] Any correction by the clerk of court must be authenticated by his signature and, where it is authorised by the court, it must record the name of the judge or judges concerned and the date of such authority.[71]

7–75   The law on the matter of corrections was substantially changed by provisions in the 1980 Act and, as a consequence, some of the older cases on the subject are now of only passing interest.[72] However, other cases are still of relevance, particularly those which stress the importance of properly authenticating any corrections which are made, especially if the correction takes the form of an erasure.[73] Unauthenticated amendments or alterations should be specifically referred to and made the grounds of appeal when an appeal is taken by way of stated case if the unauthenticated alterations are to be founded on.[74]

---

[68] 1975 Act, ss. 227A(2) and 439(2).
[69] *Ibid.* subs. (3).
[70] *Ibid.* subs. (4).
[71] *Ibid.* subs. (5).
[72] See, for example, *Smith* v. *Sempill* (1910) 6 Adam 348; *Anderson* v. *Howman*, 1935 J.C. 17; *Wilson* v. *Brown*, 1947 J.C. 81; *Kelly* v. *MacLeod*, 1960 J.C. 88.
[73] *Mackenzie* v. *Gray* (1898) 2 Adam 625; *Reids* v. *Miller* (1899) 3 Adam 29; *Dunsire* v. *Bell* (1908) 5 Adam 625; *White* v. *Jeans* (1911) 6 Adam 489.
[74] *Sutherland* v. *Shiach*, 1928 J.C. 49.

CHAPTER 8

APPEAL AGAINST SENTENCE

I. APPEALS BEFORE THE PASSING OF THE 1980 ACT

8–01   Prior to the passing of the Criminal Appeal (Scotland) Act 1926, all sentences pronounced in the High Court were final and conclusive and could not be made subject to any review.[1] Sentences imposed on indictment in the sheriff court could, in certain circumstances, be brought under review by a suspension, but that procedure was abolished by the 1926 Act which created the Court of Criminal Appeal, and established a uniform right of appeal to that court in all cases on indictment, whether in the High Court or the sheriff court. Subsequent to 1926 the appeals procedure in relation to sentences imposed on indictment remained substantially unchanged until the passing of the 1980 Act.

8–02   In relation to summary cases review by stated case was first introduced by the Summary Prosecutions Appeals (Scotland) Act 1875, and the procedure provided for in that Act was subsequently adopted in a somewhat amended form as a universal mode of appeal by the Summary Jurisdiction (Scotland) Act 1908. Under the stated case procedure a right of appeal was made available to both the accused and the prosecutor, though in relation to sentence the prosecutor's right of appeal was restricted to points of law only. Like appeals under solemn procedure, review by stated case remained substantially unchanged until the introduction of extensive amendments contained in the 1980 Act.

8–03   Since this is a book about sentencing, all of what follows relates principally to appeals against sentence and, notwithstanding that many of the procedures are the same for appeals against conviction, the reader should be alive to the possibility of differences, or of additional procedures, in such cases. One of the consequences of the amendments made by the 1980 Act was to assimilate to a large extent the rules governing appeals under both solemn and summary procedure. However, to avoid tiresome cross-referencing, the two forms of appeal will be dealt with separately and in full, even though this will involve some repetition of identical provisions.

II. APPEALS UNDER SOLEMN PROCEDURE

Right of appeal

8–04   Any person convicted on indictment may appeal against the sentence passed on such conviction, or against both conviction and sentence.[2] By such an appeal a person may bring under review of the High Court any alleged miscarriage of justice in the proceedings in which he was convicted, including any alleged miscarriage of justice on the basis of the existence and significance of additional evidence which was not heard at the trial and which was not available and could not reasonably have been made available at the trial.[3] This latter provision seems unlikely, in so far as it relates to additional evidence, to be of much significance in an appeal against sentence alone, but may well be highly relevant where an appeal is taken against both conviction and sentence. However, in one reported

---

[1] *Mackintosh* v. *Lord Advocate* (1876) 3 R. (H.L.) 34.
[2] 1975 Act, s. 228(1).
[3] *Ibid.* s. 228(2); and see *Perrie, Petr.*, 1991 S.C.C.R. 475.

case,[4] the High Court, in an appeal against sentence, heard oral evidence from psychiatrists who had submitted written evidence to the trial judge.

8–05   There is no right of appeal against any sentence fixed by law.[5] However, where, on sentencing a person convicted of murder, a judge makes a recommendation under section 205A(1) of the 1975 Act as to the minimum period which should elapse before that person is released on licence, it is competent to appeal against that recommendation which, for the purposes of the appeal, is to be deemed part of the sentence passed on conviction.[6]

8–06   It is not competent to appeal to the High Court by bill of suspension against any sentence, judgment or order pronounced in any proceedings on indictment in the sheriff court.[7] It was at one time held that this rule did not apply in the case of an appeal by a witness who was sentenced for contempt of court in the course of proceedings on indictment in the sheriff court. However, the decision expressing that view has now been overruled and it is not now competent to proceed by bill of suspension in such a case, the proper mode of appeal being a petition to the *nobile officium*.[8]

Form of appeal

8–07   An important distinction exists between the procedures that must be followed in those cases where a person wishes to appeal against both conviction and sentence, and those where the appeal is against sentence alone. In the former case the appellant must, within two weeks of the final determination of the proceedings, lodge with the Clerk of Justiciary written intimation of intention to appeal, and at the same time he must send a copy of that intimation to the Crown Agent.[9] The period of time within which this must be done may be extended at any time by the High Court upon application being made for that purpose.[10] The intimation of intention to appeal must identify the proceedings and must be in as nearly as may be the form prescribed by Act of Adjournal.[11] Upon such an intimation being lodged by a person in custody, the Clerk of Justiciary must give notice of the fact to the Secretary of State.[12] Proceedings are to be deemed to be finally determined on the day on which sentence is passed in open court.[13]

8–08   Within six weeks of lodging intimation of intention to appeal or, in the case of an appeal against sentence alone, within two weeks of the passing of the sentence in open court, the convicted person may lodge a written note of appeal with the Clerk of Justiciary. In this case it is his duty to send a copy to the Crown Agent and also to the judge who presided at the trial. The Clerk of Justiciary has power to extend the above six week period

---

[4] *Duff* v. *H.M. Advocate*, 1983 S.C.C.R. 461.
[5] 1975 Act, s. 228(1), proviso.
[6] *Ibid.* s. 205A(3).
[7] *Ibid.* s. 230.
[8] *George Outram & Co. Ltd.* v. *Lees*, 1991 G.W.D. 40–2449, overruling *Butterworth* v. *Herron*, 1975 S.L.T. (Notes) 56.
[9] 1975 Act, s. 231(1).
[10] *Ibid.* s. 236B(2).
[11] *Ibid.* s. 231(2); Act of Adjournal (Consolidation) 1988, para. 84.
[12] *Ibid.* s. 231(3).
[13] *Ibid.* s. 231(4).

before its expiry,[14] but the two week period may, like the period within which intimation of intention to appeal must be lodged, be extended only upon application to the High Court.[15] On a note of appeal against sentence alone being lodged by an appellant in custody the Clerk of Justiciary must give notice of that fact to the Secretary of State.[16]

8–09　　　A note of appeal must identify the proceedings, must contain a full statement of all the grounds of appeal, and must be in as nearly as may be the form prescribed by Act of Adjournal.[17] Except by leave of the High Court on cause shown it is not competent for an appellant to found any aspect of his appeal on a ground not contained in the note of appeal.[18] It is essential that the grounds as stated in a note of appeal should adequately and clearly identify the matters which it is sought to bring under review. A failure in this respect may result in an appeal being refused.[19]

Presentation of appeal in writing

8–10　　　If an appellant desires to present his case and his argument in writing instead of orally he must intimate this desire to the Clerk of Justiciary at least four days before the diet fixed for the hearing of the appeal. At the same time he must lodge with the Clerk of Justiciary three copies of his case and argument, and send a copy to the Crown Agent. Any case or argument so presented will be considered by the High Court.[20] Unless the High Court otherwise directs, the respondent in such a case does not make a written reply but replies orally at the diet fixed for the hearing of the appeal.[21] Unless the High Court otherwise allows, an appellant who has presented his case and argument in writing will not be entitled to submit in addition an oral argument to the court in support of the appeal.[22]

Proceedings in sheriff court

8–11　　　In the case of an appeal against a sentence in the sheriff court, the sheriff clerk must furnish to the Clerk of Justiciary a certified copy of the proceedings at the trial, or must forward to him the original record of the proceedings, as may be required by the Clerk of Justiciary.[23]

Judge's report

8–12　　　As soon as is reasonably practicable after his receipt of the copy note of appeal sent to him by the Clerk of Justiciary, the judge who presided at the trial,[24] must furnish the Clerk of Justiciary with a report in writing

---

[14] 1975 Act, s. 233(1).
[15] *Ibid.* s. 236B(2).
[16] *Ibid.* s. 233(4).
[17] *Ibid.* s. 233(2); Act of Adjournal, above.
[18] *Ibid.* s. 233(3).
[19] *Campbell* v. *MacDougall*, 1991 S.C.C.R. 218; *Donaldson* v. *McNaughton*, 1991 G.W.D. 6–305; and see High Court of Justiciary Practice Note, March 29, 1985 (printed in Part III below).
[20] 1975 Act, s. 234(1).
[21] *Ibid.* s. 234(2).
[22] *Ibid.* s. 234(3).
[23] *Ibid.* s. 236.
[24] Although here, and elsewhere, references are made to "the trial," all the provisions concerned apply equally in cases where a person has been sentenced after a plea of guilty.

giving the judge's opinion on the case generally and on the grounds contained in the note of appeal. In respect of an appeal against sentence the report should state what representations were made by or on behalf of the accused, and what view the judge took of them.[25] It is not for the judge to question the relevance or specification of the grounds of appeal: he should none the less prepare a report as best he can.[26] The Clerk of Justiciary must send a copy of the report to the convicted person or his solicitor, to the Crown Agent, and, in a case referred under section 263(1) of the 1975 Act (see paragraph 8–41 below), to the Secretary of State.[27] Subject to the foregoing, the judge's report will be available only to the High Court and the parties.[28]

8–13   Where the judge's report is not furnished as soon as is reasonably practicable, the High Court may call for it to be furnished within such period as it may specify. Alternatively, if it thinks fit the High Court may hear and determine the appeal without such report.[29] The High Court may also require the judge who presided at the trial to produce any notes taken by him of the proceedings at the trial.[30]

Computation of periods

8–14   Where the last day of any period for lodging an intimation of intention to appeal, or a note of appeal, falls on a day on which the office of the Clerk of Justiciary is closed, that period is to extend to and include the next day on which the office is open.[31] As previously noted, any such period may be extended at any time by the High Court in respect of any convicted person. Application for such extension must be in as nearly as may be the form prescribed by Act of Adjournal.[32]

Signing of documents

8–15   Any intimation of intention to appeal, note of appeal, or application for extension of time, must be signed by the convicted person or by his counsel or solicitor.[33]

Disposal of applications to High Court

8–16   Generally, any application to the High Court may be made by the appellant or respondent as the case may be or by counsel on his behalf, orally or in writing. However, if the appellant is unrepresented and is in custody and is not entitled or has not obtained leave to be present before the court,[34] he must make any such application by forwarding it in writing to the Clerk of Justiciary whose responsibility it then is to take the proper steps to obtain the decision of the court on that application.[35]

---

[25] *McFadyen* v. *Tudhope*, 1986 S.C.C.R. 712.
[26] *McTaggart, Petr.*, 1987 S.C.C.R. 638; *Henry* v. *Docherty*, 1990 S.L.T. 301; 1989 S.C.C.R. 426.
[27] 1975 Act, s. 236A(1).
[28] *Ibid.* s. 236A(3).
[29] *Ibid.* s. 236A(2).
[30] *Ibid.* s. 237.
[31] *Ibid.* s. 236B(1).
[32] *Ibid.* s. 236B(2); Act of Adjournal (Consolidation) 1988, para. 84.
[33] *Ibid.* s. 236C.
[34] See para. 8–20 below.
[35] 1975 Act, s. 235.

8–17   When the High Court has heard and dealt with any application the Clerk of Justiciary must (unless it appears to him unnecessary to do so) give to the applicant (if he is in custody and has not been present at the hearing) notice of the decision of the court in relation to that application.[36]

Admission of appellant to bail
8–18   On the application of a person who has lodged an intimation of intention to appeal or a note of appeal, the High Court may, if it sees fit, admit that person to bail pending the determination of his appeal.[37] An appellant who is admitted to bail must, unless the High Court otherwise directs, appear personally in court on the day or days fixed for the hearing of his appeal. In the event of the appellant failing so to appear the court may decline to consider the appeal and may dismiss it summarily, or may consider and determine it or make such other order as it thinks fit. The foregoing power to determine the appeal is without prejudice to the provisions relating to breach of conditions contained in section 3 of the Bail etc. (Scotland) Act 1980.[38]

Notice of date of hearing
8–19   When the High Court fixes the date for the hearing of an appeal, or of an application for extension of time, the Clerk of Justiciary must give notice to the Crown Agent and to the solicitor of the appellant or applicant, or to the appellant or applicant himself if he has no known solicitor. The appellant or applicant, or his solicitor, must thereupon lodge three copies (typed or printed) of the appeal or application for the use of the court.[39] Where it is proposed that the powers of the court should be exercised by a single judge,[40] one copy only of the application to be disposed of should be lodged for the use of the judge.[41]

Presence of appellant at hearing
8–20   An appellant, notwithstanding that he is in custody, is entitled, if he wishes, to be present at the hearing of his appeal, except where the appeal is on some ground involving a question of law alone. In that case, and on any proceedings preliminary or incidental to an appeal, he is not entitled to be present except where that is provided for by Act of Adjournal, or where the High Court gives him leave to be present.[42] There is as yet no provision on this matter in an Act of Adjournal. Where an appellant has the right to be present but does not wish to do so, the court may hear the appeal in his absence.[43]

Notice of hearing to others than parties
8–21   Where an appellant or applicant is in custody and has obtained leave or

---

[36] 1975 Act, s. 260.
[37] *Ibid.* s. 238(1) and (3).
[38] *Ibid.* s. 238(2).
[39] *Ibid.* s. 239(1).
[40] See para. 8–26 below.
[41] 1975 Act, s. 239(2).
[42] *Ibid.* s. 240.
[43] *Manuel* v. *H.M.A.*, 1958 J.C. 41.

is entitled to be present at the hearing of his appeal or application, the Clerk of Justiciary must notify the appellant or applicant, the governor of the prison in which he then is, and the Secretary of State of the probable day on which the appeal or application will be heard. The Secretary of State must take steps to transfer the appellant or applicant to a prison convenient for his appearance before the High Court, at such reasonable time before the hearing as will enable him to consult his legal adviser, if any.[44]

8–22   When an appellant or applicant is entitled, or has been granted leave, to be present at any diet before the High Court or any judge thereof, for the taking of additional evidence,[45] or for an examination or investigation by a special commissioner,[46] the Clerk of Justiciary must give timeous notice to the Secretary of State in the form set out in an Act of Adjournal.[47] That notice is sufficient warrant to the Secretary of State for transmitting the appellant or applicant in custody from prison to the place where that diet or any subsequent diets are to be held, and for reconveying him thereafter to prison. The appellant or applicant is to appear at all such diets in ordinary civilian clothes.[48] The Secretary of State must arrange for a sufficient number of male and female prison officers to attend the sittings of the court.[49]

Abandonment of appeal

8–23   An appellant may abandon his appeal by lodging with the Clerk of Justiciary a notice of abandonment in as nearly as may be the form prescribed by Act of Adjournal.[50] On such notice being lodged the appeal will be deemed to have been dismissed by the court.[51] A person who has appealed against both conviction and sentence may abandon the appeal in so far as it is against conviction and may proceed with it against sentence alone.[52]

8–24   Once a notice of abandonment has been lodged it cannot be withdrawn.[53] Conversely, where an appeal against sentence has begun to be heard, the court may refuse to allow the appeal to be abandoned where the purpose in doing so is to avoid an increase in sentence.[54]

Powers which may be exercised by a single judge

8–25   The powers of the High Court to extend the time within which intimation of intention to appeal and a note of appeal may be given, to allow the appellant to be present at any proceedings in cases where he is not entitled to be present without leave, and to admit an appellant to bail,

---

[44] 1975 Act, s. 241.
[45] See para. 8–29 below.
[46] See paras. 8–29 and 8–30 below.
[47] That form was previously contained in the Act of Adjournal 1926, No. 1373. However, that Act of Adjournal was revoked by the Act of Adjournal (Consolidation) 1988, Sched. 2, and seems not to have been replaced.
[48] 1975 Act, s. 242.
[49] *Ibid.* s. 243.
[50] Act of Adjournal (Consolidation) 1988, para. 84.
[51] 1975 Act, s. 244(1).
[52] *Ibid.* s. 244(2).
[53] *Biondi* v. *H.M. Advocate*, 1967 S.L.T. (Notes) 22.
[54] *West* v. *H.M. Advocate*, 1955 S.L.T. 425.

may be exercised by any single judge of the High Court. However if the single judge refuses an application, the appellant is entitled to have the application determined by the High Court.[55] In addition to the foregoing, preliminary and interlocutory proceedings incidental to an appeal or application may be disposed of by a single judge.[56] In all proceedings before a single judge the parties may be represented and appear by a solicitor alone.[57]

Appeal against refusal of application

8–26   When an application or applications have been dealt with by a single judge under section 247 of the 1975 Act, the Clerk of Justiciary must notify to the applicant the decision in as nearly as may be the form set out in an Act of Adjournal.[58] In the event of the single judge refusing all or any of such applications the Clerk of Justiciary, on notifying such refusal to the applicant, must forward to him the prescribed form[59] to fill up and forthwith return if he desires to have the application or applications determined by the High Court as fully constituted for the hearing of appeals. If the applicant does not so desire, or does not return the form duly filled up within five days, the refusal of the application or applications by the single judge is to be final.[60]

8–27   If the applicant desires a determination by the High Court and is not legally represented, he may be present at the hearing and determination of his application. However, an applicant who is legally represented is not entitled to be present without leave of the court.[61] When an applicant duly fills up and returns to the Clerk of Justiciary within the prescribed time the form expressing a desire to be present at the hearing and determination by the court, that form is deemed to be an application for leave to be present, and the Clerk of Justiciary must take the necessary steps for placing that application before the court.[62] If that application is refused by the court, the Clerk of Justiciary must notify the applicant; if the application is granted he must notify the applicant, the governor of the prison where the applicant is in custody, and the Secretary of State.[63]

8–28   For the purpose of constituting a court of appeal, the judge who has refused any such application may sit as a member of the court, and take part in determining the application.[64]

Powers of High Court

8–29   Without prejudice to any existing power of the High Court, that court may, for the purposes of an appeal against conviction, conviction and sentence, or sentence alone:

---

[55] 1975 Act, s. 247.
[56] *Ibid.* s. 249.
[57] *Ibid.* s. 250.
[58] *Ibid.* s. 251(1); Act of Adjournal (Consolidation) 1988, para. 84.
[59] Act of Adjournal, above.
[60] 1975 Act, s. 251(2).
[61] *Ibid.* s. 251(3).
[62] *Ibid.* s. 251(4).
[63] *Ibid.* s. 251(5).
[64] *Ibid.* s. 251(6).

(a) order the production of any document or other thing connected with the proceedings;
(b) hear any additional evidence relevant to any alleged miscarriage of justice, or order such evidence to be heard by a judge of the High Court or by such other person as it may appoint for that purpose;
(c) take account of any circumstances relevant to the case which were not before the trial judge;
(d) remit to any fit person to inquire and report in regard to any matter or circumstance affecting the appeal;
(e) appoint a person with expert knowledge to act as assessor to the High Court in any case where it appears to the court that such expert knowledge is required for the proper determination of the case.[65]

8–30   In connection with the foregoing, an error in the drafting of the 1980 Act falls to be noted. Section 252 of the 1975 Act, prior to its amendment by the 1980 Act, contained in head (d) a provision allowing the reference of certain questions to a special commissioner; and detailed provisions concerning such a reference were to be found in section 253(2). That subsection, however, was repealed by the 1980 Act, and the former head (d) of section 252, along with the remainder of that section, has been replaced by the provisions set out in paragraph 8–29 above. Notwithstanding that, no amendment has been made to head (c) of section 242 which still contains a reference to "an examination or investigation by a special commissioner in terms of section 252 (*d*) of this Act."[66] It is submitted that section 242(*c*) falls to be construed as if it referred to an inquiry by a fit person in terms of what is now section 252(*d*) of the 1975 Act.

Disposal of appeals
8–31   Subject to the provisions noted below[67] for cases where it appears that the appellant was insane at the time of committing the act charged, the High Court may dispose of an appeal against conviction by (a) affirming the verdict of the trial court, or (b) setting aside the verdict of the trial court and either quashing the conviction or substituting therefor an amended verdict of guilty. An amended verdict of guilty must be one which could have been returned on the indictment before the trial court. Further, the High Court may dispose of an appeal by (c) setting aside the verdict of the trial court and granting authority to bring a new prosecution.[68] In setting aside a verdict the High Court may quash any sentence imposed on the appellant as respects the indictment, and (a) in a case where it substitutes an amended verdict of guilty, whether or not the sentence related to the verdict set aside, or (b) in any other case, where the sentence did not so relate, may pass another (but not more severe) sentence in substitution for the sentence so quashed.[69]

---

[65] 1975 Act, s. 252.
[66] See para. 8–22 above.
[67] See para. 8–33 below.
[68] 1975 Act, s. 254(1), and see s. 255 (paras. 8–34 and 8–35 below).
[69] *Ibid.* s. 254(2).

8–32　　　Subject again to the provisions for cases where it appears that the appellant was insane at the time of committing the act charged, the High Court may dispose of an appeal against sentence by (a) affirming that sentence, or (b) if the court thinks that, having regard to all the circumstances, including any additional evidence such as is mentioned in section 228(2) of the Act,[70] a different sentence should have been passed, quashing the sentence and passing another sentence whether more or less severe in substitution therefor.[71] The power to increase a sentence is on occasions used with dramatic effect, as when a sentence of two years in a young offenders' institution was increased to five years on appeal.[72]

Disposal of appeal where appellant insane

8–33　　　Where, in an appeal, it appears to the High Court that the appellant committed the act charged against him but that he was insane when he did so, the court must dispose of the appeal by (a) setting aside the verdict of the trial court and substituting therefor a verdict of acquittal on the ground of insanity, and (b) quashing any sentence imposed on the appellant as respects the indictment and ordering that he be detained in a state hospital or such other hospital as for special reasons the court may specify.[73] The provisions of section 174(4) of the 1975 Act apply to such an order.[74]

New prosecution

8–34　　　Where authority is granted under section 254(1)(c) of the 1975 Act, a new prosecution may be brought charging the accused with the same or any similar offence arising out of the same facts; and the proceedings out of which the appeal arose are not to be a bar to such new prosecution. However, no sentence may be passed on conviction under the new prosecution which could not have been passed on conviction under the earlier proceedings.[75] This does not, it is submitted, mean that no higher sentence may be passed on conviction under the new prosecution than was in fact passed originally: that would appear to be competent provided that the higher sentence could have been passed in the earlier proceedings. On the other hand, if the earlier proceedings were taken under a statute which prescribed a maximum penalty, and the new prosecution was in respect of a common law crime where the court's powers would normally be without limit, the effect of the above provisions would appear to be to impose a limit at the level of the statutory maximum.

8–35　　　A new prosecution may be brought notwithstanding that any time limit which would normally prevent its being brought has elapsed.[76] New prosecutions have, however, their own time limit, namely two months after the date on which authority to bring the prosecution was granted.[77]

---

[70] See para. 8–04 above.
[71] 1975 Act. s. 254(3).
[72] *O'Neil* v. *H.M. Advocate*, 1976 S.L.T. (Notes) 7.
[73] 1975 Act, s. 254(4).
[74] See Chap. 3 above.
[75] 1975 Act, s. 255(1).
[76] *Ibid.* s. 255(2).
[77] *Ibid.* s. 255(3).

Failure to appear at hearing

8–36   Where no appearance is made by or on behalf of an appellant at the diet appointed for the hearing of an appeal, and where no case or argument in writing has been timeously lodged, the High Court must dispose of the appeal as if it had been abandoned.[78]

Sentence in absence

8–37   The power of the High Court to pass any sentence when disposing of an appeal may be exercised notwithstanding that the appellant is for any reason not present.[79]

Time spent pending appeal

8–38   The time during which an appellant, after admission to bail, is at large pending the determination of his appeal, is not to be reckoned as part of any term of imprisonment under his sentence.[80] On the other hand, the time during which an appellant is in custody pending the determination of his appeal will be reckoned as part of any such term of imprisonment, unless the High Court gives any direction to the contrary.[81] Subject to any direction which the High Court may give to the contrary, imprisonment of an appellant will be deemed to run—

(a) if the appellant is in custody in consequence of the conviction or sentence appealed against, as from the date on which the sentence was passed;

(b) if the appellant is in custody other than in consequence of such conviction or sentence, as from the date on which his appeal was determined or abandoned;

(c) if the appellant is not in custody, as from the date on which he is received into prison under the sentence.[82]

Definition of a "sentence"

8–39   Apart from its normal meaning, the word "sentence," for the purpose of appeals under solemn procedure, includes any order of the High Court made on conviction with reference to the person convicted or his wife or children, and any recommendation of the High Court as to the making of a deportation order in the case of a person convicted; and the power of the High Court to pass a sentence includes a power to make any such order of the court or recommendation. A recommendation so made by the High Court is to have the same effect for the purposes of Articles 20 and 21 of the Aliens Order 1953 as the certificate and recommendation of the convicting court.[83]

Appeals against hospital orders

8–40   Where a hospital order, interim hospital order (but not a renewal thereof), guardianship order, or an order restricting discharge has been

---

[78] 1975 Act, s. 257.
[79] *Ibid.* s. 258.
[80] *Ibid.* s. 268(1).
[81] *Ibid.* s. 268(2).
[82] *Ibid.* s. 268(3).
[83] *Ibid.* s. 279; and see *Crolla* v. *Horne*, 1931 J.C. 42.

made by a court in respect of a person charged or brought before it, he may, without prejudice to any other form of appeal under any rule of law (or, where an interim hospital order has been made, to any right or appeal against any other order or sentence which may be imposed), appeal against that order in the same manner as against a sentence.[84]

Prerogative of mercy

8–41   Nothing in the appeal provisions of the 1975 Act affects the prerogative of mercy, but the Secretary of State on the consideration of any sentence (other than sentence of death) passed on a person who has been convicted, may, if he thinks fit, at any time refer the whole case to the High Court for hearing and determination as in the case of an appeal. The above powers of the Secretary of State may be exercised whether or not an appeal against conviction or sentence has previously been heard and determined by the High Court, and whether or not the convicted person has petitioned for the exercise of Her Majesty's mercy.[85] Subject only to the foregoing, all interlocutors and sentences pronounced by the High Court are final and conclusive and not subject to review by any court whatsoever. Further, it is incompetent to stay or suspend any execution or diligence issuing from the High Court by virtue of the powers conferred by the appeal provisions of the 1975 Act.[86]

Disqualification, forfeiture, etc.

8–42   Where, upon conviction of any person, any disqualification, forfeiture or disability attaches to such person by reason of such conviction, this is not to attach for the period of two weeks from the date of the verdict nor, in the event of appeal proceedings being commenced, until the appeal, if it is proceeded with, is determined.[87] Where, upon a conviction, any property, matters or things which are the subject of the prosecution or connected therewith are to be or may be ordered to be destroyed or forfeited, the destruction or forfeiture or the operation of any order for destruction or forfeiture is to be suspended for the same periods as in the case of disqualifications, forfeitures and disabilities.[88] Formerly, there were no comparable provisions in respect of appeals under summary procedure, but similar, though not identical, provision was introduced for summary proceedings by the Criminal Justice (Scotland) Act 1987 (see paragraph 8–52 below).

8–43   The provisions noted above do not apply in the case of an enactment which contains express provision for the suspension of a disqualification or forfeiture, or of an order for destruction or forfeiture, pending the determination of an appeal against conviction or sentence.[89]

Fines and caution

8–44   Where a person has on conviction been sentenced to payment of a fine and in default of payment to imprisonment, the person lawfully

---

[84] 1975 Act, s. 280.
[85] *Ibid.* s. 263(1) and (2).
[86] *Ibid.* s. 262.
[87] *Ibid.* s. 264(1).
[88] *Ibid.* s. 264(2).
[89] *Ibid.* s. 264(3).

authorised to receive that fine must, on receiving it, retain it until the determination of any appeal in relation thereto.[90] If a person sentenced to payment of a fine remains in custody in default of payment he is to be deemed, for the purposes of the appeal provisions of the 1975 Act, to be a person sentenced to imprisonment.[91]

8–45   Where a person has on conviction been sentenced to payment of a fine and in default of payment to imprisonment, and he intimates to the judge who presided at the trial that he is desirous of appealing against his conviction to the High Court, the judge may, by order entered on the record, appoint that person forthwith to find caution for such sum as the judge may think right to prosecute his appeal. Subject to that the judge may also order that payment of the fine is to be made at the final determination of the appeal, if that is dismissed, to the clerk of the court in which the conviction took place or otherwise as the High Court may then order.[92] If an appellant to whom the foregoing applies does not pay the fine or lodge an intimation of intention to appeal within two weeks from the date of his conviction and sentence, the Clerk of Justiciary must report that omission to the High Court or any judge thereof. The High Court or that judge, after such notice as may be deemed advisable, may find that the caution has been forfeited, and may pronounce against the cautioner decree for such sum as may be thought proper; and may issue a warrant for the apprehension of the appellant, and may commit him to prison in default of payment of his fine, or may make such other order as is thought right.[93]

8–46   An appellant who has been sentenced to the payment of a fine, and has paid it in accordance with that sentence, will, in the event of his appeal being successful, be entitled, subject to any order of the High Court, to the return of the sum or any part thereof so paid by him.[94]

Expenses

8–47   On the hearing and determination of an appeal, or any proceedings preliminary or incidental thereto, no expenses are to be allowed on either side.[95]

Appeal by Crown

8–48   The Crown has no right of appeal against a sentence imposed on a person convicted on indictment. Although certain rights of appeal are given to the Crown by the provisions of the 1980 Act, they do not affect this general rule. The Lord Advocate's reference, under section 263A of the 1975 Act, arises only where a person has been acquitted of a charge, and the right to appeal by bill of advocation (now extended to decisions of the High Court as well as the sheriff court by section 280A of the 1975

---

[90] 1975 Act, s. 265(1).
[91] *Ibid.* s. 265(2).
[92] *Ibid.* s. 265(3).
[93] *Ibid.* s. 265(5).
[94] *Ibid.* s. 265(4).
[95] *Ibid.* s. 266.

Act) is a remedy, not against sentence, but against the dismissal of a prosecution on some preliminary ground.[96]

III. APPEALS UNDER SUMMARY PROCEDURE

Right of appeal

8–49 Any person convicted in summary proceedings may appeal to the High Court against the sentence passed on that conviction, or against both conviction and sentence. The prosecutor may also appeal against a sentence passed in such proceedings, but only on a point of law.[97] Only a party to the original proceedings may pursue an appeal, and executors cannot sist themselves as parties.[98]

8–50 By such an appeal a convicted person may bring under review of the High Court any alleged miscarriage of justice in the proceedings, including any alleged miscarriage on the basis of the existence and significance of additional evidence which was not heard at the trial and which was not available and could not reasonably have been made available at the trial.[99]

Appeals against hospital orders, etc.

8–51 Where a hospital order, interim hospital order (but not a renewal thereof), guardianship order, or an order restricting discharge, has been made by a court in respect of a person charged or brought before it, he may, without prejudice to any other form of appeal under any rule of law, (or, where an interim hospital order has been made, to any right of appeal against any other order or sentence which may be imposed), appeal against that order in the same manner as against a sentence.[1]

Suspension of disqualification, forfeiture etc.

8–52 Where, upon conviction of any person, (a) any disqualification, forfeiture or disability attaches to him by reason of such conviction, or (b) any property, matters or things which are the subject of the prosecution or connected therewith are to be or may be ordered to be destroyed or forfeited, the disqualification, forfeiture or disability or, as the case may be, destruction or forfeiture are to be suspended, if the court of conviction thinks fit, pending the determination of any appeal.[2] This provision, which was inserted in the 1975 Act by the Criminal Justice (Scotland) Act 1987,[3] is similar but not identical to the comparable provision[4] in respect of appeals under solemn procedure. In particular the summary appeal provision does not stipulate a standard two-week period of non-attachment, and moreover it allows a measure of discretion to the

---

[96] See, for example, *McFadyean* v. *Stewart*, 1951 J.C. 164; *Skeen* v. *Skerret*, 1976 S.L.T. (Notes) 6; *Skeen* v. *McLaren*, 1976 S.L.T. (Notes) 14; *H.M. Advocate* v. *McCann*, 1977 J.C. 1.
[97] 1975 Act, s. 442(1).
[98] *Keane* v. *Adair*, 1941 J.C. 77.
[99] 1975 Act, s. 442(2).
[1] *Ibid*. s. 443.
[2] *Ibid*. s. 443A(1).
[3] S. 68.
[4] See para. 8–42 above.

court before which a person has been convicted. Like the solemn provisions, however, the summary provision does not apply in the case of an enactment which contains express provision for the suspension of a disqualification or forfeiture, or of an order for destruction or forfeiture, pending the determination of an appeal.[5]

Appeal procedures

8–53 Appeals against conviction and sentence, and all appeals by a prosecutor, whether against an acquittal, or against a sentence, are together subject to a detailed procedure set out in sections 444 to 453, 453D and 453E of the 1975 Act.[6] An appeal by a convicted person against sentence alone is subject to a different procedure which is set out in sections 453B to 453E of that Act.[7] This latter form of appeal is dealt with in paragraphs 8–84 to 8–91 below.

APPEALS AGAINST CONVICTION AND SENTENCE AND APPEALS BY
PROSECUTOR

Abandonment of appeal against conviction

8–54 A person who has appealed against both conviction and sentence may abandon the appeal in so far as it is against conviction and may proceed with it against sentence alone. Procedure for this is prescribed by Act of Adjournal.[8]

Manner and time of appeal

8–55 An appeal against conviction and sentence, or an appeal against sentence by a prosecutor is by application for a stated case. That application must (a) be made within one week of the final determination of the proceedings, (b) contain a full statement of all the matters which the appellant desires to bring under review and, where the appeal is also against sentence, a statement of that fact, and (c) be signed by the appellant or his solicitor and lodged with the clerk of court. A copy of the application must, within the period of one week, be sent by the appellant to the respondent or the respondent's solicitor.[9] In calculating the period of one week the date of the determination of the judge is not counted,[10] and an application posted on the last day of the period has been held to be timeous, although it was not received by the clerk of court until later.[11] An application must be in writing, and may not be submitted orally.[12]

8–56 For the purposes of the foregoing, summary proceedings are to be deemed to be finally determined on the day on which sentence is passed in open court. However, where, in relation to an appeal against conviction, or a prosecutor's appeal against an acquittal, sentence is deferred, they are to be deemed finally determined on the day on which sentence is first

---

[5] 1975 Act, s. 443A(2).
[6] *Ibid*. s. 442A(1).
[7] *Ibid*. s. 442B.
[8] *Ibid*. s. 442A(2); Act of Adjournal (Consolidation) 1988, para. 127.
[9] *Ibid*. s. 444(1); Act of Adjournal (Consolidation) 1988, para. 127.
[10] *Hutton* v. *Garland*, (1884) 5 Couper 274; *Smith* v. *Gray*, 1925 J.C. 8.
[11] *Smith* v. *Gray*, above.
[12] *Smith* v. *Gray*, above.

so deferred in open court.[13] It is submitted that, in the event of such an appeal being disposed of in a manner which permitted the court subsequently to pass sentence, a further appeal would then be competent against that sentence.

8–57 The clerk of court must enter in the record of the proceedings the date when an application for a stated case was lodged.[14] Thereafter, a limited right is given to an appellant to amend any matter stated in his application, or to add a new matter. He may do so at any time within three weeks after the issue of a draft stated case, or within any further period allowed by the High Court under section 448(6) of the Act. Any such amendment or addition must be intimated to the respondent or the respondent's solicitor.[15]

8–58 Without prejudice to any other power of relief which the High Court may have, where it appears to that court on application made to it that the applicant has failed to comply with any of the requirements relating to an application for a stated case, the High Court may direct that such further period of time as it may think proper be afforded to the applicant to comply with any of these requirements.[16] An application for such a direction must be made in writing to the Clerk of Justiciary and must state the grounds for the application. Notification of it must be made by the appellant or his solicitor to the clerk of the court from which the appeal is to be taken, and the clerk must thereupon transmit the complaint, documentary productions and any other proceedings in the cause to the Clerk of Justiciary.[17] The High Court will dispose of any such application in the same manner as an application to review the decision of an inferior court on a grant of bail, but has power to dispense with a hearing, and to make such inquiry in relation to the application as it may think fit. When the High Court has disposed of the application the Clerk of Justiciary must inform the clerk of the inferior court of the result.[18]

Caution by appellant

8–59 It is no longer competent to require an appellant to find caution to meet any fine and expenses imposed.[19]

Procedure where appellant in custody

8–60 If an appellant who has applied for a stated case is in custody, the court may grant bail, grant a sist of execution, and make any other interim order.[20] An application for bail must be disposed of by the court within 24 hours after such application has been made; and the appellant, if dissatisfied with the conditions imposed, or on refusal of bail, may, within 24 hours after the judgment of the court, appeal by a note of appeal

---

[13] 1975 Act, s. 451(3).
[14] *Ibid.* s. 444(1A).
[15] *Ibid.* s. 444(1B).
[16] *Ibid.* s. 444(3).
[17] *Ibid.* s. 444(4).
[18] *Ibid.* s. 444(5).
[19] 1980 Act, Sched. 3, para. 4.
[20] 1975 Act, s. 446(1).

written on the complaint and signed by himself or his solicitor. Such an appeal is to the High Court or any judge thereof.[21]

8–61   If an appellant who has been granted bail does not thereafter proceed with his appeal, the inferior court has power to grant warrant to apprehend and imprison him for such period of his sentence as at the date of his bail remained unexpired. That period will run from the date of his imprisonment under such warrant.[22] Where, however, at the time of abandonment of the appeal the person is serving a term or terms of imprisonment imposed subsequently to the conviction appealed against, the court has power to order that the sentence, or any unexpired portion of it, should run from such date as the court may think fit, not being a date later than the date on which the term or terms of imprisonment subsequently imposed expired.[23] Where a court is contemplating ordering that the sentence, or any unexpired portion of it, should run other than concurrently with any sentence imposed subsequently to the sentence appealed against, intimation should be given to the appellant to the effect that the court is proposing to consider the making of such an order, and that he should make any representations which he wishes to make in relation to it, in writing, either personally or through his solicitor. Upon considering any such representations the court may, at its discretion, decide to hold a hearing on the matter.[24]

Preparation of draft stated case

8–62   Within three weeks of the final determination of proceedings in respect of which an application is made for a stated case, a draft stated case must be prepared. Where the appeal is taken from the district court and the trial was presided over by a justice of the peace or justices of the peace, the draft case is to be prepared by the clerk of court. In any other case, the draft stated case is to be prepared by the judge who presided at the trial. As soon as the case is prepared the clerk of the court concerned must issue the draft to the appellant or his solicitor and a duplicate to the respondent or his solicitor.[25]

8–63   A stated case must be as nearly as may be in the appropriate form contained in an Act of Adjournal. It must set forth the particulars of any matters competent for review which the appellant desires to bring under the review of the High Court, and of the facts, if any, proved in the case. It must also set forth any point of law decided, and the grounds of decision.[26] Where the appeal is against sentence as well as conviction, care should be taken to ensure that the case sets out any facts relevant to sentence, and the considerations upon which the particular sentence was

---

[21] 1975 Act, s. 446(2). From time to time difficulties arise in relation to the time limits prescribed for the disposal of bail applications (*cf.* 1975 Act, ss. 28 and 298), the problem being whether the 24 hours begins to run from the moment when a bail petition is presented to the clerk of court or from the moment when it is first presented to the judge. Although the former interpretation has been contended for, it is now clear that the latter one is more consistent with the words of the statute: see *H.M. Advocate* v. *Keegan*, 1981 S.L.T. (Notes) 35.

[22] *Ibid.* s. 446(4).

[23] *Ibid.* s. 446(5).

[24] *Proudfoot* v. *Wither*, 1990 S.L.T. 742; 1990 S.C.C.R. 96.

[25] 1975 Act, s. 447(1).

[26] *Ibid.* s. 447(2); Act of Adjournal (Consolidation) 1988, para. 127.

arrived at. It is not for the court which is asked to state a case to consider, and form a view on, the relevancy of the appellant's grounds of appeal. The court is obliged to state a case in such circumstances, leaving questions of relevancy for consideration by the High Court.[27]

8–64   A stated case should set out fully the facts proved and not the evidence on which these facts are based[28]; and the facts proved should be set forth in the case itself and not in a separate document.[29] The grounds of a decision should be stated distinctly in a stated case,[30] particularly where evidence has been disallowed.[31] If, for special reasons, a disqualification from holding a driving licence is imposed for less than the statutory period required under the Road Traffic Acts, the grounds of indulgence should be clearly set out in the stated case.[32]

Adjustment and signature of case

8–65   Subject to a power of relief given to the High Court,[33] within three weeks of the issue of the draft stated case each party must cause to be transmitted to the court and to the other parties or their solicitors a note of any adjustments he proposes should be made to the draft case, or must intimate that he has no such proposal. Any proposed adjustments must relate to evidence heard (or purported to have been heard) at the trial and not to additional evidence under section 442(2) of the Act.[34] Subject to the same power of relief, if the period of three weeks has expired and the appellant has not lodged adjustments and has failed to intimate that he has no adjustments to propose, he will be deemed to have abandoned his appeal, whereupon the same consequences will follow as in the case of a person granted bail who does not thereafter proceed with his appeal.[35]

8–66   If adjustments are proposed, or if the judge desires to make any alterations to the draft case, there must be a hearing for the purpose of considering such adjustments or alterations, unless the appellant has, or has been deemed to have, abandoned his appeal. That hearing must take place within one week of the expiry of the three week period mentioned above, or of such further period as the High Court may have allowed.[36] The foregoing provision for a hearing in all cases where adjustments are proposed was introduced by the 1980 Act in response to criticisms that, in some cases, proposed adjustments were being ignored by judges. The consequence of the way in which the provision has been drafted would appear to be that a hearing must be held even in a case where the judge and all the parties are perfectly content that a proposed adjustment should be incorporated in the stated case. No doubt from time to time judges and parties may agree to dispense with a formal hearing in such cases, but they will apparently be acting in contravention of the statutory

---

[27] *McTaggart Petr.*, 1987 S.C.C.R. 638.
[28] *Gordon* v. *Hansen* (1914) 7 Adam 441; *Waddell* v. *Kinnaird*, 1922 J.C. 40; *Pert* v. *Robinson*, 1955 S.L.T. 23.
[29] *MacKenna* v. *Dunn*, 1918 2 S.L.T. 66; *Cockburn* v. *Gordon*, 1928 J.C. 87.
[30] *Lyon* v. *Don Brothers, Buist & Co.*, 1944 J.C. 1.
[31] *Falconer* v. *Brown* (1893) 1 Adam 96.
[32] *Campbell* v. *Sinclair*, 1938 J.C. 127.
[33] See para. 8–70 below.
[34] 1975 Act, s. 448(1); and see para. 8–50 above.
[35] *Ibid.* s. 448(2); and see para. 8–61 above.
[36] *Ibid.* s. 448(2A).

provisions if they do so. The mandatory nature of the provision about hearings is emphasised by the further provision that, where a party neither attends nor secures that he is represented at a hearing the hearing must nevertheless proceed[37]: consequently, it would seem that, in the admittedly unlikely event of neither party being present or represented, a judge is required to hold a hearing by himself!

8–67 Where at a hearing any adjustment proposed by a party (and not withdrawn) is rejected by the judge, or any alteration to the draft case proposed by the judge is not accepted by all parties, that fact must be recorded in the minute of the proceedings of the hearing.[38] Within two weeks of the date of the hearing or, where there is no hearing, within two weeks of the expiry of the original three week period, the judge must (unless the appellant has been deemed to have abandoned his appeal) state and sign the case. He must append to the case (a) any adjustment which is rejected by him, a note of any evidence rejected by him which is alleged to support that adjustment and the reasons for his rejection of that adjustment and evidence; and (b) a note of the evidence upon which he bases any finding in fact challenged, on the basis that it is unsupported by the evidence, by a party at the hearing.[39]

8–68 Where the judge by whom a person was convicted dies before signing the case, or is precluded by illness or other cause from doing so, it is competent for the convicted person to present a bill of suspension to the High Court and to bring under the review of that court any matter which might have been brought under review by stated case.[40]

8–69 As soon as a stated case is signed the clerk of court must send the case to the appellant or his solicitor and a duplicate thereof to the respondent or his solicitor, and he must transmit the complaint, productions and any other proceedings to the Clerk of Justiciary.[41] Subject again to any power of relief granted to the High Court, within one week of receiving the case the appellant or his solicitor must cause it to be lodged with the Clerk of Justiciary.[42] If the appellant or his solicitor fails to comply with the above requirement the appellant will be deemed to have abandoned his appeal.[43]

Application to High Court for extension of time

8–70 Without prejudice to any other power of relief which the High Court may have, where it appears to that court, on application made to it, that the applicant has failed to comply with any of the time limits relating to the notification of adjustments or the lodging of the case with the Clerk of Justiciary, the High Court may direct that such further period of time as it may think proper be afforded to the applicant to comply with any such requirement.[44] Such an application must be made in writing to the Clerk

---

[37] 1975 Act, s. 448(2B).
[38] *Ibid.* s. 448(2C).
[39] *Ibid.* s. 448(2D).
[40] *Ibid.* s. 444(2).
[41] *Ibid.* s. 448(3).
[42] *Ibid.* s. 448(4).
[43] *Ibid.* s. 448(5).
[44] *Ibid.* s. 448(6).

of Justiciary and must state the grounds for the application.[45] The High Court will dispose of the application in the same manner as an application to review the decision of an inferior court on a grant of bail, but has power to dispense with a hearing, and to make such inquiry in relation to the application as it may think fit. When the High Court has disposed of the application the Clerk of Justiciary must inform the clerk of the inferior court of the result.[46] A sheriff principal also has power to extend time limits where that is necessary because a judge is temporarily absent from duty for any cause (see paragraph 8–72 below).

Abandonment of appeal
8–71   An appellant may at any time prior to lodging the case with the Clerk of Justiciary abandon his appeal by minute signed by himself or his solicitor, written on the complaint or lodged with the clerk of the inferior court, and intimated to the respondent or his solicitor. Such abandonment is without prejudice to any other competent mode of appeal, review, advocation or suspension.[47] Subject to section 453A of the 1975 Act (appeal by bill of suspension or advocation on ground of miscarriage of justice), once the case has been lodged with the Clerk of Justiciary the appellant will be held to have abandoned any other mode of appeal which might otherwise have been open to him.[48] Exceptionally, however, in such circumstances a petition to the *nobile officium* may be considered.[49]

Computation of time
8–72   If any period of time relating to appeals expires on a Saturday, Sunday or court holiday prescribed for the relevant court, the period is to be extended to expire on the next day which is not a Saturday, Sunday or such court holiday.[50] Where a judge against whose judgment an appeal is taken is temporarily absent from duty for any cause, the sheriff principal of the sheriffdom concerned may extend any period specified in sections 447(1) (preparation of draft case), 448(2A) (holding of hearing on proposed adjustments and alterations) and 448(2D) (stating and signing of case). Such extension may be for such period as the sheriff principal considers reasonable.[51] For the purposes of the statutory rules relating to the application for, and preparation of, a stated case (sections 444(1)(*a*) and 447(1)), summary proceedings are to be deemed to be finally determined on the day on which sentence is passed in open court. However, where sentence is deferred, and the appeal is against conviction or, at the instance of the prosecutor, against an acquittal, summary proceedings are to be deemed to be finally determined on the day on which sentence is first so deferred in open court.[52]

---

[45] 1975 Act, s. 448(7).
[46] *Ibid.* s. 448(8).
[47] *Ibid.* s. 449(1); and see *Kay* v. *Local Authority of Kelso* (1876) 3 Couper 305.
[48] *Ibid.* s. 449(2).
[49] *Patrick McCloy, Petr.*, 1971 S.L.T. (Notes) 32.
[50] 1975 Act, s. 451(1).
[51] *Ibid.* s. 451(2).
[52] *Ibid.* s. 451(3). It is not immediately clear why this provision is made applicable to a case where the appeal is at the instance of the prosecutor against an acquittal since, presumably, there will have been no opportunity in such a case for the court to defer sentence.

Hearing of appeal

8–73   A stated case will be heard by the High Court on such date as it may fix.[53] Where an appellant, in his application for a stated case, refers to an alleged miscarriage of justice, but in stating a case the inferior court is unable to take that allegation into account, the High Court may nevertheless have regard to the allegation at the hearing.[54] Generally, except by leave of the High Court on cause shown, it is not competent for an appellant to found any aspect of his appeal on a matter not contained in his application (or in a duly made amendment or addition to that application).[55] Where an appeal is against sentence on the basis that no notice of penalties was served on the appellant, the proper course is to appeal against sentence by note of appeal and not to appeal by stated case.[56]

8–74   Without prejudice to any existing power of the High Court, that court may in hearing a stated case:

   (a) order the production of any document or other thing connected with the proceedings;
   (b) hear any additional evidence relevant to any alleged miscarriage of justice or order such evidence to be heard by a judge of the High Court or by such other person as it may appoint for that purpose;
   (c) take account of any circumstances relevant to the case which were not before the trial judge[57];
   (d) remit to any fit person to inquire and report in regard to any matter or circumstance affecting the appeal[58];
   (e) appoint a person with expert knowledge to act as assessor to the High Court in any case where it appears to the court that such expert knowledge is required for the proper determination of the case;
   (f) take account of any matter proposed in any adjustment rejected by the trial judge and of the reasons for such rejection;
   (g) take account of any evidence contained in a note of the evidence upon which a judge bases any finding of fact challenged by a party.[59]

Additionally, the High Court may at the hearing remit the stated case back to the inferior court to be amended and returned.[60]

Disposal of stated case appeal

8–75   Apart from the procedure appropriate in cases where the offender appears to have been insane at the time of the commission of the offence,[61] the High Court may dispose of a case by:

---

[53] 1975 Act, s. 452(1).
[54] *Ibid.* s. 452(2).
[55] *Ibid.* s. 452(3).
[56] *Cowan* v. *Guild*, 1991 S.C.C.R. 424.
[57] *Cf. Hogg* v. *Heatlie*, 1962 S.L.T. 38, where the High Court obtained a social inquiry report when none had been before the trial judge.
[58] *Cf.* para. 8–30 above.
[59] 1975 Act, s. 452(4).
[60] *Ibid.* s. 452(5); *Penrose* v. *Bruce*, 1927 J.C. 79; *Cairney* v. *Patterson*, 1945 J.C. 120.
[61] See para. 8–91 below.

(a) remitting the cause to the inferior court with their opinion and any direction thereon;

(b) affirming the verdict of the inferior court;

(c) setting aside the verdict of the inferior court and either quashing the conviction or substituting an amended verdict of guilty. In the latter case the amended verdict must be one which could have been returned on the complaint before the inferior court; or

(d) setting aside the verdict of the inferior court and granting authority to bring a new prosecution.[62]

In an appeal against both conviction and sentence the High Court will dispose of the appeal against sentence by the exercise of the powers appropriate where the appeal is against sentence alone.[63]

8–76　　In setting aside a verdict the High Court may quash any sentence imposed on the appellant as respects the complaint, and (a) in a case where it substitutes an amended verdict of guilty, whether or not the sentence related to the verdict set aside, or (b) in any other case, where the sentence did not so relate, may pass another (but not more severe) sentence in substitution for the sentence so quashed.[64]

8–77　　Where an appeal against acquittal is sustained, the High Court may (a) convict and sentence the respondent, (b) remit the case to the inferior court with instructions to convict and sentence the respondent, who is bound to attend any diet fixed by the inferior court for such purpose, or (c) remit the case to the inferior court with their opinion thereon. The High Court must not in any case increase the sentence beyond the maximum sentence which could have been passed by the inferior court.[65]

8–78　　The High Court has power in an appeal to award such expenses both in the High Court and in the inferior court as it may think fit.[66]

New prosecution

8–79　　Where authority is granted by the High Court, a new prosecution may be brought charging the accused with the same or any similar offence arising out of the same facts. The proceedings out of which the stated case arose are not a bar to such prosecution. However, no sentence may be passed on conviction under the new prosecution which could not have been passed on conviction under the earlier proceedings.[67] This last provision may be of particular importance in summary courts where different statutes may impose differing maximum penalites. Thus, for example, if a person were convicted in a new prosecution of an offence of police assault under section 41 of the Police (Scotland) Act 1967, the earlier proceedings having been in respect of an assault at common law, the court could not avail itself of the extended sentencing powers conferred in respect of the statutory offence. It follows that, in all cases of

---

[62] 1975 Act, s. 452A(1); for new prosecution see paras. 8–79 and 8–80 below.

[63] *Ibid.* s. 452A(2); and see para. 8–89 below.

[64] *Ibid.* s. 452A(3).

[65] *Ibid.* s. 452A(4). The reason for the proviso at the end of s. 452A(4) is not clear. That subsection deals with appeals against acquittal where, *ex hypothesi*, there can be no sentence capable of being increased. It may be that the proviso is in fact intended to refer back to s. 452A(2), but in that event it is surely misplaced: *cf.* s. 453C(1).

[66] *Ibid.* s. 452A(5).

[67] *Ibid.* s. 452B(1).

new prosecutions, care should be taken to ascertain the nature of the earlier proceedings before sentence is passed.

8–80   A new prosecution may be brought notwithstanding that any time limit for the commencement of such proceedings, other than the one expressly provided for in relation to new prosecutions, has elapsed.[68] Proceedings in a new prosecution must be commenced within two months of the date on which authority to bring the prosecution was granted. For this purpose proceedings are to be deemed to be commenced on the date on which a warrant to apprehend or to cite the accused is granted, where such warrant is executed without unreasonable delay. In any other case the proceedings are to be deemed to be commenced on the date on which the warrant is executed.[69] Where the two months elapse and no new prosecution has been brought, the order of the High Court setting aside the verdict is to have the effect, for all purposes, of an acquittal.[70]

Consent by prosecutor to set aside conviction

8–81   Where an appeal has been taken by stated case against conviction, or against conviction and sentence, or by suspension or otherwise, and the prosecutor, on the appeal being intimated to him, is not prepared to maintain the judgment appealed against, he may consent to the conviction and sentence being set aside, either in whole or in part. This should be done by a minute signed by him and written on the complaint or lodged with the clerk of court. The minute must set forth the ground on which the prosecutor is of opinion that the judgment cannot be maintained.[71] This provision does not authorise a prosecutor to purport to reverse a sheriff on a question of law, that being a matter solely for the High Court.[72]

8–82   A copy of a minute by a prosecutor must be sent by him to the appellant or his solicitor, and the clerk of court must thereupon ascertain from the appellant or his solicitor whether he desires to be heard by the High Court before the appeal is disposed of. The clerk must note on the record whether or not the appellant so desires, and must thereafter transmit the complaint and relative proceedings to the Clerk of Justiciary.[73] On receipt of these the Clerk of Justiciary must lay them before any judge of the High Court, either in court or in chambers, and the judge, after hearing parties if they desire to be heard, or without hearing parties, may set aside the conviction either in whole or in part, or may refuse to set aside the conviction. If he sets aside the conviction he may award to the appellant expenses not exceeding £40. If he refuses to set aside the conviction the proceedings must be returned to the clerk of the inferior court when the appellant will be entitled to proceed with his appeal in the same way as if it had been marked on the date when the complaint and proceedings are

---

[68] 1975 Act, s. 452B(2).
[69] *Ibid.* s. 452B(3).
[70] *Ibid.* s. 452B(4).
[71] *Ibid.* s. 453(1).
[72] *O'Brien* v. *Adair*, 1947 J.C. 180.
[73] 1975 Act, s. 453(2).
[74] *Ibid.* s. 453(3).

returned to the clerk of the inferior court.[74] The preparation of a draft stated case is delayed pending the decision of the High Court.[75]

8–83 The power to consent to a conviction and sentence being set aside is exercisable, where the appeal is by stated case, at any time within two weeks after the receipt by the prosecutor of the draft stated case, and, where the appeal is by suspension, at any time within two weeks after the service on the prosecutor of the bill of suspension.[76] In so far as it relates to appeals by stated case the foregoing provision is a little puzzling because it appears to imply that a prosecutor may not avail himself of the power to consent to a conviction being set aside until after the draft stated case has been issued. On the other hand the general purpose of these provisions is to save expense and delay,[77] and both subsections (1) and (4) of section 453 (paragraphs 8–81 and 8–82, above) clearly contemplate the procedure being initiated before a draft case is prepared. Perhaps the provisions in subsection (5) do no more than prescribe a point after which the procedure will no longer be competent.

APPEALS AGAINST SENTENCE ALONE

Note of appeal

8–84 An appeal against sentence alone by a person convicted in summary proceedings is by note of appeal. The note must state the ground of appeal and must, within one week of the passing of the sentence, be lodged with the clerk of the court from which the appeal is to be taken.[78]

8–85 On receipt of the note of appeal the clerk of court must send a copy of the note to the respondent or his solicitor, and obtain a report from the judge who sentenced the convicted person.[79] No statutory form is prescribed for the judge's report: it should, however, fully narrate any facts pertaining to the offence which are relevant to the sentence, describe the substance of any plea in mitigation submitted by or on behalf of the convicted person, and explain the reasoning behind the sentence that was imposed. A court is obliged to prepare a report in an appeal against sentence even where the grounds of appeal stated by the appellant are unspecific.[80]

8–86 Within two weeks of the passing of the sentence against which the appeal is taken the clerk of court must send to the Clerk of Justiciary the note of appeal together with the judge's report, a certified copy of the complaint, the minute of proceedings and any other relevant documents. He must also send copies of the report to the appellant and respondent or their solicitors. The above period of two weeks may, however, be extended for such period as is considered reasonable by the sheriff principal of the sheriffdom in which the judgment was pronounced. The sheriff principal may exercise that power in cases where a judge is

---

[75] 1975 Act, s. 453(4).

[76] *Ibid.* s. 453(5).

[77] *O'Brien* v. *Adair*, above.

[78] 1975 Act, s. 453B(1) and (2). If inadequate grounds are stated, the appeal may be refused: *Campbell* v. *MacDougall*, 1991 S.C.C.R. 218.

[79] *Ibid.* s. 453B(3).

[80] *Henry* v. *Docherty*, 1990 S.L.T. 301; 1989 S.C.C.R. 426; *cf. McTaggart, Petr.*, 1987 S.C.C.R. 638, referred to in para. 8–63 above.

temporarily absent from duty for any cause.[81] Where the judge's report is not furnished within any of the periods mentioned above, the High Court may extend the period or, if it thinks fit, hear and determine the appeal without such report.[82]

8-87 An appellant proceeding by way of note of appeal may at any time prior to the hearing of the appeal abandon his appeal by minute, signed by himself or his solicitor. That minute must be lodged with the clerk of court in a case where the note has not yet been sent to the Clerk of Justiciary, and in any other case with the Clerk of Justiciary. In all cases the minute must be intimated to the respondent.[83]

8-88 Many of the provisions of the 1975 Act relating to stated cases also apply to appeals by note of appeal. These are the provisions of section 444 relating to an allowance by the High Court of further time to lodge an appeal,[84] and the provisions of section 446 (procedure where appellant in custody), section 450 (record of procedure on appeal), and section 452(4)(*a*) to (*e*) (powers of High Court at hearing of appeal).[85]

Disposal of appeal by note of appeal

8-89 An appeal against sentence by note of appeal will be heard by the High Court on such date as it may fix, and the High Court may dispose of the appeal by (a) affirming the sentence, or (b) if the court thinks that, having regard to all the circumstances, including any additional evidence, a different sentence should have been passed, quashing the sentence and passing another sentence, whether more or less severe, in substitution therefor. The court may not, however, increase the sentence beyond the maximum sentence which could have been passed by the inferior court.[86] The High Court has power in an appeal by note of appeal to award such expenses both in the High Court and in the inferior court as it may think fit.[87]

Procedure where appellant is liable to imprisonment or detention

8-90 Where, following an appeal other than one at the instance of the prosecutor, the appellant remains liable to imprisonment or detention under the sentence of the inferior court or is so liable under a sentence passed in the appeal proceedings, the High Court has certain powers. Where at the time of disposal of the appeal the appellant was at liberty on bail, it has power to grant warrant to apprehend and imprison (or detain) the appellant for a term, to run from the date of such apprehension, not longer than that part of the term or terms of imprisonment (or detention) specified in the sentence brought under review which remained unexpired at the date of liberation. Where at the time of disposal of the appeal the appellant is serving a term or terms of imprisonment (or detention) imposed in relation to a conviction subsequent to the conviction in respect of which the conviction or sentence appealed against

---

[81] 1975, Act, s. 453B(4).
[82] *Ibid*. s. 453B(5).
[83] *Ibid*. s. 453B(7).
[84] *Ibid*. s. 453B(6).
[85] *Ibid*. s. 453B(8).
[86] *Ibid*. s. 453C(1).
[87] *Ibid*. s. 453C(2).

was imposed, the High Court may exercise the like powers in relation to him as may be exercised, in relation to an appeal which has been abandoned, by a court of summary jurisdiction in pursuance of section 446(5) of the 1975 Act (see paragraph 8–61 above).[88]

Disposal of appeal where appellant insane

8–91   In relation to any appeal by a convicted person under summary procedure the High Court, where it appears to it that the appellant committed the act charged against him but that he was insane when he did so, must dispose of the appeal by (a) setting aside the verdict of the inferior court and substituting therefor a verdict of acquittal on the ground of insanity, and (b) quashing any sentence imposed on the appellant as respects the complaint and ordering that he be detained in a state hospital or such other hospital as for special reasons the court may specify.[89] The provisions of section 174(4) of the 1975 Act are to apply to such an order for detention in hospital; that is to say the order is to have the like effect as a hospital order together with an order restricting the person's discharge, made without limitation of time.[90] The fact that it was found necessary in relation to summary appeals to make reference to section 174 (which is in the part of the 1975 Act dealing with solemn procedure) lends weight to the view expressed elsewhere in this book[91] that the Act contains no provision for a court of summary jurisdiction to deal with the case of a person who is found to have been insane at the time of commission of the offence.

IV. SUSPENSION

8–92   Suspension is a process, which is now effectively confined to summary procedure, whereby an illegal or improper warrant, conviction or judgment issued by an inferior court may be reviewed and set aside by the High Court. It has been held[92] not to be a suitable mode of review in cases where the more appropriate method of appeal is by stated case, and has been said to be truly appropriate "where the relevant circumstances are instantly or almost instantly verifiable and the point sought to be raised is raised promptly, a crisp issue of say, jurisdiction, competency, oppression, or departure from the canons of natural justice."[93] Suspension is now expressly declared by statute[94] to be available against a conviction in cases where a miscarriage of justice in the proceedings is alleged and where an appeal by stated case would be incompetent or would in the circumstances be inappropriate. As has been seen (paragraph 8–68 above) it is also competent, in a case where the judge dies before signing a stated case or is precluded by illness or other cause from doing so, to present a bill of suspension so as to bring under review

---

[88] 1975 Act, ss. 452A(6) and 453C(3).
[89] *Ibid*. s. 453D(1).
[90] *Ibid*. s. 453D(2).
[91] Paras. 3–09 and 3–10.
[92] *O'Hara* v. *Mill*, 1938 J.C. 4; *James Y. Keanie Ltd.* v. *Laird*, 1943 J.C. 73.
[93] *Fairley* v. *Muir*, 1951 J.C. 56, *per* Lord Justice-General at p. 60.
[94] 1975 Act, s. 453A.

any matter that might have been brought under review by stated case. That, of course, will include an appeal against sentence where there is also an appeal against conviction. It will not, however, include an appeal against sentence alone, since such an appeal now proceeds, not by stated case, but by note of appeal.

8–93   In general, where an appeal is to be taken against sentence alone, it may be said that a bill of suspension will rarely be appropriate,[95] except where there has been some fundamental incompetence or irregularity of procedure,[96] or clearly oppressive conduct on the part of the judge.[97] Suspension cannot be used as a means of obtaining probation or other reports which were not called for by the judge.[98] On the other hand, matters incidental to sentencing, such as a remand in custody while reports are being prepared, may properly be made the subject of a suspension.[99] It was at one time held that, notwithstanding the provisions of section 230 of the 1975 Act, it is competent to proceed by way of suspension in the case of a witness sentenced for contempt of court in the course of proceedings on indictment in the sheriff court. However, the decision expressing that view has now been overruled, and it is not now competent to proceed by bill of suspension in such a case. The proper mode of appeal is by a petition to the *nobile officium*.[1] A suspension may also be brought by a person other than the prosecutor or the accused where that person has been affected by, for example, an order for forfeiture of his goods.[2]

V. GROUNDS ON WHICH A SENTENCE MAY BE OVERTURNED

Solemn jurisdiction

8–94   On an appeal against sentence the High Court may quash the sentence of the inferior court and pass another sentence whether more or less severe in substitution therefor. The court may take that course if it thinks that, having regard to all the circumstances, a different sentence should have been passed.[3] These powers, which are substantially the same as those introduced by the Criminal Appeal (Scotland) Act 1926, have been construed as meaning that a sentence may be reduced if it is clearly excessive, or increased if it is clearly inadequate. The court's power to increase sentences has been used on several occasions.[4]

8–95   A sentence is unlikely to be reduced as being excessive merely because it is somewhat higher than that which the High Court would itself have

---

[95] *Galloway* v. *Smith*, 1974 S.L.T. (Notes) 63; and see *Cowan* v. *Guild*, 1991 S.C.C.R. 424.
[96] *Smith* v. *Sempill* (1910) 6 Adam 348; *McRory* v. *Findlay* (1911) 6 Adam 417; *Anderson* v. *Begg* (1907) 5 Adam 387.
[97] *Blair* v. *Hawthorn*, 1945 J.C. 17.
[98] *Farquhar* v. *Burrell*, 1955 J.C. 66.
[99] *Morrison* v. *Clark*, 1962 S.L.T. 113.
[1] *George Outram & Co. Ltd.* v. *Lees*, 1991 G.W.D. 40–2449, overruling *Butterworth* v. *Herron*, 1975 S.L.T. (Notes) 56.
[2] *Loch Lomond Sailings Ltd.* v. *Hawthorn*, 1962 J.C. 8; *Semple & Sons* v. *Macdonald*, 1963 J.C. 90.
[3] 1975 Act, s. 254(3).
[4] *Boyle* v. *H.M. Advocate*, 1949 S.L.T. (Notes) 41; *Connelly* v. *H.M. Advocate*, 1954 J.C. 90; *O'Neil* v. *H.M. Advocate*, 1976 S.L.T. (Notes) 7.

imposed. For a reduction to be justified the sentence must go beyond what is necessary and customary in a case of that kind.[5] Although the test on appeal—and indeed most written grounds of appeal echo this—is whether the sentence appealed against is excessive, some of the cases suggest that it might equally well be expressed as whether the sentence is appropriate having regard to the circumstances of the particular case. However the test is described, the High Court's power to reduce a sentence is clearly a wide one, and, although what is sometimes referred to as "tinkering with a sentence" has been judicially disapproved of, there may sometimes be a fairly fine dividing line between that and a proper exercise of the court's powers.

8–96   It is to be noted that, prior to the passing of the 1980 Act, the High Court had power, where an appeal was against conviction only, to reduce or increase the sentence in like manner as in an appeal against sentence.[6] That power, which was on one occasion construed as enabling the court to increase a sentence beyond the maximum which could have been imposed by the sheriff,[7] was removed by the amended section 254 of the 1975 Act introduced by the 1980 Act. The position now is that, where an appeal is against conviction alone, the High Court may vary the sentence only where it sets aside the verdict of the inferior court; and in that case, while it may quash the sentence originally passed, it may not pass another which is more severe.[8]

Summary jurisdiction

8–97   Prior to the passing of the 1980 Act it was well established that the High Court would interfere with a sentence passed by a court of summary jurisdiction only if it could be shown that that sentence was harsh and oppressive.[9] The Thomson Committee,[10] however, took the view that it was undesirable to have different tests for summary and solemn procedure, and their recommendation on that matter was given statutory effect in the new section 453C of the 1975 Act which was introduced by the 1980 Act. That section describes the powers of the High Court, in an appeal against sentence in summary proceedings, in the same words as are used in section 254 in relation to solemn appeals, with only this minor difference that, in section 453C, there is a proviso to the effect that the court must not in any (summary) case increase the sentence beyond the maximum sentence which could have been passed by the inferior court. Subject to that, the position now is that summary appeals against sentence fall to be determined by the same criteria that have previously been in use in relation to solemn appeals.

The role of the appeal court

8–98   Many examples are to be found in Chapter 11, below, of cases where the High Court has exercised, or has declined to exercise, its powers to

---

[5] *O'Reilly* v. *H.M. Advocate*, 1943 J.C. 23; *Dewar* v. *H.M. Advocate*, 1945 J.C. 5; *Moar* v. *H.M. Advocate*, 1949 J.C. 31; *Cawthorne* v. *H.M. Advocate*, 1968 J.C. 32.

[6] Criminal Appeal (Scotland) Act 1926, s. 2(3).

[7] *Connelly* v. *H.M. Advocate*, above.

[8] 1975 Act, s. 254(2).

[9] *Stewart* v. *Cormack*, 1941 J.C. 73; *Fleming* v. *Macdonald*, 1958 J.C. 1.

[10] *Criminal Appeals in Scotland (Third Report)*, 1977, Cmnd. 7005, Chap. 16.

vary a sentence on appeal. As those cases demonstrate, much will turn on the individual facts and circumstances of each case. However, a few general comments on the role and practice of the High Court may be made here.

8–99 First, although upon one view the role of the High Court is, and should be, limited to that of correcting sentences which, for one reason or another, were wrong at the time of their imposition, it is clear that, from time to time, the court is prepared to acknowledge that a particular sentence was entirely appropriate at the time when it was imposed but nonetheless to vary it downwards in the light of changed circumstances between that date and the date of the appeal.[11] While a purist might argue that this is to confuse the functions of a court of appeal and a court of review, a pragmatist would no doubt retort that this kind of flexibility is necessary in order to secure fairness and justice.

8–100 Second, from time to time the High Court will disturb a sentence not necessarily because it is excessive but because it has been arrived at on the basis of considerations which are irrelevant or improper. In such cases the High Court will regard the question of sentence as being at large, and may in fact reimpose the same sentence albeit upon different, and proper, considerations. The topic of irrelevant and improper considerations is dealt with more fully in Chapter 9 below.[12]

8–101 Third, and finally, note may be taken of the fact that increasingly the High Court is adopting the practice in certain cases of continuing an appeal, often for a prolonged period, and often for the purpose of allowing an appellant to demonstrate that he can be of good behaviour.[13] The alternative practice of allowing the appeal and deferring sentence for a period is also used on occasions. It is not entirely clear why one practice should be preferred to the other unless it be on the basis that, where a sentence is quashed and sentence is then deferred, the court is accepting that the original sentence was excessive, whereas, when the appeal is continued, the court is in effect saying that its view about the appropriateness of the original sentence will depend on the offender's behaviour during the period of continuation.

---

[11] See, for example, *McLean* v. *MacDougall*, 1989 S.C.C.R. 625.
[12] See para. 9–40.
[13] See, for example, *Paxton* v. *McDonald*, 1990 G.W.D. 33–1917.

Part II

Sentencing in Practice

CHAPTER 9

THE SENTENCING PROCESS

THE JUDGE'S TASK

9–01 When a judge comes to determine the appropriate disposal in a particular case he must consider and weigh in the balance several or, on occasions, many factors. He must (although he may not consciously think of it in every case) decide what his sentencing objectives are, both in general and in relation to the particular case. He must consider the aggravating and mitigating factors bearing both on the particular crime or offence and on the particular offender. He may have to consider background information relating to the offender. And he will have to consider carefully the advantages and disadvantages of all the different disposals which are available to him. This and the following chapter attempt to describe all of those factors, and to say something about how they relate to each other.

9–02 Before attempting this task it must be said that the person who seeks to enunciate established sentencing principles in Scotland will derive only limited assistance from the reported, or unreported, decisions of the appeal court. This is partly because, in appeals against sentence, it is customary for the judges to say no more than is strictly necessary for the disposal of the case. More importantly, it is because the Scottish appeal court has traditionally adopted a pragmatic and individualised approach to questions of sentence, and has always tended to decide cases on their own facts and circumstances rather than on the basis of any declared principles. By contrast the Court of Appeal (Criminal Division) in England seems to be prepared to lay down principles to be applied in

177

particular types of case with the result that it has proved possible there to describe a comprehensive approach to sentencing based almost entirely on reported appeal cases.[1] While the English approach no doubt has the merit of providing judges with reasonably clear guidelines when dealing with individual cases, it may equally be an approach which would inhibit some of the flexibility which is a feature of the Scottish system. What follows, however, is not an attempt to perform the task that the appeal court has eschewed for nearly 70 years. Rather, it is an attempt merely to describe the factors which are, or may be, present in the sentencing process, and to offer some comment on the way in which those factors may be regarded.

SENTENCING OBJECTIVES

General approach

9-03   If one were to ask a random selection of people in the street what objectives they thought judges should have in mind when sentencing convicted offenders, one would probably receive nearly as many answers as there were people. If one were to ask the same question of a random selection of judges, one might receive the same number of answers, but the judges might add that the objectives may vary from case to case, and that sometimes there may be more than a single objective in mind in the one case. That is no doubt true, but the problem is that, faced with the same or similar cases, different judges might consider different objectives to be important, and so might arrive at different results. That of course can contribute to disparity of sentences, for the existence of which there is now some convincing evidence.[2] Equally, there are probably occasions when a false parity is achieved, that is to say when different judges make the same sentencing decision, but with quite different objectives in mind. All of that is no doubt largely inevitable so long as sentencing decisions are made by human beings and not by computers, and one may perhaps be forgiven for supposing that computers might produce at least as many anomalous results as human judges. Nonetheless, disparity or inconsistency in sentencing is now perceived as a matter of concern in many parts of the world,[3] and it is clearly something which judges should be at pains to avoid, or at least reduce, so far as that is possible. For the present, however, judges probably take a fairly broad approach to the objectives which they are hoping to achieve, and it is those considerations which will now be dealt with. The following are probably the main objectives which from time to time, and in varying proportions, figure in sentencing decisions. No special significance is intended by the order in which they are presented.

---

[1] See, for example, Thomas, *Current Sentencing Practice*. The practice of offering general sentencing guidance in cases on appeal is also followed by appeal courts in other countries such as, for example, Canada and New Zealand.

[2] For a survey of some of that evidence, see Hood and Sparks, *Key Issues in Criminology*, Chap. 5; and see also Ashworth, *Sentencing and Penal Policy*, Chap. 1. From another jurisdiction, see *Sentencing Reform, A Canadian Approach* (Report of the Canadian Sentencing Commission, 1987), Chap. 3.

[3] For example, the topic of "Consistency in Sentencing" was on the agenda of a meeting of Commonwealth Law Ministers held in New Zealand in 1990.

Punishment

9–04   Punishment has for long been an accepted aim of sentencing though it would now be generally recognised that there must be some restriction on its use in that it must be fair and broadly in proportion to the gravity of the offence. Furthermore, there are now several international agreements and conventions prohibiting the use of cruel and unnatural punishments. While punishment may sometimes be seen as an objective on its own it will more often be regarded as going hand in hand with some other objective such as deterrence, or protection of the public. To some extent punishment, as a sentencing aim, is a form of retribution, and the two are sometimes seen as synonymous. Retribution, however, is frequently described by penologists in terms which encompass a wish to make an offender atone, or make amends, to society at large for the harm he has done. Most judges would probably see punishment as distinct from retribution in that sense, and might consider a fine or, in certain circumstances, imprisonment as pure punishment whereas a community service order would be seen more as a form of retribution.

Protection of public

9–05   This is an objective which seeks to secure that for as long as may be necessary the public will be protected from the criminal activity of a particular offender. It is an objective which may be sought in various ways. At one extreme it may involve some form of incapacitation and, since the ultimate incapacitation, the death penalty, is no longer available, will take the form of a very long prison sentence or a long period of detention in a state hospital. At the other extreme it may be sought by some form of supervision, such as probation, in the expectation that the supervision will inhibit criminal activity in the short term while the probation experience will in the long term result in a beneficial change of behaviour. While this latter means of trying to achieve the aim of public protection is perfectly tenable in theory, research and common experience have shown that in practice it frequently fails to achieve its objective; and consequently, if certain protection of the public is what is wanted, that will only be achieved by a period of incarceration. However, given that few offenders commit offences every day of the week, or even every week in the year, a short prison sentence is unlikely to afford much protection to the public. Accordingly, it is suggested that, unless the incarceration is going to be of at least a reasonably long duration, it cannot be justified on the ground of achieving public protection, whatever other justification it may have.

Deterrence

9–06   Deterrence is a common aim of sentencing, and the objective may be to secure individual deterrence, or general deterrence, or both. That is to say, the purpose may be to deter only the particular individual from further acts of crime, or it may be more widely to deter others from indulging in the same or similar kinds of criminal activity. It is suggested that, while the aim of individualised deterrence may often be a perfectly valid one since it can be based on extensive and detailed information about the particular offender, the aim of general deterrence is of much more dubious validity. There is unquestionably considerable popular faith in the value and effectiveness of general deterrence as a sentencing objective, but there is little or no evidence to support the view that a particular kind of sentencing policy, or a well-publicised exemplary sentence, has any significant effect on the kind of criminal behaviour in issue. All of this is not to say, however, that a declared intention of seeking general deterrence, expressed at the time when a sentence is imposed, may not have some merit albeit for different reasons (see paragraph 9–07 below).

Denunciation

9–07   When, for example, a murderer is given a life sentence, or a terrorist is given a long, determinate, sentence of imprisonment, it may be as much a part of the judge's intention not only to achieve the protection of the public, and to punish the offender, but also, by the nature of the sentence, to express society's abhorrence of that particular kind of crime. Although most marked in the case of more serious crimes the objective is equally valid in the case of some less serious ones. Strictly, in such cases, the sentence speaks for itself in terms of denunciation, but it is not uncommon for judges, when passing sentence, to use words which express the public condemnation that is implicit in the sentence. That may be coupled with an expressed desire to achieve the aim of general deterrence and, although the sentence may not achieve that aim, the judge is certainly reinforcing thereby the general tone of denunciation. Although one can readily understand the desire on the part of a judge to show his condemnation of a particularly repellent crime, it may be asked whether that is a proper objective of sentencing. Or, to put the question in another way, to whom is the denunciation being addressed? If it is to the offender, it may well be argued that, if his sentence is a substantial one, he is more likely to be aware of the obvious realisation of the aims of punishment or public protection. If it is to the public at large, it may be argued that the denunciation, if it has any value in itself, should be equally effective even if no punishment were to be inflicted on the offender. The answer to those questions lies partly in the fact that cases which call for denunciation are likely also to call for punishment as well. Moreover, it is submitted that judges have a duty to promote respect for the law, and to seek to maintain public confidence in the way that the law is administered. Just as a law cannot be effective unless it has the assent of a majority of the public, so also a legal system, including its judges and their sentences, must have the confidence of a majority of the public if it is to survive. That does not mean, of course, that judges, in passing sentences, must always pander to public whims or prejudices: nor does it mean that judges must always be looking over their shoulders to make sure that their decisions do not conflict with public opinion. What it does mean, however, is that in appropriate cases judges may, and indeed should, do and say things which reflect and reinforce public concern and condemnation. This may involve, when such a course is otherwise appropriate, the imposition of a severe sentence, but it need not: an expression of condemnation may, in the context that has been described, be equally effective even when a more lenient sentence is being imposed.

Rehabilitation

9–08   As an objective of sentencing, rehabilitation has taken some hard knocks in recent years. While reform may be achieved as a reaction to some sentences which are imposed with another objective in mind, such as punishment, the majority of research evidence indicates that those sentences which are intended to secure rehabilitation by some form of treatment are not very successful in doing so. Thus "treatment" by training in a penal establishment is no longer accorded the confidence which it formerly received; and it is perhaps symptomatic of that decline in confidence that the borstal sentence, which had its origins in aspirations about treatment and training, was abolished in Scotland by the Criminal Justice (Scotland) Act 1980. Since that time prison administrators in Scotland have been reformulating the aims and objectives of the Scottish Prison Service. Those aims now concentrate on providing, within penal establishments, all possible opportunities for prisoners to learn new skills and to mend their ways: but the Prison Service no longer expects that courts will send offenders to prison for the purpose of rehabilitation. Prisons may seek to encourage rehabilitation, but they are content that courts should use imprisonment primarily for other purposes, such as punishment or public protection.[4] Probation undoubtedly has a rehabilitative purpose, but its long-term success in achieving that purpose is not impressive given the recidivism rates among those who have been subject to probation orders. Accordingly, while probation may commend itself in certain cases for other reasons, it is suggested that it ought not to be regarded primarily as a means of achieving lasting rehabilitation. On the whole, therefore, rehabilitation must be regarded as a very uncertain aim of sentencing, and not too much hope should be placed on sentences which are intended to realise that aim. On the other hand, there are those who do respond satisfactorily to, for example, a probation order, and it would clearly be unwise to abandon their use simply because they cannot guarantee a high rate of success, particularly since their success rate is at least no worse than that of any other form of sentence.

Restitution

9–09   In the 1970s and 1980s increasing attention was given to the role of the victim in the criminal justice process, and courts are now encouraged, whenever possible, to pursue the aim of providing some restitution to the victims of crime. Very often, of course, other sentencing aims will have to take precedence, but quite often it may be possible to combine the aim of restitution with, for example, that of punishment. Thus, a court which is minded to impose a financial penalty on an offender (and thereby punish him by an enforced deprivation of financial resources) may direct that some, or all, of that financial penalty should be paid as compensation to the victim of the offence in question. That will still be a punishment so far as the offender is concerned, but it will simultaneously achieve the objective of restitution in relation to the victim.

---

[4] See, for example, Scottish Prison Service, *Opportunity and Responsibility*, 1990.

Economy of resources

9–10   This will always be a subsidiary objective, and in many cases may have to be ignored entirely. However, in cases where there is a reasonable alternative open to a judge, for example between imprisonment and a fine, it is probably reasonable to consider the best use of scarce public resources when deciding which of the two sentences to impose.

Reduction of crime

9–11   Although it has occasionally been suggested that the reduction of crime is an all-embracing, and perhaps even the main, objective of sentencing,[5] it ought to be remembered that in fact sentences are imposed by courts of law in only a very small proportion of all the crimes and offences which are actually committed. This is because of the cumulative effect of initial non-reporting by the public, low police clear-up rates, diversionary procedures, non-prosecution of child offenders, findings of not guilty, and so on.[6] Consequently, it is suggested that sentences imposed by courts are likely to have only a limited impact on general levels of offending, and that much more is likely to be achieved in that regard by improved crime reduction measures within the community.

FACTORS WHICH MAY INFLUENCE SENTENCE

The approach to sentencing

9–12   Apart from a general awareness of the objectives which sentences may be intended to achieve, a judge must also consider many other factors in order to determine, first, the type of sentence which is appropriate for a particular case and, second, the level of severity with which the chosen sentence should be applied. Sometimes, in books such as this, an attempt is made to group those factors under headings such as "aggravating" or "mitigating." This is often less than a wholly satisfactory way of dealing with the subject since many of those factors may assume either of these descriptions depending on the facts of a particular case. What follows, therefore, is an attempt to describe the considerations that may influence a sentencing decision, and to show, where appropriate, how these may tend to be aggravating or mitigating in particular circumstances. It should be added that there is an inevitable amount of overlap between some of the matters which are to be described.

Character of crime or offence

9–13   Some crimes and offences will be more or less grave because of special circumstances peculiar to their commission, or to the victim, or to the offender. These will be dealt with shortly. In general, however, crimes and offences can be classified as more or less grave, or more or less trivial, by reason of their own type or character, and this classification may have some bearing on the appropriate kind and level of sentence. In more extreme cases this relativity is easy to see, and probably not open to any dispute. Thus, no doubt, all would agree that an armed robbery is very

---

[5] See, for example, Walker, *Sentencing in a Rational Society*, p. 38.
[6] See the analysis by Ashworth in "Criminal Justice and Deserved Sentences" [1989] Crim.L.R. 340.

much more grave than petty shoplifting. The distinction, however, may not be so easy when one moves away from such obvious extremes. Thus, is the theft of some foodstuffs from a supermarket more or less grave than a breach of the peace? The easy answer to that question is that much will depend on the value of the foodstuffs on the one hand and, on the other hand, the exact circumstances of the particular breach of the peace. That of course is true, but even once those matters are determined the question may still not be an easy one to answer; and for a judge in, say, a busy sheriff court, who may have to determine sentence in several score such cases in a day, the matter of comparability and proportionality of sentences is one of considerable concern. Of course, many other factors will also have a bearing on the decisions, and an apparent disparity, or lack of proportionality, between sentences for different offences may well be explained by, for example, the fact that one offender had a long record whereas the other had an otherwise impeccable character. Even allowing for such distinctions, however, the fact remains that there will be a need for some sort of assessment of the relative gravity of crimes and offences, if only as a base on which to build or from which to subtract the other relevant factors. How one is to arrive at this assessment is not a matter of law, and the answer will not be found in decided cases.[7] It can, in the end, be no more than a subjective decision based on personal experience and judgment.

Harm done, or harm intended

9–14   Normally, an offence will be regarded as more grave, and therefore more aggravated, the greater the amount of harm done. This approach is sometimes reflected in statute where, for example, section 1 of the Road Traffic Act 1988 (causing death by reckless driving) carries a maximum sentence of five years' imprisonment, whereas section 2 (reckless driving) carries a maximum of only two years' imprisonment.[8] The same approach is also to be found in the common law where, for example, a distinction is drawn between simple assault and an aggravated assault such as one to severe injury, a distinction which will frequently be reflected by the former type of assault being prosecuted summarily whereas the latter is prosecuted on indictment. This approach can, of course, be justified to a large extent on the retributive principle of sentencing—the greater the harm done, the greater the amount of retribution which must be exacted. Against that, however, it may be asked why an offender should be

---

[7] In some jurisdictions, for example the federal jurisdiction in the U.S.A. and in the jurisdiction of several of the American States, there are now detailed statutory provisions listing the relative gravity of different kinds of offence. In other jurisdictions, for example New Zealand, there is more general statutory guidance to the effect that, as a rule, courts should regard offences of violence as being more grave than offences against property; and a similar approach has recently been taken for England and Wales in the Criminal Justice Act 1991. There is no comparable statutory guidance in Scotland.

[8] Under the Road Traffic Act 1991 the word "reckless" in these offences will be replaced by the word "dangerous." It is to be noted, however, that a court is not permitted to take account of the consequences of an offence where those consequences are not themselves part of the offence. Thus, it is improper, when sentencing for a careless driving offence, to take account of the fact that a death was caused as a result of that careless driving: *McCallum* v. *Hamilton*, 1986 S.L.T. 156; 1985 S.C.C.R. 368; *Sharp* v. *H.M. Advocate*, 1987 S.C.C.R. 179.

punished more severely simply because his unlawful act has had serious consequences (which may have been either fortuitous or even unintentional in the strict sense), while another offender who may have intended such harm but in fact failed to achieve it may be punished less severely. Some examples will serve to illustrate this problem.

9-15   Suppose that two offenders each push a glass into the face of a victim. In each case their intention, though perhaps not precisely rationalised, is exactly the same. In one case the victim happily escapes with a few minor scratches whereas in the other case the victim loses the sight of an eye. The retributive approach would no doubt suggest that the offender in the second case should receive a more severe sentence than the other, but is that not to attach undue weight to the, in a sense, fortuitous consequences of the act? Again, suppose that two housebreakers go off about their unlawful business. One breaks into a house at random and is fortunate enough to find, and remove, a large amount of valuable property. The second breaks into a house where he has reason to believe that there is a large amount of valuable property, but in fact he is mistaken and leaves with only a few items of little worth. Should any distinction be made in the approach to sentencing these two men? The retributivist would say yes, but to many people it may seem at least as acceptable to have regard to the actual character of the offence (as distinct from its consequences), and to the intention of the offender. This is in effect to distinguish between one aspect of the gravity of the offence and the culpability of the offender. This is a perfectly proper distinction to make, and indeed, in the ultimate example of causing physical harm, namely homicide, it is a distinction which can be taken into account before the stage of sentencing is reached, by reducing a charge of murder to one of culpable homicide. Thus, in all cases save murder, where the sentence is fixed by law, it is possible and appropriate for a court to consider both the amount of harm done, and the actual culpability of the offender, when determining sentence. What effect either of those considerations will have on the actual sentence will, however, be a matter of judgment depending on all the circumstances of a particular case.

Culpability

9-16   Apart from the foregoing, other considerations affecting culpability may arise so as to have some influence on sentence. The age and sex of an offender, or the age and sex of a victim, may be of some significance in determining an offender's culpability. Thus, a middle-aged female shoplifter may be less culpable than a young, adult male who commits a similar crime (though it must be added that the female menopausal delinquent is perhaps less common than pleas in mitigation might tend to suggest). Again an assault and robbery committed against someone who is elderly and infirm may properly be taken as inferring a greater degree of culpability than if the victim had been young and active. In rather the same way, relationship, or lack of it, between an offender and his victim may be an element bearing on culpability. So, an unprovoked attack on a total stranger may be seen as more blameworthy than an attack committed on an acquaintance or a relative, at least if, in the latter case, there is evidence to show a previous history of mutual antagonism and conflict.

9–17   Culpability is also a matter which may be of importance when a court is dealing with a multiplicity of offenders who have all been convicted of the same charge. Very often the amount of blame attaching to each may vary quite substantially, and this may properly be taken into account in determining the appropriate sentence for each offender. This has come to be known as "comparative justice" or the "comparative principle." Apart from relative culpability differences in offenders' criminal records may also require that joint offenders should be sentenced differently, and this has been stressed by the High Court on a number of occasions.[9] Where financial penalties are involved, the same principle applies if the means of several joint offenders are significantly different.[10] However, the High Court will not disturb a sentence which is itself appropriate simply on the ground that a co-accused received a sentence which was too low,[11] and, if a judge is sentencing one of two co-accused, the other having already been sentenced by another judge to what the second judge regards as too lenient a sentence, that second judge is not thereby obliged to impose what he considers to be an inadequate sentence.[12]

9–18   A final aspect of culpability which falls to be noted concerns any special status which the offender may have, and in respect of which the offence has been committed. Examples of this are thefts of mail by Post Office employees, or frauds and embezzlements committed by professional persons such as accountants or solicitors. In such cases a more severe sentence than would otherwise be appropriate will often be imposed, and the question must be asked why this should be the case. It cannot be with the aim of individual deterrence since in most of these cases the offender will have been ruined by the conviction, and it will be most unlikely that he will ever again be in a position to commit such a crime. Sometimes, when imposing such a sentence, judges will express it as being with the aim of general deterrence. But, set against the, fortunately, good record that there is in this country of integrity on the part of public officials and professional men and women, it is doubtful whether a more severe sentence than would normally be appropriate is necessary in the interests of general deterrence. Instead, it is submitted, the justification for such a sentence is to be found in the greater culpability which attaches to one who abuses a position of special trust, or who departs from the high standards of those in public or professional service.

Prevalence

9–19   The fact that a particular type of crime or offence is especially prevalent, either generally or in a particular area, may be a reason, in the interests of general deterrence, for imposing a more severe, exemplary, sentence than would otherwise be appropriate.[13] Since, however, the

---

[9] *Donnelly* v. *MacKinnon*, 1985 S.C.C.R. 391; *Skilling* v. *McLeod*, 1987 S.C.C.R. 245; *Allan* v. *H.M. Advocate*, 1990 S.C.C.R. 226.

[10] *Scott* v. *Lowe*, 1990 S.C.C.R. 15.

[11] *Lam* v. *H.M. Advocate*, 1988 S.C.C.R. 347; *Smith* v. *H.M. Advocate*, 1990 S.C.C.R. 251.

[12] *Forrest* v. *H.M. Advocate*, 1988 S.C.C.R. 481.

[13] See, for example, *Blair* v. *Hawthorn*, 1945 J.C. 17, *per* Lord Justice-General at 20; *Campbell* v. *Johnston*, 1981 S.C.C.R. 179; *MacCreadie* v. *Walkingshaw*, 1990 S.C.C.R. 761; *Murray* v. *McGlennan*, 1991 S.C.C.R. 18; but, as an example of a case where an exemplary sentence was held not to be appropriate, see *Ruddy* v. *Wilson*, 1988 S.C.C.R. 193.

deterrent effectiveness of such an approach may be open to question (see paragraph 9–06 above), it is suggested that this factor should be approached with some caution. Moreover, a judge must take care that he has proper evidence concerning the prevalence of a particular crime before he takes any note of it in his approach to sentencing. In some cases he may be aware that a particular crime is occurring with undesirable frequency simply because of the number of times that it has to be dealt with in his own court. Or again, he may become aware of the increasing incidence of a particular crime from information contained in properly authenticated statistics. On the other hand, he must beware of forming a view that is based on information, such as newspaper reports and articles, which may be biased and unreliable, or of drawing conclusions, even from official statistics, which may not be justified by the figures in question.

General or local concern

9–20   Closely allied to the foregoing is the existence of general or local concern in relation to some particular type of law-breaking. So far as this is concerned it may be stated that, when considering sentence, the normal limitations on judicial knowledge do not apply, and judges are entitled to be aware of, and to take account of, public opinion and public concern where this is generally known to exist. Once again, however, care should be taken that any concern which is to be taken into account should be widespread and general, whether locally or nationally, and not merely a reflection of the views of a possibly small group of people who may be particularly vocal, or have good access to the media. Thus, for example, in recent times public concern about violence at sporting occasions, in particular at football matches, could properly be taken as general and widespread, it not only having been very widely reported in the press and elsewhere but also having been, on several occasions, the subject of debate in Parliament.[14]

Previous criminal record

9–21   There is no doubt that an offender's previous criminal record is an important factor in sentencing.[15] Having said that, it is necessary to see exactly how the existence of previous convictions, or their absence, may or should affect a sentencing decision. It is often assumed that the existence of previous convictions is an aggravating factor, and that their absence is a mitigating factor; but it is submitted that, put that way, this may be a somewhat misleading view. If, for example, one assumes that the gravity of a particular offence is such as to require a prison sentence within a certain range, one may reasonably say that an offender with a bad record should receive a sentence at the upper end of that range. But if, conversely, one is to say that an offender with no previous convictions thereby has a mitigating factor in his favour and, because of that, should receive a sentence at the lower end of the range, one is by implication

---

[14] See, for example, *Blues* v. *MacPhail*, 1982 S.C.C.R. 247; *McGivern* v. *Jessop*, 1988 S.C.C.R. 511.

[15] Previous record is in future to play a much less significant part in the sentencing of offenders in England and Wales: see Criminal Justice Act 1991, s. 29.

saying that somewhere in the middle of the range is a sort of norm to which one may add, or from which one may subtract, depending on the offender's record. In saying that, however, one is inevitably also saying that the norm for any particular offence is the sentence appropriate to an offender with some, but not too many, previous convictions. That is plainly not an acceptable conclusion, but it arises only if one regards a good or bad record as representing opposite ends of the swing of a pendulum. It is submitted that it is more sensible to regard record as a progressive factor, in the way that it is treated in many statutory provisions whereby a certain maximum sentence is prescribed for a first offence, whereas a higher maximum is permitted for a second or subsequent offence. Thus, when dealing with a first offender, a judge may properly limit his attention to the range of disposals at the lower end of the scale of sentencing severity, and progressively move up that scale when dealing with offenders with a previous criminal record. Looked at this way, previous good character is not so much a mitigating factor but rather an essentially neutral one, whereas previous bad record is certainly an aggravating factor.

9–22 What is the justification for treating the existence of previous convictions as an aggravating factor? An offender must not, in effect, be sentenced twice for past offences but, provided that is kept clearly in mind, there are, it is submitted, two main reasons why previous convictions may properly be regarded as an aggravating factor. In the first place, if one is seeking to achieve the aim of individual deterrence, they may demonstrate that previous attempts have been made to realise that objective, that they have obviously failed, and that a different, though not necessarily a more severe, sentence may now be appropriate. In the second place, if one is seeking to apply the retributivist theory, they may demonstrate simply that the offender is a repeated breaker of the law, and that a more severe punishment is now appropriate. It is important to keep the above distinction clearly in mind because, if one's principal aim is to try to achieve individual deterrence, it would be perfectly reasonable, even where an offender had on previous occasions been fined, or even imprisoned, to consider a disposal such as probation on the occasion of a subsequent offence. On the other hand, if the case were considered to be one that called for retributive measures, then in such circumstances a judge would be obliged to think only in terms of a larger fine or a longer period of imprisonment. A perusal of the reported cases in Scotland suggests that it is the retributive approach to previous convictions which most often finds favour there.

9–23 Formerly it was competent for a prosecutor to libel only those previous convictions which were "cognate" with the current offence, but now all previous offences may be libelled, though it is common for a prosecutor to exercise a measure of discretion in this and to exclude from a schedule of previous convictions those which are either very old or those which are of a trivial character. The disappearance of the cognate rule regarding previous convictions is consistent with modern thinking which recognises the plural nature of deviancy; and it would be unthinkable now that an offender on, say, an assault charge should be presented as being a first offender if in fact he has several previous convictions for theft. On the other hand, a previous conviction for the same, or a similar, offence will generally be regarded as more serious, or more aggravating, than previous convictions for dissimilar offences.

9–24   Apart from their possible aggravating effect, previous convictions may also indicate a particular line of inquiry which ought to be investigated before sentence is decided upon. Thus, repetitive theft from shops, suddenly embarked upon by the middle-aged or elderly, may suggest the desirability of obtaining a social inquiry report. So, too, the existence of a previous conviction which resulted in some sort of psychiatric disposal may indicate that a psychiatric report should be obtained. Apart from suggesting a particular form of inquiry, an offender's previous record may also indicate the likely success or failure of particular forms of disposal. Thus, a court may be slow to consider a probation order as being an appropriate disposal where the offender has previously been placed on probation but was subsequently sentenced for a breach of that order.

Provocation

9–25   It is not within the scope of this work to consider what may or may not amount to provocation. The purpose of this section is merely to consider the effect, if any, which the existence of provocation may have upon the sentence to be passed on the person thus provoked. The first point to be noted concerns the circumstances in which the judge will come to have the issue of provocation properly before him at the stage of passing sentence. Where there has been a summary trial, and the question of provocation has been put in issue in the course of the trial, the presiding judge will have been able to form his own view as to whether or not provocation has been established and, if so, how great was that provocation. In passing sentence thereafter he may, it is submitted, proceed upon his own assessment of the degree of provocation, and give that such weight in his sentence as he thinks proper. Where the trial has been before a jury, however, the position may be somewhat different. In returning a verdict of guilty it is competent for a jury to say something like "guilty under provocation," and they may indeed be invited to return such a verdict by defence counsel or solicitor. In such a case, it is submitted, the judge would be bound to take that into account when determining sentence, to such extent as he thought proper, notwithstanding that he himself may not agree with the rider attached to the verdict. Conversely, if a jury were invited to add such a rider and did not do so, the judge would be precluded from taking provocation into account, even if he himself was of the view that the act had been committed under provocation.

9–26   Apart from the foregoing fairly clear-cut situations, cases may arise where the defence counsel or solicitor will, for perfectly proper tactical reasons, seek an outright acquittal on the basis of, for example, a special defence of self-defence, and will refrain from mentioning to a judge or, particularly, a jury the possibility of a verdict of guilty under provocation. If, in such a case, the jury returns a simple verdict of guilty, and the issue of provocation is thereafter raised in the plea in mitigation, may the judge then take cognisance of it? It is submitted that it would be proper for him to do so, notwithstanding that it was not put in issue during the trial, provided that he is satisfied that the plea is supported by evidence which was led at the trial, and provided that such evidence is of a kind that the jury may be taken not to have rejected in arriving at their verdict.

9–27   Assuming that an issue of provocation is properly before the court at the stage of passing sentence, what effect should it have upon that sentence? That, of course, will depend entirely on the nature and extent of the provocation, and on the nature of the crime or offence of which the offender has been convicted. It may also depend on other factors such as the offender's previous record. If the crime is a very serious one, or if the provocation is slight, it may have no effect on sentence at all. So too, if the offender has previous convictions for the same type of offence, the mitigating effect of provocation may be substantially diminished. Such cases apart, however, the fact that a crime or offence was committed under provocation will generally be seen as a mitigating factor which will permit the court to take a more lenient course than would otherwise have been appropriate. This may result in a shorter sentence of imprisonment, or a smaller fine, or may permit a sentence of a different type altogether, such as a non-custodial rather than a custodial one.

9–28   If effect is given to the existence of provocation in any of the ways described, the judge may, in passing sentence, indicate to the offender that this has been done by stating expressly the sentence which he would otherwise have imposed. There is not, it is thought, any recognised practice in this, and some judges will prefer merely to say, in general terms, that account has been taken of the plea of provocation in arriving at the sentence which is being passed. Whichever course is followed, it is submitted that it is desirable that a judge should by some means indicate whether or not some weight is being attached to the plea since, if he does not do so, difficulties may arise in the event of an appeal.

Effect of drink or drugs

9–29   It is often submitted, in purported mitigation of sentence, that, at the time of commission of the offence, the offender was under the influence of drugs or alcohol. The question in such cases is whether, in determining sentence, any account should be taken of that. There is no simple answer to that question since much will depend on the whole facts and surrounding circumstances of each case. However, some general observations may be ventured.

9–30   At one extreme there are sometimes cases where the evidence and other information available to the judge may satisfy him that the offender is chronically addicted to alcohol or drugs, and that his law-breaking, often of a repetitive though possibly minor character, is closely related to, if not directly caused by, that addiction. Not infrequently in such cases the judge may consider that a prison sentence would be appropriate, not so much because of the nature or gravity of the immediate offence but simply because it is the latest in a long line of similar offences. He may, however, be invited to explore, by obtaining a psychiatric report, the possibility of adopting a course which would require, or at least permit, the offender to obtain some treatment for his addiction. Courts may be unwilling to consider such a disposal, at least in cases where that would in effect involve an offender having to attend for treatment on a non-voluntary basis. This attitude on the part of the courts may be influenced by the view which for some years was thought to prevail in medical circles to the effect that treatment for either alcohol or drug addiction is unlikely to offer any hope of success unless it is undertaken voluntarily by someone who has a commitment to make it succeed. However, there now appears to be some evidence to suggest that this is not necessarily the case and that in some instances enforced attendance for treatment may actually be more successful than voluntary treatment, especially where the person concerned is faced with a disagreeable alternative such as being sent to prison.[16] Accordingly, it is suggested that in appropriate cases a court should not automatically reject the possibility of treatment simply because the offender shows no inclination to seek treatment on a voluntary basis.

9-31   At the other extreme is the sort of case where the offence itself is of a grave or very grave character. Although it is by no means unknown for serious crimes to be committed by those who are alcoholics or drug addicts, it is more likely that any intoxication that may be mentioned as having contributed to the commission of such crimes will be represented as having been of a more isolated and occasional character. In such cases it is probable that, whatever the alcohol or drugs background of the offender, the court will take the view that the sentence must be determined by reference to considerations such as the gravity of the offence, the amount of harm done, or the protection of the public, and will take no account, at least by way of mitigation, of the fact that the commission of the crime may have been influenced by an over-consumption of drink or drugs.

9-32   Between the two extremes that have been mentioned there will be a range of cases of varying gravity where over-indulgence in drugs or, especially, alcohol may be put forward as an explanation, if not an excuse. Different approaches may be possible here, depending on the circumstances. On the one hand, the information available to the court may show that the offender frequently commits offences when drunk: in such a case the court may well consider that the offender's drunkenness is, so far from being a mitigating factor, if anything an aggravating one on the basis that, in the light of previous experience, he should have known better than to drink to excess yet again. On the other hand, there may be cases where a person of previously good character commits an uncharacteristic offence while under the influence of drink. If, in such a case, the court can be satisfied that the offence was brought about in large measure because the alcohol had lessened or removed the offender's normal inhibitions, it may be appropriate to impose a more lenient sentence than might otherwise be called for.

Effect of sentence on offender, his family, or associates

9-33   From time to time a court may be invited not to impose a particular sentence, particularly one of imprisonment, because of the effect that this would have on the offender himself, or on his family, or on his associates. In relation to the offender himself this submission may be put forward, for example, on the ground that his health is such that he could not

---

[16] See Gordon, "Drugs and Criminal Behaviour," and Chick, "Treatment and Control: Alcohol," in Bluglass and Bowden, eds., *Principles and Practice of Forensic Psychiatry*, pp. 897, 929.

withstand the rigours of a prison sentence, or that the crime of which he has been convicted is of such a character (*e.g.* sexual molestation of children) that he is likely to receive rough treatment at the hands of fellow prisoners. In relation to the offender's family the submission may be that the offender is the sole support of an elderly relative, or that his wife is unwell and, if he were to be incarcerated, his children might have to be taken into care. In relation to the offender's associates the submission may be that the offender's continuing freedom is crucial to some business enterprise and, if he were to be sent to prison, that enterprise might fail with consequent unemployment for innocent third parties.

9–34   These are all factors to which the court will give such weight as it thinks proper, having regard to all the other factors which must be taken into account in any particular case. Two points may, however, be made. The first is that, if submissions of the sort exemplified above are made in relation to the likely effect of imprisonment on the offender himself, it is as well to bear in mind, firstly, that all penal establishments have their own medical and, to varying degrees, hospital facilities, and secondly that provision exists under the Prison Rules to isolate any prisoner who may be at risk if in association with others. The second, and more general, point is that submissions of this sort should be scrutinised with care to ensure that they are adequately supported by facts and are not merely the result of an offender's personal, and unverified, instructions to his counsel or solicitor.

Effect of plea of guilty

9–35   In England and Wales there is a virtually universal practice of allowing a discount on the sentence which would otherwise have been imposed in cases where there has been a plea of guilty.[17] However, it has been held that such a practice is objectionable in Scotland in that it involves offering an accused person an inducement to plead guilty rather than to go to trial, and it may disable a judge from exercising his discretion fully and freely in a particular case.[18]

9–36   It is to be noted, however, that what the High Court described as objectionable in the case of *Strawhorn* was a *practice* of giving a discount for a plea of guilty. That does not, it is submitted, mean that a court must never impose a lower sentence on account of a plea of guilty. Whether that will be appropriate, however, will always depend on the circumstances of a particular case and, it is suggested, on the extent to which a plea of guilty is itself a reflection of a mitigating circumstance, such as genuine remorse, or has truly mitigating consequences, such as avoiding the need for young children to give evidence in court.[19]

Background information about the defender

9–37   During the last few decades it has become increasingly clear that the causes of criminal behaviour, in so far as they can be determined at all, are complex, diverse and plural. With that realisation has come a growing

---

[17] See, for example, *R.* v. *Williams* [1983] Crim.L.R. 693.
[18] *Strawhorn* v. *McLeod*, 1987 S.C.C.R. 413.
[19] *Khaliq* v. *H.M. Advocate*, 1984 S.C.C.R. 212; *Sweeney* v. *H.M. Advocate*, 1990 G.W.D. 25–1385.

awareness that, in determining sentences, attention must be paid in many cases to the whole background of the offender—social, economic, educational, medical, psychiatric, etc. The reason for this, it may be said, is twofold. In the first place, information on these matters may enable a judge, even where he is not considering a custodial sentence, to select one form of non-custodial sentence as being more likely than another to curb or inhibit future criminal behaviour by the offender concerned. In the second place, where a custodial sentence is being contemplated, such information may persuade the judge that a non-custodial measure could be used instead. So far as cases falling into the latter category are concerned there has been a growing statutory insistence in recent years that background information *must* be obtained before a custodial sentence can be imposed.

9–38   Information about an offender will be obtained in reports from various professional people, notably social workers, doctors and psychiatrists. Less frequently reports may be obtained from others such as teachers, educational psychologists, ministers of religion, and so on. Many of these reports will contain expressions of opinion and, although a judge is not bound to accept such opinions,[20] he must consider them carefully. Certain medical disposals, however, may not be made unless the doctors or psychiatrists concerned express certain opinions.[21]

9–39   Social inquiry reports are sometimes called for and used simply as repositories of factual information about the offender. However, a good social inquiry report should also contain the considered views of the social worker on a range of matters including the offender's present attitude to his offence, and his likely response to various possible disposals. Social inquiry reports, and their content and purpose, have been considered over the years not only by writers in learned journals but also by many committees, notably the Departmental Committee on the Probation Service (the Morison Committee),[22] the Inter-departmental Committee on the Business of the Criminal Courts (the Streatfield Committee),[23] and the Advisory Council on the Penal System.[24] Most recently in Scotland national objectives and standards for social work services within the criminal justice system were published by the Scottish Office in 1990. Those standards relate, among other things, to social inquiry reports, to probation, and to community service.

FACTORS WHICH SHOULD *NOT* INFLUENCE SENTENCE

9–40   From time to time judges have, when determining sentence, taken account of certain factors which the High Court has subsequently held to be irrelevant, inappropriate, or incompetent. It is not easy to distil the decided cases into a set of principles since many of those cases turn very much on their own facts. What follows, therefore, merely describes briefly the decided cases with, in some instances, some accompanying

---

[20] See *Scott and Anr.* v. *MacDonald*, 1961 S.L.T. 257.
[21] See Chap. 3 above.
[22] Report, 1962, H.M.S.O.
[23] Report, 1961, H.M.S.O.
[24] Report, *Young Adult Offenders*, 1974, H.M.S.O.

comment. It is unlikely that the cases which have been decided to date contain an exhaustive list of the factors which should *not* influence sentence: no doubt others will appear in the future, and in any event some of the present cases are likely to be overtaken by changes to be introduced by the Road Traffic Act 1991 (see Part III below). However, it is thought that the following list gives a fairly clear indication of the sort of considerations which judges should not rely on when determining sentence:

(1) Where a person is convicted under the Road Traffic Acts of failing to report an accident, it is improper, when determining the sentence for that offence, to take account of the fact that the offender had been drinking, he not having been convicted of a drink/driving charge.[25]

(2) When sentencing on a charge of careless driving it is improper to take account of the fact that a death was caused by that driving except to the extent that the consequences of the incident may shed light on the quality of the driving.[26]

(3) It is improper to sentence on the basis that a conviction of failing to provide a specimen for analysis under the Road Traffic Acts should always attract more than a minimum period of disqualification provided for by statute.[27]

(4) When sentencing for a drink/driving offence it is improper to increase the penalty because the offence occurred at New Year during the course of a government campaign against drink/driving.[28]

(5) When sentencing for a drink/driving offence it is improper to take into account the manner in which the accused's vehicle was being driven at the relevant time.[29]

(6) Where an offender is convicted of causing death by reckless driving and of driving with more than the permitted amount of alcohol, it is improper to take account of the consumption of alcohol when sentencing on the charge of causing death by reckless driving.[30]

(7) Where a person is convicted of driving with more than the permitted amount of alcohol, it is wrong to sentence as if he had been convicted of driving while unfit.[31]

(8) When sentencing a person convicted of careless driving, it is

---

[25] *McNamee* v. *Carmichael*, 1985 S.C.C.R. 289.

[26] *McCallum* v. *Hamilton*, 1986 S.L.T. 156; 1985 S.C.C.R. 368; *Sharp* v. *H.M. Advocate*, 1987 S.C.C.R. 179.

[27] *Hynd* v. *Guild*, 1986 S.C.C.R. 406.

[28] *Liddell* v. *McNaughton*, 1987 S.C.C.R. 437.

[29] *Lindsay* v. *Jessop*, 1987 S.C.C.R. 512.

[30] *Anderson* v. *H.M. Advocate*, 1987 S.C.C.R. 529; *Hamilton* v. *H.M. Advocate*, 1991 S.C.C.R. 282; but see *Donnelly* v. *Hamilton*, 1987 S.C.C.R. 313.

[31] *Mercer* v. *Wilson*, 1988 S.C.C.R. 214. However, the case of *McParland* v. *Wilson*, 1988 S.C.C.R. 158 (which held that it is wrong to take an offender's state of intoxication into account when sentencing for failure to provide a specimen for analysis) was expressly disapproved by a bench of five judges in *Hawthorn* v. *Jessop*, 1991 S.C.C.R. 674. It may therefore be that the approach taken by the High Court in *Mercer* is now open to doubt.

wrong to apply a higher standard, and therefore a more severe sentence, where that person is a professional driver.[32]

(9)   When sentencing an offender who has a previous conviction a judge is not entitled to rely on his own recollection of the circumstances surrounding that conviction.[33]

(10) Where a person is convicted of possessing unclassified video cassettes, it is wrong to sentence him on the basis that the cassettes were pirated.[34] This is another example which shows the importance of sentencing only in respect of the actual offence charged, and only on the basis of facts which are relevant to that charge (*cf.* sub-paragraphs (1), (5), (6) and (7) above).

(11) Where an offender's means are limited it is improper to imprison him simply because he is unable to pay a fine of a size which the court would otherwise consider to be appropriate.[35]

(12) Where a person is convicted of a breach of the peace committed in breach of a matrimonial interdict, he should be sentenced for the breach of the peace and not for breach of interdict.[36]

(13) In a prosecution under the Licensing (Scotland) Act 1976 for selling alcohol out of hours it is improper, when deciding on sentence, to take account of the fact that there have been previous *complaints* against the licence holder.[37] Presumably previous *convictions* would be different.

(14) It is wrong for a victim to be asked for views as to the sentence which ought to be imposed. The responsibility for sentence rests on the judge alone.[38]

(15) Where a common law crime is paralleled by an analogous statutory offence, and the maximum penalty for the statutory offence is increased, it is improper, when sentencing for the common law crime, to take that increase into account where it only came into effect *after* the date of commission of the common law crime.[39]

(16) On a charge of escaping from custody it is wrong to calculate a sentence of imprisonment by reference to the loss of remission which the court considers that the offender ought to suffer.[40]

(17) In a case involving possession of drugs it is improper for the court to invite the accused to identify his suppliers, and then to impose a more severe sentence when the accused declines to do so.[41]

(18) Where goods to a certain value are stolen (and recovered), it is inappropriate to fix the level of a fine by reference to that value.[42] It is submitted, however, that if (a) goods or money representing an ascertainable profit to the offender have been stolen and have

---

[32] *Ross* v. *Houston*, 1991 S.C.C.R. 102.
[33] *Brown* v. *Guild*, 1988 S.C.C.R. 6.
[34] *Higgins* v. *Carmichael*, 1988 S.C.C.R. 17.
[35] *Milligan* v. *Jessop*, 1988 S.C.C.R. 137.
[36] *Friend* v. *Normand*, 1988 S.C.C.R. 232.
[37] *Canavan* v. *Carmichael*, 1989 S.C.C.R. 480.
[38] *H.M. Advocate* v. *McKenzie*, 1990 S.L.T. 28; 1989 S.C.C.R. 587.
[39] *Reid* v. *H.M. Advocate*, 1990 S.C.C.R. 83.
[40] *Salmon* v. *H.M. Advocate*, 1991 S.C.C.R. 628.
[41] *Isdale* v. *Scott*, 1991 S.C.C.R. 491.
[42] *Donnelly* v. *Wilson*, 1991 S.C.C.R. 545.

not been recovered, and (b) the means of the offender are such as to permit it, a court would be entitled to impose a fine of an amount which would at least cancel the profit made by the offender.

CHAPTER 10

THE USE OF PARTICULAR SENTENCES

Introduction

10–01 Apart from general sentencing objectives, and the various factors which have been mentioned in Chapter 9, a court must also, when determining sentence, take into account the special characteristics, and advantages and disadvantages, of the different types of sentence themselves. Sometimes a consideration of different types of sentence will raise issues of a somewhat difficult moral nature. For example, if a judge considers it appropriate in a particular case to seek to achieve the objectives of punishment and/or denunciation, he may consider that this can be done either by the imposition of a moderate term of imprisonment or by the imposition of a large fine. But a large fine is appropriate only where the offender has the means to pay it and, if he does not have such means, the term of imprisonment may appear to be the only course open to the court unless it changes its sentencing objectives. That would mean, however, that for identical offences a rich man might escape imprisonment whereas a poor man would not. In fact the High Court has held that in such a case the proper course is to impose a fine commensurate with the offender's means on the basis that a modest fine is as much of a punishment for a poor man as a larger fine would be for one who is richer: it is not appropriate to imprison simply because an offender does not have the means to pay a fine of an amount which the court considers to be necessary in order properly to mark the gravity of the offence.[1]

10–02   Although this chapter is primarily concerned with the practical characteristics of certain sentences, some of the moral dilemmas, such as the one noted above, which occasionally face judges when passing sentence will not be overlooked. Not all types of sentence will be mentioned in what follows, but only those which most frequently present specific problems.

DEFERRED SENTENCE

Reasons for deferring sentence
10–03   Although, of course, not strictly a sentence, the use of the power to defer sentence until a later date merits some consideration. In so far as a generalisation can be made, it may be said that this power is normally used for one of three reasons. The first is where the court wishes to allow some time to elapse so that a specific fact relevant to sentence may be established. This might happen, for example, where an offender stated to the court that he expected shortly to ascertain some fact having a bearing on his future, such as the obtaining of a particular job, acceptance into a course of further education, or acceptance into the armed services. It might also arise where, for example, an offender with a history of alcoholism or drug addiction could satisfy the court that he had commenced, or was about to commence, a course of treatment for that addiction, and the court was anxious to discover the outcome of that treatment. Again, it may frequently arise where the court wishes to ascertain the outcome of, for example, a trial which the offender is shortly to undergo in respect of some other charge or charges. Since factors such as these might well influence the choice of sentence in a particular case, a court will often defer sentence until they have been ascertained. The second common reason for deferring sentence is to allow an offender the opportunity of showing that he can for a period, which may be quite prolonged, keep out of further trouble. The third common reason is to give an offender the opportunity to do something specific such as making restitution. The first of the foregoing reasons probably requires no further elaboration, but the other two merit greater consideration.

---

[1] *Milligan* v. *Jessop*, 1988 S.C.C.R. 137.

Deferred sentence for good behaviour

10-04   When sentence is deferred to allow an offender the opportunity of showing that he can keep out of further trouble the underlying, and often explicit, understanding will normally be that he will be dealt with less severely than would otherwise be appropriate if he does what is expected of him. Several questions often arise in this context. In what circumstances may such a course be considered appropriate? For how long should sentence be deferred? To what extent, if at all, should a judge indicate the probable outcome of the case in the event of the offender keeping, or not keeping, out of trouble for the period involved? How should a case be disposed of at the end of the period of deferment? Although the precise answers to these questions will depend on the circumstances of each case, some general answers may be ventured.

When may deferred sentence for good behaviour be appropriate?

10-05   The gravity of the particular offence and the past criminal record of the offender will usually have some bearing on the appropriateness of this form of disposal and, in general, the more grave the offence and the worse the previous record, the less likely it is that this course will commend itself to the court. However, where a court is faced with an offence, even quite a grave one, which seems totally out of character for an otherwise blameless offender, a deferred sentence may be appropriate as a means of establishing that the offence is truly an isolated lapse and not merely the first step in a criminal career.[2] Similarly, where an offender has a long criminal record but pleads convincingly and with vigour that he now at last intends to "go straight," the court may be disposed to give him a chance to prove his good intentions. Another related situation where a deferred sentence may be considered appropriate is where, subsequent to the offence but prior to conviction, an offender has been made the subject of a probation order in respect of a different offence. In such a case the court may wish to see the offender's response to the probation order before determining sentence, and may defer sentence for a period for that purpose. In such a case a court will often ask for a social inquiry report to be available at the end of the deferred period.

10-06   Two other circumstances fall to be noted where a deferred sentence for good behaviour may be thought to be appropriate. One is where such a disposal may benefit third parties by reason of its deterrent effect. An example of this would be the case of a man convicted of assaulting his wife: the threat of dire consequences might be effective to prevent a repetition during the period of deferment. The second circumstance is where a court wishes to make a probation or community service order but is advised that, because of over-stretched resources, the social work department in question is unable to accommodate such an order for the time being. This used to be a frequent problem in some courts but, with the introduction of 100 per cent. central funding of such services between 1989 and 1991 and the simultaneous introduction of national standards governing their provision, it should be less of a problem in the future. Nonetheless, it is a problem which may still arise from time to time, and it

---

[2] Sentence has been deferred for good behaviour even in a case of attempted murder: *McPherson* v. *H.M. Advocate*, 1986 S.C.C.R. 278.

is submitted that, when it does, deferment of sentence for good behaviour over a period of a few months, possibly with a view to making a probation order at the end of that period,[3] may be a reasonable disposal.

10–07 Many other circumstances may suggest the desirability of deferring sentence for good behaviour, but the examples that have been given provide some indication of the character which such circumstances are likely to possess. It should be added, however, that sentence should not be deferred for good behaviour simply because a judge cannot think of anything better to do. From time to time social inquiry reports recommend deferment of sentence in circumstances which seem to suggest that the writer of the report is simply unwilling to face the challenge of trying to put together a constructive non-custodial disposal. Judges should, it is submitted, guard against the risk of being swayed by such siren songs.

The length of the deferred period

10–08 The length of the period during which sentence is to be deferred will depend on many factors, not least the precise purposes for which sentence is being deferred in a given case. In good behaviour cases, however, it may be said that there can be disadvantages in deferring sentence for a very long period. Firstly, there is the practical disadvantage that the offender may forget the date of the diet for sentence, and so fail to turn up; and secondly, and more importantly, once an offence becomes very old and stale it will often seem to a court to be unreasonable to impose a severe sentence, even where an offender has committed a further offence in the interim. If, for any reason, a lengthy deferment for good behaviour is thought to be desirable, it may be preferable to break it up into shorter periods by deferring sentence on more than one occasion. To some extent, however, the force of these comments is reduced by the power to accelerate a deferred diet where an offender has been convicted of a subsequent offence.[4]

What should be said when sentence is deferred?

10–09 When a court defers sentence for an offender to be of good behaviour an indication will normally be given that he will be dealt with less severely if he complies with the condition of the deferment. On occasions some judges have been known to make this indication quite specific by saying, for example, that, if the offender is not convicted during the period of deferment, he will be fined such-and-such an amount but, if he is so convicted, he will go to prison for such-and-such a period. This is not a desirable practice for two reasons. Firstly, it may give the impression that the court is striking some sort of bargain with the offender which would be improper. Secondly, and perhaps more importantly, such a practice makes no allowance either for the type or frequency of conviction that may occur during the period of deferment, or for any changes in the offender's personal circumstances that may have taken place during the

---

[3] Under summary procedure it is competent to make a probation order after a period of deferred sentence notwithstanding that in such a case the offender has been convicted: 1975 Act, ss. 384(1), 432(1).

[4] *Ibid.* ss. 219, 432.

same period, all of which might have a considerable bearing on the type and severity of sentence that might ultimately prove to be appropriate. If a judge states in terms what a sentence will be in the event of an offender being, or not being, of good behaviour during a period of deferment, he is effectively tying his own hands when he ultimately comes to pass sentence; and that is both undesirable and improper.[5] It is certainly proper, and may be useful, for a judge to give a general indication of the type of sentence that he may wish to consider in the event of the offender acquiring subsequent convictions, especially convictions of a certain character, and to say that a more lenient view will be taken if such convictions do not occur: but, it is submitted, it is preferable that a judge should not go further than that.

Action at end of period of deferred sentence
10–10 The action to be taken by a court at the end of a period when sentence has been deferred for good behaviour will of course depend on the nature of the offender's behaviour during that period and on the whole surrounding circumstances at the time when sentence falls to be pronounced. Thus, every case will have to be disposed of according to its own particular facts and circumstances. However, some general observations can be made—

(1) To justify a more severe sentence, such as a custodial one, at the end of the deferred period it may not be necessary that the offender should have committed further offences during that period: a continuing irresponsibility of attitude in respect of the original offence may suffice.[6]

(2) If an indication is given by the court, at the time of deferring sentence, that a custodial sentence will not ultimately be imposed if the offender is of good behaviour, and he is in fact of good behaviour, then a custodial sentence should not be imposed notwithstanding that the offence in question is a very serious one such as attempted murder.[7]

(3) If a special condition such as repayment of stolen money, has been attached to a deferred sentence, and that condition has been obtempered, a custodial sentence is likely to be inappropriate.[8]

(4) Where an offender has been of good behaviour throughout a period of deferred sentence, a fine is not necessarily an inappropriate penalty at the end of that period if the case is such that the offender could otherwise have expected a custodial sentence.[9]

(5) On the other hand, the fact that an offender has been of good behaviour and has had the disposal of a case hanging over him for a prolonged period may justify a very lenient sentence such as an admonition.[10]

---

[5] *Cassidy* v. *Wilson*, 1989 S.C.C.R. 6.
[6] *Colquhoun* v. *H.M. Advocate*, 1985 S.C.C.R. 396.
[7] *McPherson* v. *H.M. Advocate*, 1986 S.C.C.R. 278.
[8] *Islam* v. *H.M. Advocate*, 1989 S.C.C.R. 109.
[9] *Meighan* v. *Jessop*, 1989 S.C.C.R. 208; *Linton* v. *Ingram*, 1989 S.C.C.R. 487.
[10] *Maxwell* v. *MacPhail*, 1990 S.C.C.R. 738.

(6) There is no rule against a court proceeding to pass sentence at the end of a period of deferment even if the case is still subject to an appeal against conviction, and it is probably preferable that the court should do so.[11]

Deferment of sentence for a specific purpose

10–11   Many of the comments that have just been made in relation to good behaviour cases apply equally to cases where sentence is deferred for a specific purpose, such as restitution or repayment, but these latter cases display certain special features which require some separate comment.

10–12   Very often, in cases of embezzlement, fraud and theft, a court will be asked to defer sentence to allow the offender to repay the amount wrongfully obtained. The purpose of such a suggestion, of course, is to seek to mitigate the offence to some extent and thereby to secure a more lenient sentence: and there is no doubt that repayment or restitution will often have that effect. However, it is suggested that in such cases a court may wish to distinguish between two situations. One is where the primary purpose of the repayment, in the eyes of the court, is to secure restitution for the victim of the crime, and the other is where the primary purpose, in the eyes of the offender, is to demonstrate, or at least to appear to be demonstrating, remorse for what he has done. Sometimes both of these features may be present in the same case and, so far as mitigation is concerned, each may secure the same result. However, the weight to be attached to each may have some bearing on whether or not the court considers it appropriate to defer sentence in the first place. Thus, if the court's primary desire is to secure the payment of compensation to a victim, it may, in appropriate cases,[12] decide that the best course is simply to make a compensation order, with or without any other penalty; and indeed it is suggested that in such cases a compensation order will generally be preferable to deferring sentence for repayment since all the enforcement procedures applicable to a fine will then be available to the court in the event of non-payment.

10–13   One factor which may influence a court's decision whether or not to defer sentence will be whether or not, prior to that stage, the offender has taken any steps to commence repayment. If the case is one which has gone to trial it will not, of course, be surprising—nor should it subsequently prejudice the accused—if no such steps have been taken. In cases where a plea of guilty is tendered, however, the position may be rather different. In many such cases it is clear that there has never been any intention to do other than plead guilty, and indeed this may even be founded on as a mitigating factor in its own right. Yet, it will often transpire in such cases that the day of sentence is the first occasion when the offender has shown any desire to make repayment. In such circumstances, it is submitted, few judges will have much confidence in the genuineness of the expressed desire, and will see it merely as an attempt to postpone the day of reckoning.

10–14   Closely allied to the foregoing are the means of the offender. While it may be one thing for an offender who is in regular and well paid

---

[11] *McRobbie* v. *H.M. Advocate*, 1990 S.C.C.R. 767.
[12] See para. 10–50 *et seq.* below.

employment to offer to repay even a large sum of money, it is quite another thing for a person who has, say, fraudulently obtained social security benefits of £1,000, to offer to repay that amount within a relatively short period while he is still in receipt of no income other than state benefits. Quite apart from the fact that many judges may feel it is no part of their function to act as debt collectors for government departments or large corporations, there would seem to be little advantage in deferring sentence in such a case since the prospects of payment (and the experience of many judges would tend to confirm this) are very remote.

10–15   This sort of case, however, can pose the kind of moral problem that was mentioned earlier. Is it consistent with justice that the rich or even reasonably rich man should be allowed to mitigate his guilt, and therefore presumably receive a lesser sentence, whereas the poor man may, simply because of his poverty, be denied that opportunity and receive a more severe and unmitigated sentence? It is possible to answer that question by saying that any restitution which is made by the rich man ought properly to be seen as part of the total penalty which he is required to pay, with the result that there may not be any great disparity between the two cases at the end of the day; but the poor man may well retort that it is not much of a penalty to require restitution from a person who, by definition, can well afford it anyway. Moreover, the practical consequence in such cases may well be that the person who makes restitution will receive a non-custodial sentence whereas the person who cannot do so will be sent to prison. A better answer to the question is that in truth it is more hypothetical than real. In practice very few cases are so identical in all their circumstances (with the exception only of the wealth of the offender) as to pose the kind of dilemma that has been suggested, and often it is possible for a judge to dispose of cases in different ways upon criteria which have nothing to do with the offender's means. Having said that, however, judges must be mindful to keep a fair and just balance between cases which are similar, even if not identical, and to take care that richer offenders are not permitted, by the use of the deferred sentence, to buy themselves out of the normal consequences of their misdeeds.

Sentence to be imposed by judge who deferred sentence initially

10–16   On several occasions recently the High Court has expressed the view that, where sentence has been deferred, the ultimate disposal of that case should be undertaken by the same judge as deferred sentence in the first place.[13] The reasons for this are obvious. The judge who deferred sentence initially will know why he did so, and will know what indication, if any, he gave as to possible sentence at the end of the deferred period. Moreover, if sentence was deferred following upon conviction at the end of a trial, the judge who presided at the trial will know the whole background to the case better than would be possible for anyone else.

10–17   In many instances the course desiderated by the High Court should be capable of achievement without difficulty. In small sheriff courts, for example, where the resident sheriff regularly undertakes criminal

---

[13] *Islam* v. *H.M. Advocate*, 1989 S.C.C.R. 109; *Main* v. *Jessop*, 1989 S.C.C.R. 437; *Beattie* v. *McGlennan*, 1990 S.C.C.R. 497.

business on certain days of the week, there should be little difficulty about assigning as the end of a period of deferment a date when that sheriff is unlikely to be on leave and will be sitting for the disposal of criminal business; and in that event problems are likely to arise only where there is an unforeseen absence caused, for example, by illness. In larger courts, however, it may not be so easy to ensure that a sheriff who deferred sentence will be available to hear the case at the end of the deferred period. The sheriff in question may be assigned to civil business on that day, and it will at best be inconvenient for him to sit in a criminal court in order to dispose of one deferred sentence case. More seriously, sentence may have been deferred by a temporary or floating sheriff who may find himself at the opposite end of the country on the date when sentence falls to be imposed.

10–18   The High Court has all along recognised that there may be occasions when it is simply impossible or at least impracticable for sentence to be passed by the judge who originally deferred sentence. Nevertheless, it is clear that every effort should be made to follow the approved practice. To that end it is submitted that, where difficulties present themselves, thought should be given to the possibility of calling a deferred sentence case before one judge simply in order that he can further defer sentence for a short period to a date when it is known that the original judge will be available.

10–19   There will, however, remain a few instances where sentence will have to be imposed by a judge other than the one who deferred sentence initially. Clearly in such a case the sentencing judge will be better able to deal with the case if he can be given some idea of why sentence was deferred in the first place and of whether the judge who took that course gave any indication to the offender of the possible, or likely, outcome at the end of the deferred period. To meet that need it is suggested that it is good practice for a judge who defers sentence to write a brief note covering those points, to be kept with the papers for future reference. Indeed, this practice can be advantageous even where sentence is ultimately dealt with by the judge who deferred sentence initially: after a prolonged period even he may find it helpful to be reminded of what was in his mind when sentence was originally deferred.

Circumstances in which deferred sentence not appropriate

In recent times the High Court has noted two circumstances where it is not appropriate to use the power to defer sentence. The first is where, following upon conviction or a plea of guilty, a court wishes to continue a case in order to obtain reports. In such a case the proper course is to adjourn the case in terms of the power conferred by sections 179 or 380 of the 1975 Act; and the fact that those sections allow a maximum adjournment of only three weeks at a time does not permit a court to defer sentence instead simply in order to achieve an adjournment for a longer period.[14]

10–21   The second circumstance in which it has recently been held to be inappropriate to defer sentence is where that is done merely as a device to

---

[14] *H.M. Advocate* v. *Clegg*, 1990 S.C.C.R. 293; *McRobbie* v. *H.M. Advocate*, 1990 S.C.C.R. 767.

allow a sentence of imprisonment to be imposed at a later date in the belief that a consecutive sentence of imprisonment could not competently be imposed on the date when sentence originally fell to be passed.[15]

PROBATION ORDERS

Reasons for choosing probation as disposal

10–22   The probation order is probably the disposal by which a judge most clearly expresses the aim of individual crime reduction, as distinct from aims like punishment, retribution, or general deterrence. In saying this, however, it must be stated that for some years there was considerable disagreement among social scientists, social workers, probation officers and others about how a probation order should be operated, about what its objectives should be, and about what a court's expectations might reasonably be when such an order is made. Moreover, for many years probation orders represented a form of disposal where the court had the least information about, and little or no control over, what would happen to the offender after the disposal had been pronounced. Although a court is required by statute to explain the effect of a probation order to an offender before such an order is made, the statute itself defines a probation order as no more than "an order requiring the offender to be under supervision."[16] What the court sometimes does not know, and therefore cannot explain to the offender, is what form that supervision will take, how intensive it will be, and what view the supervising officer will take of his role in relation to the offender and the probation order.

10–23   In 1991, however, national standards for probation were introduced in Scotland, and it is possible that they may remove some of the problems and uncertainties which previously existed. Under those standards, for example, a social worker is required to make clear in a social inquiry report what form of supervision is envisaged if a probation order is being recommended. If a particularly intensive form of probation is contemplated, this should also be clearly explained in the report. Furthermore, it will be possible under the national standards for a court to ask for a progress report during the course of a probation order, and to receive a final report when an order comes to an end. If the promise of the national standards is fulfilled courts should be in a better position than was formerly the case not only to make an informed choice of probation as a disposal but also to explain to an offender what such an order is likely to entail.

The length of the order

10–24   The length of a probation order may be anything from six months to three years, and questions may arise as to how long an order should be in any particular case. As with any other form of disposal much will depend on the circumstances in each case, but consideration will have to be given to the extent and duration of any social work intervention that may be indicated as desirable in the social inquiry report, and to the length of time during which the court considers it appropriate to keep the offender

---

[15] *Young* v. *McGlennan*, 1990 S.C.C.R. 373.
[16] 1975 Act, ss. 183, 384.

subject to a measure of supervision and individual deterrence. A well prepared social inquiry report is likely to offer a suggestion as to the appropriate length for any probation order that is being recommended but, whether that is the case or not, the ultimate decision as to the length of an order is for the court alone. In general it may be said that it is probably better to make a probation order too long rather than too short because in the former case it is always open to the supervising officer to apply to the court for an early discharge of the order if it appears to be no longer necessary to keep it in existence.

FINES

When appropriate

10–25 The fine is the most commonly used form of sentence, particularly for cases prosecuted summarily, and is probably used for a much wider range of offences than any other form of disposal. At present it is used for about 80 per cent. of all the cases coming before the courts. Thus, at one extreme, a fine may be imposed for a minor regulatory offence related to the use of a motor vehicle and, at the other extreme, it may be imposed for a quite serious offence of violence or dishonesty. In terms of general sentencing aims and objectives the fine clearly satisfies the aim of punishment, and may also satisfy the aim of individual deterrence in that an offender who has on one occasion suffered a deprivation of financial resources through the imposition of a fine may think twice about exposing himself to a similar penalty on a future occasion. It seems unlikely that fines are of much effect in terms of general deterrence except perhaps in the relatively few instances where high, exemplary fines are well publicised by the media. Even then there is little evidence to show that such fines have much general deterrent effect in relation to common law offences such as crimes of violence, though they may be more effective in relation to certain regulatory offences such as speeding and other road traffic offences. It is arguable, however, that in the latter category of cases a fear of disqualification from driving may be more effective as a deterrent than the fear of incurring even a large fine.

The amount of the fine

10–26 Since a fine is a disposal which punishes by means of deprivation of financial resources it is necessary, in the interests both of absolute and of comparative justice, to ensure that richer and poorer offenders, who have committed broadly similar offences, are dealt with in a way which renders them liable to roughly the same *quality* of punishment; and that is why courts are required, when determining the amount of a fine, to "take into consideration, amongst other things, the means of the offender so far as is known to the court."[17] Thus, for example, if two offenders, are to be fined in respect of broadly similar offences, and one has a free income of £400 per week and no dependents to support while the other has a free income of only £100 per week and supports a wife and children, equity (and the

---

[17] 1975 Act. s. 395(1). It has been held that this requirement extends to corporate offenders as well as individuals: *Andrew Redpath & Son* v. *MacNeill*, 1990 G.W.D. 25–1423.

statutory provision referred to above) would indicate that the former should receive a higher fine than the latter.

10–27   To say that, however, is to beg three important questions. First, is it fair or correct to assume that, for a given offence involving a given degree of culpability, there is, as it were, a normative fine of a certain amount appropriate for an offender of average means, with the result that a court is free to fix a fine above or below that norm depending on the means of the actual offender? Or, alternatively, is it more correct to proceed on the basis that, for a given offence involving a given degree of culpability, there is an appropriate level of fine which can be reduced for those of limited means but which cannot be increased simply because a particular offender is richer than average? Second, to what extent should consideration be given to the means of an offender when dealing with offences, particularly of a regulatory character, where a tariff approach to sentence has traditionally been adopted? And third, to what extent can or should a deficiency in an offender's means be taken note of simply by allowing a longer period for payment of a fine rather than by reducing its amount? Each of these questions will be examined in turn.

A normative level of fine?

10–28   So far as the first of the above questions is concerned, it is not one which the High Court in Scotland has yet had to answer, though the Court of Appeal in England has expressed the view that it is improper to impose a fine which is higher than would otherwise be appropriate simply because the offender is more affluent than the average.[18] It is true that the High Court has approved of a decision in which, in a case where several offenders on the same complaint were equally blameworthy, a sheriff imposed fines representing in each case five weeks' income.[19] In that case, however, the sheriff was not striking a norm and fining other offenders above and below it: he was merely seeking to ensure that equally blameworthy offenders would all suffer an equivalent, though not identical, deprivation of resources.

10–29   To an extent the sheriff in *Scott* v. *Lowe* was applying, within existing law and practice, the approach which is inherent in day or unitary fine systems such as have been in use for many years in countries such as Germany and Sweden, and which will shortly be introduced throughout England and Wales under provisions contained in the Criminal Justice Act 1991. In essence such systems are ones in which fines are expressed not as total sums of money but as a multiple of, on the one hand, a unit representing the amount which a given offender can reasonably contribute to a fine on a daily or weekly basis and, on the other hand, a number which reflects the gravity of the particular offence and the offender's degree of culpability. An attempt was made to introduce a similar system in Scotland in the Bill which eventually became the Law Reform (Miscellaneous Provisions) (Scotland) Act 1990, but the provisions in question were dropped during the Bill's passage through

---

[18] *R.* v. *Fairbairn* (1980) 2 Cr.App.R. (S.) 315. It is to be noted that the High Court appears to have given some support to the view that an affluent offender may be able to escape an otherwise deserved sentence of imprisonment by paying a substantial fine: *McLean* v. *MacDougall*, 1989 S.C.C.R. 625.

[19] *Scott* v. *Lowe*, 1990 S.C.C.R. 15.

Parliament, and it is not known when, or if, such provisions may be reintroduced.

10–30   Although at first sight a unitary fine system appears to favour the view that fines may rise or fall in relation to the amount appropriate for an offender of average means, that is not in fact the case. Most such systems, including the one tentatively proposed for introduction in Scotland, set a ceiling on the amount of a unit with the result that even a very rich offender cannot have the amount of his unitary liability assessed at more than that maximum level. The reason for doing this, coupled with a fixed maximum for the *number* of units that can be imposed for a given offence, is to ensure that in no case will a fine exceed the maximum permissible for that offence. Bearing in mind that, regardless of an offender's means, the maximum fine for a given offence should be imposed only for the worst possible example of that offence,[20] this seems to lead to the conclusion that the starting point ought not to be some sort of normative fine which is appropriate for an offender of average means. Rather, the starting point ought to be the maximum fine for the offence in question on the assumption that it reflects both the most grave example of that offence and an offender who is reasonably able to pay a fine of that amount. From that starting point it follows that in any other case a fine should be fixed in the first instance having regard to the relative gravity of the offence in question and the culpability of the particular offender. That fine can then be modified downwards to reflect the means of that offender, but should not be increased since, *ex hypothesi*, it already reflects that level of fine which is appropriate for an offender of above average means. This sort of approach has been expressly approved by the Court of Appeal in England,[21] and it is submitted that it is an approach which it is proper to adopt in Scotland.

Tariff and non-tariff fines

10–31   For a range of regulatory offences, such as certain road traffic offences, it has been traditional in Scotland for some courts to adopt a tariff structure for fining. Thus, for example, speeding offences may attract a fine calculated at so much for each mile per hour that the offender was above the particular speed limit in question. This approach to fining does not ostensibly take into consideration the means of individual offenders, but for so long as the resultant fines are relatively small this probably does not matter too much; and in any event growing provision for fixed penalties appears to give some legislative support for the view that, at the lower end of the scale, all offenders can be treated in the same way regardless of their individual means. Furthermore, a tariff structure such as the one sometimes adopted for speeding cases can produce a fair distinction between different degrees of culpability.[22] However, it must be stressed that the statutory provision requiring consideration to be given to the means of the offender is of general application, and it is accordingly suggested that it must be borne in mind in all cases, and particularly when a tariff approach is likely to produce a fine which is

---

[20] See para. 10–38 below.
[21] *R.* v. *Cleminson* (1985) 7 Cr.App.R. (S.) 128.
[22] But see comments on such an approach in para. 11–62 *et seq.* below.

more than merely nominal. In many instances, of course, a court will have no knowledge about an offender's means since there is no obligation on an offender to provide such information. This is particularly likely to be so in the case of many minor and regulatory offences where an offender may simply tender a plea of guilty in writing. Since a court is obliged to take an offender's means into consideration only so far as these are known to the court, it is submitted that a court is entitled to ignore an offender's means when no information is supplied about them by him or on his behalf.

Time to pay as a method of recognising an offender's means

10–32   Since a court is empowered to allow an offender time within which to pay a fine, or more particularly to allow him to pay it by instalments, it is clear that this has some bearing on the court's duty to give consideration to an offender's means when fixing the amount of a fine. At its simplest this means that, if two offenders are convicted of the same offence and one has free income of £200 per week while the other has free income of only £100 per week, a court could in theory fulfil its statutory obligation by fining both offenders the same amount but allowing the second offender to pay the fine at half the weekly rate (or in twice the time) allowed to the first offender. In fact this approach on its own can never produce an absolutely exact or just formula,[23] and it is submitted that the proper approach is for a court to regard the amount of a fine and the time allowed to pay it as a package both parts of which can be adjusted so as to produce a result which, without attaining mathematical precision, is fair and just both for the offender in question and in relation to other offenders whose means are different. Several recently reported cases appear to suggest that the approach of the High Court has been to regard the total amount of a fine and the arrangements for payment as elements which must be looked at together when deciding whether or not a particular fine is excessive.[24]

10–33   The length of time over which a fine is to be paid by instalments should not be unreasonably long. However, there is no general rule to the effect that a fine should be of an amount which can be paid within one year[25]; and there are several examples where the High Court has approved, or imposed, fines which would require considerably longer than one year for payment.[26] It is to be noted that there used to be a rule in England that fines should be of an amount which could be paid within one year.[27] However, that rule has now been departed from.[28]

---

[23] See Black, "Fine Tuning," 1986 S.L.T. (News) 185.
[24] *White* v. *Hamilton*, 1987 S.C.C.R. 12; *Brown* v. *Carmichael*, 1987 S.C.C.R. 183; *Hamilton* v. *Scott*, 1987 S.C.C.R. 188; *Thomson* v. *Allan*, 1987 S.C.C.R. 201; *Buchan* v. *McNaughton*, 1990 S.C.C.R. 13; *Scott* v. *McGlennan*, 1990 S.C.C.R. 537.
[25] *Johnston* v. *Lockhart*, 1987 S.C.C.R. 537.
[26] *Lambert* v. *Tudhope*, 1982 S.C.C.R. 144; *White* v. *Hamilton*, above; *Buchan* v. *McNaughton*, above; but see *Storie* v. *Scott*, 1990 S.C.C.R. 284 (a case relating to a compensation order where four years for payment was held to be excessive); *Paterson* v. *McGlennan*, 1991 S.C.C.R. 616 (90 weeks for payment of a fine was held to be excessive).
[27] *R.* v. *Knight* (1980) 2 Cr.App.R. (S.) 82.
[28] *R.* v. *Oliver* (1989) 153 J.P. 369.

Improper considerations

10–34   In determining the amount of a fine it is improper to take certain considerations into account. A court is not entitled to have regard to the possibility that a fine may subsequently be remitted in whole or in part under the powers contained in section 395A of the 1975 Act, and for that reason to fix a fine of an amount which is not otherwise justified.[29] It is also inappropriate and unrealistic to select a large fine on the assumption that the offender will be able to pay it by borrowing on the reversionary interest in his house.[30]

Amount of fine when fixed penalty previously offered

10–35   For some years it has been possible for a wide range of offences to be dealt with under fixed penalty procedure, and from time to time questions may arise as to the level of fine which is appropriate where an offender has been offered, but has declined to pay, a fixed penalty and is subsequently convicted in court either of the offence itself or, in some instances, of a related offence such as failing to pay the fixed penalty. It seems reasonable that in such cases any fine should be larger than the fixed penalty if only to punish the offender's intransigence in failing to pay the fixed penalty. However, the question then is: by how much is it reasonable to enlarge the penalty which would otherwise have been payable?

10–36   Given that Parliament has seen fit to provide for fairly modest sums as fixed penalties it would seem to be reasonable to expect that any fine for the offence in question, or for failing to pay the fixed penalty, would not be very much greater than the amount of the penalty itself (unless, of course, the proceedings in court disclosed particularly aggravating features which were not apparent at the time when the fixed penalty was offered). Unfortunately, in the very few reported cases where this issue has been before the High Court very different approaches have been adopted, and no clear statement of policy has been enunciated. In *McInnes* v. *Allan*[31] the accused pled guilty to having failed to furnish a statement of ownership in respect of an unpaid fixed penalty of £10 for a parking infringement. He was fined £100 but on appeal the fine was reduced to £25. Although that decision appears to suggest that the court favoured a fine representing two and a half times the fixed penalty, in fact the figure was not arrived at on that basis, and the court's decision was largely influenced by the fact that the justice had drawn improper inferences from the offender's profession (a lawyer). In *Taylor* v. *Cardle*[32] the offender pled guilty to speeding at 58 miles per hour in an area where the speed limit was 30 miles per hour. He had previously been offered, but failed to pay, a fixed penalty of £24. He was fined £280 and his appeal against sentence was refused save in respect of the amount of instalment payments. Although the contrast between that fine and the earlier fixed penalty was before the High Court in the ground of appeal no reference to that was made in the judgment which merely concluded that the justice

---

[29] *McCandless* v. *MacDougall*, 1987 S.C.C.R. 206.
[30] *Da Costa* v. *Lockhart*, High Court, November 6, 1990, unreported.
[31] 1987 S.C.C.R. 99.
[32] 1988 S.C.C.R. 450.

had been entitled to impose a fine of that size. (It will be noted that the fine in this case appears to represent a tariff of £10 for each mile per hour over the speed limit).

10–37   On balance the foregoing cases appear to suggest that a court is not required to inhibit itself in any way (other than by having regard to an offender's means) when determining the amount of a fine in a case where there has been an earlier offer of a fixed penalty. However, the question has not yet been explicitly addressed by the High Court, and for the moment it remains the view of this author that in such a case the amount of a fine ought not as a general rule to exceed the amount of the fixed penalty to too significant an extent.

The use of maximum fines

10–38   A statutory maximum fine, just like a statutory maximum term of imprisonment, sets the upper limit of a court's powers in respect of the offence to which that maximum applies. In practice, maximum penalties should be used very sparingly. It has been said of maximum penalties that they ought "to be regarded as the limit set on the powers of the court when dealing with the gravest type of offence which the legislature contemplated as likely to arise in practice ... if in the early stages maximum, or nearly maximum, penalties are imposed in cases where few or no features of aggravation are present, there is a grave risk that, if and when much more serious cases later arise, the court may find itself powerless to exercise that just discrimination in the award of penalties which is indispensable to the due adminstration of criminal justice."[33] This passage which, it is thought,[34] still represents an authoritative statement on the way in which maximum penalties should be regarded, appears in effect to be making two separate, though related, points. The first is that, where a maximum penalty is provided for, it should be seen as being appropriate for the worst possible example of the type of offence in question. Since it is probably impossible to predict with any accuracy what would constitute the worst possible example of any kind of offence, it follows that generally a maximum penalty will rarely in practice be used.

10–39   The second point which emerges from the statement that has been quoted is that, in fixing the level of a fine, a court must be mindful of the need to allow a reasonable leeway both above and below so as to cater for other cases which are either more or less grave. Although in the passage quoted this point was made in relation to maximum penalties, it is valid as a general proposition regardless of the maximum penalty provided, and equally in cases on indictment where there is no limit to the amount of a fine.

Cumulo fines

10–40   Although it is competent in certain circumstances to impose a *cumulo* fine in respect of several charges in a complaint,[35] this should as a rule be

---

[33] *Edward & Sons* v. *McKinnon*, 1943 J.C. 156, *per* L.J.C. Cooper at 168.
[34] See, for example, *McCandless* v. *MacDougall*, 1987 S.C.C.R. 206; *Shields* v. *H.M. Advocate*, 1987 S.C.C.R. 706.
[35] 1975 Act, s. 430(3); and see para. 7–45 *et seq.* above.

done only where, in the event of an appeal against conviction, all of the charges will stand or fall together.[36] If this is not the situation, and an appeal against conviction is successful in respect of some, but not all, of the charges, it will be difficult, if not impossible, for the High Court to determine an appropriate sentence in respect of the remaining charges.

10–41   There will, however, from time to time be cases where, although for the reasons just given it may not be appropriate to impose a *cumulo* fine, nonetheless a *cumulo* approach to fining may be desirable. A typical example is the case of the motorist who is convicted of a string of offences under the Motor Vehicles (Construction and Use) Regulations. Few judges would agree with the view that unlawful acts should come "cheaper by the dozen," but in the sort of case mentioned an accumulation of the fines appropriate for each offence may well produce a total which is quite out of proportion to the culpability of the offender. In such a case, it is submitted, it may therefore be proper to regard the individual charges as being essentially the manifestations of a single offence (although it does not appear as such in any statute), namely the driving of a generally unroadworthy vehicle. So viewed the court can determine a total fine appropriate to the totality of the offence and then, as necessary, apportion that fine to the individual charges. Although the case given as an example is a fairly common one, the same approach may be used in other cases, even of crimes or offences at common law, where the individual charges are truly incidents in a single course of conduct, or parts of a single piece of unlawful behaviour.

Balance between different offences

10–42   There is one further matter which merits consideration in relation to the use of the fine; and that is the balance which should exist between the level of fines imposed for one kind of offence and the level of fines imposed for others. This is a matter which frequently exercises judges in summary courts (where the great majority of fines are imposed), particularly if, in the course of the same day, they are required to impose fines for a wide range of offences. The same problem, of course, also arises in relation to custodial disposals but, so far as fines are concerned, the problem may readily be illustrated by considering, on the one hand, road traffic offences and, on the other hand, crimes of dishonesty or minor violence. To some extent the problem arises because most road traffic offenders do not regard themselves as criminals, and many of them will feel aggrieved if they are fined £200 for, say, careless driving when, in the case called immediately before theirs, a person has been fined the same amount for shoplifting or for a breach of the peace. A short answer to this sort of problem is that, if a realistic scale of penalties is to be applied in relation to the offence of careless driving, these penalties may inevitably on occasions equal, or even exceed, the fines imposed for minor common law offences, particularly if it is borne in mind that many minor cases of shoplifting involve the taking of goods of little value (all of which are often recovered), many minor breaches of the peace involve quite trivial disturbances, and in both cases the offenders are often people

---

[36] *Paisley Ice Rink* v. *Hill*, 1944 J.C. 158; *Seaton* v. *Allan*, 1973 J.C. 24; *Caringi* v. *H.M. Advocate*, 1989 S.C.C.R. 223.

of very limited means. To answer thus, however, is perhaps to do no more than to say that each case must be judged according to its own facts and circumstances. That, of course, is always necessary, but to say no more than that is to ignore the real danger that a range of penalties for one kind of offence may become unacceptably out of step with the penalties which are imposed for other kinds of offence. It is therefore submitted that judges should always be aware of the desirability of examining from time to time the relationship between the fines which they impose for one kind of offence and the fines which they impose for others in order to make sure that the level of fines for one is not out of step with that for another.

COMMUNITY SERVICE ORDERS

Background

10–43　Community service was first introduced in Scotland some two years before the passing of the Community Service by Offenders (Scotland) Act 1978. What happened was that, on an experimental basis, arrangements were made in four areas whereby courts could add to a probation order a condition that the offender should perform a number of hours of unpaid work of service to the community. By the time the Act of 1978 came to be passed it had been found that there were in some cases practical advantages in linking a community service requirement to a probation order. Consequently, the Act not only contains provision for direct community service orders, on the English model, but also expressly authorises the probation linked practice of the experimental period.

10–44　The introduction of community service was first recommended in the United Kingdom in the report of the Wootton Committee,[37] and statutory effect was given to part of that recommendation in the Criminal Justice Act 1972.[38] In general it may be said that the Wootton Committee saw community service as being capable of satisfying three sentencing objectives, namely punishment, reformation, and the constructive use of resources. As to punishment, it would enable the court in appropriate cases to encroach upon what would otherwise be an offender's free time and to oblige him to apply that time to a socially useful purpose. Any element of punishment, however, would be of an entirely constructive character in that it would not only involve work that was of potential benefit to the community at large, but it might also, by its very nature, have some reformative effect on the offender himself. Lastly, if it were used as an alternative to imprisonment, it would assist in relieving the pressures on already over-crowded prisons while not necessarily involving the expenditure of other capital resources.

When community service may be appropriate

10–45　For many years after community service orders were first introduced there was considerable debate as to the circumstances in which they are appropriate. Many people, including in particular social workers and

---

[37] Advisory Council on the Penal System, *Non-custodial and Semi-custodial Penalties*, 1970 H.M.S.O.

[38] Interestingly, the Wootton Committee recommended the introduction of both the direct order and the probation linked order, but only the former of these recommendations has been enacted for England and Wales.

probation officers, argued that they should be used only in cases where a court would otherwise have imposed a custodial sentence. Others, including in particular many judges, argued that in some instances they might be appropriate as an alternative to some other non-custodial sentence. It is no longer necessary to examine that debate further since, by section 61(3) of the Law Reform (Miscellaneous Provisions) (Scotland) Act 1990,[39] a community service order may now be imposed only as an alternative to a custodial sentence.[40]

10–46 Subject, then, to the fact that a community service order should be made only where a court would otherwise have imposed a custodial sentence, what are the cases where community service may be appropriate, and what may determine whether a direct order, or a probation linked order, should be made? To some extent the answer to the first part of that question depends on the availability of resources in that any social work department may be able to accommodate only a certain number of community service cases at a time. However, the recent introduction of 100 per cent. central government funding for community service ought to remove, or at least alleviate, that problem. Given that community service orders are now a direct alternative to custody it follows that they will be appropriate in cases of at least moderate gravity. Within that range of cases, however, community service may not always be a suitable disposal. It is probably not suitable in the case of sex offenders, in the case of those suffering from some form of mental disturbance, in the case of many who are elderly, and in the case of many suffering from an addiction to drugs or alcohol. More generally, it is probably not suitable in any case where there is reason to doubt the offender's commitment to undertaking and completing the work given to him. In all cases where community service is being considered as a disposal it is advisable, and in some instances necessary,[41] that the court should obtain a report as to suitability before any order is made. Although practice varies from area to area, that report will often be prepared, at least in part, by a social worker with special responsibility for, and experience of, community service, and should give an indication of the factors pointing towards or against community service.

10–47 The social inquiry report will normally also give some indication as to whether the case is one appropriate for a community service order on its own, or for a requirement linked to a probation order. In this matter also opinion and practice may vary among social workers and judges in different parts of the country. Probably, however, there would be some agreement that, in general, a probation linked requirement may be appropriate in cases where there appears to be a need for social work counselling and case work in addition to the community service requirement, whereas the direct order may be appropriate in cases where there is no such obvious need. Moreover, since a community service order may be made only where a court would otherwise have imposed a

---

[39] Amending s. 1(1) of the Community Service by Offenders (Scotland) Act 1978.
[40] It is to be noted that this requirement applies only in respect of community service orders made under s. 1 of the 1978 Act, and does not apply where a requirement to perform unpaid work is attached to a probation order under s. 7 of that Act: see para. 1–18 *et seq.* above.
[41] Community Service by Offenders (Scotland) Act 1978, s. 1(2)(*c*).

custodial sentence, whereas there is no such restriction in respect of a probation linked requirement, it follows that community service orders should be reserved for cases which are more grave in character and probation linked requirements for those which are less grave.

The length of the order

10–48   Under either of the options a court may order between 40 and 240 hours of work to be performed. The exact number to be ordered is entirely at the discretion of the judge but it may be submitted that, as with maximum fines,[42] the maximum number of hours should be seen as appropriate for the most serious type of case in which community service is likely to be ordered.[43]

Appropriate action when community service order not performed

10–49   Where an offender has failed to comply with the terms of a community service order and is brought before the court for breach of that order, questions may arise as to how he or she should then be dealt with. Although in one case[44] the High Court approved the view that "the successful implementation of non-custodial options in the law depends upon it being clearly understood that in cases of default the sanction of custody will be applied,"[45] the court has also substituted a fine for a period of detention,[46] and in another case, with reluctance, quashed a term of imprisonment and instead increased the number of hours under the community service order.[47] For the future it may be that, since community service orders are now to be used only in cases where a court would otherwise have imposed a custodial sentence, the sanction for breach of an order is more likely to be the custodial sentence which would otherwise have been imposed in the first instance.

COMPENSATION ORDERS

Background

10–50   The power to make compensation orders was introduced in Scottish criminal courts by the Criminal Justice (Scotland) Act 1980.[48] Under that Act an order may be made against any convicted person requiring him to pay compensation for any personal injury, loss or damage caused (whether directly or indirectly) by the acts which constituted the offence.[49] As with fines, an offender's means must be taken into account when determining the amount of a compensation order,[50] and, if the offender has insufficient means to pay both a fine and a compensation order, the court is directed to give preference to the latter.[51]

---

[42] See paras. 10–38, 10–39 above.
[43] See, for example, *Brown* v. *Normand*, 1988 S.C.C.R. 229.
[44] *Dunsmure* v. *Lowe*, 1990 S.C.C.R. 524.
[45] *Ibid.* p. 525.
[46] *Rankin* v. *McGlennan*, 1990 S.C.C.R. 607.
[47] *Simpson* v. *H.M. Advocate*, 1990 S.C.C.R. 680.
[48] Ss. 58 to 67.
[49] S. 58(1).
[50] S. 59(1).
[51] S. 61.

When a compensation order is appropriate

10–51   Subject to an offender's means, and possibly subject to the nature of any other sentence being imposed on the offender at the same time (see paragraphs 10–54, 10–55 below), a compensation order is likely to be appropriate in any case where a person has suffered injury, loss or damage as the result of a criminal act. Given that few, if any, victims of crime are likely to pursue a civil action for damages against an offender, a compensation order is capable of providing a quick and effective means of alternative redress. In cases of personal injury where the amount of compensation falls below the minimum figure at which the Criminal Injuries Compensation Board will make an award[52] a compensation order may be the only effective way of compensating a victim; and even in cases where total compensation is likely to exceed that minimum figure a court may well consider that at least some of that compensation should be paid by the offender rather than out of public funds. In such a case the C.I.C.B. will simply make up the difference. However, a court should not make a compensation order in respect of personal injury in circumstances where an award by the C.I.C.B. would not be competent.[53]

10–52   As a general rule a court is unlikely to consider a compensation order in cases where the calculation of any loss or damage is likely to be complex or lengthy since a criminal court is not well suited to conducting an inquiry of a kind which is more appropriate for a civil proof. Even in apparently simple cases, however, a court should be careful to ensure that it has adequate and reliable information on which to base an assessment of an appropriate figure for compensation. The need for care may be particularly apparent in, for example, cases of vandalism or malicious mischief where, at the time of conviction, there may only be a rough estimate of the likely cost of repairs. Very often such estimates prove to be wide of the mark, and in such cases, if a court is minded to make a compensation order, there may be something to be said for deferring sentence for a short period in order to obtain an accurate statement of the cost.

10–53   In recent years the High Court has given some indication of circumstances where a compensation order may, or may not, competently be used. A compensation order is not competent in respect of alarm caused by the commission of a breach of the peace since alarm alone does not sound in damages.[54] On the other hand it has been held to be competent to make a compensation order not only in respect of damage caused to a motor car but also in respect of the inconvenience caused to its owner.[55] It has also been held to be competent to make a compensation order in favour of an 11-year-old boy who was injured by a firework where the offender was convicted under the Explosives Act 1875 of selling gunpowder to a person under the age of 16.[56]

---

[52] Currently £750.
[53] *Brown* v. *Normand*, 1988 S.C.C.R. 229, where the complainer had provoked the assault upon himself; but see *McPhail* v. *Hamilton*, 1991 G.W.D. 24–1375.
[54] *Smillie* v. *Wilson*, 1990 S.L.T. 582, 1990 S.C.C.R. 133.
[55] *Stewart* v. *H.M. Advocate*, 1982 S.C.C.R. 203.
[56] *Carmichael* v. *Siddique*, 1985 S.C.C.R. 145.

Compensation order coupled with imprisonment

10–54   Section 58(1) of the 1980 Act provides that a compensation order may be made "instead of or in addition to dealing with [the offender] in any other way." Accordingly, it is clearly competent to combine such an order with a sentence of imprisonment. In practice this is seldom done, no doubt because few offenders will have the resources to pay a compensation order while they are actually in prison, and because it will often seem unreasonable to expect an offender to start paying compensation after a custodial sentence has come to an end. However, it is competent to postpone the payment of a compensation order until after a custodial sentence has been completed,[57] and the only limitation on so doing appears to be the statutory provision in the 1980 Act that, in assessing an offender's means for the purpose of determining whether to make a compensation order and for the purpose of determining the amount of any such order, no account is to be taken of earnings contingent upon his obtaining employment after release from custody.[58] However, in such a case it appears to be proper to proceed on the basis that the offender will be in receipt of social security benefits after his release.[59]

10–55   Given the fact that a compensation order may be made in addition to any other penalty, it also appears to be competent to make such an order even when a maximum sentence of imprisonment (whether for the offence or the court) is being imposed.[60] In that event, however, a question may arise as to how any such order is to be enforced bearing in mind that the maximum power of imprisonment for the offence, or as the case may be the court in question, has already been exhausted. In *Fraser* v. *Herron*,[61] where an offender was sentenced to three months' imprisonment (the statutory maximum for the offence) and a fine, it was held to be incompetent to impose imprisonment in default of payment of the fine since the total imprisonment would then exceed the court's powers. That case has never been overruled, but more recently the High Court appears to have taken the view (without referring to *Fraser* v. *Herron*) that, where there is default in paying a fine which has been imposed in addition to a maximum custodial sentence, any imprisonment in respect of that default would be imprisonment for failure to pay the fine, and not imprisonment for the original offence: in other words the two are quite separate, and exhaustion of the court's power of imprisonment in respect of the offence does not necessarily bar it from imprisoning for a failure to pay the fine.[62] It is not easy to reconcile *Fraser* v. *Herron* with the later authority, and it is therefore suggested that courts, and particularly summary courts, should consider carefully before

---

[57] See, for example, *Collins* v. *Lowe*, 1990 S.C.C.R. 605.
[58] 1980 Act, s. 59(1).
[59] *Collins* v. *Lowe*, above.
[60] *Clark* v. *Cardle*, 1989 S.C.C.R. 92.
[61] 1968 J.C. 1; 1968 S.L.T. 149.
[62] *Beattie* v. *H.M. Advocate*, 1986 S.C.C.R. 605. This was a drugs case, and the problem which arose here was subsequently covered by the 1975 Act, s. 193B(5), inserted by the Law Reform (Miscellaneous Provisions) (Scotland) Act 1985, s. 39, by virtue of which in drug cases imprisonment in default of payment of a fine imposed on indictment is to be consecutive to any other imprisonment imposed in the same proceedings (see now 1987 Act, s. 44).

ordering imprisonment in default of payment of a fine or compensation order where that has been imposed in addition to a maximum custodial sentence. Any such fine or compensation order can, however, competently be enforced by civil diligence.[63]

The amount of a compensation order, and time for payment

10–56   As with the fine, consideration must be given to the means of an offender when determining the amount of a compensation order.[64] Unlike the fine, consideration is also to be given to the means of an offender when determining whether to make a compensation order at all.[65] Presumably the reason for this added requirement is that the fine is a penalty which a court may choose entirely at its discretion. By contrast, a compensation order can only be made where quantifiable loss, injury or damage has been established; and in some instances a court may conclude that the amount necessary to compensate for that loss, injury or damage is so far beyond an offender's means as to make it unrealistic to order the payment of any compensation at all.

10–57   Subject to the foregoing, it is submitted that, in relation to assessing the amount of a compensation order, many of the observations made earlier in this chapter in relation to fines are equally relevant and applicable.[66] As with fines it is suggested that, where time is allowed for payment of a compensation order, the total period should not be so long as to be oppressive.[67] Where payment of compensation is made a condition of a probation order, payment must be completed not more than 18 months after the making of the order.[68]

CUSTODIAL SENTENCES

Reasons for imposing a custodial sentence

10–58   A custodial sentence is the most severe sentence available to courts in Scotland and, as such, it clearly satisfies the aims of punishment and retribution. When the sentence is a lengthy one it will also satisfy, if appropriate, the aim of public protection. It does not necessarily follow, however, that a long custodial sentence should be capable of being justified, even in part, on grounds of public protection. For a particularly heinous crime such as culpable homicide a long sentence may be amply justified on grounds of punishment and retribution alone even in circumstances where the offender is not thought to represent any continuing risk to the public.[69] On the other hand, considerations of public safety and protection may sometimes justify a longer custodial sentence than would otherwise be warranted by reference to the gravity of the offence alone.

10–59   Few people would now support the view that a custodial sentence

---

[63] *Fraser* v. *Herron*, see n. 61 above.
[64] 1980 Act, s. 59(1).
[65] *Ibid.*
[66] See paras. 10–26 to 10–33.
[67] *Storie* v. *Scott*, 1990 S.C.C.R. 284, where four years was held to be too long.
[68] 1975 Act, ss. 183(5C), 384(5C).
[69] See, for example, *Turner* v. *H.M. Advocate*, 1990 G.W.D. 22–1234, noted in para. 11–22 below.

should be imposed with the aim of rehabilitating the offender. In the days when borstal institutions existed for young offenders their aim was expressly to try to rehabilitate the young persons who were sent to them and, even if they were not always successful in achieving that aim, their existence and their purpose meant that courts could, and did, impose borstal sentences for rehabilitative purposes. In the case of other penal establishments the Prison Rules had stated for many years that the "purposes of training and treatment of convicted prisoners shall be to establish in them the will to lead a good and useful life on discharge, and to fit them to do so." Thus, for many decades offenders of all ages were given custodial sentences at least in part upon the view that they would thereby be reformed and become better citizens. For at least the last 20 years, however, these views have found fewer and fewer adherents. This is not the place to examine in detail why this should have been so. Suffice it to say that growing overcrowding in prisons, and increased reconviction rates for those released from prison, have both played a part. The result is that today it is almost certainly unwise and unrealistic to seek to justify the imposition of a custodial sentence on the ground that it may reform or rehabilitate the offender.

10–60   What, then, of deterrence? Can custodial sentences be justified on the ground that they may be effective either as a general, or at least an individual, deterrent? So far as general deterrence is concerned it has already been remarked[70] that there is little evidence to show that a policy of exemplary sentences has much effect in deterring others from committing the same, or similar, crimes. Certainly, the very high sentences imposed by the High Court for drug offences in the last 10 years or so seem to have done little to stem the frequency of such offending (although those sentences may well be justifiable on other grounds). On the other hand, the impositition of a custodial sentence, and particularly a first custodial sentence, may be thought likely to have some effect in deterring the individual concerned from further law-breaking. It is to be noted, however, that the High Court has disapproved of the use of very short custodial sentences for this purpose,[71] and has shown a reluctance to confirm a first custodial sentence for offences of only moderate gravity.[72]

The use of custodial sentences

10–61   Apart from the various statutory restrictions relating to the use of custodial sentences, which are dealt with elsewhere in this book,[73] there are also certain other limitations which should be borne in mind. Most of these apply equally to other penalties such as fines, and have already been explained in detail earlier in this chapter.[74] For example, maximum

---

[70] Para. 9–06 above.

[71] *Kinney* v. *Tudhope*, 1985 S.C.C.R. 393; *McKenzie* v. *Lockhart*, 1986 S.C.C.R. 663. For some years courts in England and Wales appear to have taken the view that it is the immediate fact of imprisonment ("the clang of the gates") which is most likely to act as an individual deterrent, with the result that very short custodial sentences can sometimes be justified on that ground: *cf. R.* v. *Bibi*, (1980) 71 Cr.App.R. 360.

[72] See, for example, *Hamilton* v. *Hillary*, 1986 S.C.C.R. 114; *Gordon* v. *Hamilton*, 1987 S.C.C.R. 146.

[73] See Chap. 2 above.

[74] Para. 10–25 *et seq.* above.

sentences should be reserved for the worst examples of a given offence; and care should be taken to ensure that the level of sentence imposed for one class of offence is reasonably in proportion to the level of sentence for other offences.

10–62   Since a custodial sentence is the most severe sentence available to the courts, it will normally be used for offences of at least moderate gravity. It should not be used in a case where a fine would otherwise be appropriate simply because the offender does not have the means to pay a fine of a size which the court regards as necessary to mark the gravity of the offence,[75] though, *per contra*, it appears that an affluent offender may be able to escape an otherwise deserved sentence of imprisonment by paying a large fine instead.[76] On the other hand, a custodial sentence may be appropriate even for a relatively trivial offence where the offender has a substantial record for the same or similar offences.[77]

---

[75] *Milligan* v. *Jessop*, 1988 S.C.C.R. 137.
[76] *McLean* v. *MacDougall*, 1989 S.C.C.R. 625.
[77] See, for example, the cases noted in para. 11–73 *et seq*. below.

CHAPTER 11

SENTENCE FOR PARTICULAR OFFENCES

Introduction

11–01   In this chapter an attempt is made to offer some guidance on the choice of sentence for particular offences by reference to cases which have been decided on appeal by the High Court during the last few years. Essentially, therefore, this chapter is concerned with the exercise of sentencing discretion rather than with substantive law. Before going further, however, some words of caution are desirable.

11–02   Unlike appeal courts in some other jurisdictions (for example, the Court of Appeal, Criminal Division, in England) the High Court in Scotland has never sought to offer general sentencing guidelines or to set a sentencing tariff for certain kinds of offence. Indeed, the High Court has often been at pains to state that every case must be considered according to its own particular facts and circumstances. Accordingly, what follows is not an attempt to set out approved guidelines or a tariff of general application. On the other hand an analysis of a large number of decided cases may, it is suggested, be of some assistance to judges who have to pass sentence in similar cases. It is with that thought in mind that this chapter has been prepared.

11–03   A second point which should be borne in mind is that, since the High Court is considering on appeal only those cases where the sentences are alleged to be excessive or inappropriate, there is at least a possibility that sentencing levels as reflected in the decisions of that court may actually be somewhat higher than the norm for similar offences. An offender who receives a sentence which is lower than one which has previously been approved by the High Court may be less likely to expose it to scrutiny by appeal, particularly bearing in mind the High Court's power to increase, as well as to reduce, sentences on appeal; and there may be many cases where that is the position.

11–04   A third point which should be borne in mind is that in many instances the reports of sentencing appeals do not fully disclose all the material facts and considerations which may have been before both the sentencing court and the High Court on appeal. This is particularly, and inevitably, so in those cases which are reported only in *Green's Weekly Digest*. Consequently, when comparing a case which is mentioned hereafter in this chapter with a case in which sentence falls to be imposed it should be remembered that in some instances the report, and even more so the narratives given in this chapter, may be somewhat sketchy and may fail to disclose all the relevant facts.

11–05   In this chapter an attempt has been made to take account of all the relevant sentencing decisions during the last six years or so whether in the Justiciary Reports, the *Scots Law Times*, or the *Scottish Criminal Case Reports*. Earlier decisions are cited only where they appear to lay down an approach which is still likely to be followed, or where they have been expressly disapproved by a more recent decision. In general it is suggested that earlier cases (only a very few of which have in any event been reported) are unlikely to offer a very reliable guide to sentencing today given the changes in social attitudes and perceptions which inevitably occur over a period of time. So far as cases reported in *Green's Weekly Digest* are concerned, only a limited number are mentioned in this chapter. That publication performs a useful service by listing in digested form practically all of the sentencing appeal cases decided by the High Court: but very many of these cases are quite similar to each other and, it is thought, little would be gained by referring here, for example, to scores of cases in which a sentence of around six months' imprisonment was upheld for crimes of theft by housebreaking committed by offenders with multiple previous convictions. In such instances only a few examples have been selected by way of illustration. In other instances, for example cases of assault, the circumstances of individual cases are so varied that it would not be possible to give a wholly comprehensive account of the approach taken by the High Court without referring to just about every case which is recorded in *Green's Weekly Digest*. In such instances, therefore, a selection of cases is offered in the belief that this presents a fair and balanced picture of current sentencing practice. An attempt has been made, however, to identify all those cases in which a particular approach to sentencing or a particular sentencing principle has been stated or confirmed.

11–06   In what follows the various offences which are under consideration are arranged in alphabetical order; and for each offence the cases which are referred to are arranged so far as possible in chronological order.

ASSAULT

(1) Simple assault
11–07   Even assaults which are not aggravated by being to severe injury, permanent disfigurement, or danger of life, can take many forms and involve many degrees of culpability. Consequently, the sentence range for simple assaults can be very wide. However, some recurring features in the approach of the High Court can be identified. The court has, for example, shown some reluctance, in the absence of particularly aggravating circumstances, to confirm a custodial sentence on an offender who has not previously undergone such a sentence (see, for example, *Hamilton* v. *Hillary* (1986); *Dick* v. *Jessop* (1989); *McCardle* v. *Douglas* (1989), below). On the other hand, examples can also be found where the High Court has upheld custodial sentences even on first, or virtually first, offenders convicted of simple assault (*Cooney* v. *Lockhart* (1986); *McCurdy* v. *MacKinnon* (1987); *Stirling* v. *Stewart* (1988); *Murchie* v. *McGlennan* (1990)). In many instances where custodial sentences have been affirmed on appeal the cases have displayed some particularly aggravating features such as having involved an unprovoked attack on a total stranger (*McQuarrie* v. *H.M. Advocate* (1988)), having involved an attack (albeit to minimal physical injury) on a prosecution witness immediately after the conclusion of a trial (*Furlong* v. *H.M. Advocate* (1988)), or having involved an assault on a public servant, such as a bus driver (*Ferguson* v. *Lowe* (1989)).
11–08   Subject to the foregoing comments the following cases are offered as illustrations of decisions involving convictions for simple assault.

11–08a   **Aitken** v. **Wilson**, 1986 G.W.D. 4–61.
The accused was convicted of assault by butting and kicking to injury. As a result the complainer had to stay off work for three weeks. The accused had seven previous convictions of which two were on indictment. Six months' imprisonment was held not to be excessive.

11–08b   **Hamilton** v. **Hillary**, 1986 S.C.C.R. 114.
The accused was convicted of assault by punching and kicking, causing the victim to suffer bruising and the loss of two teeth. The accused had three previous convictions for breach of the peace and one for assault, all dealt with by small fines. On appeal a sentence of 60 days' imprisonment was replaced by a fine of £500, the court observing that "we are reluctant to send a man to prison for the first time even for a grave offence of this sort."

11–08c   **Cooney** v. **Lockhart**, 1986 G.W.D. 5–93.
The accused, aged 17, was convicted of assault by punching and kicking. He was married, his wife was expecting a baby, and he was a first offender. The attack was an unprovoked one on an innocent person in a public street. A sentence of three months' detention was upheld on appeal.

11–08d **Gibson** v. **Tudhope**, 1986 S.C.C.R. 508.
A police officer was convicted of assaulting a youth in the back of a police van, striking his head against the side of the van and striking him on the knee to his injury. A fine of £500 was held not to be excessive.

11–08e **McCurdy** v. **MacKinnon**, 1987 S.C.C.R. 267.
The accused was convicted of assault by punching and kicking, the victim being at the time 15 years of age. The accused had only one previous conviction, a fine of £10 for assault in 1984. A sentence of three months' detention was upheld on appeal.

11–08f **O'Neill** v. **Wilson**, 1987 G.W.D. 9–271.
The accused was convicted of assault to injury, the injury being a cut requiring five stitches. He had a lengthy previous record but had been out of serious trouble since 1975. The assault had been on a noisy neighbour who had disturbed the accused's hyperactive child. Given the absence of recent record, and the mitigating circumstances, the High Court reduced the sentence of six months' imprisonment to one of three months

11–08g **McQuarrie** v. **H.M. Advocate**, 1988 S.C.C.R. 209.
The accused was convicted of assaulting a 19-year-old girl, who was a total stranger to him, by punching and kicking her while she was in a cubicle in the ladies' toilet of a leisure club. The girl suffered some cuts and bruises, was very shocked, and continued to suffer psychological injury. The accused had several previous convictions including two for assault. A sentence of one year's imprisonment was upheld on appeal, the court observing that it "might well be described as unduly lenient."

11–08h **English** v. **Wilson**, 1988 G.W.D. 17–730.
The accused was convicted of assault by throwing a tumbler at one man which missed him and hit another to his injury. The accused had a minor record, but was sentenced to three months' imprisonment. On appeal that sentence was quashed, and consideration was given to the alternative of community service. The court held that the sheriff had misled himself by treating the case as being equivalent to an assault with a broken glass: in the circumstances a custodial sentence was not necessary.

11–08i **Furlong** v. **H.M. Advocate**, 1988 S.C.C.R. 452.
Having just been convicted after a summary trial of attempted shoplifting, the accused, on leaving the court building, saw one of the shop assistants who had given evidence against him. He assaulted her by leaning against her and twisting his foot on her foot. A sentence of two years' imprisonment was upheld on appeal.

11–08j **Mays** v. **Brown**, 1988 S.C.C.R. 549.
The accused was convicted of assaulting a water bailiff by throwing a lamp at him. He was fined £250 but on appeal the fine was increased to £500. Both this case and the case of *Furlong*, above, indicate that the High Court takes a serious view of those who commit assaults on persons who, in their various ways, are performing a public duty in connection with the enforcement of the law or the prosecution of crime.

11–08k **Stirling** v. **Stewart**, 1988 S.C.C.R. 619.
The accused, who were aged 16, were convicted of assaulting, by

punching and kicking, an American serviceman in Dunoon. Such attacks were prevalent in the area, and sentences of 30 days' detention were upheld on appeal.

11–08l   Dick *v*. Jessop, 1989 S.C.C.R. 258.
The accused, aged 25, was convicted of assault by kicking on the head while the complainer was on the ground. The accused was in good employment and had not previously been convicted of assault or given a custodial sentence. A sentence of two months' imprisonment was quashed on appeal with a fine of £500 being substituted.

11–08m   McCardle *v*. Douglas, 1989 S.C.C.R. 262.
The accused, aged 17, was convicted of assault by kicking on the head while the complainer was on the ground. The accused was in employment and had not previously been convicted of assault or given a custodial sentence. A sentence of 30 days' detention was quashed on appeal with a compensation order for £200 being substituted.

11–08n   Ferguson *v*. Lowe, 1989 S.C.C.R. 281.
The accused, who was aged 17 at the time of the offence, had no previous convictions (though he had subsequently been convicted of a minor assault and two breaches of the peace), was convicted of assaulting a bus driver by knocking him down and punching and kicking him repeatedly. He was sentenced to 60 days' detention and on appeal it was held that the sheriff had exercised his discretion properly.

11–08o   Forrest *v*. H.M. Advocate, 1989 G.W.D. 28–1265.
The accused was convicted of assault by presenting knives at his cohabitee and her baby, threatening to kill them, and jabbing the cohabitee during a domestic dispute. He was sentenced to 18 months' imprisonment. On appeal it was held that a custodial sentence was inevitable, but the sentence was reduced to one of nine months' imprisonment.

11–08p   Murchie *v*. McGlennan, 1990 S.C.C.R. 533.
The accused, who were both first offenders, broke into the complainer's house and assaulted him to his injury with a cricket bat and a meat tenderiser. At the time the complainer was awaiting trial on a charge of using lewd and libidinous practices towards the second accused's child. The assault had been planned, and the accused had armed themselves before breaking into the complainer's house. Sentences of three months' imprisonment were upheld on appeal.

11–08q   McLean *v*. H.M. Advocate, 1990 G.W.D. 32–1844.
The accused, who had a long record of violence, was convicted of assaulting his own father by repeatedly punching him to his injury. On appeal it was held that a sentence of six months' imprisonment was not excessive.

11–08r   F.P.C. *v*. Lowe, 1990 S.C.C.R. 755.
The accused pled guilty to assaulting two of his children by striking them, in one case with an electric cable. He was sentenced to four months' imprisonment but, on appeal, it was urged that probation was appropriate because it was in the interests of the children that he should

be under continuing social work supervision. By the time of his appeal he had already served two months of his sentence. The appeal was allowed, and two years' probation substituted.

(2) Aggravated assault

11–09   Aggravated assaults, that is to say assaults to severe injury, permanent disfigurement, or danger of life, will normally attract more severe sentences than simple assaults to injury. The High Court has stated on several occasions that a custodial sentence is inevitable in cases where a weapon is used (see, for example, *Hart* v. *H.M. Advocate* (1981); *Robb* v. *H.M. Advocate* (1987); *Leonard* v. *H.M. Advocate* (1989); *O'Hare* v. *H.M. Advocate* (1989), below). However, where an offence of violence is entirely out of character a non-custodial disposal may be appropriate notwithstanding the use of a weapon (*McDonald* v. *H.M. Advocate* (1989)); and, in cases where the accused has been convicted of assault for the first time, a shorter custodial sentence than would otherwise be appropriate may be permissible (*Verbees* v. *H.M. Advocate* (1989)). Where an assault has taken place in a domestic situation, and is unlikely to recur, a non-custodial sentence may be appropriate (*McMillan* v. *H.M. Advocate* (1991)).

11–10   Where a serious assault has been carefully planned and master-minded, a court may be entitled to take the view that the organiser should bear a heavier responsibility than those who actually carried out the assault, and should be sentenced accordingly (*Ming* v. *H.M. Advocate* (1990)). Although stated in relation to a charge of serious assault, it is suggested that this principle could apply in relation to other crimes and offences. For example, the organiser of a major theft might, on the basis of this principle, deserve a more severe sentence than those who actually carried out the crime.

11–11   Subject to the foregoing comments the following cases are illustrations of decisions involving convictions for aggravated assault.

11–11a   **Hart** v. **H.M. Advocate**, 1981 S.C.C.R. 286.
The accused was convicted of an assault with a knife, though the resultant injuries were not in fact very severe. He was sentenced to three years' detention. His appeal against sentence was refused, the court stating that a sentence of three years' imprisonment was "at the very bottom end of the scale of sentences appropriate for such offences."

11–11b   **Pollock** v. **H.M. Advocate**, 1986 G.W.D. 2–24.
The accused, aged 19, was convicted of assault to severe injury, permanent disfigurement and impairment of vision by striking the complainer on the face with a glass tumbler. He was a first offender and had a favourable social inquiry report. A sentence of nine months' detention was sustained on appeal, the court observing that the sentence was inevitable in view of the gravity of the offence.

11–11c   **McArthur** v. **H.M. Advocate**, 1987 G.W.D. 2–52.
The accused was convicted of assault by butting the complainer on the face, kicking him, seizing hold of him, and striking his head against a footpath all to his injury and permanent disfigurement. The accused had no history of violence, was employed and engaged to be married, and

argued that he had been severely provoked. His appeal against a sentence of nine months' imprisonment was refused, the court observing that, but for the mitigating factors, including the provocation, a sentence of nine months' imprisonment would have been regarded as absurdly low.

11–11d **Newman** *v.* **H.M. Advocate**, 1987 G.W.D. 5–143.
The accused pled guilty to, *inter alia*, a charge of assault to severe injury involving the use of weapons and causing the complainer to have 26 stitches to his head. The accused had not himself carried a weapon but he had a bad record including a conviction for culpable homicide. His appeal against a sentence of five years' imprisonment on the assault charge was refused.

11–11e **Walker** *v.* **H.M. Advocate**, 1987 S.C.C.R. 345.
The accused was convicted of assault to severe injury on a nine-month-old child. On appeal a sentence of four years' imprisonment was reduced to one of three years on the grounds that the accused was of low intelligence and had been left in a situation where there was no one capable of restraining him.

11–11f **Patterson** *v.* **H.M. Advocate**, 1987 G.W.D. 11–360.
The accused was convicted of assault to severe injury by striking the complainer on the face with a glass. He had an insignificant criminal record, was generally of good character, and had a good record for work and for contributions to the community. Despite all that the sheriff concluded that a custodial sentence was inevitable and imposed a sentence of nine months' imprisonment. On appeal the High Court held that it was impossible to disturb the sheriff's conclusion.

11–11g **Robb** *v.* **H.M. Advocate**, 1987 G.W.D. 39–1421.
The accused was convicted of assault with a knife and assault to severe injury and permanent disfigurement, and was sentenced *in cumulo* to two years' imprisonment. On appeal the High Court stated that, where a weapon is used in an assault, a custodial sentence is required. However, in view of certain mitigating factors present in this case the sentence was reduced to one of 12 months' imprisonment.

11–11h **Kane** *v.* **H.M. Advocate**, 1988 G.W.D. 11–458.
The accused was convicted of assault to severe injury and permanent disfigurement with a tumbler. He had a bad record including five previous convictions for assault. His appeal against a sentence of two years' imprisonment was refused, it being observed that a remit to the High Court for sentence would have been justified. (At that time two years' imprisonment was the maximum which could be imposed in the sheriff court on indictment.)

11–11i **Lam** *v.* **H.M. Advocate**, 1988 S.C.C.R. 347.
The accused was convicted of assault to severe injury and danger of life. He had been one of a gang of four who carried out a Triad-inspired attack on the owner of a restaurant using long knives and a bar. A sentence of 10 years' detention was upheld on appeal. (See *Ming* v. *H.M. Advocate*, below.)

11–11j **McDonald** *v.* **H.M. Advocate**, 1989 G.W.D. 2–60.
The accused was convicted of assault to severe injury and permanent disfigurement with a tumbler. He was a first offender, aged 29, and had recently obtained employment. He was married with two children and had favourable reports and references. On appeal a sentence of 18 months' imprisonment was quashed and a fine of £1,000 and a compensation order of £750 were substituted. It was observed that the original sentence would have been appropriate in most cases, but the accused had acted entirely out of character and was unlikely to commit the same crime again.

11–11k **Leonard** *v.* **H.M. Advocate**, 1989 G.W.D. 13–544.
The accused was convicted of assault to severe injury by punching, kicking and stabbing. She had previous convictions, but none for violence, and had not previously undergone a custodial sentence. Under reference to *Hart* v. *H.M. Advocate* (1981) (see above) the High Court upheld a sentence of nine months' imprisonment.

11–11l **O'Hare** *v.* **H.M. Advocate**, 1989 G.W.D. 16–672.
The accused was convicted of assault by stabbing in the chest to permanent disfigurement. An appeal against a sentence of 18 months' imprisonment was refused, it being observed that this was the minimum sentence for such an assault.

11–11m **Verbees** *v.* **H.M. Advocate**, 1989 G.W.D. 25–1079.
The accused was convicted of assault to injury and permanent disfigurement by punching, kicking, butting to the head and pushing against a wall. He had previous convictions for dishonesty but not for violence. On appeal a sentence of nine months' imprisonment was reduced to one of six months' imprisonment on the basis that this was appropriate for a first conviction for assault.

11–11n **Munro** *v.* **H.M. Advocate**, 1989 G.W.D. 25–1080.
The accused, aged 18, was convicted of assault to severe injury by striking two people on the face with a broken glass. He had previous convictions for assault, including to severe injury. On appeal it was held that six years' detention was not excessive.

11–11o **Ming** *v.* **H.M. Advocate**, 1990 G.W.D. 27–1545.
The accused was convicted of assault to severe injury and danger of life, having planned and organised, but not taken part in, the assault described in *Lam* v. *H.M. Advocate* (above). A sentence of 11 years' imprisonment was upheld on appeal, it being observed that the court was entitled to hold that the organiser of such a crime bore a heavier responsibility than those who carried it out. Where a sentence of 10 years' imprisonment on one of the perpetrators had been affirmed on appeal, a sentence of 11 years' imprisonment for the organiser was not excessive.

11–11p **Reilly** *v.* **H.M. Advocate**, 1990 G.W.D. 32–1845.
The accused was convicted of assault with a bar stool and a broken tumbler causing six lacerations one of which required 22 stitches and another 19 stitches which would leave permanent scarring. He had a largely non-analogous record, and was sentenced to three years' imprisonment. On appeal it was held that this was not excessive.

11–11q	**McMillan** v. **H.M. Advocate**, 1991 S.C.C.R. 20.
The accused pleaded guilty to choking his wife with a piece of cable so that she became unconscious, to her injury and danger of life. He was 48 years of age at the time, and a first offender. The offence was committed after he had been drinking, and it was probable that the pressure on the complainer's neck had not been sustained for more than half a minute. The accused was in regular employment and, since the incident, had left the area where his wife lived. On appeal against a sentence of three years' imprisonment it was held that the offence was unlikely to recur, and was special in that it arose in a domestic situation from which the offender had since removed himself. The appeal was allowed, and a period of community service was substituted for the term of imprisonment.

ASSAULT AND ROBBERY

11–12	The High Court has consistently taken a very serious view of the crime of assault and robbery, particularly in cases which have involved the use of weapons. Although the absence of significant or analogous previous convictions has on occasions persuaded the court to reduce sentences for assault, including even aggravated assault, it seems that this is not a factor to which much, if any, weight is attached where an assault is associated with a robbery (see, for example, *McGuire* v. *H.M. Advocate* (1987); *Clive* v. *H.M. Advocate* (1989); *McCafferty* v. *H.M. Advocate* (1990); *Lannan* v. *H.M. Advocate* (1991); *Willets* v. *H.M. Advocate* (1991), below). Likewise, the fact that only a very small amount of property is stolen seems to have little effect in mitigating sentence (*McGann* v. *H.M. Advocate* (1987)). On the other hand, the theft of property of considerable value may justify an even more severe sentence (*Barrie* v. *H.M. Advocate* (1987)). It also seems to be clear that the court will approve of very substantial custodial sentences in cases where doctors are assaulted and robbed after being called out by a hoax telephone call, notwithstanding that any physical injuries are minor or even non-existent (*McIntyre* v. *H.M. Advocate* (1989); *Bulloch* v. *H.M. Advocate* (1989)).

11–13	The following are illustrative examples of the High Court's approach to sentence in cases of assault and robbery.

11–13a	**McCann** v. **H.M. Advocate**, 1987 G.W.D. 10–329.
The accused was convicted of a charge of robbery in a betting shop in which a pickaxe handle was brandished at the occupants, a fire extinguisher was activated against them, an attempt was made to force open a door, windows were broken, and the occupants were put in a state of fear and alarm. In fact the accused stole only £3.72. His appeal against a sentence of four years' imprisonment was refused, the court observing that the sentence could have been longer.

11–13b	**Watson** v. **H.M. Advocate**, 1987 G.W.D. 12–409.
The accused pled guilty to a charge of robbery armed with batons at a filling station. A sentence of six years' imprisonment was upheld on appeal.

11–13c	**Barrie** v. **H.M. Advocate**, 1987 G.W.D. 12–410.
The accused was convicted of theft of a motor car followed by an armed

robbery in which a loaded pistol was presented to security guards, and £40,000 was stolen. None of the money was recovered. The accused had a substantial record including a previous sentence of seven years' detention for assault and robbery. A sentence of 18 years' imprisonment was upheld on appeal.

11–13d   **Park** *v.* **H.M. Advocate**, 1987 G.W.D. 17–638.
The accused was convicted, along with another, of assault and attempted robbery. Using a realistic imitation firearm they had attempted to rob a taxi driver at 12.30 a.m. in a deserted area. A sentence of 15 months' imprisonment was upheld on appeal, the court observing that the sheriff might have erred on the side of leniency.

11–13e   **McGuire** *v.* **H.M. Advocate**, 1987 G.W.D. 28–1077.
The accused was convicted of assault and robbery involving the presentation of a knife and the theft of £1,350. A co-accused was convicted of assault and robbery involving the presentation of an imitation firearm and the theft of £1,000. The co-accused was 17 years of age and had never received a custodial sentence or previously appeared on indictment. It appeared that the robbery had taken place in order to obtain money for drugs. Sentences of eight years' imprisonment and detention respectively were upheld on appeal.

11–13f   **Clive** *v.* **H.M. Advocate**, 1989 G.W.D. 2–62.
The accused was convicted of breaking into a cottage during the night, threatening a couple with a knife, and demanding money with further threats. The accused had only one previous conviction in 1982. A sentence of two years' imprisonment was upheld on appeal.

11–13g   **Dickson** *v.* **Hamilton**, 1989 G.W.D. 12–496.
The accused, aged 16 and a first offender, was convicted of assaulting a 77-year-old lady, knocking her down, pulling her handbag, and attempting to rob her. He was sentenced to three months' detention, and on appeal the court stated that the sheriff had not erred in concluding that a custodial sentence was the only appropriate one in this case.

11–13h   **Brockwell** *v.* **H.M. Advocate**, 1989 G.W.D. 24–1032.
The accused was convicted of assault and robbery in a building society. He had threatened the employees and pointed a gun which had not in fact been loaded. He had numerous summary convictions for theft and other offences, but none for violence. On appeal against a sentence of 10 years' imprisonment the court stated that that sentence was higher than normal in the absence of exceptional circumstances; and in view of the accused's record the sentence was reduced to one of seven years' imprisonment.

11–13i   **McIntyre** *v.* **H.M. Advocate**, 1989 S.C.C.R. 34.
The accused pled guilty to assault and robbery. He and a co-accused had lured a doctor to a common close in Aberdeen by means of a hoax telephone call, and lay in wait for him with their faces masked. When he arrived they threatened him with sticks and demanded his medical bags (which contained, among other things, drugs), and these were handed over. A sentence of seven years' imprisonment was upheld on appeal, it being observed that this was the minimum that could properly be

imposed, and that it was only with hesitation that the sentence was not increased.

11–13j **Bulloch** *v.* **H.M. Advocate**, 1989 G.W.D. 26–1148.
The accused was convicted of assaulting a doctor with a baseball bat and robbing her of her bags and drugs, having made a hoax call for assistance. In upholding a sentence of eight years' imprisonment the court observed that even that sentence might be considered inadequate for an offence of the gravest possible character.

11–13k **McCafferty** *v.* **H.M. Advocate**, 1990 G.W.D. 35–1995.
The accused was convicted of assault and attempted robbery by presenting, along with a companion, a firearm or imitation firearm at persons in a public house. The accused had a record for crimes of dishonesty. In fact nobody was injured and nothing was gained by the robbers thanks to prompt action by others. In refusing an appeal against a sentence of seven years' imprisonment the court observed that the sentence would not have been excessive even if the accused had been a first offender.

11–13l **Lannan** *v.* **H.M. Advocate**, 1991 S.C.C.R. 969.
The accused, who was a first offender, pleaded guilty to assault and robbery. At about 9 p.m. the accused and his co-accused, who were both masked, went into a small corner shop which sold liquor. They threatened the employees in the shop with a knife, and as a result were handed about £230 from the till. The trial judge took the view that shops which remain open late are a soft target for crimes of this kind, and that an exemplary sentence was called for. A sentence of three years' imprisonment was imposed, and was upheld on appeal.

11–13m **Willets** *v.* **H.M. Advocate**, 1991 S.C.C.R. 976.
The accused, who were aged 16 and 15 at the time of the offence, pleaded guilty to assaulting a shopkeeper and robbing her of about £20 of money. They had threatened her with a replica handgun and a hammer. They were also charged with a contravention of section 17 of the Firearms Act 1968. They were sentenced to 18 months' detention on the assault and robbery charge, and to an additional six months on the statutory charge. Appeals against sentence were refused, the High Court observing that these types of crime must attract severe punishment.

ATTEMPTED MURDER

11–14 By its nature a conviction of attempted murder will nearly always attract a substantial custodial sentence, and this is likely to be so even where the offender has little or no previous criminal record (see, for example, *Mullen* v. *H.M. Advocate* (1989) below). On the other hand there may occasionally be a case which presents such extenuating circumstances that even a non-custodial sentence can properly be considered (see, for example, *W.* v. *H.M. Advocate* (1989)).

11–15 The following cases are illustrative of the High Court's approach in recent years.

11–15a **Sievwright** *v*. **H.M. Advocate**, 1986 G.W.D. 2–29.
The accused was convicted of attempted murder having supplied a knife to a co-accused and having encouraged him to make a vicious attack on a sleeping man. A sentence of nine years' imprisonment was held not to be excessive.

11–15b **Cummings** *v*. **H.M. Advocate**, 1987 G.W.D. 5–144.
The accused was convicted of attempted murder having threatened to kill the complainer and having stabbed him in the body with a knife to his severe injury. In refusing his appeal against a sentence of six years' imprisonment the High Court observed that a longer sentence might well have been imposed for an attack of this nature.

11–15c **Mullen** *v*. **H.M. Advocate**, 1989 G.W.D. 22–918.
The accused was convicted, along with a co-accused, of two charges of attempted murder involving an assault with a sword to severe injury and danger of life. One of the accused, who had a good working record and no previous convictions, had wielded the weapon while the other had not wielded the weapon but had a bad record. Both were sentenced to eight years' imprisonment, and appeals against sentence were refused.

11–15d **Craig** *v*. **H.M. Advocate**, 1989 G.W.D. 25–1091.
The accused was convicted of attempted murder by discharging a loaded shotgun at the body of the complainer to severe injury and danger of life. In upholding a sentence of 12 years' imprisonment the High Court observed that, but for the appellant's age (22) and lack of record for violence, the sentence would have been increased to 15 years or life.

11–15e **W.** *v*. **H.M. Advocate**, 1989 S.C.C.R. 461.
The accused, a 22-year-old married woman, was convicted of attempted murder of her two-year-old daughter by holding a pillow over her face. A sentence of five years' imprisonment was imposed but on appeal, and after obtaining a further social inquiry report, the High Court quashed that sentence and placed the accused on probation for three years. The incident in question was apparently entirely out of character, and the court described this as a "highly unusual case."

11–15f **McDonald** *v*. **H.M. Advocate**, 1990 G.W.D. 20–1124.
The accused was convicted of attempted murder by stabbing an innocent victim eight times causing multiple wounds and the collapse of a lung which required hospital treatment for five days. A sentence of nine years' imprisonment was upheld on appeal, the court observing that, in view of the sustained and vicious attack, it could be viewed as lenient.

ATTEMPT TO PERVERT THE COURSE OF JUSTICE

11–16 Any attempt to pervert the course of justice is a serious crime and, as such, is likely to merit a severe sentence. Where the crime involves threatening prosecution witnesses it is likely to result in a substantial custodial sentence, and a similar, though lesser, sentence may be justifiable in the not uncommon case where a person gives a false name in order to avoid prosecution. In other cases, however, mitigating circumstances may substantially reduce the seriousness of a particular offence.

11–17   The following cases are illustrative of the High Court's approach.

11–17a   **MacLean v. Mackenzie**, 1986 S.C.C.R. 482.
The accused, who was a 39-year-old first offender, was convicted of attempting to pervert the course of justice by making telephone calls threatening witnesses in a forthcoming trial in which her sons were charged with assault. The sheriff imposed a sentence of 60 days' imprisonment in view of the gravity of the offence and, on appeal, that sentence was upheld, the court observing that in such a case the decision whether or not to impose imprisonment was a matter for the discretion of the sheriff.

11–17b   **Christie v. Jessop**, 1988 G.W.D. 3–103.
The accused was convicted of attempting to pervert the course of justice by giving a false name (but the correct address) when charged with road traffic offences. He had a bad record but had largely kept out of trouble since 1982. In upholding a sentence of three months' imprisonment the High Court observed that such an offence had to attract a significant penalty.

11–17c   **Ball v. MacGillivray**, 1989 G.W.D. 19–798.
The accused was convicted of attempting to pervert the course of justice by giving a false name to the police. The sheriff considered that he had been attempting to avoid suspicion of being involved with others in more serious offences, and imposed a sentence of 30 days' imprisonment. On appeal that sentence was quashed and an admonition substituted. The complaint against the appellant on the more serious charge had been departed from and accordingly the considerations taken into account by the sheriff were irrelevant, and in any event the appellant had been held in custody for four months on that complaint.

11–17d   **Gallagher v. H.M. Advocate**, 1989 G.W.D. 28–1266.
The accused was convicted of attempting to pervert the course of justice by menacing and threatening witnesses with physical harm if they gave evidence. A sentence of four years' imprisonment was held not to be excessive.

11–17e   **McKee v. H.M. Advocate**, 1990 G.W.D. 4–188.
The accused was convicted of attempting to pervert the course of justice by menacing a potential witness and placing him in a state of fear and alarm. A sentence of three years' imprisonment was held not to be excessive.

11–17f   **Craig v. McGlennan**, 1990 G.W.D. 4–190.
The accused was convicted of attempting to pervert the course of justice by giving false information to the police about the driver of a car in order to protect his fiancee. He was sentenced to three months' imprisonment but on appeal the High Court quashed that sentence and substituted a fine of £200 on the basis of the circumstances of the case and because the accused's previous convictions were not very recent.

11–17g   **Davidson v. H.M. Advocate**, 1990 S.C.C.R. 699.
The accused, who was sentenced to a total of five years' imprisonment on drugs charges, was also sentenced to an additional 12 months'

imprisonment on a charge of attempting to pervert the course of justice, he having conspired with a co-accused to concoct a false alibi. The false alibi was persisted in for only one day. On appeal it was held that the sentence on that charge was excessive, and it was reduced to one of six months' imprisonment.

BAIL ACT OFFENCES

11–18 Convictions for offences under the Bail, etc. (Scotland) Act 1980 are very common nowadays. Frequently such convictions are in addition to other convictions on the same complaint or indictment and, where custodial sentences are being imposed, it is customary and, it is submitted, appropriate to make the sentence for the Bail Act offence consecutive to any other sentence then being imposed.

11–19 There remains, however, a question as to the level of sentence which should be imposed for Bail Act contraventions, and in particular as to the circumstances in which the maximum sentence ought to be imposed. The two cases detailed below illustrate the approach of the High Court to that question. Questions may also arise, where there are convictions on more than a single Bail Act charge, as to whether or not sentences for those charges should be consecutive to each other. Those questions are considered in the general context of consecutive sentences in paragraph 7–53 above.

11–20 The following are the reported cases on the use of the maximum sentence for a contravention of the Bail Act.

11–20a **Baird** *v.* **Lockhart**, 1986 S.C.C.R. 514.
The accused was convicted of attempted housebreaking and of a contravention of section 3(1) of the Bail Act in that the former crime was committed while he was on bail. The accused had no previous convictions for contraventions of the Bail Act, but he was sentenced to three months' imprisonment on that charge (the maximum) consecutive to a sentence of six months' imprisonment on the charge of attempted housebreaking. On appeal the sentence of three months' imprisonment was reduced to one of one month's imprisonment, the court observing that to impose the maximum sentence for the first time that an accused has contravened section 3(1) of the Bail Act is, save in the most exceptional circumstances, to impose an excessive sentence.

11–20b **Montgomery** *v.* **H.M. Advocate**, 1987 S.C.C.R. 264.
The accused was convicted of three contraventions of the Misuse of Drugs Act 1971 and of two contraventions of section 3(1) of the Bail Act by committing those offences in breach of two separate bail orders. In respect of the Bail Act offences she was sentenced to three months' imprisonment on each charge. She had no previous convictions for contraventions of the Bail Act. In upholding these sentences the High Court distinguished *Baird* v. *Lockhart* (above) on the basis that, in the present case, the appellant had committed three serious offences while on bail, whereas in *Baird* only one offence had been committed.

BREACH OF THE PEACE

11–21   Breach of the peace is a simple but compendious offence which can embrace incidents of disorderly behaviour ranging from the relatively trivial to the very serious. As a result sentences can vary between admonitions or small fines and substantial periods of imprisonment. Since so much will depend on the precise circumstances of individual cases, it is unlikely to be helpful to cite a selection of cases where this or that sentence has been approved or disapproved by the High Court. However, a very few examples may be helpful to show the approach which has been taken both in a case where the facts were relatively unusual and in cases where the facts are all too common. These are as follows.

11–21a   **Donaghy** *v.* **Tudhope**, 1985 S.C.C.R. 118.
The accused, along with three other men, was convicted of breach of the peace by climbing to the top of cranes on a building site and there displaying banners as part of a "peace" demonstration. Their activities prevented work being carried on at the site and annoyed persons employed there. The accused was sentenced to 60 days' imprisonment, and appealed on the ground that his action had been motivated by social conscience. The High Court dismissed the appeal stating that it was not concerned with the appellant's motive in committing the offence which was a grave one of its kind.

11–21b   **Worsfold** *v.* **Walkingshaw**, 1987 S.C.C.R. 17.
The accused was convicted of breach of the peace by swearing at a police officer and a police cadet who had approached him to warn him that his car was illegally parked. A fine of £100 was reduced on appeal to one of £25, the court observing that the offence to which the accused had pled guilty was not the kind of breach of the peace which merited so high a fine as £100.

11–21c   **McGivern** *v.* **Jessop**, 1988 S.C.C.R. 511.
The accused, aged 19 and with one previous conviction for breach of the peace, was convicted of breach of the peace by taunting rival football supporters and shouting and swearing. A sentence of three months' detention was upheld on appeal, the court observing that conduct of this kind is liable to lead to very serious consequences and must be severely discouraged.

CULPABLE HOMICIDE

11–22   Like attempted murder, culpable homicide is a crime which, by its nature, will generally attract a very substantial custodial sentence. However, again like attempted murder, it is also a crime where occasionally the circumstances may justify considerable leniency. The illustrative cases which follow are intended to provide examples across the spectrum.

11–22a   **Mowles** *v.* **H.M. Advocate**, 1986 S.C.C.R. 117.
The accused was convicted of culpable homicide and sentenced to five years' imprisonment. The circumstances were that the accused was asked

by a friend to help to get two men out of a friend's house. The accused brought with him a defective shotgun which could not be fired by pressing the trigger but could be discharged accidentally if it were knocked against. The accused, having tried the trigger, believed the gun to be unloaded. When he reached the house he pointed the gun through the window at the men inside at which point someone took hold of the barrel, the gun went off, and the deceased was killed. On appeal it was held that the sentence was excessive in light of the appellant's reasonable belief that the gun was unloaded. The sentence was quashed, and a sentence of six months' detention was substituted. (In this case the High Court distinguished the case of *H.M. Advocate* v. *A.B.* (1887) 15 R.(J.) 30; 1 White 532, where in somewhat similar circumstances the accused was dismissed without penalty on the ground that in the present case there was an assault by presenting the weapon at the deceased.)

11–22b   Hillis v. **H.M. Advocate**, 1987 G.W.D. 11–364.
The accused and his cousin pled guilty to culpable homicide by striking the deceased with golf clubs. They had been chased and assaulted before reaching the accused's home and the deceased had then arrived outside to challenge them to a fight. They went to confront him taking the golf clubs "just in case." It was accepted that the fatal blow would not normally have caused severe injury and that both accused had expressed deep remorse. On appeal, and having regard to the whole circumstances, a sentence of seven years' imprisonment was reduced to one of four years' imprisonment.

11–22c   McLean v. **H.M. Advocate**, 1987 G.W.D. 17–639.
The accused was convicted of the culpable homicide of his wife by stabbing her with a knife (having originally been charged with murder). He had previously obtained two knives with which to threaten his wife who had been nagging at him continually. His appeal against a sentence of 12 years' imprisonment was refused, the court observing that the trial judge had been fully entitled to form the view that to obtain two knives indicated a high degree of culpability and callousness, and that he had been entitled to regard the offence as falling within the higher range of culpable homicide.

11–22d   Scott v. **H.M. Advocate**, 1988 G.W.D. 2–63.
The accused was convicted of culpable homicide involving the use of a knife. The deceased was unarmed, and the attack was unprovoked. A sentence of eight years' imprisonment was upheld on appeal.

11–22e   Munro v. **H.M. Advocate**, 1990 G.W.D. 5–259.
The accused was convicted of culpable homicide arising from a savage assault involving a fatal blow to the neck with a knife. On appeal it was held that a sentence of 10 years' imprisonment was not excessive notwithstanding that the accused had a minor record, there was a history of disagreement with the deceased, the deceased was a larger man, and the accused had had a lot to drink at the time.

11–22f   Potter v. **H.M. Advocate**, 1990 G.W.D. 21–1172.
The accused was convicted of the culpable homicide of his estranged wife by stabbing her nine times in an unprovoked incident. Since his

diminished responsibility through emotional turmoil and stress had already been taken into account in the reduction of the conviction from murder to culpable homicide, a sentence of nine years' imprisonment was held on appeal not to be excessive.

11–22g **Turner** *v*. **H.M. Advocate**, 1990 G.W.D. 22–1234.
Although there would be no significant danger to the public if the accused were to be released under supervision, the gravity of the offence had to be recognised and a sentence of five years' imprisonment for culpable homicide by discharging a loaded shotgun was upheld on appeal.

11–22h **L.T.** *v*. **H.M. Advocate**, 1990 S.C.C.R. 540.
Having been charged with murder, the accused was convicted of the culpable homicide of her two sons (aged 10 and 3) by setting fire to their home. On her appeal against a sentence of 10 years' imprisonment the High Court considered the possibility of a life sentence but, having heard psychiatric evidence, concluded that it was important for the appellant to have a goal to look forward to, and that she could only have such a goal if her sentence allowed her to calculate an expected release date. Consequently, the sentence originally imposed was appropriate and not excessive.

CULPABLY AND RECKLESSLY ENDANGERING LIFE AND HEALTH

11–23 There have been two significant cases in recent years in which the High Court was required to consider the appropriate sentence for the offence of culpably and recklessly endangering life and health. Both involved the supply by shopkeepers of solvents to be used for what is popularly known as "glue sniffing."

11–23a **Khaliq** *v*. **H.M. Advocate**, 1984 S.C.C.R. 212.
Two men were convicted of culpably and recklessly endangering the life and health of certain children by supplying them with glue sniffing kits. The men were unaware at the time that what they were doing was criminal. The trial judge took the view that their conduct merited a severe punitive and exemplary sentence and, having regard to the fact that the prosecution had been taken in the High Court, imposed sentences of three years' imprisonment. On appeal it was held (1) that it was wrong to be influenced by the fact that the prosecution had been taken in the High Court, (2) that the sentences gave insufficient weight to the appellants' belief that they were not acting illegally, and (3) that insufficient weight had been given to the fact that pleas of guilty had been tendered partly to avoid the children in question having to give evidence. The sentences were reduced to two years' imprisonment.

11–23b **Ulhaq** *v*. **H.M. Advocate**, 1990 S.C.C.R. 593.
The accused was convicted of culpably and recklessly endangering the lives of various adults by supplying them with a quantity of solvents. He was sentenced to two years' imprisonment, the sheriff taking the view that the age of the recipients was not relevant to sentence. On appeal, and distinguishing *Khaliq*, above, the court took the view that the age of the recipients *was* relevant to sentence. Moreover, in the present case, and unlike the situation in the earlier case, the accused had merely supplied

the solvents on their own, and not glue sniffing kits. Accordingly the sentence was quashed and 200 hours' community service were substituted.

DRUG OFFENCES

11–24 Since the early 1980s, when prosecutions for drug-related offences became common in Scottish courts, the High Court has consistently taken the view that such offences call for severe sentences. Although the court has recently tended to take a lenient view of cases involving simple possession of small amounts of cannabis (see, for example, *Grundison* v. *Brown* (1987); *Simpson* v. *Hamilton* (1988); *Anderson* v. *Lees* (1990), below—but see also *Kenmure* v. *Lowe* (1990)), it is clear that much more substantial penalties are considered appropriate for possession of larger amounts, especially where the possession is for the purpose of supplying to others, and even more so where that is done on a commercial basis. It now seems that a sentence of around four to five years' imprisonment is common in such cases (see, for example, *Varley* v. *H.M. Advocate* (1985); *McGowan* v. *H.M. Advocate* (1987); *McGregor* v. *H.M. Advocate* (1989)). In some cases, however, much higher sentences have been imposed (see, for example, *Lyall* v. *H.M. Advocate* (1990)). The High Court has recently made it clear that a serious view will be taken in cases involving the supply of drugs to persons in prison (see *Kerr* v. *H.M. Advocate* (1991)).

11–25 So far as Class A drugs (*e.g.* heroin, cocaine) are concerned, the approach of the High Court has not tended to leniency, even for cases of simple possession. For example, sentences of 21 months' imprisonment (*Money* v. *H.M. Advocate* (1988)) and three years' imprisonment (*Campbell* v. *H.M. Advocate* (1986)) have been upheld in simple possession cases, and in cases of supplying the court has said that four years' imprisonment is the minimum appropriate sentence (*Mullady* v. *H.M. Advocate* (1988)). An exemplary sentence of imprisonment may be appropriate for the possession of even a small amount of cocaine where the offence is the first of its kind in a particular district (*McCreadie* v. *Walkingshaw* (1990)).

11–26 Subject to the foregoing comments the following cases are offered as illustrations of the High Court's approach to sentencing for drug offences. For convenience the cases are arranged in relation to (1) Class A drugs, and (2) Class B drugs.

(1) Class A drugs

11–26a **McWilliams** v. **H.M. Advocate**, 1985 S.C.C.R. 419.
The accused pled guilty to supplying heroin to another. Both persons were addicts and the accused had shared his "fix." A sentence of three years' imprisonment was held on appeal to be severe but not excessive.

11–26b **Dowell** v. **H.M. Advocate**, 1986 G.W.D. 5–96.
The accused was convicted of being concerned in the supply of heroin. A sentence of 10 years' imprisonment and a fine of £1,000 were upheld on appeal.

11–26c **Campbell** v. **H.M. Advocate**, 1986 S.C.C.R. 403.
The accused was sentenced to three years' imprisonment for possession of cocaine. On appeal this was held not to be excessive.

11–26d **Andrew** v. **H.M. Advocate**, 1987 G.W.D. 11–366.
The accused pled guilty to possessing diamorphine with intent to supply to another. The quantity involved was relatively small and it was said that the accused intended to supply only to his co-accused. On appeal a sentence of four years' imprisonment was upheld, it being observed that a commercial dealer might receive a much longer sentence.

11–26e **Wilson** v. **H.M. Advocate**, 1987 G.W.D. 12–406.
The accused was convicted of dealing in a small quantity of heroin. It was accepted that he was an addict who dealt in small quantities to obtain money to feed his addiction. On appeal a sentence of seven years' imprisonment was reduced to four years, the Crown having accepted that the level of dealing was at the bottom of the scale.

11–26f **Walker** v. **H.M. Advocate**, 1987 S.C.C.R. 379.
The accused was convicted of possession of heroin and of Class B drugs with intent to supply. She had two previous convictions in 1977 for possessing drugs, and was sentenced to one year's imprisonment on each charge, the sentences to be consecutive. On appeal it was held that the sentences were inadequate for a person with previous drug convictions, and each sentence was increased to one of two years' imprisonment, but to run concurrently. The learned editor of *Scottish Criminal Case Reports*, in his commentary on this case, suggests that from the point of view of the appellant this might be described as a Pyrrhic defeat.

11–26g **Mullady** v. **H.M. Advocate**, 1988 S.C.C.R. 113.
The accused, who had previous convictions though none for drug offences, was convicted of possessing a quantity of lysergide, a Class A drug, valued at about £100, with intent to supply, and with offering to supply lysergide to a named person. He was sentenced to four years' detention on each offence, the sentences to be concurrent, and on appeal it was held that a sentence of four years is the minimum which is appropriate for trafficking in such drugs.

11–26h **Money** v. **H.M. Advocate**, 1988 S.C.C.R. 127.
The accused was convicted of possessing 580 milligrammes of heroin and was sentenced to 21 months' imprisonment. On appeal it was held that this sentence was severe but not excessive.

11–26i **Cunningham** v. **H.M. Advocate**, 1988 S.C.C.R. 514.
The accused was convicted of possessing a small quantity of heroin and other drugs (worth about £25) with intent to supply. It appears that the supply was of a non-commercial kind. On appeal it was held that a sentence of six months' imprisonment was not excessive. This case seems to be at the bottom end of sentencing severity for such an offence: *cf. Mullady* v. *H.M. Advocate*, above.

11–26j **Montes** v. **H.M. Advocate**, 1990 G.W.D. 32–1851.
The accused, along with another, was convicted on charges of importing and supplying cocaine with a street value of £2 million. On appeal it was held that a total sentence of 20 years' imprisonment was not excessive.

11–26k **McCreadie *v*. Walkingshaw**, 1990 S.C.C.R. 761.
The accused pleaded guilty to possessing cocaine, cannabis resin and amphetamine. The amount of cocaine was 0.1 gramme. The sheriff took the view that, as this was the first charge of possessing cocaine in the jurisdiction, it was important to impose a deterrent and exemplary sentence. He accordingly imposed a sentence of six months' imprisonment on that charge. An appeal against sentence was refused on the basis that this was not a case in which it would be appropriate to interfere with the sheriff's exercise of his discretion.

(2) Class B drugs
11–26l **Varley *v*. H.M. Advocate**, 1985 S.C.C.R. 55.
The accused was convicted of possessing, with intent to supply, cannabis resin with a street value of £2,500. On appeal a sentence of four years' imprisonment was held not to be excessive.

11–26m **Miller *v*. H.M. Advocate**, 1985 S.C.C.R. 314.
The accused, who was the mother of small children, was convicted of supplying a small amount of cannabis and of possession of cannabis to a value of between £360 and £600 with intent to supply. Having regard to the personal circumstances of the accused, a sentence of four years' imprisonment was reduced on appeal to one of three years' imprisonment.

11–26n **McNab *v*. H.M. Advocate**, 1986 S.C.C.R. 230.
The accused was convicted of offering to supply a small quantity of cannabis resin, with a value of about £40. On appeal it was held that a sentence of nine months' imprisonment was not excessive.

11–26o **McNeill *v*. H.M. Advocate**, 1986 S.C.C.R. 288.
The accused was convicted of importing about two-thirds of a ton of cannabis, and possession of cannabis, and was sentenced to 12 years' imprisonment. On appeal it was held that this was not excessive.

11–26p **McIntosh *v*. H.M. Advocate**, 1986 S.C.C.R. 496.
The accused was convicted of being concerned in the supply of cannabis resin, the evidence suggesting that the supply in question was on a large scale. On appeal it was held that a sentence of seven years' imprisonment was not excessive.

11–26q **Grundison *v*. Brown**, 1987 S.C.C.R. 186.
The accused, a first offender, pled guilty to possessing 226 milligrammes of cannabis resin, with a value of about 50 pence. On appeal it was held that a fine of £100 was excessive: an admonition was substituted.

11–26r **Wright *v*. Houston**, 1987 S.C.C.R. 674.
The accused was convicted of possessing cannabis resin with intent to supply, and of permitting cannabis to be smoked in his house. He had about £75 worth of the drug in his possession and also £360 of money. On appeal against concurrent sentences of 12 months' imprisonment it was held that the sentences were not excessive, the court observing that repeated warnings had been given by the courts about the serious view taken of offences of possession with intent to supply.

11–26s **McGowan** v. **H.M. Advocate**, 1987 G.W.D. 23–846.
The accused was convicted of various charges relating to the possession and supply of cannabis with a value of £1,850. On appeal it was held that sentences totalling four years' imprisonment were not excessive.

11–26t **Bennett** v. **H.M. Advocate**, 1987 G.W.D. 24–881.
The accused was convicted of possessing a Class B drug, with a value of £750, with intent to supply. On appeal a sentence of five years' imprisonment was held not to be excessive.

11–26u **Simpson** v. **Hamilton**, 1988 S.C.C.R. 163.
The accused, a first offender, pled guilty to possessing a very small amount of cannabis resin. On appeal it was held that a fine of £125 was excessive: an admonition was substituted (*cf. Grundison* v. *Brown*, above, but see *Cleland* v. *McLeod* and *Kenmure* v. *Lowe*, below).

11–26v **Cleland** v. **McLeod**, 1988 S.C.C.R. 509.
The accused, who were first offenders, were convicted of possessing 197 milligrammes and 1.2 grammes respectively of cannabis, and were each fined £125. Their appeals against sentence were refused.

11–26w **Hemphill** v. **H.M. Advocate**, 1989 S.C.C.R. 433.
The accused, who had no previous convictions for drug offences, was convicted of possessing 334 milligrammes of cannabis resin with intent to supply. On appeal a sentence of three years' imprisonment was held not to be excessive.

11–26x **McGregor** v. **H.M. Advocate**, 1989 G.W.D. 22–916.
The accused was convicted of possessing cannabis resin, with a street value of £5,600, with intent to supply. He had one previous conviction for possession and several for dishonesty and bail offences, and had just been released from prison. On appeal it was held that a sentence of five years' imprisonment was not excessive.

11–26y **Hudson** v. **H.M. Advocate**, 1990 S.C.C.R. 200.
The accused was convicted of possessing 426.48 grammes of cannabis with intent to supply. It appeared that the supply was not commercial but only to friends. On appeal it was held that a sentence of four years' imprisonment was not excessive. The facts in this case were similar to those in *Varley* v. *H.M. Advocate*, above, and it appears that the High Court's approach in such cases has remained consistent over a period of five years.

11–26z **Anderson** v. **Lees**, 1990 G.W.D. 3–122.
The accused, a 16-year-old first offender, was convicted of possessing cannabis with a value of £2. He had no independent means, but was fined £50. On appeal it was held that this was excessive, and an admonition was substituted.

11–26aa **Kenmure** v. **Lowe**, 1990 S.C.C.R. 367.
The accused, a first offender, was found guilty of possessing 1.17 grammes of cannabis, and was fined £40. In the course of the appeal the court was expressly referred to the cases of *Grundison* v. *Brown* and *Simpson* v. *Hamilton*, above, and made it clear that these cases are not to

be regarded as laying down a tariff. The appeal against sentence was refused.

11–26ab **Kennedy** *v*. **H.M. Advocate**, 1990 S.C.C.R. 417.
The accused was convicted of possessing small quantities of cannabis and lysergide, and was sentenced to 18 months' imprisonment. On appeal this was held to be excessive and a sentence of nine months' imprisonment was substituted.

11–26ac **Lyall** *v*. **H.M. Advocate**, 1990 G.W.D. 22–1237.
The accused was convicted of possessing 12 kilogrammes of cannabis resin, and of being concerned in its supply to others. He was the dominant leader of a highly organised drug-running operation. On appeal it was held that a sentence of 10 years' imprisonment was not excessive.

11–26ad **Kerr** *v*. **H.M. Advocate**, 1991 S.C.C.R. 774.
The accused was convicted of supplying £7 worth of cannabis resin and nine buprenorphine tablets (a Class C drug) to a prisoner whom he was visiting. He was sentenced to concurrent sentences of two years' and 18 months' imprisonment. On appeal it was held that the charges were very serious indeed notwithstanding the small quantities involved, and the appeal against sentence was refused (*cf. Ogilvie* v. *H.M. Advocate*, 1991 G.W.D. 37–2249).

Embezzlement and Fraud

11–27 Embezzlement and fraud may conveniently be grouped together for present purposes since they are both crimes which may involve elements of deception or breach of trust. The seriousness of such crimes can vary from the relatively trivial to the very grave, and consequently it would be impossible to set out appropriate types and amounts of sentence for all their different manifestations. However, the approach of the High Court in cases heard on appeal in recent years offers some guidance as to the factors which may properly be taken either as aggravating or as mitigating the seriousness of particular cases.

11–28 The fact that the proceeds of a fraud or embezzlement have been repaid to the victim prior to the date when an accused appears for sentence has been regarded as a significant mitigating factor in several cases (see, for example, *Dolan* v. *H.M. Advocate* (1986): *White* v. *H.M. Advocate* (1987); *Donaldson* v. *H.M. Advocate* (1987), below). Likewise, the fact that no loss has in fact been suffered by the victim may also be a mitigating factor (*MacDonald* v. *H.M. Advocate* (1986)).

11–29 In cases involving professional people, such as solicitors or accountants, defence lawyers often put forward as a mitigating factor the fact that the accused will in any event suffer other and different penalties by virtue of loss of reputation and inability to work in a professional capacity in future. It seems that, where the amount involved is substantial and has not been repaid, such additional penalties carry little weight (*Cameron* v. *H.M. Advocate* (1988); *Jeffrey* v. *H.M. Advocate* (1990)).

11–30 Where a crime of embezzlement or fraud has been persisted in over a prolonged period this is likely to be regarded as an aggravating factor (*Paterson* v. *H.M. Advocate* (1987); *Gray* v. *H.M. Advocate* (1991)), and as such it may counterbalance any mitigating factors, such as lack of previous criminal record, which are also present (*MacRae* v. *H.M. Advocate* (1987)).

11–31   In the absence of particularly aggravating factors the fact that an accused has no relevant criminal record may be a relevant mitigating factor, especially if other mitigating factors such as repayment are also present (*MacDonald* v. *H.M. Advocate* (1986); *White* v. *H.M. Advocate* (1987)). By contrast, the presence of a relevant record may be an aggravating factor (*Cameron* v. *H.M. Advocate* (1987)). The mere fact that an accused is a first offender may not of itself be regarded as a mitigating factor (*Ashgar* v. *H.M. Advocate* (1986)), and that may be particularly so where aggravating factors such as persistence are also present (*MacRae* v. *H.M. Advocate* (1987)). However, even in such a case a good background and a favourable community service report may indicate that a disposal other than a custodial one is appropriate (*Craig* v. *Lees* (1990)). The fact that a very large amount of money is involved need not necessarily be a particularly aggravating factor (*Simpson* v. *H.M. Advocate* (1988)).

11–32   A final point which should be made here is that from time to time it may be open to the prosecutor to charge a fraud either at common law or under a statute (for example, legal aid legislation). If he chooses the former course a court's sentencing powers may be significantly greater than they would have been if the offence had been charged under the statute. In that event, while there is no rule of law which states that the sentence should not exceed that provided for the statutory offence, it may at least be prudent and fair to keep the statutory maximum in mind when determining the appropriate sentence (*McGhee* v. *H.M. Advocate* (1987)). It is to be noted, however, that, where the maximum sentence for a comparable statutory offence has been increased after the date of commission of the common law offence in question, it is improper to take account of that increase when determining the appropriate sentence (*Reid* v. *H.M. Advocate*, 1990 S.C.C.R. 83, and see paragraph 9–40 above).

11–33   The following cases are examples which illustrate the general observations made above.

11–33a **Ashgar** *v.* **H.M. Advocate**, 1986 G.W.D. 2–31.
A 57-year-old first offender pled guilty to obtaining nearly £7,000 by various fraudulent representations to insurance companies, and to attempting to obtain a further £4,500 in total. This was held to be a deliberate, calculated and ingenious fraud and, in the circumstances, a sentence of six months' imprisonment was held not to be excessive notwithstanding that a community service place was available.

11–33b **MacDonald** *v.* **H.M. Advocate**, 1986 G.W.D. 3–48.
The accused, a first offender, was convicted of embezzling a sum of £7,147, and was fined £3,500 with the alternative of six months' imprisonment. The money had been used for short-term finance of building works, and at the end of the day the person from whom the money was embezzled sustained no loss and received interest on the money in question. The accused himself made no gain. In those

circumstances, and in view of a favourable social inquiry report, the court allowed an appeal against sentence and substituted a fine of £1,000.

11–33c **Rosie** *v.* **Hamilton**, 1986 G.W.D. 4–62.
The accused pled guilty to two charges, one of making a false report to the police that his house had been broken into and that property worth nearly £5,000 had been stolen, and the other of attempting to defraud an insurance company of the alleged loss. The accused had a bad record for crimes of dishonesty, but that record had come to an end with his marriage in 1979. He was sentenced to concurrent sentences of 90 days' and four months' imprisonment and, on appeal, it was held that these were not excessive in view of the accused's record and the detailed planning behind the offences.

11–33d **Dolan** *v.* **H.M. Advocate**, 1986 S.C.C.R. 564.
The accused, who was employed as an accountant by a local authority, embezzled over £23,000 in a period of six months. The money had been put into building society accounts, and had been repaid before the accused appeared in court. He was sentenced to 15 months' imprisonment but, on appeal, it was held that a custodial sentence was not necessary, and a fine of £3,000 was substituted. This case was followed in *White* v. *H.M. Advocate* (noted below).

11–33e **Cameron** *v.* **H.M. Advocate**, 1987 G.W.D. 1–19.
The accused pled guilty to a charge of fraud involving 12 separate incidents, over a period of eight days, of obtaining goods to a total value of £840 by fraudulently operating another person's cheque book. He had extensive previous convictions including similar offences, and had determinedly persisted in his conduct. In those circumstances it was held that a sentence of nine months' imprisonment was not excessive.

11–33f **Paterson** *v.* **H.M. Advocate**, 1987 G.W.D. 3–86.
The accused pled guilty to a charge of defrauding a crippled and trusting old man on 32 occasions over a period of 14 months to a total value of £7,915. On appeal it was held that a sentence of 12 months' imprisonment was not excessive.

11–33g **Dickson** *v.* **H.M. Advocate**, 1987 G.W.D. 9–279.
The accused, along with a co-accused, pled guilty to several charges involving fraudulently obtaining goods and services to values of £90,000 and £170,000, and to obtaining a loan of £64,000 to buy a house on the basis of false information. On appeal it was held that a sentence of six years' imprisonment was not excessive.

11–33h **White** *v.* **H.M. Advocate**, 1987 S.C.C.R. 73.
The accused, an architect, pled guilty to charges of theft and fraud involving around £20,000. He was sentenced to 18 months' imprisonment but appealed on the basis that he was a first offender, had a record of service to the community, was deeply ashamed, had experienced punishment by being struck off as an architect, and had, by the time of the appeal, repaid the money involved. In view of the repayment the sentence was quashed and a fine of £4,000 was substituted.

11–33i   **Donaldson** *v*. **H.M. Advocate**, 1987 G.W.D. 12–402.
The accused pled guilty to two charges, one involving fraudulently persuading a building society to lend £85,000, and the other involving a false claim to an insurance company in respect of allegedly stolen property to a value of £5,000. He was sentenced to five years' imprisonment but, on appeal, that was reduced to three years' imprisonment on the basis that all the money had been repaid to the building society and all the "stolen" items were available for sale.

11–33j   **McGhee** *v*. **H.M. Advocate**, 1987 S.C.C.R. 702.
The accused was convicted of obtaining legal aid by a common law fraud. He was fined £5,000. The maximum fine for the corresponding statutory offence was £1,000. On appeal his fine was reduced to £1,000.

11–33k   **MacRae** *v*. **H.M. Advocate**, 1987 S.C.C.R. 712.
The accused, who was a first offender aged 52, defrauded the DHSS of £3,500 over a period of two years by concealing the fact that his wife was working. Despite a good social inquiry report it was held on appeal that a sentence of nine months' imprisonment was not excessive.

11–33l   **Cameron** *v*. **H.M. Advocate**, 1988 G.W.D. 18–787.
The accused, who was a solicitor, was convicted of three charges of embezzlement to a total value of some £25,000. The recovery of some of that money was expected, but there would still be a substantial shortfall. On appeal against a sentence of two years' imprisonment it was accepted that, in view of the accused's calling and the high degree of trust expected from a person in her position, a custodial sentence was inevitable: and the appeal was refused.

11–33m   **Simpson** *v*. **H.M. Advocate**, 1988 G.W.D. 34–1429.
The accused was convicted of embezzling some £447,000, and was sentenced to four years' imprisonment. He received little direct financial benefit, although part of the money was applied to a shop of which he was a partner. His wife suffered from a malignant tumour, and spent most of her life in a wheelchair. In the circumstances it was concluded on appeal that the sentence was excessive. It was reduced to one of two years' imprisonment.

11–33n   **Currie** *v*. **Jessop**, 1989 G.W.D. 19–802.
The accused, a first offender aged 57, was convicted of obtaining £14,000 more than he was entitled to in benefits by making false statements regarding his earnings. He was unable to repay the money and was sentenced to three months' imprisonment. Despite the accused's circumstances and health, the sheriff considered that there was no alternative to custody because of the amount involved. An appeal against sentence was refused.

11–33o   **Craig** *v*. **Lees**, 1990 G.W.D. 5–260.
The accused, who was a first offender, was convicted of fraudulently obtaining £6,672.88 from the DHSS over a period of three years, and was sentenced to three months' imprisonment. He had led an otherwise blameless and useful life in the community, and there was a favourable community service report. On appeal it was held that the sheriff had not applied the proper test that no other disposal was appropriate. The

sentence of imprisonment was quashed and 150 hours' community service was substituted.

11–33p   Jeffrey *v*. H.M. Advocate, 1990 G.W.D. 11–579.
The accused, a solicitor, obtained £251,420 from a bank by falsely representing that clients required bridging loans on seven occasions spread over a period in excess of one year. The net amount of loss was £136,000. On appeal it was held that a sentence of five years' imprisonment was not excessive since the accused had taken advantage of his professional status and the trust of the bank's officers.

11–33q   Gray *v*. H.M. Advocate, 1991 G.W.D. 6–314.
The accused, who was a chartered accountant, duped 20 small investors over a period of seven years, and embezzled some £61,900 from them. On appeal it was held that a sentence of two years' imprisonment was not only not excessive but was lenient.

11–33r   McLean *v*. H.M. Advocate, 1991 S.C.C.R. 972.
The accused, who was a motor trader, pleaded guilty to seven charges of selling cars with false odometer readings. As a result he had received an increase in the price of each car, averaging about £700 per car. He was sentenced to nine months' imprisonment, and his appeal against sentence was refused, the court observing that public interest and confidence in the motor trade required that a serious view be taken of such offences.

Possession of Offensive Weapon

11–34   The High Court has consistently taken the view that contraventions of section 1 of the Prevention of Crime Act 1953 are serious offences, and that courts should endeavour by their sentences to deter people from carrying offensive weapons in public places. However, the court has also made it clear that every case must be considered according to its own facts and circumstances, and that it is wrong to adopt, or to come close to adopting, a policy that every contravention of the Act must be met by a custodial sentence (see *Jacobs* v. *Wilson* (1989), below). The following cases illustrate how different facts and circumstances can justify different sentences.

11–34a   Addison *v*. MacKinnon, 1983 S.C.C.R. 52.
The accused was convicted of possessing a four-foot-long piece of wood with a jagged edge which he waved about while shouting gang slogans. He was a first offender and was described in the social inquiry report as a quiet and pleasant boy. On appeal against a sentence of three months' detention it was held that not enough attention had been given to the fact that the accused was a first offender. The sentence of detention was quashed and a fine of £100 was substituted.

11–34b   O'Rourke *v*. Lockhart, 1984 S.C.C.R. 322.
The accused was seen by the police running in the street, bleeding at the mouth, and brandishing a knife. According to him he had been assaulted by others and had gone home and collected the knife. His previous record included six convictions for breach of the peace. He was sentenced to 60 days' imprisonment. On appeal it was held that too little attention had

been paid to the antecedents of the offence, and too much to previous record. The sentence of imprisonment was quashed and a fine of £250 was substituted. (The court in this appeal was a particularly authoritative one, consisting of the Lord Justice-General (Lord Emslie), the Lord Justice-Clerk (Lord Wheatley), and Lord Ross.)

11–34c **Smith** v. **Wilson**, 1987 S.C.C.R. 191.
The accused, who was a first offender, pled guilty to having a flick knife with him in a car. Despite favourable reports the sheriff imposed a sentence of three months' imprisonment on the view that it was the responsibility of the court to deter those who are minded to carry knives as weapons, and to demonstrate emphatically that carrying a knife will not be tolerated. On appeal the court considered that in this case, unlike the situation in *Addison* v. *MacKinnon*, above, the sheriff had given full and adequate reasons for deciding that a custodial sentence was necessary. The appeal was refused.

11–34d **Kane** v. **H.M. Advocate**, 1988 S.C.C.R. 585.
Following arrest on a theft charge the accused was found to have a Stanley knife in an inside pocket. In respect of the charge of possessing an offensive weapon he was sentenced to four months' detention consecutive to a sentence of two years' detention for the theft. An appeal against sentence was refused.

11–34e **Jacobs** v. **Wilson**, 1989 S.C.C.R. 9.
The accused, who was a first offender, pled guilty to having a butcher's knife with a 10-inch blade in his possession in the street at 4 a.m. He stated that he had been chased by two youths, had run into the house and come out with the knife, whereupon the youths had run off. The sheriff, referring to *Smith* v. *Wilson*, above, sentenced the accused to three months' imprisonment. On appeal it was held (1) that the sheriff might be seen as having fettered his discretion and had come close to suggesting that all contraventions of the 1953 Act should be dealt with by a custodial sentence; and (2) that *Smith* v. *Wilson* was distinguishable because the weapon in the present case was not *per se* offensive, and by the time of the accused's arrest the need to use it had disappeared. The sentence of imprisonment was quashed, and an order for 120 hours' community service was substituted. (The facts of this case may be compared with those of *O'Rourke* v. *Lockhart*, above, though that case was not referred to in the opinion of the court.)

RAPE AND OTHER SEXUAL OFFENCES

11–35 For crimes of rape, as for other serious offences, a substantial custodial sentence will normally be the only appropriate penalty. A sentence of three years' imprisonment for that crime has been described as "lenient" (see *Henry* v. *H.M. Advocate* (1988), below), while particularly aggravating circumstances such as the use of excessive violence (*Martin* v. *H.M. Advocate* (1987)), or the fact that the victim was very young (*Martin* v. *H.M. Advocate* (1989); *Sweeney* v. *H.M. Advocate* (1990)) may justify sentences of up to 10 years' imprisonment.

11–36 Sexual offences other than rape can take many forms and so attract many kinds of disposal. At one extreme a minor case of indecent exposure may merit no more than a small fine (in the absence of indications that psychiatric treatment may be desirable), while at the other extreme gross sexual abuse, albeit falling short of rape, may justify a sentence on a par with that appropriate for serious cases of rape (*O.* v. *H.M. Advocate* (1989)). It is not possible within the confines of a book such as this to give examples of every kind of sexual offence, but the illustrations which follow may offer some guidance as to the way in which a representative range of offences has been dealt with. Cases of rape are listed first, followed by cases involving other sexual offences.

(1) Rape

11–36a   **Martin** v. **H.M. Advocate**, 1987 G.W.D. 17–642.
The accused was convicted of the repeated rape of a woman involving violence, threats, and the use of a knife. In the circumstances it was held that a sentence of 10 years' imprisonment could not be regarded as excessive.

11–36b   **Henry** v. **H.M. Advocate**, 1988 G.W.D. 18–789.
The accused was convicted of the rape of a friend of his wife. Both the complainer and the accused's wife were members of a close church community, and it was at the insistence of the church leaders that the matter was reported. The complainer would not herself have reported the offence, and it was suggested that her distress was at the committal of adultery rather than rape. In refusing an appeal against a sentence of three years' imprisonment it was held that the unusual circumstances were reflected in the lenient sentence imposed by the trial judge.

11–36c   **Doherty** v. **H.M. Advocate**, 1988 G.W.D. 39–1616.
The accused was convicted of the rape of a 19-year-old girl and was sentenced to seven years' imprisonment. He had not been in serious trouble before, had not used any weapon, and there was no evidence of material injury to the complainer. However, the trial judge described the rape as amounting to a brutal, prolonged and sadistic act. On appeal it was held that the sentence was severe but not excessive.

11–36d   **Martin** v. **H.M. Advocate**, 1989 G.W.D. 13–559.
The accused was convicted of using lewd and libidinous behaviour towards, and the attempted rape of, a 10-year-old girl. His appeal against a sentence of seven years' imprisonment was refused, the court observing that the charges were extremely serious particularly with regard to the complainer's age and the accused's actings.

11–36e   **Sweeney** v. **H.M. Advocate**, 1990 G.W.D. 25–1385.
The accused was convicted of lewd and libidinous practices and two charges of rape involving a continuous course of conduct for over a year with children aged seven and four. In imposing a sentence of 10 years' imprisonment the trial judge described the case as one of the worst cases of sexual abuse of children he had had to deal with, and said that he would have imposed 12 years had the accused not pled guilty to avoid the children having to give evidence. On appeal it was held that the sentence was not excessive.

(2) Other sexual offences

11–36f　**Penman** v. **MacPhail**, 1987 S.C.C.R. 563.

The accused was convicted of indecently assaulting another man by feeling his private parts while they were both in a motor lorry. He was fined £500 and appealed against sentence arguing that a social inquiry report recommendation in favour of probation should have been followed. The court held that there were no good reasons for saying that the accused required the advice or help of a social worker, and that the sheriff had been right to take the view that the accused ought to be seen to receive an immediate and appropriate penalty which would mark the gravity of the offence.

11–36g　**Mitchell** v. **Carmichael**, 1988 S.C.C.R. 222.

The accused, a 23-year-old first offender in employment, was convicted of indecently assaulting a 16-year-old girl, who was a stranger to him, in the street. He pulled her to the ground and placed his hand inside her trousers and blouse, but she sustained no injury. On appeal against a sentence of 60 days' imprisonment it was held that the accused did not deserve a custodial sentence since he had a stable background, a permanent job, and no previous convictions. A fine of £500 was substituted.

11–36h　**Curley** v. **H.M. Advocate**, 1989 G.W.D. 23–958.

The accused was convicted of indecent assault involving pushing the complainer to the floor, threatening her, sitting on her, removing her clothing, handling her, and forcing her to masturbate him. His record included a five-year sentence for robbery and a seven-year sentence for culpable homicide. On appeal against a sentence of 10 years' imprisonment it was held that the assault was a particularly revolting one, but that 10 years was more appropriate to a violent rape. Sentence was reduced to one of six years' imprisonment.

11–36i　**O.** v. **H.M. Advocate**, 1989 G.W.D. 26–1154.

The accused, a 53-year-old first offender, was convicted of lewd, indecent and libidinous behaviour involving the gross abuse, between 1970 and 1976, of his daughters, then aged one and a half and eight years old, respectively. On appeal it was held that a sentence of seven years' imprisonment was not excessive.

ROAD TRAFFIC OFFENCES

11–37　Since this chapter is primarily concerned with the discretionary aspects of sentencing no attempt is made here to deal with those aspects of sentencing for road traffic offences which are primarily, or wholly, matters of law, for example what may or may not amount to special reasons for not endorsing or not disqualifying. Such matters are dealt with in Chapter 5 above. On the other hand, matters which are primarily, though not necessarily exclusively, matters of discretion such as, for example, what may or may not amount to "exceptional hardship" in "totting-up" disqualification cases are dealt with in this part of this chapter.

11–38　In what follows common road traffic offences are dealt with separately.

Since many of the cases which are cited involve offences committed prior to the coming into force of the consolidating road traffic statutes in 1988, offences are for convenience referred to by their popular names, such as "careless driving" or "speeding," rather than by the statutory provisions under which they arise. Furthermore, all the cases which are listed below involve offences under the law prior to the Road Traffic Act 1991. It is thought that most of them will continue to be of relevance even under the new law when it comes into force.

(1) Causing death by reckless driving

11–39   The reported cases relating to causing death by reckless driving sharply focus two issues which arise in relation to other road traffic offences as well. These are the use of maximum penalties, and the propriety of taking into account the fact that an offender had been drinking prior to committing a road traffic offence not itself associated with the consumption of alcohol.

11–40   So far as the use of maximum penalties is concerned it has been held that they should be imposed only for the worst possible cases (see *Earnshaw* v. *H.M. Advocate* (1981); *Shields* v. *H.M. Advocate* (1987); *Mahmood* v. *H.M. Advocate* (1988), below). Logically, this is an impossible test since a court can never be sure that a given case, however bad, is actually the worst possible example of that particular offence. It is therefore submitted that in practice a court should consider imposing a maximum sentence only where the circumstances of the offence are very bad indeed, or possibly where the offence is a bad one of its kind and the offender has analogous previous convictions.

11–41   So far as the consumption of alcohol is concerned the High Court has said on many occasions that, when sentencing for an offence which is not itself a drink-related one, it is improper to take alcohol into account and to increase the sentence for that reason. This is particularly so where there is no evidence about the consumption of alcohol, and the court is merely speculating that it may have played a part in the commission of the offence (see, for example, *Brown* v. *McLeod*, 1981 S.C.C.R. 254, a case of failing to stop after an accident). However, the court has also held that it is improper to allow the consumption of alcohol to influence sentence for a non-drink-related offence even where there is evidence about the consumption of alcohol or there is a conviction for a separate drink-driving offence committed on the same occasion (*Cooper* v. *H.M. Advocate* (1982); *Anderson* v. *H.M. Advocate* (1987), below).

11–42   With all respect to the High Court the logic of this approach is not immediately apparent. In relation to other offences, such as assault, courts at all levels, including the High Court, frequently say that the consumption of alcohol prior to committing the offence is not merely not a mitigating factor but may indeed be an aggravation. By the same token if a driver, by the consumption of alcohol, has voluntarily put himself in a position where he is more likely to drive recklessly or carelessly, it is difficult to see why a court should be obliged to close its eyes to that aspect of the offence. Indeed, even the High Court itself appears to have been prepared to contemplate the possibility of making a distinction between cases where drink is involved and those where it is not (see *Mahmood* v.

H.M. Advocate, below, distinguishing *Shields* v. *H.M. Advocate*; and see *Hawthorn* v. *Jessop*, 1991 S.C.C.R. 674).

11–43   Probably the best explanation for the approach generally adopted by the High Court is that, since drink-related offences may themselves be prosecuted and punished under the Road Traffic Acts, it would be improper and unfair to put a person at risk of, in effect, being punished twice for the same offence. Indeed, the court has also held that, when sentencing for a drink-related offence, it is improper to take into account the manner of the offender's driving (*Lindsay* v. *Jessop*, 1987 S.C.C.R. 512; but *cf. Hawthorn* v. *Jessop*, above). In the result, then, the position is that drink-related offences must be considered on their own with, as a rule, no notice being taken of the offender's driving, and driving offences, such as reckless or careless driving, must also be considered on their own with no notice being taken of any alcohol consumed by the offender prior to the commission of that offence. However, it is suggested that, because of the enforced separation of the two kinds of offence, it would be reasonable for a court to consider imposing consecutive sentences where drink and driving offences occurring at the same time are charged on the same indictment or complaint notwithstanding the general rule that sentences for offences arising out of the same incident ought to be concurrent (see paragraph 7–52, above).

11–44   So far as the type and level of sentence for causing death by reckless driving are concerned, the normal consequence of a conviction is likely to be a custodial sentence. However, the length of that sentence appears to be influenced to a considerable extent by whether or not a case is prosecuted in the High Court. For cases prosecuted in the High Court sentences of two and three years' imprisonment have been approved on appeal whereas for cases prosecuted in the sheriff court sentences of nine or 12 months' imprisonment have been reduced on appeal to six months notwithstanding that—at least so far as can be discerned from the reports—the quality of recklessness and, needless to say, the consequences of that recklessness are not obviously very different.

11–45   The following cases are illustrative of the comments made in the foregoing paragraphs.

11–45a   **Earnshaw** *v.* **H.M. Advocate**, 1981 S.C.C.R. 279.
A driver drove an articulated lorry down a hill and took a left-hand bend so fast that he lost control and collided with a car causing the death of three occupants. He was sentenced to five years' imprisonment (the maximum) and was disqualified for 10 years. On appeal it was held that his speed was just above that at which control would be lost. Consequently, his recklessness had not been of the highest degree, and the sentence of imprisonment was reduced to three years.

11–45b   **Cooper** *v.* **H.M. Advocate**, 1982 S.C.C.R. 87.
By driving recklessly the accused caused the death of a close friend. An averment in the indictment of impairment through alcohol was withdrawn, but evidence was led of a blood alcohol concentration of 113 milligrammes per 100 millilitres of blood. Taking the view that alcohol had affected what took place the sheriff imposed a sentence of 12 months' imprisonment and disqualified the accused for six years. On appeal it was held that the sheriff had misdirected himself in his view of the part played

by alcohol. The sentence of imprisonment was quashed and a fine of £1,000 was substituted.

11–45c **Salusbury-Hughes** *v.* **H.M. Advocate**, 1987 S.C.C.R. 38.
The accused, aged 25 and with no significant previous convictions, was convicted of causing death by reckless driving. He had been giving some friends a lift and drove along a winding road erratically and at speeds between 60 and 80 m.p.h., ignoring requests from a passenger to slow down. He approached a dangerous bend at such speeds, went on to the wrong side of the road, and collided head-on with another car, killing one of his own passengers, and injuring everyone else in the two cars. On appeal it was held that a sentence of four months' imprisonment could not on any view be regarded as excessive.

11–45d **Anderson** *v.* **H.M. Advocate**, 1987 S.C.C.R. 529.
The accused, aged 23, was convicted of causing death by reckless driving, and also of driving with more than the prescribed limit of alcohol in his blood. He had driven at speeds in excess of 100 m.p.h. as a result of which his car went out of control, travelled along the top of a dyke, and overturned throwing a friend, who was a passenger in the car, on to the road. His friend was killed. In passing a sentence of nine months' imprisonment on the charge of causing death by reckless driving the sheriff made it clear that, in doing so, he was taking account of the alcohol in the accused's blood. On appeal it was held that the sheriff had not been entitled to take that matter into account, and the sentence was reduced to one of six months' imprisonment. (This case has been followed in other cases involving offences other than causing death by reckless driving, for example, *McParland* v. *Wilson*, 1988 S.C.C.R. 158; *Brown* v. *Wither*, 1990 G.W.D. 5–276; but see *Hawthorn* v. *Jessop*, 1991 S.C.C.R. 674, and para. 11–54 *et seq.* below.)

11–45e **Shields** *v* **H.M. Advocate**, 1987 S.C.C.R. 706.
The accused was convicted of causing death by reckless driving, and of driving while unfit through drink or drugs. He had driven at speeds of up to 60 m.p.h. in a built-up area, failed to take a slight left-hand bend, and crossed the road and struck and killed a pedestrian on or near the pavement. On appeal against a sentence of five years' imprisonment on the charge of causing death by reckless driving it was held that the maximum sentence should be confined to the worst possible cases, and that this case did not fall into that category. The sentence was reduced to one of three years' imprisonment.

11–45f **Mahmood** *v.* **H.M. Advocate**, 1988 G.W.D. 31–1343.
The accused was convicted of causing death by reckless driving and was sentenced to five years' imprisonment. He had driven at between 50 and 70 m.p.h. in Bishopton and had knocked down and killed a nine-year-old girl on a zebra crossing. He was 22 years of age and had worked to build up a business. He had one previous conviction for assault but had favourable references. On appeal it was held that the trial judge had not referred to the accused's personal circumstances. Furthermore, on comparison with *Shields* v. *H.M. Advocate*, above, where drink was involved, two years' imprisonment was the appropriate sentence.

11–45g   **Douglas** *v.* **H.M. Advocate**, 1990 S.C.C.R. 188.
The accused was convicted of causing death by reckless driving having overtaken a lorry in bad weather and collided with an oncoming car, killing its driver. On appeal against a sentence of 12 months' imprisonment it was held that the sheriff had erred in regarding this as an example of recklessness at the upper scale of such conduct, and the sentence was reduced to one of six months' imprisonment.

11–45h   **Ross** *v.* **H.M. Advocate**, 1991 S.C.C.R. 781.
The accused, who was 28 years of age, was convicted of causing the deaths of two young boys by reckless driving. Some two miles after attempting to overtake in the face of oncoming traffic, the accused took a bend at excessive speed and collided with an oncoming car in which the two young boys were passengers. The social inquiry report recommended community service, but the accused was sentenced to one year's imprisonment with 10 years' disqualification and an order to resit the driving test. An appeal against sentence was refused.

11–45i   **Russell** *v.* **H.M. Advocate**, 1991 S.C.C.R. 790.
The accused, a first offender aged 19, was convicted of causing the death of a girl aged 12 who was crossing the road in a built-up area. She was struck by a car driven by the accused at a speed in excess of 58 m.p.h. The social inquiry report recommended community service, but the accused was sentenced to one year's detention. He was also disqualified for five years, and ordered to resit the driving test. On appeal it was held that the sentence of detention was not excessive. However, it was also held that, having regard to the absence of previous convictions and the substantial penalty of detention, no good purpose would be served by a period of disqualification as long as five years. The disqualification was reduced to two years, and the order to resit the driving test was quashed.

(2) Reckless driving

11–46   Reckless driving on its own, and which has not caused a death, is normally prosecuted summarily with the result that the usual penalties are short periods of imprisonment or fines, and periods of disqualification. The penalty in a given case will of course depend on the particular facts and circumstances of that case but, it is submitted, it is rare to find a case of reckless (as opposed to careless) driving which does not attract some period of disqualification even where that is discretionary rather than obligatory. (Under Part 1 of Schedule 2 to the Road Traffic Offenders Act 1988 disqualification for a reckless driving offence is obligatory only where that offence has been committed within three years of a previous conviction under section 1 or section 2 of the Road Traffic Act 1988.)

11–47   The following examples give an indication of the sentences which have been approved by the High Court in recent years for offences of reckless driving.

11–47a   **Weston** *v.* **Houston**, 1988 G.W.D. 5–214.
The accused was convicted of reckless driving involving a 13-mile chase with a police vehicle along the M74 at speeds of up to 105 m.p.h. He was fined £100 and disqualified for one year, and appealed against the

disqualification on the ground that insufficient weight had been given to the fact that he ran an accident recovery service, was on call 24 hours a day, and was the only holder in south-west Scotland of certain licences for the recovery of heavy goods vehicles and chemical carriers. The appeal was refused on the basis that these matters had been before the sheriff, and that the accused's appalling driving justified the disqualification.

11–47b   **Cameron** *v.* **Jessop**, 1988 G.W.D. 8–340.
The accused was convicted of taking and driving away a motor vehicle, and of reckless driving involving a 30-mile chase by the police during which time the accused attempted to ram the police and forced others off the road. Holding that this was one of the worst cases to come up for a long time the court, in respect of the reckless driving charge, refused an appeal against a sentence of six months' detention and disqualification for 10 years.

11–47c   **Gale** *v.* **Walkingshaw**, 1988 G.W.D. 9–383.
The accused, who had previous convictions in 1984 for speeding and for failing to stop after an accident, was convicted of reckless driving. He had driven at excessive speeds and with "complete disregard to the public," had failed to stop at a police road check, and had caused a police officer to jump out of his way. He was fined £1,200 and disqualified for 18 months. In refusing his appeal the court held that in all the circumstances, including the need for a deterrent sentence for failing to stop at the road check, the sentence was not excessive: the accused might have received a custodial sentence.

11–47d   **Rowan** *v.* **Howdle**, 1989 G.W.D. 15–656.
The accused was convicted of reckless driving involving driving a motorcycle at speeds of up to 115 m.p.h. He was fined £250 and disqualified for one year. On appeal the court held that the sheriff's approach to disqualification could not be criticised in view of the seriousness of the charge, the excessive speeds, the accused's lack of experience, and the nature of the road.

11–47e   **Kelly** *v.* **Webster**, 1989 G.W.D. 38–1777.
The accused was convicted of reckless driving. He had been chased by the police for over 100 miles at speeds up to 90 m.p.h., committing numerous offences on the way, and had passed through three police road blocks. He was sentenced to four months' imprisonment, and was disqualified for three years and ordered to resit the driving test. On appeal it was held that those sentences were not excessive, the sheriff having taken account of the fact that the accused was a first offender by not imposing the maximum sentence.

11–47f   **Noblett** *v.* **Valentine**, 1990 G.W.D. 17–982.
The accused, a 22-year-old first offender, was convicted of reckless driving, and was fined £350 and disqualified for two years. While attempting to overtake in the face of oncoming traffic she had cut in front of the leading car, hit the kerb, lost control, and collided with two oncoming cars, seriously injuring herself and another driver. On appeal it was held that the sentence was substantial but not excessive.

11–47g   **Morrison** v. **Valentine**, 1990 S.C.C.R. 692.
The accused had been sitting in his car with another man's wife when her husband came on the scene. After an altercation the accused drove off with the husband on the bonnet of his car, trying to stop him. After about 30 yards the husband slid off sustaining some injury. The accused was fined £100 and disqualified for six months but, on appeal, it was held that, in the unusual circumstances of the case, disqualification was excessive, and 10 penalty points were substituted.

11–47h   **Ross** v. **H.M. Advocate**, 1991 S.C.C.R. 105.
The accused pleaded guilty to 15 charges of theft of or from cars and to a charge of reckless driving. The reckless driving occurred when he was driving a stolen car and was trying to escape from a pursuing police car. He drove in the middle of a narrow country road at speeds of 70 and 90 m.p.h., causing other vehicles to swerve to avoid a collision. He also drove at high speed through a residential estate where children were playing. He was sentenced to two years' detention on the theft charges and to a further six months' detention on the reckless driving charge. His appeal against sentence was refused, it being observed that the reckless driving charge might well have merited a much longer sentence.

(3) Careless driving
11–48   Since careless driving is an offence for which a court may, at its discretion, impose disqualification from driving, it is important to have some awareness of the circumstances in which that penalty may be appropriate. In that regard the High Court has stated on several occasions in recent years that disqualification is appropriate only in more than usually serious cases (see, for example, *Malpas* v. *Hamilton* (1988); *Griffin* v. *McLeod* (1989); *Jenkins* v. *Docherty* (1990), below).

11–49   It is also now clear that the critical factor for determining penalty in careless driving cases is the nature and quality of the offender's driving and not the consequences of that driving, save to the extent that the consequences of the driving may relevantly illuminate its nature and quality. This is particularly so where a consequence of the driving has been the death of another road user (*McCallum* v. *Hamilton* (1986); *Sharp* v. *H.M. Advocate* (1987); *Pringle* v. *Allan* (1987); *Watson* v. *Jessop* (1990)).

11–50   In the case of offences such as careless driving, where disqualification is a discretionary penalty, it seems to have become normal practice in recent years for the High Court to increase the financial penalty on occasions where a discretionary period of disqualification is being quashed or reduced on appeal (see, for example, *Saunders* v. *MacGillivray* (1985); *Livingstone* v. *Smith* (1988); *Haworth* v. *Carnegie* (1990); *Ballantine* v. *Carmichael* (1990); *Urquhart* v. *Hingston* (1990)). The court has also given limited approval to the converse situation, that is to say increasing a period of disqualification where an offender's limited means preclude the imposition of a fine of sufficient amount to mark the gravity of the offence (*Lee* v. *Brown* (1990)). Since the practice of increasing a fine to compensate for not disqualifying now appears to be commonplace in the High Court when hearing appeals, it is submitted that a judge at first instance should be entitled to adopt the same approach. Thus, if he was persuaded in a border-line case not to impose disqualification, he would be entitled to impose a higher than normal fine; and if, in a case where he was in any event going to impose disqualification, the offender's means were insufficient to allow a fine commensurate with the gravity of the offence, he would be entitled to impose a larger than normal period of disqualification.

11–51   The ratio for the foregoing approach appears to be fairly clear and satisfactory. It is that, since in appropriate cases a fine and a period of disqualification are together the total penalty for an offence such as careless driving, the way in which these two elements are allocated towards that total penalty can be flexible, and can take account of the circumstances of a particular offence or, more importantly, a particular offender. However, it is submitted that courts must use this approach to total penalty with some care since in all cases the amount of a fine ought not to exceed what it is reasonable for a particular offender to pay having regard to his means so far as these are known to the court. Consequently, if a court is minded to increase the amount of a fine to compensate for some leniency in the matter of disqualification, it should do so only with due regard to the particular offender's means. For the foregoing reasons it is also submitted that courts should be cautious about following the approach approved, albeit tentatively, in the case of *Lee* v. *Brown* (above). If a particular offender's means are insufficient to entitle a court to impose a fine above a certain amount, it is arguable that for that offender a fine of that amount is as much of a penalty as a larger fine would be for an offender whose means are greater. If that is right, there seems to be some injustice in saying that the poorer offender requires a longer period of disqualification than his richer brother just because the court is precluded from imposing a higher fine.

11–52   The following cases are illustrative of the observations made in the foregoing paragraphs.

11–52a **Donaldson** v. **Aitchison**, 1985 S.C.C.R. 43.
The accused was convicted of careless driving involving pulling out to overtake a number of cars and forcing an oncoming car to brake and swerve to avoid a collision. She had seven-and-a-half years' driving experience and a clean licence. Unknown to the sheriff the lack of a licence was likely to affect her ability to accept a promoted post which she hoped to obtain. On appeal against a fine of £150 and disqualification for six months it was held that the offence merited disqualification, but that in view of the accused's personal circumstances the period should be reduced to three months.

11–52b **Melville** v. **Lockhart**, 1985 S.C.C.R. 242.
The accused, a 23-year-old first offender, pled guilty to driving carelessly in that he drove a car at speeds of up to 80 m.p.h. in a 40 m.p.h. limit, failed to stop when directed to do so by the police, and drove on the wrong side of the road. His explanation was that he was returning from a wedding at which he had had a small amount to drink and that he panicked on seeing the police car because he needed his licence for a car-hiring business he had recently started. On appeal against a disqualification for three years it was held that an act of such total irresponsibility justified protecting the public against its recurrence and

that, althought the period of disqualification was long, it was not excessive.

11–52c   Saunders *v*. MacGillivray, 1985 S.C.C.R. 385.

The accused, who was a professional lorry driver with one previous conviction for careless driving and two for speeding, pled guilty to careless driving by overtaking another vehicle on the approach to a blind corner, so causing a collision between that vehicle and one coming from the opposite direction. The sheriff took the view that the offence was at the top limit of careless driving, and had it in mind to disqualify the accused for three to six months. In the light of representations that disqualification would lead to the appellant losing his job he restricted the period of disqualification to two months, and imposed a fine of £100. On appeal it was held that while it might have been difficult to say that a significant period of disqualification would have been wrong, the sheriff had exercised his discretion irrationally by limiting the disqualification to two months, and that the protection afforded to the public by such a disqualification was small in relation to the accused's loss of livelihood. The fine and disqualification were both quashed and a fine of £400 and an endorsement with five penalty points were substituted. (This seems to be the first reported example of the High Court increasing a fine where disqualification is quashed.)

11–52d   Rodger *v*. Wilson, 1986 S.C.C.R. 260.

The accused, who had previous convictions for road traffic offences one of which, in 1975, resulted in a period of disqualification of seven years, pled guilty to careless driving involving losing control of his car which then crossed the road and struck a rocky outcrop beyond the pavement on the far side of the road. The car was then reversed and abandoned by the accused. On appeal against disqualification for 12 months it was held that, given the accused's record, a period of disqualification was necessary, but that a period of 12 months was excessive. The period was reduced to one of six months.

11–52e   McCallum *v*. Hamilton, 1986 S.L.T. 156; 1985 S.C.C.R. 368.

The accused was charged on summary complaint that he had driven a car without due care and attention and had collided with another car which then mounted the footpath striking and injuring one pedestrian and striking and fatally injuring another. The relevancy of the averments relating to the consequences of the collision were challenged, but the sheriff repelled the objection. On appeal it was held, Lord Robertson dissenting, that the word "fatally" should be deleted from the complaint since otherwise it might be thought that the fact that death had resulted from the driving was a factor to be considered in determining the appropriate sentence, which would be an improper consideration.

11–52f   Pringle *v*. Allan, 1987 G.W.D. 6–198.

The accused pled guilty to careless driving and was fined £250 and disqualified for one year. On appeal he submitted that the sheriff should not have taken into account that he had earlier taken drink or that the collision had killed one of his passengers. The appeal was allowed. Only the standard of driving was relevant and the accused had not been charged with a drink related offence. For a bad case of careless driving four months' disqualification was appropriate.

11–52g **Sharp** *v.* **H.M. Advocate**, 1987 G.W.D. 12–431.
The accused was charged with contravention of section 1 or alternatively section 3 of the Road Traffic Act 1972. He was found guilty on the careless driving charge and was fined £250 and disqualified for one year. In imposing the sentence the sheriff had had regard to the death of the victim. On appeal it was held, following *McCallum* v. *Hamilton*, above, that this was improper, and the period of disqualification was reduced to six months.

11–52h **Malpas** *v.* **Hamilton**, 1988 S.C.C.R. 546.
The accused, a first offender, was convicted of careless driving following an incident where she struck a pedestrian with her car. The pedestrian was seriously injured and subsequently died. She was fined £200 and disqualified for six months. On appeal against the disqualification the court observed that "it is only in a more than usually serious case of a contravention of the section that disqualification will be imposed." The order for disqualification was quashed and an order made for endorsement with five penalty points.

11–52i **McCrone** *v.* **Normand**, 1988 S.C.C.R 551.
The accused was convicted of careless driving consisting of reversing a mobile shop into an area used by children as a playground. He collided with, and killed, a 16-month-old child who was playing behind his vehicle. He was not disqualified but appealed against a fine of £400. In reducing the fine to £100 the court observed that the sheriff might have allowed himself to be influenced by the fact that a death had resulted, which was wrong, and further that the driving in this case did not fall below the standard of a reasonably prudent motorist to a very large degree.

11–52j **Griffen** *v.* **McLeod**, 1989 G.W.D. 15–654.
In this case it was held that three months' disqualification was appropriate in a careless driving case where a high degree of lack of care had been shown.

11–52k **Owens** *v.* **McNaughtan**, 1990 S.C.C.R. 355.
The accused, who had a clean licence, pled guilty to careless driving after losing control of his car on a left-hand bend in bad weather and colliding with two cars on his wrong side of the road. He was fined £500 and his licence was endorsed with nine penalty points. On appeal it was held that the fine was not excessive, but that, although this was a bad piece of driving, that had been taken into account to some extent by the size of the fine, and accordingly the number of penalty points was reduced to seven.

11–52l **Jenkins** *v.* **Docherty**, 1990 G.W.D. 13–713.
The accused was convicted of careless driving involving moving his bus forward while a traffic light was still red, causing a minor collision with a van. In quashing a disqualification for six months and substituting endorsement with seven penalty points, the court observed that this case was at the lower end of careless driving cases, and disqualification was therefore inappropriate.

11–52m Watson v. Jessop, 1990 G.W.D. 29–1688.
The accused was convicted of careless driving consisting of failing to stop at a give way sign and causing a serious accident. In allowing an appeal against the imposition of nine penalty points, and reducing the number to six, the court observed that the justice had wrongly taken into account the consequences of the offence rather than the culpability of it.

(The following cases, though, not involving careless driving offences, are offered as further examples where the High Court has increased a fine on removing a disqualification or reducing the number of penalty points, and vice versa. These cases are noted briefly.)

11–52n Livingstone v. Smith, 1988 S.C.C.R. 468.
Fine of £75 and endorsement with eight penalty points: on appeal penalty points reduced to five and fine increased to £150.

11–52o Haworth v. Carnegie, 1990 G.W.D. 16–917.
Fine of £250 and disqualification for six months: on appeal disqualification quashed, three penalty points substituted, and fine increased to £400.

11–52p Ballantine v. Carmichael, 1990 G.W.D. 27–1576.
Fine of £75 and disqualification for six months: on appeal disqualification quashed, nine penalty points substituted, and fine increased to £250.

11–52q Lee v. Brown, 1990 G.W.D. 28–1635.
Held on appeal that 18 months' disqualification for a drink driving offence was not excessive. The sheriff was entitled, in taking into account the accused's ability to pay a monetary penalty, to impose more than the minimum disqualification instead of increasing the monetary penalty.

11–52r Urquhart v. Hingston, 1990 G.W.D. 28–1641.
Fine of £100 and disqualification for six months: on appeal disqualification quashed, three penalty points substituted, and fine increased to £400.

(4) Drink related offences

11–53   The main sentencing problems in connection with drink related offences appear to concern the use of imprisonment; disqualification for more than the minimum period in cases where disqualification is obligatory; and the use of disqualification at all in cases where it is only discretionary. Cases decided by the High Court in recent years offer some guidance on all of those matters.

11–54   In determining whether or not imprisonment is appropriate for a drink related offence much will depend on the nature of the offence charged, the gravity of the particular offence, and the accused's previous record particularly, but not necessarily, for analogous offences. Where the offence charged is one of driving with excess alcohol it has been said to be wrong to equiparate it with the offence of driving while unfit (see *Mercer* v. *Wilson* (1988), below). It has also been held to be inappropriate to take account of the consumption of alcohol where the charge is one of failing to provide a specimen (*McParland* v. *Wilson* (1988)), but that case has since been disapproved (*Hawthorn* v. *Jessop* (1991)). So far as previous record is concerned it has been held that a very bad record, albeit not for road traffic offences, may justify a custodial sentence (*Goldie* v. *Tudhope* (1986)). The High Court has upheld a sentence of imprisonment for a first offender even where the offence was not particularly serious of its kind (*Donnelly* v. *Hamilton* (1987)). However, as a general rule the High Court tends to uphold a sentence of imprisonment only where the offender has previous analogous convictions, and where these are quite recent (*Doolan* v. *Lockhart* (1987); *Shirlaw* v. *Wilson* (1988); *Giordano* v. *Carmichael* (1990); *Marshall* v. *Carmichael* (1990); *Weddle* v. *Carmichael* (1991)). However, the ability to pay a large fine may enable an offender to escape an otherwise deserved sentence of imprisonment (*McLean* v. *MacDougall* (1989)).

11–55   In cases where a minimum disqualification for 12 months is obligatory, questions may sometimes arise as to the circumstances in which it may be appropriate to impose more than that minimum period of disqualification. Where a person has a serious drink problem a disqualification substantially in excess of the minimum may be appropriate but disqualification for life is probably inappropriate except perhaps in a case where the accused refuses to acknowledge the existence of the problem (*Beattie* v. *Ingram* (1986), distinguishing *Wiseman* v. *Hillary* (1981)). In cases involving driving with an excess of alcohol in the blood the amount of that excess may justify a disqualification for more than the minimum period (*Harvie* v. *Cardle* (1986); *Doolan* v. *Lockhart* (1987)). On the other hand, where the circumstances of the offence do not disclose any danger to the public, it has been held to be inappropriate to disqualify for more than the minimum period notwithstanding that the alcohol level was more than twice the permitted level (*Wright* v. *Tudhope* (1986)). At first sight the foregoing authority appears to be at odds with the case of *Lindsay* v. *Jessop* (1987 S.C.C.R. 512) where the High Court held that it was improper for a sheriff, when sentencing on a charge of driving with excess alcohol, to take account of the accused's bad driving and so increase the period of disqualification. If the absence of danger is a reason for not imposing more than the minimum disqualification, it is difficult to see why bad driving should not have the opposite effect. However, that apparent conflict appears to have been resolved, at least up to a point, in the later case of *Robertson* v. *Wilson* (1988 G.W.D. 15–678) where the court appears to have stated that, where an accused is very substantially over the limit, a court is entitled to conclude that the risks created by his driving were of a general nature and to take them into account. Even where the charge is one of failing to provide specimens for analysis rather than of driving with an excess of alcohol a period of disqualification longer than the minimum may be justified if there is evidence that the accused was heavily intoxicated at the material time (*Jamsheed* v. *Walkingshaw* (1989); *Hawthorn* v. *Jessop* (1991)). In the absence of such evidence it may be inappropriate to disqualify for more than the minimum period (*Hynd* v. *Guild* (1986), but see *Reynolds* v. *Tudhope* (1987)).

11–56   So far as the relevance of previous convictions is concerned the High Court has adopted much the same position in relation to periods of disqualification as in relation to the imposition of imprisonment, that is to say that previous convictions, albeit analogous, which are more than 10 years old ought not to influence the length of the period of disqualification (*Lockerby* v. *MacDougall* (1988); *Macpherson* v. *Ingram* (1990)).

11–57   In respect of cases where disqualification is merely discretionary there appears to be little general guidance from the High Court. However, the court had said that it is the "usual practice" to impose penalty points rather than disqualification for offences of failing to give a roadside breath test (*MacMillan* v. *Scott* (1988)).

11–58   The following cases are illustrative of the comments made in the foregoing paragraphs. For convenience they are arranged in the same order as those paragraphs, that is to say (a) cases dealing with imprisonment, (b) cases dealing with disqualification for more than the minimum period, and (c) cases dealing with discretionary disqualification.

(a) Cases dealing with imprisonment

11–58a   **Goldie** v. **Tudhope**, 1986 S.C.C.R. 414.
The accused pled guilty to failing to provide specimens of breath for analysis. He had a large number of previous convictions which had led on eight occasions to custodial sentences. But he had no previous convictions for road traffic offences. Taking the view that the accused was committed to a life of lawbreaking the sheriff imposed the maximum sentence of six months' imprisonment. On appeal it was held that the sheriff was entitled to treat the offence as an illustration of the behaviour of someone who cares nothing for the observance of the law in general, but that he had gone too far in imposing the maximum sentence which was reduced to one of three months' imprisonment.

11–58b   **Donnelly** v. **Hamilton**, 1987 S.C.C.R. 313.
The accused, a 53-year-old first offender, pled guilty to driving with about twice the permitted amount of alcohol. Taking the view that this was a case of a man consciously driving a vehicle after consuming a considerable quantity of alcohol with foreseeable consequences, the sheriff imposed a sentence of three months' imprisonment and disqualification for a period of three years. On appeal it was held that the sheriff was entitled to impose that sentence, and the appeal was refused.

11–58c   **Doolan** v. **Lockhart**, 1987 G.W.D. 12–434.
The accused pled guilty to driving with about one-and-a-half times the permitted amount of alcohol. He had been convicted of three previous contraventions of the same section of the Road Traffic Act since 1985. An appeal against a sentence of six months' imprisonment, disqualification for 10 years, and an order to resit the driving test was described as being without merit.

11–58d   **McParland** v. **Wilson**, 1988 S.C.C.R. 158.
The accused, a first offender, pled guilty to failing to provide specimens of breath for analysis. The accused's solicitor informed the court that the accused had had a considerable amount to drink and knew that he should not have been driving. On appeal against a sentence of three months' imprisonment it was held that the sheriff had misdirected himself by having regard to the accused's consumption of alcohol and that

imprisonment was inappropriate. A fine of £100 was substituted. (This case has now been disapproved: see *Hawthorn* v. *Jessop* (1991) below.)

11–58e **Mercer** v. **Wilson**, 1988 S.C.C.R. 214.
The accused pled guilty to driving with an alcohol level about three times the prescribed limit. He had no significant record and a social inquiry report recommended a fine. He was sentenced to three months' imprisonment and, in his report to the High Court, the sheriff referred to the dangers of driving while under the influence of drink. On appeal it was held that the sheriff had wrongly approached this case as if he were dealing with a case of driving while unfit through drink or drugs, and that he had paid insufficient attention to the accused's background. The sentence of imprisonment was quashed, and the case was continued for a community service report.

11–58f **Shirlaw** v. **Wilson**, 1988 S.C.C.R. 225.
The accused pled guilty to driving with an alcohol level more than three times the prescribed limit. He had a previous conviction for the same offence in 1974. He was sentenced to three months' imprisonment and was disqualified for four years. On appeal it was held that the sentence was excessive having regard to the accused's circumstances and to the fact that his previous conviction was more than 10 years old. A fine of £750 and disqualification for three years were substituted.

11–58g **McLean** v. **MacDougall**, 1989 S.C.C.R. 625.
The accused pled guilty to driving with excess alcohol (nearly three times the limit). He had a previous conviction for a similar offence in 1986. At the date of sentence he was unemployed. He was sentenced to 60 days' imprisonment and was disqualified for six years. By the date of his appeal he had obtained employment at an annual salary of £10,000 which he would lose if imprisoned. In allowing the appeal against the sentence of imprisonment, and substituting a fine of £1,000, the High Court expressly stated that no criticism could be made of the reasoning and the conclusion reached by the sheriff, but that the accused's changed circumstances justified the appeal being allowed. (This appears to be an extreme example of the High Court operating as a court of review rather than as a court of appeal (see para. 8–99 above). The case also appears to support the view that at first instance a wealthier offender might be able to avoid a deserved sentence of imprisonment by paying a large fine instead; but presumably the High Court would not normally support such a policy.)

11–58h **Marshall** v. **Carmichael**, 1990 S.C.C.R. 58.
The accused pled guilty to driving with an alcohol level about three times the prescribed limit. He had analogous previous convictions in 1973 and 1976, and was sentenced to six months' imprisonment. On appeal it was held that the sentence was excessive since the last conviction was more than 13 years earlier. A sentence of 150 hours' community service was substituted.

11–58i **Giordano** v. **Carmichael**, 1990 S.C.C.R. 61.
The accused pled guilty to driving with an alcohol level of just under three times the prescribed limit. She had previous convictions for the same offence in 1981 and 1983, and was sentenced to 60 days' imprisonment.

On appeal it was held that the sheriff had been entitled to impose that sentence having regard to the recent analogous convictions and the quantity of alcohol involved in the present charge.

11–58j   **Weddle** *v*. **Carmichael**, 1991 S.C.C.R. 64.
The accused pled guilty to failing to provide specimens for analysis. He had previous convictions for drink/driving offences in 1984 and 1985. He was a family man and was in employment, earning £23,000 a year. A sentence of three months' imprisonment was upheld on appeal, the court observing that courts must take a strong and firm view about drink/ driving offences.

(b) Cases dealing with disqualification for more than the minimum period

11–58k   **Wiseman** *v*. **Hillary**, 1981 S.C.C.R. 103.
The accused pled guilty to driving with nearly three times the permitted amount of alcohol. He had one previous conviction for a similar offence. A medical report described him as having been an excessive drinker for four years who would not seek medical advice. A disqualification for life was held not to be harsh and oppressive, it being observed that he could apply for restoration of his driving licence after five years if by then he could show that he was no longer likely to be a danger to the public.

11–58l   **Beattie** *v*. **Ingram**, 1986 S.C.C.R. 38.
The accused pled guilty to driving with slightly more than the permitted amount of alcohol. He had a serious drink problem but, although he had held a driving licence for 17 years, he had no previous road traffic convictions. An appeal against a disqualification for life was allowed, and disqualification for six years was substituted. The case of *Wiseman* v. *Hillary*, above, was distinguished on the basis that in the present case the accused was making a determined, and apparently successful, effort to control his drinking problem. Account was also taken of the absence of previous convictions and the small amount of excess over the permitted alcohol limit.

11–58m   **Harvie** *v*. **Cardle**, 1986 S.C.C.R. 41.
The accused pled guilty to driving with more than twice the permitted amount of alcohol. He had been driving for about a year at the time. On appeal against a disqualification for two years it was held that this was not excessive given the circumstances of the offence.

11–58n   **Hynd** *v*. **Guild**, 1986 S.C.C.R. 406.
The accused pled guilty to failing to provide specimens of breath for analysis. There was no evidence as to the accused's actual state of intoxication at the time but the sheriff took the view that the offence must attract more than the minimum disqualification so as not to place the offender in a better position than someone who gave samples which contained twice the permitted level and who would be disqualified for more than the minimum period. He disqualified the accused for two years. On appeal it was held that the sheriff's approach was totally erroneous; that each case must be looked at in the light of all the relevant circumstances; and that in the present case there were no factors

justifying disqualification in excess of the minimum period of one year (*cf. Reynolds* v. *Tudhope*, below).

11–58o Wright v. **Tudhope**, 1986 S.C.C.R. 431.
The accused pled guilty to driving with more than twice the permitted amount of alcohol. The circumstances did not disclose any danger to the public. An appeal against a disqualification for two years was allowed, and a disqualification for one year was substituted. The ground on which the appeal was allowed related in part to the accused's personal circumstances and in part to the fact that there was nothing in the justice's report to suggest that the way in which the accused was driving his vehicle at the time constituted a danger to the public.

11–58p Reynolds v. **Tudhope**, 1987 S.C.C.R. 340.
The accused pled guilty to failing to provide specimens of breath for analysis. The stipendiary magistrate disqualified for 18 months on the ground that "this type of quite deliberate action is heard about far too often in these courts." On appeal it was held that the magistrate was entitled to take the view he did. The case of *Hynd* v. *Guild*, above, was distinguished by the court.

11–58q Lindsay v. **Jessop**, 1987 S.C.C.R. 512.
The accused pled guilty to driving with between three and four times the permitted level of alcohol. The procurator fiscal told the sheriff that the accused's car had nearly collided with a bus and had also nearly struck two persons on a pedestrian crossing at which he failed to stop. The sheriff took account of the nature of the driving and disqualified the accused for three years. On appeal it was held that, in taking account of the nature of the accused's driving, the sheriff had taken into account a consideration which should not have been before him since there was no charge of reckless or careless driving. The court considered that the matter of disqualification was at large; that a period of disqualification in excess of the minimum was appropriate having regard to the level of alcohol; and that a period of two years should be substituted. (This case is distinguished in *Robertson* v. *Wilson*, below. For the converse situation, *i.e.* the impropriety of considering consumption of alcohol when sentencing for reckless driving, see *Cooper* v. *H.M. Advocate*, 1982 S.C.C.R. 87; *Anderson* v. *H.M. Advocate*, 1987 S.C.C.R. 529, noted in para. 11–45 above.)

11–58r Robertson v. **Wilson**, 1988 G.W.D. 15–678.
The accused was convicted of careless driving and of driving with four-and-a-half times the permitted level of alcohol. He was admonished on the careless driving charge, and on the drink charge he was sentenced to three months' imprisonment and disqualified for three years. On appeal he submitted, by reference to *Lindsay* v. *Jessop*, above, that the sheriff had been unduly influenced by factors relevant only to the careless driving charge. Although the court allowed the appeal in relation to the sentence of imprisonment, *Lindsay* v. *Jessop* was distinguished in that, since the accused was four-and-a-half times over the limit, the sheriff was entitled to conclude that the risks created by his driving were of a general nature and to take them into account.

11–58s **Lockerby** *v*. **MacDougall**, 1988 S.C.C.R. 471.
The accused pled guilty to driving with about one-and-a-half times the permitted level of alcohol. He had a previous conviction for the same offence just over 10 years earlier. The sheriff imposed a disqualification for two years partly because the level of alcohol was more than just marginally over the limit, and partly because of the previous conviction. On appeal the court held that the level of alcohol, although more than marginally over the limit, was not *per se* sufficiently high to justify a longer period than the minimum; and that the previous conviction was too old to justify being taken into account. A period of one year's disqualification was substituted. (This case was followed in *Macpherson* v. *Ingram*, below.)

11–58t **Jamsheed** *v*. **Walkingshaw**, 1989 S.C.C.R. 75.
The accused pled guilty to failing to provide specimens of breath for analysis, to reckless driving, and to resisting the police. He had been seen driving erratically at excessive speed, and his appearance when stopped by the police indicated that he was heavily intoxicated. On the charge of failing to provide specimens he was fined £500 and disqualified for three years. On appeal it was held that the sheriff had been entitled to take into account the evidence about the accused's state of intoxication, and the appeal against sentence was refused.

11–58u **Macpherson** *v*. **Ingram**, 1990 S.C.C.R. 452.
The accused pled guilty to driving with about three times the permitted level of alcohol. He had a previous conviction for a drink/driving offence just over 10 years earlier. The sheriff indicated that he would normally have imposed a two-year disqualification, but in view of the previous conviction he imposed disqualification for three years. On appeal, and by reference to *Lockerby* v. *MacDougall*, above, the court quashed the disqualification and substituted a period of two years.

11–58v **Hawthorn** *v*. **Jessop**, 1991 S.C.C.R. 674.
The accused, who had no previous road traffic convictions, was convicted of failing to provide specimens of breath for analysis. Evidence was given that the accused was very drunk and, taking that into account, the sheriff disqualified him for three years. In his appeal against that disqualification the accused sought to rely on *McParland* v. *Wilson* (1988) above, but a bench of five judges disapproved of that case and held that the intention of Parliament would be frustrated if a court was to be unable to gauge the gravity of the offence by reference to evidence of the extent of the accused's unfitness to drive or of his intoxication. The cases of *Hynd* v. *Guild* (1986) and *Jamsheed* v. *Walkingshaw* (1989), above, were approved, and *Cooper* v. *H.M. Advocate*, (1982) and *Anderson* v. *H.M. Advocate* (1987), also above, were distinguished.

(c) Cases dealing with discretionary disqualification

11–58w **MacMillan** *v*. **Scott**, 1988 S.C.C.R. 219.
The accused pled guilty to failing to provide a specimen of breath for a roadside test, an offence for which disqualification is discretionary and not obligatory. He was fined £100 and disqualified for six months. On appeal it was held that there was no reason for the sheriff deviating from

"the usual practice" of imposing penalty points in such a case. The disqualification was quashed and endorsement with four penalty points was substituted.

(5) Driving while disqualified

11–59   The offence of driving while disqualified is always regarded as a serious one involving, as it does, a conscious flouting of an order of the court. Consequently, even a first offence of driving while disqualified may attract a substantial penalty (see, for example, *Elrick* v. *Jessop* (1990), below), and, where the offence is committed only a short time after a disqualification has been imposed, a custodial sentence may be appropriate, even for a first offence of driving while disqualified (*McMullen* v. *Lockhart* (1987)). Where an offender has previous convictions for the same offence, a custodial sentence appears to be the normal outcome (see the other cases noted below).

11–60   The following cases are illustrative of the approach taken by the High Court in recent years.

11–60a **McGivern** v. **H.M. Advocate**, 1986 G.W.D. 2–38.
     The accused pled guilty to a charge of driving while disqualified. He had 10 previous convictions for the same offence, and was sentenced to 15 months' imprisonment and disqualified for life. On appeal it was accepted that the maximum sentence for this offence is 12 months' imprisonment. The sentence of imprisonment was reduced to one of 12 months to take account of that, but otherwise the appeal was refused.

11–60b **McMullen** v. **Lockhart**, 1987 G.W.D. 1–46.
     The accused was convicted of, among other things, driving while disqualified, he having been disqualified only two months earlier. An appeal against a sentence of 30 days' detention and disqualification for five years was refused, the court observing that the the sheriff had been entitled to conclude that the accused was an utterly heedless young man.

11–60c **Courtney** v. **McKinnon**, 1987 G.W.D. 1–47.
     The accused was convicted of driving while disqualified and was sentenced to four months' imprisonment. He had been disqualified for five years for a similar offence five months previously. He claimed that imprisonment would have disastrous consequences for his wife (with whom he was in business) and family, and pointed to a favourable social inquiry report. His appeal against sentence was refused, the court observing that a second offence so soon after a previous conviction could hardly result in a sentence other than custodial.

11–60d **Cherry** v. **Walkingshaw**, 1989 S.C.C.R. 256.
     The accused pled guilty to driving while disqualified. He had a previous conviction for the same offence in relation to which he had been given a suspended sentence of imprisonment some three months previously. An appeal against a sentence of two months' imprisonment was refused, the court expressing the view that the legislature might wish to consider whether the penalties which this offence attracts are adequate.

11–60e **Lamont** v. **H.M. Advocate**, 1990 G.W.D. 5–280.
     The accused was convicted of driving while disqualified. He had three

previous convictions for the same offence, two of which had resulted in custodial sentences. An appeal against a sentence of 12 months' imprisonment, a fine of £250, and disqualification for 10 years was refused.

11–60f **Elrick** *v.* **Jessop**, 1990 G.W.D. 24–1361.
The accused was convicted of driving while disqualified. He had two previous convictions for driving with more than the permitted amount of alcohol. He had promised to take his 10-year-old son to a football match but the travel arrangements had fallen through at short notice. He decided to drive the short distance of three or four miles rather than disappoint his son. He was fined £1,000 and disqualified for seven years. On appeal it was held that this was not excessive, the accused having made a deliberate and conscious decision to drive in the full knowledge that he would be committing two statutory offences (the second being that of driving without insurance).

(6) Failing to stop after an accident, and failing to report an accident
11–61 A series of cases reported in the last 10 years has laid down a number of principles to be taken into account by a court which is considering the possibility of imposing disqualification for these offences. Rather than describing each case individually, it is sufficient to list those principles as follows.

(a) Although in such cases a court will often suspect that the driver has been drinking, it is improper to speculate that that is the case, and to disqualify as a result (*Brown* v. *McLeod*, 1981 S.C.C.R. 254; *Croll* v. *Smith*, 1982 S.C.C.R. 292; *McNamee* v. *Carmichael*, 1985 S.C.C.R. 289).

(b) If no acceptable explanation is offered as to why an offender failed to stop, or to report the accident, a disqualification may be justified (*Corps* v. *Lowe*, 1990 G.W.D. 23–990; *Eagleson* v. *McGlennan*, 1990 G.W.D. 23–991).

(c) Considerations of morality are not relevant in fixing the penalty for an offence whose object is the provision of information (*Morrison* v. *Haughney*, 1984 S.C.C.R. 315).

(d) If failure to stop is attributable to panic, but is then followed by a course of active concealment, a charge of failing to report the accident may be much more serious than the charge of failing to stop (*Morrison* v. *Haughney*, above).

(e) If failing to stop after an accident is an offence which is prevalent, disqualification may be justified (*Paterson* v. *MacNeill*, 1982 S.C.C.R. 141).

(f) If the failure to stop deprives a property owner of a chance to arrange reparation, disqualification may be justified (*Croll* v. *Smith*, above).

(g) If, however, a driver stops and gives at least some information from which he can be identified, disqualification may be inappropriate (*Lawson* v. *Ingram*, 1981 S.C.C.R. 240).

(h) If an offender can pray in aid substantial mitigating factors of a personal nature, disqualification may be inappropriate (*Kindlen* v.

Smith, 1981 S.C.C.R. 19; *Jackson* v. *Smith*, 1982 S.C.C.R. 138; *Thomas* v. *Lowe*, 1991 S.C.C.R. 943).

(7) Speeding

11–62   As a general rule the two matters which will be of primary concern to a court dealing with a speeding offence will be the amount of the fine that is to be imposed, and whether or not to impose a period of disqualification. As to the amount of the fine it is not uncommon for courts to apply a tariff of so much per mile per hour that the offender was driving over the permitted maximum speed. In the interests of maintaining consistency of approach as between drivers who have exceeded the limit by differing amounts this seems to have much to commend it; and, although the High Court has never expressly stated a view on this, it has sustained a fine which appears to have been calculated on the basis of £10 for each mile per hour that the offender was over the limit (see *Taylor* v. *Cardle* (1988), below). However, courts should, it is submitted, be wary of adopting rigid practices which may hamper their discretion and disable them from adequately considering the facts and circumstances of individual cases (*cf. Hynd* v. *Guild*, 1986 S.C.C.R. 406, noted in paragraph 11–58, above). Moreover, it is submitted that a tariff scale which is appropriate for one speed limit may be inappropriate for another. For example, an offence of driving at 20 miles per hour over the limit where that limit is 30 miles per hour may be much more serious than an offence of exceeding a 70 miles per hour limit by the same amount, and consequently it may not be appropriate to impose identical fines in these two cases.

11–63   So far as disqualification is concerned the High Court has shown a reluctance to sustain such sentences, and appears to have taken the view that penalty points are normally the appropriate sentence unless, by an accumulation of such points, the offender has exposed himself to a "totting-up" disqualification (*Longmuir* v. *Carmichael* (1990), or where a period of disqualification is justifiable as a deterrent and exemplary sentence (*Leslie* v. *McNaughton* (1991)).

11–64   The following cases are offered as illustrations of the foregoing observations.

11–64a   **Buchan** v. **Ingram**, 1987 S.C.C.R. 509.
The accused pled guilty to driving at 99 m.p.h. in a 60 m.p.h. area, and was fined £50 and disqualified for six months. He had one previous conviction for speeding, in 1984, and was a salesman who needed to travel by car and who would lose his job if disqualified. On appeal the disqualification was quashed and an endorsement with three penalty points was substituted.

11–64b   **Perryman** v. **MacDougall**, 1988 S.C.C.R. 24.
The accused pled guilty to driving at 107 m.p.h. on a stretch of the A74 road where the speed limit was 70 m.p.h. He was 21 years of age, recently married with a baby, and needed a driving licence for his job. He was fined £100 and disqualified for six months. On appeal it was held that a period of disqualification was required in the public interest but that the period selected by the sheriff was excessive in light of its consequences on the accused and his family. Disqualification for three months was substituted.

11–64c   **Clark** *v*. **MacDougall**, 1988 S.C.C.R. 53.
The accused pled guilty to driving at 110 m.p.h. on a stretch of the A74 road where the speed limit was 70 m.p.h. He was a first offender who employed 15 people and needed his licence for his business. He was fined £100 and disqualified for three months. On appeal it was held that the hardship caused by the disqualification was out of proportion to the public advantage which a short period of disqualification would attract. The disqualification was quashed and endorsement with three penalty points was substituted. The point of distinction between this case and that of *Perryman* v. *MacDougall*, above (which does not seem to have been cited to the court—possibly because it had not by then been reported) appears to be that in this case disqualification would have had serious consequences not only for the accused but also for his business and employees.

11–64d   **Taylor** *v*. **Cardle**, 1988 S.C.C.R. 450.
The accused pled guilty to driving at 58 m.p.h. in an area where the speed limit was 30 m.p.h. He had one previous conviction for an analogous offence in 1983, and had been offered the opportunity to pay a fixed penalty of £24. He was fined £280 (which appears to represent £10 for each mile per hour over the limit), and an appeal against that sentence was refused, though some adjustment was made to the arrangements for paying by instalments.

11–64e   **Longmuir** *v*. **Carmichael**, 1990 S.C.C.R. 522.
The accused pled guilty to driving at 47 m.p.h. in an area where the speed limit was 30 m.p.h. He had two previous convictions for speeding as a result of which there were six penalty points endorsed on his licence. He was fined £50 and disqualified for six months, and appealed against the disqualification. In imposing the disqualification the sheriff had expressed the view that he regarded a third speeding conviction within a few years as a serious matter. However, the court quashed the disqualification, observing that Parliament has laid down that in the normal case for a speeding offence a fine and penalty points will be appropriate unless the number of points exceeds 12. In any event, in this case there did not seem to be any particular reason why the accused should have been disqualified. Endorsement with three penalty points was substituted.

11–64f   **Murray** *v*. **McGlennan**, 1991 S.C.C.R. 18.
The accused, a first offender, who earned £177 per week, pled guilty to driving at 85 m.p.h. in a 60 m.p.h. limit. He was fined £250 and, in his report, the sheriff stated that speeding was rife on the stretch of road in question. On appeal it was held that in the circumstances the sheriff was entitled to impose a severe penalty, even on first offenders, and the appeal was refused.

11–64g   **Leslie** *v*. **McNaughton**, 1991 S.C.C.R. 32.
The accused pled guilty to driving at 104 m.p.h. in a 70 m.p.h. limit. He was fined £300 and disqualified for six months, the sheriff referring in his report to the prevalence of speeding and fatal accidents on the stretch of road in question. On appeal it was held that it is competent to impose a short period of disqualification in a suitable case for

punitive and deterrent purposes. However, in the present case mitigating circumstances indicated that disqualification for six months was too long, and the period was reduced to three months.

11–64h **Patrick *v*. McGlennan**, 1991 S.C.C.R. 100.
The accused pled guilty to driving at 73 m.p.h. in a 50 m.p.h. limit. Taking account of the prevalence of accidents on the stretch of road in question the justice imposed a fine of £250. On appeal it was held that, although a judge can take into account local knowledge, it must be done with moderation and discretion. The fine was reduced to £75. (It is a little difficult to reconcile this decision with *Murray* v. *McGlennan*, above, the offences in each case having occurred on virtually the same stretch of the A77 road.)

(8) Disqualification under "totting-up" provisions
11–65 Section 19 of the Transport Act 1981 (now section 35 of the Road Traffic Offenders Act 1988) introduced a new totting-up procedure under which offenders against the Road Traffic Acts fall to be disqualified for a minimum period of six months when the number of qualifying points on their driving licences amounts to 12 or more. The new procedure has given rise to many appeals to the High Court, especially in relation to what does or does not amount to "exceptional" hardship as a ground for refraining from imposing what is otherwise an obligatory disqualification. Cases dealing with that matter are noted later.

11–66 There have also been a few appeals which have helped to clarify some of the other parts of the legislation, and their effect can best be noted by setting out some principles and rules of law which courts must follow when dealing with such cases. These are as follows.

(a) It is incompetent to make a totting-up disqualification consecutive to any other disqualification imposed on the same occasion (*Middleton* v. *Tudhope*, 1986 S.C.C.R. 241).

(b) When representations are made to a court to the effect that the court ought not to impose an otherwise obligatory disqualification, it is for the accused to put proper material before the court so that it can be satisfied or otherwise as to the validity of the submissions; and, where an appeal follows, the sentencing judge should state clearly in his report to the High Court what representations were made to him, and explain what view he took of them (*McFadyen* v. *Tudhope*, 1986 S.C.C.R. 712).

(c) When a request is made by an accused to allow a proof in mitigation, and that request is concurred in by the procurator fiscal, it is incumbent on the court to allow it to take place (*Kyle* v. *McNaughton*, 1990 S.C.C.R. 450).

(d) When considering the imposition, or the length, of a totting-up disqualification a court should not use that disqualification to mark the gravity of the instant offence. The proper course is to determine the appropriate penalty for the offence and then, if the penalty involves the endorsement of penalty points such as to bring the offender within the totting-up provisions, to consider the question of disqualification under those provisions (*Briggs* v. *Guild*, 1987 S.C.C.R. 141; *Gray* v. *Jessop*, 1988 S.C.C.R. 71).

11–67   In the reports of the last two cases mentioned above the learned editor of the *Scottish Criminal Case Reports* sets out the terms of subsection (6) of the statutory provision which provides that, in considering a possible totting-up disqualification, "no account is to be taken of (*a*) any circumstances that are alleged to make the offence or any of the offences not a serious one." However, that provision is not referred to in the opinion of the court in either of the cases, and it is submitted that the provision in question has nothing to do with the decision reached by the court in those cases. Subsection (6) sets out certain matters which a court is prohibited from taking into account when considering whether or not there are circumstances which *mitigate* the normal consequences of the conviction, that is to say obligatory disqualification. By contrast, in the cases cited above the court is in effect saying that, where there are circumstances which *aggravate* the offence of which a person has been convicted, they must be taken into account in the penalty for that offence and not in the fact, or the length, of a consequential totting-up disqualification.

11–68   Consistently with the foregoing analysis the High Court appears to have taken the view that it is permissible to have regard to the gravity of the instant offence when considering whether or not to impose more than the minimum totting-up disqualification (*Snowie* v. *MacPhail*, 1988 G.W.D. 15–674; *Thomson* v. *Lowe*, 1990 G.W.D. 22–1260). By contrast, and in terms of subsection (6), it is not permissible to have regard to the mitigating nature or circumstances of the instant offence, or of those earlier offences in respect of which penalty points were imposed, when considering whether or not to reduce the length of an otherwise obligatory period of disqualification (*Kaye* v. *Wilson*, 1990 G.W.D. 19–1090; *Pitts* v. *Whitelaw*, 1991 G.W.D. 17–1065, not following *Wibberley* v. *Walkingshaw*, 1990 G.W.D. 7–389).

11–69   The provision in subsection (6) which has consistently caused the greatest trouble since its introduction in 1981 is the one which states that no account is to be taken under subsection (2) of "(*b*) hardship, other than exceptional hardship." In the first edition of this book it was tentatively suggested "that the word 'exceptional' is not merely a synonym for 'severe,' but imports a degree of hardship that would be altogether out of the ordinary." Recent cases decided on appeal by the High Court appear to confirm that view.

11–70   From an early stage it was clearly established that loss of employment consequential upon a totting-up disqualification will not of itself be enough to constitute exceptional hardship. In the case of *Allan* v. *Barclay* (1986), see below, which thereafter came to be cited as the leading authority on this topic, the court stated: "if it is to be contended that there will be exceptional hardship following from the loss of a licence, it will be necessary to demonstrate not only that the particular accused may lose his employment, but that associated with that loss of employment are certain other circumstances which may involve reflected hardship of a serious kind upon the accused's business, or his family, or his long-term future prospects."

11–71   While *Allan* v. *Barclay* is still the leading authority in relation to the principles which are to be applied, it is clear that the High Court is now taking a stricter view as to what circumstances, in addition to loss of employment, can properly be regarded as amounting to exceptional hardship (see, for example, *Coldwell* v. *Jessop* (1990), below). Moreover, it also appears that the High Court is increasingly reluctant to interfere with a lower court's discretion on those matters provided that the lower court has considered all relevant circumstances and has exercised its discretion in a proper manner (*Bibby* v. *MacDougall* (1990); *Coldwell* v. *Jessop* (1990)).

11–72   At the end of the day every case must depend on its own facts and circumstances, and accordingly no absolute list of the factors which will, or will not, constitute exceptional hardship can be prepared. However, the following cases may give some indication of what has, or has not, been held to amount to exceptional hardship in recent years. In referring to earlier cases it should be borne in mind that, as noted above, the High Court is now adopting a stricter line than was formerly the case. For convenience the factors relied upon in each case are simply expressed in note form.

11–72a   **Stephens** v. **Gibb**, 1984 S.C.C.R 195.
Loss of employment; would have to sell house. Held that exceptional hardship established.

11–72b   **North** v. **Tudhope**, 1985 S.C.C.R. 161.
Accused in business on his own as a haulage contractor with single lorry which he drove himself; business would fold, but he would still require to pay hire purchase instalments on lorry; inability to pay mortgage on house; bank overdraft of £1,000. Held that exceptional hardship established.

11–72c   **Allan** v. **Barclay**, 1986 S.C.C.R. 111.
Loss of employment; that would jeopardise house mortgage and repayment of bank loan to furnish house; trying to get back on feet after loss of job. Held that exceptional hardship established.

11–72d   **Railton** v. **Houston**, 1986 S.C.C.R. 428.
Loss of employment; inability to pay mortgage with possible loss of house; this would affect accused and his four children since little prospect of obtaining alternative employment. Held that exceptional hardship established.

11–72e   **Holden** v. **MacPhail**, 1986 S.C.C.R. 486.
Loss of employment; inability to pay mortgage with possible loss of house. Held, distinguishing *Stephens* v. *Gibb*, above, as a very special case, that exceptional hardship not established.

11–72f   **Robinson** v. **Aitchison**, 1986 S.C.C.R. 511.
Businessman whose hours were such that could not obtain services of a hired driver; nature of business such that would collapse if licence lost; this would make it impossible to meet financial commitments and lead to six full-time employees losing their jobs. Held that exceptional hardship established. (This case was applied in similar circumstances in *Nolan* v. *Carmichael*, 1989 G.W.D. 25–1121.)

11–72g   **McFadyen** v. **Tudhope**, 1986 S.C.C.R. 712.
Businessman who employed three persons; accused the only one of the

four with a driving licence; disqualification would end the business with consequent loss of jobs by employees and likely loss of accused's own family home. Held that exceptional hardship established.

11–72h   **Richardson** v. **MacPhail**, 1988 S.C.C.R. 27.
Loss of employment; consequent inability to pay mortgage with likely loss of house. Held that exceptional hardship not established.

11–72i   **Gray** v. **Jessop**, 1988 S.C.C.R. 71.
Loss of employment; consequent inability to pay mortgage, leading to loss of house; inability to repay a loan to his employer; probable break-up of marriage which had run into difficulties. Held, with some hesitation, that exceptional hardship established.

11–72j   **Bibby** v. **MacDougall**, 1990 S.C.C.R. 121.
Would jeopardise employment and that of other persons employed by the company of which accused was managing director; hardship would be caused to accused's family. Held that, in deciding that any hardship was not exceptional, the sheriff had taken into account all the matters canvassed in *Allan* v. *Barclay*, above, and had not erred in his conclusion.

11–72k   **Coldwell** v. **Jessop**, 1990 S.C.C.R. 224.
Would lose job as sales director of a firm of which assumed as a partner seven years earlier; company would go to the wall and jobs of 150 employees would be in jeopardy; mortgage payments of £800; wife would have to walk along a poorly lit road; would experience difficulty in visiting mother who lived alone. Held that "the court is now taking a much more strict view of this type of case than when *Allan* v. *Barclay* was decided. The fact of the matter is, the appellant here had nine penalty points for various road traffic offences and if he was going to take the risk of speeding and being caught again then the consequences must have been clear to him. He must have known very well that the next time he committed an offence he would incur all sorts of hardship. In our view the magistrate has proceeded perfectly properly in deciding this matter and we are not prepared to interfere with his discretion." The appeal against disqualification was refused.

11–72l   **Clumpas** v. **Ingram**, 1991 S.C.C.R. 223.
Business would be adversely affected and this would involve difficulties for other people. Held that exceptional hardship not established.

11–72m   **McLaughlin** v. **Docherty**, 1991 S.C.C.R. 227.
Self-employed consulting engineer with cash flow problem and large overdraft. Responsible for finding work for three self-employed sub-contractors who would be likely to lose their employment. Held that exceptional hardship established, and disqualification for six months reduced to three months.

11–72n   **Marshall** v. **MacDougall**, 1991 S.C.C.R. 231.
Business would collapse leading to loss of employment for accused, his wife, and five employees, and to loss of servicing for customers. Held that exceptional hardship established. Disqualification quashed and fine of £150 increased to £400.

THEFT (INCLUDING THEFT BY HOUSEBREAKING AND RESET)

11–73   As with many other offences, crimes of theft can take many forms and can reflect a large range of degrees of gravity. Consequently it is not possible to offer any detailed guidance as to the sentence which may be appropriate in a given case. However, decisions by the High Court give certain indications as to factors which may aggravate or mitigate the seriousness of such offences, and they may offer some guidance as to general approach.

11–74   The absence of significant previous record, and in particular the absence of any previous custodial sentence, may be a mitigating factor and may be enough to avoid the necessity of a custodial sentence (see, for example, *Logan* v. *Douglas* (1986); *Bowman* v. *MacDougall* (1987), below). Conversely, the existence of a substantial previous record will usually be a significant aggravating factor, even where the value of stolen property is small, and is likely to justify a custodial sentence (*McKinnon* v. *Carmichael* (1987); *Stace* v. *McNaughton* (1987); *Adamson* v. *H.M. Advocate* (1988); *Forrest* v. *H.M. Advocate* (1988); *Reid* v. *Webster* (1990)).

11–75   Where an offence has been carefully planned, that factor may outweigh any mitigation arising from the fact that the offence was committed by a virtual first offender (*Crilley* v. *MacDougall* (1986); *McCusker* v. *H.M. Advocate* (1988)). Where the value of stolen property is substantial, a substantial sentence may be justified even in the absence of a significant record (*Marsden* v. *H.M. Advocate* (1988)). On the other hand, even in such a case the youth of the offender and other circumstances may allow a much more lenient approach to be adopted (*Havlin* v. *H.M. Advocate* (1990)). Where the circumstances of the offence are particularly mean and despicable, a substantial sentence may be appropriate (*Allan* v. *O'Brien* (1991)).

11–76   As in cases of fraud and embezzlement, repayment of money that has been stolen may be a mitigating factor (*White* v. *H.M. Advocate* (1987)). Where a theft involves a breach of trust, that will generally lead to a more severe sentence than would otherwise be the case (*Smith* v. *H.M. Advocate* (1989); *Marshall* v. *H.M. Advocate* (1989)).

11–77   The following cases are illustrations of the foregoing observations.

11–77a   **Crilley** *v.* **MacDougall,** 1986 S.C.C.R. 587.
The accused, along with a co-accused, pled guilty to 11 charges of theft by forcing open lockfast telephone coin boxes, to one charge of attempting to do so, and to one charge of being found with the intention of doing so, contrary to section 57 of the Civic Government (Scotland) Act 1982. They both had previous convictions but one had not been convicted of theft since 1960, and the other had not been so convicted since 1972. One had never been in custody, and the other had been in Borstal in 1973. On appeal against sentences of three months' imprisonment it was held that, as the accused had formed themselves into a team, had acquired the necessary tools to commit the offences, had caused considerable damage and had put the telephones out of action, the sheriff was correct in holding that the gravity of the offences made a custodial disposal the only appropriate one.

11–77b   Logan v. Douglas, 1986 S.C.C.R. 590.
The accused pled guilty to breaking into a house while the householder was asleep and stealing certain articles with a value of £74. No previous convictions were libelled against him but the social inquiry report revealed minor convictions for theft in 1979 and 1986. He had not previously received a custodial sentence. At the time of sentence the accused had a number of debts and was paying off a fine, but by the time of his appeal he had no outstanding liabilities, was again in employment, and had become reconciled with his family. An appeal against a sentence of 60 days' imprisonment was allowed, and a fine of £200 was substituted.

11–77c   Bowman v. MacDougall, 1987 S.C.C.R. 14.
The accused was a haulage contractor and a first offender. He pled guilty to resetting four wheels and tyres said to have a second-hand value of about £980. The tyres came from vehicles owned by other haulage contractors and were used by the accused on his own vehicles. On appeal against a fine of £1,500 it was held that the offence was serious and that the penalty must be sufficient to deter the accused and others, and must make it plain to the accused that his conduct would not be tolerated, but that in the circumstances the fine imposed was excessive. A fine of £750 was substituted.

11–77d   White v. H.M. Advocate, 1987 S.C.C.R. 73.
The accused, an architect, pled guilty to charges of theft and fraud involving the appropriation of more than £19,000. At the time of sentence it was said that he had prospects of being able to repay the sums involved, but the sheriff took the view that these prospects were not sufficiently positive for him to consider deferring sentence for repayment, and he sentenced the accused to 18 months' imprisonment. By the time the appeal was heard the accused had in fact repaid all the money, and the court accordingly quashed the sentence of imprisonment and imposed instead a fine of £4,000. In taking that decision the court stated that it was following the line previously adopted in similar cases, including in particular *Dolan* v. *H.M. Advocate*, 1986 S.C.C.R. 564 (noted at para. 11–33 above).

11–77e   Bennett v. Tudhope, 1987 S.C.C.R. 203.
The accused, a first offender, was convicted of resetting a shotgun and of possessing it without the appropriate certificate under the Firearms Act 1968. The sheriff took the view that the danger of stolen shotguns getting into the wrong hands was such that anyone involved in their reset must be dealt with severely, and he imposed a sentence of three months' imprisonment. On appeal it was held that the sheriff's view was correct, and the appeal was refused.

11–77f   McKinnon v. Carmichael, 1987 G.W.D. 2–59.
The accused, who had 25 previous convictions, nine of which were for crimes of dishonesty, pled guilty to stealing two Braun hair curlers from a supermarket. An appeal against a sentence of six months' imprisonment was refused, it being observed that the sentence was as severe as it ought to have been in the circumstances.

11–77g   **Stace** *v.* **McNaughton**, 1987 G.W.D. 13–455.

The accused was convicted, along with two others, of stealing three jumpers from a shop. The crime was premeditated, well planned, and determinedly carried out. The offence was committed within six months of the accused being released on licence from detention on a sentence of 15 months for assault and robbery. There was an unfavourable social inquiry report. In those circumstances an appeal against a sentence of six months' detention was refused.

11–77h   **Adamson** *v.* **H.M. Advocate**, 1988 G.W.D. 2–66.

The accused, who had a substantial record for housebreaking and who was currently serving a three-year sentence for assault and robbery, was convicted of eight charges of theft by housebreaking, two of reset, and a contravention of the Bail Act. He was sentenced to 18 months' detention consecutive to his current sentence, and his appeal against sentence was refused.

11–77i   **Marsden** *v.* **H.M. Advocate**, 1988 G.W.D. 3–114.

The accused was convicted of breaking into a shop and stealing over £28,000 worth of clothing. His last conviction for dishonesty was in 1980, and he had recently married. On appeal against a sentence of 18 months' imprisonment it was held that this was a serious and planned theft, and that the sentence was not excessive.

11–77j   **McCusker** *v.* **H.M. Advocate**, 1988 S.C.C.R. 235.

The accused, aged 25 and with no previous convictions except for minor road traffic offences, was convicted of theft by housebreaking, along with others, of over 119,000 cigarettes. A social inquiry report suggested a community service assessment but the sheriff imposed a sentence of four months' imprisonment, mainly because of the seriousness of the offence which he described as carefully planned and professionally executed. An appeal against sentence was refused.

11–77k   **Forrest** *v.* **H.M. Advocate**, 1988 S.C.C.R. 481.

The accused, aged 19 and with previous convictions for dishonesty, was convicted along with a much older man of theft by housebreaking at the home of an 86-year-old lady. An appeal against a sentence of 15 months' detention was refused notwithstanding that the co-accused had been sentenced to nine months' imprisonment by a different sheriff. (For observations on comparative justice, see para. 9–17 above.)

11–77l   **Smith** *v.* **H.M. Advocate**, 1989 G.W.D. 14–597.

The accused, a first offender and a postman, was convicted of appropriating 300 postal packets which he "could not be bothered" delivering. An appeal against a sentence of nine months' imprisonment was refused, it being observed that for a grave breach of trust over a period of time the sentence was justified.

11–77m   **Marshall** *v.* **H.M. Advocate**, 1989 G.W.D. 26–1160.

The accused, a post office employee with no previous convictions, was convicted of stealing a number of postal packets and wilfully detaining or delaying 173 others. An appeal against a sentence of six months' imprisonment was refused.

11–77n **Reid** *v.* **Webster**, 1990 G.W.D. 21–1177.
The accused, who had a long record and who had only been out of prison for two months, was convicted of stealing four shirts from a shop. An appeal against a sentence of six months' imprisonment was refused.

11–77o **Havlin** *v.* **H.M. Advocate**, 1990 S.C.C.R. 467.
The accused and another, who were both aged 16 at the time and first offenders, pled guilty to theft by housebreaking of property worth £15,000 from a department store. All the property was recovered. The sheriff took the view that, because of the value of the items stolen, the only appropriate sentence was a custodial one, and he sentenced each accused to nine months' detention. On appeal the court concluded, apparently because the accused were young first offenders, that custodial sentences were inappropriate. Those sentences were quashed, and the cases were continued for community service reports.

11–77p **Allan** *v.* **O'Brien**, 1991 G.W.D. 35–2141.
The accused was convicted of two charges of theft by housebreaking. On the first charge he had broken into the house of a retired shepherd and had stolen his life savings of £1,600. On the second charge he had broken into the house of an elderly lady, terrifying her, and had ransacked the house for valuables. He was sentenced to concurrent sentences of three months' detention on these charges, and appealed against the sentences to the High Court. That court expressed the view that the sentences were insufficient since the accused had a previous conviction to be taken into account, and since the offences were mean and despicable. The offences had to be dealt with severely, and two concurrent sentences of six months were substituted.

Part III

Sentencing Statutes and Subordinate Legislation

SENTENCING STATUTES AND SUBORDINATE LEGISLATION

In this Part the main statutory provisions affecting sentencing, both in primary and in secondary legislation, are set out. It has not been practicable, however, to set out *every* statutory provision which has something to do with sentencing, and in particular those provisions which set out the penalties for specific statutory offences have not been included. It is hoped, however, that the following pages will provide a helpful accompaniment to the main text.

The statutes and other provisions which are reproduced in whole or in part are as follows:

[1] Criminal Procedure (Scotland) Act 1975

(1975 c. 21)

An Act to consolidate certain enactments relating to criminal
procedure in Scotland   [8th May 1975]

NOTE
[1] Some of the following provisions are prospectively amended by provisions in the
Criminal Justice Act 1991 (see pp. 495 to 503 below).

PART I

SOLEMN PROCEDURE

Jurisdiction

. . . . . .

Jurisdiction and powers of courts of solemn jurisdiction

2.—(1) The jurisdiction and powers of all courts of solemn jurisdiction,
except in so far as the same may be altered or modified by any future Act,
shall remain as at the commencement of this Act.

(2) The sheriff shall, without prejudice to any other or wider power
conferred by statute, not be entitled, on the conviction on indictment of
an accused person, to pass a sentence of imprisonment for a term
exceeding three years.

(3) Subject to subsection (4) below, where under any enactment passed
or made before the commencement of section 58 of the Criminal Justice
(Scotland) Act 1987 an offence is punishable on conviction on indictment
by imprisonment for a term exceeding two years but the enactment either
expressly or impliedly restricts the power of the sheriff to impose a
sentence of imprisonment for a term exceeding two years, it shall be
competent for the sheriff to impose a sentence of imprisonment for a term
exceeding two but not exceeding three years.

(4) Nothing in subsection (3) above shall authorise the imposition by
the sheriff of a sentence in excess of the sentence specified by the
enactment as the maximum sentence which may be imposed on
conviction of the offence.

. . . . . .

PROCEDURE PRIOR TO TRIAL

Arrest, judicial examination, custody, bail, etc.

• • • • • •

Remand and committal of persons under 21

[1] **23.**—(1) Where a court remands or commits for trial or for sentence a person under 21 years of age who is charged with or convicted of an offence and is not released on bail, then, except as otherwise expressly provided by this section, the following provisions shall have effect, that is to say—

(*a*) subject to the following paragraph, if he is under 16 years of age the court shall commit him to the local authority in whose area the court is situated, and the authority shall have the duty of placing him in a suitable place of safety chosen by the authority instead of committing him to prison:

(*b*) if he is a person of over 16 years of age, or a child under 16 years of age but over 14 years of age who is certified by the court to be unruly or depraved, and the court has been notified by the Secretary of State that a remand centre is available for the reception from that court of persons of his class or description, he shall be committed to a remand centre instead of being committed to prison [; but the court shall not so certify a child unless such conditions as the Secretary of State may by order made by statutory instrument prescribe are satisfied in relation to the child.][2]

(2) Where any person is committed to a local authority or to a remand centre under any provision of this Act, that authority or centre shall be specified in the warrant, and he shall be detained by the authority or in the centre for the period for which he is committed or until he is liberated in due course of law.

(3) Where any person has been committed to a local authority under any provision of this Act, the court by which he was committed, if the person so committed is not less than 14 years of age and it appears to the court that he is unruly or depraved, may revoke the commitment and commit the said person—

(*a*) if the court has been notified that a remand centre is available for the reception from that court of persons of his class or description, to a remand centre; and

(*b*) if the court has not been so notified, to a prison; [but a commitment shall not be so revoked unless such conditions as the Secretary of State may by order made by statutory instrument prescribe are satisfied in relation to the said person.][2]

(4) Where, in the case of a person under 16 years of age who has been committed to prison or to a remand centre under this section, the sheriff is satisfied that his detention in prison or a remand centre is no longer necessary, he may revoke the commitment and commit the person to the local authority in whose area the court is situated, and the authority shall have the duty of placing him in a suitable place of safety.

NOTES
[1] See the National Health Service (Scotland) Act 1978, s. 16A, substituted by the Health

Services Act 1980, s. 4(2). This section came into force on January 6, 1992: see para. 7–17, n. 48a, above.
² Words in square brackets added (*prosp.*) by the Children Act 1975, s. 70.

Committal of children to custody in place of safety
24.—(1) Any court, on remanding or committing for trial a child who is not liberated on bail shall, instead of committing him to prison, commit him to the local authority in whose area the court is situated to be detained in a place of safety chosen by the local authority for the period for which he is remanded or until he is liberated in due course of law.

Provided that in the case of a child over 14 years of age it shall not be obligatory on the court so to commit him if the court certifies that he is of so unruly a character that he cannot safely be so committed or that he is of so depraved a character that he is not a fit person to be so detained [; but the court shall not so certify a child unless such conditions as the Secretary of State may by order made by statutory instrument prescribe are satisfied in relation to the child.]¹

(2) A commitment under this section may be varied, or, in the case of a child over 14 years of age, who proves to be of so unruly a character that he cannot safely be detained in such custody, or to be of so depraved a character that he is not a fit person to be so detained, revoked, by the court which made the order, or if application cannot conveniently be made to that court, by a sheriff sitting summarily having jurisdiction in the place where the court which made the order sat, and if it is revoked the child may be committed to prison [; but a commitment shall not be so revoked unless such conditions as the Secretary of State may by order made by statutory instrument prescribe are satisfied in relation to the child.]¹

NOTE
¹ Words in square brackets added (*prosp.*) by the Children Act 1975, s. 70.

Power to court to commit to hospital a person suffering from mental disorder
25.—(1) Where a court remands or commits for trial a person charged with any offence who appears to the court to be suffering from mental disorder, and the court is satisfied that a hospital is available for his admission and suitable for his detention, the court may, instead of remanding him in custody, commit him to that hospital.

¹ (2) Where any person is committed to a hospital as aforesaid, the hospital shall be specified in the warrant and, if the responsible medical officer is satisfied that he is suffering from mental disorder of a nature or degree which warrants his admission to a hospital under Part V of the Mental Health (Scotland) Act 1984, he shall there be detained for the period for which he is remanded or the period of committal, unless before the expiration of that period he is liberated in due course of law.

(3) When the responsible medical officer has examined the person so detained he shall report the result of that examination to the court and, where the report is to the effect that the person is not suffering from mental disorder of such a nature or degree as aforesaid, the court may commit him to any prison or other institution to which he might have been committed had he not been committed to hospital or may otherwise deal with him according to law.

(4) No person shall be committed to a hospital under this section except on the written or oral evidence of a medical practitioner.

NOTE
[1] As amended by the Mental Health (Scotland) Act 1984, Sched. 3, para. 24.

． ． ． ． ． ．

Notice of previous convictions

Notice of previous convictions

68.—(1) No mention shall be made in the indictment of previous convictions, nor shall extracts of previous convictions be included in the list of productions annexed to the indictment.

(2) If the prosecutor desires to place before the court any previous conviction, he shall cause to be served on the accused along with the indictment a notice in the form of Form No. 1 of Schedule 7 to the Criminal Justice (Scotland) Act 1949 or in the form set out in an Act of Adjournal under this Act or as nearly as may be in such form, and any conviction set forth in that notice shall be held to apply to the accused unless he gives, in accordance with subsection (3) of this section, written intimation objecting to such conviction on the ground that it does not apply to him or is otherwise inadmissible.

[1] (3) Intimation objecting to a conviction under subsection (2) of this section shall be given, at least five clear days before the trial diet, to the Crown Agent, where the accused is cited to the High Court for the trial diet, or to the procurator fiscal of the district to the court of which the accused is cited for the trial diet where the case is to be tried in the sheriff court; and where the accused pleads guilty at any diet, no objection to any such conviction shall be entertained unless the accused has, at least two clear days before that diet, given intimation to the procurator fiscal of the district to the court of which the accused is cited for that diet.

(4) Where notice is given by the accused under section 102 of this Act of his intention to plead guilty and the prosecutor desires to place before the court any previous conviction, he shall cause to be served on the accused along with the indictment a notice in the form of Form No. 1 of Schedule 7 to the Criminal Justice (Scotland) Act 1949 or in the form set out in an Act of Adjournal under this Act or as nearly as may be in such form, and any conviction set forth in that notice shall be held to apply to the accused unless within two days after service of the notice he gives to the procurator fiscal written intimation objecting to such conviction on the ground that it does not apply to him or is otherwise inadmissible.

NOTE
[1] As amended by the Criminal Justice (Scotland) Act 1980, Scheds. 4 and 8.

． ． ． ． ． ．

Accelerated trial

Procedure where accused desires to plead guilty
¹ **102.**—(1) Where the accused intimates in writing to the Crown Agent
that he intends to plead guilty and desires to have his case disposed of at
once, the accused may be served with an indictment (unless one has
already been served) and a notice to appear at a diet of the appropriate
court not less than four clear days after the date of the notice; and it shall
not be necessary to lodge or give notice of any list of witnesses or
productions.
    (2) In subsection (1) above, "appropriate court" means—
        (*a*) in a case where at the time of the intimation mentioned in that
            subsection an indictment had not been served, either the High
            Court or the sheriff court; and
        (*b*) in any other case, the court specified in the notice served under
            section 75 of this Act on the accused.
    (3) If at any such diet the accused pleads not guilty to the charge or
pleads guilty only to a part of the charge, and the prosecutor declines to
accept such restricted plea, the diet shall be deserted *pro loco et tempore*,
and thereafter the cause may proceed in accordance with the other
provisions of this Part of this Act except that in a case mentioned in
paragraph (*b*) of subsection (2) above the court may postpone the trial
diet and the period of such postponement shall not count towards any
time limit applying in respect of the case.

NOTE
¹ Substituted by the Criminal Justice (Scotland) Act 1980, s. 16.

First diet

. . . . . .

Remit to High Court for sentence
¹ **104.**—(1) Where at any diet in proceedings on indictment in the
sheriff court, sentence falls to be imposed but the sheriff holds that any
competent sentence which he can impose is inadequate so that the
question of sentence is appropriate for the High Court, he shall—
        (*a*) endorse upon the record copy of the indictment a certificate of the
            plea or the verdict (as the case may be);
        (*b*) by interlocutor written on such record copy remit the convicted
            person to the High Court for sentence; and
        (*c*) append to such interlocutor a note of his reasons for such remit;
and such remit shall be sufficient warrant to bring the accused before the
High Court for sentence and shall remain in force until the convicted
person is sentenced.
    ² (1A) Where under any enactment an offence is punishable on
conviction on indictment by imprisonment for a term exceeding three
years but the enactment either expressly or impliedly restricts the power
of the sheriff to impose a sentence of imprisonment for a term exceeding
three years, it shall be competent for the sheriff to remit the convicted
person to the High Court for sentence under subsection (1) above; and it

shall be competent for the High Court to pass any sentence which it could have passed if the person had been convicted before it.

(2) When the Clerk of Justiciary receives the record copy of the indictment he shall send a copy of the note of reasons to the convicted person or his solicitor and to the Crown Agent.

(3) Subject to subsection (2) above, the note of reasons shall be available only to the High Court and the parties.

NOTES
[1] Substituted by the Criminal Justice (Scotland) Act 1980, Sched. 4.
[2] Inserted by the Criminal Justice (Scotland) Act 1987, s. 58(2).

• • • • • •

Procedure at trial

• • • • • •

Laying of previous convictions before judge

161.—(1) Previous convictions shall not be laid before the presiding judge until the prosecutor move for sentence, and in that event the prosecutor shall lay before the judge a copy of the notice referred to in subsection (2) or (4) of section 68 of this Act.

(2) On the conviction of the accused it shall be competent for the court to amend a notice of previous convictions so laid by deletion or alteration for the purpose of curing any error or defect therein:

Provided that no such amendment shall be made to the prejudice of the accused.

(3) Where any such intimation as is mentioned in section 68 of this Act is given by the accused, it shall be competent to prove any previous conviction included therein in the manner set forth in section 162 of this Act, and the provisions of the said section shall apply accordingly.

(4) Any conviction which is admitted in evidence by the court shall be entered in the record of the trial.

(5) Nothing in this section or in section 68 of this Act shall prevent evidence of previous convictions being led in any case where such evidence is competent in support of a substantive charge.

Extract convictions to be received and manner of proof

162.—(1) An extract conviction of any crime committed in any part of the United Kingdom, bearing to be under the hand of the officer in use to give out such extract conviction, shall be received in evidence without being sworn to by witnesses.

(2) It shall be competent to prove by a witness or witnesses such previous convictions, or any facts relevant to the admissibility of the same, although the name of any such witness is not included in the list served on the accused; and the accused shall be entitled to examine witnesses in regard thereto.

(3) An official of any prison in which the accused may have been confined on such conviction shall be a competent and sufficient witness to prove the application thereof to the accused, although he may not have been present in court at the trial to which such conviction relates.

Extract conviction to be issued by clerk having record copy of indictment

163. Where the accused is convicted on indictment in the sheriff court of any crime and an extract of that conviction is subsequently required in evidence, such extract shall be issued by the clerk of the court having the custody of the record copy of the indictment although the plea of the accused may have been taken and the sentence on him pronounced in another court.

Proof of previous convictions by fingerprints

164.—(1) A previous conviction may be proved against any person in any criminal proceedings by the production of such evidence of the conviction as is mentioned in this section and by showing that his fingerprints and those of the person convicted are the fingerprints of the same person.

(2) A certificate purporting to be signed by or on behalf of the Chief Constable of Strathclyde or the Commissioner of Police of the Metropolis, containing particulars relating to a conviction extracted from the criminal records kept by the person by or on whose behalf the certificate is signed, and certifying that the copies of the fingerprints contained in the certificate are copies of the fingerprints appearing from the said records to have been taken in pursuance of regulations for the time being in force under section 11 of the Prisons (Scotland) Act 1952, or under section 16 of the Prison Act 1952, from the person convicted on the occasion of the conviction or on the occasion of his last conviction, shall be sufficient evidence of the conviction or, as the case may be, of his last conviction and of all preceding convictions and that the copies of the fingerprints produced on the certificate are copies of the fingerprints of the person convicted.

(3) Where a person has been apprehended and detained in the custody of the police in connection with any criminal proceedings, a certificate purporting to be signed by the chief constable concerned or a person authorised on his behalf, certifying that the fingerprints produced thereon were taken from him while he was so detained, shall be sufficient evidence in those proceedings that the fingerprints produced on the certificate are the fingerprints of that person.

(4) A certificate purporting to be signed by or on behalf of the governor of a prison or of a remand centre in which any person has been detained in connection with any criminal proceedings, certifying that the fingerprints produced thereon were taken from him while he was so detained, shall be sufficient evidence in those proceedings that the fingerprints produced on the certificate are the fingerprints of that person.

(5) A certificate purporting to be signed by or on behalf of the Chief Constable of Strathclyde, and certifying that the fingerprints, copies of which are certified as aforesaid by or on behalf of the Chief Constable or the Commissioner of Police of the Metropolis to be copies of the fingerprints of a person previously convicted and the fingerprints certified by or on behalf of a chief constable or a governor as aforesaid, or otherwise shown, to be the fingerprints of the person against whom the previous conviction is sought to be proved, are the fingerprints of the same person, shall be sufficient evidence of the matters so certified.

(6) The method of proving a previous conviction authorised by this section shall be in addition to any other method of proving the conviction.

Procedure at trial involving children

. . . . . .

Power of court, in respect of certain offences against a child, to refer child to reporter
[1] **168.** Any court by or before which a person is convicted of having committed any offence—

(a) under section 21 of the Children and Young Persons (Scotland) Act 1937;

(b) mentioned in Schedule 1 to this Act; or

(c) in respect of a female person aged 17 years or over which constitutes the crime of incest,

may refer—

(i) the child in respect of whom the offence mentioned in paragraph (a) or (b) above has been committed; or

(ii) any child who is, or who is likely to become, a member of the same household as the person who has committed the offence mentioned in paragraph (b) or (c) above,

to the reporter of the local authority in whose area the child resides and certify that the said offence shall be a ground established for the purposes of Part III of the Social Work (Scotland) Act 1968.

NOTE
[1] As amended by the Criminal Justice (Scotland) Act 1980, Sched. 7.

. . . . . .

Welfare of child
172. Every court in dealing with a child who is brought before it as an offender shall have regard to the welfare of the child and shall in a proper case take steps for removing him from undesirable surroundings.

Reference and remit of children's cases by courts to children's hearings
[1] **173.**—(1) Where a child who is not subject to a supervision requirement is charged with an offence and pleads guilty to, or is found guilty of, that offence the court—

(a) instead of making an order on that plea or finding, may remit the case to the reporter of the local authority to arrange for the disposal of the case by a children's hearing; or

(b) on that plea or finding may request the reporter of the local authority to arrange a children's hearing for the purposes of obtaining their advice as to the treatment of the child.

(2) Where a court has acted in pursuance of paragraph (b) of the foregoing subsection, the court, after consideration of the advice received from the children's hearing may, as it thinks proper, itself dispose of the case or remit the case as aforesaid.

(3) Where a child who is subject to a supervision requirement is charged with an offence and pleads guilty to, or is found guilty of, that offence the court dealing with the case if it is—

(*a*) the High Court, may; and

(*b*) the sheriff court, shall,

request the reporter of the local authority to arrange a children's hearing for the purpose of obtaining their advice as to the treatment of the child, and on consideration of that advice may, as it thinks proper, itself dispose of the case or remit the case as aforesaid.

(4) Where a court has remitted a case to the reporter under this section, the jurisdiction of the court in respect of the child shall cease, and his case shall stand referred to a children's hearing.

(5) Nothing in the provisions of this section shall apply to a case in respect of an offence the sentence for which is fixed by law.

NOTE

[1] As amended by the Criminal Justice (Scotland) Act 1980, Sched. 7.

Procedure at trial of persons suffering from mental disorder

Insanity in bar of trial or as the ground of acquittal

174.—(1) Where any person charged on indictment with the commission of an offence is found insane so that the trial of that person upon the indictment cannot proceed, or if in the course of the trial of any person so indicted it appears to the jury that he is insane, the court shall direct a finding to that effect to be recorded.

(2) Where in the case of any person charged as aforesaid evidence is brought before the court that that person was insane at the time of doing the act or making the omission constituting the offence with which he is charged and the person is acquitted, the court shall direct the jury to find whether the person was insane at such time as aforesaid, and to declare whether the person was acquitted by them on account of his insanity at that time.

(3) Where the court has directed that a finding be recorded in pursuance of subsection (1) of this section, or where a jury has declared that a person has been acquitted by them on the ground of his insanity in pursuance of the last foregoing subsection the court shall order that the person to whom that finding or that acquittal relates shall be detained in a State hospital or such other hospital as for special reasons the court may specify.

[1] (4) An order for the detention of a person in a hospital under this section shall have the like effect as a hospital order (within the meaning of section 175(3) of this Act) together with a restriction order, made without limitation of time; and where such an order is given in respect of a person while he is in the hospital, he shall be deemed to be admitted in pursuance of, and on the date of, the order.

(5) Where it appears to a court that it is not practicable or appropriate for the accused to be brought before it for the purpose of determining whether he is insane so that his trial cannot proceed, then, if no objection to such a course is taken by or on behalf of the accused, the court may order that the case be proceeded with in his absence.

NOTE

[1] As amended with effect from 30th September 1984 by the Mental Health (Amendment) (Scotland) Act 1983, Sched. 2, para. 30.

Interim hospital orders

¹ **174A.**—(1) Where a person is convicted in the High Court or the sheriff court of an offence punishable with imprisonment (other than an offence the sentence for which is fixed by law) and the court before or by which he is convicted is satisfied on the written or oral evidence of two medical practitioners (complying with the provisions of subsection (2) of this section and section 176 of this Act)—

(*a*) that the offender is suffering from mental disorder within the meaning of section 1(2) of the Mental Health (Scotland) Act 1984; and

(*b*) that there is reason to suppose—

(i) that the mental disorder from which the offender is suffering is such that it may be appropriate for a hospital order to be made in his case; and

(ii) that, having regard to the provisions of section 175(4) of this Act, the hospital to be specified in any such hospital order may be a State hospital,

the court may, before making a hospital order or dealing with the offender in some other way, make an order (to be known as "an interim hospital order") authorising his admission to and detention in a State hospital or such other hospital as for special reasons the court may specify in the order:

Provided that where under any enactment the offender is remitted by the sheriff to the High Court for sentence the power to make an order under this subsection in relation to the offender shall be exercisable by the High Court.

(2) Of the medical practitioners whose evidence is taken into account under subsection (1) of this section at least one shall be employed at the hospital which is to be specified in the order.

(3) An interim hospital order shall not be made in respect of an offender unless the court is satisfied that the hospital which is to be specified in the order, in the event of such an order being made by the court, is available for his admission thereto within 28 days of the making of such an order.

(4) Where a court makes an interim hospital order it shall not make any other order for detention or impose a fine or pass sentence of imprisonment or make a probation order or a community service order in respect of the offence, but may make any other order which it has power to make apart from this section.

(5) The court by which an interim hospital order is made may include in the order such direction as it thinks fit for the conveyance of the offender to a place of safety and his detention therein pending his admission to the hospital within the period of 28 days referred to in subsection (3) of this section.

(6) An interim hospital order—

(*a*) shall be in force for such period, not exceeding 12 weeks, as the court may specify when making the order; but

(*b*) may be renewed for further periods of not more than 28 days at a time if it appears to the court on the written or oral evidence of the responsible medical officer that the continuation of the order is warranted;

but no such order shall continue in force for more than six months in all and the court shall terminate the order if it makes a hospital order in respect of the offender or decides, after considering the written or oral evidence of the responsible medical officer, to deal with the offender in some other way.

(7) An interim hospital order may be renewed under subsection (6) of this section without the offender being brought before the court if he is represented by counsel or a solicitor and his counsel or solicitor is given an opportunity of being heard.

(8) If an offender absconds from a hospital in which he is detained in pursuance of an interim hospital order, or while being conveyed to or from such a hospital, he may be arrested without warrant by a constable and shall, after being arrested, be brought as soon as practicable before the court which made the order; and the court may thereupon terminate the order and deal with him in any way in which it could have dealt with him if no such order had been made.

(9) When an interim hospital order ceases to have effect in relation to an offender the court may deal with him in any way (other than by making a new interim hospital order) in which it could have dealt with him if no such order had been made.

(10) The power conferred on the court by the provisions of this section is without prejudice to the power of the court under section 180(1) of this Act to remand a person in order that an inquiry may be made into his physical or mental condition.

NOTE
[1] Inserted by the Mental Health (Amendment) (Scotland) Act 1983, s. 34(*a*), and as amended by the Mental Health (Scotland) Act 1984, Sched. 3, para. 25, both with effect from 30th September 1984.

Power of court to order hospital admission or guardianship
[1] **175.**—(1) Where a person is convicted in the High Court or the sheriff court of an offence, other than an offence the sentence for which is fixed by law, punishable by that court with imprisonment, and the following conditions are satisfied, that is to say—
  (*a*) the court is satisfied, on the written or oral evidence of two medical practitioners (complying with the provisions of section 176 of this Act) that the grounds set out in section 17(1) or, as the case may be, the ground set out in section 36(*a*) of the Mental Health (Scotland) Act 1984 apply in relation to the offender, and
  (*b*) the court is of opinion, having regard to all the circumstances including the nature of the offence and the character and antecedents of the offender, and to the other available methods of dealing with him, that the most suitable method of disposing of the case is by means of an order under this section,
the court may by order authorise his admission to and detention in such hospital as may be specified in the order or, as the case may be, place him under the guardianship of such local authority or of such other person approved by a local authority as may be so specified:

Provided that, where his case is remitted by the sheriff to the High Court for sentence under any enactment, the power to make an order under this subsection shall be exercisable by that court.

(2) Where it appears to the prosecutor in any court before which a person is charged with an offence that the person may be suffering from mental disorder, it shall be the duty of such prosecutor to bring before the court such evidence as may be available of the mental condition of that person.

(3) An order for the admission of a person to a hospital (in this Act, referred to as "a hospital order") shall not be made under this section in respect of an offender unless the court is satisfied that that hospital, in the event of such an order being made by the court, is available for his admission thereto within 28 days of the making of such an order.

(4) A State hospital shall not be specified in a hospital order in respect of the detention of a person unless the court is satisfied, on the evidence of the medical practitioners which is taken into account under paragraph (*a*) of subsection (1) of this section, that the offender, on account of his dangerous, violent or criminal propensities, requires treatment under conditions of special security, and cannot suitably be cared for in a hospital other than a State hospital.

(5) An order placing a person under the guardianship of a local authority or of any other person (in this Act referred to as "a guardianship order") shall not be made under this section unless the court is satisfied (*a*) after taking into consideration the evidence of a mental health officer, that it is necessary in the interests of the welfare of the person that he should be placed under guardianship; and (*b*) that that authority or person is willing to receive that person into guardianship.

(6) A hospital order or guardianship order shall specify the form of mental disorder, being mental illness or mental handicap or both, from which, upon the evidence taken into account under paragraph (*a*) of subsection (1) of this section, the offender is found by the court to be suffering; and no such order shall be made unless the offender is described by each of the practitioners, whose evidence is taken into account as aforesaid, as suffering from the same form of mental disorder, whether or not he is also described by either of them as suffering from the other form.

(7) Where an order is made under this section, the court shall not pass sentence of imprisonment or impose a fine or make a probation order or a community service order in respect of the offence, but may make any other order which the court has power to make apart from this section; and for the purposes of this subsection "sentence of imprisonment" includes any sentence or order for detention.

NOTE
[1] As amended with effect from 30th September 1984 by the Mental Health (Amendment) (Scotland) Act 1983, Sched. 2, para. 31, and the Mental Health (Scotland) Act 1984, Sched. 3, para. 26. Extended by the Contempt of Court Act 1981, s. 15(3).

Requirements as to medical evidence
[1] **176.**—[2] (1) Of the medical practitioners whose evidence is taken into account under sections 174A(1) and 175(1)(*a*) of this Act, at least one shall be a practitioner approved for the purposes of section 20 or 39 of the Mental Health (Scotland) Act 1984 by a Health Board as having special experience in the diagnosis or treatment of mental disorder.

[3] (1A) Written or oral evidence given for the purposes of the said

section 175(1)(*a*) shall include a statement as to whether the person giving the evidence is related to the accused and of any pecuniary interest which that person may have in the admission of the accused to hospital or his reception into guardianship.

(2) For the purposes of the said section 175(1)(*a*) a report in writing purporting to be signed by a medical practitioner may, subject to the provisions of this section, be received in evidence without proof of the signature or qualifications of the practitioner; but the court may, in any case, require that the practitioner by whom such a report was signed be called to give oral evidence.

(3) Where any such report as aforesaid is tendered in evidence, otherwise than by or on behalf of the accused, then—

(*a*) if the accused is represented by counsel or solicitor, a copy of the report shall be given to his counsel or solicitor;

(*b*) if the accused is not so represented, the substance of the report shall be disclosed to the accused or, where he is a child under 16 years of age, to his parent or guardian if present in court;

(*c*) in any case, the accused may require that the practitioner by whom the report was signed be called to give oral evidence, and evidence to rebut the evidence contained in the report may be called by or on behalf of the accused;

and where the court is of opinion that further time is necessary in the interests of the accused for consideration of that report, or the substance of any such report it shall adjourn the case.

(4) For the purpose of calling evidence to rebut the evidence contained in any such report as aforesaid, arrangements may be made by or on behalf of an accused person detained in a hospital for his examination by any medical practitioner, and any such examination may be made in private.

NOTES
[1] Extended by the Contempt of Court Act 1981, s. 15(3).
[2] As amended with effect from 30th September 1984 by the Mental Health (Amendment) (Scotland) Act 1983, Sched. 2, para. 32, and the Mental Health (Scotland) Act 1984, Sched. 3, para. 27.
[3] Inserted in relation to proceedings commenced on or after 30th September 1984 by the Mental Health (Amendment) (Scotland) Act 1983, s. 35(*a*): see *ibid*. Sched. 1, para. 12.

Supplementary provisions as to hospital orders
[1] **177.** The court by which a hospital order is made may give such directions as it thinks fit for the conveyance of the patient to a place of safety and his detention therein pending his admission to the hospital within the period of 28 days referred to in section 175(3) of this Act; but a direction for the conveyance of a patient to a residential establishment provided by a local authority under Part IV of the Social Work (Scotland) Act 1968 shall not be given unless the court is satisfied that that authority is willing to receive the patient therein.

NOTE
[1] Extended by the Contempt of Court Act 1981, s. 15(3).

Power of court to restrict discharge from hospital
[1] **178.**—(1) Where a hospital order is made in respect of a person, and it

appears to the court, having regard to the nature of the offence with which he is charged, the antecedents of the person and the risk that as a result of his mental disorder he would commit offences if set at large, that it is necessary for the protection of the public from serious harm so to do, the court may, subject to the provisions of this section, further order that the person shall be subject to the special restrictions set out in section 62(1) of the Mental Health (Scotland) Act 1984, either without limit of time or during such period as may be specified in the order.

(2) An order under this section (in this Act referred to as "a restriction order") shall not be made in the case of any person unless the medical practitioner approved by the Health Board for the purposes of section 20 or 39 of the Mental Health (Scotland) Act 1984, whose evidence is taken into account by the court under section 175(1)(*a*) of this Act, has given evidence orally before the court.

(3) Where a restriction order is in force in respect of a patient, a guardianship order shall not be made in respect of him; and where the hospital order relating to him ceases to have effect by virtue of section 60(4) of the Mental Health (Scotland) Act 1984 on the making of another hospital order that order shall have the same effect in relation to the restriction order as the previous hospital order, but without prejudice to the power of the court making that other hospital order to make another restriction order to have effect on the expiration of the previous such order.

NOTE
[1] As amended by the Mental Health (Amendment) (Scotland) Act 1983, s. 22(2) and Sched. 2, para. 33, and the Mental Health (Scotland) Act 1984, Sched. 3, para. 28.

CONVICTION AND SENTENCE

Adjournment and remand

Power of court to adjourn a case before sentence
[1] **179.** It is hereby declared that the power of a court to adjourn the hearing of a case includes power, after a person has been convicted or the court has found that he committed the offence and before he has been sentenced or otherwise dealt with, to adjourn the case for the purpose of enabling inquiries to be made or of determining the most suitable method of dealing with his case and where the court so adjourns the case it shall remand the accused in custody or on bail or ordain him to appear at the adjourned diet: provided that a court shall not for the purpose aforesaid adjourn the hearing of a case for any single period exceeding three weeks.

(2) An accused who is remanded under this section may appeal against the refusal of bail or against the conditions imposed within 24 hours of his remand, by note of appeal presented to the High Court, and the High Court, either in court or in chambers, may, after hearing parties—
   (*a*) review the order appealed against and either grant bail on such conditions as it thinks fit or ordain the accused to appear at the adjourned diet; or
   (*b*) confirm the order.

NOTE

[1] As amended by the Bail, etc. (Scotland) Act 1980, s. 5, and the Criminal Justice (Scotland) Act 1980, Sched. 7. Saved by the Criminal Justice (Scotland) Act 1987, s. 2(1).

Remand for inquiry into physical or mental condition

180.—(1) Without prejudice to any powers exercisable by a court under the last foregoing section, where a person is charged before a court with an offence punishable with imprisonment, and the court is satisfied that he did the act or made the omission charged but is of opinion that an inquiry ought to be made into his physical or mental condition before the method of dealing with him is determined, the court shall remand him in custody or on bail for such period or periods, no single period exceeding three weeks, as the court thinks necessary to enable a medical examination and report to be made.

[1] (2) Where a person is remanded on bail under this section, it shall be a condition of the order granting bail that he shall—

(*a*) undergo a medical examination by a duly qualified medical practitioner or, where the inquiry is into his mental condition and the order granting bail so specifies, two such practitioners; and

(*b*) for the purpose attend at an institution or place, or on any such practitioner specified in the order granting bail and, where the inquiry is into his mental condition, comply with any directions which may be given to him for the said purpose by any person so specified or by a person of any class so specified;

and, if arrangements have been made for his reception, it may be a condition of the order granting bail that the person shall, for the purpose of the examination, reside in an institution or place specified as aforesaid, not being an institution or place to which he could have been remanded in custody, until the expiry of such period as may be so specified or until he is discharged therefrom, whichever first occurs.

(3) [Repealed by the Bail, etc. (Scotland) Act 1980, Sched. 2.]

(4) On exercising the powers conferred by this section the court shall—

(*a*) where the person is remanded in custody, send to the institution or place in which he is detained, and

(*b*) where the person is released on bail, send to the institution or place at which or the person by whom he is to be examined,

a statement of the reasons for which the court is of opinion that an inquiry ought to be made into his physical or mental condition, and of any information before the court about his physical or mental condition.

[2] (5) A person remanded under this section may appeal against the refusal of bail or against the conditions imposed within 24 hours of his remand, by note of appeal presented to the High Court, and the High Court, either in court or in chambers, may after hearing parties—

(*a*) review the order and grant bail on such conditions as it thinks fit; or

(*b*) confirm the order.

NOTES

[1] As amended by the Bail, etc. (Scotland) Act 1980, s. 6 and Sched. 1.

[2] Added by the Bail, etc. (Scotland) Act 1980, s. 6.

Admonition and discharge

Admonition

181. A court may, if it appears to meet the justice of the case, dismiss with an admonition any person found guilty by the court of any offence.

Absolute discharge

[1] **182.** Where a person is convicted of an offence (other than an offence the sentence for which is fixed by law) the court, if it is of opinion, having regard to the circumstances, including the nature of the offence and the character of the offender, that it is inexpedient to inflict punishment and that a probation order is not appropriate may, instead of sentencing him, make an order discharging him absolutely.

NOTE

[1] See the Licensed Premises (Exclusion of Certain Persons) Act 1980, s. 1(2)(*c*) and the Criminal Justice (Scotland) Act 1980, s. 2(5).

Probation

Probation

[1] **183.**—[1a] (1) Subject to subsection (1A) below, where a person is convicted of an offence (other than an offence the sentence for which is fixed by law), the court, if it is of opinion having regard to the circumstances, including the nature of the offence and the character of the offender and having obtained a report as to the circumstances and character of the offender, that it is expedient to do so, may instead of sentencing him make a probation order, that is to say an order requiring the offender to be under supervision for a period to be specified in the order of not less than six months nor more than three years.

(1A) A court shall not make a probation order under subsection (1) above unless it is satisfied that suitable arrangements for the supervision of the offender can be made by the local authority in whose area he resides or is to reside.

(2) A probation order shall be as nearly as may be in the form prescribed by Act of Adjournal, and shall name the local authority area in which the offender resides or is to reside and the order shall make provision for the offender to be under the supervision of an officer of the local authority of that area, or, where the offender resides or is to reside in a local authority area in which the court has no jurisdiction the court shall name the appropriate court (being such a court as could have been named in any amendment of the order in accordance with the provisions of Schedule 5 to this Act) in the area of residence or intended residence, and the court last mentioned shall require the local authority for that area to arrange for the offender to be under the supervision of an officer of that authority.

(3) Subject to the provisions of Schedule 5 to this Act relating to probationers who change their residence, an offender in respect of whom a probation order is made shall be required to be under the supervision of an officer of the local authority as aforesaid.

[2] (4) Subject to the provisions of the next following section, a probation order may in addition require the offender to comply during the whole or

any part of the probation period with such requirements as the court, having regard to the circumstances of the case, considers (*a*) conducive to securing the good conduct of the offender or to preventing a repetition by him of the offence or the commission of other offences or (*b*) where the probation order is to include such a requirement as is mentioned in subsection (5A) or (5B) below, conducive to securing or preventing the aforesaid matters.

(5) Without prejudice to the generality of the last foregoing subsection, a probation order may include requirements relating to the residence of the offender:

Provided that—

    (*a*) before making an order containing any such requirements, the court shall consider the home surroundings of the offender; and

    (*b*) where the order requires the offender to reside in any institution or place, the name of the institution or place and the period for which he is so required to reside shall be specified in the order, and that period shall not exceed beyond 12 months from the date of the requirement or beyond the date when the order expires.

[3] (5A) Without prejudice to the generality of subsection (4) above, where a court which is considering making a probation order—

    (*a*) is satisfied that the offender is of or over 16 years of age and has committed an offence punishable with imprisonment and that the conditions for the making of a community service order under the Community Service by Offenders (Scotland) Act 1978 specified in paragraphs (*a*) and (*c*) of section 1(2) of that Act have been met;

    (*b*) has been notified by the Secretary of State that arrangements exist for persons who reside in the locality where the offender resides, or will be residing when the probation order comes into force, to perform unpaid work as a requirement of a probation order; and

    (*c*) is satisfied that provision can be made under the arrangements mentioned in paragraph (*b*) above for the offender to perform unpaid work under the probation order,

it may include in the probation order, in addition to any other requirement, a requirement that the offender shall perform unpaid work for such number of hours (being in total not less than 40 nor more than 240) as may be specified in the probation order; and the said Act of 1978 shall apply to a probation order including such a requirement as it applies to a community service order, but as if—

    (i) subsections (1), (2)(*b*) and (*d*) and (4)(*b*) of section 1 and sections 4, 6 and 6A were omitted;

    (ii) in section 1(5) for the words "subsection (1) above" there were substituted the words "subsection (5A) of section 183 or, as the case may be, 384 of the 1975 Act"; and

    (iii) any other necessary modifications were made.

(5B) Without prejudice to the generality of subsection (4) above, where a court is considering making a probation order it may include in the probation order, in addition to any other requirement, a requirement that the offender shall pay compensation either in a lump sum or by instalments for any personal injury, loss or damage caused (whether directly or indirectly) by the acts which constituted the offence; and the following provisions of the Criminal Justice (Scotland) Act 1980 shall apply to such a requirement as if any reference in them to a compensation order included a reference to a requirement to pay compensation under this subsection—

section 58(2) and (3);

section 59 (except the proviso to subsection (1) and subsection (2));

section 60;

section 62;

section 64 (except paragraph (a));

section 67.

(5C) Where the court imposes a requirement to pay compensation under subsection (5B) above—

(*a*) it shall be a condition of a probation order containing such a requirement that payment of the compensation shall be completed not more than 18 months after the making of the order or not later than two months before the end of the period of probation whichever first occurs;

(*b*) the court, on the application of the offender or the officer of the local authority responsible for supervising the offender, may vary the terms of the requirement, including the amount of any instalments, in consequence of any change which may have occurred in the circumstances of the offender; and

(*c*) in any proceedings for breach of a probation order where the breach consists only in the failure to comply with a requirement to pay compensation, a document purporting to be a certificate signed by the clerk of the court for the time being having jurisdiction in relation to the order that the compensation or, where payment by instalments has been allowed, any instalment has not been paid shall be sufficient evidence of such breach.

[4] (6) Before making a probation order, the court shall explain to the offender in ordinary language the effect of the order (including any additional requirements proposed to be inserted therein under subsection (4), (5), (5A), (5B) or (5C) of this section or under the next following section) and that if he fails to comply therewith or commits another offence during the probation period he will be liable to be sentenced for the original offence and the court shall not make the order unless the offender expresses his willingness to comply with the requirements thereof.

(7) The clerk of the court by which a probation order is made or of the appropriate court, as the case may be, shall cause copies thereof to be given to the officer of the local authority who is to supervise the probationer, to the probationer, and to the person in charge of any institution or place in which the probationer is required to reside under the probation order.

NOTES
[1] See the Licensed Premises (Exclusion of Certain Persons) Act 1980, s. 1(2)(*c*) and the Criminal Justice (Scotland) Act 1980, s. 2(5). As amended by the Criminal Justice (Scotland) Act 1987, s. 65, and the Law Reform (Miscellaneous Provisions) (Scotland) Act 1990, s. 61(1).
[1a] As amended by the Criminal Justice (Scotland) Act 1987, Sched. 1, para. 10.

² As amended by the Community Service by Offenders (Scotland) Act 1978, s. 7(*a*).
³ Added by the Community Service by Offenders (Scotland) Act 1978, s. 7(*b*), and as amended by the Criminal Justice Act 1982, Sched. 13, para. 3.
⁴ As amended by the Community Service by Offenders (Scotland) Act 1978, s. 7(*c*).

Probation orders requiring treatment for mental condition
¹ **184.**—(1) Where the court is satisfied, on the evidence of a registered medical practitioner approved for the purposes of section 20 or 39 of the Mental Health (Scotland) Act 1984, that the mental condition of an offender is such as requires and may be susceptible to treatment but is not such as to warrant his detention in pursuance of a hospital order under Part VI of that Act, or under this Act, the court may, if it makes a probation order, include therein a requirement that the offender shall submit, for such period not extending beyond 12 months from the date of the requirement as may be specified therein, to treatment by or under the diréction of a registered medical practitioner with a view to the improvement of the offender's mental condition.

(2) The treatment required by any such order shall be such one of the following kinds of treatment as may be specified in the order, that is to say—

(*a*) treatment as a resident patient in a hospital within the meaning of the Mental Health (Scotland) Act 1984, not being a State hospital within the meaning of the Act;

(*b*) treatment as a non-resident patient at such institution or place as may be specified in the order; or

(*c*) treatment by or under the direction of such registered medical practitioner as may be specified in the order;

but except as aforesaid the nature of the treatment shall not be specified in the order.

(3) A court shall not make a probation order containing such a requirement as aforesaid unless it is satisfied that arrangements have been made for the treatment intended to be specified in the order, and, if the offender is to be treated as a resident patient, for his reception.

(4) [Repealed by the Mental Health (Amendment) (Scotland) Act 1983, s. 36(1) and Sched. 3.]

(5) Where the medical practitioner by whom or under whose direction a probationer is receiving any of the kinds of treatment to which he is required to submit in pursuance of a probation order is of opinion—

(*a*) that the probationer requires, or that it would be more appropriate for him to receive, a different kind of treatment (whether in whole or in part) from that which he has been receiving, being treatment of a kind which subject to subsection (5A) of this section could have been specified in the probation order; or

(*b*) that the treatment (whether in whole or in part) can be more appropriately given in or at a different institution or place from that where he has been receiving treatment in pursuance of the probation order,

he may, subject to subsection (5B) of this section, make arrangements for the probationer to be treated accordingly.

(5A) Arrangements made under subsection (5) of this section may provide for the probationer to receive his treatment (in whole or in part) as a resident patient in an institution or place notwithstanding that it is not one which could have been specified in that behalf in the probation order.

(5B) Arrangements shall not be made under subsection (5) of this section unless—

(*a*) the probationer and any officer responsible for his supervision agree;

(*b*) the treatment will be given by or under the direction of a registered medical practitioner who has agreed to accept the probationer as his patient; and

(*c*) where such treatment entails the probationer's being a resident patient, he will be received as such.

(6) Where any such arrangements as are mentioned in subsection (5) of this section are made for the treatment of a probationer—

(*a*) any officer responsible for the probationer's supervision shall notify the appropriate court of the arrangements; and

(*b*) the treatment provided for by the arrangements shall be deemed to be treatment to which he is required to submit in pursuance of the probation order.

(7) Subsections (2), (3) and (4) of section 176 of this Act shall apply for the purposes of this section as if for the reference in the said subsection (2) to section 175(1)(*a*) of this Act there were substituted a reference to subsection (1) of this section.

(8) Except as provided by this section, a court shall not make a probation order requiring a probationer to submit to treatment for his mental condition.

NOTE
[1] As amended by the Mental Health (Amendment) (Scotland) Act 1983, s. 36 and Sched. 3, and the Mental Health (Scotland) Act 1984, Sched. 3, para. 29.

Discharge and amendment of probation orders
   185.—(1) The provisions of Schedule 5 to this Act shall have effect in relation to the discharge and amendment of probation orders.

(2) Where, under section 186 of this Act, a probationer is sentenced for the offence for which he was placed on probation, the probation order shall cease to have effect.

Failure to comply with requirement of probation order
[1] **186.**—[1a] (1) If, on information on oath from

(*a*) the officer supervising the probationer,

(*b*) the director of social work of the local authority whose officer is supervising the probationer; or

(*c*) an officer appointed by the director of social work to act on his behalf for the purposes of this subsection,

it appears to the court by which the order was made or to the appropriate court that the probationer has failed to comply with any of the requirements of the order, that court may issue a warrant for the arrest of the probationer, or may, if it thinks fit, instead of issuing such a warrant in the first instance, issue a citation requiring the probationer to appear before the court at such time as may be specified in the citation.

(2) If it is proved to the satisfaction of the court before which a probationer appears or is brought in pursuance of the last foregoing

subsection that he has failed to comply with any of the requirements of the probation order, the court may—
[2] (*a*) except in the case of a failure to comply with a requirement to pay compensation and without prejudice to the continuance in force of the probation order, impose a fine not exceeding level 3 on the standard scale; or
   (*b*) (i) where the probationer has been convicted for the offence for which the order was made, sentence him for that offence;
       (ii) where the probationer has not been so convicted, convict him and sentence him as aforesaid; or
   (*c*) vary any of the requirements of the probation order, so however that any extension of the probation period shall terminate not later than three years from the date of the probation order; or
[3] (*d*) without prejudice to the continuance in force of the probation order, in a case where the conditions required by the Community Service by Offenders (Scotland) Act 1978 are satisfied, make a community service order, and the provisions of that Act shall apply to such an order as if the failure to comply with the requirement of the probation order were the offence in respect of which the order had been made.

(3) A fine imposed under this section in respect of a failure to comply with the requirements of a probation order shall be deemed for the purposes of any enactment to be a sum adjudged to be paid by or in respect of a conviction or a penalty imposed on a person summarily convicted.

(4) A probationer who is required by a probation order to submit to treatment for his mental condition shall not be deemed for the purpose of this section to have failed to comply with that requirement on the ground only that he had refused to undergo any surgical, electrical or other treatment if, in the opinion of the court, his refusal was reasonable having regard to all the circumstances.

(5) Without prejudice to the provisions of section 187 of this Act, a probationer who is convicted of an offence committed during the probation period shall not on that account be liable to be dealt with under this section for failing to comply with any requirement of the probation order.

NOTES
[1] As amended by the Criminal Justice (Scotland) Act 1980, s. 46.
[1a] As amended by the Law Reform (Miscellaneous Provisions) (Scotland) Act 1990, s. 61(2).
[2] As amended by the Criminal Justice Act 1982, Sched. 7 and the Criminal Justice (Scotland) Act 1987, s. 65(5).
[3] Added by the Community Service by Offenders (Scotland) Act 1978, s. 8.

Commission of further offence
187.—(1) If it appears to the court by which a probation order has been made (or to the appropriate court) that the probationer to whom the order relates has been convicted by a court in any part of Great Britain of an offence committed during the probation period and has been dealt with for that offence, the first-mentioned court (or the appropriate court) may issue a warrant for the arrest of the probationer, or may, if it thinks

fit, instead of issuing such a warrant in the first instance issue a citation requiring the probationer to appear before that court at such time as may be specified in the citation, and on his appearance or on his being brought before the court, the court may, if it thinks fit, deal with him under section 186(2)(*b*) of this Act.

(2) Where a probationer is convicted by the court which made the probation order (or by the appropriate court) of an offence committed during the probation period, that court may, if it thinks fit, deal with him under section 186(2)(*b*) of this Act for the offence for which the order was made as well as for the offence committed during the period of probation.

Probation orders relating to persons residing in England

[1] **188.**—(1) Where the court by which a probation order is made under section 183 of this Act (not being a probation order including a requirement that the offender shall perform unpaid work) is satisfied that the offender has attained the age of 17 years and resides or will reside in England, subsection (2) of the said section shall not apply to the order, but the order shall contain a requirement that he be under the supervision of a probation officer appointed for or assigned to the petty sessions area in which the offender resides or will reside; and that area shall be named in the order.

(2) Where a probation order has been made under section 183 of this Act and the court in Scotland by which the order was made or the appropriate court is satisfied that the probationer has attained the age of 17 years and proposes to reside or is residing in England, the power of that court to amend the order under Schedule 5 to this Act shall include power to insert the provisions required by subsection (1) of this section; and the court may so amend the order without summoning the probationer and without his consent.

(3) A probation order made or amended by virtue of this section may, notwithstanding section 184(8) of this Act, include a requirement that the probationer shall submit to treatment for his mental condition, and—

(*a*) subsections (1), (3) and (7) of the said section 184 and section 3(2) of the Powers of Criminal Courts Act 1973 (all of which regulate the making of probation orders which include any such requirement) shall apply to the making of an order which includes any such requirement by virtue of this subsection as they apply to the making of an order which includes any such requirement by virtue of section 184 of this Act and section 3 of the said Act of 1973 respectively; and

(*b*) subsections (4) to (6) of section 3 of the said Act of 1973 (functions of supervising officer and medical practitioner where such a requirement has been imposed) shall apply in relation to a probationer who is undergoing treatment in England in pursuance of a requirement imposed by virtue of this subsection as they apply in relation to a probationer undergoing such treatment in pursuance of a requirement imposed by virtue of that section.

(4) Sections 185(1) and 186(1) of this Act shall not apply to any order made or amended under this section; but subject as hereinafter provided the provisions of the Powers of Criminal Courts Act 1973 (except section

8 of that Act) shall apply to the order as if it were a probation order made under section 2 of that Act:

Provided that section 6(2)(*a*), (3)(*d*) and (6) of that Act shall not apply to any such order and section 6(4) and (5) of that Act shall have effect respectively in relation to any such order as if for the first reference in section 6(4) to the Crown Court there were substituted a reference to a court in Scotland and as if for the second such reference therein and for both such references in section 6(5) there were substituted references to the court in Scotland by which the probation order was made or amended under this section.

(5) If it appears on information to a justice acting for the petty sessions area for which the supervising court within the meaning of the Powers of Criminal Courts Act 1973 acts that a person in whose case a probation order has been made or amended under this section has been convicted by a court in any part of Great Britain of an offence committed during the period specified in the order, he may issue a summons requiring that person to appear, at the place and time specified therein, before the court in Scotland by which the probation order was made or, if the information is in writing and on oath, may issue a warrant for his arrest, directing that person to be brought before the last-mentioned court.

(6) If a warrant for the arrest of a probationer issued under section 187 of this Act by a court is executed in England, and the probationer cannot forthwith be brought before that court, the warrant shall have effect as if it directed him to be brought before a magistrates' court for the place where he is arrested; and the magistrates' court shall commit him to custody or release him on bail (with or without sureties) until he can be brought or appear before the court in Scotland.

(7) The court by which a probation order is made or amended in accordance with the provisions of this section shall send three copies of the order to the clerk to the justices for the petty sessions area named therein, together with such documents and information relating to the case as it considers likely to be of assistance to the court acting for that petty sessions area.

(8) Where a probation order which is amended under subsection (2) of this section is an order to which the provisions of this Act apply by virtue of section 10 of the Powers of Criminal Courts Act 1973 (which relates to probation orders under that Act relating to persons residing in Scotland) then, notwithstanding anything in that section or this section, the order shall, as from the date of the amendment, have effect in all respects as if it were an order made under section 2 of that Act in the case of a person residing in England.

NOTE
[1] As amended by the Community Service by Offenders (Scotland) Act 1978, Sched. 2, para. 2.

Further provisions as to probation orders
189.—(1) Where the court by which a probation order is made under section 183 of this Act or subsection (6) of this section is satisfied that the person to whom the order relates is under the age of 17 years and resides or will reside in England, subsection (2) of the said section 183 shall not apply to the order but the order shall name the petty sessions area in

which that person resides or will reside and the court shall send notification of the order to the clerk to the justices for that area.

(2) Where a probation order has been made under section 183 of this Act or subsection (6) of this section and the court which made the order or the appropriate court is satisfied that the person to whom the order relates is under the age of 17 years and proposes to reside or is residing in England, the power of that court to amend the order under Schedule 5 to this Act shall include power, without summoning him and without his consent, to insert in the order the name of the petty sessions area aforesaid; and where the court exercises the power conferred on it by virtue of this subsection it shall send notification of the order to the clerk aforesaid.

(3) A court which sends a notification to a clerk in pursuance of the foregoing provisions of this section shall send to him with it three copies of the probation order in question and such other documents and information relating to the case as it considers likely to be of assistance to the juvenile court mentioned in the following subsection.

(4) It shall be the duty of the clerk to whom a notification is sent in pursuance of the foregoing provisions of this section to refer the notification to a juvenile court acting for the petty sessions area named in the order, and on such a reference the court—

(a) may make a supervision order under the Children and Young Persons Act 1969 in respect of a person to whom the notification relates; and

(b) if it does not make such an order, shall dismiss the case.

(5) A supervision order made by virtue of the last foregoing subsection shall not include a requirement authorised by section 12 of the said Act of 1969 unless the supervised person is before the court when the supervision order is made, and in relation to a supervision order made by virtue of that subsection—

(a) section 15 of that Act shall have effect as if, in subsection (4), paragraph (b) and the words following it were omitted; and

(b) section 17(a) of that Act shall have effect as if the second reference to the supervision order were a reference to the probation order in consequence of which the supervision order is made;

and when a juvenile court disposes of a case referred to it in pursuance of the last foregoing subsection, the probation order in consequence of which the reference was made shall cease to have effect.

(6) The court which, in pursuance of subsection (1) of section 73 of the Social Work (Scotland) Act 1968, considers a case referred to it in consequence of a notification under paragraph (i) of that subsection (which relates to a case in which a person subject to a supervision order made by virtue of this section moves to Scotland)—

(a) may, if it is of opinion that the person to whom the notification relates should continue to be under supervision, make a probation order in respect of him for a period specified in the order; and

(b) if it does not make such an order, shall dismiss the case;

and when the court disposes of a case in pursuance of this subsection the supervision order aforesaid shall cease to have effect.

(7) Notwithstanding any provision to the contrary in section 183 of this Act, a probation order made by virtue of the last foregoing subsection

which includes only requirements having the like effect as any requirement or provision of the supervision order to which the notification relates may be made without summoning the person to whom the notification relates and without his consent, and shall specify a period of supervision which shall expire not later than the date on which that supervision order would have ceased to have effect by the effluxion of time; and, except as aforesaid, the provisions of this Act shall apply to that probation order.

(8) In this and the last foregoing section "petty sessions area" has the same meaning as in the said Act of 1969.

Supplementary provisions as to probation

190.—(1) Any court, on making a probation order, may, if it thinks that such a course is expedient for the purpose of the order, require the offender to give security for his good behaviour.

(2) Security may be given under the foregoing subsection by consignation with the clerk of the court or by entering into an undertaking to pay the amount, but not otherwise, and such security may be forfeited and recovered in like manner as caution.

Effects of probation and absolute discharge

[1] **191.**—(1) Subject as hereinafter provided, a conviction of an offence for which an order is made placing the offender on probation or discharging him absolutely shall be deemed not to be a conviction for any purpose other than the purposes of the proceedings in which the order is made and of laying it before a court as a previous conviction in subsequent proceedings for another offence:

Provided that where an offender, being not less than 16 years of age at the time of his conviction of an offence for which he is placed on probation as aforesaid, is subsequently sentenced under this Act for that offence, the provisions of this subsection shall cease to apply to the conviction.

(2) Without prejudice to the foregoing provisions of this section, the conviction of an offender who is placed on probation or discharged absolutely as aforesaid shall in any event be disregarded for the purposes of any enactment which imposes any disqualification or disability upon convicted persons, or authorises or requires the imposition of any such disqualification or disability.

(3) The foregoing provisions of this section shall not affect—

(a) any right of any such offender as aforesaid to appeal against his conviction; or

(b) the operation, in relation to any such offender, of any enactment which was in force as at the commencement of section 9(3)(b) of the Criminal Justice (Scotland) Act 1949 and is expressed to extend to persons dealt with under section 1(1) of the Probation of Offenders Act 1907 as well as to convicted persons.

(4) Where a person charged with an offence has at any time previously been placed on probation or discharged absolutely in respect of the commission by him of an offence it shall be competent, in the proceedings

for that offence, to bring before the court the probation order or order of absolute discharge in like manner as if the order were a conviction.

NOTE
[1] As amended by the Criminal Justice (Scotland) Act 1980, Sched. 8. See the Licensed Premises (Exclusion of Certain Persons) Act 1980, s. 1(2)(c). Excluded by the Road Traffic Offenders Act 1988, s. 46(3).

Probation reports
192. Where a report by an officer of a local authority is made to any court (other than a court whose procedure is regulated by rules made under section 366(2) of this Act) with a view to assisting the court in determining the most suitable method of dealing with any person in respect of an offence, a copy of the report shall be given by the clerk of the court to the offender or his solicitor:

Provided that if the offender is under 16 years of age and is not represented by counsel or a solicitor, a copy of the report need not be given to him but shall be given to his parent or guardian if present in court.

Penalties for statutory offences

Power to mitigate penalties
[1] **193.** In proceedings in respect of the contravention of any statute or order, where each contravention involves any of the following punishments, namely, imprisonment, the imposition of a fine, the finding of caution for good behaviour or otherwise, either singly or in combination with imprisonment or fine, the court shall have in addition to any other powers conferred by Act of Parliament the following powers, *viz.*:—

(1) to reduce the period of imprisonment:
[2] (2) to substitute for imprisonment (either with or without caution for good behaviour, not exceeding the prescribed sum within the meaning of section 289B of this Act and a period of 12 months) a fine:

(3) to substitute the finding of caution not exceeding the prescribed sum within the meaning of section 289B of this Act and the period of 12 months for a fine or imprisonment:

(4) to reduce the amount of any fine:

(5) to dispense with the finding of caution:

Provided that,
    (i) where any Act carries into effect a treaty, convention, or agreement with a foreign state, and such treaty, convention, or agreement stipulates for a fine of minimum amount, the court shall not be entitled by virtue of this section to reduce the amount of such fine below that minimum amount;
    (ii) this section shall not apply to proceedings taken under any Act relating to any of Her Majesty's regular or auxiliary forces.

NOTES
[1] As amended by the Criminal Justice (Scotland) Act 1980, s. 46 and Sched. 8.
[2] Extended by the Companies Act 1948, s. 188(7).

Fines on conviction on indictment to be without limit
[1] **193A.**—(1) Where a person convicted on indictment of any offence (whether triable only on indictment or triable either on indictment or summarily other than by virtue of section 457A(4) of this Act) would, apart from this subsection, be liable to a fine of or not exceeding a specified amount, he shall by virtue of this subsection be liable to a fine of any amount.

(2) Where any Act confers a power by subordinate instrument to make a person liable on conviction on indictment of any offence mentioned in subsection (1) above to a fine or a maximum fine of a specified amount, or which shall not exceed a specified amount, the fine which may be provided in the exercise of that power shall by virtue of this subsection be a fine of an unlimited amount.

NOTE
[1] Added by the Criminal Law Act 1977, Sched. 11, para. 1, and as amended by the Criminal Justice (Scotland) Act 1980, Sched. 7, and the Criminal Justice Act 1982, Sched. 15, para. 17.

Fines

Application of summary procedure provisions relating to fines
[1] **194.**—(1) The provisions of Part II of this Act specified in subsection (2) below shall, subject to any necessary modifications, apply in relation to solemn proceedings as they apply in relation to summary proceedings.
(2) The provisions mentioned in subsection (1) above are—
   section 395(1) (means of offender to be taken into account);
   section 395A (power to remit fines);
   section 396 (time for payment);
   section 397 (further time for payment);
   section 398 (reasons for default);
   section 399 (payment by instalments);
   section 400 (supervision pending payment of fine);
   section 401(2) and (3) (supplementary provisions);
   section 403 (transfer of fine orders);
   section 404 (action of clerk of court on transfer of fine order);
   section 406 (substitution of custody for imprisonment where child defaults on fine);
   section 407 (maximum period of imprisonment for non-payment of fine);
   section 408 (discharge from imprisonment to be specified);
   section 409 (payment of fine in part by prisoner);
   section 411 (recovery by civil diligence);
   Schedule 7 (application of sums paid as part of fine under section 409).

NOTE
[1] Substituted by the Criminal Justice (Scotland) Act 1980, s. 47. Applied to compensation orders by *ibid.*, s. 66. See the Criminal Justice (Scotland) Act 1987, s. 44.

. . . . . .

Fines, etc., may be enforced in other district
[1] **196.**—(1) Any sentence or decree for any fine or expenses pronounced by any sheriff court may be enforced against the person or effects of any party against whom any such sentence or decree shall have been awarded in any other sheriff court district, as well as in the district where such sentence or decree is pronounced:

Provided that such sentence or decree, or an extract thereof, shall be first produced to and indorsed by the sheriff of such other district competent to have pronounced such sentence or decree in such other district.

(2) A fine imposed by the High Court shall be remitted for enforcement to, and shall be enforceable as if it had been imposed by—

(*a*) where the person upon whom the fine was imposed resides in Scotland, the sheriff for the district where that person resides;

(*b*) where that person resides outwith Scotland, the sheriff before whom he was brought for examination in relation to the offence for which the fine was imposed.

NOTE
[1] As amended by the Criminal Justice (Scotland) Act 1980, s. 48. Applied to compensation orders by *ibid.* s. 66. Applied by the Criminal Justice (Scotland) Act 1987, s. 7(1).

. . . . . .

Fines payable to H.M. Exchequer
[1] **203.** Any fine imposed in the High Court upon the accused, and upon a juror for non-attendance, and any forfeiture for non-appearance of a party, witness or juror in the High Court shall be payable to and recoverable by the proper officer in Exchequer for Her Majesty's use, unless in a case where the High Court shall, by the sentence awarding the said fine, order the same or any part thereof to be otherwise disposed of.

NOTE
[1] Applied by the Criminal Justice (Scotland) Act 1987, s. 7(1). See the Prevention of Terrorism (Temporary Provisions) Act 1989, Sched. 4, para. 11(4).

. . . . . .

Imprisonment, etc.

Punishment for murder
[1] **205.**—(1) Subject to subsections (2) and (3) below, a person convicted of murder shall be sentenced to imprisonment for life.

[2] (2) Where a person convicted of murder is under the age of 18 years he shall not be sentenced to imprisonment for life but to be detained without limit of time and shall be liable to be detained in such place, and under such conditions, as the Secretary of State may direct.

[2] (3) Where a person convicted of murder has attained the age of 18 years but is under the age of 21 years he shall not be sentenced to imprisonment for life but to be detained in a young offenders institution and shall be liable to be detained for life.

NOTES
[1] Substituted by the Criminal Justice (Scotland) Act 1980, s. 43.
[2] See the Prisons (Scotland) Act 1989, s. 26(1).

Recommendation as to minimum period of detention for person convicted of murder

[1] **205A.**—[2] (1) On sentencing any person convicted of murder a judge may make a recommendation as to the minimum period which should elapse before, under section 26 of the Prisons (Scotland) Act 1989, the Secretary of State releases that person on licence.

(2) When making a recommendation under subsection (1) above, the judge shall state his reasons for so recommending.

(3) Notwithstanding the proviso to subsection (1) of section 228 of this Act it shall be competent to appeal under paragraph (*b*) or (*c*) of that subsection against a recommendation made under subsection (1) above; and for the purposes of such appeal (including the High Court's power of disposal under section 254(3)(*b*) of this Act) the recommendation shall be deemed part of the sentence passed on conviction.

NOTES
[1] Inserted by the Criminal Justice (Scotland) Act 1980, s. 43.
[2] As amended by the Prisons (Scotland) Act 1989, Sched. 2, para. 11, with effect from 16th February 1990.

Detention of children convicted on indictment

[1] **206.** Subject to section 205 of this Act, where a child is convicted and the court is of the opinion that no other method of dealing with him is appropriate, it may sentence him to be detained for a period which it shall specify in the sentence; and the child shall during that period be liable to be detained in such place and on such conditions as the Secretary of State may direct.

NOTE
[1] Substituted for former s. 206(1) by the Prisons (Scotland) Act 1989, Sched. 2, para. 12, with effect from 16th February 1990. Subss. (2)–(7) repealed by *ibid.*, Sched. 3. See also *ibid.*, s. 31.

Detention of young offenders

[1] **207.**—(1) It shall not be competent to impose imprisonment on a person under 21 years of age.

(2) Subject to section 205(2) and (3) of this Act and to subsections (3) and (4) below a court may impose detention (whether by way of sentence or otherwise) on a person, who is not less than 16 but under 21 years of age, where but for subsection (1) above the court would have power to impose a period of imprisonment; and the period of detention imposed under this section on any person shall not exceed the maximum period of imprisonment which might otherwise have been imposed.

(3) The court shall not under subsection (2) above impose detention on a person unless it is of the opinion that no other method of dealing with him is appropriate; and the court shall state its reasons for that opinion, and, except in the case of the High Court, those reasons shall be entered in the record of proceedings.

(4) To enable the court to form an opinion under subsection (3) above, it shall obtain (from an officer of a local authority or otherwise) such

information as it can about the offender's circumstances; and it shall also take into account any information before it concerning the offender's character and physical and mental condition.

² (5) A sentence of detention imposed under this section shall be a sentence of detention in a young offenders institution.

³ (11) Section 18 (functions of Parole Board), section 24 (remission for good conduct) and sections 22, 26, 28 and 29 (release on licence) of the Prisons (Scotland) Act 1989 shall apply to a person sentenced under this section as those enactments apply to a person sentenced to a period of imprisonment.

NOTES
¹ Substituted by the Criminal Justice (Scotland) Act 1980, s. 45. Restricted by the Repatriation of Prisoners Act 1984, Sched. 1, para. 4(2). See the Prisons (Scotland) Act 1989, s. 32. The Criminal Justice Act 1988, Sched. 9, para. 6 provides: "An offender who was ordered to be detained in a detention centre on a date before the commencement of section 124(1) of this Act [1st November 1988] shall, if the order has not expired at the commencement of that section, be treated for all purposes of detention, release and supervision as if he had been sentenced to detention for the like term in a young offenders institution."
² Substituted for subss. (5)–(10) by the Criminal Justice Act 1988, s. 124(1) and Sched. 9, para. 6.
³ As amended by the Prisons (Scotland) Act 1989, Sched. 2, para. 13, with effect from 16th February 1990.

. . . . . .

Recall to young offenders institution on re-conviction
¹ **212.**—² (1) Where a person sentenced to detention under section 207 of this Act, being under supervision after his release from such detention, is convicted of an offence punishable with imprisonment, the court may, except where the person convicted is subject to a licence granted under section 60(1) or section 61 of the Criminal Justice Act 1967 or section 22(1) or section 26 of the Prisons (Scotland) Act 1989, make an order for his recall.

(2) An order for the recall of a person made as aforesaid shall have the like effect as an order for recall made by the Secretary of State under section 32 of the said Act of 1989.

NOTES
¹ As amended by the Criminal Justice (Scotland) Act 1980, Sched. 7, para. 38, and (with effect from 16th February 1990) the Prisons (Scotland) Act 1989, Sched. 2, para. 14. Saved by the 1989 Act, s. 21(3).
² As amended by the Criminal Justice (Scotland) Act 1987, Sched. 1, para. 11.

. . . . . .

Return to prison in case of breach of supervision
¹ **214.**—(1) If, on sworn information laid by or on behalf of the Secretary of State, it appears to the sheriff that a person, being under supervision under section 30 of the Prisons (Scotland) Act 1989, has failed to comply with any of the requirements imposed on him by his notice of supervision, the sheriff may issue a warrant for the arrest of that person or may, if he thinks fit, instead of issuing such a warrant in the first

instance, issue a citation requiring the person to appear before him at such time as may be specified in the citation.

(2) If it is proved to the satisfaction of the sheriff before whom a person appears or is brought in pursuance of the last foregoing subsection that the person has failed to comply with any of the requirements of the notice of supervision, the sheriff shall, unless having regard to all the circumstances of the case, he considers it unnecessary or inexpedient to do so, order that he be sent back to prison for such term as may be specified in that order, not exceeding whichever is the shorter of the following, that is to say—

(a) a period of three months;

(b) a period equal to so much of the period of twelve months referred to in section 30(4) of the said Act of 1989 as was unexpired on the date on which proceedings were commenced.

(3) Subject to the following provisions of this section, Part II of this Act shall apply in relation to proceedings for an order as aforesaid as it applies in relation to proceedings in respect of a summary offence, and references in Part II of this Act to an offence, trial, conviction or sentence shall be construed accordingly.

(4) Proceedings for an order under subsection (2) of this section may be brought before a sheriff having jurisdiction in the area in which the supervising officer carries out his duties.

(5) A warrant issued for the purposes of proceedings for an order under subsection (2) above may, if the person laying the information so requests, bear an endorsement requiring any constable charged with its execution to communicate with the Secretary of State before arresting the person under supervision if the constable finds that that person is earning an honest livelihood or that there are other circumstances which ought to be brought to the notice of the Secretary of State.

(6) Where a person while under supervision under section 30 of the said Act of 1989 is convicted of an offence for which the court has power to pass sentence of imprisonment, the court may, instead of dealing with him in any other manner, make such an order as could be made by a sheriff under subsection (2) of this section in proceedings for such an order.

(7) The Secretary of State may at any time release from prison a person who has been sent back to prison under subsection (2) or (6) of this section; and the provisions of this section and of section 30 of the said Act of 1989 shall apply to a person released by virtue of this subsection, subject to the following modifications:—

(a) that the period of 12 months referred to in subsection (4) of the said section 30 shall be calculated from the date of his original release; and

(b) in relation to any further order for sending him back to prison under this section the period referred to in subsection (2)(a) of this section shall be reduced by any time during which he has been detained by virtue of the previous order.

(8) In any proceedings, a certificate purporting to be signed by or on behalf of the Secretary of State and certifying—

(a) that a notice of supervision was given to any person in the terms specified in the certificate and on the date so specified; and

(*b*) either that no notice has been given to him under subsection (5) of
section 30 of the said Act of 1989 or that a notice has been so given
in the terms specified in the certificate,
shall be sufficient evidence of the matters so certified; and the fact that a
notice of supervision was given to any person shall be sufficient evidence
that he was a person to whom the said section 30 applies.

(9) For the purposes of Part III of the Criminal Justice Act 1961, a
person who has been sent back to prison under subsection (2) or (6) of this
section, and has not been released again, shall be deemed to be serving
part of his original sentence, whether or not the term of that sentence has
in fact expired.

NOTE
[1] As amended by the Prisons (Scotland) Act 1989, Sched. 2, para. 15, with effect from
16th February 1990. This section is not yet in force: see s. 464(4).

Legal custody
[1] **215.** Any person required or authorised by or under this Act or any
other enactment or any subordinate instrument to be taken to any place,
or to be detained or kept in custody shall, while being so taken or
detained or kept, be deemed to be in legal custody.

NOTE
[1] Substituted by the Criminal Justice (Scotland) Act 1980, Sched. 7 and as amended by
the Criminal Justice (Scotland) Act 1987, Sched. 1, para. 12.

Miscellaneous provisions as to conviction, sentence, etc.

. . . . . .

Form of sentence
217.—(1) In any case the sentence to be pronounced shall be
announced by the judge in open court and shall be entered in the record in
the form now in use in the High Court, and it shall not be necessary to
read the entry of the sentence from the record.

(2) In recording sentences of imprisonment, it shall be sufficient to
minute the term of imprisonment to which the court sentenced the panel,
without specifying the prison in which the sentence is to be carried out;
and such entries of sentences, signed by the clerk of court, shall be full
warrant and authority for all execution to follow thereon, and for the
clerk to issue extracts thereof for carrying the same into execution or
otherwise.

(3) In extracting sentences of imprisonment, the extract may be in the
form set out in an Act of Adjournal under this Act or as nearly as may be
in such form.

Consideration of time spent in custody
[1] **218.** A court, in passing a sentence of imprisonment or detention on a
person for any offence, shall, in determining the period of imprisonment
or detention, have regard to any period of time spent in custody by that
person on remand awaiting trial or sentence.

NOTE
[1] As amended by the Criminal Justice (Scotland) Act 1980, Scheds. 7, para. 40, and 8.

Deferred sentence
  [1] **219.**—(1) It shall be competent for a court to defer sentence after conviction for a period and on such conditions as the court may determine.

(2) If it appears to the court by which sentence on a person has been deferred under subsection (1) above that that person has been convicted, during the period of deferment, by a court in any part of Great Britain of an offence committed during that period and has been dealt with for that offence, the first mentioned court may issue a warrant for the arrest of that person, or may, instead of issuing such a warrant in the first instance, issue a citation requiring him to appear before it at such time as may be specified in the citation; and on his appearance or on his being brought before the court it may deal with him in any manner in which it would be competent for it to deal with him on the expiry of the period of deferment.

(3) Where a court which has deferred sentence under subsection (1) above on a person convicts that person of another offence during the period of deferment, it may deal with him for the original offence in any manner in which it would be competent for it to deal with him on the expiry of the period of deferment, as well as for the offence committed during the said period.

NOTE
[1] As amended by the Criminal Justice (Scotland) Act 1980, s. 54 and saved by the Criminal Justice (Scotland) Act 1987, s. 2(1).

· · · · · ·

Forfeiture of property
  [1] **223.**—(1) Where a person is convicted of an offence and the court which passes sentence is satisfied that any property which was in his possession or under his control at the time of his apprehension—
    (*a*) has been used for the purpose of committing, or facilitating the commission of, any offence; or
    (*b*) was intended by him to be used for that purpose,
that property shall be liable to forfeiture, and any property forfeited under this section shall be disposed of as the court may direct.

(2) Any reference in this section to facilitating the commission of an offence shall include a reference to the taking of any steps after it has been committed for the purpose of disposing of any property to which it relates or of avoiding apprehension or detection.

NOTE
[1] See the Criminal Justice (Scotland) Act 1987, s. 5(3)(*b*). Excluded by the Telecommunications Act 1984, Sched. 3, para. 3(*b*).

Warrant of search for forfeited articles
  224. Where a court has made an order for the forfeiture of an article, the court or any justice may, if satisfied on information on oath—
    (*a*) that there is reasonable cause to believe that the article is to be found in any place or premises; and

(*b*) that admission to the place or premises has been refused or that a
refusal of such admission is apprehended,
issue a warrant of search which may be executed according to law.

. . . . . .

Correction of entries
[1] **227A.**—(1) Subject to the provisions of this section, it shall be
competent to correct an entry in—
  (*a*) the record of proceedings in a solemn prosecution; or
  (*b*) the extract of a sentence passed or an order of court made in such
    proceedings,
in so far as that entry constitutes an error of recording or is incomplete.
  (2) Such entry may be corrected—
    (*a*) by the clerk of the court, at any time before either the sentence
      (or order) of the court is executed or, on appeal, the
      proceedings are transmitted to the Clerk of Justiciary;
    (*b*) by the clerk of the court, under the authority of the court which
      passed the sentence or made the order, at any time after the
      execution of the sentence (or order) of the court but before
      such transmission as is mentioned in paragraph (*a*) above; or
    (*c*) by the clerk of the court under the authority of the High Court
      in the case of a remit under subsection (4)(*b*) below.
  (3) A correction in accordance with paragraph (*b*) or (*c*) of subsection
(2) above shall be intimated to the prosecutor and to the former accused
or his solicitor.
  (4) Where, during the course of an appeal, the High Court becomes
aware of an erroneous or incomplete entry, such as is mentioned in
subsection (1) above, the court—
    (*a*) may consider and determine the appeal as if such entry were
      corrected; and
    (*b*) either before or after the determination of the appeal, may remit
      the proceedings to the court of first instance for correction in
      accordance with subsection (2)(*c*) above.
  (5) Any correction under subsections (1) and (2) above by the clerk of
the court shall be authenticated by his signature and, if such correction is
authorised by a court, shall record the name of the judge or judges
authorising such correction and the date of such authority.

NOTE
[1] Inserted by the Criminal Justice (Scotland) Act 1980, s. 20.

APPEAL

Procedure prior to hearing

Right of appeal
[1] **228.**—(1) Any person convicted on indictment may appeal in
accordance with the provisions of this Part of this Act, to the High
Court—
  (*a*) against such conviction;

(*b*) against the sentence passed on such conviction; or

(*c*) against both such conviction and such sentence:

Provided that there shall be no appeal against any sentence fixed by law.

(2) By an appeal under subsection (1) of this section, a person may bring under review of the High Court any alleged miscarriage of justice in the proceedings in which he was convicted, including any alleged miscarriage of justice on the basis of the existence and significance of additional evidence which was not heard at the trial and which was not available and could not reasonably have been made available at the trial.

NOTE

[1] Substituted by the Criminal Justice (Scotland) Act 1980, Sched. 2. Applied by the Criminal Justice (Scotland) Act 1987, s. 2(2) and (3).

* * * * * *

Bill of suspension not competent

230. It shall not be competent to appeal to the High Court by bill of suspension against any conviction, sentence, judgment or order pronounced in any proceedings on indictment in the sheriff court.

Intimation of intention to appeal

[1] **231.**—(1) Subject to section 236B(2) of this Act and to section 2(2) of the Criminal Justice (Scotland) Act 1987 (postponed confiscation orders), where a person desires to appeal under section 228(1)(*a*) or (*c*) of this Act he shall, within two weeks of the final determination of the proceedings, lodge with the Clerk of Justiciary written intimation of intention to appeal and send a copy to the Crown Agent.

(2) Such intimation shall identify the proceedings and be in as nearly as may be the form prescribed by Act of Adjournal under this Act.

(3) On such intimation being lodged by a person in custody, the Clerk of Justiciary shall give notice thereof to the Secretary of State.

(4) Subject to subsection (5) below, for the purposes of subsection (1) above and section 270(2) of this Act, proceedings shall be deemed finally determined on the day on which sentence is passed in open court; except that, where in relation to an appeal under section 228(1)(*a*) of this Act sentence is deferred under section 219 of this Act, they shall be deemed finally determined on the day on which sentence is first so deferred in open court.

(5) Without prejudice to subsection (2) of section 2 of the said Act of 1987, the reference in subsection (4) above to "the day on which sentence is passed in open court" shall, in relation to any case in which, under subsection (1) of that section, a decision has been postponed for a period, be construed as a reference to the day on which that decision is made (whether or not a confiscation order is then made or any other sentence is then passed).

NOTE

[1] Substituted by the Criminal Justice (Scotland) Act 1980, Sched. 2, and as amended by the Criminal Justice (Scotland) Act 1987, s. 45(6).

* * * * * *

Note of appeal
¹ **233.**—(1) Subject to section 236B (2) of this Act, within six weeks of lodging intimation of intention to appeal or, in the case of an appeal against sentence alone, within two weeks of the passing of the sentence in open court, the convicted person may lodge a written note of appeal with the Clerk of Justiciary who shall send a copy to the judge who presided at the trial and to the Crown Agent: Provided that the first mentioned period may be extended, before expiry thereof, by the Clerk of Justiciary.

(2) Such a note shall identify the proceedings, contain a full statement of all the grounds of appeal and be in as nearly as may be the form prescribed by Act of Adjournal under this Act.

(3) Except by leave of the High Court on cause shown it shall not be competent for an appellant to found any aspect of his appeal on a ground not contained in the note of appeal.

(4) On a note of appeal against sentence alone being lodged by an appellant in custody the Clerk of Justiciary shall give notice thereof to the Secretary of State.

NOTE
¹ Substituted by the Criminal Justice (Scotland) Act 1980, Sched. 2.

Presentation of appeal in writing
¹ **234.**—(1) If an appellant desires to present his case and his argument in writing instead of orally he shall intimate this desire to the Clerk of Justiciary at least four days before the diet fixed for the hearing of the appeal and, at the same time, shall lodge with the Clerk of Justiciary three copies of his case and argument; at the same time, he shall also send a copy thereof to the Crown Agent. Any case or argument so presented shall be considered by the High Court.

(2) Unless the High Court shall otherwise direct, the respondent, in a case to which this section applies, shall not make a written reply to the case and argument in writing, but shall reply orally thereto at the diet fixed for the hearing of the appeal or application for leave to appeal.

(3) Unless the High Court shall otherwise allow, an appellant who has presented his case and argument in writing shall not be entitled to submit in addition an oral argument to the court in support of the appeal.

NOTE
¹ As amended by the Criminal Justice (Scotland) Act 1980, Scheds. 2 and 8.

Applications may be made orally or in writing
235. Except where otherwise provided in this Part of this Act, any application to the High Court may be made by the appellant or respondent as the case may be or by counsel on his behalf, orally or in writing, but in regard to such applications if the appellant is unrepresented and is in custody and is not entitled or has not obtained leave to be present before the court, he shall make any such application by forwarding the same in writing to the Clerk of Justiciary who shall take the proper steps to obtain the decision of the court thereon.

Proceedings in sheriff court to be furnished
¹ **236.** In the case of an appeal against a conviction or sentence in a

sheriff court, the sheriff clerk shall furnish to the Clerk of Justiciary a certified copy of the proceedings at the trial, or shall forward to him the original record of the proceedings, as may be required by the Clerk of Justiciary.

NOTE
[1] As amended by the Criminal Justice (Scotland) Act 1980, Scheds. 2 and 8.

Judge's report
[1] **236A.**—(1) As soon as is reasonably practicable after his receipt of the copy note of appeal sent to him under section 233(1) of this Act, the judge who presided at the trial shall furnish the Clerk of Justiciary with a report in writing giving the judge's opinion on the case generally and on the grounds contained in the note of appeal; and the Clerk of Justiciary shall send a copy of the report to the convicted person or his solicitor, to the Crown Agent, and, in a case referred under section 263(1) of this Act, to the Secretary of State.

(2) Where the judge's report is not furnished as mentioned in subsection (1) above, the High Court may call for such report to be furnished within such period as it may specify or, if it thinks fit, hear and determine the appeal without such report.

(3) Subject to subsection (1) above, the report of the judge shall be available only to the High Court and the parties.

NOTE
[1] Inserted by the Criminal Justice (Scotland) Act 1980, Sched. 2.

Computation of periods
[1] **236B.**—(1) Where the last day of any period mentioned in sections 231(1) and 233(1) of this Act falls on a day which the office of the Clerk of Justiciary is closed, such period shall extend to and include the next day on which such office is open.

(2) Any period mentioned in section 231(1) or 233(1) of this Act may be extended at any time by the High Court in respect of any convicted person; and application for such extension may be made under this subsection and shall be in as nearly as may be the form prescribed by Act of Adjournal under this Act.

NOTE
[1] Inserted by the Criminal Justice (Scotland) Act 1980, Sched. 2.

Signing of documents
[1] **236C.** Any intimation of intention to appeal, note of appeal or application in terms of section 236B (2) of this Act shall be signed by the convicted person or by his counsel or solicitor.

NOTE
[1] Inserted by the Criminal Justice (Scotland) Act 1980, Sched. 2.

Note of proceedings
[1] **237.** The High Court where hearing an appeal under this Part of this Act may require the judge who presided at the trial to produce any notes taken by him of the proceedings at the trial.

NOTE
[1] Substituted by the Criminal Justice (Scotland) Act 1980, Sched. 2.

. . . . . .

Clerk to give notice of date of hearing
[1] **239.**—(1) When the High Court fixes the date for the hearing of an appeal, or of an application under section 236B (2) of this Act, the Clerk of Justiciary shall give notice to the Crown Agent and to the solicitor of the appellant or applicant, or to the appellant or applicant himself if he has no known solicitor, and the latter shall thereupon lodge three copies (typed or printed) of the said appeal or application for the use of the court.

(2) Where it is proposed that the powers of the court shall be exercised by a single judge under the provisions of section 247 of this Act, one copy only of the application to be disposed of shall be lodged by the solicitor of the applicant for the use of the judge.

NOTE
[1] As amended by the Criminal Justice (Scotland) Act 1980, Scheds. 2 and 8.

Appellant may be present at hearing
[1] **240.** An appellant, notwithstanding that he is in custody, shall be entitled to be present if he desires it, on the hearing of his appeal, except where the appeal is on some ground involving a question of law alone, but, in that case and on any proceedings preliminary or incidental to an appeal, shall not be entitled to be present, except where it is provided by Act of Adjournal that he shall have the right to be present, or where the High Court gives him leave to be present.

NOTE
[1] As amended by the Criminal Justice (Scotland) Act 1980, Scheds. 2 and 8.

Notice to authorities, etc., of date of hearing
[1] **241.** Where an appellant or applicant is in custody and has obtained leave or is entitled to be present at the hearing of his appeal or application, the Clerk of Justiciary shall notify the appellant or applicant, the Governor of the prison in which the appellant or applicant then is, and the Secretary of State of the probable day on which the appeal or application will be heard. The Secretary of State shall take steps to transfer the appellant or applicant to a prison convenient for his appearance before the High Court, at such reasonable time before the hearing as shall enable him to consult his legal adviser, if any.

NOTE
[1] As amended by the Criminal Justice (Scotland) Act 1980, Sched. 7.

Notice to Prison Commissioners of attendance of appellant at hearing
[1] **242.** When an appellant or applicant is entitled, or has been granted leave to be present at any diet—
(a) before the High Court or any judge thereof, or
(b) for the taking of additional evidence before a person appointed for the purpose under section 252(b) of this Act, or

(c) for an examination or investigation by a special commissioner in terms of section 252(d) of this Act,

the Clerk of Justiciary shall give timeous notice to the Secretary of State in the form set out in an Act of Adjournal under the Criminal Appeal (Scotland) Act 1926 or under this Act or as nearly as may be in such form, which notice shall be sufficient warrant to the Secretary of State for transmitting the appellant or applicant in custody from prison to the place where said diet or any subsequent diets are to be held and for reconveying him to prison at the conclusion of the said diet and any subsequent diets. The appellant or applicant shall appear at all such diets in ordinary civilian clothes.

NOTE
[1] As amended by the Criminal Justice (Scotland) Act 1980, Sched. 7.

• • • • • •

Abandonment of appeal
[1] **244.**—(1) An appellant may abandon his appeal by lodging with the Clerk of Justiciary a notice of abandonment in as nearly as may be the form prescribed by Act of Adjournal under this Act; and on such notice being lodged the appeal shall be deemed to have been dismissed by the court.

(2) A person who has appealed against both conviction and sentence may abandon the appeal in so far as it is against conviction and may proceed with it against sentence alone.

NOTE
[1] Substituted by the Criminal Justice (Scotland) Act 1980, Sched. 2. See S.I. 1981 No. 386.

Procedure at hearing

• • • • • •

Powers which may be exercised by a single judge
[1] **247.** The powers of the High Court under this Part of this Act to extend the time within which intimation of intention to appeal and note of appeal may be given, to allow the appellant to be present at any proceedings in cases where he is not entitled to be present without leave, and to admit an appellant to bail, may be exercised by any judge of the High Court in the same manner as they may be exercised by the High Court, and subject to the same provisions; but, if the judge refuses an application on the part of the appellant to exercise any such power in his favour, the appellant shall be entitled to have the application determined by the High Court.

NOTE
[1] As amended by the Criminal Justice (Scotland) Act 1980, Scheds. 2 and 8.

Single judge may act wherever convenient
248. A judge of the High Court sitting under the provisions of section 247 of this Act may sit and act wherever convenient.

Interlocutory proceedings

249. Subject to the provisions of section 247 of this Act and without prejudice thereto, preliminary and interlocutory proceedings incidental to any appeal or application may be disposed of by a single judge.

Representation before single judge

250. In all proceedings before a judge under section 247 of this Act, and in all preliminary and interlocutory proceedings and applications except such as are heard before the full court, the parties thereto may be represented and appear by a solicitor alone.

Appeal against refusal of application

[1] **251.**—(1) When an application or applications have been dealt with by a judge of the High Court, under section 247 of this Act, the Clerk of Justiciary shall notify to the applicant the decision in the form set out in an Act of Adjournal under the Criminal Appeal (Scotland) Act 1926 or under this Act or as nearly as may be in such form.

(2) In the event of such judge refusing all or any of such applications, the Clerk of Justiciary on notifying such refusal to the applicant shall forward to him the prescribed form to fill up and forthwith return if he desires to have his said application or applications determined by the High Court as fully constituted for the hearing of appeals under this Part of this Act. If the applicant does not so desire, or does not return within five days to the Clerk the form duly filled up by him, the refusal of his application or applications by such judge shall be final.

(3) If the applicant desires a determination by the High Court as aforesaid and is not legally represented, he may be present at the hearing and determination by the High Court of his said application:

Provided that an applicant who is legally represented shall not be entitled to be present without leave of the court.

(4) When an applicant duly fills up and returns to the Clerk of Justiciary within the prescribed time the said form expressing a desire to be present at the hearing and determination by the court of the applications mentioned in this section, the said form shall be deemed to be an application by the applicant for leave to be so present, and the Clerk of Justiciary, on receiving the said form, shall take the necessary steps for placing the said application before the court.

(5) If the said application to be present is refused by the court, the Clerk of Justiciary shall notify the applicant; and if the said application is granted, he shall notify the applicant and the Governor of the prison wherein the applicant is in custody and the Secretary of State.

(6) For the purpose of constituting a Court of Appeal, the judge who has refused any such application may sit as a member of such court, and take part in determining such application.

NOTE
[1] As amended by the Criminal Justice (Scotland) Act 1980, Sched. 7. See S.I. 1981 No. 356.

Powers of High Court

[1] **252.** Without prejudice to any existing power of the High Court, that court may for the purposes of an appeal under section 228(1) of this Act—

(a) order the production of any document or other thing connected with the proceedings;

(b) hear any additional evidence relevant to any alleged miscarriage of justice or order such evidence to be heard by a judge of the High Court or by such other person as it may appoint for that purpose;

(c) take account of any circumstances relevant to the case which were not before the trial judge;

(d) remit to any fit person to enquire and report in regard to any matter or circumstance affecting the appeal;

(e) appoint a person with expert knowledge to act as assessor to the High Court in any case where it appears to the court that such expert knowledge is required for the proper determination of the case.

NOTE
[1] Substituted by the Criminal Justice (Scotland) Act 1980, Sched. 2.

. . . . . .

Disposal of appeals
[1] **254.**—(1) The High Court may, subject to subsection (4) below, dispose of an appeal against conviction by—

(a) affirming the verdict of the trial court;

(b) setting aside the verdict of the trial court and either quashing the conviction or substituting therefor an amended verdict of guilty:
Provided that an amended verdict of guilty must be one which could have been returned on the indictment before the trial court; or

(c) setting aside the verdict of the trial court and granting authority to bring a new prosecution in accordance with section 255 of this Act.

(2) In setting aside, under subsection (1) above, a verdict the High Court may quash any sentence imposed on the appellant as respects the indictment, and—

(a) in a case where it substitutes an amended verdict of guilty, whether or not the sentence related to the verdict set aside; or

(b) in any other case, where the sentence did not so relate,
may pass another (but not more severe) sentence in substitution for the sentence so quashed.

(3) The High Court may, subject to subsection (4) below, dispose of an appeal against sentence by—

(a) affirming such sentence; or

(b) if the court thinks that, having regard to all the circumstances, including any additional evidence such as is mentioned in section 228(2) of this Act, a different sentence should have been passed, quashing the sentence and passing another sentence whether more or less severe in substitution therefor.

(4) In relation to any appeal under section 228(1) of this Act, the High Court shall, where it appears to it that the appellant committed the act charged against him but that he was insane when he did so, dispose of the appeal by—

(*a*) setting aside the verdict of the trial court and substituting therefor a verdict of acquittal on the ground of insanity; and

(*b*) quashing any sentence imposed on the appellant as respects the indictment and ordering that he be detained in a state hospital or such other hospital as for special reasons the court may specify.

(5) The provisions of subsection (4) of section 174 of this Act shall apply to an order under subsection (4)(*b*) above as they apply to an order under that section.

NOTE
[1] Substituted by the Criminal Justice (Scotland) Act 1980, Sched. 2.

Supplementary provisions where High Court authorises new prosecution

[1] **255.**—(1) Where authority is granted under section 254(1)(*c*) of this Act, a new prosecution may be brought charging the accused with the same or any similar offence arising out of the same facts; and the proceedings out of which the appeal arose shall not be a bar to such new prosecution:

Provided that no sentence may be passed on conviction under the new prosecution which could not have been passed on conviction under the earlier proceedings.

(2) A new prosecution may be brought under this section, notwithstanding that any time limit (other than the time limit mentioned in subsection (3) below), for the commencement of such proceedings has elapsed.

(3) Proceedings in a prosecution under this section shall be commenced within two months of the date on which authority to bring the prosecution was granted; and for the purposes of this subsection proceedings shall, in a case where such warrant is executed without unreasonable delay, be deemed to be commenced on the date on which a warrant to apprehend or to cite the accused is granted, and shall in any other case be deemed to be commenced on the date on which the warrant is executed.

(4) Where the two months mentioned in subsection (3) above elapse and no new prosecution has been brought under this section, the order under section 254(1)(*c*) of this Act setting aside the verdict shall have the effect, for all purposes, of an acquittal.

NOTE
[1] Substituted by the Criminal Justice (Scotland) Act 1980, Sched. 2.

. . . . . .

Failure to appear at hearing

[1] **257.** Where no appearance is made by or on behalf of an appellant at the diet appointed for the hearing of an appeal and where no case or argument in writing has been timeously lodged, the High Court shall dispose of the appeal as if it had been abandoned.

NOTE
[1] As amended by the Criminal Justice (Scotland) Act 1980, Scheds. 2 and 8.

Appellant may be sentenced in absence

258. The power of the High Court to pass any sentence under this Part of this Act may be exercised notwithstanding that the appellant is for any reason not present.

. . . . . .

Further provisions as to appeals

Prerogative of mercy

[1] **263.**—(1) Nothing in this Part of this Act shall affect the prerogative of mercy, but the Secretary of State on the consideration of any conviction of a person or the sentence (other than sentence of death) passed on a person who has been convicted, may, if he thinks fit, at any time, and whether or not an appeal against such conviction or sentence has previously been heard and determined by the High Court, refer the whole case to the High Court and the case shall be heard and determined, subject to any directions the High Court may make, as if it were an appeal under this Part of this Act.

[2] (2) The power of the Secretary of State under this section to refer to the High Court the case of a person convicted shall be exercisable whether or not that person has petitioned for the exercise of Her Majesty's mercy.

NOTES
[1] As amended by the Criminal Justice (Scotland) Act 1980, Scheds. 2 and 8. See the Legal Aid (Scotland) Act 1986, s. 25(5)(*b*), and the Criminal Justice Act 1988, s. 133.
[2] As amended by the Criminal Justice (Scotland) Act 1987, Sched. 2.

. . . . . .

Disqualification, forfeiture, etc.

[1] **264.**—(1) Where upon conviction of any person, any disqualification, forfeiture or disability attaches to such person by reason of such conviction, such disqualification, forfeiture or disability shall not attach for the period of two weeks from the date of the verdict against such person nor, in the event of an intimation of intention to appeal (or in the case of an appeal under section 228(1)(*b*) of this Act a note of appeal) being lodged under this Part of this Act, until such appeal, if it is proceeded with, is determined.

(2) Where, upon a conviction, any property, matters or things which are the subject of the prosecution or connected therewith are to be or may be ordered to be destroyed or forfeited, the destruction or forfeiture or the operation of any order for destruction or forfeiture thereof shall be suspended for the period of two weeks after the date of the verdict in the trial, and, in the event of an intimation of intention to appeal (or in the case of an appeal under section 228(1)(*b*) of this Act a note of appeal) being lodged under this Part of this Act, shall be further suspended until such appeal, if it is proceeded with, is determined.

[2] (3) Subsections (1) and (2) above do not apply in respect of any disqualification, forfeiture or, as the case may be, destruction or

forfeiture or order for destruction or forfeiture under or by virtue of any enactment which contains express provision for the suspension of such disqualification, forfeiture or, as the case may be, destruction or forfeiture or order for destruction or forfeiture pending the determination of any appeal against conviction or sentence.

NOTES
[1] As amended by the Criminal Justice (Scotland) Act 1980, Scheds. 2 and 8.
[2] Added by the Criminal Justice (Scotland) Act 1987, s. 68(2).

Fines and caution
[1] **265.**—(1) Where a person has on conviction been sentenced to payment of a fine and in default of payment to imprisonment, the person lawfully authorised to receive such fine shall, on receiving the same, retain it until the determination of any appeal in relation thereto.

(2) If a person sentenced to payment of a fine remains in custody in default of payment of the fine he shall be deemed, for the purposes of this Part of this Act, to be a person sentenced to imprisonment.

(3) Where a person has on conviction been sentenced to payment of a fine and in default of such payment to imprisonment, and he intimates to the judge who presided at the trial that he is desirous of appealing against his conviction to the High Court, the judge may, by order entered on the record, appoint such person forthwith to find caution for such sum as the judge may think right, to prosecute his appeal; and, subject thereto, may also so order that payment of the said fine shall be made at the final determination of the appeal, if the same be dismissed, to the clerk of the court in which the conviction took place or otherwise as the High Court may then order.

(4) An appellant who has been sentenced to the payment of a fine, and has paid the same in accordance with such sentence, shall, in the event of his appeal being successful, be entitled, subject to any order of the High Court, to the return of the sum or any part thereof so paid by him.

(5) If an appellant to whom subsection (3) of this section applies does not pay the fine or lodge an intimation of intention to appeal within two weeks from the date of his conviction and sentence, the Clerk of Justiciary shall report such omission to the High Court or any judge thereof who, after such notice as they or he may deem advisable, may find that the aforesaid caution has been forfeited, and may pronounce against the cautioner decree for such sum as they or he may think proper and may issue a warrant for the apprehension of the appellant and may commit him to prison in default of payment of his fine, or may make such other order as they or he may think right.

NOTE
[1] As amended by the Criminal Justice (Scotland) Act 1980, Scheds. 2 and 8.

• • • • • •

Reckoning of time spent pending appeal
[1] **268.**—(1) Subject to subsection (2) below, where an appellant is admitted to bail under section 238 of this Act the period beginning with the date of his admission to bail and ending on the date of his readmission

to prison in consequence of the determination or abandonment of his appeal shall not be reckoned as part of any term of imprisonment under this sentence.

(2) The time during which an appellant is in custody pending the determination of his appeal, including any period spent in custody in consequence of the recall of his bail, shall, subject to any direction which the High Court may give to the contrary, be reckoned as part of any term of imprisonment under his sentence.

(3) Subject to any direction which the High Court may give to the contrary, imprisonment of an appellant—

(*a*) who is in custody in consequence of the conviction or sentence appealed against shall be deemed to run as from the date on which the sentence was passed;

(*b*) who is in custody other than in consequence of such conviction or sentence shall be deemed to run or to be resumed as from the date on which his appeal was determined or abandoned;

(*c*) who is not in custody shall be deemed to run or to be resumed as from the date on which he is received into prison under the sentence.

(4) In this section references to a prison and imprisonment shall include respectively references to a young offenders institution, detention centre or place of safety and to detention in such institution, centre or place of safety, and any reference to a sentence shall be construed as a reference to a sentence passed by the court imposing sentence or by the High Court on appeal as the case may require.

NOTE
[1] As amended by the Criminal Justice (Scotland) Act 1980, Sched. 7, para. 46, and the Criminal Justice (Scotland) Act 1987, Sched. 1, para. 14.

· · · · · ·

Appeals against hospital orders, etc.
[1] **280.** Where a hospital order, interim hospital order (but not a renewal thereof), guardianship order or an order restricting discharge has been made by a court in respect of a person charged or brought before it, he may, without prejudice to any other form of appeal under any rule of law (or, where an interim hospital order has been made, to any right of appeal against any other order or sentence which may be imposed), appeal against that order in the same manner as against sentence.

NOTE
[1] As amended by the Criminal Justice (Scotland) Act 1980, Sched. 2, and the Mental Health (Amendment) (Scotland) Act 1983, s. 34(*b*).

· · · · · ·

[1] PART II

SUMMARY PROCEDURE

NOTE
[1] Applied by the Transport Act 1982, s. 40(4).

Jurisdiction

. . . . . .

Jurisdiction of inferior courts

284. The jurisdiction and powers of all courts of summary jurisdiction, except in so far as the same may be altered or modified by any future Act shall remain as at the commencement of this Act and the district court shall, without prejudice to any other or wider powers conferred by statute, be entitled to exercise power on convicting of a common law offence—

(*a*) to award imprisonment for any period not exceeding 60 days;

[1] (*b*) to impose a fine not exceeding level 4 on the standard scale;

[1] (*c*) to ordain the accused (in lieu of or in addition to such imprisonment or fine) to find caution for good behaviour for any period not exceeding six months and to an amount not exceeding level 4 on the standard scale;

(*d*) failing payment of such fine or on failure to find such caution, to award imprisonment in accordance with section 407 of this Act:

Provided that in no case shall the total imprisonment exceed 60 days.

NOTE
[1] As amended by the Criminal Law Act 1977, Sched. 11, para. 3, and the Criminal Justice Act 1982, Sched. 7. Extended by the Animal Health Act 1981, s. 92(2).

. . . . . .

Summary powers of sheriff

289. The sheriff shall, without prejudice to any other or wider powers conferred by statute, have power on convicting any person of a common law offence—

[1] (*a*) to impose a fine not exceeding the prescribed sum (within the meaning of section 289B below);

[1] (*b*) to ordain the accused to find caution for good behaviour for any period not exceeding 12 months and to an amount not exceeding the prescribed sum (within the meaning of section 289B below), such caution being either in lieu of or in addition to a fine or in addition to imprisonment as hereafter in this section mentioned;

(*c*) failing payment of such fine, or on failure to find such caution, to award imprisonment in accordance with section 407 of this Act;

(*d*) to award imprisonment, for any period not exceeding three months.

NOTE
[1] As amended by the Criminal Law Act 1977, Sched. 11, para. 4.

Amendment relating to penalties (and mode of trial) for offences made triable only summarily

[1] **289A.**—(1) The enactments specified in column 2 of Schedule 7A to this Act (which relate to the modes of trial of, and the maximum penalties for, the offences which are by section 283A of this Act made triable only summarily) shall so far as they relate to Scotland have effect subject to the amendments specified in column 3 of that Schedule.

(2) The said amendments have the effect of altering the maximum penalties available on summary conviction of those offences as well as making alterations consequential on their becoming triable only summarily; and in that Schedule column 4 shows the present maximum penalties by way of fine or imprisonment on summary conviction and on conviction on indictment, and column 5 shows the new maximum penalties resulting from amendments.

NOTE
[1] Added by the Criminal Law Act 1977, Sched. 11, para. 5.

Penalties on summary conviction for offences triable either summarily or on indictment

[1] **289B.**—(1) Where an offence created by a relevant enactment may be tried either on indictment or summarily, the penalty or maximum penalty on summary conviction shall, to the extent that it included, immediately before the commencement of section 55 of the Criminal Justice Act 1982, a penalty or maximum penalty mentioned in column 1 of the Table below, be amended so as to substitute as a maximum penalty the corresponding penalty set forth in column 2 thereof (unless provision is expressly made by any enactment for a larger penalty or maximum penalty on summary conviction)—

Column 1	*Column 2*
Penalty or maximum penalty at commencement of section 55 of Criminal Justice Act 1982	*New maximum penalty*
1. Fine (other than a fine specified in paragraph 3 below, or a fine in respect of each period of a specified length during which a continuing offence is committed).	1. Fine not exceeding the prescribed sum.
2. Imprisonment for a period exceeding 3 months.	2. Imprisonment for a period not exceeding 3 months.
3. Fine in respect of a specified quantity or number of things.	3. Fine not exceeding the prescribed sum in respect of such quantity or number.
4. Fine exceeding £100 in respect of each period of a specified length during which a continuing offence is committed.	4. Fine not exceeding £100 in respect of each such period.

(2) Where, by virtue of a relevant enactment, a person summarily convicted of any offence to which subsection (1) above relates would, apart from this section, be liable to a fine or a maximum fine of one amount in the case of a first conviction and of a different amount in the case of a second or subsequent conviction, subsection (1) above shall apply irrespective of whether the conviction is a first, second or subsequent one.

(3), (4) [Repealed by the Criminal Justice (Scotland) Act 1987, Sched. 2.]

(5) Subsection (1) above is without prejudice to section 290 of this Act (six months' imprisonment competent for certain offences).

[2] (6) In this section—

"the prescribed sum" means £2,000 or such sum as is for the time being substituted in this definition by an order in force under section 289D(1) of this Act;

"relevant enactment" means an enactment contained in the Criminal Law Act 1977 or in any Act (including this Act) passed before, or in the same session as, that Act.

[3] (7) Section 289GA(1) of this Act shall not affect so much of any enactment as (in whatever words) provides for a person to be made liable, on summary conviction, to a fine or a maximum fine for each period of a specified length during which a continuing offence is committed.

[3] (8) Where an enactment to which section 289GA(1) of this Act applies provides for a person to be made liable to a penalty or maximum penalty on summary conviction of an offence triable either on indictment or summarily which includes a fine or a maximum fine in respect of a specified quantity or a specified number of things, that subsection shall apply to that fine or maximum fine.

(9) Schedule 7B to this Act shall have effect for the purpose of altering the penalties or maximum penalties available on summary conviction of the offences therein mentioned; and subsection (1) above shall not apply on summary conviction of any of the offences mentioned in paragraph 1(2) of the said Schedule 7B.

NOTES
[1] Added by the Criminal Law Act 1977, Sched. 11, para. 5. Substituted by the Criminal Justice Act 1982, s. 55(2).
[2] As amended by S.I. 1984 No. 526.
[3] As amended by the Criminal Justice (Scotland) Act 1987, Sched. 1, para. 15.

Increase of fines for certain summary offences
[1] **289C.**—(1) The enactments specified in column 2 of Schedule 7C to this Act, which relate to the maximum fines for the offences mentioned (and broadly described) in column 1 of that Schedule, shall have effect as if the maximum fine that may be imposed on summary conviction of any offence so mentioned were a fine not exceeding the amount specified in column 4 of that Schedule instead of a fine not exceeding the amount specified in column 3 of that Schedule, so however that the preceding provision shall not alter the maximum daily fine, if any, provided for by any of those enactments.

(2) This subsection applies to the following enactments (by virtue of which certain byelaws may make persons contravening the byelaws liable on summary conviction to a fine not exceeding £20), namely—

(*a*) section 203 of the Local Government (Scotland) Act 1973 (offences against byelaws) but (the provisions of section 462(11) of this Act notwithstanding) not that section as applied to byelaws made under any provision contained in a local or private Act other than by a local authority; and (*b*) [Repealed by the Weights and Measures Act 1985, Sched. 13, Pt. I, with effect from 30th January 1986.]

² (3) In the enactments to which subsection (2) above applies for any reference to £20 there shall be substituted a reference to £50; and any provision in force at the coming into force of this subsection which—

(*a*) is contained in any byelaw made by virtue of any enactment to which subsection (2) above applies; and

(*b*) specifies £20 as the maximum fine which may be imposed on summary conviction in respect of a contravention of, or offence under, any byelaw mentioned in that provision,

shall have effect as if it specified £50 instead (but with no change by virtue of this subsection in the maximum daily fine, if any, for which it provides).

(4) This subsection applies to any pre-1949 enactment (however framed or worded) which—

(*a*) as regards any summary offence makes a person liable on conviction thereof to a fine of, or not exceeding, a specified amount less than £50 which has not been altered since the end of 1948 (and is not altered by this Act); or

(*b*) confers power by subordinate instrument to make a person as regards any summary offence (whether or not created by the instrument), liable on conviction thereof to a fine of, or a maximum fine of, less than £50 which has not been altered since the end of 1948 (and is not altered by this Act):

Provided that this subsection does not apply to any offence to which section 457A(1)(*b*) of this Act applies (offences triable only summarily other than by virtue of express provision).

(5) Every enactment to which subsection (4) above applies shall have effect as if for the specified amount less than £50 there mentioned there were substituted:—

(*a*) £25 if the specified amount is less than £20; or

(*b*) £50 if the specified amount is not less than £20.

(6) Where, by virtue of any enactment to which subsection (4) above applies by virtue of paragraph (*a*) of that subsection, a person convicted of a summary offence would, apart from this section, be liable to a fine, or maximum fine, of one amount in the case of a first conviction and of a different amount in the case of a second or subsequent conviction, subsection (5) above shall apply separately in relation to each specified amount less than £50, even if this produces the same instead of different amounts for different convictions.

(7) Subsection (4) above does not apply to so much of any enactment as (in whatever words) makes a person liable or provides for a person to be made liable, on summary conviction, to a fine or a maximum fine for each period of a specified length during which a continuing offence is committed.

(7A) Where an enactment to which subsection (4) above applies provides or confers a power to provide for, on conviction of an offence triable only summarily, a fine or a maximum fine in respect of a specified quantity or a specified number of things, "the specified amount" for the purposes of subsection (5) above is the fine or maximum fine so provided or for which provision may be made.

(8) In subsection (4) above "pre-1949 enactment" means an enactment

passed before 1st January 1949 or an enactment passed on or after that date which (whether directly or, through successive re-enactments, indirectly) re-enacts with or without modification an enactment passed before that date.

(9) In this section "enactment" does not include an enactment contained in an order, regulation or other instrument made under an Act.

NOTES
[1] Added by the Criminal Law Act 1977, Sched. 11, para. 5. As amended by the Criminal Justice Act 1982, s. 55(3).
[2] See the Weights and Measures Act 1985, Sched. 11, para. 24.

Power to alter sums specified in certain provisions
[1] **289D.**—(1) If it appears to the Secretary of State that there has been a change in the value of money since the relevant date, he may by order substitute for the sum or sums for the time being specified in the provisions mentioned in subsection (1A) below such other sum or sums as appear to him justified by the change.

(1A) The provisions referred to in subsection (1) above are—
(*a*) section 289B(6) of this Act;
(*b*) section 289G(2) of this Act;
(*c*) section 407(1A) of this Act;
(*d*) section 435(*e*) of this Act;
(*e*) section 453(3) of this Act;
(*f*), (*g*) [Repealed by the Criminal Justice (Scotland) Act 1987, Sched. 2.]

(1B) In subsection (1) above "relevant date" means—
(*a*) in relation to the first order made under that subsection, 29th July 1977 (the date of the passing of the Criminal Law Act 1977); and
(*b*) in relation to each subsequent order, the date of the previous order.

(2), (3) [Repealed by the Criminal Justice (Scotland) Act 1987, Sched. 2.]

(3A) [Inserted by the Criminal Justice (Scotland) Act 1980, Sched. 7, para. 50; repealed by the Criminal Justice Act 1982, s. 53(*c*) and Sched. 16.]

[2] (4) An order under subsection (1) above—
(*a*) shall be made by statutory instrument subject to annulment in pursuance of a resolution of either House of Parliament and may be revoked by a subsequent order thereunder; and
(*b*) without prejudice to Schedule 14 to the Criminal Law Act 1977, shall not affect the punishment for an offence committed before that order comes into force.

NOTES
[1] Added by the Criminal Law Act 1977, Sched. 11, para. 5. Saved by the Criminal Justice (Scotland) Act 1980, s. 7(2). As amended by the Criminal Justice (Scotland) Act 1980, Scheds. 7 and 8, and the Criminal Justice Act 1982, ss. 53, 55(4) and Sched. 16.
[2] As amended by the Criminal Justice (Scotland) Act 1987, Sched. 2.

Penalties for first and subsequent convictions of summary offences to be the same
[1] **289E.**—(1) Subject to subsections (2) to (4) and (6) below, this section applies where any Act—

(*a*) makes a person liable on conviction of an offence triable only summarily to a penalty or a maximum penalty; or

(*b*) confers a power by subordinate instrument to make a person liable on conviction of an offence triable only summarily (whether or not created by the instrument) to a penalty or a maximum penalty

which is different in the case of a second or subsequent conviction from the penalty or maximum penalty provided or for which provision may be made in the case of a first conviction.

(2) Where the penalty or maximum penalty for an offence to which section 457A(1)(*b*) of this Act applies has not been altered by any enactment passed or made after 29th July 1977 (the date of the passing of the Criminal Law Act 1977), this section applies as if the amount referred to in subsection (5)(*a*) below were the greatest amount to which a person would have been liable on any conviction immediately before that date.

(3) Where any Act—

(*a*) provides or confers a power to provide for a penalty or a maximum penalty which would, but for the operation of section 289C(5) of this Act, be different in the case of a second or subsequent conviction from the penalty or maximum penalty provided for or for which provision may be made in the case of a first conviction; and

(*b*) otherwise fulfils the conditions of subsection (1) above;

this section applies to that penalty or maximum penalty as if the amount referred to in subsection (5)(*a*) below were the greatest amount to which a person would have been liable or could have been made liable on any conviction immediately before the commencement of the said section 289C.

(4) This section does not apply to—

(*a*) section 290 of this Act (imprisonment for certain offences);

(*b*) section 78 of the Criminal Justice (Scotland) Act 1980 (vandalism); or

(*c*) an enactment mentioned in Schedule 7D to this Act.

(5) Where this section applies the maximum penalty to which a person is or may be made liable by or under the Act in the case of any conviction shall be either or both of—

(*a*) a fine not exceeding the greatest amount;

(*b*) imprisonment for a term not exceeding the longest term (if any)

to which an offender would have been liable or could have been liable on any conviction (whether the first or a second or subsequent conviction) by or under the Act immediately before the commencement of this section.

(6) This section does not affect the penalty which may be imposed in respect of an offence committed before it comes into force.

NOTE
[1] Inserted by the Criminal Justice Act 1982, s. 54. Section 56(2) of the Criminal Justice Act 1988 provides:

"Section 289E of the Criminal Procedure (Scotland) Act 1975 (penalties for first and subsequent convictions of summary offences to be the same) shall have effect as if the references in it to an Act included references to an instrument and the reference in subsection (5) to the commencement of the section were a reference, in relation to an instrument conferring a power such as is mentioned in subsection (1), to the coming into force of this section."

Increase of fines for certain summary offences

[1] **289F.**—(1) Subject to subsections (2) to (7) and (9) below, this section applies where any Act passed on or before 29th July 1977 (the date of the passing of the Criminal Law Act 1977)—

(*a*) makes a person liable on conviction of an offence triable only summarily to a fine or a maximum fine which is less than £1,000; or

(*b*) confers a power by subordinate instrument to make a person liable on conviction of an offence triable only summarily (whether or not created by the instrument) to a fine or a maximum fine which is less than £1,000, or a fine or a maximum fine which shall not exceed an amount of less than £1,000,

and the fine or maximum fine which may be imposed or, as the case may be, for which the subordinate instrument may provide has not been altered by—

(i) section 289A of this Act;

(ii) section 289C of this Act (except where section 289E(3) of this Act applies);

(iii) section 30(3) of the Criminal Law Act 1977;

(iv) an enactment passed or made after 29th July 1977 and before the commencement of this section.

(2) In the case of an offence to which section 457A(1)(*b*) of this Act applies, paragraphs (i) to (iii) of subsection (1) above do not apply and the fine or the maximum fine referred to in subsection (8) below is the fine or the maximum fine for the offence immediately before 29th July 1977 as amended, where applicable, by section 289E of this Act.

(3) This section also applies where any enactment—

(*a*) is contained in a consolidation Act passed after 29th July 1977 and before the commencement of this section; and

(*b*) otherwise fulfils the conditions of subsection (1) above as amended by subsection (2) above where it applies; and

(*c*) is a re-enactment (with or without modification) of an enactment passed on or before that date.

(4) Subject to subsection (9) below, where an Act provides or confers a power to provide for, on conviction of an offence triable only summarily, a fine or a maximum fine in respect of a specified quantity or a specified number of things, that fine or maximum fine is the fine or, as the case may be, the maximum fine for the purposes of this section.

(5) Where an Act to which this section applies provides or confers a power to provide different fines or maximum fines in relation to different circumstances or persons of different descriptions, such fines or maximum fines are to be treated separately for the purposes of this section.

(6) This section also applies where the penalties or maximum penalties provided or for which provision may be made by or under any Act on first and on second or subsequent conviction of an offence have been made the same by operation of section 289E of this Act; and in that case the fine or the maximum fine referred to in subsection (8) below is the maximum fine to which a person is or may be made liable by virtue of that section.

(7) This section does not apply in the case of—

(*a*) so much of any Act as (in whatever words) makes a person liable or provides for a person to be made liable to a fine or a

maximum fine for each period of a specified length during
which a continuing offence is committed;

(*b*) section 67(3) of the Transport Act 1962;

(*c*) sections 40(5) and 44(1) of the Road Traffic Act 1972;

(*d*) an enactment mentioned in Schedule 1 to the British Railways
Act 1977 to the extent that the enactment was amended by
section 13(1) of that Act;

(*e*) an enactment mentioned in Schedule 7D to this Act or in
Schedule 2 to the Criminal Justice Act 1982.

(8) Where this section applies, the fine or, as the case may be, the
maximum fine to which a person is or may be made liable by or under the
Act shall be increased to the amount shown in column 2 of the Table
below opposite the band in column 1 within which the fine or the
maximum fine referred to in subsection (1) above falls.

Column 1	*Column 2*
Fine or maximum fine	*Increased amount*
Under £25	£25
Under £50 but not less than £25	£50
Under £200 but not less than £50	£200
Under £400 but not less than £200	£500
Under £1,000 but not less than £400	£1,000

(9) Where an Act to which this section applies provides or confers a
power to provide for, on conviction of an offence triable only summarily,
a fine or a maximum fine in respect of a specified quantity or a specified
number of things but also provides or confers a power to provide for an
alternative fine or maximum fine as regards the offence, subsection (8)
above shall have effect to increase—

(*a*) the alternative fine; and

(*b*) any amount that the Act provides or confers a power to provide for
as the maximum which a fine as regards the offence may not
exceed,

as well as the fine or maximum fine which it has effect to increase by virtue
of subsection (4) above.

(10) This section does not affect the penalty which may be imposed in
respect of an offence committed before it comes into force.

NOTE
[1] Inserted by the Criminal Justice Act 1982, s. 54.

The standard scale: amendment of enactments
[1] **289G.**—(1) There shall be a standard scale of fines for offences triable
only summarily, which shall be known as "the standard scale".

[2] (2) The standard scale is as follows—

Standard Scale	
Level	*Amount*
1	£50
2	£100

Level	*Amount*
3	£400
4	£1,000
5	£2,000

(3) Any reference in any enactment (whether passed or made before or after the passing of the Criminal Justice Act 1982) to a specified level on the standard scale shall be construed as referring to the amount which corresponds to that level on the standard scale referred to in subsection (2) above.

(4) Subject to subsection (8) below, where—

    (*a*) an enactment to which subsection (5) below applies either—

        (i) makes a person liable on conviction of an offence triable only summarily (whether created by that enactment or otherwise) to a fine or a maximum fine; or

        (ii) confers a power by subordinate instrument to make a person liable on conviction of an offence triable only summarily (whether or not created by the instrument) to a fine or a maximum fine;

        and

    (*b*) the amount of the fine or the maximum fine is, whether by virtue of that enactment or otherwise, an amount shown in the second column of the standard scale,

for the reference in the enactment to the amount of the fine or maximum fine there shall be substituted a reference to the level on the standard scale shown in the first column thereof as corresponding to the amount in the second column thereof referred to in paragraph (*b*) above.

(5) This subsection applies to an enactment in any Act (including this Act) passed before the commencement of this section.

(6) Subject to subsection (7) below, where an Act provides or confers a power to provide for, on conviction of an offence triable only summarily, a fine or a maximum fine in respect of a specified quantity or a specified number of things, that fine or maximum fine is the fine, or as the case may be, the maximum fine for the purposes of this section.

(7) Where an Act provides or confers a power to provide for, on conviction of an offence triable only summarily, a fine or a maximum fine in respect of a specified quantity or a specified number of things but also provides or confers a power to provide for an alternative fine or maximum fine as regards the offence, the fine or the maximum fine for the purposes of this section is—

    (*a*) the alternative fine; and

    (*b*) any amount that the Act provides or confers a power to provide for as the maximum which a fine as regards the offence may not exceed,

as well as the fine or maximum fine referred to in subsection (6) above.

(8) Subsection (4) above does not apply to—

    (*a*) an enactment mentioned in Schedule 2 to the Companies Act 1980;

    (*b*) the Companies Act 1981; or

    (*c*) so much of any Act as (in whatever words) makes a person liable or provides for a person to be made liable to a fine or a maximum fine for each period of a specified length during which a continuing offence is committed.

(9) Where an enactment to which subsection (5) above applies confers a power such as is mentioned in subsection (4)(*a*)(ii) above, the power shall be construed as a power to make a person liable to a fine or, as the case may be, a maximum fine of the amount corresponding to the level on the standard scale to which the enactment refers by virtue of subsection (4) above or of a lesser amount.

(10) Subject to subsection (12) below, where under a relevant subordinate instrument the fine or maximum fine on conviction of a summary offence specified in the instrument is an amount shown in the second column of the standard scale, the reference in the instrument to the amount of the fine or maximum fine shall be construed as a reference to the level in the first column of the standard scale corresponding to that amount.

(11) In subsection (10) above, "relevant subordinate instrument" means any instrument made by virtue of an enactment after 30th April 1984 and before the commencement of section 66 of the Criminal Justice (Scotland) Act 1987.

(12) Subsection (10) above shall not affect so much of any instrument as (in whatever words) makes a person liable on summary conviction to a fine not exceeding a specified amount for each period of a specified length during which a continuing offence is continued after conviction or the occurrence of any other specified event.

(13) Where there is—

(*a*) under any enactment (however framed or worded) contained in an Act passed before the commencement of section 66 of the Criminal Justice (Scotland) Act 1987,

(*b*) under any instrument (however framed or worded) made by virtue of such an enactment,

a power to provide by subordinate instrument that a person, as regards any summary offence (whether or not created by the instrument) shall be liable on conviction to a fine, a person may be so made liable to a fine not exceeding a specified level on the standard scale.

(14) Subsection (13) above has effect in relation to exercises of powers before as well as after the commencement of section 66 of the Criminal Justice (Scotland) Act 1987.

NOTES
[1] Inserted by the Criminal Justice Act 1982, s. 54. New subss. (10)–(14) inserted by the Criminal Justice (Scotland) Act 1987, s. 66(1).
[2] As amended by S.I. 1984 No. 526.
[3] Amended by the Criminal Justice Act 1988. Sched. 15, para. 49.

Statutory maximum as penalty in respect of summary conviction for offences in subordinate instruments

[1] **289GA.**—(1) Where there is, under any enactment (however framed or worded) contained in an Act passed before the commencement of section 66 of the Criminal Justice (Scotland) Act 1987, a power by subordinate instrument to create a criminal offence triable either on indictment or summarily, the maximum fine which may, in the exercise of the power, be authorised on summary conviction shall, by virtue of this

section, be the statutory maximum (unless some larger maximum fine can be authorised on summary conviction of such an offence by virtue of an enactment other than this subsection).

(2) Where there is, under any enactment (however framed or worded) contained in an Act passed before the commencement of section 66 of the Criminal Justice (Scotland) Act 1987, a power to create offences triable either on indictment or summarily by subordinate instrument, the maximum fine on summary conviction for such an offence may be expressed as a fine not exceeding the statutory maximum.

(3) Subsections (1) and (2) above shall have effect in relation to any exercise of such power before as well as after the commencement of section 66 of the Criminal Justice (Scotland) Act 1987.

(4) Where an offence created by a subordinate instrument made before the commencement of section 66 of the Criminal Justice (Scotland) Act 1987 may be tried either on indictment or summarily, the maximum fine which may be imposed on summary conviction shall by virtue of this subsection be the statutory maximum (unless the offence is one for which by virtue of the instrument a larger maximum fine may be imposed on summary conviction).

(5) Where a person summarily convicted of any offence to which subsection (4) above relates would, apart from this section, be liable to a fine or to a maximum fine of an amount in the case of a first conviction and of a different amount in the case of a second or subsequent conviction, subsection (4) above shall apply irrespective of whether the conviction is a first, second or subsequent one.

(6) Subsection (4) above shall not affect so much of any instrument as (in whatever words) makes a person liable on summary conviction to a fine not exceeding a specified amount for each period of a specified length during which a continuing offence is continued after conviction or the occurrence of any other specified event.

(7) Nothing in this section shall affect the punishment for an offence committed before the commencement of section 66 of the Criminal Justice (Scotland) Act 1987.

NOTE
[1] Inserted by the Criminal Justice Act 1987, s. 66(2).

Exceptionally high maximum fines
[1] **289GB.**—(1) The Secretary of State may by order amend an enactment or subordinate instrument specifying a sum to which this subsection applies so as to substitute for that sum such other sum as appears to him—
  (*a*) to be justified by a change in the value of money appearing to him to have taken place since the last occasion on which the sum in question was fixed; or
  (*b*) to be appropriate to take account of an order altering the standard scale which has been made or is proposed to be made.

(2) Subsection (1) above applies to any sum which—
  (*a*) is higher than level 5 on the standard scale; and
  (*b*) is specified as the fine or the maximum fine which may be imposed on conviction of an offence which is triable only summarily.

(3) The Secretary of State may by order amend an enactment or subordinate instrument specifying a sum to which this subsection applies so as to substitute for that sum such other sum as appears to him—

(*a*) to be justified by a change in the value of money appearing to him to have taken place since the last occasion on which the sum in question was fixed; or

(*b*) to be appropriate to take account of an order made or proposed to be made altering the statutory maximum.

(4) Subsection (3) above applies to any sum which—

(*a*) is higher than the statutory maximum; and

(*b*) is specified as the maximum fine which may be imposed on summary conviction of an offence triable either on indictment or summarily.

(5) An order under this section—

(*a*) shall be made by statutory instrument subject to annulment in pursuance of a resolution of either House of Parliament; and

(*b*) shall not affect the punishment for an offence committed before that order comes into force.

(6) In this section—

"enactment" includes an enactment contained in an Act passed after the Criminal Justice (Scotland) Act 1987; and

"subordinate instrument" includes an instrument made after the passing of that Act.

NOTE
[1] Inserted by the Criminal Justice Act 1987, s. 66(2).

Fines under secondary subordinate instruments—Scotland

[1] **289GC.**—(1) This section applies to any instrument (however framed or worded) which—

(*a*) was made before 11th April 1983 (the date of commencement of Part IV of the Criminal Justice Act 1982);

(*b*) confers on any authority other than a harbour authority a power by subordinate instrument to make a person, as regards any summary offence (whether or not created by the latter instrument), liable on conviction to a maximum fine of a specified amount not exceeding £1,000,

but does not affect so much of any such instrument as (in whatever words) confers a power by subordinate instrument to make a person liable on conviction to a fine for each period of a specified length during which a continuing offence is continued.

(2) The maximum fine to which a subordinate instrument made by virtue of an instrument to which this section applies may provide that a person shall be liable on conviction of a summary offence is—

(*a*) if the specified amount is less than £25, level 1 on the standard scale;

(*b*) if it is £25 or more but less than £50, level 2;

(*c*) if it is £50 or more but less than £200, level 3;

(*d*) if it is £200 or more but less than £400, level 4; and

(*e*) if it is £400 or more, level 5.

(3) Subject to subsection (5) below, where an instrument to which this

section applies confers a power by subordinate instrument to make a person, as regards a summary offence, liable on conviction to a fine in respect of a specified quantity or a specified number of things, that fine shall be treated for the purposes of this section as being the maximum fine to which a person may be made liable by virtue of the instrument.

(4) Where an instrument to which this section applies confers a power to provide for different maximum fines in relation to different circumstances or persons of different descriptions, the amount specified as those maximum fines are to be treated separately for the purposes of this section.

(5) Where an instrument to which this section applies confers a power by subordinate instrument to make a person, as regards a summary offence, liable on conviction to a fine in respect of a specified quantity or a specified number of things but also confers a power by subordinate instrument to make a person, as regards such an offence, liable on conviction to an alternative fine, this section shall have effect in relation—

(*a*) to the alternative fine; and

(*b*) to any amount that the instrument specifies as the maximum fine for which a subordinate instrument made in the exercise of the power conferred by it may provide,

as well as in relation to the fine mentioned in subsection (3) above.

NOTE
[1] Inserted by the Criminal Justice Act 1988, s. 56.

Fines on summary conviction for offences under subordinate instruments—conversion to references to levels on scale

[1] **289GD.**—(1) Where an instrument which was made under an enactment on or after 11th April 1983 but before the commencement of section 54 of the Criminal Justice Act 1988 confers on any authority other than a harbour authority a power by subordinate instrument to make a person liable on summary conviction to a fine of an amount shown in the second column of the standard scale, as that scale had effect when the instrument was made, a reference to the level in the first column of the standard scale which then corresponded to that amount shall be substituted for the reference in the instrument conferring the power to the amount of the fine.

(2) This section shall not affect so much of any instrument as (in whatever words) makes a person liable on summary conviction to a maximum fine not exceeding a specified amount for each period of a specified length during which a continuing offence is continued.

NOTE
[1] Inserted by the Criminal Justice Act 1988, s. 54.

Schedule 7D
[1] **289H.**—(1) The enactments specified in column 1 of Schedule 7D to this Act, which relate to the penalties or the maximum penalties for the offences mentioned in those enactments, shall be amended in accordance with the amendments specified in column 2 of that Schedule, which have the effect of altering the penalties on summary conviction of the said

offences and placing the fines on a level on the standard scale; and in that Schedule column 3 shows the penalties or, as the case may be, maximum penalties in force immediately before the commencement of this section and column 4 shows the penalties or, as the case may be, maximum penalties resulting from the amendments.

(2) Subsection (1) above does not affect the penalty which may be imposed in respect of an offence committed before it comes into force.

NOTE
[1] Inserted by the Criminal Justice Act 1982, s. 54.

When six months' imprisonment competent
290. Where a person is convicted by the sheriff of—
  (*a*) a second or subsequent offence inferring dishonest appropriation of property, or attempt thereat, or
  (*b*) a second or subsequent offence inferring personal violence,
he may, without prejudice to any wider powers conferred by statute, be sentenced to imprisonment for any period not exceeding six months.

. . . . . .

Procedure prior to trial

. . . . .

Committal of children to custody in place of safety
[1] **297.**—(1) Any court, on remanding or committing for trial a child who is not liberated on bail shall, instead of committing him to prison, commit him to the local authority in whose area the court is situated to be detained in a place of safety chosen by the local authority for the period for which he is remanded or until he is liberated in due course of law.

Provided that in the case of a child over 14 years of age it shall not be obligatory on the court so to commit him if the court certifies that he is of so unruly a character that he cannot safely be so committed or that he is of so depraved a character that he is not a fit person to be so detained; [but the court shall not so certify a child unless such conditions as the Secretary of State may by order made by statutory instrument prescribe are satisfied in relation to the child.][2]

(2) A commitment under this section may be varied, or, in the case of a child over 14 years of age, who proves to be of so unruly a character that he cannot safely be detained in such custody, or to be of so depraved a character that he is not a fit person to be so detained, revoked, by the court which made the order, or if application cannot conveniently be made to that court, by a sheriff sitting summarily having jurisdiction in the place where the court which made the order sat, and if it is revoked the child may be committed to prison; [but a commitment shall not be so revoked unless such conditions as the Secretary of State may by order made by statutory instrument prescribe are satisfied in relation to the child.][2]

NOTES
[1] See the National Health Service (Scotland) Act 1978, s. 16A.
[2] Words in square brackets added (*prosp.*) by the Children Act 1975, s. 70.

• • • • • •

Remand and committal of persons under 21
[1] **329.**—[2] (1) Where a court remands or commits for trial or for sentence a person under 21 years of age who is charged with or convicted of an offence and is not released on bail or ordained to appear, then, except as otherwise expressly provided by this section, the following provisions shall have effect, that is to say—
  (*a*) subject to the following paragraph, if he is under 16 years of age the court shall commit him to the local authority in whose area the court is situated, and the authority shall have the duty of placing him in a suitable place of safety chosen by the authority instead of committing him to prison;
  (*b*) if he is a person of over 16 years of age, or a child under 16 years of age but over 14 years of age who is certified by the court to be unruly or depraved, and the court has been notified by the Secretary of State that a remand centre is available for the reception from that court of persons of his class or description, he shall be committed to a remand centre instead of being committed to prison [; but the court shall not so certify a child unless such conditions as the Secretary of State may by order made by statutory instrument prescribe are satisfied in relation to the child.][1]
  (2) Where any person is committed to a local authority or to a remand centre under any provision of this Act, that authority or centre shall be specified in the warrant, and he shall be detained by the authority or in the centre for the period for which he is committed or until he is liberated in due course of law.
  (3) Where any person has been committed to a local authority under any provision of this Act, the court by which he was committed, if the person so committed is not less than 14 years of age and it appears to the court that he is unruly or depraved, may revoke the commitment and commit the said person—
  (*a*) if the court has been notified that a remand centre is available for the reception from that court of persons of his class or description, to a remand centre; and
  (*b*) if the court has not been so notified, to a prison [but a commitment shall not be so revoked unless such conditions as the Secretary of State may by order made by statutory instrument prescribe are satisfied in relation to the said person.][3]
  (4) Where, in the case of a person under 16 years of age who has been committed to prison or to a remand centre under this section, the sheriff is satisfied that his detention in prison or remand centre is no longer necessary, he may revoke the commitment and commit the person to the local authority in whose area the court is situated, and the authority shall have the duty of placing him in a suitable place of safety.

NOTES
[1] This section came into force on January 6, 1992: see para. 7–17, n. 48a, above.

[2] As amended by the Criminal Justice (Scotland) Act 1987, s. 62(2).
[3] Words in square brackets added (*prosp.*) by the Children Act 1975, s. 70.

Power of court to commit to hospital a person suffering from mental disorder

330.—(1) Where a court remands or commits for trial a person charged with any offence who appears to the court to be suffering from mental disorder, and the court is satisfied that a hospital is available for his admission and suitable for this detention, the court may, instead of remanding him in custody, commit him to that hospital.

[1] (2) Where any person is committed to a hospital as aforesaid, the hospital shall be specified in the warrant and, if the responsible medical officer is satisfied that he is suffering from mental disorder of a nature or degree which warrants his admission to a hospital under Part V of the Mental Health (Scotland) Act 1984, he shall there be detained for the period for which he is remanded or the period of committal, unless before the expiration of that period he is liberated in due course of law.

(3) When the responsible medical officer has examined the person so detained he shall report the result of that examination to the court and, where the report is to the effect that the person is not suffering from mental disorder of such a nature or degree as aforesaid, the court may commit him to any prison or other institution to which he might have been committed had he not been committed to hospital or may otherwise deal with him according to law.

(4) No person shall be committed to a hospital under this section except on the written or oral evidence of a medical practitioner.

NOTE
[1] As amended by the Mental Health (Scotland) Act 1984, Sched. 3, para. 31.

· · · · · ·

Offences by companies, etc.

333. With regard to the summary prosecution of offences committed by a company, association, incorporation or body of trustees, the following provisions shall, without prejudice to any other or wider powers conferred by statute, apply:—

(*a*) proceedings may be taken against the company, association, incorporation or body of trustees in their corporate capacity, and in that event any penalty imposed shall be recovered by civil diligence in manner hereinafter provided; or

(*b*) proceedings may be taken against an individual representative of such company, association or incorporation as follows:—

    (i) in the case of an ordinary company or firm, any one of the partners thereof, or the manager or the person in charge or locally in charge of the affairs thereof, may be dealt with as if he was the person offending;

    (ii) in the case of an association, incorporation or incorporated company, the managing director or the secretary or other person in charge, or locally in charge, of the affairs thereof, may be dealt with as if he was the person offending;

    (iii) the offence shall be deemed to be the offence of such company, association or incorporation.

Trial Procedure

. . . . . .

Punishment of witness for contempt
[1] **344.**—[2] (1) If a witness in a summary prosecution shall wilfully fail to attend after being duly cited, or unlawfully refuse to be sworn, or after the oath has been administered to him refuse to answer any question which the court may allow, or to produce documents in his possession when required by the court, or shall prevaricate in his evidence, he shall be deemed guilty of contempt of court and be liable to be summarily punished forthwith for such contempt by a fine not exceeding level 3 on the standard scale or by imprisonment for any period not exceeding 21 days.

(2) Where such punishment as aforesaid is summarily imposed, the clerk of court shall enter in the record of the proceedings the acts constituting the contempt or the statements forming the prevarication.

(3) The foregoing provisions of this section shall be without prejudice to the prosecutor proceeding by way of formal complaint for any such contempt where such summary punishment, as above mentioned, is not imposed.

(4) Any witness who, after being duly cited in accordance with section 315 of this Act—

(a) fails without reasonable excuse, after receiving at least 48 hours' notice, to attend for precognition by a prosecutor at the time and place mentioned in the citation served on him, or

(b) refuses when so cited to give information within his knowledge regarding any matter relative to the commission of the offence in relation to which such precognition is taken,

shall be liable to the like punishment as is provided in the foregoing provisions of this section.

NOTES
[1] As amended by the Criminal Justice (Scotland) Act 1980, s. 46 and Sched. 7.
[2] As amended by the Criminal Justice Act 1982, Sched. 7.

. . . . . .

Previous convictions
356.—(1) A previous conviction may not be libelled as an aggravation of an offence.

(2) Where a person is convicted of an offence, the court may have regard to any previous conviction in respect of that person in deciding on the disposal of the case.

(3) Nothing in this section shall affect the sentence which a court may pass on a second or subsequent conviction.

Laying of previous convictions before court
[1] **357.**—[2] (1) Where the accused in a summary prosecution has been previously convicted of any offence and the prosecutor has decided to lay a previous conviction before the court, the following provisions shall have effect:—

(*a*) a notice in the form, as nearly as may be, of Form No. 2 or 3 of Part III of Schedule 2 to the Summary Jurisdiction (Scotland) Act 1954 or of the appropriate form in an Act of Adjournal under this Act setting forth the previous conviction shall be served on the accused with the complaint where he is cited to a diet, and where he is in custody the complaint and such a notice shall be served on him before he is asked to plead;

(*b*) the previous conviction shall not be laid before the judge until he is satisfied that the charge is proved;

(*c*) if a plea of guilty is tendered or if, after a plea of not guilty, the accused is convicted the prosecutor shall lay the notice referred to in paragraph (*a*) of this subsection before the judge, and

(i) in a case where the plea of guilty is tendered in writing the accused shall be deemed to admit any previous conviction set forth in the notice, unless he expressly denies it in the writing by which that plea is tendered;

(ii) in any other case the judge or the clerk of court shall ask the accused whether he admits the previous conviction,

and if such admission is made or deemed to be made it shall be entered in the record of the proceedings;

(*d*) it shall not be necessary for the prosecutor to produce extracts of any previous convictions so admitted;

(*e*) where the accused does not admit any such previous conviction, the prosecutor unless he withdraws the conviction shall adduce evidence in proof thereof either then or at any other diet;

(*f*) a copy of any notice served on the accused under this subsection shall be entered in the record of the proceedings.

(2) A conviction, or an extract conviction of any offence committed in any part of the United Kingdom, bearing to be under the hand of the officer in use to give out such extract conviction, shall be received in evidence without being sworn to by witnesses. An official of any prison in which the accused may have been confined on such conviction shall be a competent and sufficient witness to prove the application thereof to the accused, although such official may not have been present in court at the trial to which such conviction relates. The provision shall be without prejudice to any other competent mode of proving a conviction and the application thereof to the accused.

(3) Where in any court a book of record is kept of the convictions in the court containing the like particulars as are inserted in an extract conviction, and where at the end of each day's proceedings the entries in such book are certified as correct by the judge or clerk of court, such entries shall, in any proceeding in that court, be accepted as evidence of such convictions.

(4) Where the accused in a summary prosecution is convicted of any offence and also of any aggravation by previous conviction, and is again accused of any offence in regard to which such conviction may be competently used as an aggravation, the production of the prior conviction, or an extract thereof, setting forth the particulars of the previous convictions therein libelled, shall be admissible and sufficient evidence to prove against the accused all the previous convictions and aggravations therein set forth.

(5) Nothing in this section shall prevent evidence of previous convictions being led *in causa* where such evidence is competent in support of a substantive charge.

NOTES
[1] As amended by the Criminal Justice (Scotland) Act 1980, s. 40. See S.I. 1978 No. 834.
[2] Excluded by the Road Traffic Offenders Act 1988, ss. 31(2) and 32(6).

Proof of previous convictions by fingerprints

358.—(1) A previous conviction may be proved against any person in any criminal proceedings by the production of such evidence of the conviction as is mentioned in this section and by showing that his fingerprints and those of the person convicted are the fingerprints of the same person.

(2) A certificate purporting to be signed by or on behalf of the Chief Constable of Strathclyde or the Commissioner of Police of the Metropolis, containing particulars relating to a conviction extracted from the criminal records kept by the person by or on whose behalf the certificate is signed, and certifying that the copies of the fingerprints contained in the certificate are copies of the fingerprints appearing from the said records to have been taken in pursuance of regulations for the time being in force under section 11 of the Prisons (Scotland) Act 1952, or under section 16 of the Prison Act 1952, from the person convicted on the occasion of the conviction or on the occasion of his last conviction, shall be sufficient evidence of the conviction or, as the case may be, of his last conviction and of all preceding convictions and that the copies of the fingerprints produced on the certificate are copies of the fingerprints of the person convicted.

(3) Where a person has been apprehended and detained in the custody of the police in connection with any criminal proceedings, a certificate purporting to be signed by the chief constable concerned or a person authorised on his behalf, certifying that the fingerprints produced thereon were taken from him while he was so detained, shall be sufficient evidence in those proceedings that the fingerprints produced on the certificate are the fingerprints of that person.

(4) A certificate purporting to be signed by or on behalf of the governor of a prison or of a remand centre in which any person has been detained in connection with any criminal proceedings, certifying that the fingerprints produced thereon were taken from him while he was so detained, shall be sufficient evidence in those proceedings that the fingerprints produced on the certificate are the fingerprints of that person.

(5) A certificate purporting to be signed by or on behalf of the Chief Constable of Strathclyde, and certifying that the fingerprints, copies of which are certified as aforesaid by or on behalf of the Chief Constable or the Commissioner of Police of the Metropolis to be copies of the fingerprints of a person previously convicted and the fingerprints certified by or on behalf of a chief constable or a governor as aforesaid, or otherwise shown, to be the fingerprints of the person against whom the previous conviction is sought to be proved, are the fingerprints of the same person, shall be sufficient evidence of the matter so certified.

(6) The method of proving a previous conviction authorised by this section shall be in addition to any other method of proving the conviction.

. . . . . .

Procedure at trial involving children

. . . . . .

Welfare of child

371. Every court in dealing with a child who is brought before it as an offender shall have regard to the welfare of the child and shall in a proper case take steps for removing him from undesirable surroundings.

Reference and remit of children's cases by courts to children's hearings

372.—(1) Where a child who is not subject to a supervision requirement is charged with an offence and pleads guilty to, or is found guilty of, that offence the court—

(*a*) instead of making an order on that plea or finding, may remit the case to the reporter of the local authority to arrange for the disposal of the case by a children's hearing; or

(*b*) on that plea or finding may request the reporter of the local authority to arrange a children's hearing for the purposes of obtaining their advice as to the treatment of the child.

(2) Where a court has acted in pursuance of paragraph (*b*) of the foregoing subsection, the court, after consideration of the advice received from the children's hearing may, as it thinks proper, itself dispose of the case or remit the case as aforesaid.

(3) Where a child who is subject to a supervision requirement is charged with an offence and pleads guilty to, or is found guilty of, that offence the court shall request the reporter of the local authority to arrange a children's hearing for the purpose of obtaining their advice as to the treatment of the child, and on consideration of that advice may, as it thinks proper, itself dispose of the case or remit the case as aforesaid.

(4) Where a court has remitted a case to the reporter under this or the next following section, the jurisdiction of the court in respect of the child or person shall cease, and his case shall stand referred to a children's hearing.

(5) Nothing in the provisions of this or the next following section shall apply to a case in respect of an offence the sentence for which is fixed by law.

Reference and remit of cases of certain young persons by courts to children's hearings

373. Where a person who is not subject to a supervision requirement but is a person over the age of 16, and is not within six months of attaining the age of 18, is charged summarily with an offence and pleads guilty to, or has been found guilty of, that offence the court on that plea or finding may request the reporter of the local authority to arrange a children's hearing for the purpose of obtaining their advice as to the treatment of the person, and on consideration of that advice, the court may, as it thinks proper, itself dispose of the case or, where the hearing have so advised, remit the case to the reporter of the local authority for the disposal of the case by a children's hearing.

· · · · · ·

Procedure at Trial of Persons suffering from Mental Disorder

Insanity in bar of trial

375.—(1) Subject to the following provisions of this section, any rule of law relating to insanity standing in bar of trial shall apply in the case of a person charged summarily in the sheriff court as it would apply if that person were charged on indictment.

(2) Where, in the case of any person charged summarily in the sheriff court, the court is satisfied that the person is insane so that the trial of that person cannot proceed, the court shall direct a finding to that effect, and the reasons for that finding, to be recorded, and shall deal with him in the manner provided by section 376(2) of this Act.

(3) It shall not be competent for a person charged as aforesaid to found on a plea of insanity standing in bar of trial unless, before the first witness for the prosecution is called, he gives notice to the prosecutor of the plea and of the witnesses by whom he proposes to maintain it; and where notice as aforesaid has been given, the court shall, if the prosecutor so moves, adjourn the case.

(4) Where it appears to a court that it is not practicable or appropriate for the accused to be brought before it for the purpose of determining whether he is insane so that his trial cannot proceed, then, if no objection to such a course is taken by or on behalf of the accused, the court may order that the case be proceeded with in his absence.

Interim hospital orders

[1] **375A.**—(1) Where, in the case of any person charged summarily in the sheriff court—

    (*a*) the person is convicted of an offence punishable by that court with imprisonment (other than an offence the sentence for which is fixed by law); or

    (*b*) the sheriff is satisfied that the person did the act or made the admission charged but does not convict him,

and the sheriff is satisfied on the written or oral evidence of two medical practitioners (complying with the provisions of subsection (3) of this section and section 377 of this Act)—

    (*a*) that the offender is suffering from mental disorder within the meaning of section 1(2) of the Mental Health (Scotland) Act 1984; and

    (*b*) that there is reason to suppose—

        (i) that the mental disorder from which the offender is suffering is such that it may be appropriate for a hospital order to be made in his case; and

        (ii) that, having regard to the provisions of section 376(7) of this Act, the hospital to be specified in any such hospital order may be a State hospital,

the court may, before making a hospital order or dealing with the offender in some other way, make an order (to be known as "an interim hospital order") authorising his admission to and detention in a State hospital or such other hospital as for special reasons the court may specify in the order.

(2) Where a person is remitted to the sheriff court from the district court under section 376(4) of this Act, the sheriff court may, if it is satisfied as in subsection (1) of this section, make an interim hospital order in relation to that person.

(3) Of the medical practitioners whose evidence is taken into account under subsection (1) of this section at least one shall be employed at the hospital which is to be specified in the order.

(4) An interim hospital order shall not be made in respect of an offender unless the court is satisfied that the hospital which is to be specified in the order, in the event of such an order being made by the court, is available for his admission thereto within 28 days of the making of such an order.

(5) Where a court makes an interim hospital order it shall not make any other order for detention or impose a fine or pass sentence of imprisonment or make a probation order or a community service order in respect of the offence, but may make any other order which it has power to make apart from this section.

(6) The court by which an interim hospital order is made may include in the order such direction as it thinks fit for the conveyance of the offender to a place of safety and his detention therein pending his admission to the hospital within the period of 28 days referred to in subsection (4) of this section.

(7) An interim hospital order—

(*a*) shall be in force for such period, not exceeding 12 weeks, as the court may specify when making the order; but

(*b*) may be renewed for further periods of not more than 28 days at a time if it appears to the court on the written or oral evidence of the responsible medical officer that the continuation of the order is warranted;

but no such order shall continue in force for more than six months in all and the court shall terminate the order if it makes a hospital order in respect of the offender or decides, after considering the written or oral evidence of the responsible medical officer, to deal with the offender in some other way.

(8) The power of renewing an interim hospital order may be exercised without the offender being brought before the court if he is represented by counsel or a solicitor and his counsel or solicitor is given an opportunity of being heard.

(9) If an offender absconds from a hospital in which he is detained in pursuance of an interim hospital order, or while being conveyed to or from such a hospital, he may be arrested without warrant by a constable and shall, after being arrested, be brought as soon as practicable before the court which made the order; and the court may thereupon terminate the order and deal with him in any way in which it could have dealt with him if no such order had been made.

(10) When an interim hospital order ceases to have effect in relation to an offender the court may deal with him in any way (other than by making

a new interim hospital order) in which it could have dealt with him if no such order had been made.

(11) The power conferred on the court by the provisions of this section is without prejudice to the power of the court under section 381(1) of this Act to remand a person in order that an inquiry may be made into his physical or mental condition.

NOTE
[1] Inserted by the Mental Health (Amendment) (Scotland) Act 1983, s. 34(*c*), and as amended by the Mental Health (Scotland) Act 1984, Sched. 3, para. 32, both with effect from 30th September 1984.

Power of court to order hospital admission or guardianship
[1] **376.**—(1) Where a person is convicted in the sheriff court of an offence, other than an offence the sentence for which is fixed by law, punishable by that court with imprisonment, and the following conditions are satisfied, that is to say—

(*a*) the court is satisfied, on the written or oral evidence of two medical practitioners (complying with the provisions of section 377 of this Act) that the grounds set out in section 17(1) or, as the case may be, the ground set out in section 36(*a*) of the Mental Health (Scotland) Act 1984 apply in relation to the offender; and

(*b*) the court is of opinion, having regard to all the circumstances including the nature of the offence and the character and antecedents of the offender, and to the other available methods of dealing with him, that the most suitable method of disposing of the case is by means of an order under this section,

the court may by order authorise his admission to and detention in such hospital as may be specified in the order or, as the case may be, place him under the guardianship of such local authority or of such other person approved by a local authority as may be so specified.

(2) Where a person is charged summarily in the sheriff court with an act or omission as an offence and a finding has been recorded in respect of that person under section 375(2) of this Act, the court shall make such an order for his admission to and detention in a hospital as may be made under the foregoing subsection.

(3) Where in the case of a person charged as aforesaid the court would have power, on convicting him, to make an order under subsection (1) of this section, then if it is satisfied that the person did the act or made the omission charged, the court may, if it thinks fit, make such an order without convicting him.

(4) Where a person is charged before a court of summary jurisdiction, other than a sheriff court, with any act or omission constituting an offence punishable with imprisonment, the court, if it appears to it that that person may be suffering from mental disorder, shall remit him to the sheriff court in the manner provided by section 286 of this Act, and the sheriff court shall, on any such remit being made, have the like power to make an order under subsection (1) of this section in respect of him as if he had been charged before that court with the said act or omission as an offence, or in dealing with him may exercise the like powers as the court making the remit.

(5) Where it appears to the prosecutor in any court before which a

person is charged with an offence that the person may be suffering from mental disorder, it shall be the duty of such prosecutor to bring before the court such evidence as may be available of the mental condition of that person.

(6) An order for the admission of a person to a hospital (in this Act referred to as "a hospital order") shall not be made under this section in respect of an offender or of a person to whom subsection (3) of this section applies unless the court is satisfied that that hospital, in the event of such an order being made by the court, is available for his admission thereto within 28 days of the making of such an order.

(7) A State hospital shall not be specified in a hospital order in respect of the detention of a person unless the court is satisfied, on the evidence of the medical practitioners which is taken into account under paragraph (*a*) of subsection (1) of this section, that the offender, on account of his dangerous, violent or criminal propensities, requires treatment under conditions of special security, and cannot suitably be cared for in a hospital other than a State hospital.

(8) An order placing a person under the guardianship of a local authority or of any other person (in this Act referred to as "a guardianship order") shall not be made under this section unless the court is satisfied (*a*) after taking into consideration the evidence of a mental health officer, that it is necessary in the interests of the welfare of the person that he should be placed under guardianship; and (*b*) that that authority or person is willing to receive that person into guardianship.

(9) A hospital order or guardianship order shall specify the form of mental disorder, being mental illness or mental handicap or both, from which, upon the evidence taken into account under paragraph (*a*) of subsection (1) of this section, the offender is found by the court to be suffering; and no such order shall be made unless the offender is described by each of the practitioners, whose evidence is taken into account as aforesaid, as suffering from the same form of mental disorder, whether or not he is also described by either of them as suffering from the other form.

(10) Where an order is made under this section, the court shall not pass sentence of imprisonment or impose a fine or make a probation order or a community service order in respect of the offence, but may make any other order which the court has power to make apart from this section; and for the purposes of this subsection "sentence of imprisonment" includes any sentence or order for detention.

NOTE
[1] As amended with effect from 30th September 1984 by the Mental Health (Amendment) (Scotland) Act 1983, Sched. 2, para. 34, and the Mental Health (Scotland) Act 1984, Sched. 3, para. 33. Extended by the Contempt of Court Act 1981, s. 15(3), (5).

Requirements as to medical evidence
[1] **377.**—[2] (1) Of the medical practitioners whose evidence is taken into account under sections 375A(1) and 376(1)(*a*) of this Act, at least one shall be a practitioner approved for the purposes of section 20 or 39 of the Mental Health (Scotland) Act 1984 by a Health Board as having special experience in the diagnosis or treatment of mental disorder.
[3] (1A) Written or oral evidence given for the purposes of the said

section 376(1)(*a*) shall include a statement as to whether the person giving the evidence is related to the accused and of any pecuniary interest which that person may have in the admission of the accused to hospital or his reception into guardianship.

(2) For the purposes of the said section 376(1)(*a*) a report in writing purporting to be signed by a medical practitioner may, subject to the provisions of this section, be received in evidence without proof of the signature or qualifications of the practitioner; but the court may, in any case, require that the practitioner by whom such a report was signed be called to give oral evidence.

(3) Where any such report as aforesaid is tendered in evidence, otherwise than on behalf of the accused, then—

(*a*) if the accused is represented by counsel or solicitor, a copy of the report shall be given to his counsel or solicitor;

(*b*) if the accused is not so represented, the substance of the report shall be disclosed to the accused or, where he is a child under 16 years of age, to his parent or guardian if present in court;

(*c*) in any case, the accused may require that the practitioner by whom the report was signed be called to give oral evidence, and evidence to rebut the evidence contained in the report may be called by or on behalf of the accused;

and where the court is of opinion that further time is necessary in the interests of the accused for consideration of that report, or the substance of any such report, it shall adjourn the case.

(4) For the purpose of calling evidence to rebut the evidence contained in any such report as aforesaid, arrangements may be made by or on behalf of an accused person detained in a hospital for his examination by any medical practitioner, and any such examination may be made in private.

NOTES
[1] Extended by the Contempt of Court Act 1981, s. 15(3).
[2] As amended with effect from 30th September 1984 by the Mental Health (Amendment) (Scotland) Act 1983, Sched. 2, para. 35, and the Mental Health (Scotland) Act 1984, Sched. 3, para. 34.
[3] Inserted in relation to proceedings commenced on or after 30th September 1984 by the Mental Health (Amendment) (Scotland) Act 1983, s. 35(*b*): see *ibid.*, Sched. 1, para. 12.

Supplementary provisions as to hospital orders
[1] **378.** The court by which a hospital order is made may give such directions as it thinks fit for the conveyance of the patient to a place of safety and his detention therein pending his admission to the hospital within the period of 28 days referred to in section 376(6) of this Act; but a direction for the conveyance of a patient to a residential establishment provided by a local authority under Part IV of the Social Work (Scotland) Act 1968 shall not be given unless the court is satisfied that that authority is willing to receive the patient therein.

NOTE
[1] Extended by the Contempt of Court Act 1981, s. 15(3).

Power of court to restrict discharge from hospital
[1] **379.**—(1) Where a hospital order is made in respect of a person, and it

appears to the court, having regard to the nature of the offence with which he is charged, the antecedents of the person and the risk that as a result of his mental disorder he would commit offences if set at large, that it is necessary for the protection of the public from serious harm so to do, the court may, subject to the provisions of this section, further order that the person shall be subject to the special restrictions set out in section 62(1) of the Mental Health (Scotland) Act 1984, either without limit of time or during such period as may be specified in the order.

(2) An order under this section (in this Act referred to as "a restriction order") shall not be made in the case of any person unless the medical practitioner approved by the Health Board for the purposes of section 20 or 39 of the Mental Health (Scotland) Act 1984, whose evidence is taken into account by the court under section 376(1)(*a*) of this Act, has given evidence orally before the court.

(3) Where a restriction order is in force in respect of a patient, a guardianship order shall not be made in respect of him; and where the hospital order relating to him ceases to have effect by virtue of section 62(1) of the Mental Health (Scotland) Act 1984 on the making of another hospital order, that order shall have the same effect in relation to the restriction order as the previous hospital order, but without prejudice to the power of the court making that other hospital order to make another restriction order to have effect on the expiration of the previous such order.

NOTE
[1] Extended by the Contempt of Court Act 1981, s. 15(3). As amended with effect from 30th September 1984 by the Mental Health (Amendment) (Scotland) Act 1983, s. 22(2) and Sched. 2, para. 36, and the Mental Health (Scotland) Act 1984, Sched. 3, para. 35.

CONVICTION AND SENTENCE

Adjournment and remand

Power of a court to adjourn case before sentence
[1] **380.**—(1) It is hereby declared that the power of a court to adjourn the hearing of a case includes power, after a person has been convicted or the court has found that he committed the offence and before he has been sentenced or otherwise dealt with, to adjourn the case for the purpose of enabling inquiries to be made or of determining the most suitable method of dealing with his case and where the court so adjourns the case it shall remand the accused in custody or on bail or ordain him to appear at the adjourned diet;

Provided that a court shall not for the purpose aforesaid adjourn the hearing of a case for a single period exceeding three weeks.

[2] (2) An accused who is remanded under this section may appeal against the refusal of bail or against the conditions imposed within 24 hours of his remand by note of appeal presented to the High Court, and the High Court, either in court or in chambers, may, after hearing parties—

(*a*) review the order appealed against and either grant bail on such conditions as it thinks fit or ordain the accused to appear at the adjourned diet; or (*b*) confirm the order.

NOTES
¹ As amended by the Bail etc. (Scotland) Act 1980, s. 5(*a*), and the Criminal Justice (Scotland) Act 1980, Sched. 7.
² Added by the Bail etc. (Scotland) Act 1980, s. 5(*b*).

Remand for inquiry into physical or mental condition
381.—(1) Without prejudice to any powers exercisable by a court under the last foregoing section, where a person is charged before a court with an offence punishable with imprisonment, and the court is satisfied that he did the act or made the omission charged but is of opinion that an inquiry ought to be made into his physical or mental condition before the method of dealing with him is determined, the court shall remand him in custody or on bail for such period or periods, no single period exceeding three weeks, as the court thinks necessary to enable a medical examination and report to be made.
¹ (2) Where a person is remanded on bail under this section, it shall be a condition of the order granting bail that he shall—
   (*a*) undergo a medical examination by a duly qualified medical practitioner or, where the inquiry is into his mental condition and the order granting bail so specifies, two such practitioners; and
   (*b*) for the purpose attend at an institution or place, or on any such practitioner specified in the order granting bail and, where the inquiry is into his mental condition, comply with any directions which may be given to him for the said purpose by any person so specified or by a person of any class so specified;
and if arrangements have been made for his reception, it may be a condition of the order granting bail that the person shall, for the purpose of the examination, reside in an institution or place specified as aforesaid, not being an institution or place to which he could have been remanded in custody, until the expiry of such period as may be so specified or until he is discharged therefrom, whichever first occurs.
(3) [Repealed by the Bail etc. (Scotland) Act 1980, s. 6(*a*).]
(4) On exercising the powers conferred by this section the court shall—
   (*a*) where the person is remanded in custody, send to the institution or place in which he is detained, and
   (*b*) where the person is released on bail, send to the institution or place at which or the person by whom he is to be examined,
a statement of the reasons for which the court is of opinion that an inquiry ought to be made into his physical or mental condition, and of any information before the court about his physical or mental condition.
² (5) A person remanded under this section may appeal against the refusal of bail or against the conditions imposed within 24 hours of his remand, by note of appeal presented to the High Court, and the High Court, either in court or in chambers, may after hearing parties—
   (*a*) review the order and grant bail on such conditions as it thinks fit; or
   (*b*) confirm the order.

NOTES
¹ As amended by the Bail etc. (Scotland) Act 1980, s. 6 and Sched. 1, para. 9.
² Added by the Bail etc. (Scotland) Act 1980, s. 6(*b*).

Admonition and discharge

Admonition

382. A court of summary jurisdiction may, if it appears to meet the justice of the case, dismiss with an admonition any person found guilty by the court of any offence.

Absolute discharge

[1] **383.** Where a person is charged before a court of summary jurisdiction with an offence (other than an offence the sentence for which is fixed by law) and the court is satisfied that he committed the offence, the court, if it is of opinion, having regard to the circumstances, including the nature of the offence and the character of the offender, that it is inexpedient to inflict punishment and that a probation order is not appropriate may, without proceeding to conviction, make an order discharging him absolutely.

NOTE
[1] See the Bail etc. (Scotland) Act 1980, s. 4(3), the Licensed Premises (Exclusion of Certain Persons) Act 1980, ss. 1(2)(c) and 4(2) and the Criminal Justice (Scotland) Act 1980, s. 2(5).

Probation

Probation

[1] **384.**—[2] (1) Subject to subsection (1A) below, where a person is charged before a court of summary jurisdiction with an offence (other than an offence the sentence for which is fixed by law) and the court is satisfied that he committed the offence, the court, if it is of opinion having regard to the circumstances, including the nature of the offence and the character of the offender and having obtained a report as to the circumstances and character of the offender, that it is expedient to do so, may, without proceeding to conviction (except in a case to which section 432 of this Act applies), make a probation order, that is to say an order requiring the offender to be under supervision for a period to be specified in the order of not less than six months nor more than three years.

(1A) A court shall not make a probation order under subsection (1) above unless it is satisfied that suitable arrangements for the supervision of the offender can be made by the local authority in whose area he resides or is to reside.

(2) A probation order shall be as nearly as may be in the form prescribed by Act of Adjournal, and shall name the local authority area in which the offender resides or is to reside and the order shall make provision for the offender to be under the supervision of an officer of the local authority of that area, or, where the offender resides or is to reside in a local authority area in which the court has no jurisdiction the court shall name the appropriate court (being such a court as could have been named in any amendment of the order in accordance with the provisions of Schedule 5 to this Act) in the area of residence or intended residence, and the court last mentioned shall require the local authority for that area to arrange for the offender to be under the supervision of an officer of that authority.

(3) Subject to the provisions of Schedule 5 to this Act relating to probationers who change their residence, an offender in respect of whom a probation order is made shall be required to be under the supervision of an officer of the local authority as aforesaid.

[3] (4) Subject to the provisions of the next following section, a probation order may in addition require the offender to comply during the whole or any part of the probation period with such requirements as the court having regard to the circumstances of the case, considers (*a*) conducive to securing the good conduct of the offender or to preventing a repetition by him of the offence or the commission of other offences or (*b*) where the probation order is to include such requirement as is mentioned in subsection (5A) or (5B) below, conducive to securing or preventing the aforesaid matters.

(5) Without prejudice to the generality of the last foregoing subsection, a probation order may include requirements relating to the residence of the offender:

Provided that—

> (*a*) before making an order containing any such requirements the court shall consider the home surroundings of the offender; and
>
> (*b*) where the order requires the offender to reside in any institution or place, the name of the institution or place and the period for which he is so required to reside shall be specified in the order, and that period shall not extend beyond 12 months from the date of the requirement or beyond the date when the order expires.

[4] (5A) Without prejudice to the generality of subsection (4) above, where a court which is considering making a probation order—

> (*a*) is satisfied that the offender is of or over 16 years of age and has committed an offence punishable with imprisonment and that the conditions for the making of a community service order under the Community Service by Offenders (Scotland) Act 1978 specified in paragraphs (*a*) and (*c*) of section 1(2) of that Act have been met;
>
> (*b*) has been notified by the Secretary of State that arrangements exist for persons who reside in the locality where the offender resides, or will be residing when the probation order comes into force, to perform unpaid work as a requirement of a probation order; and
>
> (*c*) is satisfied that provision can be made under the arrangements mentioned in paragraph (*b*) above for the offender to perform unpaid work under the probation order,

it may include in the probation order, in addition to any other requirement, a requirement that the offender shall perform unpaid work for such number of hours (being a total of not less than 40 nor more than 240) as may be specified in the probation order; and the said Act of 1978 shall apply to a probation order including such a requirement as it applies to a community service order, but as if—

> (i) subsections (1), (2)(*b*) and (*d*) and (4)(*b*) of section 1 and sections 4, 6 and 6A were omitted;
>
> (ii) in section 1(5) for the words "subsection (1) above" there were substituted the words "subsection (5A) of section 183 or, as the case may be, 384 of the 1975 Act"; and

(iii) any other necessary modifications were made.

⁵ (5B) Without prejudice to the generality of subsection (4) above, where a court is considering making a probation order it may include in the probation order, in addition to any other requirement, a requirement that the offender shall pay compensation either in a lump sum or by instalments for any personal injury, loss or damage caused (whether directly or indirectly) by the acts which constituted the offence; and the following provisions of the Criminal Justice (Scotland) Act 1980 shall apply to such a requirement as if any reference in them to a compensation order included a reference to a requirement to pay compensation under this subsection—

> section 58(2) and (3);
> section 59 (except the proviso to subsection (1) and subsection (3));
> section 60;
> section 62;
> section 64 (except paragraph (a));
> section 67.

⁵ (5C) Where the court imposes a requirement to pay compensation under subsection (5B) above—

(a) it shall be a condition of a probation order containing such a requirement that payment of the compensation shall be completed not more than 18 months after the making of the order or not later than two months before the end of the period of probation whichever first occurs;

(b) the court, on the application of the offender or the officer of the local authority responsible for supervising the offender, may vary the terms of the requirement, including the amount of any instalments, in consequence of any change which may have occurred in the circumstances of the offender; and

(c) in any proceedings for breach of a probation order where the breach consists only in the failure to comply with a requirement to pay compensation, a document purporting to be a certificate signed by the clerk of the court for the time being having jurisdiction in relation to the order that the compensation or, where payment by instalments has been allowed, any instalment has not been paid shall be sufficient evidence of such breach.

(6) Before making a probation order, the court shall explain to the offender in ordinary language the effect of the order (including any additional requirements proposed to be inserted therein under subsection (4), (5), (5A), (5B) or (5C) of this section or under the next following section) and that if he fails to comply therewith or commits another offence during the probation period he will be liable to be convicted of and sentenced for the original offence and the court shall not make the order unless the offender expresses his willingness to comply with the requirements thereof.

(7) The clerk of the court by which a probation order is made or of the appropriate court, as the case may be, shall cause copies thereof to be given to the officer of the local authority who is to supervise the probationer, to the probationer, and to the person in charge of any institution or place in which the probationer is required to reside under the probation order.

NOTES
[1] See the Bail etc. (Scotland) Act 1980, s. 4(3), the Licensed Premises (Exclusion of Certain Persons) Act 1980, ss. 1(2)(c) and 4(2), and the Criminal Justice (Scotland) Act 1980, s. 2(5). As amended by the Criminal Justice (Scotland) Act 1987, s. 65, and the Law Reform (Miscellaneous Provisions) (Scotland) Act 1990, s. 61(1).
[2] As amended by the Criminal Justice (Scotland) Act 1980, s. 53 and the Criminal Justice (Scotland) Act 1987, Sched. 1, para. 10.
[3] As amended by the Community Service by Offenders (Scotland) Act 1978, s. 7(a).
[4] Added by the Community Service by Offenders (Scotland) Act 1978, s. 7(b), and as amended by the Criminal Justice Act 1982, Sched. 13, para. 3.
[5] Inserted by the Criminal Justice (Scotland) Act 1987, s. 65.

Probation orders requiring treatment for mental condition

[1] **385.**—(1) Where the court is satisfied, on the evidence of a registered medical practitioner approved for the purposes of section 20 or 39 of the Mental Health (Scotland) Act 1984, that the mental condition of an offender is such as requires and may be susceptible to treatment but is not such as to warrant his detention in pursuance of a hospital order under Part VI of that Act, or under this Act, the court may, if it makes a probation order, include therein a requirement that the offender shall submit, for such period not extending beyond 12 months from the date of the requirement as may be specified therein, to treatment by or under the direction of a registered medical practitioner with a view to the improvement of the offender's mental condition.

(2) The treatment required by any such order shall be such one of the following kinds of treatment as may be specified in the order, that is to say—

(a) treatment as a resident patient in a hospital within the meaning of the Mental Health (Scotland) Act 1984, not being a State hospital within the meaning of that Act;

(b) treatment as a non-resident patient at such institution or place as may be specified in the order; or

(c) treatment by or under the direction of such registered medical practitioner as may be specified in the order;

but except as aforesaid the nature of the treatment shall not be specified in the order.

(3) A court shall not make a probation order containing such a requirement as aforesaid unless it is satisfied that arrangements have been made for the treatment intended to be specified in the order, and, if the offender is to be treated as a resident patient, for his reception.

(4) [Repealed by the Mental Health (Amendment) (Scotland) Act 1983, s. 36(1) and Sched. 3.]

(5) Where the medical practitioner by whom or under whose direction a probationer is receiving any of the kinds of treatment to which he is required to submit in pursuance of a probation order is of opinion—

(a) that the probationer requires, or that it would be more appropriate for him to receive, a different kind of treatment (whether in whole or in part) from that which he has been receiving, being treatment of a kind which subject to subsection (5A) of this section could have been specified in the probation order; or

(b) that the treatment (whether in whole or in part) can be more appropriately given in or at a different institution or place from that

where he has been receiving treatment in pursuance of the probation order,
he may, subject to subsection (5B) of this section, make arrangements for the probationer to be treated accordingly.

(5A) Arrangements made under subsection (5) of this section may provide for the probationer to receive his treatment (in whole or in part) as a resident patient in an institution or place notwithstanding that it is not one which could have been specified in that behalf in the probation order.

(5B) Arrangements shall not be made under subsection (5) of this section unless—

(a) the probationer and any officer responsible for his supervision agree;

(b) the treatment will be given by or under the direction of a registered medical practitioner who has agreed to accept the probationer as his patient; and

(c) where such treatment entails the probationer's being a resident patient, he will be received as such.

(6) Where any such arrangements as are mentioned in subsection (5) of this section are made for the treatment of a probationer—

(a) any officer responsible for the probationer's supervision shall notify the appropriate court of the arrangements; and

(b) the treatment provided for by the arrangements shall be deemed to be treatment to which he is required to submit in pursuance of the probation order.

(7) Subsections (2), (3) and (4) of section 377 of this Act shall apply for the purposes of this section as if for the reference in the said subsection (2) to section 376(1)(a) of this Act there were substituted a reference to subsection (1) of this section.

(8) Except as provided by this section, a court shall not make a probation order requiring a probationer to submit to treatment for his mental condition.

NOTE
[1] As amended with effect from 30th September 1984 by the Mental Health (Amendment) (Scotland) Act 1983, s. 36 and Sched. 3, and the Mental Health (Scotland) Act 1984, Sched. 3, para. 36.

Discharge and amendment of probation orders
386.—(1) The provisions of Schedule 5 to this Act shall have effect in relation to the discharge and amendment of probation orders.

(2) Where, under section 387 of this Act, a probationer is sentenced for the offence for which he was placed on probation, the probation order shall cease to have effect.

Failure to comply with requirement of probation order
[1] **387.**—[1a] (1) If, on information on oath from

(a) the officer supervising the probationer,

(b) the director of social work of the local authority whose officer is supervising the probationer; or

(c) an officer appointed by the director of social work to act on his behalf for the purposes of this subsection,

it appears to the court by which the order was made or to the appropriate court that the probationer has failed to comply with any of the requirements of the order, that court may issue a warrant for the arrest of the probationer, or may, if it thinks fit, instead of issuing such a warrant in the first instance, issue a citation requiring the probationer to appear before the court at such time as may be specified in the citation.

(2) If it is proved to the satisfaction of the court before which a probationer appears or is brought in pursuance of the foregoing subsection that he has failed to comply with any of the requirements of the probation order, the court may—

[2] (*a*) except in the case of a failure to comply with a requirement to pay compensation and without prejudice to the continuance in force of the probation order, impose a fine not exceeding level 3 on the standard scale; or

(*b*) (i) where the probationer has been convicted for the offence for which the order was made, sentence him for that offence;
(ii) where the probationer has not been so convicted, convict him and sentence him as aforesaid; or

(*c*) vary any of the requirements of the probation order, so however that any extension of the probation period shall terminate not later than three years from the date of the probation order; or

[3] (*d*) without prejudice to the continuance in force of the probation order, in a case where the conditions required by the Community Service by Offenders (Scotland) Act 1978 are satisfied, make a community service order, and the provisions of that Act shall apply to such an order as if the failure to comply with the requirement of the probation order were the offence in respect of which the order had been made.

(3) A fine imposed under this section in respect of a failure to comply with the requirements of a probation order shall be deemed for the purposes of any enactment to be a sum adjudged to be paid by or in respect of a conviction of a penalty imposed on a person summarily convicted.

(4) A probationer who is required by a probation order to submit to treatment for his mental condition shall not be deemed for the purpose of this section to have failed to comply with that requirement on the ground only that he has refused to undergo any surgical, electrical or other treatment if, in the opinion of the court, his refusal was reasonable having regard to all the circumstances.

(5) Without prejudice to the provisions of section 388 of this Act, a probationer who is convicted of an offence committed during the probation period shall not on that account be liable to be dealt with under this section for failing to comply with any requirement of the probation order.

NOTES

[1] As amended by the Criminal Justice (Scotland) Act 1980, s. 46.

[1a] As amended by the Law Reform (Miscellaneous Provisions) (Scotland) Act 1990, s. 61(2).

[2] As amended by the Criminal Justice Act 1982, Sched. 7 and the Criminal Justice (Scotland) Act 1987, s. 65(5).

[3] Added by the Community Service by Offenders (Scotland) Act 1978, s. 8.

Commission of further offence

388.—(1) If it appears to the court by which a probation order has been made (or to the appropriate court) that the probationer to whom the order relates has been convicted by a court in any part of Great Britain of an offence committed during the probation period and has been dealt with for that offence, the first-mentioned court (or the appropriate court) may issue a warrant for the arrest of the probationer, or may, if it thinks fit, instead of issuing such a warrant in the first instance issue a citation requiring the probationer to appear before that court at such time as may be specified in the citation, and on his appearance or on his being brought before the court the court may, if it thinks fit, deal with him under section 387(2)(*b*) of this Act.

(2) Where a probationer is convicted by the court which made the probation order (or by the appropriate court) of an offence committed during the probation period, that court may, if it thinks fit, deal with him under section 387(2)(*b*) of this Act for the offence for which the order was made as well as for the offence committed during the period of probation.

Probation orders relating to persons residing in England

[1] **389.**—(1) Where the court by which a probation order is made under section 384 of this Act (not being a probation order including a requirement that the offender shall perform unpaid work) is satisfied that the offender has attained the age of 17 years and resides or will reside in England, subsection (2) of the said section shall not apply to the order, but the order shall contain a requirement that he be under the supervision of a probation officer appointed for or assigned to the petty sessions area in which the offender resides or will reside, and that area shall be named in the order.

(2) Where a probation order has been made under section 384 of this Act and the court in Scotland by which the order was made or the appropriate court is satisfied that the probationer has attained the age of 17 years and proposes to reside or is residing in England, the power of that court to amend the order under Schedule 5 to this Act shall include power to insert the provisions required by subsection (1) of this section; and the court may so amend the order without summoning the probationer and without his consent.

(3) A probation order made or amended by virtue of this section may, notwithstanding section 385(8) of this Act, include a requirement that the probationer shall submit to treatment for his mental condition, and

   (*a*) subsections (1), (3) and (7) of the said section 385 and section 3(2) of the Powers of Criminal Courts Act 1973 (all of which regulate the making of probation orders which include any such requirement) shall apply to the making of an order which includes any such requirement by virtue of this subsection as they apply to the making of an order which includes any such requirement by virtue of section 385 of this Act and section 3 of the said Act of 1973 respectively; and

   (*b*) subsections (4) to (6) of section 3 of the said Act of 1973 (functions of supervising officer and medical practitioner where such a requirement has been imposed) shall apply in relation to a probationer who is undergoing treatment in England in pursuance of a requirement imposed by virtue of this subsection as they apply in relation to a probationer undergoing such treatment in pursuance of a requirement imposed by virtue of that section.

(4) Sections 386(1) and 387(1) of this Act shall not apply to any order made or amended under this section; but subject as hereinafter provided the provisions of the Powers of Criminal Courts Act 1973 (except section 8 of that Act) shall apply to the order as if it were a probation order made under section 2 of that Act:

Provided that section 6(2)(*a*), (3)(*d*) and (6) of that Act shall not apply to any such order and section 6(4) and (5) of that Act shall have effect respectively in relation to any such order as if for the first reference in section 6(4) to the Crown Court there were substituted a reference to a court in Scotland and as if for the second such reference therein and for both such references in section 6(5) there were substituted references to the court in Scotland by which the probation order was made or amended under this section.

(5) If it appears on information to a justice acting for the petty sessions area for which the supervising court within the meaning of the Powers of Criminal Courts Act 1973 acts that a person in whose case a probation order has been made or amended under this section has been convicted by a court in any part of Great Britain of an offence committed during the period specified in the order, he may issue a summons requiring that person to appear, at the place and time specified therein, before the court in Scotland by which the probation order was made or, if the information is in writing and on oath, may issue a warrant for his arrest, directing that person to be brought before the last-mentioned court.

(6) If a warrant for the arrest of a probationer issued under section 388 of this Act by a court is executed in England, and the probationer cannot forthwith be brought before that court, the warrant shall have effect as if it directed him to be brought before a magistrates' court for the place where he is arrested; and the magistrates' court shall commit him to custody or release him on bail (with or without sureties) until he can be brought or appear before the court in Scotland.

(7) The court by which a probation order is made or amended in accordance with the provisions of this section shall send three copies of the order to the clerk to the justices for the petty sessions area named therein, together with such documents and information relating to the case as it considers likely to be of assistance to the court acting for that petty sessions area.

(8) Where a probation order which is amended under subsection (2) of this section is an order to which the provisions of this Act apply by virtue of section 10 of the Powers of Criminal Courts Act 1973 (which relates to probation orders under that Act relating to persons residing in Scotland) then, notwithstanding anything in that section or this section, the order shall, as from the date of the amendment, have effect in all respects as if it were an order made under section 2 of that Act in the case of a person residing in England.

NOTE
[1] As amended by the Community Service by Offenders (Scotland) Act 1978, Sched. 2, para. 3.

Further provisions as to probation orders

390.—(1) Where the court by which a probation order is made under section 384 of this Act or subsection (6) of this section is satisfied that the person to whom the order relates is under the age of 17 years and resides or will reside in England, subsection (2) of the said section 384 shall not apply to the order but the order shall name the petty sessions area in which that person resides or will reside and the court shall send notification of the order to the clerk to the justices for that area.

(2) Where a probation order has been made under section 384 of this Act or subsection (6) of this section, and the court which made the order or the appropriate court is satisfied that the person to whom the order relates is under the age of 17 years and proposes to reside or is residing in England, the power of that court to amend the order under Schedule 5 to this Act shall include power, without summoning him and without his consent, to insert in the order the name of the petty sessions area aforesaid; and where the court exercises the power conferred on it by virtue of this subsection it shall send notification of the order to the clerk aforesaid.

(3) A court which sends a notification to a clerk in pursuance of the foregoing provisions of this section shall send to him with it three copies of the probation order in question and such other documents and information relating to the case as it considers likely to be of assistance to the juvenile court mentioned in the following subsection.

(4) It shall be the duty of the clerk to whom a notification is sent in pursuance of the foregoing provisions of this section to refer the notification to a juvenile court acting for the petty sessions area named in the order, and on such a reference the court—

(*a*) may make a supervision order under the Children and Young Persons Act 1969 in respect of a person to whom the notification relates; and

(*b*) if it does not make such an order, shall dismiss the case.

(5) A supervision order made by virtue of the last foregoing subsection shall not include a requirement authorised by section 12 of the said Act of 1969 unless the supervised person is before the court when the supervision order is made, and in relation to a supervision order made by virtue of that subsection—

(*a*) section 15 of that Act shall have effect as if, in subsection (4), paragraph (*b*) and the words following it were omitted; and

(*b*) section 17(*a*) of that Act shall have effect as if the second reference to the supervision order were a reference to the probation order in consequence of which the supervision order is made;

and when a juvenile court disposes of a case referred to it in pursuance of the last foregoing subsection, the probation order in consequence of which the reference was made shall cease to have effect.

(6) The court which, in pursuance of subsection (1) of section 73 of the Social Work (Scotland) Act 1968, considers a case referred to it in consequence of a notification under paragraph (*b*) of that subsection (which relates to a case in which a person subject to a supervision order made by virtue of this section moves to Scotland)—

(*a*) may, if it is of opinion that the person to whom the notification relates should continue to be under supervision, make a probation order in respect of him for a period specified in the order; and

(b) if it does not make such an order, shall dismiss the case;

and when the court disposes of a case in pursuance of this subsection the supervision order aforesaid shall cease to have effect.

(7) Notwithstanding any provision to the contrary in section 384 of this Act, a probation order made by virtue of the last foregoing sub-section which includes only requirements having the like effect as any requirement or provision of the supervision order to which the notification relates may be made without summoning the person to whom the notification relates and without his consent, and shall specify a period of supervision which shall expire not later than the date on which that supervision order would have ceased to have effect by the effluxion of time; and, except as aforesaid, the provisions of this Act shall apply to that probation order.

(8) In this and the last foregoing section, "petty sessions area" has the same meaning as in the said Act of 1969.

Supplementary provisions as to probation

391.—(1) Any court, on making a probation order, may, if it thinks that such a course is expedient for the purpose of the order, require the offender to give security for his good behaviour.

(2) Security may be given under the foregoing subsection by consignation with the clerk of the court or by entering into an undertaking to pay the amount, but not otherwise, and such security may be forfeited and recovered in like manner as caution.

Effects of probation and absolute discharge

[1] **392.**—(1) Subject as hereinafter provided, a conviction of an offence for which an order is made placing the offender on probation or discharging him absolutely shall be deemed not to be a conviction for any purpose other than the purposes of the proceedings in which the order is made and of laying it before a court as a previous conviction in subsequent proceedings for another offence:

Provided that where an offender, being not less than 16 years of age at the time of his conviction of an offence for which he is placed on probation as aforesaid, is subsequently sentenced under this Act for that offence, the provisions of this subsection shall cease to apply to the conviction.

(2) Without prejudice to the foregoing provisions of this section, the conviction of an offender who is placed on probation or discharged absolutely as aforesaid shall in any event be disregarded for the purposes of any enactment which imposes any disqualification or disability upon convicted persons, or authorises or requires the imposition of any such disqualification or disability.

(3) The foregoing provisions of this section shall not affect—

(a) any right of any such offender as aforesaid to appeal against his conviction; or

(b) the operation, in relation to any such offender, of any enactment which was in force as at the commencement of section 9(3)(b) of the Criminal Justice (Scotland) Act 1949 and is expressed to extend to persons dealt with under section 1(1) of the Probation of Offenders Act 1907 as well as to convicted persons.

(4) Where an offender is placed on probation or discharged absolutely by a court of summary jurisdiction, he shall have the like right of appeal against the finding that he committed the offence as if that finding were a conviction.

(5) Where a person charged with an offence has at any time previously been placed on probation or discharged absolutely in respect of the commission by him of an offence, it shall be competent, in the proceedings for that offence, to bring before the court the probation order or order of absolute discharge in like manner as if the order were a conviction.

NOTE
[1] As amended by the Criminal Justice (Scotland) Act 1980, Sched. 8. See the Licensed Premises (Exclusion of Certain Persons) Act 1980, s. 1(2)(c). Excluded by the Road Traffic Offenders Act 1988, s. 46(3).

Probation reports
393. Where a report by an officer of a local authority is made to any court (other than a court whose procedure is regulated by rules made under section 366(2) of this Act) with a view to assisting the court in determining the most suitable method of dealing with any person in respect of an offence, a copy of the report shall be given by the clerk of the court to the offender or his solicitor:

Provided that if the offender is under 16 years of age and is not represented by counsel or a solicitor, a copy of the report need not be given to him but shall be given to his parent or guardian if present in court.

Penalties for Statutory Offences

Power to mitigate penalties
394. In a summary prosecution for the contravention of any statute or order, where such contravention involves any of the following punishments, namely, imprisonment, the imposition of a fine, the finding of caution for good behaviour or otherwise, either singly or in combination with imprisonment or fine, the court shall have in addition to any other powers conferred by Act of Parliament the following powers, *viz*:—

(*a*) to reduce the period of imprisonment:
[1] (*b*) to substitute for imprisonment a fine which in the case of an offence triable either summarily or on indictment shall not exceed the prescribed sum (within the meaning of section 289B above), and in the case of an offence triable only summarily shall not exceed level 4 on the standard scale (in either case, with or without caution for good behaviour, not exceeding the amount and the period competent under this Part of this Act):
(*c*) to substitute the finding of caution as provided for in this Part of this Act for a fine or imprisonment:
(*d*) to reduce the amount of any fine:
(*e*) to dispense with the finding of caution:

Provided that—
>   (i) where any Act carries into effect a treaty, convention or agreement with a foreign state, and such treaty, convention or agreement stipulates for a fine of minimum amount, the court shall not be entitled by virtue of this section to reduce the amount of such fine below that minimum amount;
>   (ii) this section shall not apply to proceedings taken under any Act relating to any of Her Majesty's regular or auxiliary forces.

NOTE
[1] Substituted by the Criminal Law Act 1977, Sched. 11, para. 7, and as amended by the Criminal Justice Act 1982, Sched. 7.

Fines

Provisions as to fines
[1] **395.**—[1a] (1) A court of summary jurisdiction in determining the amount of any fine to be imposed on an offender shall take into consideration, amongst other things, the means of the offender so far as known to the court.

[2] (2) Where a court of summary jurisdiction imposes a fine on an offender, the court may order him to be searched, and any money found on him on apprehension or when so searched or when taken to prison or to a young offenders institution in default of payment of the fine, may, unless the court otherwise directs, be applied towards payment of the fine, and the surplus if any shall be returned to him:

Provided that the money shall not be so applied if the court is satisfied that it does not belong to the person on whom it was found or that the loss of the money will be more injurious to his family than his imprisonment or detention.

[2] (3) When a court of summary jurisdiction, which has adjudged that a sum of money shall be paid by an offender, shall consider that any money found on the offender on apprehension, or after he has been searched by order of the court, should not be applied towards payment of such sum, the court shall make a direction in writing to that effect which shall be written on the extract of the sentence which imposes the fine before the same is issued by the clerk of the court.

[2] (4) An accused may make an application to such a court either orally or in writing, through the governor of the prison in whose custody he may be at the time, that any sum of money which shall have been found on his person should not be applied in payment of the fine adjudged to be paid by him.

[2] (5) A person who alleges that any money found on the person of an offender is not the property of the offender, but belongs to such person, may apply to such court either orally or in writing for a direction that such money should not be applied in payment of the fine adjudged to be paid, and the court after enquiry may so direct.

[2] (6) A court of summary jurisdiction, which has adjudged that a sum of money shall be paid by an offender, may order the attendance in court of the offender, if he is in prison, for the purpose of ascertaining the ownership of money which shall have been found on his person.

[2] (7) A notice in the form, as nearly as may be, of the appropriate form

contained in an Act of Adjournal under this Act, addressed to the governor of the prison in whose custody an offender may be at the time, signed by the judge of a court of summary jurisdiction shall be a sufficient warrant to the governor of such prison for conveying the offender to the court.

NOTES
[1] As amended by the Criminal Justice (Scotland) Act 1980, Sched. 7, para. 60.
[1a] Excluded by the Criminal Justice (Scotland) Act 1987, s. 56(9)(*b*). See also *ibid.*, s. 44.
[2] Applied to compensation orders by the Criminal Justice (Scotland) Act 1980, s. 66.

Power to remit fines
    [1,2] **395A.**—(1) A fine may at any time be remitted in whole or in part by—
      (*a*) in a case where a transfer of fine order under section 403 of this Act is effective and the court by which payment is enforceable is, in terms of the order, a court of summary jurisdiction in Scotland, that court; or
      (*b*) in any other case, the court which imposed the fine or (where that court was the High Court) by which payment was first enforceable.
    (2) Where the court remits the whole or part of a fine after imprisonment has been imposed under section 396(2) or (4) of this Act, it shall also remit the whole period of imprisonment or, as the case may be, reduce the period by an amount which bears the same proportion to the whole period as the amount remitted bears to the whole fine.
    (3) The power conferred by subsection (1) above shall be exercisable without requiring the attendance of the accused.

NOTES
[1] Inserted by the Criminal Justice (Scotland) Act 1980, s. 49.
[2] Applied (with modifications) to compensation orders by the Criminal Justice (Scotland) Act 1980, s. 66. Subs. (2) excluded by the Criminal Justice (Scotland) Act 1987, s. 56(9)(*b*).

Time for payment
    [1] **396.**—(1) Where a court of summary jurisdiction has imposed a fine on an offender or ordered him to find caution, the court shall, subject to the provisions of the next following subsection, allow him at least seven days to pay the fine or the first instalment thereof or, as the case may be, to find caution; and any reference in this and the next following section to a failure to pay a fine or other like expression shall include a reference to a failure to find caution.
    [2] (2) If on the occasion of the imposition of a fine—
      (*a*) the offender appears to the court to possess sufficient means to enable him to pay the fine forthwith; or
      (*b*) on being asked by the court whether he wishes to have time for payment, he does not ask for time; or
      (*c*) if he fails to satisfy the court that he has a fixed abode; or
      (*d*) the court is satisfied for any other special reason that no time should be allowed for payment,
the court may refuse him time to pay the fine and, if the offender fails to pay, may exercise its power to impose imprisonment and, if it does so, shall state the special reason for its decision.
    (3) In all cases where time is not allowed by a court of summary

jurisdiction for payment of a fine, the reasons of the court for not so allowing time shall be stated in the extract of the finding and sentence as well as in the finding and sentence itself.

(4) Where time is allowed for payment of a fine or payment by instalments is ordered, a court of summary jurisdiction shall not, on the occasion of the imposition of a fine, impose imprisonment in the event of a future default in paying the fine or an instalment thereof unless the offender is before it and the court determines that, having regard to the gravity of the offence or to the character of the offender, or to other special reason, it is expedient that he should be imprisoned without further inquiry in default of payment; and where a court so determines, it shall state the special reason for its decision.

(5) Where a court of summary jurisdiction has imposed imprisonment in accordance with the provisions of the last foregoing subsection, then, if at any time the offender asks the court to commit him to prison, the court may do so notwithstanding subsection (1) of this section.

(6) Nothing in the foregoing provisions of this section shall affect any power of a court of summary jurisdiction to order a fine to be recovered by civil diligence.

(7) Where time has been allowed for payment of a fine imposed by a court of summary jurisdiction, the court may, subject to any rules under this Part of this Act, on an application by or on behalf of the offender, and after giving the prosecutor an opportunity of being heard, allow further time for payment.

NOTES
[1] Applied to compensation orders by the Criminal Justice (Scotland) Act 1980, s. 66 and applied to confiscation orders by the Criminal Justice (Scotland) Act 1987, s. 7(2). Subss. (1)–(6) excluded by *ibid.*, s. 56(9)(*b*).
[2] See the Criminal Justice (Scotland) Act 1980, s. 41. See also the Legal Aid (Scotland) Act 1986, s. 23(1)(*b*).

Application for further time for payment of fine
[1] **397.**—[2] (1) An application by an offender for further time in which to pay a fine adjudged to be paid by him by a court of summary jurisdiction, or of instalments thereof, shall be made to that court, except in a case where a transfer of fine order shall have been made under section 403 of this Act, under section 90 of the Magistrates' Courts Act 1980 or under section 104A of the Magistrates' Courts Act (Northern Ireland) 1964, in which case the application shall be made to the court specified in the transfer order, or to the court specified in the last transfer order where there is more than one transfer.

(2) A court to which an application is made under the foregoing subsection shall allow further time for payment of the fine or of instalments thereof, unless it is satisfied that the failure of the offender to make payment has been wilful or that the offender has no reasonable prospect of being able to pay if further time is allowed.

(3) An application made under this section to a court of summary jurisdiction may be made orally or in writing.

NOTES
[1] Applied to compensation orders by the Criminal Justice (Scotland) Act 1980, s. 66 and applied to confiscation orders by the Criminal Justice (Scotland) Act 1987, s. 7(2).

[2] As amended by the Criminal Law Act 1977, Sched. 11, para. 8 and the Magistrates' Courts Act 1980, Sched. 7, para. 136.

Restriction on imprisonment after fine or caution

[1] **398.**—(1) Where a court of summary jurisdiction has imposed a fine or ordered the finding of caution without imposing imprisonment in default of payment, it shall not impose imprisonment on an offender for failing to make payment of the fine, unless on an occasion subsequent to that sentence the court has enquired into in his presence the reason why the fine has not been paid; but this subsection shall not apply where the offender is in prison.

(2) A court of summary jurisdiction may, for the purpose of enabling enquiry to be made under this section—

(a) issue a citation requiring the offender to appear before the court at a time and place appointed in the citation; or

(b) issue a warrant of apprehension.

(3) On the failure of the offender to appear before the court in response to a citation under this section, the court may issue a warrant of apprehension.

(4) A warrant of apprehension issued by a court of summary jurisdiction under subsection (2) of this section shall be in the form, as nearly as may be, of the appropriate form contained in an Act of Adjournal under this Act.

(5) The minute of procedure in relation to an enquiry into the means of an offender under this section shall be in the form, as nearly as may be, of the appropriate form contained in an Act of Adjournal under this Act.

NOTE
[1] As amended by the Criminal Justice (Scotland) Act 1980, Sched. 7. Applied to compensation orders by *ibid.*, s. 66 and applied to confiscation orders by the Criminal Justice (Scotland) Act 1987, s. 7(2).

Payment by instalments

[1] **399.**—(1) Without prejudice to the operation of section 396(2) of this Act, where a court of summary jurisdiction has imposed a fine on an offender, the court may, of its own accord or on the application of the offender, order payment of that fine by instalments of such amounts and at such time as it may think fit.

(2) Where the court has ordered payment of a fine by instalments it may—

(a) allow further time for payment of any instalment thereof;

(b) order payment thereof by instalments of lesser amounts or at longer intervals, than those originally fixed.

(3) The powers conferred by subsection (2) above shall be exercisable without requiring the attendance of the accused.

NOTE
[1] As amended by the Criminal Justice (Scotland) Act 1980, Scheds. 7 and 8. Applied to compensation orders by *ibid.*, s. 66 and applied to confiscation orders by the Criminal Justice (Scotland) Act 1987, s. 7(2).

Supervision pending payment of fine

[1] **400.**—(1) Where an offender has been allowed time for payment of a

fine by a court of summary jurisdiction, the court may, either on the occasion of the imposition of the fine or on a subsequent occasion, order that he be placed under the supervision of such person as the court may from time to time appoint for the purpose of assisting and advising the offender in regard to payment of the fine.

(2) An order made in pursuance of the foregoing subsection shall remain in force so long as the offender to whom it relates remains liable to pay the fine or any part of it unless the order ceases to have effect or is discharged under the next following subsection.

(3) An order under this section shall cease to have effect on the making of a transfer of fine order under section 403 of this Act in respect of the fine or may be discharged by the court that made it without prejudice, in either case, to the making of a new order.

(4) Where an offender under 21 years of age has been allowed time for payment of a fine by a court of summary jurisdiction, the court shall not order the form of detention appropriate to him in default of payment of the fine unless he has been placed under supervision in respect of the fine or the court is satisfied that it is impracticable to place him under supervision.

(5) Where a court, being satisfied as aforesaid, orders the detention of a person under 21 years of age without an order under this section having been made, the court shall state the grounds on which it is so satisfied.

(6) Where an order under this section is in force in respect of an offender, the court shall not impose imprisonment in default of the payment of the fine unless the court has, before so doing, taken such steps as may be reasonably practicable to obtain from the person appointed for the supervision of the payment of his fine a report, which may be oral, on the offender's conduct and means, and shall consider any report so obtained in addition, in a case where an enquiry is required by section 398 of this Act, to that enquiry.

(7) When a court of summary jurisdiction shall have made an order under subsection (1) of this section placing an offender under the supervision of another person, a notice shall be sent by the clerk of the court to such an offender in the form, as nearly as may be, of the appropriate form contained in an Act of Adjournal under this Act.

(8) The person appointed to supervise such an offender shall communicate with him with a view to assisting and advising him in regard to payment of the fine, and unless the same or any instalment thereof shall have been paid to the clerk of the court within the time allowed by the court for payment, the person so appointed shall report to the court without delay after the expiry of such time, as to the conduct and means of the offender.

NOTE
[1] Applied to compensation orders by the Criminal Justice (Scotland) Act 1980, s. 66 and applied to confiscation orders by the Criminal Justice (Scotland) Act 1987, s. 7(2).

Supplementary provisions as to payment of fine
[1] **401.**—(1) Where under the provisions of section 396 or 400 of this Act a court is required to state a special reason for its decision or the grounds on which it is satisfied that it is undesirable or impracticable to place an offender under supervision, the reason or, as the case may be, the

grounds shall be entered in the record of the proceedings along with the finding and sentence.

(2) Any reference in the sections last mentioned to imprisonment shall be construed, in the case of an offender on whom by reason of his age imprisonment may not lawfully be imposed, as a reference to the lawful form of detention in default of payment of a fine appropriate to that person, and any reference to prison shall be construed accordingly.

(3) Where a warrant has been issued for the apprehension of an offender for non-payment of a fine, the offender may, notwithstanding section 412 of this Act, pay such fine in full to a constable; and the warrant shall not then be enforced and the constable shall remit the fine to the clerk of court.

NOTE
[1] As amended by the Criminal Justice (Scotland) Act 1980, Sched. 7. Applied to compensation orders by *ibid.*, s. 66 and applied to confiscation orders by the Criminal Justice (Scotland) Act 1987, s. 7(2).

Fines, etc., may be enforced in another district
[1] **402.** Any sentence or decree for any fine or expenses pronounced by any sheriff court or district court may be enforced against the person or effects of any party against whom any such sentence or decree shall have been awarded in any other sheriff court district, as well as in the district where such sentence or decree is pronounced:

Provided that such sentence or decree, or an extract thereof, shall be first produced to and indorsed by the sheriff or justice of such other district competent to have pronounced such sentence or decree in such other district.

NOTE
[1] Applied to compensation orders by the Criminal Justice (Scotland) Act 1980, s. 66 and applied to confiscation orders by the Criminal Justice (Scotland) Act 1987, s. 7(2).

Transfer of fine orders
[1] **403.**—[2] (1) Where a court of summary jurisdiction has imposed a fine on a person convicted of an offence and it appears to the court that he is residing—

(a) within the jurisdiction of another court of summary jurisdiction in Scotland, or

(b) in a petty sessions area or petty sessions district in England and Wales, or

(c) in any petty sessions district in Northern Ireland,

the court may order that payment of the fine shall be enforceable by that other court of summary jurisdiction or in that petty sessions area, as the case may be.

[3] (2) An order under this section (in this section referred to as a transfer of fine order) shall specify the court by which or the petty sessions area or petty sessions district in which payment is to be enforceable and, where the court to be specified in a transfer of fine order is a court of summary jurisdiction, it shall, in any case where the order is made by the sheriff court, be a sheriff court.

(3) Where a transfer of fine order is made with respect to any fine under

this section, any functions under any enactment relating to that sum which, if no such order had been made, would have been exercisable by the court which made the order or by the clerk of that court shall cease to be so exercisable.

[3,4] (4) Where a transfer of fine order under this section, section 90 of the Magistrates' Courts Act 1980 or section 104A of the Magistrates' Courts Act (Northern Ireland) 1964 specifies a court of summary jurisdiction in Scotland, that court and the clerk of that court shall have all the like functions under this Part of this Act in respect of the fine or the sum in respect of which that order was made (including the power to make any further order under this section) as if the fine or the sum were a fine imposed by that court and as if any order made under this section, the said Act of 1980 or the said Act of 1964 in respect of the fine or the sum before the making of the transfer of fine order had been made by that court:

Provided that for the purpose of determining the period of imprisonment which may be imposed under this Part of this Act by any court having jurisdiction in respect of a sum adjudged to be paid by a conviction of a magistrates' court acting for a petty sessions area, section 407 of this Act shall have effect as if for the Table set out in subsection (1) of that section there were substituted the Table set out in paragraph 1 of Schedule 4 to the said Act of 1980.

(5) [Repealed by the Criminal Law Act 1977, Sched. 13.]

[5] (6) Where a transfer of fine order under section 90 of the Magistrates' Courts Act 1980, section 104A of the Magistrates' Courts Act (Northern Ireland) 1964 or this section provides for the enforcement by a sheriff court in Scotland of a fine imposed by the Crown Court, the proviso to subsection (4) of this section shall not apply, but the term of imprisonment which may be imposed under this Part of this Act shall be the term fixed in pursuance of section 31 of the Powers of Criminal Courts Act 1973 by the Crown Court or a term which bears the same proportion to the term so fixed as the amount of the fine remaining due bears to the amount of the fine imposed by that court, notwithstanding that the term exceeds the period applicable to the case under section 407 of this Act.

NOTES
[1] Applied to compensation orders by the Criminal Justice (Scotland) Act 1980, s. 66. See the Magistrates' Courts Act 1980, s. 91. Applied to confiscation orders by the Criminal Justice (Scotland) Act 1987, s. 7(2).
[2] Repealed in part and amended by the Criminal Law Act 1977, Sched. 13.
[3] As amended by the Criminal Law Act 1977, Sched. 7, para. 2.
[4] As amended by the Magistrates' Courts Act 1980, Sched. 7, para. 137. Repealed in part by the Criminal Law Act 1977, Sched. 13.
[5] As amended by the Criminal Law Act 1977, Sched. 7, para. 2 and the Magistrates' Courts Act 1980, Sched. 7, para. 137. Excluded by the Criminal Justice (Scotland) Act 1987, s. 56(9)(*b*).

Action of clerk of court on transfer of fine orders
[1] **404.**—(1) Where a court of summary jurisdiction makes a transfer of fine order under section 403 of this Act, the clerk of the court shall send to the clerk of the court specified in the order a notice in the form, as nearly as may be, of the appropriate form contained in an Act of Adjournal under this Act, and shall at the same time send to that clerk a statement of the offence of which the offender was convicted, and of the steps if any

which shall have been taken to recover the fine, and shall give him such further information if any as, in his opinion, is likely to assist the court specified in the order in recovering the fine.

(2) In the case of a further transfer of fine order the clerk of the court which shall have made the order shall send to the clerk of the court by which the fine was imposed a copy of the notice which shall have been sent to the clerk of the court specified in the order.

(3) The clerk of the court specified in a transfer of fine order shall, as soon as may be after he has received the notice prescribed in subsection (1) of this section, send an intimation to the offender in the form, as nearly as may be, of the appropriate form contained in an Act of Adjournal under this Act.

(4) The clerk of the court specified in a transfer of fine order shall remit or otherwise account for any payment received in respect of the fine, to the clerk of the court by which the fine was imposed, and if the sentence shall have been enforced otherwise than by payment of the fine, he shall inform the clerk of that court how the sentence was enforced.

NOTE
[1] Applied to compensation orders by the Criminal Justice (Scotland) Act 1980, s. 66 and applied to confiscation orders by the Criminal Justice (Scotland) Act 1987, s. 7(2).

. . . . . .

Substitution of custody for imprisonment where a child defaults on fine
[1] **406.** Where a child would, if he were an adult, be liable to be imprisoned in default of payment of any fine, damages or expenses, the court may, if it considers that none of the other methods by which the case may legally be dealt with is suitable, order that the child be detained for such period, not exceeding one month, as may be specified in the order in a place chosen by the local authority in whose area the court is situated.

NOTE
[1] Applied to compensation orders by the Criminal Justice (Scotland) Act 1980, s. 66 and applied to confiscation orders by the Criminal Justice (Scotland) Act 1987, s. 7(2). Excluded by *ibid.*, s. 56(9)(*b*).

Period of imprisonment for non-payment of fine
[1] **407.**—(1) Subject to sections 396 to 401 of this Act—
    (*a*) a court of summary jurisdiction may, when imposing a fine, impose a period of imprisonment in default of payment; or
   [2] (*b*) where no order has been made under paragraph (*a*) above and a person fails to pay a fine, or any part or instalment of a fine, by the time ordered by the court (or, where section 396(2) of this Act applies, immediately) the court may impose a period of imprisonment for such failure either with immediate effect or to take effect in the event of the person failing to pay the fine or any part or instalment of it by such further time as the court may order,
whether or not the fine is imposed under an enactment which makes provision for its enforcement or recovery.
[2,3] (1A) Subject to the following subsections of this section, the

maximum period of imprisonment which may be imposed under subsection (1) above or for failure to find caution, shall be as follows—

Amount of Fine or of Caution	Maximum Period of Imprisonment
Not exceeding £50	7 days
Exceeding £50 but not exceeding £100	14 days
Exceeding £100 but not exceeding £400	30 days
Exceeding £400 but not exceeding £1,000	60 days
Exceeding £1,000 but not exceeding £2,000	90 days
Exceeding £2,000 but not exceeding £5,000	6 months
Exceeding £5,000 but not exceeding £10,000	9 months
Exceeding £10,000 but not exceeding £20,000	12 months
Exceeding £20,000 but not exceeding £50,000	18 months
Exceeding £50,000 but not exceeding £100,000	2 years
Exceeding £100,000 but not exceeding £250,000	3 years
Exceeding £250,000 but not exceeding £1 million	5 years
Exceeding £1 million	10 years

[2] (1B) Where an offender is fined on the same day before the same court for offences charged in the same complaint or in separate complaints, the amount of the fine shall, for the purposes of this section, be taken to be the total of the fines imposed.

(1C) Where a court has imposed a period of imprisonment in default of payment of a fine, and—

(*a*) an instalment of the fine is not paid at the time ordered; or

(*b*) part only of the fine has been paid within the time allowed for payment,

the offender shall be liable to imprisonment for a period which bears to the period so imposed the same proportion, as nearly as may be, as the amount outstanding at the time when warrant is issued for imprisonment of the offender in default bears to the original fine.

[2] (1D) Where no period of imprisonment in default of payment of a fine has been imposed and—

(*a*) an instalment of the fine is not paid at the time ordered; or

(*b*) part only of the fine has been paid within the time allowed for payment,

the offender shall be liable to imprisonment for a maximum period which bears, as nearly as may be, the same proportion to the maximum period of imprisonment which could have been imposed by virtue of the Table in subsection (1A) above in default of payment of the original fine as the amount outstanding at the time when he appears before the court bears to the original fine.

[2] (2) If in any sentence or extract sentence the period of imprisonment inserted in default of payment of a fine or on failure to find caution is in excess of that competent under this Part of this Act, such period of imprisonment shall be reduced to the maximum period under this Part of this Act applicable to such default or failure, and the judge who pronounced the sentence shall have power to order the sentence or extract to be corrected accordingly.

(3) The periods of imprisonment set forth in subsection (1A) of this section shall apply to the non-payment of any sum imposed as aforesaid

by a court of summary jurisdiction under a statute or order passed or made before the first day of June 1909, notwithstanding that that statute or order fixes any other period of imprisonment.

[2] (4) The provisions of this section shall be without prejudice to the operation of section 409 of this Act.

(5) Where in any case—

(*a*) the sheriff considers that the imposition of imprisonment for the number of years for the time being specified in section 2(2) of this Act would be inadequate; and

(*b*) the maximum period of imprisonment which may be imposed under subsection (1) above (or under that subsection as read with either or both of sections 66(2) of the Criminal Justice (Scotland) Act 1980 and 7(2) of the Criminal Justice (Scotland) Act 1987) exceeds that number of years,

he shall remit the case to the High Court for sentence.

NOTES

[1] As amended by the Criminal Justice (Scotland) Act 1980, s. 50 and Sched. 7. See the Magistrates' Courts Act 1980, s. 91(2). As amended by the Criminal Justice (Scotland) Act 1987, s. 67, applied to confiscation orders by *ibid.*, s. 7(2) and excluded (except subs. (1)(*b*)) by *ibid.*, s. 56(9)(*b*).

[2] Applied (with modifications) to compensation orders by the Criminal Justice (Scotland) Act 1980, s. 66. As amended by the Law Reform (Miscellaneous Provisions) (Scotland) Act 1990, Sched. 8, para. 27(3).

[3] As amended by S.I. 1984 No. 526, and by the Law Reform (Miscellaneous Provisions) (Scotland) Act 1985, s. 40, with effect from 30th December 1985. For transitional provision see *ibid.*, Sched. 3, para. 4.

Discharge from imprisonment to be specified

[1] **408.** All warrants of imprisonment for payment of a fine, or for finding of caution, shall specify a period at the expiry of which the person sentenced shall be discharged, notwithstanding such fine shall not have been paid, or caution found.

NOTE

[1] Applied to compensation orders by the Criminal Justice (Scotland) Act 1980, s. 66 and applied to confiscation orders by the Criminal Justice (Scotland) Act 1987, s. 7(2). Excluded by *ibid.*, s. 56(9)(*b*).

Payment of fine in part by prisoner

[1] **409.**—(1) Where a person committed to prison or otherwise detained for failure to pay a fine imposed by a court of summary jurisdiction pays to the governor of the prison, under conditions prescribed by rules made under the Prisons (Scotland) Act 1952, any sum in part satisfaction of the fine, the term of imprisonment shall be reduced (or as the case may be further reduced) by a number of days bearing as nearly as possible the same proportion to such term as the sum so paid bears to the amount of the fine outstanding at the commencement of the imprisonment:

Provided that the day on which any sum is paid shall not be regarded as a day served by the prisoner as part of the said term of imprisonment.

(2) In this section references to a prison and to the governor thereof shall include respectively references to any other place in which a person may be lawfully detained in default of payment of a fine, and to an officer in charge thereof.

(3) Provision may be made by Act of Adjournal for the application of sums paid under this section and for any matter incidental thereto.

(4) The provisions of Schedule 7 to this Act shall apply for the purposes of this section.

NOTE
[1] As amended by the Criminal Justice (Scotland) Act 1980, Sched. 7. Applied to compensation orders by *ibid.*, s. 66 and applied to confiscation orders by the Criminal Justice (Scotland) Act 1987, s. 7(2). Excluded by *ibid.*, s. 56(9)(*b*).

. . . . . .

Recovery by civil diligence
[1] **411.**—(1) Where any fine falls to be recovered by civil diligence in pursuance of this Part of this Act or in any case in which a court of summary jurisdiction may think it expedient to order a fine to be recovered by civil diligence, there shall be added to the finding of the court imposing the fine a warrant for civil diligence in a form prescribed by Act of Adjournal which shall have the effect of authorising—

(*a*) the charging of the person who has been fined to pay the fine within the period specified in the charge and, in the event of failure to make such payment within that period, the execution of an earnings arrestment and the poinding of articles belonging to him and, if necessary for the purpose of executing the poinding, the opening of shut and lockfast places;

(*b*) an arrestment other than an arrestment of earnings in the hands of his employer;

and such diligence, whatever the amount of the fine imposed, may be executed in the same manner as if the proceedings were on an extract decree of the sheriff in a summary cause.

(2) [Repealed by the Criminal Justice (Scotland) Act 1980, Sched. 8.]

[2] (3) Proceedings by civil diligence under this section may be adopted at any time after the imposition of the fine to which they relate:

Provided that no such proceedings shall be authorised after the offender has been imprisoned in consequence of his having defaulted in payment of the fine.

NOTES
[1] As amended by the Criminal Justice (Scotland) Act 1980, s. 52 and Scheds. 7 and 8. Applied to compensation orders by *ibid.*, s. 66. As amended by the Debtors (Scotland) Act 1987, Sched. 6, para. 18. Applied to confiscation orders by the Criminal Justice (Scotland) Act 1987, s. 7(2).
[2] Excluded by the Criminal Justice (Scotland) Act 1987, s. 56(9)(*b*).

Payment of fines to be made to clerk of court
412. All fines and expenses imposed under this Part of this Act shall be paid to the clerk of court to be accounted for by him to the person entitled thereto, and it shall not be necessary to specify in any sentence the person entitled to payment of any such fine or expenses, unless where it is necessary to provide for the division of the penalty.

Residential and Borstal Training

Detention of children

[1]413.—(1) Where a child appears before the sheriff in summary proceedings and pleads guilty to, or is found guilty of, an offence to which this section applies, the sheriff may order that he be detained in residential care by the appropriate local authority for such period, not exceeding one year, as the sheriff may determine in such place (in any part of the United Kingdom) as the local authority may, from time to time, consider appropriate.

(2) This section applies to any offence in respect of which it is competent to impose imprisonment on a person of the age of 21 years or more.

(3) In this section—

"the appropriate local authority" means—

(*a*) where the child usually resides in Scotland, the regional or islands council for the area in which he usually resides;

(*b*) in any other case, the regional or islands council for the area in which the offence was committed;

"care" shall be construed in accordance with section 32(3) of the 1968 Act, and the provisions of that Act specified in section 44(5) of that Act shall apply in respect of a child who is detained in residential care in pursuance of this section as they apply in respect of a child who is subject to a supervision requirement;

"the 1968 Act" means the Social Work (Scotland) Act 1968.

(4) Where a child in respect of whom an order is made under this section is also subject to a supervision requirement within the meaning of the 1968 Act, subject to subsection (6) below, the supervision requirement shall be of no effect during any period for which he is required to be detained under the order.

(5) The Secretary of State may, by regulations[2] made by statutory instrument subject to annulment in pursuance of a resolution of either House of Parliament, make such provision as he considers necessary as regards the detention in secure accommodation (within the meaning of the 1968 Act) of children in respect of whom orders have been made under this section.

(6) Section 20A of the 1968 Act (review of children in care) shall apply to a child detained in residential care in pursuance of an order under this section as if the references to care in that section were references to care within the meaning of this section; and, without prejudice to their duty to do so by virtue of the said section 20A, the local authority may, at any time, review the case of such a child and may, in consequence of such a review and after having regard to the best interests of the child and the need to protect members of the public, release the child—

(*a*) for such period and on such conditions as they consider appropriate; or

(*b*) unconditionally,

and where a child who is released unconditionally is subject to a supervision requirement within the meaning of the 1968 Act, the effect of the supervision requirement shall, in the case of a supervision requirement imposed during the period of detention, commence or, in any other case, resume upon such release.

(7) Where a local authority consider it appropriate that a child in respect of whom an order has been made under subsection (1) above should be detained in a place in any part of the United Kingdom outside Scotland, the order shall be a like authority as in Scotland to the person in charge of the place to restrict the child's liberty to such an extent as that person may consider appropriate having regard to the terms of the order.

NOTES
[1] Substituted by the Criminal Justice (Scotland) Act 1987, s. 59(1). See also *ibid.*, s. 59(3).
[2] See S.I. 1988 No. 294.

．　．　．　．　．　．

Imprisonment, etc.

Detention of young offenders
[1] **415.**—(1) It shall not be competent to impose imprisonment on a person under 21 years of age.

(2) Subject to subsections (3) and (4) below a court may impose detention (whether by way of sentence or otherwise) on a person, who is not less than 16 but under 21 years of age, where but for subsection (1) above the court would have power to impose a period of imprisonment; and the period of detention imposed under this section on any person shall not exceed the maximum period of imprisonment which might otherwise have been imposed.

(3) The court shall not under subsection (2) above impose detention on a person unless it is of the opinion that no other method of dealing with him is appropriate; and the court shall state its reasons for that opinion, and, except in the case of the High Court, those reasons shall be entered in the record of proceedings.

(4) To enable the court to form an opinion under subsection (3) above, it shall obtain (from an officer of a local authority or otherwise) such information as it can about the offender's circumstances; and it shall also take into account any information before it concerning the offender's character and physical and mental condition.

[2] (5) A sentence of detention imposed under this section shall be a sentence of detention in a young offenders institution.

[3] (11) Section 18 (functions of Parole Board), section 24 (remission for good conduct) and sections 22, 26, 28 and 29 (release on licence) of the Prisons (Scotland) Act 1989 shall apply to a person sentenced under this section as those enactments apply to a person sentenced to a period of imprisonment.

NOTES
[1] Substituted by the Criminal Justice (Scotland) Act 1980, s. 45. Restricted by the Repatriation of Prisoners Act 1984, Sched. 1, para. 4(2). See the Prisons (Scotland) Act 1989, s. 32. The Criminal Justice Act 1988, Sched. 9, para. 6 provides:
"An offender who was ordered to be detained in a detention centre on a date before the commencement of section 124(1) of this Act [1st November 1988] shall, if the order has not expired at the commencement of that section, be treated for all purposes of detention,

release and supervision as if he had been sentenced to detention for the like term in a young offenders institution."
    [2] Substituted for subss. (5)–(10) by the Criminal Justice Act 1988, s. 124(1) and Sched. 9, para. 6.
    [3] As amended by the Prisons (Scotland) Act 1989, Sched. 2, para. 13, with effect from 16th February 1990.

. . . . . .

Recall to young offenders institution on re-conviction

[1] **421.**—(1) Where a person sentenced to detention under section 415 of this Act, being under supervision after his release from such detention is convicted of an offence punishable with imprisonment, the court may, except where the person convicted is subject to a licence granted under section 60(1) or section 61 of the Criminal Justice Act 1967 or section 22(1) or section 26 of the Prisons (Scotland) Act 1989, make an order for his recall.

(2) An order for the recall of a person made as aforesaid shall have the like effect as an order for a recall made by the Secretary of State under section 32 of the said Act of 1989.

NOTE
    [1] As amended by the Criminal Justice (Scotland) Act 1980, Sched. 7, para. 67, the Criminal Justice Act 1982, Sched. 15, para. 18 and Sched. 16, and (with effect from 16th February 1990) the Prisons (Scotland) Act 1989, Sched. 2, para. 14. Saved by the 1989 Act, s. 21(3).

. . . . . .

Return to prison in case of breach of supervision

[1] **423.**—(1) If, on sworn information laid by or on behalf of the Secretary of State, it appears to the sheriff that a person, being under supervision under section 30 of the Prisons (Scotland) Act 1989, has failed to comply with any of the requirements imposed on him by his notice of supervision, the sheriff may issue a warrant for the arrest of that person or may, if he thinks fit, instead of issuing such a warrant in the first instance, issue a citation requiring the person to appear before him at such time as may be specified in the citation.

(2) If it is proved to the satisfaction of the sheriff before whom a person appears or is brought in pursuance of the foregoing subsection that the person has failed to comply with any of the requirements of the notice of supervision, the sheriff shall, unless having regard to all the circumstances of the case, he considers it unnecessary or inexpedient to do so, order that he be sent back to prison for such term as may be specified in that order, not exceeding whichever is the shorter of the following, that is to say—

(*a*) a period of three months;
(*b*) a period equal to so much of the period of 12 months referred to in section 30(4) of the said Act of 1989 as was unexpired on the date in which proceedings were commenced.

(3) Subject to the following provisions of this section, this Part of this Act shall apply in relation to proceedings for an order as aforesaid as it

applies in relation to proceedings in respect of a summary offence, and references in this Part of this Act to an offence, trial, conviction or sentence shall be construed accordingly.

(4) Proceedings for an order under subsection (2) of this section may be brought before a sheriff having jurisdiction in the area in which the supervising officer carries out his duties.

(5) A warrant issued for the purposes of proceedings for an order under subsection (2) above may, if the person laying the information so requests, bear an endorsement requiring any constable charged with its execution to communicate with the Secretary of State before arresting the person under supervision if the constable finds that that person is earning an honest livelihood or that there are other circumstances which ought to be brought to the notice of the Secretary of State.

(6) Where a person while under supervision under section 30 of the said Act of 1989 is convicted of an offence for which the court has power to pass sentence of imprisonment, the court may, instead of dealing with him in any other manner, make such an order as could be made by a sheriff under subsection (2) of this section in proceedings for such an order.

(7) The Secretary of State may at any time release from prison a person who has been sent back to prison under subsection (2) or (6) of this section and the provisions of this section and of section 30 of the said Act of 1989 shall apply to a person released by virtue of this subsection, subject to the following modifications:

(a) that the period of 12 months referred to in subsection (4) of the said section 30 shall be calculated from the date of his original release; and

(b) in relation to any further order for sending him back to prison under this section, the period referred to in subsection (2)(a) of this section shall be reduced by any time during which he has been detained by virtue of the previous order.

(8) In any proceedings, a certificate purporting to be signed by or on behalf of the Secretary of State and certifying—

(a) that a notice of supervision was given to any person in the terms specified in the certificate and on the date so specified; and

(b) either that no notice has been given to him under subsection (5) of section 30 of the said Act of 1989 or that a notice has been so given in the terms specified in the certificate,

shall be sufficient evidence of the matters so certified; and the fact that a notice of supervision was given to any person shall be sufficient evidence that he was a person to whom the said section 30 applies.

(9) For the purposes of Part III of the Criminal Justice Act 1961, a person who has been sent back to prison under subsection (2) or (6) of this section, and has not been released again, shall be deemed to be serving part of his original sentence, whether or not the term of that sentence has in fact expired.

NOTE
[1] As amended by the Prisons (Scotland) Act 1989, Sched. 2, para. 15, with effect from 16th February 1990. This section is not yet in force: see s. 464(4).

Detention in precincts of court

[1] **424.** Where a court of summary jurisdiction has power to impose imprisonment or detention on an offender it may, in lieu of so doing, order that the offender be detained within the precincts of the court or at any police station, till such hour, not later than eight in the evening on the day on which he is convicted, as the court may direct:

Provided that before making an order under this section a court shall take into consideration the distance between the proposed place of detention and the offender's residence (if known to, or ascertainable by, the court), and shall not make any such order under this section as would deprive the offender of a reasonable opportunity of returning to his residence on the day on which the order is made.

NOTE

[1] As amended by the Criminal Justice (Scotland) Act 1980, Sched. 7, para. 68.

No imprisonment for less than five days

425.—(1) No person shall be sentenced to imprisonment by a court of summary jurisdiction for a period of less than five days.

(2) Where a court of summary jurisdiction has power to impose imprisonment on an offender, it may, if any suitable place provided and certified as hereinafter mentioned is available for the purpose, sentence the offender to be detained therein, for such period not exceeding four days as the court thinks fit, and an extract of the finding and sentence shall be delivered with the offender to the person in charge of the place where the offender is to be detained and shall be a sufficient authority for his detention in that place in accordance with the sentence.

(3) The expenses of the maintenance of offenders detained under this section shall be defrayed in like manner as the expenses of the maintenance of prisoners under the Prisons (Scotland) Act 1952.

(4) The Secretary of State may, on the application of any police authority, certify any police cells or other similar places provided by the authority to be suitable places for the detention of persons sentenced to detention under this section, and may by statutory instrument make regulations for the inspection of places so provided, the treatment of persons detained therein and generally for carrying this section into effect.

(5) No place certified under this section shall be used for the detention of females unless provision is made for their supervision by female officers.

(6) In this section the expression "police authority" means a regional or islands council, except that where there is an amalgamation scheme under the Police (Scotland) Act 1967 in force it means a joint police committee.

(7) Until 16th May 1975 the last foregoing subsection shall have effect as if, for the words "regional or islands council" there were substituted the words "council of a county or of a burgh which maintains a separate police force."

Legal custody

[1] **426.** Any person required or authorised by or under this Act or any other enactment or any subordinate instrument to be taken to any place,

or to be detained or kept in custody shall, while being so taken or detained or kept, be deemed to be in legal custody.

NOTE
[1] Substituted by the Criminal Justice (Scotland) Act 1980, Sched. 7 and as amended by the Criminal Justice (Scotland) Act 1987, Sched. 1, para. 12.

Miscellaneous provisions as to conviction, sentence, etc.

. . . . . .

"Conviction" and "sentence" not to be used in relation to a child
429. The words "conviction" and "sentence" shall not be used in relation to children dealt with summarily and any reference in any enactment, whether passed before or after the commencement of this Act, to a person convicted, a conviction or a sentence shall in the case of a child be construed as including a reference to a person found guilty of an offence, a finding of guilt or an order made upon such a finding as the case may be.

Forms of finding and sentence
430.—(1) The finding and sentence of any order of a court of summary jurisdiction, as regards both offences at common law and offences under any statute or order, shall be entered in the record of the proceedings in the form, as nearly as may be, of the appropriate form contained in Part V of Schedule 2 to the Summary Jurisdiction (Scotland) Act 1954 or in an Act of Adjournal under this Act, which shall be sufficient warrant for all execution thereon and for the clerk of court to issue extracts containing such executive clauses as may be necessary for implement thereof; and, when imprisonment forms part of any sentence or other judgment, warrant for the apprehension and interim detention of the accused pending his being committed to prison shall, where necessary, be implied.

(2) Where a fine imposed by a court of summary jurisdiction is paid at the bar it shall not be necessary for the court to refer to the period of imprisonment applicable to the non-payment thereof.

(3) Where several charges at common law or under any statute or order are embraced in one complaint, a cumulo fine may be imposed in respect of all or any of such charges of which the accused is convicted.

(4) A sentence following on a conviction by a court of summary jurisdiction may be framed so as to take effect on the expiry of any previous sentence which at the date of such conviction the accused is undergoing.

Consideration of time spent in custody
[1] **431.** A court, in passing a sentence of imprisonment or detention on a person for any offence, shall, in determining the period of imprisonment or detention, have regard to any period of time spent in custody by that person on remand awaiting trial or sentence.

NOTE
[1] As amended by the Criminal Justice (Scotland) Act 1980, Sched. 7, para. 70.

Deferred sentence

[1] **432.**—(1) It shall be competent for a court to defer sentence after conviction for a period and on such conditions as the court may determine; and the fact that the accused has been convicted shall not prevent the court from making, in due course, a probation order under section 384 of this Act.

(2) If it appears to the court by which sentence on a person has been deferred under subsection (1) above that that person has been convicted, during the period of deferment, by a court in any part of Great Britain of an offence committed during that period and has been dealt with for that offence, the first mentioned court may issue a warrant for the arrest of that person, or may, instead of issuing such a warrant in the first instance, issue a citation requiring him to appear before it at such time as may be specified in the citation; and on his appearance or on his being brought before the court it may deal with him in any manner in which it would be competent for it to deal with him on the expiry of the period of deferment.

(3) Where a court which has deferred sentence under subsection (1) above on a person convicts that person of another offence during the period of deferment, it may deal with him for the original offence in any manner in which it would be competent for it to deal with him on the expiry of the period of deferment, as well as for the offence committed during the said period.

NOTE
[1] As amended by the Criminal Justice (Scotland) Act 1980, ss. 53 and 54.

Sentence in open court

433. Every sentence imposed by a court of summary jurisdiction shall unless otherwise provided be pronounced in open court in the presence of the accused, but need not be written out or signed in his presence.

Further provision as to sentence

[1] **434.**—(1) It shall be competent at any time before imprisonment has followed on a sentence for the court to alter or modify it; but no higher sentence than that originally pronounced shall be competent.

(2) The signature of the judge or clerk of court to any sentence shall be sufficient also to authenticate the findings on which such sentence proceeds.

(3) The power conferred by subsection (1) of this section to alter or modify a sentence shall be exercisable without requiring the attendance of the accused.

NOTE
[1] As amended by the Criminal Justice (Scotland) Act 1980, Sched. 8.

Expenses

[1] **435.** The following provisions shall have effect with regard to the award of expenses in a summary prosecution:—

(a) expenses may be awarded to or against a private prosecutor but shall not be awarded against any person prosecuting in the public interest unless the statute or order under which the prosecution is brought expressly or impliedly authorises such an award;

(*b*) the finding regarding expenses shall be stated in the sentence or judgment disposing of the case;

(*c*) expenses awarded to the prosecutor shall be restricted to the fees set forth in Schedule 3 to the Summary Jurisdiction (Scotland) Act 1954;

(*d*) the court may award expenses against the accused without imposing any fine or may direct the expenses incurred by the prosecutor, whether public or private, to be met wholly or partly out of any fine imposed;

(*e*) expenses awarded against the accused, where the fine or fines imposed do not exceed £400, shall not exceed £100:

Provided that if it appears to the court that the reasonable expenses of the prosecutor's witnesses together with the other expenses exceed the sum of £100, the court may direct the expenses of those witnesses to be paid wholly or partly out of the fine;

(*f*) where a child is himself ordered by a sheriff sitting summarily to pay expenses in addition to a fine, the amount of the expenses so ordered to be paid shall in no case exceed the amount of the fine;

(*g*) any expenses awarded shall be recoverable by civil diligence in accordance with section 411 of this Act.

NOTE
[1] As amended by the Criminal Justice (Scotland) Act 1980, s. 46 and S.I. 1984 No. 526.

Forfeiture of property
[1] **436.**—(1) Where a person is convicted of an offence and the court which passes sentence is satisfied that any property which was in his possession or under his control at the time of his apprehension—

(*a*) has been used for the purpose of committing, or facilitating the commission of, any offence; or

(*b*) was intended by him to be used for that purpose,

that property shall be liable to forfeiture, and any property forfeited under this section shall be disposed of as the court may direct.

(2) Any reference in this section to facilitating the commission of an offence shall include a reference to the taking of any steps after it has been committed for the purpose of disposing of any property to which it relates or of avoiding apprehension or detection.

NOTE
[1] As substituted by the Criminal Justice (Scotland) Act 1980, Sched. 7, and excluded by the Telecommunications Act 1984, Sched. 3, para. 3(*b*). See the Criminal Justice (Scotland) Act 1987, s. 5(3)(*b*).

Warrant of search for forfeited articles
437. Where a court has made an order for the forfeiture of an article, the court or any justice of the peace may, if satisfied on information on oath—

(*a*) that there is reasonable cause to believe that the article is to be found in any place or premises; and

(*b*) that admission to the place or premises has been refused or that a refusal of such admission is apprehended,

issue a warrant of search which may be executed according to law; and for the purposes of this section, any reference to a justice of the peace includes a reference to the sheriff and to a magistrate.

. . . . . .

Correction of entries
[1] **439.**—(1) Subject to the provisions of this section, it shall be competent to correct an entry in—
(*a*) the record of proceedings in a summary prosecution; or
(*b*) the extract of a sentence passed or an order of court made in such proceedings,
in so far as that entry constitutes an error of recording or is incomplete.
(2) Such entry may be corrected—
(*a*) by the clerk of the court, at any time before either the sentence (or order) of the court is executed or, on appeal, the proceedings are transmitted to the Clerk of Justiciary;
(*b*) by the clerk of the court, under the authority of the court which passed the sentence or made the order, at any time after the execution of the sentence (or order) of the court but before such transmission as is mentioned in paragraph (*a*) above; or
(*c*) by the clerk of the court under the authority of the High Court in the case of a remit under subsection (4)(*b*) below.
(3) A correction in accordance with paragraph (*b*) or (*c*) of subsection (2) above shall be intimated to the prosecutor and to the former accused or his solicitor.
(4) Where, during the course of an appeal, the High Court becomes aware of an erroneous or incomplete entry, such as is mentioned in subsection (1) above, the court—
(*a*) may consider and determine the appeal as if such entry were corrected; and
(*b*) either before or after the determination of the appeal, may remit the proceedings to the court of first instance for correction in accordance with subsection (2)(*c*) above.
(5) Any correction under subsections (1) and (2) above by the clerk of the court shall be authenticated by his signature and, if such correction is authorised by a court, shall record the name of the judge or judges authorising such correction and the date of such authority.

NOTE
[1] Substituted by the Criminal Justice (Scotland) Act 1980, s. 20.

Extract sufficient warrant for imprisonment
440. Where an imprisonment is authorised by the sentence of a court of summary jurisdiction, an extract of the finding and sentence in the form, as nearly as may be, of the appropriate form contained in Part V of Schedule 2 to the Summary Jurisdiction (Scotland) Act 1954 or in an Act of Adjournal under this Act shall be a sufficient warrant for the apprehension and commitment of the accused, and no such extract shall be void or liable to be set aside on account of any error or defect in point of form.

. . . . . .

Review

Right of appeal

[1] **442.**—(1) Without prejudice to any right of appeal under section 453A of this Act—

(*a*) any person convicted in summary proceedings may appeal under this section to the High Court—

(i) against such conviction;

(ii) against the sentence passed on such conviction; or

(iii) against both such conviction and such sentence;

(*b*) the prosecutor in such proceedings may so appeal on a point of law—

(i) against an acquittal in such proceedings; or

(ii) against a sentence passed in such proceedings.

(2) By an appeal under subsection (1)(*a*) of this section or, as the case may be, against acquittal under subsection (1)(*b*) of this section, an appellant may bring under review of the High Court any alleged miscarriage of justice in the proceedings, including, in the case of an appeal under the said subsection (1)(*a*), any alleged miscarriage of justice on the basis of the existence and significance of additional evidence which was not heard at the trial and which was not available and could not reasonably have been made available at the trial.

NOTE

[1] Substituted by the Criminal Justice (Scotland) Act 1980, Sched. 3.

Method of appeal against conviction or conviction and sentence

[1] **442A.**—(1) Where a person desires to appeal under section 442(1)(*a*) (i) or (iii) or (*b*) of this Act, he shall pursue each appeal in accordance with the provisions of sections 444 to 453, 453D and 453E of this Act.

(2) A person who has appealed against both conviction and sentence, may abandon the appeal in so far as it is against conviction and may proceed with it against sentence alone, subject to such procedure as may be prescribed by Act of Adjournal under this Act.

NOTE

[1] Inserted by the Criminal Justice (Scotland) Act 1980, Sched. 3.

Method of appeal against sentence alone

[1] **442B.** Where a person desires to appeal against sentence alone, under section 442(1)(*a*)(ii) of this Act, he shall pursue such appeal in accordance with the provisions of sections 453B to 453E of this Act:

Provided that nothing in this section shall prevent a convicted person from proceeding by way of a bill of suspension in respect of any alleged fundamental irregularity relating to the imposition of the sentence.

NOTE

[1] Inserted by the Criminal Justice (Scotland) Act 1980, Sched. 3.

Appeals against hospital orders, etc.

[1] **443.** Where a hospital order, interim hospital order (but not a renewal thereof), guardianship order or an order restricting discharge has been made by a court in respect of a person charged or brought before it, he

may, without prejudice to any other form of appeal under any rule of law, (or, where an interim hospital order has been made, to any right of appeal against any other order or sentence which may be imposed), appeal against that order in the same manner as against sentence.

NOTE
[1] As amended by the Bail etc. (Scotland) Act 1980, Sched. 1, the Criminal Justice (Scotland) Act 1980, Sched. 3 and with effect from 30th September 1984 by the Mental Health (Amendment) (Scotland) Act 1983, s. 34(*d*).

Suspension of disqualification, forfeiture etc.
[1] **443A.**—(1) Where upon conviction of any person—
  (*a*) any disqualification, forfeiture or disability attaches to him by reason of such conviction; or
  (*b*) any property, matters or things which are the subject of the prosecution or connected therewith are to be or may be ordered to be destroyed or forfeited,
if the court before which he was convicted thinks fit, the disqualification, forfeiture or disability or, as the case may be, destruction or forfeiture or order for destruction or forfeiture shall be suspended pending the determination of any appeal against conviction or sentence.

(2) Subsection (1) above does not apply in respect of any disqualification, forfeiture or, as the case may be, destruction or forfeiture or order for destruction or forfeiture under or by virtue of any enactment which contains express provision for the suspension of such disqualification, forfeiture or, as the case may be, destruction or forfeiture or order for destruction or forfeiture pending the determination of any appeal against conviction or sentence.

NOTE
[1] Inserted by the Criminal Justice (Scotland) Act 1987, s. 68.

Manner and time of appeal
[1] **444.**—(1) An appeal under section 442(1)(*a*)(i) or (iii) or (*b*) of this Act shall be by application for a stated case, which application shall—
  (*a*) be made within one week of the final determination of the proceedings;
  (*b*) contain a full statement of all the matters which the appellant desires to bring under review and where the appeal is also against sentence, a statement of that fact; and
  (*c*) be signed by the appellant or his solicitor and lodged with the clerk of court;
and a copy of the application shall within the period mentioned in paragraph (*a*) above be sent by the appellant to the respondent or the respondent's solicitor.

(1A) The clerk of the court shall enter in the record of the proceedings the date when an application under subsection (1) above was lodged.

(1B) The appellant may, at any time within the period of three weeks mentioned in subsection (1) of section 448 of this Act, or within any further period afforded him by virtue of subsection (6) of that section, amend any matter stated in his application or add a new matter; and he shall intimate any such amendment, or addition, to the respondent or the respondent's solicitor.

(2) Where such an application has been made by the person convicted, and the judge by whom he was convicted dies before signing the case or is precluded by illness or other cause from doing so, it shall be competent for the convicted person to present a bill of suspension to the High Court and to bring under the review of that court any matter which might have been brought under review by stated case.

(3) Without prejudice to any other power of relief which the High Court may have, where it appears to that court on application made in accordance with the following provisions of this section, that the applicant has failed to comply with any of the requirements of subsection (1) of this section, the High Court may direct that such further period of time as it may think proper be afforded to the applicant to comply with any requirement of the aforesaid provisions.

(4) Any application for a direction under the last foregoing subsection shall be made in writing to the Clerk of Justiciary and shall state the grounds for the application, and notification of the application shall be made by the appellant or his solicitor to the clerk of the court from which the appeal is to be taken, and the clerk shall thereupon transmit the complaint, documentary productions and any other proceedings in the cause to the Clerk of Justiciary.

(5) The High Court shall dispose of any application under subsection (3) of this section in like manner as an application to review the decision of an inferior court on a grant of bail, but shall have power—

(*a*) to dispense with a hearing; and

(*b*) to make such enquiry in relation to the application as the court may think fit;

and when the High Court has disposed of the application the Clerk of Justiciary shall inform the clerk of the inferior court of the result.

(6) [Repealed by the Criminal Justice (Scotland) Act 1980, Sched. 8.]

NOTE
[1] As amended by the Bail etc. (Scotland) Act 1980, Sched. 1 and the Criminal Justice (Scotland) Act 1980, Sched. 3.

. . . . . .

Procedure where appellant in custody
[1] **446.**—(1) If an appellant under section 444 of this Act is in custody, the court may—

(*a*) grant bail;

(*b*) grant a sist of execution;

(*c*) make any other interim order.

[2] (2) An application for bail shall be disposed of by the court within 24 hours after such application has been made. The appellant, if dissatisfied with the conditions imposed or on refusal of bail, may, within 24 hours after the judgment of the court, appeal there against by a note of appeal written on the complaint and signed by himself or his solicitor, and the complaint and proceedings shall thereupon be transmitted to the Clerk of Justiciary, and the High Court or any judge thereof, either in court or in

chambers, shall, after hearing parties, have power to review the decision of the inferior court and to grant bail on such conditions as such court or judge may think fit, or to refuse bail.

(3) No clerk's fees, court fees or other fees or expenses shall be exigible from or awarded against an appellant in custody in respect of an appeal to the High Court against the conditions imposed or on account of refusal of bail by a court of summary jurisdiction.

(4) If an appellant who has been granted bail does not thereafter proceed with his appeal, the inferior court shall have power to grant warrant to apprehend and imprison him for such period of his sentence as at the date of his bail remained unexpired, such period to run from the date of his imprisonment under such warrant.

(5) Where an appellant who has been granted bail does not thereafter proceed with his appeal, the court from which the appeal was taken shall have power, where at the time of the abandonment of the appeal the person is serving a term or terms of imprisonment imposed subsequently to the conviction appealed against, to order that the sentence or, as the case may be, the unexpired portion of that sentence relating to that conviction should run from such date as the court may think fit, not being a date later than the date on which the term or terms of imprisonment subsequently imposed expired.

NOTES
[1] As amended by the Bail etc. (Scotland) Act 1980, Sched. 1, para. 10 and Sched. 2 and the Criminal Justice (Scotland) Act 1980, Sched. 3.
[2] Applied by the Extradition Act 1989, s. 10(13).

Draft stated case to be prepared
[1] **447.**—[2] (1) Within three weeks of the final determination of proceedings in respect of which an application for a stated case is made under section 444 of this Act—

(*a*) where the appeal is taken from the district court and the trial was presided over by a justice of the peace or justices of the peace, the clerk of court; or

(*b*) in any other case the judge who presided at the trial,

shall prepare a draft stated case, and the clerk of the court concerned shall forthwith issue the draft to the appellant or his solicitor and a duplicate thereof to the respondent or his solicitor.

(2) A stated case shall be in the form, as nearly as may be, of the appropriate form contained in an Act of Adjournal under this Act, and shall set forth the particulars of any matters competent for review which the appellant desires to bring under the review of the High Court and of the facts, if any, proved in the case, and any point of law decided, and the grounds of the decision.

NOTES
[1] As amended by the Criminal Justice (Scotland) Act 1980, Scheds. 3 and 8.
[2] As amended by the Law Reform (Miscellaneous Provisions) (Scotland) Act 1985, Sched. 2, para. 20.

Adjustment and signature of case
[1] **448.**—(1) Subject to subsection (6) below, within three weeks of the issue of the draft stated case under section 447 of this Act, each party shall

cause to be transmitted to the court and to the other parties or their solicitors a note of any adjustments he proposes be made to the draft case or shall intimate that he has no such proposal:

Provided that adjustments proposed shall relate to evidence heard (or purported to have been heard) at the trial and not to such additional evidence as is mentioned in section 442(2) of this Act.

(2) Subject to subsection (6) below, if the period mentioned in subsection (1) above has expired and the appellant has not lodged adjustments and has failed to intimate that he has no adjustments to propose, he shall be deemed to have abandoned his appeal; and subsection (4) of section 446 of this Act shall apply accordingly.

(2A) If adjustments are proposed under subsection (1) above or if the judge desires to make any alterations to the draft case there shall, within one week of the expiry of the period mentioned in that subsection or as the case may be of any further period afforded under subsection (6) below, be a hearing (unless the appellant has, or has been deemed to have, abandoned his appeal) for the purposes of considering such adjustments or alterations.

(2B) Where a party neither attends nor secures that he is represented at a hearing under subsection (2A) above, the hearing shall nevertheless proceed.

[2] (2C) where at a hearing under subsection (2A) above—

(*a*) any adjustment proposed under subsection (1) above by a party (and not withdrawn) is rejected by the judge; or

(*b*) any alteration proposed by the judge is not accepted by all the parties,

that fact shall be recorded in the minute of the proceedings of the hearing.

(2D) Within two weeks of the date of the hearing under subsection (2A) above or, where there is no hearing, within two weeks of the expiry of the period mentioned in subsection (1) above, the judge shall (unless the appellant has been deemed to have abandoned the appeal) state and sign the case and shall append to the case—

(*a*) any adjustment, proposed under subsection (1) above, which is rejected by him, a note of any evidence rejected by him which is alleged to support that adjustment and the reasons for his rejection of that adjustment and evidence; and

(*b*) a note of the evidence upon which he bases any finding of fact challenged, on the basis that it is unsupported by the evidence, by a party at the hearing under subsection (2A) above.

(3) As soon as the case is signed under subsection (2D) above the clerk of court—

(*a*) shall send the case to the appellant or his solicitor and a duplicate thereof to the respondent or his solicitor; and

(*b*) shall transmit the complaint, productions and any other proceedings in the cause to the Clerk of Justiciary.

(4) Subject to subsection (6) below, within one week of receiving the case the appellant or his solicitor, as the case may be, shall cause it to be lodged with the Clerk of Justiciary.

(5) Subject to subsection (6) below, if the appellant or his solicitor fails to comply with subsection (4) above the appellant shall be deemed to

have abandoned the appeal; and subsection (4) of section 446 of this Act shall apply accordingly.

(6) Without prejudice to any other power of relief which the High Court may have, where it appears to that court on application made in accordance with the following provisions of this section, that the applicant has failed to comply with any of the requirements of subsection (1) or (4) of this section, the High Court may direct that such further period of time as it may think proper be afforded to the applicant to comply with any requirement of the aforesaid provisions.

(7) Any application for a direction under the last foregoing subsection shall be made in writing to the Clerk of Justiciary and shall state the grounds for the application.

(8) The High Court shall dispose of any application under subsection (6) of this section in like manner as an application to review the decision of an inferior court on a grant of bail, but shall have power—

(*a*) to dispense with a hearing; and

(*b*) to make such enquiry in relation to the application as the court may think fit;

and when the High Court has disposed of the application the Clerk of Justiciary shall inform the clerk of the inferior court of the result.

(9) [Repealed by the Criminal Justice (Scotland) Act 1980, Sched. 8.]

NOTES

[1] As amended by the Bail etc. (Scotland) Act 1980, Sched. 1 and the Criminal Justice (Scotland) Act 1980, Sched. 3.

[2] As amended by the Law Reform (Miscellaneous Provisions) (Scotland) Act 1985, Sched. 4, with effect from 30th December 1985.

Abandonment of appeal

[1] **449.**—(1) An appellant in an appeal such as is mentioned in section 444(1) of this Act may at any time prior to lodging the case with the Clerk of Justiciary abandon his appeal by minute signed by himself or his solicitor written on the complaint or lodged with the clerk of the inferior court, and intimated to the respondent or the respondent's solicitor, but such abandonment shall be without prejudice to any other competent mode of appeal, review, advocation or suspension.

(2) Subject to section 453A of this Act, on the case being lodged with the Clerk of Justiciary, the appellant shall be held to have abandoned any other mode of appeal which might otherwise have been open to him.

NOTE

[1] As amended by the Criminal Justice (Scotland) Act 1980, Sched. 3 and S.I. 1981 No. 386. See S.I. 1981 No. 386.

Record of procedure in appeal

[1] **450.** On an appeal such as is mentioned in section 444(1) of this Act being taken the clerk of court shall record on the complaint the different steps of procedure in the appeal, and such record shall be evidence of the dates on which the various steps of procedure took place. The forms of procedure in appeals shall be as nearly as may be in accordance with the forms contained in an Act of Adjournal under this Act.

NOTE
[1] As amended by the Criminal Justice (Scotland) Act 1980, Sched. 3 and S.I. 1981 No. 386.

Computation of time
[1] **451.**—(1) If any period of time specified in any provision of this Part of this Act relating to appeals expires on a Saturday, Sunday or court holiday prescribed for the relevant court, the period shall be extended to expire on the next day which is not a Saturday, Sunday or such court holiday.

(2) Where a judge against whose judgment an appeal is taken is temporarily absent from duty for any cause, the sheriff principal of the sheriffdom in which the court at which the judgment was pronounced is situated may extend any period specified in sections 447(1) and 448(2A) and (2D) of this Act for such period as he considers reasonable.

(3) For the purposes of sections 444(1)(a) and 447(1) of this Act, summary proceedings shall be deemed to be finally determined on the day on which sentence is passed in open court; except that, where in relation to an appeal under section 442(1)(a)(i) or (b)(i) of this Act sentence is deferred under section 432 of this Act, they shall be deemed finally determined on the day on which sentence is first so deferred in open court.

NOTE
[1] Substituted by the Criminal Justice (Scotland) Act 1980, Sched. 3. See S.I. 1981 No. 386.

Hearing of appeal
[1] **452.**—(1) A stated case under this Part of this Act shall be heard by the High Court on such date as it may fix.

(2) For the avoidance of doubt, where an appellant, in his application under section 444(1) of this Act (or in a duly made amendment or addition to that application), refers to an alleged miscarriage of justice, but in stating a case under section 448(2D) of this Act the inferior court is unable to take the allegation into account, the High Court may nevertheless have regard to the allegation at a hearing under subsection (1) above.

(3) Except by leave of the High Court on cause shown, it shall not be competent for an appellant to found any aspect of his appeal on a matter not contained in his application under section 444(1) of this Act (or in a duly made amendment or addition to that application).

(4) Without prejudice to any existing power of the High Court, that court may in hearing a stated case—
(a) order the production of any document or other thing connected with the proceedings;
(b) hear any additional evidence relevant to any alleged miscarriage of justice or order such evidence to be heard by a judge of the High Court or by such other person as it may appoint for that purpose;
(c) take account of any circumstances relevant to the case which were not before the trial judge;
(d) remit to any fit person to enquire and report in regard to any matter or circumstance affecting the appeal;

    (*e*) appoint a person with expert knowledge to act as assessor to the High Court in any case where it appears to the court that such expert knowledge is required for the proper determination of the case;

    (*f*) take account of any matter proposed in any adjustment rejected by the trial judge and of the reasons for such rejection;

    (*g*) take account of any evidence contained in a note of evidence such as is mentioned in section 448(2D) of this Act.

(5) The High Court may at the hearing remit the stated case back to the inferior court to be amended and returned.

NOTE
[1] Substituted by the Criminal Justice (Scotland) Act 1980, Sched. 3.

Disposal of stated case appeal
[1] **452A.**—(1) The High Court may, subject to section 453D(1) of this Act, dispose of a stated case by—

    (*a*) remitting the cause to the inferior court with their opinion and any direction thereon;

    (*b*) affirming the verdict of the inferior court;

    (*c*) setting aside the verdict of the inferior court and either quashing the conviction or substituting therefor an amended verdict of guilty:

        Provided that an amended verdict of guilty must be one which could have been returned on the complaint before the inferior court; or

    (*d*) setting aside the verdict of the inferior court and granting authority to bring a new prosecution in accordance with section 452B of this Act.

(2) In an appeal against both conviction and sentence the High Court shall, subject to section 453D(1) of this Act, dispose of the appeal against sentence by exercise of the power mentioned in section 453C(1) of this Act.

(3) In setting aside, under subsection (1) above, a verdict the High Court may quash any sentence imposed on the appellant as respects the complaint, and—

    (*a*) in a case where it substitutes an amended verdict of guilty, whether or not the sentence related to the verdict set aside; or

    (*b*) in any other case, where the sentence did not so relate,

may pass another (but not more severe) sentence in substitution for the sentence so quashed.

(4) Where an appeal against acquittal is sustained, the High Court may—

    (*a*) convict and sentence the respondent;

    (*b*) remit the case to the inferior court with instructions to convict and sentence the respondent, who shall be bound to attend any diet fixed by the inferior court for such purpose; or

    (*c*) remit the case to the inferior court with their opinion thereon:

Provided that the High Court shall not in any case increase the sentence beyond the maximum sentence which could have been passed by the inferior court.

(5) The High Court shall have power in an appeal under this Part of this Act to award such expenses both in the High Court and in the inferior court as it may think fit.

(6) Where, following an appeal (other than an appeal under section 442(1)(*a*)(ii) or 442(1)(*b*) of this Act), the appellant remains liable to imprisonment or detention under the sentence of the inferior court, or is so liable under a sentence passed in the appeal proceedings the High Court shall have power where at the time of disposal of the appeal the appellant—

(*a*) was at liberty on bail, to grant warrant to apprehend and imprison (or detain) the appellant for a term, to run from the date of such apprehension, not longer than that part of the term or terms of imprisonment (or detention) specified in the sentence brought under review which remained unexpired at the date of liberation;

(*b*) is serving a term or terms of imprisonment (or detention) imposed in relation to a conviction subsequent to the conviction appealed against, to exercise the like powers in regard to him as may be exercised, in relation to an appeal which has been abandoned, by a court of summary jurisdiction in pursuance of section 446(5) of this Act.

NOTE
[1] Inserted by the Criminal Justice (Scotland) Act 1980, Sched. 3.

Supplementary provisions where High Court authorises new prosecution

[1] **452B.**—(1) Where authority is granted under section 452A(1)(*d*) of this Act, a new prosecution may be brought charging the accused with the same or any similar offence arising out of the same facts; and the proceedings out of which the stated case arose shall not be a bar to such prosecution:

Provided that no sentence may be passed on conviction under the new prosecution which could not have been passed on conviction under the earlier proceedings.

(2) A new prosecution may be brought under this section, notwithstanding that any time limit (other than the time limit mentioned in subsection (3) below) for the commencement of such proceedings has elapsed.

(3) Proceedings in a prosecution under this section shall be commenced within two months of the date on which authority to bring the prosecution was granted; and for the purposes of this subsection proceedings shall, in a case where such warrant is executed without unreasonable delay, be deemed to be commenced on the date on which a warrant to apprehend or to cite the accused is granted, and shall in any other case be deemed to be commenced on the date on which the warrant is executed.

(4) Where the two months mentioned in subsection (3) above elapse and no new prosecution has been brought under this section, the order under section 452(1)(*d*) of this Act setting aside the verdict shall have the effect, for all purposes, of an acquittal.

NOTE
[1] Inserted by the Criminal Justice (Scotland) Act 1980, Sched. 3.

Consent by prosecutor to set aside conviction

[1] **453.**—(1) Where an appeal has been taken under section 442(1)(*a*)(i) or (iii) of this Act or by suspension or otherwise, and the prosecutor, on the appeal being intimated to him, is not prepared to maintain the judgment appealed against, he may by a minute signed by him and written on the complaint or lodged with the clerk of court consent to the conviction and sentence being set aside, either in whole or in part. Such minute shall set forth the grounds on which the prosecutor is of opinion that the judgment cannot be maintained.

(2) A copy of any minute under the foregoing subsection shall be sent by the prosecutor to the appellant or his solicitor, and the clerk of court shall thereupon ascertain from the appellant or his solicitor whether he desires to be heard by the High Court before the appeal is disposed of, and shall note on the record whether or not the appellant so desires, and shall thereafter transmit the complaint and relative proceedings to the Clerk of Justiciary.

(3) The Clerk of Justiciary on receipt of a complaint and relative proceedings under the last foregoing subsection shall lay them before any judge of the High Court, either in court or in chambers, and such judge, after hearing parties if they desire to be heard, or without hearing parties, may set aside the conviction either in whole or in part and award expenses to the appellant not exceeding £40, or may refuse to set aside the conviction, in which case the proceedings shall be returned to the clerk of the inferior court, and the appellant shall then be entitled to proceed with his appeal in the same way as if it had been marked on the date when the complaint and proceedings are returned to the clerk of the inferior court.

(4) Where proceedings are taken under this section, the preparation of the draft stated case shall be delayed pending the decision of the High Court.

(5) The power conferred by this section to consent to a conviction and sentence being set aside shall be exercisable—

(*a*) where the appeal is by stated case, at any time within two weeks after the receipt by the prosecutor of the draft stated case; and

(*b*) where the appeal is by suspension at any time within two weeks after the service on the prosecutor of the bill of suspension.

NOTE
[1] As amended by the Criminal Justice (Scotland) Act 1980, s. 46 and Sched. 3, and S.I. 1984 No. 526.

Appeal by bill of suspension or advocation on ground of miscarriage of justice

[1] **453A.**—(1) Notwithstanding section 449(2) of this Act, a party to a summary prosecution may, where an appeal under section 442 of this Act would be incompetent or would in the circumstances be inappropriate, appeal to the High Court, by bill of suspension against a conviction, or as the case may be by advocation against an acquittal, on the ground of an alleged miscarriage of justice in the proceedings:

Provided that where the alleged miscarriage of justice is referred to in an application, under section 444(1) of this Act, for a stated case as regards the proceedings (or in a duly made amendment or addition to that application) an appeal under subsection (1) above shall not proceed without the leave of the High Court until the appeal to which the application relates has been finally disposed of or abandoned.

(2) Sections 452(4)(*a*) to (*e*), 452A(1)(*d*), 452A(3) and 452B of this Act shall apply to appeals under this section as they apply to appeals such as are mentioned in section 444(1) of this Act.

(3) The foregoing provisions of this section shall be without prejudice to any rule of law relating to bills of suspension or advocation in so far as such rule of law is not inconsistent with those provisions.

NOTE
[1] Inserted by the Criminal Justice (Scotland) Act 1980, Sched. 3.

Appeals against sentence only
[1] **453B.**—(1) An appeal under section 442(1)(*a*)(ii) of this Act shall be by note of appeal, which shall state the ground of appeal.

(2) The note of appeal shall, within one week of the passing of the sentence, be lodged with the clerk of the court from which the appeal is to be taken.

(3) The clerk of court on receipt of the note of appeal shall—

(*a*) send a copy of the note to the respondent or his solicitor; and

(*b*) obtain a report from the judge who sentenced the convicted person.

(4) The clerk of court shall within two weeks of the passing of the sentence against which the appeal is taken—

(*a*) send to the Clerk of Justiciary the note of appeal, together with the report mentioned in subsection (3)(*b*) above, a certified copy of the complaint, the minute of proceedings and any other relevant documents; and

(*b*) send copies of that report to the appellant and respondent or their solicitors:

Provided that the sheriff principal of the sheriffdom in which the judgment was pronounced may, where a judge is temporarily absent from duty for any cause, extend the period of two weeks specified in this subsection for such period as the sheriff principal considers reasonable.

(5) Where the judge's report is not furnished within the period mentioned in subsection (4) above, the High Court may extend such period or, if it thinks fit, hear and determine the appeal without such report.

(6) Subsections (3), (4) and (5) of section 444 of this Act shall apply where an appellant fails to comply with the requirement of subsection (2) above as they apply where an applicant fails to comply with any of the requirements of subsection (1) of that section.

(7) An appellant under section 442(1)(*a*)(ii) of this Act may at any time prior to the hearing of the appeal abandon his appeal by minute, signed by himself or his solicitor, lodged—

(*a*) in a case where the note of appeal has not yet been sent under subsection (4)(*a*) above to the Clerk of Justiciary, with the clerk of court;

(*b*) in any other case, with the Clerk of Justiciary, and intimated to the respondent.

(8) Sections 446, 450 and 452(4)(*a*) to (*e*) of this Act shall apply to

appeals under section 442(1)(*a*)(ii) of this Act as they apply to appeals under section 442(1)(*a*)(i) or (iii) of this Act.

NOTE
[1] Inserted by the Criminal Justice (Scotland) Act 1980, Sched. 3. See S.I. 1981 No. 386.

Disposal of appeal by note of appeal
[1] **453C.**—(1) An appeal against sentence by note of appeal shall be heard by the High Court on such date as it may fix, and the High Court may, subject to section 453D(1) of this Act, dispose of such appeal by—
　　(*a*) affirming the sentence; or
　　(*b*) if the court thinks that, having regard to all the circumstances, including any additional evidence such as is mentioned in section 442(2) of this Act, a different sentence should have been passed, quashing the sentence and passing another sentence, whether more or less severe, in substitution therefor:
Provided that the court shall not in any case increase the sentence beyond the maximum sentence which could have been passed by the inferior court.

(2) The High Court shall have power in an appeal by note of appeal to award such expenses both in the High Court and in the inferior court as it may think fit.

(3) Where, following an appeal under section 442(1)(*a*)(ii) of this Act, the appellant remains liable to imprisonment or detention under the sentence of the inferior court or is so liable under a sentence passed in the appeal proceedings, the High Court shall have power where at the time of disposal of the appeal the appellant—
　　(*a*) was at liberty on bail, to grant warrant to apprehend and imprison (or detain) the appellant for a term, to run from the date of such apprehension, not longer than that part of the term or terms of imprisonment (or detention) specified in the sentence brought under review which remained unexpired at the date of liberation; or
　　(*b*) is serving a term or terms of imprisonment (or detention) imposed in relation to a conviction subsequent to the conviction in respect of which the sentence appealed against was imposed, to exercise the like powers in regard to him as may be exercised, in relation to an appeal which has been abandoned, by a court of summary jurisdiction in pursuance of section 446(5) of this Act.

NOTE
[1] Inserted by the Criminal Justice (Scotland) Act 1980, Sched. 3.

Disposal of appeal where appellant insane
[1] **453D.**—(1) In relation to any appeal under section 442(1)(*a*) of this Act, the High Court shall, where it appears to it that the appellant committed the act charged against him but that he was insane when he did so, dispose of the appeal by—
　　(*a*) setting aside the verdict of the inferior court and substituting therefor a verdict of acquittal on the ground of insanity; and
　　(*b*) quashing any sentence imposed on the appellant as respects the

complaint and ordering that he be detained in a state hospital or such other hospital as for special reasons the court may specify.

(2) The provisions of subsection (4) of section 174 of this Act shall apply to an order under subsection (1)(*b*) above as they apply to an order under that section.

NOTE
[1] Inserted by the Criminal Justice (Scotland) Act 1980, Sched. 3.

Failure of appellant who has been granted bail to appear personally

[1] **453E.** Where an appellant has been granted bail, whether his appeal is under this Part of this Act or otherwise, he shall appear personally in court at the diet appointed for the hearing of the appeal. If he does not appear the High Court shall either—

(*a*) dispose of the appeal as if it had been abandoned (in which case subsection (4) of section 446 of this Act shall apply accordingly); or

(*b*) on cause shown permit the appeal to be heard in his absence.

NOTE
[1] Inserted by the Criminal Justice (Scotland) Act 1980, Sched. 3.

Convictions not to be quashed on certain grounds

454.—(1) No conviction, sentence, judgment, order of court or other proceeding whatsoever under this Part of this Act shall be quashed for want of form or, where the accused had legal assistance in his defence, shall be suspended or set aside in respect of any objections to the relevancy of the complaint, or to the want of specification therein, or to the competency or admission or rejection of evidence at the trial in the inferior court, unless such objections shall have been timeously stated at the trial by the solicitor of the accused.

(2) [Repealed by the Criminal Justice (Scotland) Act 1980, Scheds. 3 and 8.]

．　．　．　．　．　．

PART III

GENERAL

．　．　．　．　．

Construction of enactments referring to sentence of detention

[1] **458.** In any enactment, any reference to a sentence of imprisonment as including a reference to a sentence of any other form of detention shall be construed as including a reference to a sentence of detention under section 207 or 415 of this Act.

NOTE
[1] As amended by the Criminal Justice (Scotland) Act 1980, Sched. 7, para. 73.

Construction of enactments referring to detention

[1] **459.** In any enactment, any reference to imprisonment as including

any other form of detention shall be construed as including a reference to detention under section 207 or 415 of this Act.

NOTE
[1] As amended by the Criminal Justice (Scotland) Act 1980, Sched. 7, para. 74.

. . . . . .

Interpretation
462.—(1) In this Act, except where the context otherwise requires, the following expressions shall have the meanings hereby respectively assigned to them—

. . . . . .

[3] "fine" includes (*a*) any pecuniary penalty (but not a pecuniary forfeiture or pecuniary compensation) and (*b*) an instalment of a fine;

. . . . . .

[5] "impose detention" or "impose imprisonment" means pass a sentence of detention or imprisonment, as the case may be, or make an order for committal in default of payment of any sum of money or for contempt of court;

. . . . . .

[8] "sentence" whether of detention or of imprisonment, means a sentence passed in respect of a crime or offence and does not include an order for committal in default of payment of any sum of money or for contempt of court.

NOTES
[3] As amended by the Criminal Law Act 1977, Sched. 11, para. 10, and by the Criminal Justice Act 1982, Sched. 15, para. 19.
[5] As amended by the Criminal Justice (Scotland) Act 1980, Sched. 7.
[8] As amended by the Criminal Justice (Scotland) Act 1980, Sched. 7.

. . . . . .

SCHEDULES

. . . . . .

Sections 183, 185, 384 and 386   SCHEDULE 5

DISCHARGE AND AMENDMENT OF PROBATION ORDERS

Discharge

1. A probation order may on the application of the officer supervising the probationer or of the probationer be discharged—
    (*a*) by the appropriate court, or
    (*b*) if no appropriate court has been named in the original or in any amending order, by the court which made the order.

Amendment

2.—(1) If the court by which a probation order was made, or the appropriate court is satisfied that the probationer proposes to change or has changed his residence from the area of a local authority named in the order to another area of a local authority, the court may, and if application is made in that behalf by the officer supervising the probationer shall, by order, amend the probation order by—

(a) substituting for the area named therein that other area, and

(b) naming the appropriate court to which all the powers of the court by which the order was made shall be transferred and shall require the local authority for that other area to arrange for the probationer to be under the supervision of an officer of that authority.

(2) The court to be named as the appropriate court in any amendment of a probation order in pursuance of the last foregoing subparagraph shall be a court exercising jurisdiction in the place where the probationer resides or is to reside and shall be a sheriff court or district court according to whether the probation order was made by a sheriff court or district court: Provided that—

(i) if there is no district court exercising jurisdiction in the said place the court to be so named shall be the sheriff court; and

(ii) if the probation order contains requirements which in the opinion of the court cannot be complied with unless the probationer continues to reside in the local authority area named in the order, the court shall not amend the order as aforesaid, unless in accordance with the following provisions of this Schedule, it cancels those requirements or substitutes therefor other requirements which can be so complied with.

(3) Where a probation order is amended under this paragraph, the clerk of the court amending it shall send to the clerk of the appropriate court four copies of the order together with such documents and information relating to the case as the court amending the order considers likely to be of assistance to the appropriate court, and the clerk of that court shall send one copy of the probation order to the local authority of the substituted local authority area and two copies to the officer supervising the probationer one of which the supervising officer shall give to the probationer.

(4) The foregoing provisions of this paragraph shall, in a case where the probation order was made by the High Court, have effect subject to the following modifications—

(a) the court shall not name an appropriate court, but may substitute for the local authority named in the order, the local authority for the area in which the probationer is to reside;

(b) the Clerk of Justiciary shall send to the director of social work of that area in which the probationer is to reside three copies of the amending order together with such documents and information relating to the case as is likely to be of assistance to the director, and the director shall send two copies of the amending order to the officer supervising the probationer, one of which the supervising officer shall give to the probationer.

3. Without prejudice to the provisions of the last foregoing paragraph, the court by which a probation order was made or the appropriate court may, upon application made by the officer supervising the probationer or by the probationer, by order amend a probation order by cancelling any of the requirements thereof or by inserting therein (either in addition to or in substitution of any such requirement) any requirement which could be included in the order if it were then being made by that court in accordance with the provisions of sections 183, 184, 384 and 385 of this Act: Provided that—

(a) the court shall not amend a probation order by reducing the probation period, or by extending that period beyond the end of three years from the original order;

(b) the court shall not so amend a probation order that the probationer is thereby required to reside in any institution or place, or to submit to treatment for his mental condition, for any period or periods exceeding 12 months in all;

(c) the court shall not amend a probation order by inserting therein a requirement that the probationer shall submit to treatment for his mental condition unless the amending order is made within three months after the date of the original order.

4. Where the medical practitioner by whom or under whose direction a probationer is

being treated for his mental condition in pursuance of any requirement of the probation order is of opinion—

(a) in the treatment of the probationer should be continued beyond the period specified in that behalf in the order; or

(b) that the probationer needs a different kind of treatment (whether in whole or in part) from that which he has been receiving in pursuance of the probation order, being treatment of a kind which could have been specified in the probation order but to which the probationer or his supervising officer has not agreed under subsection (5B) of section 184 or, as the case may be, 385 of this Act; or

(c) that the probationer is not susceptible to treatment; or

(d) that the probationer does not require further treatment,

or where the practitioner is for any reason unwilling to continue to treat or direct the treatment of the probationer, he shall make a report in writing to the effect to the officer supervising the probationer and the supervising officer shall apply to the court which made the order or to the appropriate court for the variation or cancellation of the requirement.

NOTE

[1] As amended with effect from 30th September 1984 by the Mental Health (Amendment) (Scotland) Act 1983, s.36(4).

General

5. Where the court which made the order or the appropriate court proposes to amend a probation order under this Schedule, otherwise than on the application of the probationer, it shall cite him to appear before the court; and the court shall not amend the probation order unless the probationer expresses his willingness to comply with the requirements of the order as amended:

Provided that this paragraph shall not apply to an order cancelling a requirement of the probation order or reducing the period of any requirement, or substituting a new area of a local authority for the area named in the probation order.

6. On the making of an order discharging or amending a probation order, the clerk of the court shall forthwith give copies of the discharging or amending order to the officer supervising the probationer; and the supervising officer shall give a copy to the probationer and to the person in charge of any institution in which the probationer is or was required by the order to reside.

Community Service by Offenders (Scotland) Act 1978

(1978 c. 49)

An Act to make provision as respects the performance of unpaid work by persons convicted or placed on probation in Scotland; and for connected purposes.   [31st July 1978]

Community service orders

1.—[1] (1) Subject to the provisions of this Act, where a person of or over 16 years of age is convicted of an offence punishable by imprisonment, other than an offence the sentence for which is fixed by law, the court may, instead of imposing on him a sentence of, or including, imprisonment or any other form of detention, make an order (in this Act referred to as "a community service order") requiring him to perform unpaid work for such number of hours (being in total not less than 40 nor more than 240) as may be specified in the order.

(2) A court shall not make a community service order in respect of any offender unless—

(a) the offender consents;

(b) the court has been notified by the Secretary of State that arrangements exist for persons who reside in the locality in which the offender resides, or will be residing when the order comes into force, to perform work under such an order;

(c) the court is satisfied, after considering a report by an officer of a local authority about the offender and his circumstances, and, if the court thinks it necessary, hearing that officer, that the offender is a suitable person to perform work under such an order; and

(d) the court is satisfied that provision can be made under the arrangements mentioned in paragraph (b) above for the offender to perform work under such an order.

(3) A copy of the report mentioned in subsection (2)(c) above shall be supplied to the offender or his solicitor.

(4) Before making a community service order the court shall explain to the offender in ordinary language—

(a) the purpose and effect of the order and in particular the obligations on the offender as specified in section 3 of this Act;

(b) the consequences which may follow under section 4 of this Act if he fails to comply with any of those requirements; and

(c) that the court has under section 5 of this Act the power to review the order on the application either of the offender or of an officer of the local authority in whose area the offender for the time being resides.

(5) The Secretary of State may by order direct that subsection (1) above shall be amended by substituting, for the maximum or minimum number of hours specified in that subsection as originally enacted or as

subsequently amended under this subsection, such number of hours as may be specified in the order; and an order under this subsection may specify a different maximum or minimum number of hours for different classes of case.

(6) An order under subsection (5) above shall be made by statutory instrument, but no such order shall be made unless a draft of it has been laid before, and approved by a resolution of, each House of Parliament; and any such order may be varied or revoked by a subsequent order under that subsection.

(7) Nothing in subsection (1) above shall be construed as preventing a court which makes a community service order in respect of any offence from—

(a) imposing any disqualification on the offender;

(b) making an order for forfeiture in respect of the offence;

(c) ordering the offender to find caution for good behaviour.

NOTE
[1] As amended by the Law Reform (Miscellaneous Provisions) (Scotland) Act 1990, s. 61(3).

Further provisions about community service orders

2.—(1) A community service order shall—

(a) specify the locality in which the offender resides or will be residing when the order comes into force;

(b) require the local authority in whose area the locality specified under paragraph (a) above is situated to appoint or assign an officer (referred to in this Act as "the local authority officer") who will discharge the functions assigned to him by this Act; and

(c) state the number of hours of work which the offender is required to perform.

(2) Where, whether on the same occasion or on separate occasions, an offender is made subject to more than one community service order, or to both a community service order and a probation order which includes a requirement that that offender shall perform any unpaid work, the court may direct that the hours of work specified in any of those orders shall be concurrent with or additional to those specified in any other of those orders, but so that at no time shall the offender have an outstanding number of hours of work to perform in excess of the maximum provided for in section 1(1) of this Act.

(3) Upon making a community service order the court shall—

(a) give a copy of the order to the offender;

(b) send a copy of the order to the director of social work of the local authority in whose area the offender resides or will be residing when the order comes into force; and

(c) where it is not the appropriate court, send a copy of the order (together with such documents and information relating to the case as are considered useful) to the clerk of the appropriate court.

Obligations of persons subject to community service orders

3.—(1) An offender in respect of whom a community service order is in force shall—

(a) report to the local authority officer and notify him without delay of any change of address or in the times, if any, at which he usually works; and

(*b*) perform for the number of hours specified in the order such work at such times as the local authority officer may instruct.

(2) Subject to section 5(1) of this Act, the work required to be performed under a community service order shall be performed during the period of 12 months beginning with the date of the order; but, unless revoked, the order shall remain in force until the offender has worked under it for the number of hours specified in it.

(3) The instructions given by the local authority officer under this section shall, so far as practicable, be such as to avoid any conflict with the offender's religious beliefs and any interference with the times, if any, at which he normally works or attends a school or other educational establishment.

Failure to comply with requirements of community service orders

4.—(1) If at any time while a community service order is in force in respect of any offender it appears to the appropriate court, on evidence on oath from the local authority officer, that that offender has failed to comply with any of the requirements of section 3 of this Act (including any failure satisfactorily to perform the work which he has been instructed to do), that court may issue a warrant for the arrest of that offender, or may, if it thinks fit, instead of issuing a warrant in the first instance issue a citation requiring that offender to appear before that court at such time as may be specified in the citation.

(2) If it is proved to the satisfaction of the court before which an offender appears or is brought in pursuance of subsection (1) above that he has failed without reasonable excuse to comply with any of the requirements of the said section 3, that court may—

[1] (*a*) without prejudice to the continuance in force of the order, impose on him a fine not exceeding level 3 on the standard scale;

(*b*) revoke the order and deal with that offender in any manner in which he could have been dealt with for the original offence by the court which made the order if the order had not been made; or

(*c*) subject to section 1(1) of this Act, vary the number of hours specified in the order.

NOTE
[1] As amended by the Criminal Justice Act 1982, Sched. 7.

Amendment and revocation of community service orders, and substitution of other sentences

5.—(1) Where a community service order is in force in respect of any offender and, on the application of that offender or of the local authority officer, it appears to the appropriate court that it would be in the interests of justice to do so having regard to circumstances which have arisen since the order was made, that court may—

(*a*) extend, in relation to the order, the period of 12 months specified in section 3(2) of this Act;

(*b*) subject to section 1(1) of this Act, vary the number of hours specified in the order;

(*c*) revoke the order; or

(*d*) revoke the order and deal with the offender for the original offence in any manner in which he could have been dealt with for that offence by the court which made the order if the order had not been made.

(2) If the appropriate court is satisfied that the offender proposes to change, or has changed, his residence from the locality for the time being specified under section 2(1)(*a*) of this Act to another locality and—

(*a*) that court has been notified by the Secretary of State that arrangements exist for persons who reside in that other locality to perform work under community service orders; and

(*b*) it appears to that court that provision can be made under those arrangements for him to perform work under the order;

that court may, and on the application of the local authority officer shall, amend the order by substituting that other locality for the locality for the time being specified in the order; and the provisions of this Act shall apply to the order as amended.

(3) Where the court proposes to exercise its powers under subsection (1)(*a*), (*b*) or (*d*) above otherwise than on the application of the offender, it shall issue a citation requiring him to appear before the court and, if he fails to appear, may issue a warrant for his arrest.

Community service orders relating to persons residing in England or Wales

[1] **6.**—(1) Where a court is considering the making of a community service order under section 1(1) of this Act and it is satisfied that the offender has attained the age of 16 years and resides, or will be residing when the order comes into force, in England or Wales, then—

(*a*) the said section 1 shall have effect as if for paragraphs (*b*) and (*d*) of subsection (2) there were substituted the following paragraphs—

"(*b*) where the offender is under the age of 17 years, the court has been notified by the Secretary of State that arrangements exist for persons of the offender's age who reside in the petty sessions area in which the offender resides, or will be residing when the order comes into force, to perform work under community service orders made under section 14 of the Powers of Criminal Courts Act 1973;

(*d*) it appears to that court that provision can be made for the offender to perform work under the order made under subsection (1) above under the arrangements which exist in the petty sessions area in which he resides or will be residing for persons to perform work under community service orders made under section 14 of the Powers of Criminal Courts Act 1973;";

and as if for the words "such an order" in paragraph (*c*) of the said subsection (2) there were substituted the words "a community service order";

(*b*) the order shall specify that the unpaid work required to be performed by the order shall be performed under the arrangements mentioned in section 1(2)(*d*) of this Act as substituted by paragraph (*a*) above.

(2) Where a community service order has been made under the said section 1(1) and—

(*a*) the appropriate court is satisfied that the offender has attained the age of 16 years and proposes to reside or is residing in England or Wales;

(*b*) where the offender is under the age of 17 years, that court has been notified by the Secretary of State that arrangements exist for persons of the offender's age who reside in the petty sessions area in which the offender proposes to reside or is residing to perform work under community service orders made under section 14 of the Powers of Criminal Courts Act 1973; and

(*c*) it appears to that court that provision can be made for the offender to perform work under the order made under the said section 1(1) under the arrangements which exist in the petty sessions area in which he proposes to reside or is residing for persons to perform work under community service orders made under section 14 of the Powers of Criminal Courts Act 1973,

it may amend the order by specifying that the unpaid work required to be performed by the order shall be performed under the arrangements mentioned in paragraph (*c*) of this subsection.

(2A) A community service order made under section 1(1) of this Act as amended by this section or amended in accordance with this section shall—

(*a*) specify the petty sessions area in England or Wales in which the offender resides or will be residing when the order or the amendment comes into force; and

(*b*) require the probation committee for that area to appoint or assign a probation officer who will discharge in respect of the order the functions in respect of community service orders conferred on relevant officers by the Powers of Criminal Courts Act 1973.

(3) [Repealed by the Criminal Justice Act 1982, Sched. 16.]

NOTE
[1] As amended by the Criminal Justice Act 1982, Sched. 13, para. 4.

Community service orders relating to persons residing in Northern Ireland
 [1] **6A.**—(1) Where a court is considering the making of a community service order under section 1(1) of this Act and it is satisfied that the offender has attained the age of 17 years and resides, or will be residing when the order comes into force, in Northern Ireland, then—

(*a*) the said section 1 shall have effect as if, in subsection (2) thereof—
  (i) paragraph (*b*) were omitted;
  (ii) for paragraph (*d*) there were substituted the following paragraph—
      "(*d*) it appears to the court that provision can be made by the Probation Board for Northern Ireland for him to perform work under such an order;";

(*b*) the order shall specify that the unpaid work required to be performed by the order shall be performed under the provision made by the Probation Board for Northern Ireland and referred to in section 1(2)(*d*) of this Act as substituted by paragraph (*a*) above.

(2) Where a community service order has been made under the said section 1(1) and—

(*a*) the appropriate court is satisfied that the offender has attained the age of 17 years and proposes to reside or is residing in Northern Ireland; and

(*b*) it appears to that court that provision can be made by the Probation Board for Northern Ireland for him to perform work under the order made under the said section 1(1),

it may amend the order by specifying that the unpaid work required to be performed by the order shall be performed under the provision made by the Probation Board for Northern Ireland and referred to in paragraph (*b*) of this subsection.

(3) A community service order made under section 1(1) of this Act as amended by this section or amended in accordance with this section shall—

(*a*) specify the petty sessions district in Northern Ireland in which the offender resides or will be residing when the order or the amendment comes into force; and

(*b*) require the Probation Board for Northern Ireland to select an officer who will discharge in respect of the order the functions in respect of community service orders conferred on the relevant officer by the Treatment of Offenders (Northern Ireland) Order 1976.

NOTE
[1] Inserted by the Criminal Justice Act 1982, Sched. 13, para. 5.

Community service orders relating to persons residing in England or Wales or Northern Ireland—general

[1] **6B.**—(1) Where a community service order is made or amended in the circumstances specified in section 6 or 6A of this Act, the court which makes or amends the order shall send three copies of it as made or amended to the home court, together with such documents and information relating to the case as it considers likely to be of assistance to that court.

(2) In this section—
"home court" means—

(*a*) if the offender resides in England or Wales, or will be residing in England or Wales at the relevant time, the magistrates' court acting for the petty sessions area in which he resides or proposes to reside; and

(*b*) if he resides in Northern Ireland, or will be residing in Northern Ireland at the relevant time, the court of summary jurisdiction acting for the petty sessions district in which he resides or proposes to reside; and

"the relevant time" means the time when the order or the amendment to it comes into force.

(3) A community service order made or amended in the circumstances specified in section 6 or 6A of this Act shall be treated, subject to the following provisions of this section, as if it were a community service order made in the part of the United Kingdom in which the offender resides, or will be residing at the relevant time; and the legislation relating to community service orders which has effect in that part of the United Kingdom shall apply accordingly.

(4) Before making or amending a community service order in those circumstances the court shall explain to the offender in ordinary language—

    (*a*) the requirements of the legislation relating to community service orders which has effect in the part of the United Kingdom in which he resides or will be residing at the relevant time;

    (*b*) the powers of the home court under that legislation, as modified by this section; and

    (*c*) its own powers under this section,

and an explanation given in accordance with this section shall be sufficient without the addition of an explanation under section 1(4) of this Act.

(5) The home court may exercise in relation to the community service order any power which it could exercise in relation to a community service order made by a court in the part of the United Kingdom in which the home court exercises jurisdiction, by virtue of the legislation relating to such orders which has effect in that part of the United Kingdom except—

    (*a*) a power to vary the order by substituting for the number of hours' work specified in it any greater number than the court which made the order could have specified;

    (*b*) a power to revoke the order; and

    (*c*) a power to revoke the order and deal with the offender for the offence in respect of which it was made in any manner in which he could have been dealt with for that offence by the court which made the order if the order had not been made.

(6) If at any time while legislation relating to community service orders which has effect in one part of the United Kingdom applies by virtue of subsection (3) above to a community service order made in another part—

    (*a*) it appears to the home court—

        (i) if that court is in England or Wales, on information to a justice of the peace acting for the petty sessions area for the time being specified in the order; or

        (ii) if it is in Northern Ireland, upon a complaint being made to a justice of the peace acting for the petty sessions district for the time being specified in the order,

    that the offender has failed to comply with any of the requirements of the legislation applicable to the order; or

    (*b*) it appears to the home court on the application of—

        (i) the offender; or

        (ii) if that court is in England and Wales, the relevant officer under the Powers of Criminal Courts Act 1973; or

        (iii) if that court is in Northern Ireland, the relevant officer under the Treatment of Offenders (Northern Ireland) Order 1976,

    that it would be in the interests of justice to exercise a power mentioned in subsection (5)(*b*) or (*c*) above,

the home court may require the offender to appear before the court by which the order was made.

(7) Where an offender is required by virtue of subsection (6) above to appear before the court which made a community service order, that court—

(*a*) may issue a warrant for his arrest; and

(*b*) may exercise any power which it could exercise in respect of the community service order if the offender resided in the part of the United Kingdom where the court has jurisdiction,

and any enactment relating to the exercise of such powers shall have effect accordingly.

NOTE
[1] Inserted by the Criminal Justice Act 1982, Sched. 13, para. 5.

Requirement that probationer shall perform unpaid work

7. [Amendments to the Criminal Procedure (Scotland) Act 1975, ss. 183 and 384, are given effect in the print of that Act, *supra*.]

Community service order may be made after failure to comply with requirement of probation order

8. [Amendments to the Criminal Procedure (Scotland) Act 1975, ss. 186 and 387, are given effect in the print of that Act, *supra*.]

Grants in respect of community service facilities

9. [Inserts a new s. 27A in the Social Work (Scotland) Act 1968.]

Rules

10.—(1) The Secretary of State may make rules for regulating the performance of work under community service orders or probation orders which include a requirement that the offender shall perform unpaid work.

(2) Without prejudice to the generality of subsection (1) above, rules under this section may—

(*a*) limit the number of hours' work to be done by a person under such an order on any one day;

(*b*) make provision as to the reckoning of time worked under such orders;

(*c*) make provision for the payment of travelling and other expenses in connection with the performance of work under such orders;

(*d*) provide for records to be kept of the work done by any person under such an order.

(3) Rules under this section shall be made by statutory instrument subject to annulment in pursuance of a resolution of either House of Parliament.

Annual reports to be laid before Parliament

11. The Secretary of State shall lay before Parliament each year, or incorporate in annual reports he already makes, a report of the working of community service orders.

Interpretation

12.—(1) In this Act—

"the 1975 Act" means the Criminal Procedure (Scotland) Act 1975;

"the appropriate court" means—

(*a*) where the relevant community service order has been made by the High Court, the High Court;

(*b*) in any other case, the court having jurisdiction in the locality for the time being specified in the order under section 2(1)(*a*) of this Act, being a sheriff or district court according to whether the order has been made by a sheriff or a district court, but in a case where the order has been made by a district court and there is no district court in that locality, the sheriff court;

"local authority" means a regional or islands council.

(2) Except where the context otherwise requires, expressions used in this Act and in the 1975 Act shall have the same meanings in this Act as in that Act.

(3) Except where the context otherwise requires, any reference in this Act to any enactment is a reference to it as amended, and includes a reference to it as extended or applied, by or under any other enactment, including this Act.

Financial provisions

13. There shall be defrayed out of money provided by Parliament any increase attributable to the provisions of this Act in the sums payable out of such money under any other Act.

Minor and consequential amendments

14. The enactments specified in Schedule 2 to this Act shall have effect subject to the amendments there specified, being minor amendments and amendments consequential on the provisions of this Act.

Short title, commencement and extent

15.—(1) This Act may be cited as the Community Service by Offenders (Scotland) Act 1978.

(2) This Act shall come into force on such a day as the Secretary of State may appoint by order made by statutory instrument; and different days may be appointed under this subsection for different provisions of this Act or for different purposes, or for the purposes of the same provision in relation to different classes of case.

(3) Any order under subsection (2) above may make such transitional provision as appears to the Secretary of State to be expedient in connection with the provisions thereby brought into force.

(4) Subject to subsection (5) below, this Act extends to Scotland only.

[1] (5) Section 6B and this section extend to England, Wales and Northern Ireland.

NOTE
[1] As amended by the Criminal Justice Act 1982, Sched. 13, para. 6.

SCHEDULE 1

COMMUNITY SERVICE ORDERS MADE OR AMENDED BY VIRTUE OF SECTION 6

[Repealed by the Criminal Justice Act 1982, Sched. 10.]

SCHEDULE 2

MINOR AND CCONSEQUENTIAL AMENDMENTS

[Amendments to Acts reprinted in this work are shown in the prints of those Acts.]

Criminal Justice (Scotland) Act 1980

(1980 c. 62)

An Act to make further provision as regards criminal justice in Scotland; and for connected purposes. [13th November 1980]

PART III

PENALTIES

. . . . . .

Restriction on passing sentence of imprisonment or detention on person not legally represented

41.—(1) A court shall not pass a sentence of imprisonment or of detention in respect of any offence, nor impose imprisonment, or detention, under section 396(2) of the 1975 Act in respect of failure to pay a fine, on an accused who is not legally represented in that court and has not been previously sentenced to imprisonment or detention by a court in any part of the United Kingdom, unless the accused either—

(a) applied for legal aid and the application was refused on the ground that he was not financially eligible; or

(b) having been informed of his right to apply for legal aid, and having had the opportunity, failed to do so.

⁰ (2) The court shall, for the purpose of determining whether a person has been previously sentenced to imprisonment or detention by a court in any part of the United Kingdom—

(a) disregard a previous sentence of imprisonment which, having been suspended, has not taken effect under section 23 of the Powers of Criminal Courts Act 1973 or under section 19 of the Treatment of Offenders Act (Northern Ireland) 1968;

(b) construe detention as meaning—

(i) in relation to Scotland, detention in a young offenders institution or detention centre;

¹ (ii) in relation to England and Wales, a sentence of youth custody, borstal training or detention in a young offenders institution or detention centre; and

(iii) in relation to Northern Ireland, detention in a young offenders centre.

(3) Subsection (1) above does not affect the power of a court to pass sentence on any person for an offence the sentence for which is fixed by law.

(4) In this section—

"legal aid" means legal aid for the purposes of any part of the proceedings before the court;

"legally represented" means represented by counsel or a solicitor at some stage after the accused is found guilty and before he is dealt with as referred to in subsection (1) above.

NOTES
[0] Excluded by the Criminal Justice Act 1988, s. 124(3).
[1] As amended by the Criminal Justice (Scotland) Act 1987, Sched. 1, para. 17 and the Criminal Justice Act 1988, Sched. 9, para. 5.

Restriction on passing sentence of imprisonment on person not previously so dealt with
42.—(1) A court shall not pass a sentence of imprisonment on a person of or over 21 years of age who has not been previously sentenced to imprisonment or detention by a court in any part of the United Kingdom unless the court considers that no other method of dealing with him is appropriate; and for the purpose of determining whether any other method of dealing with such a person is appropriate the court shall obtain (from an officer of a local authority or otherwise) such information as it can about the offender's circumstances; and it shall also take into account any information before it concerning the offender's character and physical and mental condition.

(2) Where a court of summary jurisdiction passes a sentence of imprisonment on any such person as is mentioned in subsection (1) above, the court shall state the reason for its opinion that no other method of dealing with him is appropriate, and shall have that reason entered in the record of the proceedings.

(3) Subsections (2) and (3) of section 41 of this Act shall apply for the purposes of this section as they apply for the purposes of that section.

. . . . . .

Recovery of fine or caution by civil diligence
[1] **52.** Where proceedings by civil diligence for recovery of a fine or caution are adopted, imprisonment for non-payment of the fine or for failure to find such caution shall remain competent, and such proceedings by civil diligence may be authorised after the court has imposed imprisonment for (or in the event of) the non-payment or the failure but before imprisonment has followed such imposition; and accordingly in section 411 of the 1975 Act—

[Amendments made to the Criminal Procedure (Scotland) Act 1975, s. 411 are shown in the print of that Act.]

NOTE
[1] Excluded by the Criminal Justice (Scotland) Act 1987, s. 56(9)(*b*).

. . . . . .

PART IV

COMPENSATION BY OFFENDERS

Compensation order against convicted person
[1] **58.**—(1) Subject to subsection (3) below, where a person is convicted

of an offence the court, instead of or in addition to dealing with him in any other way, may make an order (in this Act referred to as "a compensation order") requiring him to pay compensation for any personal injury, loss or damage caused (whether directly or indirectly) by the acts which constituted the offence:

Provided that it shall not be competent for a court to make a compensation order—

> (a) where, under section 182 of the 1975 Act, it makes an order discharging him absolutely;
> (b) where, under section 183 of that Act, it makes a probation order; or
> (c) at the same time as, under section 219 or 432 of that Act, it defers sentence.

[2] (2) Where, in the case of an offence involving the dishonest appropriation, or the unlawful taking and using, of property or a contravention of section 175(1) of the Road Traffic Act 1972 (taking motor vehicle without authority, etc.) the property is recovered, but has been damaged while out of the owner's possession, that damage (however and by whomsoever it was in fact caused) shall be treated for the purposes of subsection (1) above as having been caused by the acts which constituted the offence.

[2] (3) No compensation order shall be made in respect of—

> (a) loss suffered in consequence of the death of any person; or
> (b) injury, loss or damage due to an accident arising out of the presence of a motor vehicle on a road, except such damage as is treated, by virtue of subsection (2) above, as having been caused by the convicted person's acts.

NOTES
[1] See the Criminal Justice Act 1988, s. 116.
[2] Applied by the Criminal Procedure (Scotland) Act 1975, ss. 183 and 384.

Amount of compensation order
[2] **59.**—(1) In determining whether to make a compensation order against any person, and in determining the amount to be paid by any person under such order, the court shall take into consideration his means so far as known to the court:

Provided that where the person is serving, or is to serve, a period of imprisonment or detention no account shall be taken, in assessing such means, of earnings contingent upon his obtaining employment after release.

(2) In solemn proceedings there shall be no limit on the amount which may be awarded under a compensation order.

[1] (3) In summary proceedings—

> (a) a sheriff, or a stipendiary magistrate appointed under section 5 of the District Courts (Scotland) Act 1975, shall have power to make a compensation order awarding in respect of each offence an amount not exceeding the prescribed sum (within the meaning of section 289B of the Criminal Procedure (Scotland) Act 1975);
> (b) a judge of a district court (other than such stipendiary magistrate) shall have power to make a compensation order

awarding in respect of each offence an amount not exceeding
level 4 on the standard scale.

NOTES
[1] As amended by the Criminal Justice Act 1982, Sched. 7.
[2] Applied (except proviso to subs. (1)) by the Criminal Procedure (Scotland) Act 1975, ss.
183 and 384.

Payment under compensation order
[1] **60.**—(1) Payment of any amount under a compensation order shall be
made to the clerk of the court who shall account for the amount to the
person entitled thereto.

(2) Only the court shall have power to enforce a compensation order.

NOTE
[1] Applied by the Criminal Procedure (Scotland) Act 1975, ss. 183 and 384.

Guidance as to whether compensation order or fine should be preferred
61. Where a court considers that in respect of an offence it would be
appropriate to impose a fine and to make a compensation order but the
convicted person has insufficient means to pay both an appropriate fine
and an appropriate amount in compensation the court should prefer a
compensation order.

Precedence of compensation order over fine
[1] **62.** Where a convicted person has both been fined and had a
compensation order made against him in respect of the same offence or
different offences in the same proceedings, a payment by the convicted
person shall first be applied in satisfaction of the compensation order.

NOTE
[1] Applied by the Criminal Procedure (Scotland) Act 1975, ss. 183 and 384.

Appeal as regards compensation order
63.—(1) For the purposes of any appeal or review, a compensation
order is a sentence.

(2) Where a compensation order has been made against a person, a
payment made to the court in respect of the order shall be retained until
the determination of any appeal in relation to the order.

Review of compensation order
[1] **64.** Without prejudice to the power contained in section 395A of the
1975 Act (as applied by section 66 of this Act), at any time before a
compensation order has been complied with or fully complied with—
　　(*a*) in a case where, as respects the compensation order, a transfer of
　　　　fine order under section 403 of the 1975 Act (as applied by the said
　　　　section 66) is effective and the court by which the compensation
　　　　order is enforceable is in terms of the transfer of fine order a court
　　　　of summary jurisdiction in Scotland, that court; or
　　(*b*) in any other case, the court which made the compensation order or
　　　　(where that court was the High Court) by which the order was first
　　　　enforceable,
may, on the application of the person against whom the compensation

order was made, discharge the compensation order, or reduce the amount that remains to be paid, if it appears to the court either that the injury, loss or damage in respect of which the compensation order was made has been held in civil proceedings to be less than it was taken to be for the purposes of the compensation order or that property the loss of which is reflected in the compensation order has been recovered.

NOTE

[1] Applied (except para. (*a*)) by the Criminal Procedure (Scotland) Act 1975, ss. 183 and 384.

Acts of Adjournal

65. The High Court's power to make Acts of Adjournal under sections 282 and 457 of the 1975 Act shall include power to make rules with regard to any of the provisions of this Part of this Act, including rules relating to the award and payment, by compensation orders, of sums to persons under any legal disability.

Application of provisions relating to fines to enforcement of compensation orders

66.—(1) The provisions of the 1975 Act specified in subsection (2) below shall, subject to any necessary modifications and to the qualifications mentioned in that subsection, apply in relation to compensation orders as they apply in relation to fines; and sections 91 of the Magistrates' Courts Act 1980 and 104B of the Magistrates' Courts Act (Northern Ireland) 1964 shall be construed accordingly.

(2) The provisions mentioned in subsection (1) above are—

section 194 (application to solemn procedure of summary procedure provisions relating to fines);

section 196 (fines, etc., may be enforced in other district);

section 395(2) to (7) (application of money found on offender);

section 395A (power to remit fines), with the omission of the words "or (4)" in subsection (2) of that section;

section 396 (time for payment) with the omission of the words from "unless" to "its decision" in subsection (4) and of subsection (5) of that section;

section 397 (further time for payment);

section 398 (reasons for default);

section 399 (payment by instalments);

section 400 (supervision pending payment of fine);

section 401 (supplementary provisions), except that subsection (1) of that section shall not apply in relation to compensation orders made in solemn proceedings;

section 402 (fines, etc., may be enforced in another district);

section 403 (transfer of fine orders);

section 404 (action of clerk of court on transfer of fine order);

section 406 (substitution of custody for imprisonment where child defaults on fine);

section 407(1)(*b*), (1A), (1D), (2) and (4) (maximum period of imprisonment for non-payment of fine):

Provided that—

(*a*) a court may impose imprisonment in respect of a fine

and decline to impose imprisonment in respect of a compensation order but not *vice versa*; and

(*b*) where a court imposes imprisonment both in respect of a fine and of a compensation order the amounts in respect of which imprisonment is imposed shall, for the purposes of the said subsection (1A), be aggregated;

section 408 (discharge from imprisonment to be specified);
section 409 (payment of fine in part by prisoner);
section 411 (recovery by civil diligence); and
Schedule 7 (application of sums paid as part of fine under section 409).

Effect of compensation order on subsequent award of damages in civil proceedings

[1] **67.**—(1) This section shall have effect where a compensation order has been made in favour of any person in respect of any injury, loss or damage and a claim by him in civil proceedings for damages in respect thereof subsequently falls to be determined.

(2) The damages in the civil proceedings shall be assessed without regard to the order; but where the whole or part of the amount awarded by the order has been paid, the damages awarded in the civil proceedings shall be restricted to the amount (if any) by which, as so assessed, they exceed the amount paid under the order.

(3) Where the whole or part of the amount awarded by the order remains unpaid and damages are awarded in a judgment in the civil proceedings, then, unless the person against whom the order was made has ceased to be liable to pay the amount unpaid (whether in consequence of an appeal, or of his imprisonment for default or otherwise), the court shall direct that the judgment—

(*a*) if it is for an amount not exceeding the amount unpaid under the order, shall not be enforced; or

(*b*) if it is for an amount exceeding the amount unpaid under the order, shall not be enforced except to the extent that it exceeds the amount unpaid,

without the leave of the court.

NOTE
[1] Applied by the Criminal Procedure (Scotland) Act 1975, ss. 183 and 384.

. . . . . .

Mental Health (Scotland) Act 1984

(1984 c. 36)

An Act to consolidate the Mental Health (Scotland) Act 1960.

[12th July 1984]

PART I

APPLICATION OF ACT

Application of Act: "mental disorder"

1.—(1) The provisions of this Act shall have effect with respect to the reception, care and treatment of persons suffering, or appearing to be suffering, from mental disorder, to the management of their property and affairs, and to other related matters.

(2) In this Act—

"mental disorder" means mental illness or mental handicap however caused or manifested;

"mental impairment" means a state of arrested or incomplete development of mind not amounting to severe mental impairment which includes significant impairment of intelligence and social functioning and is associated with abnormally aggressive or seriously irresponsible conduct on the part of the person concerned; and cognate expressions shall be construed accordingly;

"severe mental impairment" means a state of arrested or incomplete development of mind which includes severe impairment of intelligence and social functioning and is associated with abnormally aggressive or seriously irresponsible conduct on the part of the person concerned; and cognate expressions shall be construed accordingly;

and other expressions have the meanings assigned to them in section 125 of this Act.

(3) No person shall be treated under this Act as suffering from mental disorder by reason only of promiscuity or other immoral conduct, sexual deviancy or dependence on alcohol or drugs.

. . . . . .

.

PART V

ADMISSION TO AND DETENTION IN HOSPITAL AND GUARDIANSHIP

Grounds for hospital admission

Patients liable to be detained in hospital

17.—(1) A person may, in pursuance of an application for admission under section 18(1) of this Act, be admitted to a hospital and there detained on the grounds that—

(a) he is suffering from mental disorder of a nature or degree which makes it appropriate for him to receive medical treatment in a hospital, and

(i) in the case where the mental disorder from which he suffers is a persistent one manifested only by abnormally aggressive or seriously irresponsible conduct, such treatment is likely to alleviate or prevent a deterioration of his condition; or

(ii) In the case where the mental disorder from which he suffers is a mental handicap, the handicap comprises mental impairment (where such treatment is likely to alleviate or prevent a deterioration of his condition) or severe mental impairment; and

(b) it is necessary for the health or safety of that person or for the protection of other persons that he should receive such treatment and it cannot be provided unless he is detained under this Part of this Act.

(2) Nothing in this Act shall be construed as preventing a patient who requires treatment for mental disorder from being admitted to any hospital or nursing home for that treatment in pursuance of arrangements made in that behalf without any application, recommendation or order rendering him liable to be detained under this Act, or from remaining in any hospital in pursuance of such arrangements if he has ceased to be so liable to be detained.

. . . . . .

Care and treatment of patients: hospital

Return and re-admission of patients absent without leave: hospital

28.—(1) Where a patient who is for the time being liable to be detained under this Part of this Act in a hospital—

(a) absents himself from the hospital without leave granted under section 27 of this Act; or

(b) fails to return to the hospital on any occasion on which, or at the expiration of any period for which, leave of absence was granted to him under that section, or upon being recalled thereunder; or

(c) absents himself without permission from any place where he is required to reside in accordance with conditions imposed on the grant of leave of absence under that section,

he may, subject to the provisions of this section, be taken into custody and returned to the hospital or place by any mental health officer, by any officer on the staff of the hospital, by any constable, or by any person authorised in writing by the managers of the hospital.

(2) Where the place referred to in subsection 1(*c*) of this section is a hospital other than the one in which the patient is for the time being liable to be detained, the references in that subsection to an officer on the staff of the hospital and to the managers of the hospital shall respectively include references to an officer on the staff of the first-mentioned hospital and to the managers of that hospital.

(3) A patient shall not be taken into custody under this section after the expiration of the period of 28 days beginning with the first day of his absence without leave and a patient who has not returned or been taken into custody under this section within the same period shall cease to be liable to be detained at the expiration of that period.

(4) A patient shall not be taken into custody under this section if the period for which he is liable to be detained is that specified in section 24(3), 25(2), or 26(3) of this Act and that period has expired.

. . . . . .

Grounds for reception into guardianship

Patients liable to be received into guardianship
36. A person may, in pursuance of an application for reception into guardianship under section 37(1) of this Act, be received into guardianship on the grounds that—
   (*a*) he is suffering from mental disorder of a nature or degree which warrants his reception into guardianship; and
   (*b*) it is necessary in the interests of the welfare of the patient that he should be so received.

. . . . . .

Supplementary

. . . . . .

Interpretation of Part V
59.—(1) In this Part of this Act the expression "responsible medical officer" means—
   (*a*) in relation to a patient who is liable to be detained in a hospital, any medical practitioner employed on the staff of that hospital who may be authorised by the managers to act (either generally or in any particular case or class of case or for any particular purpose) as the responsible medical officer;
   (*b*) in relation to a patient subject to guardianship, any medical practitioner authorised by the local authority to act (either generally or in any particular case or class of case or for any particular purpose) as the responsible medical officer.

(2) In relation to a patient who is subject to guardianship under this Part of this Act, any reference in this Act to the local authority concerned is a reference—

(*a*) where a guardianship application is effective, to the local authority to whom that application is addressed;

(*b*) where the patient has been transferred to guardianship by the managers of a hospital under section 29(1) of this Act, to the local authority who received him into guardianship or approved his guardian.

(3) In this Act the expression "absent without leave" means absent from any hospital or other place and liable to be taken into custody and returned under section 28 or 44 of this Act, and kindred expressions shall be construed accordingly.

Part VI

Detention of Patients Concerned in Criminal Proceedings etc. and Transfer of Patients Under Sentence

Provisions for compulsory detention and guardianship of patients charged with offences etc.

. . . . . .

Powers of Secretary of State in respect of patients subject to restriction orders

68.—(1) If the Secretary of State is satisfied that a restriction order in respect of a patient is no longer required for the protection of the public from serious harm, he may direct that the patient shall cease to be subject to the special restrictions set out in section 62(1) of this Act; and, where the Secretary of State so directs, the restriction order shall cease to have effect and subsection (3) of that section shall apply accordingly.

(2) At any time while a restriction order is in force in respect of a patient, the Secretary of State may, if he thinks fit, by warrant discharge the patient from hospital, either absolutely or subject to conditions; and where a person is absolutely discharged under this subsection he shall thereupon cease to be liable to be detained by virtue of the relevant hospital order, and the restriction order shall cease to have effect accordingly.

(3) The Secretary of State may, at any time during the continuance in force of a restriction order in respect of a patient who has been conditionally discharged under subsection (2) of this section, and without prejudice to his further discharge as aforesaid, by warrant recall the patient to such hospital as may be specified in the warrant; and thereupon—

(*a*) if the hospital so specified is not the hospital from which the patient was conditionally discharged, the hospital order and the restriction order shall have effect as if the hospital specified in the warrant were substituted for the hospital specified in the hospital order;

(*b*) in any case, the patient shall be treated for the purposes of section 28 of this Act as if he had absented himself without leave from the hospital specified in the warrant, and if the restriction order was made for a specified period, that period shall not in any event expire until the patient returns to the hospital or is returned to the hospital under that section.

(4) If a restriction order ceases to have effect in respect of a patient after the patient has been conditionally discharged under this section, the patient shall, unless previously recalled under the last foregoing subsection, be deemed to be absolutely discharged on the date when the order ceases to have effect, and shall cease to be liable to be detained by virtue of the relevant hospital order accordingly.

(5) The Secretary of State may, if satisfied that the attendance at any place in Great Britain of a patient who is subject to a restriction order is desirable in the interests of justice or for the purposes of any public inquiry, direct him to be taken to that place; and where a patient is directed under this subsection to be taken to any place he shall, unless the Secretary of State otherwise directs, be kept in custody while being so taken, while at that place, and while being taken back to the hospital in which he is liable to be detained.

. . . . . .

Part XI

Miscellaneous and General

. . . . . .

Interpretation

125.—(1) In this Act, unless the context otherwise requires, the following expressions have the meanings hereby respectively assigned to them, that is to say— ...

"hospital" means—

(a) any hospital vested in the Secretary of State under the National Health Service (Scotland) Act 1978;

(b) any private hospital registered under Part IV of this Act; and

(c) any State hospital;

"hospital order" and "guardianship order" have the meanings respectively assigned to them by section 175 or 376 of the Criminal Procedure (Scotland) Act 1975; ...

"managers of a hospital" means—

(a) in relation to a hospital vested in the Secretary of State under the National Health Service (Scotland) Act 1978, the health board responsible for the administration of that hospital;

(b) in relation to a private hospital registered under Part IV of this Act, the person or persons carrying on the hospital;

(c) in relation to a State hospital, the Secretary of State or, if the Secretary of State has appointed a State Hospital Management Committee to manage that hospital, that committee, or, if the management of that hospital has been delegated to a Health Board or to the Common Services Agency for the Scottish Health Service, that board or agency, as the case may be; ...

"medical treatment" includes nursing, and also includes care and training under medical supervision; ...

"patient" (except in Part IX of this Act) means a person suffering or appearing to be suffering from mental disorder; ...

"restriction order" means an order made under section 178 or 379 of the Criminal Procedure (Scotland) Act 1975; ...

(2) Unless the context otherwise requires, any reference in this Act to any other enactment is a reference thereto as amended, and includes a reference thereto as extended or applied by or under any other enactment, including this Act.

...

(4) In relation to a person who is liable to be detained or subject to guardianship by virtue of an order or direction under Part VI of this Act or under section 174, 175, 178, 375, 376 or 379 of the Criminal Procedure (Scotland) Act 1975, any reference in this Act to any enactment contained in Part V of this Act shall be construed as a reference to that enactment as it applies to that person by virtue of the said Part VI or any of the provisions of the said sections.

(5) Any reference, however expressed, in this Act to a patient admitted to or detained in, or liable to be admitted to or detained in, a hospital or received, or liable to be received, into guardianship under this Act (other than under Part V thereof) or under Part VI of this Act shall include a reference to a patient who is admitted to or detained in, or liable to be admitted to or detained in, a hospital or received or liable to be received into guardianship under the Criminal Procedure (Scotland) Act 1975.

. . . . . .

Criminal Justice (Scotland) Act 1987

(1987 c. 41)

An Act to make provision for Scotland as regards the recovery of the proceeds of drug trafficking; to make further provision as regards criminal justice in Scotland; and for connected purposes. [15th May 1987]

PART I

CONFISCATION OF PROCEEDS OF DRUG TRAFFICKING ETC.

Confiscation orders

Confiscation orders

1.—(1) Subject to the provisions of this Part of this Act, where a person is convicted in the High Court of, or is under section 104(1) of the 1975 Act remitted to that Court for sentence as regards, an offence to which this section relates the Court may, on the application of the prosecutor made when he moves for sentence (or, if the case is one so remitted, made before sentence is pronounced), make an order (in this Act referred to as a "confiscation order") requiring the person to pay such amount as the Court considers appropriate, being an amount not exceeding—

(*a*) subject to paragraph (*b*) below, what it assesses to be the value of the proceeds of the person's drug trafficking; or

(*b*) if the Court is satisfied that the property that might be realised in terms of this Part of this Act at the time the confiscation order is made has a value less than that of the proceeds of the person's drug trafficking, what it assesses to be the value of that property.

(2) This section relates to any of the following—

(*a*) an offence under section 4(2) (production, or being concerned in production, of controlled drug), 4(3) (supply of, or offer to supply, or being concerned in supply of, controlled drug), 5(3) (possession of controlled drug with intent to supply) or 20 (assisting in, or inducing commission of, certain drug related offences punishable under foreign law) of the Misuse of Drugs Act 1971;

¹(*b*) in connection with a prohibition or restriction on importation and exportation having effect by virtue of section 3 of the said Act of 1971, an offence under section 50(2) or (3) (improper importation), 68(2) (improper exportation) or 170 (fraudulent evasion of duty etc.) of the Customs and Excise Management Act 1979;

(*c*) an offence under section 43 of this Act;

420

²(*cc*) an offence under sections 12, 14 or 19 of the Criminal Justice (International Co-operation) Act 1990;

²(*d*) an offence of conspiring, inciting or attempting to commit an offence to which, by virtue of paragraph (*a*), (*b*), (*c*) or (*cc*) above, this section relates.

(3) The Court shall take account of the provisions of any order made by it under subsection (1) above in determining the amount of any fine imposed on the person as regards the offence but not in determining any other matter as regards sentence.

(4) For the purposes of any appeal or review, a confiscation order is a sentence.

(5) No enactment restricting the power of a court dealing with a person in a particular way from dealing with him also in any other way shall by reason only of the making of an order under subsection (1) above (or the postponement of a decision as regards making such an order) restrict the High Court from dealing with a person in any way the Court considers appropriate in respect of an offence to which this section relates.

(6) In this Part of this Act, "drug trafficking" means doing or being concerned in any of the following, whether in Scotland or elsewhere—

(*a*) producing or supplying a controlled drug where the production or supply contravenes section 4(1) of the said Act of 1971;

(*b*) transporting or storing such a drug where possession of it contravenes section 5(1) of that Act;

(*c*) importing or exporting such a drug where the importation or exportation is prohibited by section 3(1) of that Act;

(*d*) producing, supplying, transporting, storing, importing or exporting such a drug in contravention of a corresponding law ("corresponding law" having the meaning assigned by section 36(1) of that Act);

³ (*e*) manufacturing or supplying a scheduled substance within the meaning of section 12 of the Criminal Justice (International Co-operation) Act 1990 where the manufacture or supply is an offence under that section;

and includes, whether in Scotland or elsewhere, entering into or being otherwise concerned in an arrangement whereby—

(i) the retention or control by or on behalf of another person of the other person's proceeds of drug trafficking is facilitated, or

(ii) the proceeds of drug trafficking by another person are used to secure that funds are placed at the other person's disposal or are used for the other person's benefit to acquire property by way of investment.

NOTES
¹ As amended by the Criminal Justice Act 1988 (c. 33), s. 103, Sched. 5, para. 19, Sched. 8, para. 16.
² Inserted by the Criminal Justice (International Co-operation) Act 1990 (c. 5), ss. 31(1), 32(2), Sched. 4, para. 5(2)(*a*).
³ Inserted by the Criminal Justice (International Co-operation) Act 1990 (c. 5), ss. 31(1), 32(2), Sched. 4, para. 5(2)(*b*).

Postponed confiscation orders

2.—(1) The Court, if it considers that it requires further information before coming to any decision as regards making an order under section 1(1) of this Act, may subject to subsection (4) below postpone that decision for a period not exceeding six months after the date of conviction for the purpose of enabling that information to be obtained; but without prejudice to sections 179 and 219 of the 1975 Act may notwithstanding such postponement proceed, on the prosecutor's motion therefor, to sentence or to otherwise deal with the person in respect of the conviction:

Provided that no fine shall be imposed before the decision is taken.

(2) Where under subsection (1) above a decision has been postponed for a period, any intention to appeal under section 228 of the 1975 Act against conviction or against both conviction and any sentence passed during that period in respect of the conviction, shall be intimated under section 231(1) of that Act not within two weeks of the final determination of the proceedings but within two weeks of—

(*a*) in the case of an appeal against conviction where there has been no such sentence, the day on which the period of postponement commences;

(*b*) in any other case, the day on which such sentence is passed in open court.

(3) Notwithstanding any appeal of which intimation has been given by virtue of subsection (2) above, a person may appeal under the said section 228 against the confiscation order (if the decision is to make one) or against any other sentence passed, after the period of postponement, in respect of the conviction.

(4) If during the period of postponement—

(*a*) intimation is given by virtue of subsection (2) above by the person, the Court may, on the application of the prosecutor, extend that period to a date up to three months after the date of disposal of the appeal;

(*b*) the case is remitted under subsection (5) of section 3 of this Act, the Court may, on such application, extend that period to a date up to three months after the case is transmitted under that subsection by the Court of Session or, if there is an appeal against the decision of the Court of Session on such remit, the date of disposal of that appeal.

Assessing the proceeds of drug trafficking

3.—(1) For the purposes of this Act—

(*a*) any payments or other rewards received by a person at any time (whether before or after the commencement of section 1 of this Act) in connection with drug trafficking carried on by him or another are his proceeds of drug trafficking, and

(*b*) the value of his proceeds of drug trafficking is the aggregate of the values of the payments or other rewards.

(2) Without prejudice to section 4 of this Act the Court may, in making an assessment as regards a person under section 1(1) of this Act, make the following assumptions, except in so far as any of them may be shown to be incorrect in that person's case—

(*a*) that any property appearing to the Court—

(i) to have been held by him at any time since his conviction, or

(ii) to have been transferred to him at any time since a date six years before his being indicted,

was received by him, at the earliest time at which he appears to the Court to have held it, as a payment or reward in connection with drug trafficking carried on by him,

(*b*) that any expenditure of his since the date mentioned in paragraph (*a*)(ii) above was met out of payments received by him in connection with drug trafficking carried on by him, and

(*c*) that, for the purpose of valuing any property received or assumed to have been received by him at any time as such a reward, he received the property free of any other interests in it.

[1] (3) Subsection (2) above does not apply if the only offence by virtue of which the assessment is being made is an offence under section 43 of this Act or section 14 of the Criminal Justice (International Co-operation) Act 1990.

(4) The Court shall, in making an assessment as regards a person under section 1(1) of this Act, leave out of account any of his proceeds of drug trafficking that are shown to the court to have been taken into account in a case where a confiscation order (whether under this Act or under and within the meaning of—

(*a*) section 1 of the Drug Trafficking Offences Act 1986; or

(*b*) any corresponding provision in Northern Ireland),

has previously been made against him.

(5) Where in making an assessment as regards a person under section 1(1) of this Act the Court at any stage is of the opinion that a difficult question of law or a question of fact of exceptional complexity is involved, it may of its own accord, or on the application of the prosecutor or of the person (or on their joint application), remit the case to the Court of Session for a decision as regards that question; and the Court of Session shall on deciding the question transmit the case to the High Court.

NOTE
[1] As amended by the Criminal Justice (International Co-operation) Act 1990 (c. 5), ss. 31(1), 32(2), Sched. 4, para. 5(3).

Statements relating to drug trafficking

4.—(1) Without prejudice to section 150 of the 1975 Act, where the prosecutor has, as regards a person, moved for an order under section 1(1) of this Act the prosecutor may lodge with the clerk of court a statement as to any matters relevant to the assessment of the value of that person's proceeds of drug trafficking and if the person accepts to any extent any allegation in the statement the Court may, for the purposes of that assessment, treat that acceptance as conclusive of the matters to which it relates.

(2) Where—

(*a*) a statement is lodged under subsection (1) above, and

(*b*) the Court is satisfied that a copy of that statement has been served on the person,

the Court may require the person to indicate, within such period as the Court may specify, to what extent he accepts each allegation in the statement and, in so far as he does not accept any such allegation, to indicate the basis of such non-acceptance.

(3) If the person fails in any respect to comply with a requirement under subsection (2) above, he may be treated for the purposes of this section as accepting every allegation in the statement apart from any allegation in respect of which he has complied with the requirement.

(4) Without prejudice to section 150 of the 1975 Act, where—

(*a*) there is lodged with the clerk of court by the person a statement as to any matters relevant to determining the amount that might be realised at the time the confiscation order is made, and

(*b*) the prosecutor accepts to any extent any allegation in the statement,

the Court may, for the purposes of that determination, treat that acceptance as conclusive of the matters to which it relates.

(5) No acceptance by the person under this section that any payment or other reward was received by him in connection with drug trafficking carried on by him or another shall be admissible in evidence in any proceedings, whether in Scotland or elsewhere, in respect of an offence.

Realisable property

5.—(1) Subject to subsection (3) below, the following property is realisable in terms of this Part of this Act—

(*a*) the whole estate of a person suspected of, or charged with, an offence to which section 1 of this Act relates, being an offence in respect of which (either or both)—

(i) warrant to arrest and commit him has been granted;

(ii) a restraint order has been made against him; and

(*b*) the whole estate of a person to whom any person whose whole estate is realisable by virtue of paragraph (*a*) above has (directly or indirectly and whether in one transaction or in a series of transactions) made an implicative gift,

if the proceedings as regards the offence have not been concluded.

[1] (2) In subsection (1) above, "the whole estate of a person" means his whole estate, wherever situated, and includes—

(*a*) any income or estate vesting in the holder of the realisable property; and

(*b*) the capacity to exercise, and to take proceedings for exercising, such powers in, over or in respect of any property as might have been exercised by the holder of the realisable property for his own benefit.

(3) Property is not realisable if—

(*a*) held on trust by a person mentioned in subsection (1)(*a*) or (*b*) above for a person not so mentioned; or

(*b*) an order under—

(i) section 27 of the Misuse of Drugs Act 1971 (forfeiture orders), or

(ii) section 223 or 436 of the 1975 Act (forfeiture of property), or

(iii) section 43 of the Powers of Criminal Courts Act 1973 (deprivation orders), or

[2] (iiia) section 13(2), (3) or (4) of the Prevention of Terrorism (Temporary Provisions) Act 1989 (forfeiture orders), or

(iv) any other statutory provision providing specifically for forfeiture in relation to an offence,

is in force in respect of the property.

(4) Subject to subsection (7) below, for the purposes of sections 1(1)(*b*) and 4(4)(*a*) of this Act, the amount that might be realised at the time a confiscation order is made in respect of a person is the total value at that time of all realisable property owned, and all implicative gifts which have been made, by him; except that where there are obligations having priority at that time the amount that might be realised is the aforesaid total value less the total amount payable in pursuance of those obligations.

(5) In assessing, for the purposes of section 1(1)(*b*) of this Act, the value—

(*a*) of realisable property (other than money) owned by a person in respect of whom it proposes to make a confiscation order, the High Court shall have regard to the market value of the property at the date on which the order would be made; but it may also have regard to any security or real burden which would require to be discharged in realising the property or to any other factors which might reduce the amount recoverable by such realisation;

(*b*) of an implicative gift, the Court shall, subject to section 6(2) and (3) of this Act, take it to be—

(i) the value of the gift when received, adjusted to take account of subsequent changes in the value of money, or

(ii) where subsection (6) below applies, the value there mentioned,

whichever is the greater.

(6) If at the date on which the order would be made the recipient holds—

(*a*) the property which he received (not being cash), or

(*b*) property which, in whole or in part, directly or indirectly represents in his hands the property which he received,

the value referred to in subsection (5)(*b*)(ii) above is, subject to section 6(2) and (3) of this Act, the value at that date of the property mentioned in paragraph (*a*) above or, as the case may be, of the property mentioned in paragraph (*b*) above so far as it represents the property which he received.

(7) Without prejudice to section 47(3) of this Act, the Court may, notwithstanding subsections (5)(*b*) and (6) above, for the purposes of section 1(1)(*b*) of this Act disregard the amount (or part of the amount) of an implicative gift if it considers it improbable that such amount (or part) could be realised.

(8) For the purposes of subsection (4) above, an obligation has priority at any time if it is an obligation of the person in respect of whom the confiscation order is made to—

(*a*) pay an amount due in respect of—

(i) a fine or order (not being a confiscation order or an order mentioned in sub-paragraph (ii) below) of a court, imposed or made on conviction of an offence, where the fine was imposed or order made before the confiscation order;

(ii) a compensation order (within the meaning of the Criminal

Justice (Scotland) Act 1980), made on conviction of an offence, where such order was made before, or in the same proceedings as, the confiscation order; or
(b) pay any sum which would be included among—
    (i) the preferred debts (as defined in section 51(2) of the 1985 Act) were his estate being sequestrated in accordance with the provisions of that Act and were the date on which the confiscation order would be made the date of sequestration;
    (ii) the preferential debts (within the meaning given by section 386 of the Insolvency Act 1986) in the person's bankruptcy or winding up were that bankruptcy commencing on the date of the confiscation order or as the case may be were the winding up under an order of the court made on that date.

NOTES
[1] As amended by the Criminal Justice (International Co-operation) Act 1990 (c. 5), ss. 31(1), (3), 32(2), Sched. 4, para. 5(4), Sched. 5.
[2] Inserted by the Prevention of Terrorism (Temporary Provisions) Act 1989 (c. 4), s. 25(1), Sched. 8, para. 9.

Implicative gifts
[1] **6.**—(1) Subject to subsection (4) below, in this Part of this Act references to an "implicative gift" are references to a gift (whether made before or after the commencement of section 1 of this Act)—
(a) made not more than six years before the date on which, in respect of a person suspected of, or charged with, an offence to which section 1 of this Act relates, the warrant to arrest and commit was granted, or a restraint order was made (whichever first occurs); or
(b) made at any time if the gift was—
    (i) of property received by the giver in connection with drug trafficking carried on by him or another, or
    (ii) of property which, in whole or in part, directly or indirectly represented in the giver's hands property received by him in that connection.

(2) For the purposes of subsection (1) above, the circumstances in which a person is to be treated as making a gift shall include those of a case where he transfers an interest in property to another person, directly or indirectly, for a consideration significantly less than the value of that interest at the time of transfer. In subsection (3) below the said consideration is referred to as "consideration A" (or as "A") and the said value as "consideration B" (or as "B").

(3) In the case mentioned in subsection (2) above, section 5 of this Act shall apply as if the reference in sub-paragraph (i) of subsection (5)(b) of that section to "the value of the gift when received" were a reference to the amount by which consideration A is exceeded by consideration B and as if in sub-paragraph (ii) of the said subsection (5)(b) the reference to "the value there mentioned" were a reference to a value determined in accordance with the formula—

$$\frac{C(B-A)}{B}$$

where C is what the value referred to in the said sub-paragraph (ii) would be had the gift been an outright gift.

(4) A gift made for a charitable purpose to a person who is not an associate of the giver, being a gift which having regard to all the circumstances it was reasonable to make, is not an implicative gift.

(5) In subsection (4) above, "charitable purpose" means any charitable, benevolent or philanthropic purpose whether or not it is charitable within the meaning of any rule of law.

NOTE
[1] As amended by the Law Reform (Miscellaneous Provisions) (Scotland) Act 1990 (c. 40), Sched. 8, para. 37.

Application of provisions relating to fines to enforcement of confiscation orders

7.—(1) Sections 196 and 203 of the 1975 Act and, as applied by section 194 of that Act, the provisions of that Act specified in subsection (2) below shall, subject to the qualifications mentioned in subsection (2) below, apply in relation to confiscation orders as they apply in relation to fines; and section 91 of the Magistrates' Courts Act 1980 and Article 96 of the Magistrates' Courts (Northern Ireland) Order 1981 (provisions relating to transfer of fines from Scotland etc.) shall be construed accordingly.

(2) The provisions mentioned in subsection (1) above are—
  section 396;
  Provided that any allowance under that section (or section 397) of time (or further time) for payment shall be without prejudice to the exercise by any administrator appointed in relation to the confiscation order of his powers and duties under this Act; and the court may, pending such exercise, postpone any decision as to refusing or allowing time (or further time) for payment;
  section 397;
  section 398;
  section 399;
  Provided that any order of payment by instalments shall be without prejudice to such exercise as is above mentioned;
  section 400;
  section 401(2) and (3);
  section 403, except that for the purposes of subsections (4) and (6) of that section "confiscation order" in subsection (1) above shall be construed as including such an order within the meaning of the Drug Trafficking Offences Act 1986 or of any corresponding provision in Northern Ireland;
  section 404;
  section 406;
  section 407;
  Provided that where a court imposes a period of imprisonment both in respect of a fine and of a confiscation order the amounts in respect of which the period is imposed shall, for the purposes of subsection (1A) of that section, be aggregated:
  Provided also that before imposing a period of imprisonment to which there is a liability by virtue of that section the court shall, if an administrator has been appointed in relation to the

confiscation order, require a report from him as to whether and in what way he is likely to exercise his powers and duties under this Act and shall take that report into account; and the court may, pending such exercise, postpone any decision as to such imposition;

section 408;

section 409, except that the reference in subsection (1) of that section to the person paying a sum to the governor of the prison under conditions prescribed by rules made under the Prisons (Scotland) Act 1952 shall be construed as including a reference to an administrator appointed in relation to the confiscation order making such payment under this Act in respect of the person;

section 411, except the proviso to subsection (3):

Provided that an order for recovery by civil diligence shall not be made under the section where an administrator is appointed in relation to the confiscation order;

Schedule 7.

(3) Where in any proceedings an order has been made under section 1(1) of this Act as regards a person and a period of imprisonment or detention is imposed on him in default of payment of its amount (or as the case may be of an instalment thereof), that period shall run from the expiry of any other period of imprisonment or detention (not being one of life imprisonment or detention for life) imposed on him in the proceedings.

(4) The reference in subsection (3) above to "any other period of imprisonment or detention imposed" includes (without prejudice to the generality of the expression) a reference to such a period on default of payment of a fine (or instalment thereof); but only where that default has occurred before the warrant for imprisonment is issued for the default in relation to the order.

Restraint orders and interdict

Cases in which restraint orders may be made

8.—(1) Where—

(*a*) warrant to arrest and commit a person suspected of or charged with an offence to which section 1 of this Act relates has been granted and either—

(i) notice has been served on him calling upon him to appear at a trial diet in the High Court or at a diet of that Court fixed for the purposes of section 102 of the 1975 Act (whether or not the trial has commenced, provided that the proceedings as regards the offence have not been concluded); or

(ii) the Court of Session is satisfied that it is intended that any trial diet in respect of the suspected offence (or as the case may be the offence with which he has been charged) shall proceed in the High Court; or

(*b*) the Court of Session is satisfied that a procurator fiscal proposes to petition within 28 days for warrant to arrest and commit a person suspected of such an offence, that the suspicion is reasonable and that it is intended that any trial diet in respect of the suspected offence shall proceed in the High Court; or

(c) an interlocutor has been pronounced under section 104(1)(*b*) of the 1975 Act remitting a person to the High Court for sentence in respect of such an offence,

the Court of Session may, on the application of the Lord Advocate, make in respect of the person such order (in this Act referred to as a "restraint order") as is described in section 9 of this Act. Any such application shall be heard in chambers.

(2) Subject to subsection (3) below, the Court of Session may, at the instance of—

(*a*) the Lord Advocate, at any time vary or recall a restraint order in relation to any person or to any property;

(*b*) any person having an interest, at any time vary or recall a restraint order in relation to the person or to any property; and in particular may, on the application of a person named in a restraint order as having received an implicative gift, recall the order in relation to that person if satisfied—

(i) that he received the gift not knowing, not suspecting and not having reasonable grounds to suspect that the giver was in any way concerned in drug trafficking; and

(ii) that he is not, and has never been, an associate of the giver; and

(iii) that he would suffer hardship were the order not to be recalled.

(3) The Court of Session may, where it has recalled a restraint order under subsection (2) above, order that property of the person at whose instance it was recalled shall cease to be realisable.

(4) Rules of court may provide that any application under subsection (2) above shall be made within such period of the applicant receiving notice of the restraint order as may be specified in the rules; and in the period between such application and any decision of the Court as regards recalling that order the powers of any administrator appointed as regards property of the applicant shall be subject to the restriction that the administrator shall not realise the property.

(5) Where, a restraint order having been made by virtue of—

(*a*) paragraph (*b*) of subsection (1) above, the days mentioned in that paragraph expire without the petition having been presented; or

(*b*) paragraph (*a*), (*b*) or (*c*) of that subsection, the proceedings as regards the offence are concluded,

the Lord Advocate shall forthwith apply to the Court of Session for recall of that order and the Court shall grant the application.

Restraint orders

9.—(1) A restraint order is an order interdicting—

(*a*) the person in respect of whom it is made from dealing with his realisable property; or

(*b*) that person and any person named in the order as appearing to the Court of Session to have received from him an implicative gift from dealing with their own, or the other's, realisable property,

(whenever that property was acquired and whether it is described in the order or not); but, subject to subsection (5) below, the order may contain conditions and exceptions to which such interdict shall be subject.

(2) A restraint order shall provide for notice to be given to persons affected by the order.

(3) In subsection (1) above, the reference to "dealing with" property shall (without prejudice to the generality of the expression) be construed as including a reference—

(*a*) to making a payment in reduction of the amount of a debt; and

(*b*) to removing the property from Great Britain.

(4) If the restraint order is made by virtue of section 8(1)(*b*) of this Act, references in the foregoing provisions of this section to "realisable property" shall, in relation to any period before warrant to arrest and commit the person in respect of whom it was made is granted, be construed as references to property which would be realisable property had such warrant been granted immediately before the commencement of that period.

(5) Without prejudice to the generality of subsection (1) above, property in so far as it comprises reasonable legal expenses payable in relation to proceedings as regards the offence by virtue of which the restraint order has been made or as regards a confiscation order made on conviction thereof shall be excepted under that subsection from the interdict.

Seizure of property affected by restraint order

10.—(1) A constable or a person commissioned by the Commissioners of Customs and Excise may, for the purpose of preventing realisable property of a person subject to a restraint order (whether under this Act or under and within the meaning of the Drug Trafficking Offences Act 1986) from being removed from Great Britain, seize the property.

(2) Property seized under subsection (1) above shall be dealt with in accordance with the directions of the court which made the order.

Inhibition and arrestment of property affected by restraint order or by interdict under section 12

11.—(1) On the application of the Lord Advocate, the Court of Session may, in respect of—

(*a*) heritable realisable property in Scotland affected by a restraint order (whether such property generally or particular such property) grant warrant for inhibition against any person interdicted by the order or, in relation to that property, under section 12 of this Act;

(*b*) moveable realisable property so affected (whether such property generally or particular such property) grant warrant for arrestment if the property would be arrestable were the person entitled to it a debtor;

and, subject to the provisions of this Part of this Act, the warrant—

(i) shall have effect as if granted on the dependence of an action for debt at the instance of the Lord Advocate against the person and

may be executed, recalled, loosed or restricted accordingly;
(ii) where granted under subsection (1)(*a*) above, shall have the effect of letters of inhibition and shall forthwith be registered by the Lord Advocate in the register of inhibitions and adjudications.

(2) Section 155 of the Titles to Land Consolidation (Scotland) Act 1868 (effective date of inhibition) shall apply in relation to an inhibition for which warrant has been granted under subsection (1)(*a*) above as that section applies to an inhibition by separate letters or contained in a summons.

(3) In the application of section 158 of the said Act of 1868 (recall of inhibition) to such inhibition as is mentioned in subsection (2) above, references in that section to a particular Lord Ordinary shall be construed as references to any Lord Ordinary.

(4) That an inhibition or arrestment has been executed under subsection (1) above in respect of property shall not prejudice the exercise of an administrator's powers under or for the purposes of this Part of this Act in respect of that property.

(5) No inhibition or arrestment executed under subsection (1) above shall have effect once, or in so far as, the restraint order affecting the property in respect of which the warrant for such inhibition or arrestment has been granted has ceased to have effect in respect of that property; and the Lord Advocate shall—

(*a*) apply for the recall, or as the case may be restriction, of the inhibition or arrestment accordingly; and
(*b*) ensure that recall, or restriction, of an inhibition on such application is reflected in the register of inhibitions and adjudications.

[1] (6) The foregoing provisions of this section shall apply in relation to an order made under section 8 of the Drug Trafficking Offences Act 1986 and registered under section 28 of this Act (a "relevant order") as they apply to a restraint order; but as if—

(*a*) for any reference to the Lord Advocate there were substituted a reference to the prosecutor or, in a case where the order was made by virtue of subsection (2) of section 7 of that Act and the information in respect of the charge mentioned in that subsection has not yet been laid, to the person as regards whom the court which made the order was satisfied as is mentioned in subsection (3)(*b*) of that section;
(*b*) any reference to realisable property fell to be construed in accordance with section 5 of that Act (references in that section to the defendant, and to the time at which proceedings were instituted against him, being in such case as is mentioned in paragraph (*a*) above taken to be, respectively, references to the person as regards whom the court which made the order was satisfied as is mentioned in subsection (2) of the said section 7 and to the time immediately before the order was made);
(*c*) for any reference to a restraint order there were substituted a reference to a relevant order;
(*d*) in subsection (1)(*a*) for the words "interdicted by the order or, in relation to that property, under section 12 of this Act" there were substituted the words "with an interest in that property";

(e) in subsection (1), for the words "Part of this Act" there were substituted the word "section";

(f) in subsection (1)(i), after the word "and" there were inserted the words "subject to subsection (3A) below";

(g) after subsection (3) there were inserted the following subsection—

"(3A) Any power of the Court of Session to recall, loose or restrict inhibitions or arrestments shall, in relation to an inhibition or arrestment proceedings upon a warrant under this section and without prejudice to any other consideration lawfully applying to the exercise of the power, be exercised with a view to achieving the purposes specified in section 13 of the Drug Trafficking Offences Act 1986."; and

(h) in subsection (4)—

(i) for the reference to an administrator there were substituted a reference to a receiver; and

(ii) for the words "this Part of this Act" there were substituted the words "section 8, 11 or 12 of the said Act of 1986".

NOTE
[1] As amended by the Criminal Justice Act 1988 (c. 33), s.103, Sched. 5, para. 20, Sched. 8, para. 16.

Interdict of person not subject to restraint order

12.—(1) The Court of Session may, where it has granted a restraint order, interdict a person not subject to that order from dealing with realisable property affected by it while it is in force; and the clerk of court shall, on the restraint order being recalled, forthwith so inform each person so interdicted.

(2) Subsection (2) of section 8 of this Act applies in relation to an interdict under subsection (1) above as the said subsection (2) applies in relation to a restraint order; and subsection (3) of section 9 thereof applies in relation to subsection (1) above as the said subsection (3) applies in relation to subsection (1) of the said section 9.

(3) An interdict under subsection (1) above shall not be effective against a person unless and until he is served with a copy both of it and of the restraint order.

Administrators

Administrators

13.—(1) On the application of the Lord Advocate the Court of Session may as regards realisable property—

(a) affected by a restraint order, appoint a person to manage, or otherwise deal with, the property; or

(b) where a confiscation order has been made, appoint a person (or empower an appointee under paragraph (a) above) to realise the property,

in accordance with the Court's directions and may (whether on making the appointment or from time to time) require any person having possession of the property to give possession of it to the appointee (any such appointee being in this Act referred to as an "administrator").

(2) A requirement under subsection (1) above—

(*a*) subject to paragraph (*b*) below, may relate to the property generally or to particular such property and may be subject to such exceptions and conditions as may be specified by the Court;

(*b*) shall relate to property mentioned in paragraph (*b*) of section 5(1) of this Act only if expressly stated so to do and then only in so far as the person in whom such property is vested is named in the requirement as being subject to it.

(3) On a requirement being imposed under subsection (1) above—

(*a*) the clerk of court shall forthwith so notify—

(i) the person in respect of whom the restraint order, or as the case may be the confiscation order, has been made; and

(ii) any other person named in the requirement as being subject to it; and

(*b*) any dealing of or with such person in relation to the property shall be of no effect in a question with the administrator unless whoever dealt with the person had, at the time when the dealing occurred, no knowledge of the appointment.

(4) The Court of Session, at the instance of any person having an interest, may at any time—

(*a*) vary or withdraw a requirement imposed under subsection (1) above; or

(*b*) without prejudice to section 16 of this Act or to the powers and duties of an administrator pending a decision under this paragraph, on cause shown, remove the administrator from office.

(5) On the death or resignation of the administrator, or on his removal from office under subsection (4)(*b*) above or section 17 of this Act, the Court of Session shall appoint a new administrator. Such of the property (if any) as was, by virtue of section 14(3) of this Act, vested in the administrator who has died, resigned or been removed shall forthwith vest in the new administrator; and any requirement imposed under subsection (1) above shall, on the person subject to the requirement being notified in writing of the appointment by the appointee, apply in relation to the appointee instead of in relation to his predecessor.

(6) The administration of property by an administrator shall be deemed continuous notwithstanding any temporary vacancy in that office.

(7) Any appointment under this section shall be on such conditions as to caution as the accountant of court may think fit to impose; but the premium of any bond of caution or other security thereby required of the administrator shall be treated as part of his outlays in his actings as such.

(8) Without prejudice to section 17 of this Act, section 6 of the Judicial Factors (Scotland) Act 1889 (supervision of judicial factors) shall not apply in relation to an appointment under this section.

Functions of administrators

14.—(1) Subject to section 17 of this Act, an administrator—

(*a*) shall be entitled to take possession of, and if appointed (or empowered) under paragraph (*b*) of section 13(1) of this Act shall as soon as practicable take possession of, the property as regards which he has been appointed and of any document which both—

    (i) is in the possession or control of the person (in this section referred to as "A") in whom the property is vested (or would be vested but for an order made under subsection (3) of this section); and

    (ii) relates to the property or to A's assets, business or financial affairs;

(*b*) shall be entitled to have access to, and to copy, any document relating to the property or to A's assets, business or financial affairs and not in such possession or control as is mentioned in paragraph (*a*) above;

(*c*) may bring, defend or continue any legal proceedings relating to the property and, without prejudice to the generality of this paragraph, may sist himself in any case in the Court of Session which has been remitted under section 3(5) of this Act if the restraint order by virtue of which the administrator has been appointed interdicts the person whose case has been so remitted from dealing with the property;

(*d*) may borrow money in so far as it is necessary to do so to safeguard the property and may for the purposes of such borrowing create a security over any part of the property;

(*e*) may, if the administrator considers that to do so would be beneficial for the management or realisation of the property—

    (i) carry on any business of A;

    (ii) exercise any right of A as holder of securities in a company;

    (iii) grant a lease of the property or take on lease any other property; or

    (iv) enter into any contract, or execute any deed, as regards the property or as regards A's business;

(*f*) may, where any right, option or other power forms part of A's estate, make payments or incur liabilities with a view to—

    (i) obtaining property which is the subject of; or

    (ii) maintaining,

    the right, option or power;

(*g*) may effect or maintain insurance policies as regards the property or A's business;

(*h*) may, where A has an uncompleted title to any heritable estate, complete title thereto:

    Provided that completion of title in A's name shall not validate by accretion any unperfected right in favour of any person other than the administrator;

(*j*) may sell, purchase or exchange property or discharge any security for an obligation due to A:

    Provided that it shall be incompetent for the administrator or an associate of his to purchase any of A's property in pursuance of this paragraph;

(*k*) may claim, vote and draw dividends in the sequestration of the estate (or bankruptcy or liquidation) of a debtor of A and may accede to a voluntary trust deed for creditors of such a debtor;

(*l*) may discharge any of his functions through agents or employees:

    Provided that the administrator shall be personally liable to meet the fees and expenses of any such agent or employee out of such remuneration as is payable to the administrator by virtue of section 18(1) and (3) of this Act;

(*m*) may take such professional advice as he may consider requisite for the proper discharge of his functions;

(*n*) may at any time apply to the Court of Session for directions as regards the discharge of his functions;

(*o*) may exercise any power specifically conferred on him by the Court of Session, whether such conferral was at the time of his appointment or on his subsequent application to the Court in that regard; and

(*p*) may do anything incidental to the above powers and duties.

(2) Subject to the proviso to paragraph (*j*) of subsection (1) above—

(*a*) a person dealing with an administrator in good faith and for value shall not require to determine whether the administrator is acting within the powers mentioned in that subsection; and

(*b*) the validity of any title shall not be challengeable by reason only of the administrator having acted outwith those powers.

(3) The exercise of a power mentioned in any of paragraphs (*c*) to (*k*) above shall be in A's name except where and in so far as an order made by the Court of Session under this subsection (either on its own motion or on the application of the administrator) has vested the property in the administrator (or in his predecessor in that office).

Money received by administrator

15.—(1) Subject to subsection (2) below, all money received by an administrator in the exercise of his functions shall be deposited by him, in the name (unless vested in the administrator by virtue of subsection (3) of section 14 of this Act) of the holder of the property realised, in an appropriate bank or institution.

(2) The administrator may at any time retain in his hands a sum not exceeding £200 or such other sum as may be prescribed by the Secretary of State by regulations made by statutory instrument.

(3) In subsection (1) above, "appropriate bank or institution" means a bank or institution mentioned in section 2(1) of the Banking Act 1979 or for the time being specified in Schedule 1 to that Act.

Application of proceeds of realisation and other sums

16.—(1) Subject to subsection (2) below, sums in the hands of an administrator which are—

(*a*) proceeds of a realisation of property under section 13 of this Act, and

(*b*) other property held by the person in respect of whom the confiscation order was made,

shall first be applied in payment of such expenses as are payable under section 37(2) of this Act and then shall, after such payments (if any) as the Court of Session may direct have been made out of those proceeds and sums, be applied on the person's behalf towards the satisfaction of the confiscation order.

(2) If, after the amount payable under the confiscation order has been

fully paid, any such proceeds and sums remain in the hands of the administrator, he shall distribute them

(*a*) among such of those who held property which has been realised under this Act, and

(*b*) in such proportions,

as the Court of Session may, after giving such persons an opportunity to be heard as regards the matter, direct.

[1] (3) The receipt of any sum by a sheriff clerk on account of an amount payable under a confiscation order shall reduce the amount so payable, but the sheriff clerk shall apply the money received—

(*a*) first, in payment of any expenses to payment of which a person is entitled under section 37(2) of this Act but which were not paid to him under subsection (1) above;

(*b*) next, in payment of the administrator's remuneration and expenses;

(*c*) next, in reimbursement of any sums paid by the Lord Advocate under section 20(2) of this Act,

and the balance shall be payable and recoverable (or as the case may be disposed of) under section 203 of the 1975 Act (fines payable to H.M. Exchequer) as applied by section 7 of this Act.

NOTE
[1] As amended by the Criminal Justice Act 1988 (c. 33), s. 103, Sched. 5, para. 21 and Sched. 8, para. 16.

Supervision of administrators
17.—(1) The accountant of court shall supervise the performance by administrators of the functions conferred on them by this Act; and in particular an administrator proposing to exercise functions conferred by any of paragraphs (*c*) to (*p*) of subsection (1) of section 14 of this Act shall first obtain the consent of the accountant of court to such exercise.

(2) If it appears to the accountant of court that an administrator has, without reasonable cause, failed to perform a duty imposed on him by any provision of this Part of this Act, he shall report the matter to the Court of Session which, after giving the administrator an opportunity to be heard as regards the matter, may remove the administrator from office, censure him or make such other order as the circumstances of the case may appear to the Court to require.

Accounts and remuneration of administrator
18.—(1) The administrator shall keep such accounts in relation to his intromissions with the property as regards which he is appointed as the Court of Session may require and shall lodge these accounts with the accountant of court at such times as may be fixed by the Court in that regard; and the accountant of court shall audit the accounts and issue a determination as to the amount of outlays and, on the basis mentioned in subsection (3) below, remuneration payable to the administrator in respect of those intromissions.

(2) Not later than two weeks after the issuing of a determination under subsection (1) above, the administrator or the Lord Advocate may appeal against it to the Court of Sessions.

(3) The basis for determining the amount of remuneration payable to

the administrator shall be the value of the work reasonably undertaken by him, regard being had to the extent of the responsibilities involved.

(4) The accountant of court may authorise the administrator to pay without taxation an account in respect of legal services incurred by the administrator.

Effect of appointment under section 13 on diligence

19. Without prejudice to section 11 of this Act—
    (*a*) no arrestment or poinding of realisable property executed on or after an appointment as regards the property under section 13 of this Act shall be effectual to create a preference for the arrester or poinder and any such property so arrested or poinded, or the proceeds of sale thereof, shall be handed over to the administrator;
    (*b*) no poinding of the ground in respect of realisable property on or after such appointment shall be effectual in a question with the administrator except for the interest on the debt of a secured creditor, being interest for the current half-yearly term and arrears of interest for one year immediately before the commencement of that term;
    (*c*) it shall be incompetent on or after such appointment for any other person to raise or insist in an adjudication against the realisable property or to be confirmed as executor-creditor on that property; and
    (*d*) no inhibition on realisable property which takes effect on or after such appointment shall be effectual to create a preference for the inhibitor in a question with the administrator.

Further provision as to administrators

20.—(1) Where an administrator takes any action—
    (*a*) in relation to property which is not realisable property, being action which he would be entitled to take if it were such property,
    (*b*) believing, and having reasonable grounds for believing, that he is entitled to take that action in relation to that property,
he shall not be liable to any person in respect of any loss or damage resulting from his action except in so far as the loss or damage is caused by his negligence.

(2) Any amount due in respect of the remuneration and expenses of an administrator so appointed shall, if no sum is available to be applied in payment of it under section 16(3)(*b*) of this Act, be paid by the Lord Advocate.

Discharge of administrator

21. After an administrator has lodged his final accounts under section 18(1) of this Act, he may apply to the accountant of court to be discharged from office; and such discharge, if granted, shall have the effect of freeing him from all liability (other than liability arising from fraud) in respect of any act or omission of his in exercising the functions conferred on him by this Act.

Rules of court as regards accountant of court's supervision etc. of administrators

22. Without prejudice to section 16(i) of the Administration of Justice (Scotland) Act 1933 (power, in relation to certain statutory powers and duties, to regulate procedure etc. by Act of Sederunt), provision may be made by rules of court as regards (or as regards any matter incidental to) the accountant of court's powers and duties under this Act in relation to the functions of administrators.

Exercise of powers

Exercise of powers by Court of Session or administrator

23.—(1) The following provisions apply to the powers conferred on the Court of Session by sections 8, 11(1) to (5), 12 to 13, 16 and 24 of this Act, or on an administrator appointed under subsection (1) of the said section 13.

(2) Subject to the following provisions of this section, the powers shall be exercised with a view to making available for satisfying a confiscation order the value for the time being of realisable property held by any person by the realisation of such property.

(3) In the case of a person who holds realisable property by virtue only of having received an implicative gift, the powers shall, so far as is reasonably attainable, be exercised so as to realise, interdict dealing with, or permit the seizure or taking possession of, property of a value no greater than the value for the time being of that gift.

(4) The powers shall be exercised with a view to allowing any person other than one mentioned in paragraph (*a*) or (*b*) of section 5(1) of this Act to retain or recover the value of any property held by him.

(5) An order may be made or other action taken in respect of a debt owed by the Crown.

(6) Subject to subsection (4) above and without prejudice to the power of the Court of Session to make an exception under section 9(1) or 13(2)(*a*) of this Act for the protection of a person or his family, in exercising those powers no account shall be taken of any obligation (other than an obligation having priority, within the meaning of section 5(8) of this Act) of a person holding realisable property if that obligation conflicts with the obligations to satisfy a confiscation order.

(7) Subsections (2) to (6) of section 13 of the Drug Trafficking Offences Act 1986 (exercise of powers by High Court etc.) shall apply as regards the powers conferred on the Court of Session by sections 27 and 28, or by virtue of section 11(6), of this Act as those subsections apply as regards the powers conferred on the High Court (within the meaning that expression has in relation to England and Wales) by the sections mentioned in subsection (1) of the said section 13.

Power to facilitate realisation

24.—(1) Without prejudice to any enactment or rule of law in respect of the recording of deeds relating to heritable property or the registration on interests therein, the Court of Session, to facilitate realisation under section 13 of this Act, may—

    (*a*) order any person (in this section referred to as "A") holding an interest in property, not being such person (in this section referred

to as "B") as is mentioned in paragraph (*a*) or (*b*) of section 5(1) of this Act, to make such payment to an administrator appointed to realise estate comprising an interest of B in that property as the Court may direct and may, subject to such payment being made—
  (i) authorise the administrator to transfer B's interest to A or to discharge it in favour of A; or
  (ii) itself by order so transfer or discharge B's interest; or
(*b*) by order—
  (i) transfer A's interest to B; or
  (ii) discharge it in favour of B,
on the administrator making such payment to A out of that estate in respect of A's interest as the Court may direct.

(2) The Court may make such incidental provision in relation to any exercise of powers conferred on it by subsection (1) above as it considers appropriate; but it shall not exercise those powers without giving such persons as hold an interest in the property reasonable opportunity to make representations to it in that regard.

Variation of confiscation orders

Variation of confiscation order
25.—(1) If, on an application by a person in respect of whom a confiscation order has been made, the Court of Session is satisfied that the realisable property is inadequate for the payment of any amount remaining to be recovered under that order, the Court shall issue a certificate to that effect giving the Court's reasons for being so satisfied.

(2) For the purposes of subsection (1) above the Court of Session—
  (*a*) in the case of realisable property held by a person whose estate has been sequestrated, or who has been adjudged bankrupt in England and Wales or in Northern Ireland, shall take into account the extent to which any property held by him may be distributed among creditors; and
  (*b*) may disregard any inadequacy in the realisable property if that inadequacy appears to the Court to be attributable wholly or partly to anything done by the person for the purpose of preserving such property from realisation under this Act.

(3) Where a certificate has been issued under subsection (1) above, the person may apply to the High Court for the amount to be recovered under the order to be reduced.

(4) The High Court shall, on an application under subsection (3) above—
  (*a*) substitute for the amount to be recovered under the order such lesser amount as the High Court thinks just in all the circumstances of the case; and
  (*b*) substitute for any period of imprisonment imposed under section 407 of the 1975 Act (or period of detention imposed under section 415(2) of that Act by virtue of the said section 407) in respect of the amount to be recovered under the order a shorter period, determined in accordance with subsection (1A) of the said section 407 (as it has effect by virtue of section 7 of this Act), in respect of the lesser amount.

Compensation

Compensation

26.—(1) Subject to subsection (2) below, if proceedings are instituted against a person for an offence to which section 1 of this Act relates and either—

(*a*) the proceedings do not result in his conviction for any such offence, or

(*b*) where he is convicted of one or more such offences, the conviction or convictions concerned are quashed (and no conviction for any such offence is substituted),

the Court of Session may, on an application by a person who held property which was realisable property, order compensation to be paid to the applicant; but this subsection is without prejudice to any right which may otherwise exist to institute proceedings in respect of delictual liability disclosed by such circumstances as are mentioned in paragraphs (*a*) and (*b*) of that subsection.

(2) The Court of Session shall not order compensation to be paid under subsection (1) above in any case unless satisfied—

(*a*) that there has been some serious default on the part of a person concerned in the investigation of the offence or offences concerned, being a person mentioned in subsection (4) below, and that, but for that default, the proceedings would not have been instituted or continued; and

(*b*) that the applicant has suffered substantial loss or damage in consequence of anything done in relation to the property under section 8, 11, 12, 13 or 24 of this Act or by virtue of section 24A of the Drug Trafficking Offences Act 1986 (recognition and enforcement in England and Wales of orders and functions under this part of this Act).

(3) The amount of compensation to be paid under this section shall be such as the Court of Session thinks just in all the circumstances of the case.

(4) Compensation payable under this section shall be paid, where the person in default was—

(*a*) a constable of a police force, by the police authority or joint police committee for the police area for which that force is maintained ("constable", "police force", "police authority", "joint police committee" and "police area" having the meanings assigned to these terms by the Police (Scotland) Act 1967);

(*b*) a constable other than is mentioned in paragraph (*a*) above, but with the powers of such a constable, by the body under whose authority he acts;

(*c*) a procurator fiscal or was acting on behalf of the Lord Advocate, by the Lord Advocate; and

(*d*) a person commissioned by the Commissioners of Customs and Excise, by those Commissioners.

Reciprocal arrangements for enforcement of confiscation orders

Recognition and enforcement of orders under Drug Trafficking Offences Act 1986

27.—(1) An order to which this section applies shall, subject to this section and section 28 of this Act, have effect in the law of Scotland but shall be enforced in Scotland only in accordance with this section and that section.

(2) A receiver's functions under or for the purposes of section 8, 11 or 12 of the Drug Trafficking Offences Act 1986 shall, subject to this section and section 28 of this Act, have effect in the law of Scotland.

(3) If an order to which this section applies is registered under this section—

(a) the Court of Session shall have, in relation to its enforcement, the same power,

(b) proceedings for or with respect to its enforcement may be taken, and

(c) proceedings for or with respect to any contravention of such an order (whether before or after such registration) may be taken,

as if the order had originally been made in that Court.

(4) Nothing in this section enables any provision of an order which empowers a receiver to do anything in Scotland under section 11(3)(a) of the said Act of 1986 to have effect in the law of Scotland.

(5) The orders to which this section applies are orders of the High Court (within the meaning that expression has in relation to England and Wales)—

(a) made under section 8, 11, 12 or 30 of the said Act of 1986,

(b) relating to the exercise by that Court of its powers under those sections, or

(c) relating to receivers in the performance of their functions under section 8, 11 or 12 of that Act,

but not including an order in proceedings for enforcement of any such order.

(6) References in this section to an order under section 8 of the said Act of 1986 include references to a discharge under section 7(4) of that Act of such an order.

(7) In this section and in section 28 of this Act, "order" means any order, direction or judgment (by whatever name called).

(8) Nothing in any order of the High Court (within the meaning mentioned in subsection (5) above) under section 11(6) of the said Act of 1986 prejudices any enactment or rule of law in respect of the recording of deeds relating to heritable property in Scotland or the registration of interests in such property.

Provisions supplementary to section 27

28.—(1) The Court of Session shall, on application made to it in accordance with rules of court for registration of an order to which section 27 of this Act applies, direct that the order shall, in accordance with such rules, be registered in that Court.

(2) Subsections (1) and (3) of section 27 of this Act and subsection (1) above are subject to any provision made by rules of court—

(*a*) as to the manner in which and conditions subject to which orders to which that section applies are to be enforced in Scotland,

(*b*) for the sisting of proceedings for enforcement of such an order,

(*c*) for the modification or cancellation of the registration of such an order if the order is modified or revoked or ceases to have effect.

(3) This section and section 27 of this Act are without prejudice to any enactment or rule of law as to the effect of notice or the want of it in relation to orders of the High Court (within the meaning mentioned in section 27(5) of this Act).

(4) The Court of Session shall have the like power to make an order under section 1 of the Administration of Justice (Scotland) Act 1972 (extended power to order inspection of documents etc.) in relation to proceedings brought or likely to be brought under the Drug Trafficking Offences Act 1986 in the High Court (within the meaning mentioned in section 27(5) of this Act) as if those proceedings had been brought or were likely to be brought in the Court of Session.

(5) The Court of Session may, additionally, for the purpose of—

(*a*) assisting the achievement in Scotland of the purposes of orders to which section 27 of this Act applies, or

(*b*) assisting receivers performing functions there under or for the purposes of section 8, 11 or 12 of the said Act of 1986,

make such orders and do otherwise as seems to it appropriate.

(6) A document purporting to be a copy of an order under or for the purposes of the Drug Trafficking Offences Act 1986 by the High Court (within the meaning mentioned in section 27(5) of this Act) and to be certified as such by a proper officer of that Court shall, in Scotland, be sufficient evidence of the order.

Enforcement of Northern Ireland orders

29.—(1) Her Majesty may by Order in Council provide that, for the purposes of sections 8 to 25 and 33 to 35 of this Act, this Act shall have effect as if—

(*a*) references to confiscation orders included a reference to orders made by courts in Northern Ireland which appear to Her Majesty to correspond to confiscation orders;

(*b*) references to offences to which section 1 of this Act relates included a reference to any offence under the law of Northern Ireland (not being an offence to which that section relates) which appears to Her Majesty to correspond to such an offence; and

(*c*) such other modifications were made as may be specified in the Order in Council, being modifications which appear to Her Majesty to be requisite or desirable having regard to procedural differences which may for the time being exist between Scotland and Northern Ireland; and without prejudice to the generality of this paragraph modifications may include provision as to the circumstances in which proceedings in Northern Ireland are to be treated for the purposes of those sections as instituted or as concluded.

(2) An Order in Council under this section may provide for the sections mentioned in subsection (1) above to have effect in relation to anything

done or to be done in Northern Ireland subject to such further modifications as may be specified in the order.

(3) An Order in Council under this section may contain such incidental, consequential and transitional provisions as Her Majesty considers expedient.

(4) An Order in Council under this section shall not be made unless a draft of the order has been laid before Parliament and approved by resolution of each House of Parliament.

Enforcement of other external orders
[1] **30.**—(1) Her Majesty may by Order in Council—

(*a*) direct in relation to a country or territory outside the United Kingdom designated by the order ("a designated country") that, subject to such modifications as may be specified, this Part of this Act shall apply to external confiscation orders and to proceedings which have been or are to be instituted in the designated country and may result in an external confiscation order being made there;

(*b*) make—

(i) such provision in connection with the taking of action in the designated country with a view to satisfying a confiscation order; and

(ii) such provision as to evidence or proof of any matter for the purposes of this section and section 30A of this Act; and

(iii) such incidental, consequential and transitional provision, as appears to Her Majesty to be expedient; and

(*c*) without prejudice to the generality of this subsection, direct that in such circumstances as may be specified proceeds which arise out of action taken in the designated country with a view to satisfying a confiscation order shall be treated as reducing the amount payable under the order to such extent as may be specified.

(2) In this Part of this Act—

"external confiscation order" means an order made by a court in a designated country for the purpose of recovering payments or other rewards received in connection with drug trafficking or their value; and

"modifications" includes additions, alterations and omissions.

(3) An Order in Council under this section may make different provision for different cases or classes of case.

(4) The power to make an Order in Council under this section includes power to modify this Part of this Act in such a way as to confer power on a person to exercise a discretion.

(5) An Order in Council under this section shall not be made unless a draft of the Order has been laid before Parliament and approved by a resolution of each House of Parliament.

NOTE
[1] Substituted by the Law Reform (Miscellaneous Provisions) (Scotland) Act 1990 (c. 40), s. 63.

Registration of external confiscation orders
[1] **30A.**—(1) On an application made by or on behalf of the Government

of a designated country, the Court of Session may register an external confiscation order made there if—

(*a*) it is satisfied that at the time of registration the order is in force and not subject to appeal;

(*b*) it is satisfied, where the person against whom the order is made did not appear in the proceedings, that he received notice of the proceedings in sufficient time to enable him to defend them; and

(*c*) it is of the opinion that enforcing the order in Scotland would not be contrary to the interests of justice.

(2) In subsection (1) above "appeal" includes—

(*a*) any proceedings by way of discharging or setting aside a judgment; and

(*b*) an application for a new trial or a stay of execution.

(3) The Court of Session shall cancel the registration of an external confiscation order if it appears to the court that the order has been satisfied by payment of the amount due under it or by the person against whom it was made serving imprisonment in default of payment or by any other means.

NOTE
[1] Inserted by the Law Reform (Miscellaneous Provisions) (Scotland) Act 1990 (c. 40), s. 63.

Enforcement in England and Wales
31. The following section shall be inserted before section 25 of the Drug Trafficking Offences Act 1986—

"Recognition and enforcement of orders and functions under Part I of the Criminal Justice (Scotland) Act 1987

24A.—(1) Her Majesty may by Order in Council make such provision as Her Majesty considers expedient for the purpose—

(*a*) of enabling property in England and Wales which is realisable property for the purposes of Part I of the Criminal Justice (Scotland) Act 1987 to be used or realised for the payment of any amount payable under a confiscation order made under that Part of that Act; and

(*b*) of securing that, where no confiscation order has been made under that Part of that Act, property in England and Wales which is realisable property for the purposes of that Part of that Act is available, in the event that such an order is so made, to be used or realised for the payment of any amount payable under it.

(2) Without prejudice to the generality of the power conferred by subsection (1) above, an Order in Council under this section may—

(*a*) provide that, subject to any specified conditions—

(i)   the functions of a person appointed under section 13 of the Criminal Justice (Scotland) Act 1987; and

(ii)   such descriptions of orders made under or for the purposes of Part I of the Criminal Justice (Scotland) Act 1987 as may be specified;

shall have effect in the law of England and Wales;

(*b*) make provision—

    (i)   for the registration in the High Court of such descriptions of orders made under or for the purposes of that Part of that Act as may be specified; and

    (ii) for the High Court to have in relation to the enforcement of orders made under or for the purposes of that Part of that Act which are so registered such powers as may be specified; and

  (c) make provision as to the proof in England and Wales of orders made under or for the purposes of that Part of that Act.

(3) In subsection (2) above "specified" means specified in an Order in Council under this section.

(4) An Order in Council under this section may amend or apply, with or without modifications, any enactment.

(5) An Order in Council under this section may contain such incidental, consequential and transitional provisions as Her Majesty considers expedient.

(6) An Order in Council under this section shall not be made unless a draft of the Order has been laid before Parliament and approved by resolution of each House of Parliament.".

Order in Council as regards taking of action in designated country

32.—(1) Her Majesty may by Order in Council make such provision in connection with the taking of action in a designated country in consequence of the making of a restraint order or of a confiscation order as appears to Her Majesty to be expedient; and without prejudice to the generality of this subsection such provision may include a direction that in such circumstances as may be specified proceeds arising out of action taken in that country with a view to satisfying a confiscation order which are retained there shall nevertheless be treated as reducing the amount payable under the confiscation order to such extent as may be specified.

(2) Subsections (9)(*a*), (10), (11) and (12) of section 30 of this Act shall apply in respect of Orders in Council under this section as they apply in respect of Orders in Council under that section.

Sequestration etc. of estate comprising realisable property

Sequestration of person holding realisable property

33.—(1) Where the estate of a person who holds realisable property is sequestrated—

  (*a*) property for the time being subject to a restraint order made before the date of sequestration (within the meaning of section 12(4) of the 1985 Act); and

  (*b*) any proceeds of property realised by virtue of section 13(1) of this Act for the time being in the hands of an administrator appointed under that section,

is excluded from the debtor's estate for the purposes of that Act.

¹ (2) Where an award of sequestration has been made, the powers conferred on the Court of Session by sections 8, 11 to 13, 16, 24, 27 and 28 of this Act or on an administrator appointed under subsection (1) of the said section 13 shall not be exercised in relation to—

(*a*) property comprised in the whole estate of the debtor (within the meaning of section 31(8) of the 1985 Act); or

(*b*) any income of the debtor which has been ordered, under subsection (2) of section 32 of that Act, to be paid to the permanent trustee or any estate which, under subsection (10) of section 31 of that Act or subsection (6) of the said section 32 of that Act, vests in the permanent trustee,

and it shall not be competent to submit a claim in relation to the confiscation order to the permanent trustee in accordance with section 48 of that Act.

(3) Nothing in the 1985 Act shall be taken as restricting, or enabling the restriction of, the exercise of the powers so conferred.

(4) Where, during the period before sequestration is awarded, an interim trustee stands appointed under the proviso to section 13(1) of the 1985 Act and any property in the debtor's estate is subject to a restraint order, the powers conferred on the interim trustee by virtue of that Act do not apply to property for the time being subject to the restraint order.

(5) Where the estate of a person is sequestrated and he has directly or indirectly made an implicative gift—

(*a*) no decree shall, at any time when proceedings as regards an offence to which section 1 of this Act relates have been instituted against him and have not been concluded or when property of the person to whom the gift was made is subject to a restraint order, be granted under section 34 or 36 of the 1985 Act (gratuitous alienations and unfair preferences) in respect of the making of the gift; and

(*b*) any decree granted under either of the said sections 34 and 36 after the conclusion of the proceedings shall take into account any realisation under this Act of property held by the person to whom the gift was made.

(6) In any case in which, notwithstanding the coming into force of the 1985 Act, the Bankruptcy (Scotland) Act 1913 applies to a sequestration, subsection (2) above shall have effect as if for paragraphs (*a*) and (*b*) thereof there were substituted the following paragraphs—

"(*a*) property comprised in the whole property of the debtor which vests in the trustee under section 97 of the Bankruptcy (Scotland) Act 1913,

(*b*) any income of the bankrupt which has been ordered, under subsection (2) of section 98 of that Act, to be paid to the trustee or any estate which, under subsection (1) of that section, vests in the trustee,";

and subsection (3) above shall have effect as if, for the reference in it to the 1985 Act, there were substituted a reference to the said Act of 1913.

NOTE
[1] As amended by the Housing Act 1988 (c. 50), s. 140, Sched. 17, para. 81.

Bankruptcy in England and Wales of person holding realisable property
34.—(1) Where a person who holds realisable property is adjudged bankrupt—

(*a*) property for the time being subject to a restraint order made before the order adjudging him bankrupt, and (*b*) any proceeds of property realised by virtue of section 13(1) of this Act for the time being in the hands of an administrator appointed under that section;

is excluded from the bankrupt's estate for the purposes of Part IX of the Insolvency Act 1986.

[1] (2) Where a person has been adjudged bankrupt, the powers conferred on the Court of Session by sections 8, 11 to 13, 16, 24, 27 and 28 of this Act or on an administrator appointed under subsection (1) of the said section 13 shall not be exercised in relation to—

(*a*) property for the time being comprised in the bankrupt's estate for the purposes of the said Part IX,

(*b*) property in respect of which his trustee in bankruptcy may (without leave of the court) serve a notice under section 307, 308 or 308A of the Insolvency Act 1986 (after-acquired property and tools, clothes etc. exceeding value of reasonable replacement and certain tenancies), and

(*c*) property which is to be applied for the benefit of creditors of the bankrupt by virtue of a condition imposed under section 280(2)(*c*) of the Insolvency Act 1986.

(3) Nothing in the Insolvency Act 1986 shall be taken as restricting, or enabling the restriction of, the exercise of the powers so conferred.

(4) Where, in the case of a debtor, an interim receiver stands appointed under section 286 of the Insolvency Act 1986 and any property of the debtor is subject to a restraint order the powers conferred on the receiver by virtue of that Act do not apply to property for the time being subject to the restraint order.

(5) Where a person is adjudged bankrupt and has directly or indirectly made an implicative gift—

(*a*) no order shall, at any time when proceedings for a drug trafficking offence have been instituted against him and have not been concluded or when property of the person to whom the gift was made is subject to a restraint order, be made under section 339 or 423 of the Insolvency Act 1986 (avoidance of certain transactions) in respect of the making of the gift, and

(*b*) any order made under either of those sections after the conclusion of the proceedings shall take into account any realisation under this Act of property held by the person to whom the gift was made.

[2] (6) In any case in which a petition in bankruptcy was presented, or a receiving order or adjudication in bankruptcy was made, before the date on which the Insolvency Act 1986 came into force, subsections (2) to (5) above have effect with the following modifications—

(*a*) for references to the bankrupt's estate for the purposes of Part IX of that Act there are substituted references to the property of the bankrupt for the purposes of the Bankruptcy Act 1914,

(*b*) for references to the said Act of 1986 and to sections 280(2)(*c*), 286, 339, and 423 of that Act there are respectively substituted references to the said Act of 1914 and to sections 26(2), 8, 27 and 42 of that Act,

(*c*) the references in subsection (4) to an interim receiver appointed as there mentioned include, where a receiving order has been made, a reference to the receiver constituted by virtue of section 7 of the said Act of 1914, and

(*d*) subsection (2)(*b*).

NOTES
[1] As amended by the Housing Act 1988 (c. 50), s. 140, Sched. 7, para. 82.
[2] As amended by the Criminal Justice Act 1988 (c. 33), s. 103, Sched. 5, para. 22 and Sched. 8, para. 16.

Winding up company holding realisable property
   35.—(1) Where realisable property is held by a company and an order for the winding up of the company has been made or a resolution has been passed by the company for the voluntary winding up, the functions of the liquidator (or any provisional liquidator) shall not be exercisable in relation to—
   (*a*) property for the time being subject to a restraint order made before the relevant time, and
   (*b*) any proceeds of property realised by virtue of section 13(1) of this Act for the time being in the hands of an administrator appointed under that section.
   (2) Where, in the case of a company, such an order has been made or such a resolution has been passed, the powers conferred on the Court of Session by sections 8, 11 to 13, 16, 24, 27 and 28 of this Act or on an administrator appointed under subsection (1) of the said section 13 shall not be exercised in relation to any realisable property held by the company in relation to which the functions of the liquidator are exercisable—
   (*a*) so as to inhibit the liquidator from exercising those functions for the purpose of distributing any property held by the company to the company's creditors, or
   (*b*) so as to prevent the payment out of any property of expenses (including the remuneration of the liquidator or any provisional liquidator) properly incurred in the winding up in respect of the property.
   (3) Nothing in the Insolvency Act 1986 shall be taken as restricting, or enabling the restriction of, the exercise of the powers so conferred.
   (4) For the purposes of the application of Parts IV and V of the Insolvency Act 1986 (winding up of registered companies and winding up of unregistered companies) to a company which the Court of Session has jurisdiction to wind up, a person is not a creditor in so far as any sum due to him by the company is due in respect of a confiscation order (whether under this Act or under and within the meaning of section 1 of the Drug Trafficking Offences Act 1986 or any corresponding provision in Northern Ireland).
   (5) In this section—
   "company" means any company which may be wound up under the Insolvency Act 1986; and
   "the relevant time" means—
      (*a*) where no order for the winding up of the company has been made, the time of the passing of the resolution for voluntary winding up,
      (*b*) where such an order has been made and, before the

presentation of the petition for the winding up of the company by the court, such a resolution had been passed by the company, the time of the passing of the resolution, and

(c) in any other case where such an order has been made, the time of the making of the order.

(6) In any case in which a winding up of a company commenced, or is treated as having commenced, before the date on which the Insolvency Act 1986 came into force, subsections (2) to (5) above have effect with the substitution for references to that Act of references to the Companies Act 1985.

Property subject to floating charge

36.—(1) Where any property held subject to a floating charge by a company is realisable property and a receiver has been appointed by, or on the application of, the holder of the charge, the powers of the receiver in relation to the property so held shall not be exercisable in relation to—

(a) so much of it as is for the time being subject to a restraint order made before the appointment of the receiver, and

(b) any proceeds of property realised by virtue of section 13(1) of this Act for the time being in the hands of an administrator appointed under that section.

(2) Where, in the case of a company, such an appointment has been made, the powers conferred on the Court of Session by sections 8, 11 to 13, 16 and 24 of this Act or on an administrator appointed under subsection (1) of the said section 13 shall not be exercised in relation to any realisable property held by the company in relation to which the powers of the receiver are exercisable—

(a) so as to inhibit the receiver from exercising his powers for the purpose of distributing any property held by the company to the company's creditors, or

(b) so as to prevent the payment out of any property of expenses (including the remuneration of the receiver) properly incurred in the exercise of the receiver's powers in respect of the property.

(3) Nothing in the Insolvency Act 1986, shall be taken as restricting, or enabling the restriction of, the exercise of the powers so conferred.

(4) In this section—

"company" has the same meaning as in section 35 of this Act; and

"floating charge" includes a floating charge within the meaning given by section 462 of the Companies Act 1985 (power of incorporated company to create floating charge).

(5) In any case in which a receiver was appointed as is mentioned in subsection (1) above before the date on which the Insolvency Act 1986 came into force, subsections (2) to (4) above have effect with the substitution for references to that Act of references to the Companies Act 1985.

Insolvency practitioners dealing with property subject to restraint order

37.—(1) Without prejudice to the generality of any enactment contained in the Insolvency Act 1986 or the 1985 Act, where—

(a) any person acting as an insolvency practitioner seizes or disposes of any property in relation to which his functions are, because that property is for the time being subject to a restraint order, not exercisable; and

(*b*) at the time of the seizure or disposal he believes, and has reasonable grounds for believing, that he is entitled (whether in pursuance of a court order or otherwise) to seize or dispose of that property,

he shall not be liable to any person in respect of any loss or damage resulting from the seizure or disposal except in so far as the loss or damage is caused by the insolvency practitioner's negligence; and the insolvency practitioner shall have a lien on the property, or the proceeds of its sale, for such of his expenses as were incurred in connection with the liquidation, sequestration or other proceedings in relation to which the seizure or disposal purported to take place and for so much of his remuneration as may reasonably be assigned for his actings in connection with those proceedings.

(2) Any person who, acting as an insolvency practitioner, incurs expenses—

(*a*) in respect of such property as is mentioned in paragraph (*a*) of subsection (1) above and in so doing does not know and has no reasonable grounds to believe that the property is for the time being subject to a restraint order; or

(*b*) other than in respect of such property as is so mentioned, being expenses which, but for the effect of a restraint order, might have been met by taking possession of and realising the property,

shall be entitled (whether or not he has seized or disposed of that property so as to have a lien under that subsection) to payment of those expenses under section 16(1) or (3)(*a*) of this Act.

(3) In the foregoing provisions of this section, the expression "acting as an insolvency practitioner" shall be construed in accordance with section 388 (interpretation) of the said Act of 1986 except that for the purposes of such construction the reference in subsection (2)(*a*) of that section to a permanent or interim trustee in a sequestration shall be taken to include a reference to a trustee in a sequestration and subsection (5) of that section (which provides that nothing in the section is to apply to anything done by the official receiver) shall be disregarded; and the expression shall also comprehend the official receiver acting as receiver or manager of the property.

Investigations and disclosure of information

Order to make material available

38.—(1) The procurator fiscal may, for the purposes of an investigation into drug trafficking, apply to the sheriff for an order under subsection (2) below in relation to particular material or material of a particular description.

(2) If on such an application the sheriff is satisfied that the conditions in subsection (4) below are fulfilled, he may make an order that the person who appears to him to be in possession of the material to which the application relates shall—

(*a*) produce it to a constable or person commissioned by the Commissioners of Customs and Excise for him to take away, or

(*b*) give a constable or person so commissioned access to it,
within such period as the order may specify.

This subsection is subject to section 41(11) of this Act.

(3) The period to be specified in an order under subsection (2) above
shall be seven days unless it appears to the sheriff that a longer or shorter
period would be appropriate in the particular circumstances of the
application.

(4) The conditions referred to in subsection (2) above are—

(*a*) that there are reasonable grounds for suspecting that a specified
person has carried on, or has derived financial or other rewards
from, drug trafficking,

(*b*) that there are reasonable grounds for suspecting that the material
to which the application relates—

    (i) is likely to be of substantial value (whether by itself or together
with other material) to the investigation for the purpose of
which the application is made, and

    (ii) does not consist of or include items subject to legal privilege,
and

(*c*) that there are reasonable grounds for believing that it is in the
public interest, having regard—

    (i) to the benefit likely to accrue to the investigation if the
material is obtained, and

    (ii) to the circumstances under which the person in possession of
the material holds it,

that the material should be produced or that access to it should be
given.

[1] (5) Where the sheriff makes an order under subsection (2)(*b*) above
in relation to material on any premises he may, on the application of the
procurator fiscal, order any person who appears to him to be entitled to
grant entry to the premises to allow a constable or person commissioned
as aforesaid to enter the premises to obtain access to the material.

(6) Provision may be made by rules of court as to—

(*a*) the discharge and variation of orders under this section, and

(*b*) proceedings relating to such orders.

(7) Where the material to which an application under this section
relates consists of information contained in a computer—

(*a*) an order under subsection (2)(*a*) above shall have effect as an order
to produce the material in a form in which it can be taken away and
in which it is visible and legible, and

(*b*) an order under subsection (2)(*b*) above shall have effect as an order
to give access to the material in a form in which it is visible and
legible.

(8) An order under subsection (2) above—

(*a*) shall not confer any right to production of, or access to, items
subject to legal privilege,

(*b*) shall have effect notwithstanding any obligation as to secrecy or
other restriction upon the disclosure of information imposed by
statute or otherwise, and

(*c*) may be made in relation to material in the possession of an
authorised government department.

NOTE
[1] As amended by the Criminal Justice Act 1988 (c. 33), s. 103, Sched. 5, para. 23 and Sched. 8, para. 16.

Authority for search
39.—(1) The procurator fiscal may, for the purpose of an investigation into drug trafficking, apply to the sheriff for a warrant under this section in relation to specified premises.

(2) On such application the sheriff may issue a warrant authorising a constable, or person commissioned by the Commissioners of Customs and Excise, to enter and search the premises if the sheriff is satisfied—

(*a*) that an order made under section 38 of this Act in relation to material on the premises has not been complied with, or

(*b*) that the conditions in subsection (3) below are fulfilled, or

(*c*) that the conditions in subsection (4) below are fulfilled.

(3) The conditions referred to in subsection (2)(*b*) above are—

(*a*) that there are reasonable grounds for suspecting that a specified person has carried on, or has derived financial or other rewards from, drug trafficking, and

(*b*) that the conditions in section 38(4)(*b*) and (*c*) of this Act are fulfilled in relation to any material on the premises, and

(*c*) that it would not be appropriate to make an order under that section in relation to the material because—

   (i) it is not practicable to communicate with any person entitled to produce the material, or

   (ii) it is not practicable to communicate with any person entitled to grant access to the material or entitled to grant entry to the premises on which the material is situated, or

   (iii) the investigation for the purposes of which the application is made might be seriously prejudiced unless a constable or person commissioned as aforesaid could secure immediate access to the material.

(4) The conditions referred to in subsection (2)(*c*) above are—

(*a*) that there are reasonable grounds for suspecting that a specified person has carried on, or has derived financial or other rewards from, drug trafficking, and

(*b*) that there are reasonable grounds for suspecting that there is on the premises material relating to the specified person or to drug trafficking which is likely to be of substantial value (whether by itself or together with other material) to the investigation for the purpose of which the application is made, but that the material cannot at the time of the application be particularised, and

(*c*) that—

   (i) it is not practicable to communicate with any person entitled to grant entry to the premises, or

   (ii) entry to the premises will not be granted unless a warrant is produced, or

   (iii) the investigation for the purpose of which the application is made might be seriously prejudiced unless a constable or person commissioned as aforesaid arriving at the premises could secure immediate entry to them.

(5) Where a constable or person commissioned as aforesaid has entered premises in the execution of a warrant issued under this section, he may seize and retain any material, other than items subject to legal privilege, which is likely to be of substantial value (whether by itself or together with other material) to the investigation for the purpose of which the warrant was issued.

Interpretation of sections 38 and 39

40. In sections 38 and 39 of this Act—

"items subject to legal privilege" means—

(*a*) communications between a professional legal adviser and his client, or

(*b*) communications made in connection with or in contemplation of legal proceedings and for the purposes of these proceedings,

being communications which would in legal proceedings be protected from disclosure by virtue of any rule of law relating to the confidentiality of communications; and

"premises" includes any place and, in particular, includes—

(*a*) any vehicle, vessel, aircraft or hovercraft,

(*b*) any offshore installation within the meaning of section 1 of the Mineral Workings (Offshore Installations) Act 1971, and

(*c*) any tent or moveable structure.

Disclosure of information held by government departments

41.—(1) Subject to subsection (4) below, the Court of Session may on an application by the Lord Advocate order any material mentioned in subsection (3) below which is in the possession of an authorised government department to be produced to the Court within such period as the Court may specify.

(2) The power to make an order under subsection (1) above is exercisable if—

(*a*) the powers conferred on the Court by subsection (1) of section 8 of this Act are exercisable by virtue of paragraph (*a*) thereof, or

(*b*) those powers are exercisable by virtue of paragraph (*b*) of subsection (1) of that section and the Court has made a restraint order which has not been recalled;

but, where the power to make an order under subsection (1) above is exercisable by virtue only of paragraph (*b*) above, subsection (4) of section 9 of this Act shall for the purposes of this section apply in relation to that order as the said subsection (4) applies, for the purposes of that section, in relation to a restraint order made by virtue of paragraph (*b*) of subsection (1) of the said section 8.

(3) The material referred to in subsection (1) above is any material which—

(*a*) has been submitted to an officer of an authorised government department by a person who holds, or has at any time held, realisable property,

(*b*) has been made by an officer of an authorised government department in relation to such a person, or

(*c*) is correspondence which passed between an officer of an authorised government department and such a person;

and an order under that subsection may require the production of all such material or of a particular description of such material, being material in the possession of the department concerned.

(4) An order under subsection (1) above shall not require the production of any material unless it appears to the Court of Session that the material is likely to contain information that would facilitate the exercise of the powers conferred on the Court by section 8, 13 or 24 of this Act or on an administrator appointed under subsection (1) of the said section 13.

(5) The Court may by order authorise the disclosure to such an administrator of any material produced under subsection (1) above or any part of such material; but the Court shall not make an order under this subsection unless a reasonable opportunity has been given for an officer of the department to make representations to the Court.

(6) Material disclosed in pursuance of an order under subsection (5) above may, subject to any conditions contained in the order, be further disclosed for the purposes of the functions under this Act of the administrator or the High Court.

(7) The Court of Session may by order authorise the disclosure to a person mentioned in subsection (8) below of any material produced under subsection (1) above or any part of such material; but the Court shall not make an order under this subsection unless—

    (*a*) a reasonable opportunity has been given for an officer of the department to make representations to the Court, and

    (*b*) it appears to the Court that the material is likely to be of substantial value in exercising functions relating to drug trafficking.

(8) The persons referred to in subsection (7) above are—

    (*a*) a constable,

    (*b*) the Lord Advocate or any procurator fiscal, and

    (*c*) a person commissioned by the Commissioners of Customs and Excise.

(9) Material disclosed in pursuance of an order under subsection (7) above may, subject to any conditions contained in the order, be further disclosed for the purposes of functions relating to drug trafficking.

(10) Material may be produced or disclosed in pursuance of this section notwithstanding any obligation as to secrecy or other restriction upon the disclosure of information imposed by statute or otherwise.

(11) An order under subsection (1) above and, in the case of material in the possession of an authorised government department, an order under section 38(2) of this Act may require any officer of the department (whether named in the order or not) who may for the time being be in possession of the material concerned to comply with such order; and any such order shall be served as if the proceedings were civil proceedings against the department.

(12) The person on whom an order under subsection (1) above is served—

    (*a*) shall take all reasonable steps to bring it to the attention of the officer concerned, and

    (*b*) if the order is not brought to that officer's attention within the period referred to in subsection (1) above, shall report the reasons for the failure to the Court of Session;

and it shall also be the duty of any other officer of the department in receipt of the order to take such steps as are mentioned in paragraph (*a*) above.

Offences

Offence of prejudicing investigation

42.—(1) A person who, knowing or suspecting that an investigation into drug trafficking is taking place, does anything which is likely to prejudice the investigation is guilty of an offence.

(2) In proceedings against a person for an offence under subsection (1) above, it is a defence to prove—

(*a*) that he did not know or suspect, or have reasonable grounds to suspect, that by acting as he did he was likely to prejudice the investigation, or

(*b*) that he had lawful authority or reasonable excuse for acting as he did.

(3) A person guilty of an offence under subsection (1) above shall be liable—

(*a*) on conviction on indictment, to imprisonment for a term not exceeding five years or to a fine or to both, and

(*b*) on summary conviction, to imprisonment for a term not exceeding six months or to a fine not exceeding the statutory maximum or to both.

Offence of assisting another to retain the proceeds of drug trafficking

43.—(1) Subject to subsection (3)(*b*) below, a person shall be guilty of an offence if, knowing or suspecting that another person (in this section referred to as "A") is a person who carries on, or has carried on, or has derived financial or other rewards from, drug trafficking, he enters into, or is otherwise concerned in, an arrangement whereby—

(*a*) the retention or control, by or on behalf of A, of A's proceeds of drug trafficking is facilitated (whether by concealment, removal from the jurisdiction, transfer to nominees or otherwise); or

(*b*) A's proceeds of drug trafficking—

(i) are used to secure that funds are placed at A's disposal, or

(ii) are used for A's benefit to acquire property by way of investment.

(2) In this section, references to proceeds of drug trafficking shall be construed as including any property which, whether in whole or in part, directly or indirectly constitutes such proceeds.

(3) Where a person discloses to a constable or to a person commissioned by the Commissioners of Customs and Excise a suspicion or belief that any funds or investments are derived from or used in connection with drug trafficking or any matter on which such a suspicion or belief is based—

(*a*) the disclosure shall not be treated as a breach of any restriction imposed by contract on the disclosure of information; and

(*b*) if the disclosure relates to an arrangement entry into which, or concern in which, by the person would (but for this paragraph)

contravene subsection (1) above, he does not commit an offence under that subsection if—
 (i) the disclosure is made before, with the consent of the constable or as the case may be of the person so commissioned, he enters into, or becomes concerned in, that arrangement, or
 (ii) though made after he enters into, or becomes concerned in, that arrangement, it is made on his own initiative and as soon as it is reasonable for him to do so.

(4) In proceedings against a person for an offence under subsection (1) above, it shall be a defence to prove—
 (*a*) that he did not know or suspect that the arrangement related to any person's proceeds of drug trafficking; or
 (*b*) that he did not know or suspect that by the arrangement the retention or control by or on behalf of A of any property was facilitated or, as the case may be, that by the arrangement any property was used as mentioned in subsection (1) above; or
 (*c*) that—
 (i) he intended to disclose to a constable or to a person commissioned as aforesaid such a suspicion, belief or matter as is mentioned in subsection (3) above in relation to the arrangement, but
 (ii) there is reasonable excuse for his failure to make disclosure in accordance with paragraph (*b*) of that subsection.

(5) A person guilty of an offence under subsection (1) above shall be liable—
 (*a*) on conviction on indictment, to imprisonment for a term not exceeding 14 years or to a fine or to both; and
 (*b*) on summary conviction, to imprisonment for a term not exceeding six months or to a fine not exceeding the statutory maximum or to both.

Offences relating to controlled drugs: fines
44.—(1) Without prejudice to section 395(1) of the 1975 Act (fines) as applied by section 194 of that Act but subject to the proviso to subsection (1) of section 2 of this Act, where a person is convicted on indictment of an offence to which this section relates and sentenced in respect of that offence to a period of imprisonment or detention, the Court where—
 (*a*) paragraph (*b*) below does not apply shall, unless it is satisfied that for any reason it would be inappropriate to do so, also impose a fine;
 (*b*) it makes an order under section 1(1) of this Act as regards the person, may also impose a fine.

(2) In determining the amount of a fine imposed under paragraph (*a*) of subsection (1) above, the Court shall have regard to any profits likely to have been made by the person from the crime in respect of which he has been convicted.

(3) This section relates to the same offences as does section 1 of this Act.

(4) Where in any proceedings a fine has been imposed by virtue of subsection (1) above as regards a person and a period of imprisonment or

detention is imposed on him in default of payment of its amount (or as the case may be of an instalment thereof), that period shall run from the expiry of any other period of imprisonment or detention (not being one of life imprisonment or detention for life) imposed on him in the proceedings.

(5) The reference in subsection (4) above to "any other period of imprisonment or detention imposed" includes (without prejudice to the generality of the expression) a reference to such a period imposed on default of payment of a fine (or instalment thereof) or of a confiscation order (or instalment thereof); but only where that default has occurred before the warrant for imprisonment is issued for the default in relation to the fine imposed by virtue of subsection (1) of this section.

Minor amendments, service, notice and interpretation

Minor amendments in relation to drug trafficking

45.—(1) Section 28 of the Bankruptcy Act 1914 (effect of order of discharge) shall have effect as if amounts payable under confiscation orders were debts excepted under subsection (1)(*a*) of that section.

(2) In section 1(2)(*a*) of the Rehabilitation of Offenders Act 1974 (failure to pay fines etc., not to prevent person becoming rehabilitated) the reference to a fine or other sum adjudged to be paid by or on a conviction does not include a reference to an amount payable under a confiscation order.

(3) In subsection (4A) of section 18 of the Civil Jurisdiction and Judgments Act 1982 (exceptions as to enforcement of U.K. judgments in other parts of U.K.), at the end there shall be added the following words—

"; or as respects the enforcement in England and Wales of orders made by the Court of Session under or for the purposes of Part I of the Criminal Justice (Scotland) Act 1987".

(4) Section 281(4) of the Insolvency Act 1986 (discharge of bankrupt not to release him from liabilities in respect of fines, etc.) shall have effect as if the reference to a fine included a reference to a confiscation order.

(5) In the 1985 Act—

(*a*) in section 5(4) (interpretation)—

    (i) after the words "future debts" there shall be inserted the words "or amounts payable under a confiscation order"; and

    (ii) at the end there shall be added the words "; and in the foregoing provisions of this subsection 'confiscation order' has the meaning assigned by section 1(1) of the Criminal Justice (Scotland) Act 1987 or by section 1(8) of the Drug Trafficking Offences Act 1986";

(*b*) in section 7(1) (constitution of apparent insolvency)—

    (i) in paragraph (*b*), at the beginning there shall be inserted the words "not being a person whose property is for the time being affected by a restraint order or subject to a confiscation, or charging, order,";

    (ii) in paragraph (*c*), after the words "became due" there shall be inserted the words "or that but for his property being affected by a restraint order or subject to a confiscation, or charging, order he would be able to do so"; and

(iii) at the end there shall be added the words "In paragraph (*d*) above, "liquid debt" does not include a sum payable under a confiscation order; and in the foregoing provisions of this subsection—

"charging order" has the meaning assigned by section 9(2) of the Drug Trafficking Offences Act 1986;

"confiscation order" has the meaning assigned by section 1(1) of the Criminal Justice (Scotland) Act 1987 or by section 1(8) of the said Act of 1986; and

"restraint order" has the meaning assigned by section 9 of the said Act of 1987 or by section 8 of the said Act of 1986."; and

(*c*) section 55(2) (discharge of debtor not to release him from liabilities in respect of fines etc.) shall have effect as if the reference to a fine included a reference to a confiscation order.

(6) In section 231 of the 1975 Act (intimation of intention to appeal)—

(*a*) in subsection (1), after the words "236B(2) of this Act" there shall be inserted the words "and to section 2(2) of the Criminal Justice (Scotland) Act 1987 (postponed confiscation orders)";

(*b*) in subsection (4), at the beginning there shall be inserted the words "Subject to subsection (5) below,"; and

(*c*) after subsection (4) there shall be added the following subsection—

"(5) Without prejudice to subsection (2) of section 2 of the said Act of 1987, the reference in subsection (4) above to "the day on which sentence is passed in open court" shall, in relation to any case in which, under subsection (1) of that section, a decision has been postponed for a period, be construed as a reference to the day on which that decision is made (whether or not a confiscation order is then made or any other sentence is then passed).".

(7) In the Drug Trafficking Offences Act 1986—

(*a*) at the end of section 2(5) (assessing the proceeds of drug trafficking) there shall be inserted the words—

"References in this subsection to a confiscation order include a reference to a confiscation order within the meaning of Part I of the Criminal Justice (Scotland) Act 1987";

(*b*) in section 8 (restraint orders)—

(i) in subsection (8), for the words "the High Court has made a restraint order" there shall be substituted the words "a restraint order has been made" and at the end of that subsection there shall be added the words—

"In this subsection, the reference to a restraint order includes a reference to a restraint order within the meaning of Part I of the Criminal Justice (Scotland) Act 1987, and, in relation to such an order, "realisable property" has the same meaning as in that Part"; and

(ii) in subsection (9), for the words "court's directions" there shall be substituted the words "directions of the court which made the order";

(*c*) in section 16 (sequestration of person holding realisable property)—
    (i) in subsection (2), at the end there shall be added the words ", and it shall not be competent to submit a claim in relation to the confiscation order to the permanent trustee in accordance with section 48 of that Act."; and
    (ii) in subsection (5), in paragraph (*b*)(ii), after the word "disposal" there shall be inserted the words "and for so much of his remuneration as may reasonably be assigned for his actings in that connection"; and in paragraph (*c*), for the words "a lien for any expenses (including his remuneration) properly incurred in respect of the property" there shall be substituted the words "any such lien as is mentioned in paragraph (*b*)(ii) above";
(*d*) in section 19(2)(*b*)(ii) (compensation for loss in consequence of anything done in relation to realisable property by or in pursuance of order of Court of Session), for the words "20, 21 or 22 of this Act" there shall be substituted the words "11 (as applied by subsection (6) of that section), 27 or 28 of the Criminal Justice (Scotland) Act 1987 (inhibition and arrestment of property affected by restraint order and recognition and enforcement of orders under this Act)";
(*e*) in section 33 (power to inspect Land Register etc.)—
    (i) in subsection (2), after paragraph (*c*) there shall be inserted the words— ", or
        (*d*) the Lord Advocate or any person conducting a prosecution in Scotland on his behalf,";
    (ii) in subsection (4)—
        after the words "8 or 11 of this Act" there shall be inserted the words "or by an administrator appointed under section 13 of the Criminal Justice (Scotland) Act 1987 (comparable Scottish provisions)"; and
        in each of paragraphs (*a*) and (*b*), after the word "receiver" there shall be inserted the words "(or administrator)"; and
(*f*) in section 40(4)(*b*) (effect in Scotland), at the beginning there shall be inserted the words "section 3(6)".

Service and notice for purposes of Part I
46. Subject to the provisions of this Part of this Act, provision may be made by rules of court as to the giving of notice required for the purposes of this Part of this Act or the effecting of service so required; and different provision may be so made for different cases or classes of case and for different circumstances or classes of circumstance.

Interpretation of Part I
47.—(1) In this Part of this Act (except where the context otherwise requires)—
    "administrator" shall be construed in accordance with section 13 of this Act;

"associate" shall be construed in accordance with section 74 of the 1985 Act;

"authorised government department" means a government department which is an authorised department for the purposes of the Crown Proceedings Act 1947;

"confiscation order" has the meaning assigned by section 1(1) of this Act;

"designated country" shall be construed in accordance with section 30(2) of this Act;

"drug trafficking" has the meaning assigned by section 1(6) of this Act;

"implicative gift" shall be construed in accordance with section 6 of this Act;

"realisable property" shall be construed in accordance with section 5 of this Act;

"restraint order" has the meaning assigned by section 9 of this Act; and

"the 1985 Act" means the Bankruptcy (Scotland) Act 1985.

(2) This Part of this Act shall (except where the context otherwise requires) be construed as one with the 1975 Act.

(3) This Part of this Act applies to property whether it is situated in Scotland or elsewhere.

(4) References in this Part of this Act—

(*a*) to offences include a reference to offences committed before the commencement of section 1 of this Act; but nothing in this Act imposes any duty or confers any power on any court in or in connection with proceedings against a person for an offence to which that section relates instituted before the commencement of that section;

(*b*) to anything received in connection with drug trafficking include a reference to anything received both in that connection and in some other connection; and

(*c*) to property held by a person include a reference to property vested in the interim or permanent trustee in his sequestration or in his trustee in bankruptcy or liquidator.

(5) For the purposes of this Part of this Act (and subject to subsections (8) and (9) of section 30 of this Act), proceedings are concluded as regards an offence where—

(*a*) the trial diet is deserted *simpliciter*;

(*b*) the accused is acquitted or, under section 101 of the 1975 Act, discharged or liberated;

(*c*) the High Court sentences or otherwise deals with him without making a confiscation order and without postponing a decision as regards making such an order;

(*d*) after such postponement as is mentioned in paragraph (*c*) above, the High Court decides not to make a confiscation order;

(*e*) his conviction is quashed; or

(*f*) either the amount of a confiscation order made has been paid or there remains no liability to imprisonment in default of so much of that amount as is unpaid.

. . . . . .

¹ **Road Traffic Offenders Act 1988**

(1988 c. 53)

NOTE
¹ Many of the following provisions have been prospectively amended by provisions in the
Road Traffic Act 1991 (see pp. 478 to 494 below).

An Act to consolidate certain enactments relating to the
prosecution and punishment (including the punishment
without conviction) of road traffic offences with amendments
to give effect to recommendations of the Law Commission and
the Scottish Law Commission.

[15th November 1988]

PART I

TRIAL

•   •   •   •   •   •

Trial

•   •   •   •   •   •

Jurisdiction of district court in Scotland

10.—(1) Notwithstanding anything in any enactment or rule of law to
the contrary, a district court in Scotland may try—

    (*a*) any fixed penalty offence (within the meaning of Part III of this
       Act), and

    (*b*) any other offence in respect of which a conditional offer (within the
       meaning of sections 75 to 77 of this Act) may be sent.

(2) Subject to subsection (1) above, the district court may not try any
offence involving obligatory endorsement.

•   •   •   •   •   •

Notification of disability

22.—(1) If in any proceedings for an offence committed in respect of a
motor vehicle it appears to the court that the accused may be suffering
from any relevant disability or prospective disability (within the meaning
of Part III of the Road Traffic Act 1988) the court must notify the
Secretary of State.

(2) A notice sent by a court to the Secretary of State in pursuance of this
section must be sent in such manner and to such address and contain such
particulars as the Secretary of State may determine.

•   •   •   •   •   •

PART II

SENTENCE

Introductory

Production of licence

[1] **27.**—(1) Where a person who is the holder of a licence is convicted of an offence involving obligatory endorsement, the court must, before making any order under section 44 of this Act, require the licence [and its counterpart] to be produced to it.

(2) Where a magistrates' court—

(*a*) commits a person who is the holder of a licence to the Crown Court, under section 56 of the Criminal Justice Act 1967 or any enactment to which that section applies, to be dealt with in respect of an offence involving obligatory endorsement, and

(*b*) does not make an order in his case under section 26(1) of this Act, the Crown Court must require the licence [and its counterpart] to be produced to it.

(3) If the holder of the licence has not caused it [and its counterpart] to be delivered, or posted it [and its counterpart], in accordance with section 7 of this Act and does not produce it [and its counterpart] as required then, unless he satisfies the court that he has applied for a new licence and has not received it—

(*a*) he is guilty of an offence, and

(*b*) the licence shall be suspended from the time when its production was required until [it and its counterpart are] produced to the court and shall, while suspended, be of no effect.

(4) Subsection (3) above does not apply where the holder of the licence—

(*a*) has caused a current receipt for the licence [and its counterpart] issued under section 56 of this Act to be delivered to the clerk of the court not later than the day before the date appointed for the hearing, or

(*b*) has posted such a receipt, at such time that in the ordinary course of post it would be delivered not later than that day, in a letter duly addressed to the clerk and either registered or sent by the recorded delivery service, or

(*c*) surrenders such a receipt to the court at the hearing, and produces the licence [and its counterpart] to the court immediately on [their] return.

NOTE

[1] The words in square brackets were substituted or inserted by the Driving Licences (Community Driving Licence) Regulations 1990 (S.I. 1990 No. 144) with effect in relation to licences coming into force on or after June 1, 1990.

Penalty points to be attributed to an offence

28.—(1) Where a person is convicted of an offence involving obligatory or discretionary disqualification, the number of penalty points to be attributed to the offence, subject to subsection (2) below, is—

(*a*) in the case of an offence under a provision of the Traffic Acts specified in column 1 of Part I of Schedule 2 to this Act or an offence specified in column 1 of Part II of that Schedule, the number shown against the provision or offence in the last column or, where a range of numbers is so shown, a number falling within the range, and

(b) in the case of an offence committed by aiding, abetting, counselling or procuring, or inciting to the commission of, an offence involving obligatory disqualification, ten penalty points.

(2) Where a person is convicted of two or more such offences, the number of penalty points to be attributed to those of them that were committed on the same occasion is the number or highest number that would be attributed on a conviction of one of them.

(3) The Secretary of State may by order made by statutory instrument—

(a) alter the number of penalty points shown in subsection (1)(b) above or against a provision or offence specified in that Schedule or, where a range of numbers is shown, alter that range, and

(b) provide for different numbers to be so shown in respect of the same offence committed in different circumstances;

but no such order shall be made unless a draft of it has been laid before Parliament and approved by resolution of each House of Parliament.

Penalty points to be taken into account on conviction

[1] **29.**—(1) Where a person is convicted of an offence involving obligatory or discretionary disqualification, the penalty points to be taken into account on that occasion are (subject to subsection (2) below)—

(a) any that are to be attributed to the offence or offences of which he is convicted, and

(b) any that were on a previous occasion ordered to be endorsed on [the counterpart of] any licence held by him, unless the offender has since that occasion and before the conviction been disqualified under section 34 or 35 of this Act.

(2) If any of the offences was committed more than three years before another, the penalty points in respect of that offence shall not be added to those in respect of the other.

NOTE
[1] The words in square brackets were inserted by the Driving Licences (Community Driving Licence) Regulations 1990 (S.I. 1990 No. 144) with effect in relation to licences coming into force on or after June 1, 1990.

Penalty points: modification where fixed penalty also in question

[1] **30.**—(1) Sections 28 and 29 of this Act shall have effect subject to this section in any case where—

(a) a person is convicted of an offence involving obligatory or discretionary disqualification, and

(b) the court is satisfied that [the counterpart of] his licence has been or is liable to be endorsed under section 57 or 77 of this Act in respect of an offence (referred to in this section as the "connected offence") committed on the same occasion as the offence of which he is convicted.

(2) Subject to section 28(2) of this Act, the number of penalty points to be attributed to the offence of which he is convicted is—

    (*a*) the number of penalty points to be attributed to that offence under section 28(1) of this Act apart from this section, less

    (*b*) the number of penalty points required to be endorsed on [the counterpart of] his licence under section 57 or 77 of this Act in respect of the connected offence.

(3) For the purposes of subsection (2) above, where a range of numbers is shown in the last column of Part I of Schedule 2 to this Act against the provision of the Traffic Acts under which his offence is committed or punishable or in Part II of that Schedule against the offence of which he is convicted, the number of penalty points referred to in subsection (2)(*a*) above shall be taken to be a number falling within that range determined by the court as the number of penalty points to be attributed to the offence under section 28(1) of this Act apart from this section.

NOTE
[1] The words in square brackets were inserted by the Driving Licences (Community Driving Licence) Regulations 1990 (S.I. 1990 No. 144) with effect in relation to licences coming into force on or after June 1, 1990.

Court may take particulars endorsed on licence into consideration
[1] **31.**—(1) Where a person is convicted of an offence involving obligatory endorsement and his licence [and its counterpart are] produced to the court—

    (*a*) any existing endorsement on [the counterpart of] his licence is prima facie evidence of the matters endorsed, and

    (*b*) the court may, in determining what order to make in pursuance of the conviction, take those matters into consideration.

(2) This section has effect notwithstanding anything in sections 311(5) and 357(1) of the Criminal Procedure (Scotland) Act 1975 (requirements as to notices of penalties and previous convictions).

NOTE
[1] The words in square brackets were inserted by the Driving Licences (Community Driving Licence) Regulations 1990 (S.I. 1990 No. 144) with effect in relation to licences coming into force on or after June 1, 1990.

In Scotland, court may take extract from licensing records into account
[1] **32.**—(1) Subsections (2) to (5) below apply where a person is convicted in Scotland of an offence involving obligatory endorsement but his licence [and its counterpart are] not produced to the court.

(2) The court may, in determining what order to make in pursuance of the conviction, take into consideration (subject to subsection (3) below)—

    (*a*) particulars of any previous conviction or disqualification pertaining to him, and

    (*b*) any penalty points ordered to be endorsed on [the counterpart of] any licence held by him which are to be taken into account under section 29 of this Act,

which are specified in a document purporting to be a note of information contained in the records maintained by the Secretary of State in connection with his functions under Part III of the Road Traffic Act 1988.

(3) If the prosecutor lays before the court such a document as is mentioned in subsection (2) above, the court or the clerk of court must ask the accused if he admits the accuracy of the particulars relating to him contained in the document.

(4) Where the accused admits the accuracy of any particulars, the prosecutor need not adduce evidence in proof of those particulars, and the admission must be entered in the record of the proceedings.

(5) Where the accused does not admit the accuracy of any particulars, the prosecutor must, unless he withdraws those particulars, adduce evidence in proof of them, either then or at any other diet.

(6) This section has effect notwithstanding anything in sections 311(5) and 357(1) of the Criminal Procedure (Scotland) Act 1975 (requirements as to notices of penalties and previous convictions).

NOTE
[1] The words in square brackets were inserted by the Driving Licences (Community Driving Licence) Regulations 1990 (S.I. 1990 No. 144) with effect in relation to licences coming into force on or after June 1, 1990.

Fine and imprisonment

Fine and imprisonment
33.—(1) Where a person is convicted of an offence against a provision of the Traffic Acts specified in column 1 of Part I of Schedule 2 to this Act or regulations made under any such provision, the maximum punishment by way of fine or imprisonment which may be imposed on him is that shown in column 4 against the offence and (where appropriate) the circumstances or the mode of trial there specified.

(2) Any reference in column 4 of that Part to a period of years or months is to be construed as a reference to a term of imprisonment of that duration.

Disqualification

Disqualification for certain offences
34.—(1) Where a person is convicted of an offence involving obligatory disqualification, the court must order him to be disqualified for such period not less than 12 months as the court thinks fit unless the court for special reasons thinks fit to order him to be disqualified for a shorter period or not to order him to be disqualified.

(2) Where a person is convicted of an offence involving discretionary disqualification, the court may order him to be disqualified for such period as the court thinks fit.

(3) Where a person convicted of an offence under any of the following provisions of the Road Traffic Act 1988, that is—
   (a) section 4(1) (driving or attempting to drive while unfit),
   (b) section 5(1)(a) (driving or attempting to drive with excess alcohol), and
   (c) section 7(6) (failing to provide a specimen) where that is an offence involving obligatory disqualification,
has within the ten years immediately preceding the commission of the offence been convicted of any such offence, subsection (1) above shall

apply in relation to him as if the reference to 12 months were a reference to three years.

(4) Where a person is convicted of an offence under section 1 of the Road Traffic Act 1988 (causing death by reckless driving), subsection (1) above shall apply in relation to him as if the reference to 12 months were a reference to two years.

(5) The preceding provisions of this section shall apply in relation to a conviction of an offence committed by aiding, abetting, counselling or procuring, or inciting to the commission of, an offence involving obligatory disqualification as if the offence were an offence involving discretionary disqualification.

(6) This section is subject to section 48 of this Act.

Disqualification for repeated offences

35.—(1) Where—

(*a*) a person is convicted of an offence involving obligatory or discretionary disqualification, and

(*b*) the penalty points to be taken into account on that occasion number 12 or more,

the court must order him to be disqualified for not less than the minimum period unless the court is satisfied, having regard to all the circumstances, that there are grounds for mitigating the normal consequences of the conviction and thinks fit to order him to be disqualified for a shorter period or not to order him to be disqualified.

(2) The minimum period referred to in subsection (1) above is—

(*a*) six months if no previous disqualification imposed on the offender is to be taken into account, and

(*b*) one year if one, and two years if more than one, such disqualification is to be taken into account;

and a previous disqualification imposed on an offender is to be taken into account if it was imposed within the three years immediately preceding the commission of the latest offence in respect of which penalty points are taken into account under section 29 of this Act.

(3) Where an offender is convicted on the same occasion of more than one offence involving obligatory or discretionary disqualification—

(*a*) not more than one disqualification shall be imposed on him under subsection (1) above,

(*b*) in determining the period of the disqualification the court must take into account all the offences, and

(*c*) for the purposes of any appeal any disqualification imposed under subsection (1) above shall be treated as an order made on the conviction of each of the offences.

(4) No account is to be taken under subsection (1) above of any of the following circumstances—

(*a*) any circumstances that are alleged to make the offence or any of the offences not a serious one,

(*b*) hardship, other than exceptional hardship, or

(*c*) any circumstances which, within the three years immediately preceding the conviction, have been taken into account under that subsection in ordering the offender to be disqualified for a shorter period or not ordering him to be disqualified.

(5) References in this section to disqualification do not include a disqualification imposed under section 26 of this Act or section 44 of the Powers of Criminal Courts Act 1973 (disqualification by Crown Court where vehicle used for commission of offence).

(6) In relation to Scotland, references in this section to the court include the district court.

(7) This section is subject to section 48 of this Act.

Disqualification until test is passed

[1] **36.**—(1) Where a person is convicted of an offence involving obligatory or discretionary disqualification, the court may order him to be disqualified until he passes the test of competence to drive prescribed by virtue of section 89(3) of the Road Traffic Act 1988.

(2) That power is exercisable by the court whether or not the person convicted has previously passed that test and whether or not the court makes an order under section 34 or 35 of this Act.

(3) A disqualification by virtue of an order under subsection (1) above shall be deemed to have expired on production to the Secretary of State of evidence, in such form as may be prescribed by regulations under section 105 of the Road Traffic Act 1988, that the person disqualified has passed that test since the order was made.

(4) On the issue of a licence to a person who stands disqualified by an order under subsection (1) above, there shall be added to the [particulars of the disqualification endorsed on the counterpart of the licence] a statement that the person disqualified has passed that test since the order was made.

(5) This section is subject to section 48 of this Act.

NOTE

[1] The words in square brackets in subs. (4) were substituted by the Driving Licences (Community Driving Licence) Regulations 1990 (S.I. 1990 No. 144) with effect in relation to licences coming into force on or after June 1, 1990.

Effect of order of disqualification

37.—(1) Where the holder of a licence is disqualified by an order of a court, the licence shall be treated as being revoked with effect from the beginning of the period of disqualification.

(2) Where the holder of the licence appeals against the order and the disqualification is suspended under section 39 of this Act, the period of disqualification shall be treated for the purpose of subsection (1) above as beginning on the day on which the disqualification ceases to be suspended.

(3) Notwithstanding anything in Part III of the Road Traffic Act 1988, a person disqualified by an order of a court under section 36(1) of this Act is (unless he is also disqualified otherwise than by virtue of such an order) entitled to obtain and to hold a provisional licence and to drive a motor vehicle in accordance with the conditions subject to which the provisional licence is granted.

Appeal against disqualification

38.—(1) A person disqualified by an order of a magistrates' court under section 34 or 35 of this Act may appeal against the order in the same manner as against a conviction.

(2) A person disqualified by an order of a court in Scotland may appeal against the order in the same manner as against a sentence.

Suspension of disqualification pending appeal

39.—(1) Any court in England and Wales (whether a magistrates' court or another) which makes an order disqualifying a person may, if it thinks fit, suspend the disqualification pending an appeal against the order.

(2) The court by or before which a person disqualified by an order of a court in Scotland was convicted may, if it thinks fit, suspend the disqualification pending an appeal against the order.

(3) Where a court exercises its power under subsection (1) or (2) above, it must send notice of the suspension to the Secretary of State.

(4) The notice must be sent in such manner and to such address and must contain such particulars as the Secretary of State may determine.

. . . . . .

Power of High Court of Justiciary to suspend disqualification

41.—(1) This section applies where a person has been convicted by or before a court in Scotland of an offence involving obligatory or discretionary disqualification and has been ordered to be disqualified; and in the following provisions of this section—

(a) any reference to a person ordered to be disqualified is to be construed as a reference to a person so convicted and so ordered to be disqualified, and

(b) any reference to his sentence includes a reference to the order of disqualification and to any other order made on his conviction and, accordingly, any reference to an appeal against his sentence includes a reference to an appeal against any order forming part of his sentence.

(2) Where a person ordered to be disqualified appeals to the High Court of Justiciary, whether on appeal against a summary conviction or a conviction on indictment or his sentence, the court may, if it thinks fit, suspend the disqualification on such terms as it thinks fit.

The powers conferred by this subsection on the court may be exercised by any single judge of the court.

(3) Where, by virtue of this section, the High Court suspends the disqualification of any person, it must send notice of the suspension to the Secretary of State.

(4) The notice must be sent in such manner and to such address and must contain such particulars as the Secretary of State may determine.

Removal of disqualification

[1] **42.**—(1) Subject to the provisions of this section, a person who by an order of a court is disqualified may apply to the court by which the order was made to remove the disqualification.

(2) On any such application the court may, as it thinks proper having regard to—

(a) the character of the person disqualified and his conduct subsequent to the order,

(b) the nature of the offence, and

    (*c*) any other circumstances of the case,
either by order remove the disqualification as from such date as may be
specified in the order or refuse the application.

    (3) No application shall be made under subsection (1) above for the
removal of a disqualification before the expiration of whichever is
relevant of the following periods from the date of the order by which the
disqualification was imposed, that is—

    (*a*) two years, if the disqualification is for less than four years,

    (*b*) one half of the period of disqualification, if it is for less than 10 years
        but not less than four years,

    (*c*) five years in any other case;
and in determining the expiration of the period after which under this
subsection a person may apply for the removal of a disqualification, any
time after the conviction during which the disqualification was suspended
or he was not disqualified shall be disregarded.

    (4) Where an application under subsection (1) above is refused, a
further application under that subsection shall not be entertained if made
within three months after the date of the refusal.

    (5) If under this section a court orders a disqualification to be removed,
the court—

    (*a*) must cause particulars of the order to be endorsed on [the
        counterpart of] the licence, if any, previously held by the applicant,
        and

    (*b*) may in any case order the applicant to pay the whole or any part of
        the costs of the application.

    (6) The preceding provisions of this section shall not apply where the
disqualification was imposed by order under section 36(1) of this Act.

NOTE
[1] The words in square brackets in subs. (5) were inserted by the Driving Licences
(Community Driving Licence) Regulations 1990 (S.I. 1990 No. 144) with effect in relation
to licences coming into force on or after June 1, 1990.

Rule for determining end of period of disqualification
    43. In determining the expiration of the period for which a person is
disqualified by an order of a court made in consequence of a conviction,
any time after the conviction during which the disqualification was
suspended or he was not disqualified shall be disregarded.

Endorsement

Endorsement of licences
    44.—(1) Where a person is convicted of an offence involving obligatory
endorsement, the court must order there to be endorsed on [the
counterpart of] any licence held by him particulars of the conviction and
also—

    (*a*) if the court orders him to be disqualified, particulars of the
        disqualification, or

    (*b*) if the court does not order him to be disqualified—

        (i) particulars of the offence, including the date when it was
    committed, and

        (ii) the penalty points to be attributed to the offence.

(2) Where the court does not order the person convicted to be disqualified, it need not make an order under subsection (1) above if for special reasons it thinks fit not to do so.

(3) In relation to Scotland, references in this section to the court include the district court.

(4) This section is subject to section 48 of this Act.

NOTE
[1] The words in square brackets in subs. (1) were inserted by the Driving Licences (Community Driving Licence) Regulations 1990 (S.I. 1990 No. 144) with effect in relation to licences coming into force on or after June 1, 1990.

Effect of endorsement
[1] **45.**—(1) An order that any particulars or penalty points are to be endorsed on [the counterpart of] any licence held by the person convicted shall, whether he is at the time the holder of a licence or not, operate as an order that [the counterpart of] any licence he may then hold or may subsequently obtain is to be so endorsed until he becomes entitled under subsection (4) below to have a licence issued to him [with its counterpart] free from the particulars or penalty points.

(2) On the issue of a new licence to a person, any particulars or penalty points ordered to be endorsed on [the counterpart of] any licence held by him shall be entered on [the counterpart of] the licence unless he has become entitled under subsection (4) below to have a licence issued to him [with its counterpart] free from those particulars or penalty points.

(3) [...]

(4) [A person the counterpart of whose licence has been ordered to be endorsed is entitled to have issued to him with effect from the end of the period for which the endorsement remains effective a new licence with a counterpart free from the endorsement if] he applies for a new licence in pursuance of section 97(1) of the Road Traffic Act 1988, surrenders any subsisting licence [and its counterpart], pays the fee prescribed by regulations under Part III of that Act and satisfies the other requirements of section 97(1).

(5) An endorsement ordered on a person's conviction of an offence remains effective (subject to subsections (6) and (7) below)—
(a) if an order is made for the disqualification of the offender, until four years have elapsed since the conviction, and
(b) if no such order is made, until either—
(i) four years have elapsed since the commission of the offence, or
(ii) such an order is made.

(6) Where the offence was one under section 1 or 2 of that Act (causing death by reckless driving and reckless driving), the endorsement remains in any case effective until four years have elapsed since the conviction.

(7) Where the offence was one—
(a) under section 4(1) or 5(1)(a) of that Act (driving when under influence of drink or drugs or driving with alcohol concentration above prescribed limit), or
(b) under section 7(6) of that Act (failing to provide specimen) involving obligatory disqualification,

the endorsement remains effective until 11 years have elapsed since the conviction.

NOTE
[1] The words in square brackets in subss. (1), (2) and (4) were substituted or inserted by the Driving Licences (Community Driving Licence) Regulations 1990 (S.I. 1990 No. 144) with effect in relation to licences coming into force on or after June 1, 1990.

Subs. (3) was repealed by the Road Traffic (Driver Licensing and Information Systems) Act 1989, ss.7, 16 and Scheds. 3, para. 25 and 6, which came into force on June 1, 1990.

General

Combination of disqualification and endorsement with probation orders and orders for discharge

46.— ...

(3) Where—

(*a*) a person is charged in Scotland with an offence involving obligatory or discretionary disqualification, and

(*b*) the court makes an order in respect of the offence under section 182 or 383 (absolute discharge) or 183 or 384 (probation) of the Criminal Procedure (Scotland) Act 1975,

then, for the purposes of sections 34, 35, 36, 44 and 45 of this Act, he shall be treated as if he had been convicted of an offence of the kind in question and section 191 or, as the case may be, section 392 of that Act shall not apply.

Supplementary provisions as to disqualifications and endorsements

[1] **47.—**(1) In any case where a court exercises its power under section 34, 35 or 44 of this Act not to order any disqualification or endorsement or to order disqualification for a shorter period than would otherwise be required, it must state the grounds for doing so in open court and, if it is a magistrates' court or, in Scotland, a court of summary jurisdiction, must cause them to be entered in the register (in Scotland, record) of its proceedings.

(2) Where a court orders the endorsement of [the counterpart of] any licence held by a person it may and, if it orders him to be disqualified, must, send the [licence and its counterpart, on their] being produced to the court, to the Secretary of State; and if the court orders the endorsement but does not send the licence [and its counterpart] to the Secretary of State it must send him notice of the endorsement.

(3) Where on an appeal against any such order the appeal is allowed, the court by which the appeal is allowed must send notice of that fact to the Secretary of State.

(4) A notice sent by a court to the Secretary of State in pursuance of this section must be sent in such manner and to such address and contain such particulars as the Secretary of State may determine, and a licence [and the counterpart of a licence] so sent in pursuance of this section must be sent to such address as the Secretary of State may determine.

NOTE
[1] The words in square brackets were substituted or inserted by the Driving Licences (Community Driving Licence) Regulations 1990 (S.I. 1990 No. 144) with effect in relation to licences coming into force on or after June 1, 1990.

Exemption from disqualification and endorsement for offences against construction and use regulations

[1] **48.** Where a person is convicted of an offence under section 42(1) of the Road Traffic Act 1988 (contravention of construction and use regulations) committed in a manner described against that section in column 5 of Part I of Schedule 2 to this Act, the court must not—

(*a*) order him to be disqualified, or

(*b*) order any particulars or penalty points to be endorsed on [the counterpart of] any licence held by him,

if he proves that he did not know, and had no reasonable cause to suspect, that the facts of the case were such that the offence would be committed.

NOTE

[1] The words in square brackets were inserted by the Driving Licences (Community Driving Licence) Regulations 1990 (S.I. 1990 No. 144) with effect in relation to licences coming into force on or after June 1, 1990.

. . . . . .

Powers of district court in Scotland

50. Nothing in section 10 of this Act empowers a district court in Scotland in respect of any offence—

(*a*) to impose—

(i) a penalty of imprisonment which exceeds 60 days, or

(ii) a fine which exceeds level 4 on the standard scale, or

(*b*) to impose disqualification.

. . . . . .

PART IV

MISCELLANEOUS AND GENERAL

. . . . . .

Meaning of "offence involving obligatory endorsement"

96. For the purposes of this Act, an offence involves obligatory endorsement if it is an offence under a provision of the Traffic Acts specified in column 1 of Part I of Schedule 2 to this Act or an offence specified in column 1 of Part II of that Schedule and either—

(*a*) the word "obligatory" (without qualification) appears in column 6 (in the case of Part I) or column 3 (in the case of Part II) against the offence, or

(*b*) that word appears there qualified by conditions relating to the offence which are satisfied.

Meaning of "offence involving obligatory disqualification" and "offence involving discretionary disqualification"

97.—(1) For the purposes of this Act, an offence involves obligatory disqualification if it is an offence under a provision of the Traffic Acts specified in column 1 of Part I of Schedule 2 to this Act or an offence specified in column 1 of Part II of that Schedule and either—

(*a*) the word "obligatory" (without qualification) appears in column 5 (in the case of Part I) or column 2 (in the case of Part II) against the offence, or

(*b*) that word appears there qualified by conditions or circumstances relating to the offence which are satisfied or obtain.

(2) For the purposes of this Act, an offence involves discretionary disqualification if it is an offence under a provision of the Traffic Acts specified in column 1 of Part I of Schedule 2 to this Act or an offence specified in column 1 of Part II of that Schedule and either—

(*a*) the word "discretionary" (without qualification) appears in column 5 (in the case of Part I) or column 2 (in the case of Part II) against the offence, or

(*b*) that word appears there qualified by conditions or circumstances relating to the offence which are satisfied or obtain.

. . . . . .

Law Reform (Miscellaneous Provisions) (Scotland) Act 1990

(1990 c. 40)

An Act, as respects Scotland; ... to provide for supervised attendance as an alternative to imprisonment on default in paying a fine; ... and to make certain other miscellaneous reforms of the law.

[1st November 1990]

· · · · · ·

[1] PART IV

MISCELLANEOUS REFORMS

NOTE
[1] Pt. IV will be brought into force on a day or days to be appointed: s.75(2). Ss.61 and 62 were brought into force on 1st April 1991 by S.I. 1991 No. 850.

· · · · · ·

Treatment of offenders

· · · · · ·

Supervised attendance orders as alternative to imprisonment on fine default
62.—(1) A court may make a supervised attendance order in the circumstances specified in subsection (3) below.

(2) A supervised attendance order is an order made by a court with the consent of an offender requiring him—

(a) to attend a place of supervision for such time, being 10, 20, 30, 40, 50 or 60 hours, as is specified in the order; and

(b) during that time, to carry out such instructions as may be given to him by the supervising officer.

(3) The circumstances are where—

(a) the offender is of or over 16 years of age; and

(b) having been convicted of an offence, he has had imposed on him a fine which (or any part or instalment of which) he has failed to pay and either of the following sub-paragraphs applies—

    (i) the court, prior to the commencement of this section, has imposed on him a period of imprisonment under paragraph (a) of subsection (1) of section 407 of the Criminal Procedure (Scotland) Act 1975 (power of court, when imposing a fine, to impose also imprisonment on default) but he has not served any of that period of imprisonment;

    (ii) the court, but for this section, would also have imposed on him

474

a period of imprisonment under that paragraph or paragraph (*b*) of that subsection (power of court to impose imprisonment when a person fails to pay a fine or any part or instalment thereof); and

(*c*) the court considers a supervised attendance order more appropriate than the serving of or, as the case may be, imposition of such a period of imprisonment.

(4) Where, in respect of an offender, a court makes a supervised attendance order in circumstances where sub-paragraph (i) of paragraph (b) of subsection (3) above applies, the making of that order shall have the effect of discharging the sentence of imprisonment imposed on the offender.

(5) Schedule 6 to this Act has effect for the purpose of making further and qualifying provision as to supervised attendance orders.

(6) In this section—

"local authority" means a regional or islands council;

"place of supervision" means such place as may be determined for the purposes of a supervised attendance order by the supervising officer; and

"supervising officer", in relation to a supervised attendance order, means a person appointed or assigned under Schedule 6 to this Act by the local authority whose area includes the locality in which the offender resides or will be residing when the order comes into force.

・　・　・　・　・　・

SCHEDULES

・　・　・　・　・　・

Section 62   SCHEDULE 6

Supervised Attendance Orders: Further Provisions

1.—(1) A court shall not make a supervised attendance order in respect of any offender unless—

(*a*) the court has been notified by the Secretary of State that arrangements exist for persons who reside in the locality in which the offender resides, or will be residing when the order comes into force, to carry out the requirements of such an order.

(*b*) the court is satisfied that provision can be made under the arrangements mentioned in paragraph (*a*) above for the offender to carry out such requirements.

(2) Before making a supervised attendance order, the court shall explain to the offender in ordinary language—

(*a*) the purpose and effect of the order and in particular the obligations on the offender as specified in paragraph 3 below;

(*b*) the consequences which may follow under paragraph 4 below if he fails to comply with any of those requirements; and

(*c*) that the court has, under paragraph 5 below, the power to review the order on the application either of the offender or of an officer of the local authority in whose area the offender for the time being resides.

(3) The Secretary of State may by order direct that subsection (2) of section 62 of this Act shall be amended by substituting, for any number of hours specified in that subsection such other number of hours as may be specified in the order; and an order under this subsection

may in making such amendment specify different such numbers of hours for different classes of case.

(4) An order under paragraph (3) above shall be made by statutory instrument, but no such order shall be made unless a draft of it has been laid before, and approved by a resolution of, each House of Parliament.

2.—(1) A supervised attendance order shall—

(a) specify the locality in which the offender resides or will be residing when the order comes into force; and

(b) require the local authority in whose area the locality specified under paragraph (a) above is situated to appoint or assign a supervising officer.

(2) Where, whether on the same occasion or on separate occasions, an offender is made subject to more than one supervised attendance order, the court may direct that the requirements specified in any of those orders shall be concurrent with or additional to those specified in any other of those orders, but so that at no time shall the offender have an outstanding number of hours during which he must carry out the requirements of these orders in excess of the largest number specified in section 62 of this Act.

(3) Upon making a supervised attendance order the court shall—

(a) give a copy of the order to the offender;

(b) send a copy of the order to the director of social work of the local authority in whose area the offender resides or will be residing when the order comes into force; and

(c) where it is not the appropriate court, send a copy of the order (together with such documents and information relating to the case as are considered useful) to the clerk of the appropriate court.

3.—(1) An offender in respect of whom a supervised attendance order is in force shall report to the supervising officer and notify him without delay of any change of address or in the times, if any, at which he usually works.

(2) Subject to paragraph 5(1) below, instructions given under a supervised attendance order shall be carried out during the period of 12 months beginning with the date of the order; but, unless revoked, the order shall remain in force until the offender has carried out the instructions given under it for the number of hours specified in it.

(3) The instructions given by the supervising officer under the order shall, so far as practicable, be such as to avoid any conflict with the offender's religious beliefs and any interference with the times, if any, at which he normally works or attends a school or other educational establishment.

4.—(1) If at any time while a supervised attendance order is in force in respect of any offender it appears to the appropriate court, on evidence on oath from the supervising officer, that that offender has failed to comply with any of the requirements of paragraph 3 above or of the order (including any failure satisfactorily to carry out any instructions which he has been given by the supervising officer under the order), the court may issue a warrant for the arrest of that offender, or may, if it thinks fit, instead of issuing a warrant in the first instance issue a citation requiring the offender to appear before that court at such time as may be specified in the citation.

(2) If it is proved to the satisfaction of the court before which an offender is brought or appears in pursuance of sub-paragraph (1) above that he has failed without reasonable excuse to comply with any of the requirements of paragraph 3 above or of the order (including any failure satisfactorily to carry out any instructions which he has been given by the supervising officer under the order), the court may—

(a) revoke the order and impose such period of imprisonment as could, in respect of the original default or failure, have been imposed by the court which made the order if the order had not been made; or

(b) subject to section 62 of this Act and paragraph 2(2) above, vary the number of hours specified in the order.

(3) The evidence of one witness shall, for the purposes of sub-paragraph (2) above, be sufficient evidence.

5.—(1) Where a supervised attendance order is in force in respect of any offender and, on the application of that offender or of the supervising officer, it appears to the appropriate court that it would be in the interests of justice to do so having regard to circumstances which have arisen since the order was made, that court may—

(a) extend, in relation to the order, the period of 12 months specified in paragraph 3 above;

(b) subject to section 62 of this Act and paragraph 2(2) above, vary the number of hours specified in the order;

(c) revoke the order; or

(d) revoke the order and impose such period of imprisonment as could, in respect of the original default or failure, have been imposed by the court which made the order if the order had not been made.

(2) If the appropriate court is satisfied that the offender proposes to change, or has changed, his residence from the locality for the time being specified under paragraph 2(1)(a) above to another locality and—

(a) that court has been notified by the Secretary of State that arrangements exist for persons who reside in that other locality to carry out instructions under supervised attendance orders; and

(b) it appears to that court that provision can be made under those arrangements for him to carry out instructions under the order;

that court may, and on application of the supervising officer shall, amend the order by substituting that other locality for the locality for the time being specified in the order; and the provisions of section 62 of this Act and of this Schedule shall apply to the order as amended.

(3) Where the court proposes to exercise its powers under sub-paragraph (1)(a), (b) or (d) above otherwise than on the application of the offender, it shall issue a citation requiring him to appear before the court and, if he fails to appear, may issue a warrant for his arrest.

6.—(1) The Secretary of State may make rules for regulating the carrying out of the requirements of supervised attendance orders.

(2) Without prejudice to the generality of subsection (1) above, rules under this section may—

(a) limit the number of hours during which the requirements of an order are to be met on any one day;

(b) make provision as to the reckoning of time for the purposes of the carrying out of these requirements;

(c) make provision for the payment of travelling and other expenses in connection with the carrying out of these requirements;

(d) provide for records to be kept of what has been done by any person carrying out these requirements.

(3) Rules under this paragraph shall be made by statutory instrument subject to annulment in pursuance of a resolution of either House of Parliament.

7. The Secretary of State shall lay before Parliament each year, or incorporate in annual reports he already makes, a report of the operation of section 62 of this Act and this Schedule.

8. [Amendment to the Social Work (Scotland) Act 1968, s.27: see Parliament House Book, Division K.]

9.—(1) In this Schedule—

"the appropriate court," in relation to a supervised attendance order, means the court having jurisdiction in the locality for the time being specified in the order under paragraph 2(1)(a) above, being a sheriff or district court according to whether the order has been made by a sheriff or a district court, but in a case where the order has been made by a district court and there is no district court in that locality, the sheriff court;

"local authority" and "supervising officer" have the same meanings respectively as in section 62 of this Act.

(2) Except where the context otherwise requires, expressions used in this Schedule and in the Criminal Procedure (Scotland) Act 1975 have the same meanings in this Schedule as in that Act.

Road Traffic Act 1991

(1991 c. 40)

[This Act contains a number of provisions which add to, or modify, the provisions of the Road Traffic Act 1988 and the Road Traffic Offenders Act 1988, as described in Chapter 5 above. Since the provisions of the 1991 Act may be introduced by stages, and since in any event the provisions of the earlier legislation are likely to remain relevant for some time in respect of offences committed prior to the coming into force of the 1991 Act, Chapter 5 has been written entirely by reference to the pre-1991 law. However, a tentative commentary is offered in respect of those provisions of the 1991 Act which are set out below.]

An Act to amend the law about road traffic. [25th July 1991]

PART I

GENERAL

Driving offences

Offences of dangerous driving

1. For sections 1 and 2 of the Road Traffic Act 1988 there shall be substituted—

"Causing death by dangerous driving

1. A person who causes the death of another person by driving a mechanically propelled vehicle dangerously on a road or other public place is guilty of an offence.

Dangerous driving

2. A person who drives a mechanically propelled vehicle dangerously on a road or other public place is guilty of an offence.

Meaning of dangerous driving

2A.—(1) For the purposes of sections 1 and 2 above a person is to be regarded as driving dangerously if (and, subject to subsection (2) below, only if)—

    (*a*) the way he drives falls far below what would be expected of a competent and careful driver, and

    (*b*) it would be obvious to a competent and careful driver that driving in that way would be dangerous.

(2) A person is also to be regarded as driving dangerously for the purposes of sections 1 and 2 above if it would be obvious to a competent and careful driver that driving the vehicle in its current state would be dangerous.

(3) In subsections (1) and (2) above "dangerous" refers to danger either of injury to any person or of serious damage to property; and in determining for the purposes of those subsections what would be expected of, or obvious to, a competent and careful driver in a particular case, regard shall be had not only to the circumstances of

which he could be expected to be aware but also to any circumstances shown to have been within the knowledge of the accused.

(4) In determining for the purposes of subsection (2) above the state of a vehicle, regard may be had to anything attached to or carried on or in it and to the manner in which it is attached or carried."

Careless, and inconsiderate, driving

2. For section 3 of the Road Traffic Act 1988 there shall be substituted—

"Careless, and inconsiderate, driving

3. If a person drives a mechanically propelled vehicle on a road or other public place without due care and attention, or without reasonable consideration for other persons using the road or place, he is guilty of an offence."

Commentary. The foregoing sections introduce new offences in place of the existing offences under ss.1, 2 and 3 of the Road Traffic Act 1988. The new concept of driving "dangerously" replaces the old concept of reckless driving, and seems to have been adopted largely in order to avoid the problems which English courts have had in recent years in deciding whether "recklessness" is to be defined subjectively or objectively (see, for example, *R.* v. *Cunningham* [1957] 2 Q.B. 396; *R.* v. *Caldwell* [1982] A.C. 341; *R.* v. *Lawrence* [1982] A.C. 510). In fact, the definition of driving "dangerously" as set out in the new section 2A does not appear to be significantly different from the Scottish approach to reckless driving as explained in the leading case of *Allan* v. *Patterson*, 1980 J.C. 57; 1980 S.L.T. 77. So far as penalties are concerned, it is to be noted that an offence under section 2 of the 1988 Act will now attract obligatory disqualification (1991 Act, Sched. 2, para. 6(*b*)).

Drink and drugs

Causing death by careless driving when under influence of drink or drugs

3. Before section 4 of the Road Traffic Act 1988 there shall be inserted—

"Causing death by careless driving when under influence of drink or drugs

3A.—(1) if a person causes the death of another person by driving a mechanically propelled vehicle on a road or other public place without due care and attention, or without reasonable consideration for other persons using the road or place, and—

(*a*) he is, at the time when he is driving, unfit to drive through drink or drugs, or

(*b*) he has consumed so much alcohol that the proportion of it in his breath, blood or urine at that time exceeds the prescribed limit, or

(*c*) he is, within 18 hours after that time, required to provide a specimen in pursuance of section 7 of this Act, but without reasonable excuse fails to provide it,

he is guilty of an offence.

(2) For the purposes of this section a person shall be taken to be unfit to drive at any time when his ability to drive properly is impaired.

(3) Subsection (1)(*b*) and (*c*) above shall not apply in relation to a person driving a mechanically propelled vehicle other than a motor vehicle."

Commentary. This is a wholly new offence which will clearly entitle a court, when passing sentence, to have regard to the fact that a death has been caused by careless driving (*cf. McCallum* v. *Hamilton*, 1986 S.L.T. 156; 1985 S.C.C.R. 368, and other cases referred to in paras. 9–40 and 11–49 *et seq.* above).

There may, however, be a problem of a different kind in relation to this new offence. Under existing law it is, as a general rule, improper to take account of the consumption of alcohol when sentencing for an offence such as that of careless driving (see cases referred to in para. 9–40 above). At first sight it would seem that the new offence is worded in a way which would entitle a court to have regard to the consumption, and level of consumption, of alcohol when determining sentence since the consumption of alcohol (or drugs) is an integral part of the offence. It is not clear, however, whether, in a s.3A case, the practice of prosecutors will be simply to charge the s.3A offence on its own (with evidence about alcohol consumption etc. being led only to establish that part of the offence), or whether the practice will be to charge both the s.3A offence *and* the appropriate offence under ss.4, 5 or 7 of the 1988 Act. Judging by the terms of the 1991 Act itself the legislature appears to have contemplated that prosecutors will adopt the former of the above courses since s.24 makes provision, where an offence under s.3A is charged, enabling a court to convict, as an alternative verdict, of an offence under ss.4, 5, or 7 as appropriate. Such a provision would be unnecessary if it were intended that prosecutors should always charge both a s.3A offence and an associated charge relating only to consumption of alcohol. If it is indeed to be the practice of prosecutors to charge only a s.3A offence, without any related drink charge, it is tentatively submitted that, when sentencing for that offence, a court would be entitled to have regard to the level of consumption of alcohol as established by the evidence. However, such a course would be improper if in fact a person was convicted both under s.3A and under a related drink charge because, in that event, to take account of the level of alcohol consumption when sentencing on the s.3A charge would in effect involve sentencing the offender twice for the same offence.

•   •   •   •   •   •

Licensing of drivers

•   •   •   •   •   •

Effects of disqualification

19. For section 103 of the Road Traffic Act 1988 there shall be substituted—

"Effects of disqualification

Obtaining licence, or driving, while disqualified

103.—(1) A person is guilty of an offence if, while disqualified for holding or obtaining a licence, he—

(*a*) obtains a licence, or

(*b*) drives a motor vehicle on a road.

(2) A licence obtained by a person who is disqualified is of no effect (or, where the disqualification relates only to vehicles of a particular class, is of no effect in relation to vehicles of that class).

(3) A constable in uniform may arrest without warrant any person driving a motor vehicle on a road whom he has reasonable cause to suspect of being disqualified.

(4) Subsections (1) and (3) above do not apply in relation to disqualification by virtue of section 101 of this Act.

(5) Subsections (1)(*b*) and (3) above do not apply in relation to disqualification by virtue of section 102 of this Act.

(6) In the application of subsections (1) and (3) above to a person

whose disqualification is limited to the driving of motor vehicles of a particular class by virtue of—
> (*a*) section 102 or 117 of this Act, or
> (*b*) subsection (9) of section 36 of the Road Traffic Offenders Act 1988 (disqualification until test is passed),

the references to disqualification for holding or obtaining a licence and driving motor vehicles are references to disqualification for holding or obtaining a licence to drive and driving motor vehicles of that class."

Commentary. This new provision effects certain changes to section 103 of the Road Traffic Act 1988 (*cf.* para. 5–46 above). It is to be noted in particular that, by virtue of the new s.103(4), under-age driving will no longer be an offence under s.103.

. . . . . .

Trial

. . . . . .

Interim disqualification

25. For section 26 of the Road Traffic Offenders Act 1988 (interim disqualification on committal for sentence in England and Wales) there shall be substituted—

"**Interim disqualification**
26.— . . .
(3) Where a court in Scotland—
> (*a*) adjourns a case under section 179 or section 380 of the Criminal Procedure (Scotland) Act 1975 (for inquiries to be made or to determine the most suitable method of dealing with the offender);
> (*b*) remands a person in custody or on bail under section 180 or section 381 of the Criminal Procedure (Scotland) Act 1975 (to enable a medical examination and report to be made);
> (*c*) defers sentence under section 219 or section 432 of the Criminal Procedure (Scotland) Act 1975;
> (*d*) remits a convicted person to the High Court for sentence under section 104 of the Criminal Procedure (Scotland) Act 1975,

in respect of an offence involving obligatory or discretionary disqualification, it may order the accused to be disqualified until he has been dealt with in respect of the offence.

(4) Subject to subsection (5) below, an order under this section shall cease to have effect at the end of the period of six months beginning with the day on which it is made, if it has not ceased to have effect before that time.

(5) In Scotland, where a person is disqualified under this section where section 219 or section 432 of the Criminal Procedure (Scotland) Act 1975 (deferred sentence) applies and the period of deferral exceeds six months, subsection (4) above shall not prevent

the imposition under this section of any period of disqualification which does not exceed the period of deferral.

(6) Where a court orders a person to be disqualified under this section ("the first order"), no court shall make a further order under this section in respect of the same offence or any offence in respect of which an order could have been made under this section at the time the first order was made.

(7) Where a court makes an order under this section in respect of any person it must—

(a) require him to produce to the court any licence held by him and its counterpart, and

(b) retain the licence and counterpart until it deals with him or (as the case may be) cause them to be sent to the clerk of the court which is to deal with him.

(8) If the holder of the licence has not caused it and its counterpart to be delivered, or has not posted them, in accordance with section 7 of this Act and does not produce the licence and counterpart as required under subsection (7) above, then he is guilty of an offence.

(9) Subsection (8) above does not apply to a person who—

(a) satisfies the court that he has applied for a new licence and has not received it, or

(b) surrenders to the courts a current receipt for his licence and its counterpart issued under section 56 of this Act, and produces the licence and counterpart to the court immediately on their return.

(10) Where a court makes an order under this section in respect of any person, sections 44(1) and 47(2) of this Act and section 109(3) of the Road Traffic Act 1988 (Northern Ireland drivers' licences) shall not apply in relation to the order, but—

(a) the court must send notice of the order to the Secretary of State, and

(b) if the court which deals with the offender determines not to order him to be disqualified under section 34 or 35 of this Act, it must send notice of the determination to the Secretary of State.

(11) A notice sent by a court to the Secretary of State in pursuance of subsection (10) above must be sent in such manner and to such address and contain such particulars as the Secretary of State may determine.

(12) Where on any occasion a court deals with an offender—

(a) for an offence in respect of which an order was made under this section, or

(b) for two or more offences in respect of any of which such an order was made,

any period of disqualification which is on that occasion imposed under section 34 or 35 of this Act shall be treated as reduced by any period during which he was disqualified by reason only of an order made under this section in respect of any of those offences.

(13) Any reference in this or any other Act (including any Act passed after this Act) to the length of a period of disqualification

shall, unless the context otherwise requires, be construed as a reference to its length before any reduction under this section.

(14) In relation to licences which came into force before 1st June, 1990, the references in this section to counterparts of licences shall be disregarded."

Commentary. Section 26 of the Road Traffic Offenders Act 1988 (which did not extend to Scotland) allowed a magistrates' court, when remitting an offender to the Crown Court for sentence, to disqualify him from driving until he had been dealt with by the higher court. The new s.26 enlarges the circumstances in which an interim disqualification may be ordered in England and Wales (subss.(1) and (2)), and for the first time introduces interim disqualification in Scotland.

The general power to order interim disqualification is set out in subs.(3). It is to be noted that the power may be used in respect of an offence involving obligatory or discretionary disqualification, but that the power is itself discretionary. It would therefore appear that a court could refrain from ordering interim disqualification even in respect of an offence involving obligatory disqualification. It is suggested that this might be appropriate if, for example, a case is being adjourned, or sentence is being deferred, in order to allow a proof as to special reasons for not disqualifying at all to take place.

The combined effect of subss.(3) and (4) appears to be that an order for interim disqualification should not be expressed as an order for a fixed period of weeks or months, but should be expressed as an order for disqualification until the offender "has been dealt with in respect of the offence" (subs.(3)). However, any such order will cease to have effect after six months if it has not ceased to have effect before that time, *i.e.* by virtue of the offender being sentenced for the offence (subs.(4)).

The foregoing time limit is subject to the exception provided by subs.(5). Although not expressed with the utmost clarity, that subsection appears to provide that, where sentence is deferred for more than six months, an interim disqualification may be ordered to cover the whole period of deferment notwithstanding that that period exceeds the six month maximum required under subs.(4).

Subs.(6) in effect provides that only one order for interim disqualification may be made in respect of the same complaint or indictment.

Subss.(7), (8) and (9) contain provisions relating to the production of a licence similar to those of general application in s.27 of the Road Traffic Offenders Act 1988. The reference to the "counterpart" of a licence arises by virtue of an extension to the definition of "licence" in s.108 of the Road Traffic Act 1988 inserted by the Driving Licences (Community Driving Licence) Regulations 1990 (S.I. 1990 No. 144). The enlarged definition applies to licences issued after June 1, 1990 (*cf.* subs.(14) of the new s.26 above).

Subs.(10) provides that, where a court makes an order for interim disqualification, ss.44(1) and 47(2) of the Road Traffic Offenders Act 1988 are not to apply in relation to the order. Section 44(1) provides for the endorsement on a licence of particulars of a disqualification or of penalty points as the case may be, and s.47(2) provides for the sending to the Secretary of State of a licence which has been endorsed. The effect of subs.(10) is that there is to be no endorsement in respect of an interim disqualification but, instead, notice of the order is to be sent to the Secretary of State. It is submitted, however, that the subsection does not prohibit appropriate endorsement of an offender's licence at the stage when sentence is finally determined. This seems to be the effect of the provision that ss.44(1) and 47(2) are not to apply "in relation to the order": that does not mean that they are disapplied in relation to the final determination of sentence.

Subs.(12) in effect provides that, where an offender is ultimately disqualified for an offence or offences either directly or under the totting up provisions, he is to be given full credit for any period during which he was subject to an interim disqualification in respect of one or more of the offences. This provision is obviously intended to be fair to offenders, but it is thought that some offenders might have difficulty in remembering the duration of a period of disqualification if, say, they were to be told that they are disqualified for a period of 11 months and three days (that being one year less 28 days when an interim disqualification was in operation). It is suggested that it may be preferable in such a case, where the periods of interim and full disqualification are to be continuous, for the offender to be given the explanation that his disqualification is of one year's duration from the date when the interim disqualification was ordered.

Subs.(13) provides that as a general rule the length of a period of disqualification is to be taken as being its length before any reduction operated under subs.(12). This provision is significant in relation to, for example, other provisions which prescribe certain consequences where an earlier disqualification has been of a certain length (see, for example, s.29(4) of the 1991 Act below).

. . . . . .

Penalties

. . . . . .

Penalty points to be attributed to offences

27. For section 28 of the Road Traffic Offenders Act 1988 there shall be substituted—

"Penalty points to be attributed to an offence

28.—(1) Where a person is convicted of an offence involving obligatory endorsement, then, subject to the following provisions of this section, the number of penalty points to be attributed to the offence is—

(*a*) the number shown in relation to the offence in the last column of Part I or Part II of Schedule 2 to this Act, or

(*b*) where a range of numbers is shown, a number within that range.

(2) Where a person is convicted of an offence committed by aiding, abetting, counselling or procuring, or inciting to the commission of, an offence involving obligatory disqualification, then, subject to the following provisions of this section, the number of penalty points to be attributed to the offence is ten.

(3) Where both a range of numbers and a number followed by the words "(fixed penalty)" is shown in the last column of Part I of Schedule 2 to this Act in relation to an offence, that number is the number of penalty points to be attributed to the offence for the purposes of sections 57(5) and 77(5) of this Act; and, where only a range of numbers is shown there, the lowest number in the range is the number of penalty points to be attributed to the offence for those purposes.

(4) Where a person is convicted (whether on the same occasion or not) of two or more offences committed on the same occasion and involving obligatory endorsement, the total number of penalty points to be attributed to them is the number or highest number that would be attributed on a conviction of one of them (so that if the convictions are on different occasions the number of penalty points to be attributed to the offences on the later occasion or occasions shall be restricted accordingly).

(5) In a case where (apart from this subsection) subsection (4) above would apply to two or more offences, the court may if it thinks fit determine that that subsection shall not apply to the offences (or, where three or more offences are concerned, to any one or more of them).

(6) Where a court makes such a determination it shall state its reasons in open court and, if it is a magistrates' court, or in Scotland a

court of summary jurisdiction, shall cause them to be entered in the register (in Scotland, record) of its proceedings.

(7) The Secretary of State may by order made by statutory instrument—

(*a*) alter a number or range of numbers shown in relation to an offence in the last column of Part I or Part II of Schedule 2 to this Act (by substituting one number or range for another, a number for a range, or a range for a number),

(*b*) where a range of numbers is shown in relation to an offence in the last column of Part I, add or delete a number together with the words "(fixed penalty)", and

(*c*) alter the number of penalty points shown in subsection (2) above;

and an order under this subsection may provide for different numbers or ranges of numbers to be shown in relation to the same offence committed in different circumstances.

(8) Where the Secretary of State exercises his power under subsection (7) above by substituting or adding a number which appears together with the words "(fixed penalty)", that number shall not exceed the lowest number in the range shown in the same entry.

(9) No order shall be made under subsection (7) above unless a draft of it has been laid before and approved by resolution of each House of Parliament."

Commentary. The new s.28 largely restates the provisions of the existing s.28, albeit in rather different wording. However, there are also new provisions. Subs. (3) deals with the number of penalty points to be attributed to fixed penalty offences, and subss.(4) and (5) restate, and enlarge upon, the existing provisions in s.28(2) relating to the attribution of penalty points where a person is convicted of two or more offences committed upon the same occasion. Subs.(5) contains the most significant new provision in that it permits a court to disregard the prohibition against adding together the points for several such offences if it thinks fit to do so. However, no guidance is given as to the circumstances which might persuade a court to take such a course. If it does, however, it must state its reasons and, in the case of a court of summary jurisdiction, it must cause those reasons to be entered in the record of proceedings (subs.(6)).

Penalty points to be taken into account on conviction

28. For section 29 of the Road Traffic Offenders Act 1988 there shall be substituted—

"**Penalty points to be taken into account on conviction**

29.—(1) Where a person is convicted of an offence involving obligatory endorsement, the penalty points to be taken into account on that occasion are (subject to subsection (2) below)—

(*a*) any that are to be attributed to the offence or offences of which he is convicted, disregarding any offence in respect of which an order under section 34 of this Act is made, and

(*b*) any that were on a previous occasion ordered to be endorsed on the counterpart of any licence held by him, unless the offender has since that occasion and before the conviction been disqualified under section 35 of this Act.

(2) If any of the offences was committed more than three years before another, the penalty points in respect of that offence shall not be added to those in respect of the other.

(3) In relation to licences which came into force before 1st June, 1990, the reference in subsection (1) above to the counterpart of a licence shall be construed as a reference to the licence itself."

Commentary. The foregoing provision makes small but significant changes to the existing s.29. Under subs.(1)(*a*) an offence in respect of which an offender is disqualified under s.34 is to be disregarded when attributing penalty points for the current offence or offences. (As a counterpart to this provision the 1991 Act (Sched. 4, para. 95) amends s.35 of the Road Traffic Offenders Act 1988 so that a totting-up disqualification will in future be competent only where a person is convicted of (*a*) an offence involving discretionary disqualification and obligatory endorsement, or (*b*) an offence involving obligatory disqualification in respect of which no such disqualification is imposed.) However, under subs.(1)(*b*) only a totting-up disqualification is now to operate to stop the counting back of penalty points short of the three year limit provided for by subs.(2). The result of this appears to be that in future only a totting-up disqualification will "wipe the slate clean" (*cf.* para. 5–21 above) but, where an offender's record shows only a direct disqualification under s.34, earlier penalty points on his licence will fall to be taken into account provided that they are within the three year period.

For "counterpart" see commentary to s.25 above.

Disqualification for certain offences

29.—(1) Section 34 of the Road Traffic Offenders Act 1988 (disqualification for certain offences) shall be amended as follows.

(2) For subsection (2) there shall be substituted—

"(2) Where a person is convicted of an offence involving discretionary disqualification, and either

(*a*) the penalty points to be taken into account on that occasion number fewer than 12, or

(*b*) the offence is not one involving obligatory endorsement,

the court may order him to be disqualified for such period as the court thinks fit."

(3) In subsection (3) before paragraph (*a*) there shall be inserted—

"(*aa*) section 3A (causing death by careless driving when under the influence of drink or drugs),".

(4) For subsection (4) there shall be substituted—

"(4) Subject to subsection (3) above, subsection (1) above shall apply as if the reference to 12 months were a reference to two years—

(*a*) in relation to a person convicted of—

(i) manslaughter, or in Scotland culpable homicide, or

(ii) an offence under section 1 of the Road Traffic Act 1988 (causing death by dangerous driving), or

(iii) an offence under section 3A of that Act (causing death by careless driving while under the influence of drink or drugs), and

(*b*) in relation to a person on whom more than one disqualification for a fixed period of 56 days or more has been imposed within the three years immediately preceding the commission of the offence.

(4A) For the purposes of subsection (4)(*b*) above there shall be disregarded any disqualification imposed under section 26 of this Act or section 44 of the Powers of Criminal Courts Act 1973 or section 223A or 436A of the Criminal Procedure (Scotland) Act 1975 (offences committed by using vehicles) and any disqualification imposed in respect of an offence of stealing a motor vehicle, an offence under section 12 or 25 of the Theft Act 1968, an offence under section 178 of the Road Traffic Act 1988, or an attempt to commit such an offence."

Commentary. This provision makes certain amendments to s.34 of the Road Traffic Offenders Act 1988. The new subs.(2) limits the circumstances in which a court may exercise its power to impose a discretionary disqualification, though the reasons for that limitation are not immediately apparent. The nature of the limitation effected by subs. (2)(a) is clear; but the consequence seems to be that, where 12 or more penalty points are to be taken into account, only a totting-up disqualification will be available to the court notwithstanding that the gravity of the offence might be such that the court would otherwise have wished to impose a substantial period of discretionary disqualification.

The new subs.(2)(b) is somewhat obscure. The scheme of the Road Traffic Acts, and in particular Sched. 2 to the Road Traffic Offenders Act 1988, has been that there is no such thing as discretionary endorsement: where endorsement is competent at all it is obligatory. On that basis the new subsection would appear to relate to offences which do not attract endorsement at all. But the difficulty about that approach is that, under Sched. 2 to the 1988 Act, discretionary disqualification has not been competent in respect of any offence which does not also attract obligatory endorsement.

A tentative solution to the problem appears to be that the 1991 Act introduces a new regime of penalties for cases where a motor vehicle is used in connection with an offence which is not itself strictly a road traffic offence. Section 39 of the 1991 Act (see below) allows a court to impose a discretionary disqualification (apparently without obligatory endorsement) where a person has used a motor vehicle for the purpose of committing, or facilitating the commission of, *any* offence; and para. 31 of Sched. 2 to the 1991 Act removes the penalties of obligatory endorsement and discretionary disqualification for offences under s.178 of the Road Traffic Act 1988 (taking and driving away), presumably on the basis that in future discretionary disqualification will be available in such cases under the new s. 39.

Subs.(3) amends s.34(3) of the 1988 Act so as to add the new s.3A offence to the list of offences which will attract an obligatory disqualification for not less than three years where the offender has a previous conviction for such an offence within the preceding 10 years.

Subs.(4) enlarges the categories of offence and offender which will attract an obligatory disqualification of not less than two years. The new subs.(4)(b) is of particular interest. It is not clear why 56 days should have been selected as the qualifying period. However, since the earlier periods of disqualification need not, apparently, have been imposed in respect of offences which themselves attracted obligatory disqualification, the effect of the subsection will be that, for example, an offender who is convicted of a drink/driving offence attracting obligatory disqualification, and who has two previous convictions and disqualifications of the appropriate length (say, for speeding) within the previous three years will be liable to an obligatory disqualification for a minimum period of two years.

The new subs.(4A) excludes certain disqualifications for the purposes of subs.(4)(b). Sections 223A and 436A of the 1975 Act are new sections inserted by the 1991 Act (see s.39 below).

Courses for drink-drive offenders

30. After section 34 of the Road Traffic Offenders Act 1988 there shall be inserted—

"Reduced disqualification period for attendance on courses

34A.—(1) This section applies where—

(a) a person is convicted of an offence under section 3A (causing death by careless driving when under influence of drink or drugs), 4 (driving or being in charge when under influence of drink or drugs), 5 (driving or being in charge with excess alcohol) or 7 (failing to provide a specimen) of the Road Traffic Act 1988, and

(b) the court makes an order under section 34 of this Act disqualifying him for a period of not less than 12 months.

(2) Where this section applies, the court may make an order that the period of disqualification imposed under section 34 shall be reduced if, by a date specified in the order under this section, the offender satisfactorily completes a course approved by the Secretary of State for the purposes of this section and specified in the order.

(3) The reduction made by an order under this section in a period of disqualification imposed under section 34 shall be a period specified in the order of not less than three months and not more than one quarter of the unreduced period (and accordingly where the period imposed under section 34 is 12 months, the reduced period shall be nine months).

(4) The court shall not make an order under this section unless—

(*a*) it is satisfied that a place on the course specified in the order will be available for the offender,

(*b*) the offender appears to the court to be of or over the age of 17,

(*c*) the court has explained the effect of the order to the offender in ordinary language, and has informed him of the amount of the fees for the course and of the requirement that he must pay them before beginning the course, and

(*d*) the offender has agreed that the order should be made.

(5) The date specified in an order under this section as the latest date for completion of a course must be at least two months before the last day of the period of disqualification as reduced by the order.

(6) An order under this section shall name the petty sessions area (or in Scotland the sheriff court district or, where an order has been made under this section by a stipendiary magistrate, the commission area) in which the offender resides or will reside.

Certificates of completion of courses

34B.—(1) An offender shall be regarded for the purposes of section 34A of this Act as having completed a course satisfactorily if (and only if) a certificate that he has done so is received by the clerk of the supervising court before the end of the period of disqualification imposed under section 34.

(2) If the certificate referred to in subsection (1) above is received by the clerk of the supervising court before the end of the period of disqualification imposed under section 34 but after the end of the period as it would have been reduced by the order, the order shall have effect as if the reduced period ended with the day on which the certificate is received by the clerk.

(3) The certificate referred to in subsection (1) above shall be a certificate in such form, containing such particulars, and given by such person, as may be prescribed by, or determined in accordance with, regulations made by the Secretary of State.

(4) A course organiser shall give the certificate mentioned in subsection (1) above to the offender not later than 14 days after the date specified in the order as the latest date for completion of the course, unless the offender fails to make due payment of the fees for the course, fails to attend the course in accordance with the organiser's reasonable instructions, or fails to comply with any other reasonable requirements of the organiser.

(5) Where a course organiser decides not to give the certificate mentioned in subsection (1) above, he shall give written notice of his decision to the offender as soon as possible, and in any event not later than 14 days after the date specified in the order as the latest date for completion of the course.

(6) An offender to whom a notice is given under subsection (5) above may, within such period as may be prescribed by rules of court, apply to the supervising court for a declaration that the course organiser's decision not to give a certificate was contrary to subsection (4) above; and if the court grants the application section 34A of this Act shall have effect as if the certificate had been duly received by the clerk of the court.

(7) If 14 days after the date specified in the order as the latest date for completion of the course the course organiser has given neither the certificate mentioned in subsection (1) above nor a notice under subsection (5) above, the offender may, within such period as may be prescribed by rules of court, apply to the supervising court for a declaration that the course organiser is in default; and if the court grants the application section 34A of this Act shall have effect as if the certificate had been duly received by the clerk of the court.

(8) A notice under subsection (5) above shall specify the ground on which it is given, and the Secretary of State may by regulations make provision as to the form of notices under that subsection and as to the circumstances in which they are to be treated as given.

(9) Where the clerk of a court receives a certificate of the kind referred to in subsection (1) above, or a court grants an application under subsection (6) or (7) above, the clerk or court must send notice of that fact to the Secretary of State; and the notice must be sent in such manner and to such address, and must contain such particulars, as the Secretary of State may determine.

Provisions supplementary to sections 34A and 34B

34C.—(1) The Secretary of State may issue guidance to course organisers, or to any category of course organiser as to the conduct of courses approved for the purposes of section 34A of this Act; and—

(*a*) course organisers shall have regard to any guidance given to them under this subsection, and

(*b*) in determining for the purposes of section 34B(6) whether any instructions or requirements of an organiser were reasonable, a court shall have regard to any guidance given to him under this subsection.

(2) In sections 34A and 34B and this section—

"course organiser", in relation to a course, means the person who, in accordance with regulations made by the Secretary of State, is responsible for giving the certificates mentioned in section 34B(1) in respect of the completion of the course;

"petty sessions area" has the same meaning as in the Magistrates' Courts Act 1980;

"supervising court", in relation to an order under section 34A, means—

(*a*) in England and Wales, a magistrates' court acting for

the petty sessions area named in the order as the area where the offender resides or will reside;

(b) in Scotland, the sheriff court for the district where the offender resides or will reside or, where the order is made by a stipendiary magistrate and the offender resides or will reside within his commission area, the district court for that area.

and any reference to the clerk of a magistrates' court is a reference to the clerk to the justices for the petty sessions area for which the court acts,

(3) Any power to make regulations under section 34B or this section—

(a) includes power to make different provision for different cases, and to make such incidental or supplemental provision as appears to the Secretary of State to be necessary or expedient;

(b) shall be exercisable by statutory instrument, which shall be subject to annulment in pursuance of a resolution of either House of Parliament."

Commentary. The provisions of the inserted sections are, it is thought, self-explanatory. Initially, those provisions are to be introduced in designated court areas for an experimental period expiring at the end of 1997 (1991 Act, s.31). During the experimental period an order under the new s.34A is not to be made by virtue of a person's conviction under s.3A of the Road Traffic Act 1988 (*ibid.* s.31(4)(*a*)).

. . . . . .

Disqualification until test is passed

32. For section 36 of the Road Traffic Offenders Act 1988 there shall be substituted—

"Disqualification until test is passed

36.—(1) Where this subsection applies to a person the court must order him to be disqualified until he passes the appropriate driving test.

(2) Subsection (1) above applies to a person who is disqualified under section 34 of this Act on conviction of—

(a) manslaughter, or in Scotland culpable homicide, by the driver of a motor vehicle, or

(b) an offence under section 1 (causing death by dangerous driving) or section 2 (dangerous driving) of the Road Traffic Act 1988.

(3) Subsection (1) above also applies—

(a) to a person who is disqualified under section 34 or 35 of this Act in such circumstances or for such period as the Secretary of State may by order prescribe, or

(b) to such other persons convicted of such offences involving obligatory endorsement as may be so prescribed.

(4) Where a person to whom subsection (1) above does not apply is convicted of an offence involving obligatory endorsement, the court

may order him to be disqualified until he passes the appropriate driving test (whether or not he has previously passed any test).

(5) In this section—

"appropriate driving test" means—

(*a*) an extended driving test, where a person is convicted of an offence involving obligatory disqualification or is disqualified under section 35 of this Act,

(*b*) a test of competence to drive, other than an extended driving test, in any other case,

"extended driving test" means a test of competence to drive prescribed for the purposes of this section, and

"test of competence to drive" means a test prescribed by virtue of section 89(3) of the Road Traffic Act 1988.

(6) In determining whether to make an order under subsection (4) above, the court shall have regard to the safety of road users.

(7) Where a person is disqualified until he passes the extended driving test—

(*a*) any earlier order under this section shall cease to have effect, and

(*b*) a court shall not make a further order under this section while he is so disqualified.

(8) Subject to subsection (9) below, a disqualification by virtue of an order under this section shall be deemed to have expired on production to the Secretary of State of evidence, in such form as may be prescribed by regulations under section 105 of the Road Traffic Act 1988, that the person disqualified has passed the test in question since the order was made.

(9) A disqualification shall be deemed to have expired only in relation to vehicles of such classes as may be prescribed in relation to the test passed by regulations under that section.

(10) Where there is issued to a person a licence on the counterpart of which are endorsed particulars of a disqualification under this section, there shall also be endorsed the particulars of any test of competence to drive that he has passed since the order of disqualification was made.

(11) For the purposes of an order under this section, a person shall be treated as having passed a test of competence to drive other than an extended driving test if he passes a corresponding test conducted—

(*a*) under the law of Northern Ireland, the Isle of Man, any of the Channel Islands, another member State, Gibraltar or a designated country or territory (as defined by section 89(11) of the Road Traffic Act 1988), or

(*b*) for the purposes of obtaining a British Forces licence (as defined by section 88(8) of that Act);

and accordingly subsections (8) to (10) above shall apply in relation to such a test as they apply in relation to a test prescribed by virtue of section 89(3) of that Act.

(12) This section is subject to section 48 of this Act.

(13) The power to make an order under subsection (3) above shall be exercisable by statutory instrument; and no such order shall be

made unless a draft of it has been laid before and approved by resolution of each House of Parliament.

(14) The Secretary of State shall not make an order under subsection (3) above after the end of 2001 if he has not previously made such an order."

Commentary. The new s.36 requires a court in certain circumstances to order an offender to be disqualified until he passes the appropriate driving test. Formerly the power to order an offender to resit a driving test was entirely discretionary. The circumstances in which an offender must be disqualified until he passes the appropriate test are set out in the new subss.(2) and (3), though it is to be noted that subs.(3) is to lapse after a period of 10 years if no order is made under the subsection within that period (see new subs.(14)).

In cases where the new subs.(1) does not apply, a court may, as at present, order a person who is convicted of an offence involving obligatory endorsement to be disqualified until he passes the appropriate driving test (new subs.(4)). The existing s.36(2) provides that the comparable power under that section may be exercised whether or not the court makes an order of disqualification under ss.34 or 35, but the new section contains no comparable provision. It is submitted, however, that the new subs.(4) is worded in such a way as to allow a court to follow the former practice notwithstanding that a power to do so is not expressly conferred.

Where a person is convicted of an offence involving obligatory disqualification, or is disqualified under the totting-up provisions, and is further disqualified until he passes the driving test, the test is to be an extended one as prescribed for the purposes of s.36 (new subs.(5)). In any other case the test is to be one prescribed by virtue of s.89(3) of the Road Traffic Act 1988 (*ibid.*).

For the first time the statute gives guidance (new subs.(6)) as to the factors which a court should take note of when determining whether or not to make an order under the new subs. (4). For this purpose the court is to have regard to the safety of road users. That, it is submitted, is the underlying principle which has been applied by the High Court in Scotland in the series of cases mentioned in Chapter 5 (para. 5–44) above. It is therefore suggested that those cases will continue to offer authoritative guidance as to the circumstances in which a discretionary order for disqualification until the appropriate driving test is passed should be made.

Subsections (7) to (12) contain provisions which are consequential to those described above. It is thought that they are self-explanatory.

Short periods of disqualification

33. In section 37 of the Road Traffic Offenders Act 1988 (effect of order of disqualification) after subsection (1) there shall be inserted—

"(1A) Where—

(*a*) the disqualification is for a fixed period shorter than 56 days in respect of an offence involving obligatory endorsement, or

(*b*) the order is made under section 26 of this Act,

subsection (1) above shall not prevent the licence from again having effect at the end of the period of disqualification."

Commentary. Normally, where a person who holds a driving licence is disqualified, his licence is revoked with effect from the beginning of the period of disqualification (s.37(1)), and at the end of the period of disqualification he must apply for a new licence. Under the new subs.(1A) this will not be so in the case of short disqualifications for a fixed period shorter than 56 days, or in the case of interim disqualifications under s.26 (see 1991 Act, s.25 above). In such cases an offender's licence will again have effect at the end of the period of disqualification.

. . . . . .

Miscellaneous

. . . . . .

Forfeiture of vehicles: Scotland

37.—(1) In each of sections 223 and 436 of the Criminal Procedure (Scotland) Act 1975 (forfeiture of property) after subsection (1) there shall be inserted—

"(1A) Where a person commits an offence to which this subsection applies by—

(*a*) driving, attempting to drive, or being in charge of a vehicle, or

(*b*) failing to comply with a requirement made under section 7 of the Road Traffic Act 1988 (failure to provide specimen for analysis or laboratory test) in the course of an investigation into whether the offender had committed an offence while driving, attempting to drive or being in charge of a vehicle, or

(*c*) failing, as the driver of a vehicle, to comply with subsections (2) or (3) of section 170 of the Road Traffic Act 1988 (duty to stop and give information or report accident),

the vehicle shall be regarded for the purposes of subsection (1)(*a*) above as used for the purpose of committing the offence."

(2) In section 223 of that Act after subsection (1A) there shall be inserted—

"(1B) Subsection (1A) above applies to—

(*a*) an offence under the Road Traffic Act 1988 which is punishable with imprisonment,

(*b*) an offence of culpable homicide."

(3) In section 436 of that Act after subsection (1A) there shall be inserted—

"(1B) Subsection (1A) above applies to an offence under the Road Traffic Act 1988 which is punishable with imprisonment."

Commentary. Under the foregoing provisions it will be possible in appropriate circumstances for a court to order forfeiture of a vehicle used in connection with the crime of culpable homicide and certain offences under the Road Traffic Act 1988 (*cf.* Chapter 6, para. 6–05 above). For such an order to be competent in the case of an offence under the 1988 Act the offence must be one which is punishable with imprisonment (new subs.(1B)), and in all cases one or more of the conditions set out in the new subs.(1A)(*a*) to (*c*) must be satisfied.

It is not immediately clear what purpose is to be served by the conditions prescribed in subs.(1A). It may be that they are intended to exclude from risk of forfeiture one who aids and abets the commission of an offence, since such a person would not be "driving, attempting to drive, or . . . in charge of" the vehicle (subs.(1A)(*a*)). But, in the case of one who aids and abets, the vehicle used in the offence is unlikely to be "in his possession or under his control" at the time (1975 Act, ss.223(1) and 436(1)), so that he would be excluded from risk of forfeiture on that ground.

The provision in subs.(1A)(*c*) is at first sight obscure since hitherto offences under s.170 of the Road Traffic Act 1988 have not been punishable with imprisonment. However, a maximum of six months' imprisonment is now to be competent for such offences (1991 Act, Sched. 2, para. 29). It is not clear, however, why this particular imprisonable offence, and the one referred to in subs.(1A)(*b*), should have been singled out for particular mention.

. . . . . .

Disqualification in Scotland where vehicle used to commit offence

39. After each of sections 223 and 436 of the Criminal Procedure (Scotland) Act 1975 there shall be added sections numbered 223A and 436A in the following terms—

> **"Disqualification in Scotland where vehicle used to commit offence**
>
> .—(1) Where a person is convicted of an offence (other than one triable only summarily) and the court which passes sentence is satisfied that a motor vehicle was used for the purpose of committing or facilitating the commission of that offence, the court may order him to be disqualified for such period as the court thinks fit from holding or obtaining a licence to drive a motor vehicle granted under Part III of the Road Traffic Act 1988.
>
> (2) A court which makes an order under this section disqualifying a person from holding or obtaining a licence shall require him to produce any such licence held by him and its counterpart.
>
> (3) Any reference in this section to facilitating the commission of an offence shall include a reference to the taking of any steps after it has been committed for the purpose of disposing of any property to which it relates or of avoiding apprehension or detection.
>
> (4) In relation to licences which came into force before 1st June, 1990, the reference in subsection (2) above to the counterpart of a licence shall be disregarded."

Commentary. This provision introduces for Scottish courts a power similar to that hitherto enjoyed by the Crown Court in England and Wales under s.44 of the Powers of Criminal Courts Act 1973. The effect of the provision is that, in cases where a motor vehicle is used for the purpose of committing, or facilitating the commission of, an offence, the court may order the offender to be disqualified for such period as it thinks fit. Unlike the forfeiture provisions in ss.223 and 436 of the 1975 Act, it is not necessary that the vehicle should have been in the possession or under the control of the offender at the relevant time. It therefore appears to follow that if, for example, several co-accused were to use a motor vehicle to convey stolen property from the scene of a theft, all of them could be disqualified under this provision.

For "counterpart" see commentary to s.25 above.

. . . . . .

Criminal Justice Act 1991

(1991 c. 53)

An Act to make further provision with respect to the treatment of offenders and the position of children and young persons and persons having responsibility for them; to make provision with respect to certain services provided or proposed to be provided for purposes connected with the administration of justice or the treatment of offenders; to make financial and other provision with respect to that administration; and for connected purposes. **[25th July 1991]**

PART I

POWERS OF COURTS TO DEAL WITH OFFENDERS

. . . . . .

Orders: supplemental

. . . . . .

Reciprocal enforcement of certain orders

16. Schedule 3 to this Act shall have effect for making provision for and in connection with—

(*a*) the making and amendment in England and Wales of community orders relating to persons residing in Scotland or Northern Ireland; and

(*b*) the making and amendment in Scotland or Northern Ireland of corresponding orders relating to persons residing in England and Wales.

Financial penalties

Increase of certain maxima

17.—(1) In section 37 (standard scale of fines) of the Criminal Justice Act 1982 ("the 1982 Act") and section 289G of the Criminal Procedure (Scotland) Act 1975 (corresponding Scottish provision), for subsection (2) there shall be substituted the following subsection—

"(2) The standard scale is shown below—

Level on the scale	*Amount of fine*
1	£200
2	£500
3	£1,000
4	£2,500
5	£5,000".

(2) Part I of the Magistrates' Courts Act 1980 ("the 1980 Act") shall be amended as follows—

(*a*) in section 24(3) and (4) (maximum fine on summary conviction of young person for indictable offence) and section 36(1) and (2) (maximum fine on conviction of young person by magistrates' court), for "£400" there shall be substituted "£1,000";

(*b*) in section 24(4) (maximum fine on summary conviction of child for indictable offence) and section 36(2) (maximum fine on conviction of child by magistrates' court), for "£100" there shall be substituted "£250"; and

(*c*) in section 32(9) (maximum fine on summary conviction of offence triable either way), for "£2,000" there shall be substituted "£5,000";

and in section 289B(6) of the Criminal Procedure (Scotland) Act 1975 (interpretation), in the definition of "prescribed sum," for "£2,000" there shall be substituted "£5,000. ...."

. . . . . .

Financial penalties: supplemental

. . . . .

Default in other cases

23.— ...

(2) For the Table in section 407(1A) of the Criminal Procedure (Scotland) Act 1975 (maximum period of imprisonment for failure to pay fine or find caution) there shall be substituted the following Table—

"*Amount of fine or caution*	*Maximum period of imprisonment*
An amount not exceeding £200	7 days
An amount exceeding £200 but not exceeding £500	14 days
An amount exceeding £500 but not exceeding £1,000	28 days
An amount exceeding £1,000 but not exceeding £2,500	45 days
An amount exceeding £2,500 but not exceeding £5,000	3 months
An amount exceeding £5,000 but not exceeding £10,000	6 months
An amount exceeding £10,000 but not exceeding £20,000	12 months
An amount exceeding £20,000 but not exceeding £50,000	18 months
An amount exceeding £50,000 but not exceeding £100,000	2 years
An amount exceeding £100,000 but not exceeding £250,000	3 years

"Amount of fine or caution	Maximum period of imprisonment
An amount exceeding £250,000 but not exceeding £1 million	5 years
An amount exceeding £1 million	10 years."...

Recovery of fines etc. by deductions from income support

24.—(1) The Secretary of State may by regulations provide that where a fine has been imposed on an offender by a magistrates' court, or a sum is required to be paid by a compensation order which has been made against an offender by such a court, and (in either case) the offender is entitled to income support—

    (*a*) the court may apply to the Secretary of State asking him to deduct sums from any amounts payable to the offender by way of income support, in order to secure the payment of any sum which is or forms part of the fine or compensation; and

    (*b*) the Secretary of State may deduct sums from any such amounts and pay them to the court towards satisfaction of any such sum.

(2) The regulations may include—

    (*a*) provision that, before making an application, the court shall make an enquiry as to the offender's means;

    (*b*) provision allowing or requiring adjudication as regards an application, and provision as to appeals and reviews;

    (*c*) provision as to the circumstances and manner in which and the times at which sums are to be deducted and paid;

    (*d*) provision as to the calculation of such sums (which may include provision to secure that amounts payable to the offender by way of income support do not fall below prescribed figures);

    (*e*) provision as to the circumstances in which the Secretary of State is to cease making deductions;

    (*f*) provision requiring the Secretary of State to notify the offender, in a prescribed manner and at any prescribed time, of the total amount of sums deducted up to the time of notification; and

    (*g*) provision that, where the whole amount to which the application relates has been paid, the court shall give notice of that fact to the Secretary of State.

(3) In subsection (1) above—

    (*a*) the reference to a fine having been imposed by a magistrates' court includes a reference to a fine being treated, by virtue of section 32 of the 1973 Act, as having been so imposed; and

    (*b*) the reference to a sum being required to be paid by a compensation order which has been made by a magistrates' court includes a reference to a sum which is required to be paid by such an order being treated, by virtue of section 41 of the Administration of Justice Act 1970, as having been adjudged to be paid on conviction by such a court.

(4) In this section—

"fine" includes—

        (*a*) a penalty imposed under section 8(1) or 18(4) of the

Vehicles (Excise) Act 1971 or section 102(3)(*aa*) of the Customs and Excise Management Act 1979 (penalties imposed for certain offences in relation to vehicle excise licences);

(*b*) an amount ordered to be paid, in addition to any penalty so imposed, under sections 9, 18A or 26A of the said Act of 1971 (liability to additional duty);

(*c*) an amount ordered to be paid by way of costs which is, by virtue of section 41 of the Administration of Justice Act 1970, treated as having been adjudged to be paid on a conviction by a magistrates' court;

"income support" means income support within the meaning of the Social Security Act 1986, either alone or together with any unemployment, sickness or invalidity benefit, retirement pension or severe disablement allowance which is paid by means of the same instrument of payment;

"prescribed" means prescribed by regulations made by the Secretary of State.

(5) In the application of this section to Scotland—

(*a*) references in subsections (1) and (2) above to a magistrates' court shall be construed as references to a court; and

(*b*) in subsection (3) above, for paragraphs (*a*) and (*b*) there shall be substituted the following paragraphs—

"(*a*) the reference to a fine having been imposed by a court includes a reference to a fine being treated, by virtue of section 196(2) of the Criminal Procedure (Scotland) Act 1975, as having been so imposed; and

(*b*)the reference to a compensation order having been made by a court includes a reference to such an order being treated, by virtue of section 66 of the Criminal Justice (Scotland) Act 1980, as having been so made."

* * * * * *

SCHEDULES

* * * * * *

Section 16   SCHEDULE 3

RECIPROCAL ENFORCEMENT OF CERTAIN ORDERS

PART I

TRANSFER OF COMMUNITY ORDERS TO SCOTLAND OR NORTHERN IRELAND

Probation orders: Scotland

1.—(1) Where a court considering the making of a probation order is satisfied that the offender resides in Scotland, or will be residing there when the order comes into force, section 2 of the 1973 Act (probation orders) shall have effect as if after subsection (1) there were inserted the following subsection—

"(1A) A court shall not make a probation order in respect of any offender unless it is satisfied that suitable arrangements for his supervision can be made by the regional or islands council in whose area he resides, or will be residing when the order comes into force."

(2) Where a probation order has been made and—

(a) a magistrates' court acting for the petty sessions area specified in the order is satisfied that the offender proposes to reside or is residing in Scotland; and

(b) it appears to the court that suitable arrangements for his supervision can be made by the regional or islands council in whose area he proposes to reside or is residing,

the power of the court to amend the order under Part IV of Schedule 2 to this Act shall include power to amend it by requiring him to be supervised in accordance with arrangements so made.

(3) Where a court is considering the making or amendment of a probation order in accordance with this paragraph, Schedule 1A to the 1973 Act (additional requirements in probation orders) shall have effect as if—

(a) any reference to a probation officer were a reference to an officer of the regional or islands council in whose area the offender resides or will be residing when the order or amendment comes into force;

(b) the reference in paragraph 2(5) to the probation committee for the area in which the premises are situated were a reference to the regional or islands council for that area;

(c) paragraph 3 (requirements as to attendance at probation centre) were omitted; and

(d) the reference in paragraph 5(3) to a mental hospital were a reference to a hospital within the meaning of the Mental Health (Scotland) Act 1984, not being a State hospital within the meaning of that Act.

(4) A probation order made or amended in accordance with this paragraph shall—

(a) specify the locality in Scotland in which the offender resides or will be residing when the order or amendment comes into force; and

(b) specify as the appropriate court for the purposes of subsection (2) of section 183 or 384 of the Criminal Procedure (Scotland) Act 1975 a court of summary jurisdiction (which, in the case of an offender convicted on indictment, shall be the sheriff court) having jurisdiction in the locality specified under paragraph (a) above.

Probation orders: Northern Ireland

2.—(1) Where a court considering the making of a probation order is satisfied that the offender resides in Northern Ireland, or will be residing there when the order comes into force, section 2 of the 1973 Act shall have effect as if after subsection (1) there were inserted the following subsection—

"(1A) A court shall not make a probation order in respect of any offender unless it is satisfied that suitable arrangements for his supervision can be made by the Probation Board for Northern Ireland."

(2) Where a probation order has been made and—

(a) a magistrates' court acting for the petty sessions area specified in the order is satisfied that the offender proposes to reside or is residing in Northern Ireland; and

(b) it appears to the court that suitable arrangements for his supervision can be made by the Probation Board for Northern Ireland,

the power of the court to amend the order under Part IV of Schedule 2 to this Act shall include power to amend it by requiring him to be supervised in accordance with arrangements so made.

(3) Where a court is considering the making or amendment of a probation order in accordance with this paragraph, Schedule 1A to the 1973 Act shall have effect as if—

(a) any reference to a probation officer were a reference to a probation officer assigned to the petty sessions district in Northern Ireland in which the offender resides or will be residing when the order or amendment comes into force;

(b) the reference in paragraph 2(5) to the probation committee for the area in which the premises are situated were a reference to the Probation Board for Northern Ireland;

(c) references in paragraph 3 to a probation centre were references to a day centre within the meaning of section 2B of the Probation Act (Northern Ireland) 1950; and

(d) the reference in paragraph 5(3) to treatment as a resident patient in a mental hospital were a reference to treatment (whether as an in-patient or an out-patient) at such hospital as may be specified in the order, being a hospital within the meaning of the Health and Personal Social Services (Northern Ireland) Order 1972, approved by the Department of Health and Social Services for Northern Ireland for the purposes of section 2 of the Probation Act (Northern Ireland) 1950.

(4) A probation order made or amended in accordance with this paragraph shall specify the petty sessions district in Northern Ireland in which the offender resides or will be residing when the order or amendment comes into force.

Community service orders: Scotland

3.—(1) Where a court considering the making of a community service order is satisfied that the offender resides in Scotland, or will be residing there when the order comes into force, section 14 of the 1973 Act shall have effect as if for subsection (2A) there were substituted the following subsection—

"(2A) A court shall not make a community service order in respect of any offender unless—

(a) the court has been notified by the Secretary of State that arrangements exist for persons who reside in the locality in Scotland in which the offender resides, or will be residing when the order comes into force, to perform work under community service orders made under section 1 of the Community Service by Offenders (Scotland) Act 1978; and

(b) it appears to the court that provision can be made for him to perform work under those arrangements."

(2) Where a community service order has been made and—

(a) a magistrates' court acting for a petty sessions area for the time being specified in it is satisfied that the offender proposes to reside or is residing in Scotland;

(b) the court has been notified by the Secretary of State that arrangements exist for persons who reside in the locality in Scotland in which the offender proposes to reside or is residing to perform work under community service orders made under section 1 of the Community Service by Offenders (Scotland) Act 1978; and

(c) it appears to the court that provision can be made for him to perform work under the community service order under those arrangements,

it may amend the order by specifying that the unpaid work required to be performed by the order be so performed.

(3) A community service order made or amended in accordance with this paragraph shall—

(a) specify the locality in Scotland in which the offender resides or will be residing when the order or amendment comes into force; and

(b) require the regional or islands council in whose area the locality specified under paragraph (a) above is situated to appoint or assign an officer who will discharge in respect of the order the functions in respect of community service orders conferred on the local authority officer by the Community Service by Offenders (Scotland) Act 1978.

.   .   .   .   .   .

Combination orders: Scotland

5. Paragraphs 1 and 3 above shall apply in relation to combination orders—

(a) in so far as they impose such a requirement as is mentioned in paragraph (a) of subsection (1) of section 11 of this Act, as if they were probation orders; and

(b) in so far as they impose such a requirement as is mentioned in paragraph (b) of that subsection, as if they were community service orders.

General

6.—(1) Where a community order is made or amended in any of the circumstances specified in this Schedule, the court which makes or amends the order shall send three copies of it as made or amended to the home court, together with such documents and information relating to the case as it considers likely to be of assistant to that court.

(2) Where a community order is made or amended in any of the circumstances specified in this Schedule, then, subject to the following provisions of this paragraph—

(a) the order shall be treated as if it were a corresponding order made in the part of the United Kingdom in which the offender resides, or will be residing at the relevant time; and (*b*) the legislation relating to such orders which has effect in that part of the United Kingdom shall apply accordingly.

(3) Before making or amending a community order in those circumstances the court shall explain to the offender in ordinary language—

(*a*) the requirements of the legislation relating to corresponding orders which has effect in the part of the United Kingdom in which he resides or will be residing at the relevant time;

(*b*) the powers of the home court under the legislation, as modified by this paragraph; and

(*c*) its own powers under this paragraph,

and an explanation given in accordance with this sub-paragraph shall be sufficient without the addition of an explanation under section 2(3) or 14(5) of the 1973 Act.

(4) The home court may exercise in relation to the community order any power which it could exercise in relation to a corresponding order made by a court in the part of the United Kingdom in which the home court exercises jurisdiction, by virtue of the legislation relating to such orders which has effect in that part, except the following, namely—

(*a*) in the case of a probation order or a combination order, a power conferred by section 186(2)(*b*), 187, 387(2)(*b*) or 388 of, or paragraph 1 of Schedule 5 to, the Criminal Procedure (Scotland) Act 1975;

(*b*) in the case of a probation order, a power conferred by section 4(3)(*d*) or (4B)(*d*) or 6 of, or paragraph 1 of Schedule 2 to, the Probation Act (Northern Ireland) 1950; and

(*c*) in the case of a community service order—

(i) a power conferred by section 4(2)(*b*) or 5(1)(*c*) or (*d*) of the Community Service by Offenders (Scotland) Act 1978;

(ii) a power conferred by Article 9(3)(*a*) or (*b*) or (5)(*b*) or 10 of the Treatment of Offenders (Northern Ireland) Order 1976; or

(iii) a power to vary the order by substituting for the number of hours of work specified in it any greater number than the court which made the order could have specified.

(5) If at any time while legislation relating to corresponding orders which has effect in Scotland or Northern Ireland applies by virtue of sub-paragraph (2) above to a community order made in England and Wales—

(*a*) it appears to the home court—

(i) if that court is in Scotland, on evidence on oath from the local authority officer concerned; and

(ii) if it is in Northern Ireland, upon a complaint being made to a justice of the peace acting for the petty sessions district for the time being specified in the order, that the offender has failed to comply with any of the requirements of the legislation applicable to the order; or

(*b*) it appears to the home court on the application of the offender or—

(i) if that court is in Scotland, of the local authority officer concerned; and

(ii) if it is in Northern Ireland, of the probation officer concerned, that it would be in the interests of justice for a power conferred by paragraph 7 or 8 of Schedule 2 to this Act to be exercised,

the home court may require the offender to appear before the court which made the order.

(6) Where an offender is required by virtue of sub-paragraph (5) above to appear before the court which made the community order, that court—

(*a*) may issue a warrant for his arrest; and

(*b*) may exercise any power which it could exercise in respect of the community order if the offender resided in England and Wales,

and any enactment relating to the exercise of such powers shall have effect accordingly, and with any reference to the responsible officer being construed as a reference to the local authority or probation officer concerned.

(7) Where an offender is required by virtue of paragraph (*a*) of sub-paragraph (5) above to appear before the court which made the community order—

(*a*) the home court shall send to that court a certificate certifying that the offender has failed to comply with such of the requirements of the order as may be specified in the certificate, together with such other particulars of the case as may be desirable; and

(*b*) a certificate purporting to be signed by the clerk of the home court shall be admissible as evidence of the failure before the court which made the order.

(8) In this paragraph—

"corresponding order," in relation to a combination order, means a probation order including such a requirement as is mentioned in subsection (5A) of section 183 or 384 of the Criminal Procedure (Scotland) Act 1975;

"home court" means—

(a) if the offender resides in Scotland, or will be residing there at the relevant time, the sheriff court having jurisdiction in the locality in which he resides or proposes to reside; and

(b) if he resides in Northern Ireland, or will be residing there at the relevant time, the court of summary jurisdiction acting for the petty sessions district in which he resides or proposes to reside;

"the local authority officer concerned," in relation to an offender, means the officer of a regional or islands council responsible for his supervision or, as the case may be, discharging in relation to him the functions assigned by the Community Service by Offenders (Scotland) Act 1978;

"the probation officer concerned," in relation to an offender, means the probation officer responsible for his supervision or, as the case may be, discharging in relation to him the functions conferred by Part III of the Treatment of Offenders (Northern Ireland) Order 1976;

"the relevant time" means the time when the order or the amendment to it comes into force.

PART II

TRANSFER OF CORRESPONDING ORDERS FROM SCOTLAND

Probation orders

7.—(1) The Criminal Procedure (Scotland) Act 1975 shall be amended as follows.

(2) In each of sections 183 and 384 (which provide, respectively, for probation orders in solemn and in summary proceedings), in subsection (1A) for the words "by the local authority in whose area he resides or is to reside" there shall be substituted the following paragraphs—

"(a) in a case other than that mentioned in paragraph (b) below, by the local authority in whose area he resides or is to reside; or

(b) in a case where, by virtue of section 188(1) of this Act, subsection (2) of this section would not apply, by the probation committee for the area which contains the petty sessions area which would be named in the order."

(3) In each of sections 188 and 389 (which provide, respectively, for probation orders relating to persons residing in England being made in solemn and in summary proceedings)—

(a) in subsection (1)—

(i) for the words "that the offender shall perform unpaid work" there shall be substituted the words "which, while corresponding to a requirement mentioned in paragraph 2 or 3 of Schedule 1A to the Powers of Criminal Courts Act 1973, would if included in a probation order made under that Act fail to accord with a restriction as to days of presentation, participation or attendance mentioned in paragraph 2(4)(a) or (6)(a), or as the case may be 3(3)(a), of that Schedule;

(ii) for the word "17" there shall be substituted the word "16"

(iii) the word "and," where it secondly occurs, shall cease to have effect; and

(iv) at the end there shall be added the words "; and where the order includes a requirement that the probationer perform unpaid work for a number of hours, the number specified shall not exceed one hundred.";

(b) in subsection (2)—

(i) for the words "that the probationer has attained the age of 17 years and proposes to reside in or is residing in England" there shall be substituted the following paragraphs—

"(a) that the probationer has attained the age of 16 years;

(b) that he proposes to reside, or is residing, in England; and

(c) that suitable arrangements for his supervision can be made by the probation committee for the area which contains the petty sessions area in which he resides or will reside"; and

(ii) after the word "section," where it secondly occurs, there shall be inserted the words "or to vary any requirement for performance of unpaid work so that such hours as remain to be worked to not exceed one hundred";

(*c*) in subsection (3)—

(i) in paragraph (*a*), for the words "section 3(2) of" and "section 3 of" there shall be substituted, respectively, the words "paragraph 5(3) of Schedule 1A to" and "paragraph 5 of Schedule 1A to"; and

(ii) in paragraph (*b*), for the words "subsections (4) to (6) of section 3 of" there shall be substituted the words "sub-paragraphs (5) to (7) of paragraph 5 of Schedule 1A to";

(*d*) in subsection (4), for the words from "the Powers" to the end of the proviso there shall be substituted the words "Schedule 2 to the Criminal Justice Act 1991 shall apply to the order—

(*a*) except in the case mentioned in paragraph (*b*) below, as if that order were a probation order made under section 2 of the Powers of Criminal Courts Act 1973; and

(*b*) in the case of an order which contains a requirement such as is mentioned in subsection (5A) of section 183 or 384 of this Act, as if it were a combination order made under section 11 of the said Act of 1991:

Provided that Part III of that Schedule shall not so apply; and sub-paragraphs (3) and (4) of paragraph 3 of that Schedule shall so apply as if for the first reference in the said sub-paragraph (3) to the Crown Court there were substituted a reference to a court in Scotland and for the other references in those sub-paragraphs to the Crown Court there were substituted references to the court in Scotland."; and

(*e*) in subsection (5), for the words from "for which" to "this section" there shall be substituted the words "named in a probation order made or amended under this section that the person to whom the order relates."

(4) Sections 189 and 390 (which make further provision as to probation orders in, respectively, solemn and summary proceedings) shall cease to have effect.

Community service orders

8. Section 6 of the Community Service by Offenders (Scotland) Act 1978 (community service orders relating to persons residing in England and Wales) shall be amended as follows—

(*a*) in subsection (1)(*a*), for the words from "for paragraphs" to the end of paragraph (*b*) as substituted in section 1(2) of that Act there shall be substituted the words ", in subsection (2), paragraph (*b*) were omitted and for paragraph (*d*) there were substituted the following paragraph—";

and

(*b*) in subsection (2), paragraph (*b*) shall cease to have effect.

Supervision requirements

9. Section 72 of the Social Work (Scotland) Act 1968 (supervision of children moving to England and Wales or to Northern Ireland) shall be amended as follows—

(*a*) in subsection (1)(*b*), for the words "to a juvenile court acting for the petty sessions area" there shall be substituted the following sub-paragraphs—

"(i) in the case of residence in England and Wales, to a youth court acting for the petty sessions area (within the meaning of the Children and Young Persons Act 1969);

(ii) in the case of residence in Northern Ireland, to a juvenile court acting for the petty sessions district (within the meaning of Part III of the Magistrates' Courts (Northern Ireland) Order 1981).";

(*b*) in subsection (1A)—

(i) for the words "The juvenile court in England and Wales" there shall be substituted the words "A youth court";

(ii) after the word "12" there shall be inserted the words ", 12A, 12AA, 12B or 12C"; and

(iii) paragraph (*a*), and the word "and" immediately following that paragraph, shall cease to have effect;

(*c*) in subsection (2), for the words "The juvenile court in Northern Ireland" there shall be substituted the words "A juvenile court";

(*d*) in subsection (3), after the words "by a" there shall be inserted the words "youth court or as the case may be; and

(*e*) subsection (4) shall cease to have effect.

• • • • • •

Act of Adjournal (Consolidation) 1988

(S.I. 1988 No. 110)

[21st January 1988]

CHAPTER 1

SOLEMN PROCEDURE

PART I

PROCEDURE PRIOR TO TRIAL

. . . . . .

Interim Hospital Order

Application
62.—(1) Where the court has made or renewed an *interim* hospital order under section 174A and the responsible medical officer has intimated to the prosecutor either—
  (*a*) that he seeks a continuation of the order, or
  (*b*) that he seeks termination of the order before the date on which it would otherwise cease to have effect,
the prosecutor shall make an application in the form set out in Form 29 of Schedule 1, to the court which made the order, to renew or terminate the order, as the case may be.
  (2) Where an application is made under paragraph (1)—
  (*a*) the court shall by interlocutor in the form set out in Form 30 of Schedule 1, appoint a diet for hearing the application and where appropriate, grant warrant to authorised officers of the hospital, or officers of law, for conveyance of the offender from the hospital to the court for that diet; and
  (*b*) the clerk of court shall intimate the application and the diet to the offender or his solicitor.
  (3) Where, in an application under paragraph (1)(*a*), the court renews an *interim* hospital order before the date on which the order would otherwise cease to have effect, the period of renewal shall commence from the date on which the order would otherwise cease to have effect.
  (4) Where the court makes an order to renew or terminate an *interim* hospital order, before the date on which it would otherwise cease to have effect, the adjourned diet fixed when the previous order of the court was made shall be treated as being discharged.

. . . . . .

PART III

CONVICTION AND SENTENCE

Interruption of proceedings

74.—(1) On conviction of an accused person in solemn proceedings the presiding judge may, without adjourning those proceedings, interrupt them by—

    (*a*) considering a conviction against that person in other proceedings pending before that court for which he has not been sentenced;

    (*b*) passing sentence on that person in respect of the conviction in those other proceedings.

(2) When the judge has interrupted any proceedings under the powers contained in paragraph (1), he may in passing sentence on an accused person in respect of a conviction in those proceedings at the same time pass sentence on that person in respect of any other conviction he has considered thereunder.

(3) No interruption of any proceedings under the powers contained in paragraphs (1) and (2) shall cause the instance to fall in respect of any person accused in those proceedings or shall otherwise affect the validity of those proceedings.

. . . . . .

Form of probation order

76. A probation order shall be in the form set out in Form 35 of Schedule 1.

Compensation orders: application

77. The provisions of rules 78 to 82 apply to compensation orders made by courts against convicted persons under Part IV of the 1980 Act.

Terms of order

78. Entries shall be made in the record of proceedings by the clerk of court on the making of a compensation order, specifying the terms of the order and in particular—

    (*a*) the name of the convicted person or persons required to pay compensation;

    (*b*) the amount of compensation required to be paid by such person or persons;

    (*c*) the name of the person or persons entitled to the compensation payable;

    (*d*) where there is more than one such person, the amount of compensation each is entitled to and the priority, if any, among those persons for payment.

Information of disability

79.—(1) The prosecutor, if he knows that any person entitled to payment of compensation under a compensation order is under any legal disability, shall so inform the court immediately it makes any such order in respect of any such person, and that information shall be entered by the clerk of court in the record of proceedings.

(2) Those entries shall be authenticated by the signature of the clerk of court.

Variation

80.—(1) The judge may, at any time before a compensation order is fully complied with, and after such further enquiries as the court may order, vary the terms of the order as he thinks fit.

(2) A variation order under paragraph (1) may be made in chambers and in the absence of the parties, or any of them.

Discharge or reduction of amount

81.—(1) An application to discharge a compensation order or to reduce the amount that remains to be paid under section 64 of the 1980 Act shall be made in writing to the clerk of the court to whom application may be made in accordance with the provisions of that section.

(2) The clerk of court shall, on any such application being made to him, cause intimation of the application to be given to the prosecutor.

(3) The court to whom the application is made may dispose of the application after such enquiry as it thinks fit.

Administration where person under disability

82. Where payment of any sum is made under a compensation order to the clerk of court in respect of a person known to be under a legal disability, paragraphs (1) to (3) and (5) of rule 128 of the First Schedule to the Sheriff Courts (Scotland) Act 1907 shall apply to the administration of that sum as they apply to the administration of a sum of money paid into court in respect of damages for such a person.

Form of extract of sentence

83.—(1) This rule applies to any case where an accused person has been sentenced to a custodial sentence following upon conviction on indictment.

(2) An extract of a custodial sentence and warrant of detention and return of sentence required for any purpose in connection with any case to which this rule applies, shall be in the form set out in Form 36 of Schedule 1 and shall be signed by the clerk of court.

(3) An extract issued in accordance with the provisions of paragraph (2) above shall be warrant and authority for execution.

Forms of warrant for execution and charge for payment of fine or other financial penalty

[1] **83A.**—(1) In every extract of a sentence of a fine or other financial penalty, there shall be included a warrant for execution in the following terms:– "and the Lords [*or* sheriff] grant(s) warrant for all lawful execution hereon.".

(2) The form of charge for payment of a fine or other financial penalty to be used by a sheriff officer under section 90 of the Debtors (Scotland) Act 1987 shall be in Form 36A of Schedule 1.

NOTE
¹ Inserted by S.I. 1989 No. 1020.

PART IV

APPEAL PROCEDURE

Forms for appeal
84.—(1) For the purposes of appeals, the forms specified by number in column 3 of the Table set out below and set out under those numbers in Schedule 1 are the forms prescribed under the 1975 Act for the purposes of the sections of that Act specified in column 1 of the Table relating respectively to the matters summarised in column 2 of the Table, and shall have effect for those purposes.

TABLE

(1) No. of Section	(2) Content	(3) No. of Form
231	Intimation of intention to appeal	37
233	Note of appeal	38
236B	Application for extension of time	39
238	Application for bail pending appeal	40
244	Notice of abandonment of appeal	41
251	Notification of decision	42
251	Application for determination by High Court	43

(2) Where the Clerk of Justiciary extends the period for lodging a written note of appeal under section 233(1) he shall record the period of any such extension on the completed form of intimation of intention to appeal.

· · · · · ·

Suspension of disqualification from driving pending appeal
86.—(1) Where a person who has been disqualified from holding or obtaining a driving licence appeals against that disqualification to the Court, any application to suspend that disqualification pending the hearing of the appeal shall be made—
(*a*) if the sentencing court was the sheriff, by application to the sheriff;
(*b*) if the sentencing court was the High Court, or if an application to the sheriff under sub-paragraph (*a*) has been refused, by petition in the form set out in Form 44 of Schedule 1.
(2) An application to the sheriff under paragraph (1)(*a*) shall be in the form set out in Form 44A of Schedule 1 and shall be lodged with the sheriff clerk together with a copy of the Note of Appeal endorsed with the receipt of the Clerk of Justiciary.
(3) The sheriff clerk shall record the order made by the sheriff on the application in the minute of proceedings.
(4) A petition under paragraph (1)(*b*) shall be lodged with the Clerk of Justiciary.

(5) The petitioner or his solicitor shall, on lodging the petition, send a copy of it to—

(*a*) the Crown Agent, and

(*b*) if the sentencing court was the sheriff, if the clerk of that court.

(6) The court may order such further intimation (including intimation to the Lord Advocate) as it thinks fit, and may dispose of the application in open court or in chambers as it thinks fit.

(7) An order made by a single judge under paragraph (6) shall not be subject to review.

(8) On an order being made on the petition, the Clerk of Justiciary shall, if the sentencing court was the sheriff, send a certified copy of the order to the clerk of that court.

(9) If the order suspends the disqualification, the Clerk of Justiciary shall also send a certified copy of the order to the Secretary of State with such further information as the Secretary of State may require.

(10) The Clerk of Justiciary shall, on determination of the appeal—

(*a*) if the sentencing court was the sheriff, send the clerk of that court a certified copy of the order determining the appeal and the clerk shall, if appropriate, make the appropriate endorsement on the appellant's driving licence and intimate the disqualification;

(*b*) otherwise if the appeal against the disqualification is refused, make the appropriate endorsement on the appellant's driving licence, and intimate the disqualification.

CHAPTER 2

SUMMARY PROCEDURE

PART I

PROCEDURE PRIOR TO TRIAL

Forms

Forms of complaint and related notices

87.—(1) The form of complaint referred to in section 311(1) shall be in the form set out in Form 45 of Schedule 1.

(2) The form of notice referred to in section 311(5) shall be in the form set out in Form 46 of Schedule 1.

(3) The form of citation of the accused referred to in section 315(2) shall be in the form set out in Form 47 of Schedule 1.

(4) The form of notice of previous convictions referred to in section 357(1)(*a*) shall be in the form set out in Form 48 of Schedule 1.

Ancillary forms

88. The procurator fiscal shall send to the accused person together with the citation—

(*a*) a reply form for completion and return by him stating whether he pleads guilty or not guilty in the form set out in Form 49 of Schedule 1;

(*b*) a means form for completion and return by him in the form set out in Form 50 of Schedule 1.

. . . . . .

Interim Hospital Order

Application

112.—(1) Where the court has made or renewed an *interim* hospital order under section 375A and the responsible medical officer has intimated to the prosecutor either—

(*a*) that he seeks a continuation of the order, or

(*b*) that he seeks termination of the order before the date on which it would otherwise cease to have effect,

the prosecutor shall make an application in the form set out in Form 29 of Schedule 1 to the court which made the order, to renew or terminate the order, as the case may be.

(2) Where an application is made under paragraph (1)—

(*a*) the court shall, by interlocutor in the form set out in Form 30 of Schedule 1 appoint a diet for hearing the application and, where appropriate, grant warrant to authorised officers of the hospital, or officers of law, for conveyance of the offender from the hospital to the court for that diet; and

(*b*) the clerk of court shall intimate the application and the diet to the offender or his solicitor.

(3) Where, in an application under paragraph (1)(*a*), the court renews an *interim* hospital order before the date on which the order would otherwise cease to have effect, the period of renewal shall commence from the date on which the order would otherwise cease to have effect.

(4) Where the court makes an order to renew or terminate an *interim* hospital order before the date on which it would otherwise cease to have effect, the adjourned diet fixed when the previous order of the court was made shall be treated as being discharged.

. . . . . .

Part III

Conviction and Sentence

Interruption of proceedings

123.—(1) On conviction of an accused person in summary proceedings the judge may, without adjourning those proceedings, interrupt them by—

(*a*) considering a conviction against that person in other proceedings pending before that court for which he has not been sentenced;

(*b*) passing sentence on that person in respect of the conviction in those other proceedings.

(2) When the judge has interrupted any proceedings under the powers contained in paragraph (1), he may in passing sentence on an accused

person in respect of a conviction in those proceedings at the same time pass sentence on that person in respect of any other conviction he has considered thereunder.

(3) No interruption of any proceedings under the powers contained in paragraphs (1) and (2) shall cause the instance to fall in respect of any person accused in those proceedings or shall otherwise affect the validity of those proceedings.

Forms for fines enquiry and related matters

124.—(1) The forms set out in Forms 57 to 69 of Schedule 1 shall have effect in summary proceedings for the purpose of determining means in respect of fines and related matters.

(2) Those forms may be used for that purpose with such variations as circumstances may require.

(3) This rule does not affect the Second Schedule to the Summary Jurisdiction (Scotland) Act 1954.

Compensation orders

125.—(1) The provisions of this rule apply to compensation orders made by courts against convicted persons under Part IV of the 1980 Act.

(2) Entries shall be made in the minutes of proceedings by the clerk of court on the making of a compensation order, specifying the terms of the order and in particular—

    (*a*) the name of the convicted person or persons required to pay compensation;

    (*b*) the amount of compensation required to be paid by such person or such persons;

    (*c*) the name of the person or persons entitled to the compensation payable;

    (*d*) where there is more than one such person, the amount of compensation each is entitled to and the priority, if any, among those persons for payment.

(3) The prosecutor, if he knows that any person entitled to payment of compensation under a compensation order is under any legal disability, shall so inform the court immediately it makes any such order in respect of any such person, and that information shall be entered by the clerk of court in the minutes of proceedings.

(4) Those entries shall be authenticated by the signature of the clerk of court.

(5) The judge may, at any time before a compensation order is fully complied with, and after such further enquiries as the court may order, vary the terms of the order as he thinks fit.

(6) A variation order under paragraph (5) may be made in chambers and in the absence of the parties, or any of them.

(7) An application to discharge a compensation order or to reduce the amount that remains to be paid under section 64 of the 1980 Act shall be made in writing to the clerk of the court to whom application may be made in accordance with the provisions of that section.

(8) The clerk of court shall, on any such application being made to him, cause intimation of the application to be given to the procurator fiscal.

(9) The court to whom the application is made may dispose of the application after such inquiry as it thinks fit.

(10) Where payment of any sum is made under a compensation order to the clerk of court in respect of a person known to be under a legal disability, paragraphs (1) to (3) and (5) of rule 128 of the First Schedule to the Sheriff Courts (Scotland) Act 1907 shall apply to the administration of that sum as they apply to the administration of a sum of money paid into court in respect of damages for such a person.

Form of probation order
126. A probation order shall be in the form set out in Form 35 of Schedule 1.

Forms of warrant for execution and charge for payment of fine or other financial penalty
[1] **126A.**—(1) In every extract of a sentence of a fine or other financial penalty, there shall be included a warrant for execution in the following terms:– "and the sheriff [*or* justice(s)] grant(s) warrant for all lawful execution hereon.".

(2) The form of charge for payment of a fine or other financial penalty to be used by a sheriff officer under section 90 of the Debtors (Scotland) Act 1987 shall be in Form 36A of Schedule 1.

NOTE
[1] Inserted by S.I. 1989 No. 1020.

PART IV

APPEAL PROCEDURE

Forms for appeal
127. For the purposes of appeals in summary proceedings the forms specified by numbers in column 3 of the Table set out below and set out under those numbers in Schedule 1 are the forms prescribed under the 1975 Act for the purposes of the sections of that Act specified in column 1 of the Table relating respectively to the matters summarised in column 2 of the Table, and shall have effect for those purposes.

TABLE

(1) No. of Section	(2) Content	(3) No. of Form
442A(2)	Minute abandoning appeal against conviction only	70
444	Application for a stated case	71
447(2)	Stated case	72
449	Minute abandoning stated case	70
450	Minutes of procedure in appeal by stated case	73
453B	Minutes of procedure in note of appeal	74
451(2)	Extension of time limit by sheriff principal	75
453B(1)	Note of appeal against sentence	76
453B(4)	Extension of time limit by sheriff principal	75
453B(7)	Minute abandoning appeal	77

. . . . . .

Extension of time for appeal against sentence only

130.—(1) Where by virtue of the provisions of section 453B(6), the court makes an order extending the period within which the note of appeal shall be lodged under subsection (2) of that section, the periods mentioned in subsections (2) and (4) of that section shall run from the date which is two days after the date on which the court makes that order and not from the passing of the sentence.

(2) If the date from which an extended period runs by virtue of paragraph (1) is a Saturday, Sunday or court holiday prescribed for the relevant court, the date shall be the next date that is not a Saturday, Sunday or court holiday.

Intimation of abandonment

[1] **131.** The Clerk of Justiciary or the clerk of court, as the case may be, on the lodging with him of—

(*a*) a minute abandoning an appeal by stated case under section 449;

(*b*) a minute abandoning a note of appeal against sentence under section 453B(7),

shall notify immediately the Crown Agent or the prosecutor, as the case may be, of the lodging of the minute; and, the Clerk of Justiciary shall, where the minute is lodged with him, notify immediately the clerk of court.

NOTE
[1] As amended by S.I. 1990 No. 2106.

Suspension of disqualification from driving pending application to sentencing court

132.—(1) Where a person who has been disqualified from holding or obtaining a driving licence appeals against that disqualification by stated case under section 442, any application to suspend the disqualification shall be made together with the application to the court to state a case for the opinion of the High Court.

(2) On an application being made under paragraph (1) to suspend a disqualification, the court shall grant or refuse to grant the application within seven days of it being made.

(3) If the court refuses to grant the application and the appellant applies to the High Court to suspend the disqualification, any such application shall be made by note in the form set out in Form 80 of Schedule 1.

(4) The note shall be lodged by the appellant or his solicitor with the Clerk of Justiciary.

(5) The appellant or his solicitor shall intimate the lodging of the note to the respondent and the clerk of the court which imposed the sentence of disqualification.

(6) The clerk shall on receiving such intimation forthwith send to the Clerk of Justiciary—

(*a*) a certified copy of the complaint;

(*b*) a certified copy of the minute of proceedings.

(7) The Court may order such further intimation (including intimation

to the Lord Advocate) as it thinks fit, and may dispose of the application in open court or in chambers after such hearing as it thinks fit.

(8) On the High Court making an order on the note, the Clerk of Justiciary shall send a certified copy of the order to the clerk.

(9) If the order suspends the disqualification, the Clerk of Justiciary shall also send a certified copy of the order to the Secretary of State with such further information as the Secretary of State may require.

(10) An order made by a single judge of the High Court under this rule shall not be subject to review.

· · · · · ·

PART V

PROCEDURE IN SPECIAL SUMMARY PROCEEDINGS

Proceedings Against Children

· · · · · ·

Procedure

144. In any case where a child is brought before a court on a complaint the court—

(*a*) shall explain to the child the substance of the charge in simple language suitable to his age and understanding, and shall then ask the child whether he admits the charge;

(*b*) if the child has been brought before the court on apprehension, shall inform him that he is entitled to an adjournment of the case for not less than 48 hours;

(*c*) if the child does not admit the charge, may adjourn the case for trial to as early a diet as is fair to both parties, and in that event shall give intimation or order intimation to be given of such adjourned diet to such child and his parent or guardian: but the court may proceed to trial forthwith if the court considers this to be advisable in the interests of the child or to be necessary to secure the examination of witnesses who would not otherwise be available;

(*d*) if in any case, where the child is not represented by solicitor or counsel or assisted in his defence under rule 143, the child, instead of asking questions by way of cross-examination, makes assertions, shall then put to the witness such questions as it thinks necessary on behalf of the child and may for this purpose question the child in order to clarify any point arising out of any such assertions;

(*e*) at the close of the case for the prosecution, shall tell the child that he may give evidence or make a statement and the evidence of any witness for the defence shall be heard;

(*f*) if satisfied, after trial or otherwise, that the child has committed an offence, shall so inform the child and—

(i) he and his parent or guardian, or other representative, shall be given an opportunity of making a statement;

(ii) shall obtain such information as to the general conduct, home surroundings, school record, health and character of the child as may enable it to deal with the case in his best interests and may remand the child for such enquiry as may be necessary;

(iii) shall take into consideration any report which may be rendered to it by a local authority under section 308;

(g) may receive and consider any written report of a local authority, education authority, or registered medical practitioner without it being read aloud, provided that—

(i) the child shall be told of the substance of any part of the report bearing on his character or conduct which the court considers to be material to the disposal of the case:

(ii) the parent or guardian, or other representative shall, if present, be told the substance of any part of the report which the court considers to be material and which has reference to his character or conduct, or the character, conduct, home surroundings or health of the child; and

(iii) if the child or his parent or guardian, or other representative, having been told the substance of any part of any such report, desires to produce evidence in relation to any matter contained in it, the court, if it thinks the evidence material, shall adjourn the proceedings for the production of further evidence, and shall, if necessary, require the attendance at the adjourned hearing of the person who made the report;

(h) if it considers it necessary in the interests of the child, may require the parent or guardian, or other representative, or the child, as the case may be, to withdraw from the court;

(i) shall, unless it thinks it undesirable to do so, inform the parent or guardian, or other representative, of the manner in which it proposes to deal with the child and shall allow that person to make a statement, if he so desires.

Failure to comply with probation order

145. In any case where a child is to be brought before a court upon information given on oath that he has failed to comply with any of the requirements of a probation order—

(a) the person under whose supervision the child has been placed shall immediately on being placed on oath inform the procurator fiscal on oath of the respects in which the child has so failed to comply, as far as known to him;

(b) the citation (if any) requiring the appearance of the child shall be accompanied by a notice giving the reasons for the issue of such citation and stating in what respects it is alleged that any one or more of the requirements of the order has or have not been complied with by him, and in any case where the child has been apprehended without prior citation such notice shall be handed to him in court;

(c) the court shall explain to the child in simple language suitable to his age and understanding the effect of the notice and shall then ask him whether he admits having failed to comply with the requirements of the order as alleged; provided that, where the notice has been handed to the child in court, the court may, if it thinks it desirable, adjourn the proceedings for 48 hours before so asking him;

(*d*) if the child does not admit the alleged failure to comply with the requirements of the order, the proceedings shall thereafter be conducted and the matter shall be determined by the court in like manner as if the same were a matter which had arisen for determination upon the original complaint.

Remand

146. The court may from time to time and at any stage of a case remand a child for information to be obtained with respect to him.

. . . . . .

SCHEDULE 1

PART I

FORMS REFERRED TO IN CHAPTER I (SOLEMN PROCEDURE)

. . . . . .

Rules 62 and 112   FORM 29

APPLICATION FOR RENEWAL OR TERMINATION OF INTERIM HOSPITAL ORDER UNDER SECTION 174A(1) AND 375A(1) OF THE CRIMINAL PROCEDURE (SCOTLAND) ACT 1975

UNTO THE RIGHT HONOURABLE THE LORD JUSTICE GENERAL, LORD JUSTICE CLERK AND LORDS COMMISSIONERS OF JUSTICIARY

(or UNTO THE HONOURABLE THE SHERIFF
OF   AT   )

APPLICATION

under

Section 174A(6), 375A(7) of the Criminal
Procedure (Scotland) Act 1975

by
Her Majesty's Advocate
(or AB   Procurator Fiscal)
in respect of
CD presently a patient in
Hospital

for

Renewal (or Termination) of an *interim* hospital order

(1) On (*date*) the court made an *interim* hospital order in respect of CD (which order was renewed by the court on (*date*)).

(2) The order expires on (*date*).

(3) It is necessary to bring the case before the court before the date mentioned in paragraph 2 above for the following reasons

         (*here state reasons*).

MAY IT THEREFORE please your Lordship(s) to fix a diet for the purpose of considering this application to renew the *interim* hospital order; (and for that purpose to grant warrant to authorised officers of the hospital (or officers of the law) to bring CD before the court for said diet).

Or MAY IT THEREFORE please your Lordship(s) to fix a diet for the purpose of considering this application and further information now available with a view to making a final disposal of the case; (and for that purpose to grant warrant to authorised officers of the hospital (or officers of law) to bring CD before the court for said diet).

According to justice, etc.

(*signed*)
for Her Majesty's Advocate
(or Procurator Fiscal (Depute))

(*Plate and date*)

Rules 62 and 112   FORM 30

FORM OF ORDER FOR DIET OF HEARING AND WARRANT FOR CONVEYANCE OF OFFENDER TO COURT FOR HEARING OF APPLICATION FOR RENEWAL OR TERMINATION OF INTERIM ORDER

(*place*)   (*date*) 19

Appoints   the   day of

19   at   within

as a diet for hearing the foregoing application; Grants
warrant to (authorised officers of hospital) (officers of
law) to bring
before the court for said diet.

(*signed*)
(Lord Commissioner of Justiciary)
(Sheriff)

· · · · · ·

Rules 76 and 126   Form 35

FORM OF PROBATION ORDER

Under the Criminal Procedure (Scotland) Act 1975, Sections 183 and 384

COURT:

ON   19

OFFENDER:

Address:

Date of Birth:

The court   being satisfied that the offender has committed the offence with which he is charged
            (or)
            in view of the conviction of the offender

and being of the opinion that having regard to the circumstances, including the nature of the offence and the character of the offender, it is expedient to make a probation order containing the undernoted requirements; and the court having explained to the offender the effect of the order (including the requirements set out below), and that if he fails to comply with the order, he may be brought before the court by his supervising officer for a breach of probation and may be sentenced/dealt with for the original offence, and that, if he commits another offence during the period of the probation order, he may be dealt with likewise:

And the offender having expressed his willingness to comply with the requirements of the order:

THE COURT therefore orders that for a period of
the date hereof the offender who resides/is to reside in the local authority area of
                                                           shall be under the
supervision of an officer of that local authority allocated for the purpose/allocated for the purpose as required by the court at   in
the said local authority area; that the offender shall be notified in writing by the clerk of court of the name and official address of the officer who is to supervise him and similarly if at any time such supervision is to be undertaken by another officer of the local authority allocated for the purpose; and that the offender shall comply with the following requirements, namely—
    (1) to be of good behaviour;
    (2) to conform to the directions of the supervising officer;
    (3) to inform the supervising officer at once if he changes his residence or place of employment;
    (4) (*Here insert any additional requirements*)

                                                      Clerk of Court.

Date:

Note: of   has been allocated as supervising officer in this case.

CRIMINAL PROCEDURE (SCOTLAND) ACT 1975

EXTRACT SENTENCE, WARRANT OF DETENTION AND RETURN OF SENTENCE

Court	Judge
Accused	Date of Sentence
	Address (where known)

Date of Birth	Marital Status	Occupation

Offence(s) for which sentenced	Method of conviction Jury trial Plea Sec. 102

Sentence: The court sentenced, decerned and adjudged the said accused to be imprisoned as from this date for the period specified below and thereafter to be set at liberty

Period of Imprisonment:

Warrant: In respect of the foregoing sentence the court ordained, and hereby ordains, the said accused to be conveyed by officers of law to the Prison of

thereafter to be dealt with in due course of law.

Officers to prove conviction	

Previous record
(as per list attached)

Extracted by me ....

....

Rules 83A and 126A   [1] FORM 36A

FORM OF CHARGE FOR PAYMENT OF A FINE OR OTHER FINANCIAL PENALTY

CHARGE FOR PAYMENT OF A FINE OR OTHER FINANCIAL PENALTY
instructed by the sheriff clerk (*address*) or Clerk to the District Court (*address*)

To (*name and address of person fined or subject to the financial penalty*)

On (*date*) a fine [*or financial penalty*] (*give details and total amount of fine or other financial penalty*) was imposed on you in the High Court of Justiciary [*or* Sheriff Court *or* District Court] at (*place*)

The court authorised recovery of the fine [*or other financial penalty*] on (*date*) and an extract conviction was issued in respect of the outstanding balance of £

I, (*name and address*), sheriff officer, by virtue of the extract conviction in Her Majesty's name and authority and in the name and authority of the Lords Commissioners of Justiciary [*or* sheriff *or* justice] at (*place*), charge you to pay the total sum due within [14] days after the date of this charge to the sheriff clerk [or clerk to the District Court] (*address*)

If you do not pay this sum within [14] days you are liable to have further action taken against you.

This charge is served on you today by me (*state method of service*) and is witnessed by (*name and address of witness*)

Dated the   day of   19

(*Signed*)   (*Signed*)
Witness   Sheriff Officer

_____

NOTE
[1] Inserted by S.I. 1989 No. 1020.

Rule 84   FORM 37
(Section 231)

INTIMATION OF INTENTION TO APPEAL

HIGH COURT OF JUSTICIARY

To: Clerk of Justiciary

> Intimation of Intention to
> Appeal
> under
> Criminal Procedure (Scotland)
> Act 1975

Name of convicted person

Date of Birth

Prisoner in the Prison of

Date of final determination of the proceedings

Crime or offence to which appeal relates

Court and name of judge

Sentence

*[or as the
case may be]*

Intimation is hereby given that the above named intends to appeal to the   *[delete as
High Court against the foregoing *conviction/conviction and sentence.   appropriate]*

> *(Signed by convicted person, his Counsel or Solicitor)*
> [*Solicitor to add address and telephone number*]

(Date)

Rule 84   Form 38
(Section 233)

Note of Appeal

HIGH COURT OF JUSTICIARY

To: Clerk of Justiciary

NOTE OF APPEAL
under
Criminal Procedure (Scotland)
Act 1975

Name of convicted person

Date of Birth

Prisoner in the Prison of
                                                    [*or as the*
Date of final determination of the proceedings   *case may be*]

Crime or offence to which appeal relates

Court and name of judge

Sentence

The above named convicted person appeals against *conviction/sentence/   *[*delete as*
conviction and sentence on the following grounds:–[*here*   *appropriate*]
give full statement of all grounds of appeal].

                    (*Signed by convicted person, his Counsel or Solicitor*)
                    [*Solicitor to add address and telephone number*]
(*Date*)

Rule 84   FORM 39
(Section 236B)

APPLICATION FOR EXTENSION OF TIME

HIGH COURT OF JUSTICIARY
Application for Extension of Time under Section 236B(2) of the Criminal Procedure
(Scotland) Act 1975

UNTO THE RIGHT HONOURABLE THE LORD JUSTICE GENERAL, LORD
JUSTICE CLERK AND LORDS COMMISSIONERS OF JUSTICIARY

Name of convicted person

Date of Birth

Prisoner in the Prison of   [*or as the*
  Date of final determination of the proceedings   *case may be*]

Crime or offence to which appeal relates

Court and name of judge

Sentence

Application is hereby made for extension of time within which to: [*delete as*
    (*a*) intimate an intention to appeal against conviction   *appropriate*]
    (*b*) intimate an intention to appeal against conviction & sentence
    (*c*) lodge a note of appeal against sentence
    (*d*) lodge a note of appeal against conviction
    (*e*) lodge a note of appeal against conviction and sentence
      for the following reasons:—
      [*here fully state the reasons for the failure to lodge timeously the intimation
      of intention to appeal or note of appeal as the case may be*].

               (*Signed by convicted person, his Counsel or Solicitor*)
[*Solicitor to add address and telephone number*]   (*Date*)

. . . . . .

Rule 84
(Section 244)   FORM 41

NOTICE OF ABANDONMENT OF APPEAL

CRIMINAL APPEAL

THE CRIMINAL PROCEDURE (SCOTLAND) ACT 1975

Name of convicted person

Date of birth

Prisoner in the Prison of   [*or as the*
Crime or offence to which appeal relates   *case may be*]

Court

Sentence

I, [*name in full*]   abandon as from
this date my appeal against:
    (a) Conviction
    (b) Conviction but proceed with   [*delete as*
        my appeal against sentence   *appropriate*]
    (c) Conviction and sentence
    (d) Sentence

(*Signature*) ....
                              Appellant

[*Place and date*]

To:– The Clerk of Justiciary
     Parliament Square
     Edinburgh
     EH1 1RF

Rule 84
(Section 251)   FORM 42

NOTIFICATION OF DECISION

CRIMINAL PROCEDURE (SCOTLAND) ACT 1975

NOTIFICATION UNDER SECTION 251 TO APPLICANT OF A DECISION OF A
JUDGE UNDER SECTION 247

To: (*Name and designation*)

I hereby give notice that a judge of the High Court of Justiciary having considered your
application for:—

(a) Extension of time within which an intimation of intention
to appeal against conviction/conviction and sentence
may be lodged;

(b) Extension of time within which a note of appeal against conviction/
conviction and sentence/sentence may be lodged;   [*delete as
                                                                    appropriate*]

(c) Permission to you to be present at the hearing of any proceedings in
relation to your appeal and/or application;

(d) Admission to bail

has refused/granted the application ....
....

If you desire to have the above mentioned application(s) which has/have been refused,
determined by the High Court of Justiciary constituted as provided in the Act above
mentioned you are required to fill up the enclosed form and return it to me within five days
of its receipt by you, otherwise the decision of the single judge will be final.

....
                                                   Clerk of Justiciary
[*Date*]

Rule 84   FORM 43

APPLICATION FOR DETERMINATION BY HIGH COURT

CRIMINAL PROCEDURE (SCOTLAND) ACT 1975

REQUISITION UNDER SECTION 251 FOR DETERMINATION BY THE COURT
UNDER SECTION 247 OF APPLICATION(S) REFUSED BY A SINGLE JUDGE

To: Clerk of Justiciary

I, (*name in full*)   having received your
notification that my application(s) for:—

(a) Extension of time within which an intimation of intention
to appeal against conviction/conviction and sentence
may be lodged;

(b) Extension of time within which a note of appeal against conviction/
conviction and sentence/sentence may be lodged;

                                                          [*delete as
(c) Permission to me to be present at the hearing of any proceedings   appropriate*]
in relation to my appeal and/or application;

(d) Admission to bail;

has/have been refused hereby give notice that I desire that the said application(s) shall be
considered and determined by the High Court of Justiciary constituted as provided in the
Act above mentioned.

(*Signature*) .... Applicant

[*Date*]

Note:—If the applicant desires to be present at the hearing by the court in relation to his application(s), he should complete and sign the following:—

I, (*name in full*)
*(not being legally represented) desire to be present at the hearing of
my application(s) above mentioned.

*If legally
represented
delete these
words

(*Signature*) .... Applicant

[*Date*]

Rule 86   FORM 44

UNTO THE RIGHT HONOURABLE THE LORD JUSTICE-GENERAL, THE
LORD JUSTICE CLERK AND LORDS COMMISSIONERS OF JUSTICIARY

THE PETITION OF

presently

....

HUMBLY SHEWETH:

THAT on the   day of   19   the petitioner was convicted
in the   Court
at   and was
inter alia ordered to be disqualified for a period of   in terms
of section 93 of the Road Traffic Act 1972.

THAT on   the petitioner lodged with the Clerk of Justiciary a note of
appeal in terms of the provisions of section 233 of the Criminal Procedure (Scotland) Act
1975.

*THAT an application for suspension of the said disqualification made in terms of section
94(3) of the said Road Traffic Act was refused by the said sheriff court on the
day of   19   and that the petitioner has
served a copy of this petition on the clerk of the said sheriff court.

THAT the petitioner has served a copy of this petition on the Crown Agent.

May it therefore please your Lordships in
terms of section 94B(2) of the Road
Traffic Act 1972 to suspend the said
disqualification on such terms as your
Lordships think fit.

According to justice &c

Solicitor for petitioner

*Delete as applicable
(Sheriff Court case only)

APPLICATION TO SHERIFF FOR SUSPENSION OF ORDER FOR DISQUALIFICATION PENDING
APPEAL

A.B.
Appellant
against
HER MAJESTY'S ADVOCATE
Respondent

HUMBLY SHEWETH:

(1) THAT on the   day of   19   the Appellant was convicted
in the Sheriff Court at   and was
inter alia ordered to be disqualified for a period of   in terms
of section 93 of the Road Traffic Act 1972.

(2) THAT on   the appellant lodged with the Clerk of Justiciary
a note of appeal in terms of the provisions of section 233 of the Criminal Procedure
(Scotland) Act 1975. A copy of said note is attached hereto and is endorsed as having
been received by the Clerk of Justiciary.

(3) THAT the appellant has served a copy of this application on the procurator fiscal at

> May it therefore please your Lordships in
> terms of section 94(3) of the Road
> Traffic Act 1972 to suspend the said
> disqualification on such terms as your
> Lordships think fit.

Solicitor of appellant

(Place and date)

Part II

Forms Referred to in Chapter 2 (Summary Procedure)

. . . . . .

Rule 87 Form 48

Form of Notice of Previous Convictions

NOTICE OF PREVIOUS CONVICTIONS APPLYING TO A.B.

In the event of your being convicted of the charge(s) in the complaint it is intended to place before the court the following previous conviction(s) applying to you.

Date	Place of Trial	Court	Offence	Sentence

. . . . . .

Rule 88   Form 50

MEANS FORM

INFORMATION ABOUT YOUR MEANS   PF REF ....

You are not required by law to return this form completed but it can help you and the court.

If you are found guilty and are fined the information you give here will help the court to set an amount which you can reasonably afford and to give you the time you need to pay.

The information you give on this form will not be used for any other purpose.

If you decide to plead guilty by letter please complete this and the reply form and send them to the court.

If you decide to appear in court you may hand the form in when you appear.

If the information you have given below changes a great deal between now and the court hearing you should tell the clerk of court—he will give you another form to fill in.

PERSONAL DETAILS (Please use BLOCK CAPITALS and tick the appropriate box where required).

---

1. Your full name ....
2. Your address ....
3. Are you   Married   Single   Separated   Divorced   Widowed
4. Are you the head of your household?   Yes   No
5. How many children under 16 do you support ....
6. Is there anyone else financially dependent on you?   Yes   No
   (a) If YES what is their relationship to you ....

YOUR JOB

---

7. Are you   Employed   Unemployed   Self-employed   Other
   (a) If OTHER, please give details here ....
   (b) If EMPLOYED, please give your job here ....

YOUR WEEKLY INCOME   YOUR WEEKLY EXPENSES

You may not receive your money or pay your bills weekly. Even so please try to work out what the weekly figures would be.

	£		£
8. (a) Your usual weekly take-home pay including over-time. (If self-employed give your usual earnings)	____	9. (a) Housing (rent, rates, mortgage). (If you pay board and lodgings give the amount)	____
(b) Usual total take-home pay of other household earners	____	(b) Fuel (electricity, coal, gas, etc.)	____
(c) Total social security payments received in your household each week	____	(c) Food	____
		(d) Travel	____
(d) Total pensions received in your household each week	____	(e) Weekly cost of supporting anyone else (see question 6)	____
		(f) Other big weekly payments (such as hire purchase agreements or repayment of rent arrears)	____
Usual total WEEKLY household income	____	Usual total WEEKLY expenses	____

GENERAL DETAILS

10. If the court decides to fine you how much do you think you could afford to pay each week? £ ....

11. Please give any further information about your finances which you would like the court to know here. (You can continue over the page if you need to.)

SIGNATURE BOX

12. I declare that the information I have given in this form is true

Signed .... Date ....

. . . . . .

Rule 124   FORM 57

CITATION TO APPEAR FOR ENQUIRY

Under the Criminal Procedure (Scotland) Act 1975, Section 398

Court:

To	*(Name and designation)*		No.
			Date
			Fine
			Class of offence
			Rate of payment

Citation to attend for enquiry

on   19

at   .m.

Balance
outstanding £

In respect that you were fined as shown above, that you are in default of payment and that the outstanding balance of said fine is as shown above you are ordained to appear personally at the time and date shown above in the ....
Court at ....
for an enquiry under section 398 of the Criminal Procedure (Scotland) Act 1975.

(Place),   19   Clerk of Court

NOTES
(1) If you fail to appear personally at the enquiry court, the court may issue a warrant for your arrest.
(2) If you pay the whole outstanding balance of the fine before the enquiry court, it will not be necessary for you to appear.

. . . . . .

Rule 124   Form 60

NOTICE OF FINES SUPERVISION ORDER

Under the Criminal Procedure (Scotland) Act 1975, Section 400

Court:

To: (*Name and designation*)

In respect that a fine of £   was imposed on you by the court at
on   19   and the said fine (or balance of £   ) remains unpaid, the court today
has placed you under the supervision of
                                                                                who
will assist you and advise you on the payment of the fine for so long as the fine remains
unpaid or until the further order of court.

Payment of the fine is now to be made by weekly instalments of £   per week—first
instalment due within   days from this date.

(*Place*),   19   Clerk of Court

Copy to: Director of Social Work
        (*Address*)

· · · · · ·

Rule 124   Form 62

TRANSFER OF FINE ORDER (WITHIN SCOTLAND)

Under the Criminal Procedure (Scotland) Act 1975, Section 403

IN THE   COURT AT

(*Name*)

Date of birth:

was on   19   convicted of   (*offence*)

and was sentenced to pay a fine of £   , said fine to be paid by   19   or by
weekly instalments of £   , the first instalment to be paid on   19   ; and the
said fine or the balance of the said fine as shown in the statement annexed hereto is still
unpaid

and   imprisonment has been
fixed in the event of a future default in payment of the sum in question.

And as it appears that the said (*name*)
is now residing at

a transfer of fine order is hereby made in pursuance of section 403 of the Criminal Procedure
(Scotland) Act 1975, transferring to the   Court of

at   and to the
clerk thereof with respect of the said fine all the functions referred to in said section.

Date: 19   Judge

STATEMENT REFERRED TO

Fine	£	
Instalment(s) paid to date of transfer	£	_____
Balance due	£	_____
In instalments of	£	

Clerk of Court

Rule 124   FORM 63

TRANSFER OF FINE ORDER (TO ENGLAND AND WALES AND NORTHERN IRELAND)

Under the Criminal Procedure (Scotland) Act 1975, Section 403

IN THE   COURT AT

(*Name*)

Date of birth:

was on   19   convicted of   (*offence*)

and was sentenced to pay a fine of £   , said fine to be paid by weekly instalments
of £   , the first instalment to be paid on   19   ; and the said fine or the balance
of the said fine as shown in the statement annexed hereto is still unpaid and

imprisonment has been fixed
in the event of a future default in payment of the sum in question.

And as it appears that the said (*name*)
is now residing at

a transfer of fine order is hereby made in pursuance of section 403 of the Criminal Procedure
(Scotland) Act 1975, transferring to the

and to the clerk thereof with respect of the said fine all the functions referred to in said
section.

Date: 19   Judge

STATEMENT REFERRED TO

Fine	£	
Instalment(s) paid to date of transfer	£	_____
Balance due	£	_____
In instalments of	£	

Clerk of Court

Rule 124   Form 64

Further Transfer of Fine Order

Under the Criminal Procedure (Scotland) Act 1975, Section 403

IN THE   COURT AT
(or the Magistrates Court acting for the Petty Sessions Area of
                    or in the District of   )

(*Name*)

Date of birth:

was on   19   convicted of   (*offence*)

and was sentenced to pay a fine of £   , said fine to be paid by weekly instalments of
£   , the first instalment to be paid on   19   ; by virtue of a
transfer of fine order dated   19   , the function of the last mentioned court
and the clerk thereof with respect to that sum are exercisable by this   Court at
                          and the clerk thereof; and the said fine or the balance
of the said fine as shown in the statement annexed hereto is still unpaid and

                                        imprisonment has been fixed
in the event of a future default in payment of the sum in question.

And as it appears that the said (*name*)
is now residing at

outwith the jurisdiction of this court, a further transfer of fine order is hereby made in
pursuance of section 403 of the Criminal Procedure (Scotland) Act 1975, transferring to the

and to the clerk thereof with respect of the said fine all the functions referred to in said
section.

Date: 19   Judge

STATEMENT REFERRED TO

Fine	£	
Instalment(s) paid to date of transfer	£	_____
Balance due	£	_____
In instalments of	£	

Clerk of Court

Rule 124   FORM 65

NOTICE TO OFFENDER OF TRANSFER OF FINE ORDER

Under the Criminal Procedure (Scotland) Act 1975, Section 403

IN THE   COURT AT

TO: (*Name and designation*)

On   19   , you were convicted by the
          Court at   and were
sentenced to pay a fine of £   , said fine to be paid by   19   ; the said fine
has not been fully paid and

imprisonment has been fixed in the event of a future default in payment of the sum in
question.

NOTICE IS HEREBY GIVEN TO YOU that in consequence of a transfer of fine order
made by the   Court
at   on
          19   , the enforcement of the said fine or balance thereof due by you as shown
in the statement annexed hereto, has become a matter for this court.

Payment of the   due by you should therefore be made within the time
(or times) ordered, either by post or personally to me (*clerk of court and address*)

If you cannot pay forthwith (or by   19   ), you should at once make an
application for further time to be granted. Such an application should be made either in
person to this court or by letter addressed to me stating fully why you are unable to pay the
sum due.

                                                      Clerk of Court

NOTE: Any communications sent by post must be properly stamped.
       Cash should not be sent in an unregistered envelope.

STATEMENT REFERRED TO

Fine	£	
Instalment(s) paid to date of transfer	£	_____
Balance due	£	_____
In instalments of	£	

                                                      Clerk of Court

              .   .   .   .   .   .

Rule 127   FORM 70
(Sections 422A(2) and 449)

MINUTE ABANDONING APPEAL

SHERIFF COURT/DISTRICT COURT ....

UNDER THE CRIMINAL PROCEDURE (SCOTLAND) ACT 1975
SECTION 442A(2)/449

MINUTE OF ABANDONMENT

IN THE

APPEAL BY STATED CASE

A.B., APPELLANT v. THE PROCURATOR FISCAL, RESPONDENT

(delete where not   The said A.B. abandons his appeal as from this date against:
applicable)

    (a) conviction;

    (b) conviction and sentence;

    (c) conviction but proceeds with his appeal against sentence on the
    following ground:–*(here specify)*

Intimation of the foregoing abandonment has been made to the respondent.

                              (Signed) A.B.

                              [or C.D.

                              Solicitor for the said A.B.]
                              (address and telephone number)

(Place and date)

Rule 127   FORM 71
(Section 444)

APPLICATION FOR STATED CASE

SHERIFF COURT/DISTRICT COURT ....

UNDER THE CRIMINAL PROCEDURE (SCOTLAND) ACT 1975

APPLICATION FOR STATED CASE

PROCURATOR FISCAL v. A.B.

(1) The said *A.B./procurator fiscal craves the court to state a case for the opinion of the
High Court of Justiciary in the above proceedings in which the date of final
determination was
(date).

(2) The matters which it is desired to bring under review are:–*(here specify)*

    (a)
    (b)

(c)
(d)

*(3) The appeal is also against sentence.

*(4) The said A.B. also craves the court to (*here insert any application for bail, for interim suspension of an order for disqualification imposed under the Road Traffic Acts, or for any other interim order in terms of section 446(1) of the Criminal Procedure (Scotland) Act 1975*)

> (*Signed* *A.B./Procurator Fiscal
>
> [or C.D.
>
> Solicitor for the said A.B.]
> (*address and telephone number*)

(*Place and date*)
*Delete as appropriate

Rule 127   FORM 72

STATED CASE

IN THE   COURT AT

Case for the Opinion of the High Court of Justiciary at Edinburgh *in causa*

Appellant v.   Respondent

This is a cause (*here state concisely and without argument the nature of the cause and the facts if any admitted or proved in evidence, any objections to the admission or rejection of evidence taken in the proof, the grounds of the decision, and any other matters necessary to be stated for the information of the superior court*)

The question submitted for the opinion of the court is:—(*here state the question or questions seriatim, for the opinion of the court*)

This case is stated by me (or us)

> (*Signature of the Judge(s)*)

(*Append any additional material required by section 448(2D) of the Criminal Procedure (Scotland) Act 1975*)

> (*Initials of the Judge(s)*)

. . . . . .

Rule 127

FORM 75

EXTENSION OF PERIOD BY SHERIFF PRINCIPAL

Under the Criminal Procedure (Scotland) Act 1975

SHERIFF COURT/DISTRICT COURT, ...

PROCURATOR FISCAL *v.* A.B.

(*Place and date*), I   Sheriff Principal
of the Sheriffdom of
by virtue of the powers vested in me by section 451(2)/453B(4) of the said Act,

(*or as*   and in respect that   (*name of judge*) is temporarily absent
the case   from duty, extend the period specified, in section 447(1)/448(2A)/
may be)   448(2D)/453B(4) of the said Act so that it will now expire on   (*date*).

Signed ....

Rule 127

FORM 76

NOTE OF APPEAL AGAINST SENTENCE

Under the Criminal Procedure (Scotland) Act 1975, Section 453B

SHERIFF COURT/DISTRICT COURT, ...

NOTE OF APPEAL
against sentence
by
A.B. presently prisoner
in the Prison of

(or now residing at   )
APPELLANT
against
the Procurator Fiscal
RESPONDENT

(1) The said A.B. appeals to the High Court of Justiciary against the sentence of
passed in the above court on   (*date*)
(2) The ground of appeal is:— (*here specify*)
(3) The said A.B. also craves the court to
(*here insert any application for bail, for interim suspension of an order for
disqualification imposed under the Road Traffic Acts, or for any other interim order in
terms of section 446(1) of the Criminal Procedure (Scotland) Act 1975*).

(*Signed*) A.B.

(or C.D.

Solicitor for the said A.B.)
(*address and telephone number*)

(*Place and date*)

Rule 127   FORM 77

MINUTE OF ABANDONMENT OF APPEAL AGAINST SENTENCE

Under the Criminal Procedure (Scotland) Act 1975, Section 453B(7)

Name of Appellant

Date of birth

Prisoner in the Prison of

Crime or offence to which appeal relates

Sheriff/District Court at

Sentence

The above named appellant having lodged a note of appeal in terms of section 442(1)(*a*)(ii) of said Act abandons as from this date said appeal against sentence.

Intimation of the foregoing abandonment has been made to the respondent.

> (*Signed*) A.B.
>
> (or C.D.
>
> Solicitor for the said A.B.)

(*Place and date*)

Rule 128   FORM 78

To: Sheriff Clerk/Clerk to the District Court
      at

NOTE OF APPEAL

under
the Criminal Procedure (Scotland) Act 1975,
Section 334,
by
A.B.
residing at
(or presently a prisoner in the Prison
of   )
APPELLANT
against
the Procurator Fiscal
RESPONDENT

Date of decision appealed against:

Date of trial:

The said appellant appeals to the High Court of Justiciary in respect that

(1) (*State whether objection taken to competency or relevancy of the complaint or the proceedings and specify the terms of said objection*)

(2) (*State the decision which it is desired to bring under review by the High Court*)

(3) (*State the grounds of appeal*)

> (*Signed*) A.B.
>
> (or C.D.
>
> Solicitor for the said A.B.)
> (*address and telephone number*)

(*Place and date*)

Rule 128(11)   FORM 79

MINUTE OF ABANDONMENT OF APPEAL

To: Clerk of Justiciary

> Minute of Abandonment
> of
> Appeal under Criminal Procedure
> (Scotland) Act 1975, Section
> 334(2A)

Name of appellant ....

Name of respondent ....

Date of decision appealed against ....

Date of appeal hearing ....

The above named appellant abandons the said appeal

> (*Signed*) *A.B./Procurator Fiscal
>
> (or C.D.
>
> Solicitor for the said A.B.)
> (*address and telephone number*)

(*Place and date*)
*Delete as appropriate

Rule 132 Form 80

UNTO THE RIGHT HONOURABLE THE LORD JUSTICE GENERAL, THE LORD JUSTICE CLERK AND LORDS COMMISSIONERS OF JUSTICIARY

NOTE OF APPLICATION FOR
SUSPENSION OF DISQUALIFICATION
UNDER SECTION 94(2) OF THE
ROAD TRAFFIC ACT 1972
IN
SUMMARY COMPLAINT
I.C.

Procurator

Fiscal,

Complainer and
Respondent

against

Applicant and
Appellant

HUMBLY SHEWETH:

THAT the said applicant and appellant having been convicted on a complaint brought under the Criminal Procedure (Scotland) Act 1975 at the instance of the complainer and respondent of was on the day of 19 in the Court at fined/sentenced to

and ordered to be disqualified for a period of in terms of section 93 of the Road Traffic Act 1972.

THAT on the day of 19 the said applicant and appellant applied to the said court to state a case for the opinion of the High Court of Justiciary in terms of section 442 of the said Act of 1975.

THAT the said applicant and appellant thereafter requested the said court to suspend the said period of disqualification in terms of section 94(3) of the Road Traffic Act 1972.

THAT the said court on the day of 19 refused to suspend the said disqualification.

THAT the said applicant and appellant has served a copy of this note on the clerk of the said court and on the said respondent.

May it therefore please your Lordships in terms of section 94B(2) of the Road Traffic Act 1972 to suspend the said disqualification on such terms as your Lordships think fit.

According to justice &c

Solicitors for applicant and appellant

. . . . . .

High Court of Justiciary Practice Note

29th March 1985

*Appeals in solemn procedure and appeals against sentence in summary
   procedure*

All too often the time of the appeal court is wasted, and proper disposal
of appeals is hampered, where the grounds stated in notes of appeal are
wholly unspecific. In appeals against conviction, for example, it is
common to find grounds stated thus:
   (i) "Misdirection" without any specification whatever;
   (ii) "Insufficient evidence" without any specification of the particular
        point, if any, which is to be taken, *e.g.* the absence of
        corroboration of evidence identifying the appellant as the
        perpetrator of the crime, or an alleged insufficiency of evidence to
        establish that the crime libelled, or a crime within the scope of the
        libel, was committed;
In appeals against sentence, for example, the ground of appeal is more
often than not equally uninformative, *e.g.* "sentence excessive in the
circumstances" or merely "severity of sentence". No hint is given of the
circumstances to be relied on and it often happens that at the hearing the
court is told of allegedly relevant circumstances which, it is said, were not
before the judge or sheriff or which, it is said, the judge or sheriff ignored.

It will be appreciated that the consequence of the statement of
unspecific grounds of appeal is that the trial judge or sheriff is unable to
report upon them, and the appeal court is at a grave disadvantage in
preparing for and hearing appeals without the benefit of the observations
of the trial judge or sheriff upon the proposition which the appellant
submits to the court without notice.

This practice note is intended to remind practitioners that grounds of
appeal must be stated with sufficient specification to identify the
particular criticism of the conviction or sentence which the appellant
hopes to present at the hearing. In the case of notes of appeal lodged after
the issue of this practice note the appeal court may be expected, save in
exceptional circumstances and on cause shown, to refuse to entertain any
appeal upon any unspecific ground.

INDEX

[References are to paragraph numbers]

541